Relational Database Management

Obtaining the REQUIEM source code

The source code of the relational database System REQUIEM is available for:

- Apple Macintosh
- IBM-PC and compatible systems
- Sun
- Digital Equipment VAX (ULTRIX)

For detailed information concerning distribution, including cost and licence terms, please contact:

c/o Mike Papazoglou
Australian National University,
Department of Computer Science,
GPO Box 4,
Canberra, ACT 2601,
Australia

Relational Database Management
A Systems Programming Approach

M. Papazoglou and W. Valder

Prentice Hall

New York   London   Toronto   Sydney   Tokyo   Singapore

First published 1989 by
Prentice Hall International (UK) Ltd,
66 Wood Lane End, Hemel Hempstead,
Hertfordshire, HP2 4RG
A division of
Simon & Schuster International Group

Printed and bound in Great Britain by
BPCC Wheatons Ltd, Exeter

Library of Congress Cataloging-in-Publication Data

Papazoglou, M., 1953–
  Relational database management.

  (Prentice Hall International series in computer
  science)
  Bibliography: p.
  Includes index.
  1. Data base management. 2. Relational data bases.
I. Valder, W., 1954–   . II. Title. III. Series.
QA76.9.D3P346 1988   005.75'6   88-23185
ISBN 0-13-771866-7

British Library Cataloguing in Publication Data

Papazogolou, M.
  Relational database management: the
  systems programming approach. – (Prentice
  Hall International series in computer
  science).
  1. Relational machine-readable files
I. Title II. Valder, W.
  005.75'6

  ISBN 0-13-771866-7
  ISBN 0-13-771874-8 Pbk

---

3 4 5 6   93 92 91 90

ISBN 0-13-771866-7
ISBN 0-13-771874-8 PBK

Contents

Preface

To most people the development of a relational database system still remains a mystery as it encompasses such diverse concepts as language design, file organization and management, meta-data techniques, etc. that have traditionally been tackled separately. It is the aim of this book to elucidate such issues and tie them together by consolidating much material found scattered in research and book literature. Our purpose in writing this material was to produce a book that would be of practical use, easy to read and understand, yet not lacking in substance or completeness.

Unlike many traditional database books, this one does not attempt to survey the field of relational databases by concentrating on theoretical aspects or by presenting as many alternatives as possible. Instead the book strikes a balance between theory and practice by covering fundamental conceptual design principles and showing how to develop a fullyfledged database management system from scratch. In doing so, it reviews the major components of an experimental product and tries to consolidate the material into a systematic discipline. The book begins with a theoretical coverage of relational systems and proceeds gradually through the design stages of a system that can serve both as an example and pattern design. It demonstrates that the development of REQUIEM (RElational Query and Update Interactive SystEM) involves many aspects of information processing and systems programming, e.g. lexical analysis, parsing, view processing, and catalog interrogation, and elaborates on the entire source implementation (some 14,000 lines) of this prototype system in detail. It is worth mentioning that we are primarily addressing small and medium sized systems and that REQUIEM is at present a single-user system. Although such issues as transaction management, recovery, and concurrency control are obviously not dealt with in this book, the system offers an open-ended interface facility so that such modules can be incorporated with reasonable programming effort.

The host system for REQUIEM runs on Sun computers under the Unix operating system. However, you can port it with a little effort to a non-Unix environment: a version of REQUIEM runs on the Macintosh under the C Lightspeed compiler. The entire set of REQUIEM source files was developed in C. There are many good factors which have influenced this decision. In the following we will try to present some of them as succinctly as possible. Over the past years C has been used successfully for literally every type of programming problem – from operating systems to expert systems – and efficient compilers are available for machines ranging in power from a small personal computer to the largest mainframe. Although C is fundamentally a systems programming language it offers many attractive features such as a high degree of portability, modifiability, and access to low-level operations that are normally confined to assembly language programming. One further reason for choosing C as the vehicle for the development of REQUIEM is that it is intimately associated with Unix which has established itself as an academic standard and is well on its way to becoming an industrial standard. However, C has not only notable advantages but also some drawbacks. One of the most serious drawbacks of C is that it can sometimes be very cryptic. To remedy this situation we have tried to be as clear as possible in our code implementation. Actually, we have tried to strike a balance between instructional as well as practical programs. This makes the code implementation easier to read for those who are unfamiliar with C.

Purpose and contents of the book

Chapters 1 to 3 of the book provide a general introduction to the concepts and the theory underlying a relational DBMS. In particular, they introduce the reader to the basic concepts of database technology and data modeling. As explained, emphasis is placed on the relational data model, not only because this model forms the basis for most commercially available database systems, but also because its concepts can with a reasonable programming effort be incorporated into high-level programming languages. We hope that readers with strong backgrounds in computer systems and programming languages will bear with us when we take time to explain some of the more basic concepts. We would like to suggest that you read these sections even if they seem familiar. A common understanding of each topic is very important to the overall development of the book.

The rest of the book (excepting Chapter 16) consists of twelve chapters which have a strong practical orientation. These chapters are presented in a bottom-up fashion in accordance with the three general design levels of a realistic database system. Chapters 4–6 introduce the concepts and the implementation of the physical database level, such as access paths, indices, sequential record accessing, etc. Chapters 7–11 elaborate on the implementation of relational operators and a complete relational data language, called RQL, and show how these issues are mapped on the physical database level. Finally, Chapters 12–15 are concerned with the user level of the system and include such concepts and issues as view definition and processing, catalog interrogation, and man–machine interface. Each of the Chapters 4–14 contains a blend of conceptual design principles and implementation which allows for a better reasoning about the essence of each problem and shows how these problems are coped with both individually and collectively. All chapters come in logical sequence which implies that they would have to be read one after the other. Chapter 15 introduces some advanced user interface facilities, e.g. menus, and suggests how these systems can be integrated with the current interface of REQUIEM to make it a more user-friendly system. We consider this chapter to be an exercise or a challenge for the advanced reader. We have also included a concise list of exercises (Chapter 16), appendices that provide complete source listings, the syntax of the language, indications how to compile and load the system, working examples, and a concise glossary.

This book is intended for a broad audience. It is a book aimed at the advanced student, the researcher, and the professional. Although considered an advanced book, the concepts and techniques presented herein should be understandable to all readers having an elementary knowledge of data structures such as stacks, queues, or linked lists, and thorough knowledge of at least one high-level programming language, preferably C. Knowledge of filing systems and the like is considered to be helpful but is not essential for an understanding of the material in this book.

Finally, a word about REQUIEM and its objectives. The actual reason for implementing REQUIEM was amongst other things to provide a solid foundation for further development and experimentation with new ideas and features. For example, you can use the concepts, data structures, and parts of the code presented in this book and adapt them to your own requirements, experiment with them, try out different alternatives, and finally design your own query language by means of the methodology presented herein. We certainly hope that you will somehow adapt and improve upon the source code included in this material. We are aware of the fact that in certain instances more elegant and compact source code could be written but for teaching purposes we tried to keep implementation as simple as possible. Should you wish to port this system to another machine, operating system or C compiler, some adjustments to the header files would have to be made to cater for the machine- or compiler-specific parameters. Those definitions which are potential candidates for adjustment are appropriately indicated by comments in the source listings. If this book helps you understand the issues involved in developing and implementing a database management system, or, better still, if it helps you succeed in accomplishing such a task, then we will have met our primary objective. We would certainly be glad to receive any suggestions or comments you may have.

Use as a text

The material presented in this book addresses both advanced undergraduate and graduate level courses which have practical orientation. Although this book is mainly oriented toward database courses dealing with the development of database management systems, it could with slight adaptation provide a novel and general approach to courses on systems programming as it could be regarded as a case study in the design and development of a large software system. Some of the exercises at the end of the book are case exercises which were written exactly with this purpose in mind.

Acknowledgments

There remains only the pleasant task of acknowledging the help I have received during programming REQUIEM and writing the present book. Although I personally wrote the entire source code of the database and the major design decisions are my own, many people have contributed useful programs that are included in the distribution. I am grateful, first, to Willy Valder, co-author and consultant, for providing suggestions and the best possible solution to the most strenuous programming problems. My sincere thanks also go to James Hunt who kindly offered us his B-tree implementation and David Betz for providing us with his SDB implementation, parts of which proved to be invaluable in our implementation efforts. My special thanks and appreciation to those people who helped me with their comments and their valuable criticisms and suggestions: Dimitris Christodoulakis, Bernd Krämer, Louis Marinos, Andreas Mikes, Gillian Mikes, and Moira Norrie. I have also benefited enormously from the comments of the reviewers who did an excellent job in reviewing a very difficult and technical manuscript in the best possible manner. I am also grateful to the staff of Prentice Hall, and in particular to Helen Martin, for their valuable advice, continuous encouragement, and contributions to make this book better than any of us could have achieved individually.

Thanks to all of you for helping us to succeed in doing something which at times seemed to be quite impossible.

Mike P.Papazoglou

1

Basic Concepts of Database Management

The following chapter presents a brief introduction to the general concepts and methods which have been developed to facilitate data management. We begin with a discussion of databases, data models, and data representation. This is followed by a brief overview of the components and functionality of fullyfledged database management systems.

1.1   The database concept

Until recently the traditional approach to information system design concentrated on conventional file processing systems. File processing systems were used to reflect the data processing requirements of a particular organization. These file processing systems usually consisted of a set of programs and a set of data files. The programs were often developed individually to meet the requirements set by a particular department of the organization or even by a group of users with common interests. This consequently meant that some of the data in the files was either duplicated (data redundancy) or inconsistent as no coordination existed between files belonging to different groups of people. This in turn meant that many of the existing programs either had to be revised, or even worse, had to be completely rewritten because of a change in their data structuring requirements. In addition to these disadvantages, several other drawbacks, such as limited data sharing and poor enforcement of standards, proliferated, resulting in poor programmer productivity and requiring excessive program maintenance. Thus, file processing systems soon became unpopular and undesirable, and their inherent difficulties have promoted the development of database systems.

Unlike traditional file systems, the database approach to information system design provides a solution to these difficulties by eliminating data redundancy (if possible) and by promoting data sharing. A *database* can be perceived as a single shared pool of interrelated data, designed to meet the data processing requirements of an organization. Consequently, we can define a database as a collection of formatted data which is accessed by more than one person and/or which is used for more than one purpose.

The database might be a collection of similar data such as that relating to airline seat reservations, or it might consist of various related data such as used in an integrated accounting system. A database possesses the following two important features:

1. It provides users with an integrated view of the data.
2. It allows sharing of the data between a wide community of users.

The term *integrated database* signifies the fact that previously distinct data files have been logically organized to eliminate (or reduce) data redundancy. On the other hand, as the database itself consists of a set of files, all users in a particular organization that may require the same data item can safely share the files containing the common information.

The database approach offers a number of significant advantages in comparison with other traditional approaches. Some of these include data consistency, minimal data redundancy, data integrity, the enforcement of standards, and ease of application development. Consequently, the advent of database systems has significantly increased programmer productivity and reduced program maintenance; two of the most acute requirements facing modern software engineering systems.

1.1.1 Database management systems

A *database management system* (DBMS) is a system that provides the user with a means of communicating with the database efficiently. This implies that a DBMS is a system that provides the user with suitable and adequate facilities to define *database schemas*, i.e. a logical perception of the database, and also provides a powerful set of operations that are able to retrieve and manipulate *database instances*. A database instance is the information content of the database at a particular point in time.

Broadly speaking, the purpose of a DBMS is to provide the user with better methods of data access to increase productivity. The DBMS allows the user to formulate requests at a logical level, without regard to how the data is stored in physical files. The DBMS determines which physical files are involved in a user request, and how these files are to be accessed by referring to a stored data mapping description (schema). It then reads the required database records and converts the data obtained into the form requested by the database user. This process guarantees *data independence* which means that the file structures could be modified internally without affecting the user's perception of the data. This whole process is obviously invisible to the user; although the same logical requests posed by users on the contents of the database may result in a different set of operations on files of the database, the results of the requests would be the same.

Data independence as provided by a DBMS is very important since it guarantees that the techniques used by the physical storage of a database could be changed at will without affecting the logical structure of the data.

1.1.2 Levels of database representation

A major purpose of a database system is to provide users with an abstract view of data. That is, the database system hides certain details of how data is stored and manipulated. Thus, the starting point for the design of a database must be an abstract and general description which is to be represented in terms of the data contained in the database.

In a university environment, for example, we may be interested in modeling: (a) real world entities describing students, tutors, departments, employees, etc. and (b) a set of useful *relationships* between those entities, e.g. students studying in certain departments or tutors teaching students. Furthermore, as a database is a resource that is shared by a number of users in an organization each user may require a different view of the data included in the database. In the previous example, the teaching staff require a view of student performance data, while the administrative staff require views of financial and administrative data. These latter views are obviously more specialized than the former generalized views which require the logical description of the entire organization, i.e. the university environment.

To satisfy these needs, most contemporary database management systems permit the users to view an organization's database at three levels of abstraction: the *internal level*, the *conceptual level*, and the *external level*. The interrelationship among these levels of abstraction is depicted in Figure 1.1.

The conceptual level
The starting point for the design of a database system is some abstract and general description of that part of the universe which is to be represented by the data in the database. It is precisely the conceptual level that formulates this abstract but precise image of all the data stored in the database (including the relationships between the modeled data entities).

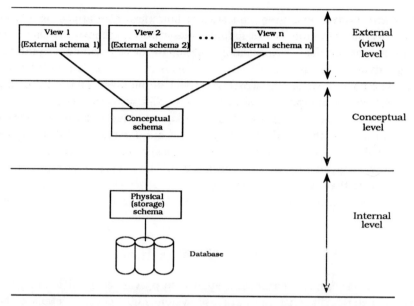

Figure 1.1 The three levels of the standard architecture for database systems.

This level describes the database in terms of a set of relatively simple structures (definitions). In fact, it entails a global, logical description of data, independent of physical data storage considerations. The implementation of these definitions normally involves complex physical level structures such as file organizations, access methods, etc. These implementation details are invisible to the user of the conceptual level. The conceptual level of abstraction is normally designed and used by qualified users, e.g. *database administrators*, who must decide how the database must be organized and what implementation should be kept in it.

The external (view) level
This represents the highest level of abstraction at which the user views only a subset of the entire database. Each user view is formulated according to the user's needs and is derived from the same database. The subset feature means that the user is able to see only those data items which were specified; this helps to preserve privacy and stop unauthorized updating. As the external level normally consists of multiple user perceptions of the data, it is usually referred to as the *view level*.

The internal level
This is the lowest level of data representation at which the DBMS specifies the physical implementation of the database. Here the database is viewed as a collection of internal records, which are normally interrelated

by specific mechanisms, e.g. indices or pointers which impact on efficiency and implementation details. At this level, complex low-level data structures are described. We describe techniques for physical data organization in Chapter 6.

The purpose of the three level architecture shown in Figure 1.1 is to provide views of the same database that are tailored to the needs of each particular database user. Another important advantage is that it provides data independence, which is considered to be a major advantage of the database approach as compared to traditional filing systems. Data independence allows various modifications to be made to the database with minor or no impact to the database users.

1.2 The main types of data model

The DBMS is based on a data model which should be considered as its underlying inherent data model. Most of the contemporary DBMSs are based completely on a specific data model, e.g. INGRES [1],* System R [2]. However, there are some exceptions to this rule if one considers the IMS [3] which is loosely based on the hierarchical model.

The term *data model* is used to define a set of rules according to which data is structured. Apart from the structuring of data, a data model must also specify the nature of operations that are allowed on the data and a possible set of integrity rules which ensure that the data in the database is accurate. The operations are traditionally related to the structures of data, i.e. operations are executed within the context provided by the structures of the data [4]. A data model comprises an integrated collection of tools for describing data, data relationships, and constraints on the context of data.

Quite a few data models have been proposed. They fall into two broad categories, *object-based* and *record-based*; distinction is made on the basis of the internal structure of the data models. They are both used to describe data at the conceptual and external levels. Record-based logical data models are used to specify the overall structure of the database, and a higher level description of the implementation [5]. Their main drawback lies in the fact that they do not provide adequate facilities for explicitly specifying constraints on the data, whereas the object-based data models lack the means of logical structure specification, but provide more semantic substance by allowing the user explicitly to specify constraints on the data. The object-based models deal with database aspects which are beyond the scope of this book. For further information and references see [6], [7], and [8]

---

*Numbers in square brackets refer to entries in the bibliography (pages 545–8).

which present a selection of articles on object-based data models and data
management systems. A comprehensive analysis of the differences between
relational and object data models can be found in [9].

There exist three principal types of record-based logical data model: the
relational data model, the *hierarchical data model*, and the *network data
model*. In the relational model data is represented as tables, in the hierarchical data model it is represented as tree graphs, and in the network
model it can be viewed as generalized graph structures. The majority of
the contemporary database systems are based on the relational paradigm,
whereas the early database systems were either based on the hierarchical
or network data models. The last two models still require the application
program or user to have knowledge of the physical database being accessed,
whereas the former provides a substantial measure of physical and logical
data independence.*

1.3   Conceptual data analysis

This section introduces the concept of *conceptual data analysis*, by which we
mean the process of gathering information and converting it into a logical
data model [10], [11]. The results of this analysis are applied to the design
of the corresponding database, and have impact on the structure of the files
underlying the database. The first step in the conceptual data analysis is
to identify data items of interest to be stored in the database and explicitly
state the *associations* between them. An association is a logical, meaningful
connection between the data items. It actually implies that the values for
the associated data items are somehow interdependent. The final step in
the conceptual data analysis is to group the data items into logical records,
and to try to make these records as independent from each other as possible
to achieve a plausible overall database design.

1.3.1   Associations between the data items

In the following we describe simple graphical methods for representing data
items and existing associations among them. Let us consider the product
entities of a rudimentary products database. Here we may identify data
items such as product number, product name, or product report. Each type
of data item is represented by an oval enclosing its name, while associations

---

*A system is said to promote logical data independence if users are insulated from
changes in the logical structure of the database.

between data items are represented by means of arrows.

Let us now examine briefly the relationships which hold between the identified data items. In a database the following types of association can be distinguished.

1. **One-to-one associations (1:1):** Supposing we have two data items characterizing product identity numbers and product names, namely *PRODUCT_NO#* and *PRODUCT_NAME*. A one-to-one association from the data item *PRODUCT_NO#* to the data item *PRODUCT_NAME* means that each *PRODUCT_NO#* corresponds exactly to one *PRODUCT_NAME*. Accordingly, the following mapping is one-to-one:

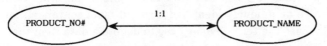

In the above representation a single arrow head points to a "one-to-one" association. Note that there is also an inverse association, namely that from the data item *PRODUCT_NAME* to the data item *PRODUCT_NO#*; this association is indicated by an arrow from *PRODUCT_NAME* to *PRODUCT_NO#*. Thus, each *PRODUCT_NAME* is associated with exactly one and only one *PRODUCT_NO#*.

2. **One-to-many associations (1:n):** Supposing now that we have two data items, namely *PRODUCT_NO#* and *PRODUCT_REPORT*. A one-to-many association from the data item *PRODUCT_NO#* to the data item *PRODUCT_REPORT* means that each product has an arbitrary number, say *n* (including zero), of product reports. This mapping is indicated by a double-headed arrow directed from the data item *PRODUCT-_NO#* to the data item *PRODUCT_REPORT*:

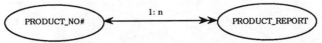

The inverse association means that each value of *PRODUCT_REPORT* is associated with exactly one value (hence the value 1 and the single arrow head in the above diagram) of *PRODUCT_NO#*.

3. **Many-to-many associations (m:n):** This type of association means that at any given instant, for each value of a data item *A*, e.g. *PRODUCT_NO#*, there can be many values of data item *B*, e.g. *WAREHOUSE*. The following diagram denotes that every product can be found in an arbitrary number, say *n*, of warehouses, and each warehouse can store an arbitrary number, say *m*, of products:

The next section illustrates how the former graphical representation can also be used when grouping the data items into logical records.

1.3.2   The grouping of data items into records

As stated previously, a *logical record* represents a collection of associated data items. To be uniquely identified a record must contain an appropriate *key*. We shall use the term *primary key* to denote a data item that is chosen by the database designer as the principal means of identifying a logical record. Hence, there exists a one-to-one association from the primary key of a record to the remaining data items in the record.

The data association diagram of Figure 1.2(a) clearly indicates that there exists such a one-to-one association from the data item *PRODUCT_NO#* to all the other data items that collectively represent the entity *PRODUCT*. Records are represented by rectangles containing the names of the data items included in the record, see Figure 1.2(b). Notice that in Figure 1.2(a) the data item *PRODUCT_NO#* is underlined to indicate the fact that it represents the sole means of identification for the record of type *PROD-UCT*. Finally, Figure 1.2(c) represents a possible instance of this particular

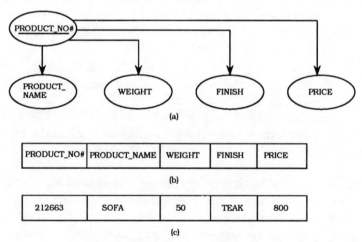

Figure 1.2 Groupings of data items.

record type. In addition to primary keys, it is quite possible that a logical record contains also *secondary keys*. Secondary keys provide the means for retrieving selected data records from a data file without having to search the entire file sequentially. For example, a secondary key for the *PRODUCT* record in Figure 1.2(b) could be the data item *PRODUCT_NAME*. We will explain how secondary keys can speed up record retrieval later in this text.

1.3.3 Associations between records

In addition to grouping the data items into records we can use the previous graphical representations to develop more complex data structures. Most of the examples in this chapter (and indeed in all subsequent chapters) are based on a single database, the suppliers-and-products database. Several views corresponding to this suppliers-and-products database are illustrated in Figure 1.3. For example, Figure 1.3(a) contains information regarding the supplier's part of the database, while Figure 1.3(b) contains information regarding the products supplied by the various suppliers. Finally, Figure 1.3(c) shows how these two views are combined to form a single integrated view.

Figures 1.3(a) and 1.3(c) assume that each supplier supplies a range of products. For reasons of simplicity it is, however, assumed that no two suppliers supply the same product. Figure 1.4 shows the results of grouping the data items of Figure 1.3(c) into logical records. We call such records logical to stress the fact that they might be made up of *fields* originating from more than one physical record, thereby demonstrating a degree of data independence. For example, the *SUPPLIER* record in Figure 1.4 consists of four data elements called its fields. As Figure 1.4 shows, there are two resulting record types, namely *SUPPLIER* and *PRODUCT*. As the association between the primary keys (*SUPPLIER_ID#* for *SUPPLIER* and *PRODUCT_NO#* for *PRODUCT*) is 1:*n*, the corresponding association between the logical records is also 1:*n*. Consequently, the types of association existing between data records are identical to those existing between data items.

Some records cannot be uniquely identified by a simple primary key that consists of a single data item. In this case, a primary key that consists of two or even more data items is required to identify the corresponding data record. Such a key is called a *composite key*. In Figure 1.5 the *ORDER_LINE* record includes a composite key consisting of *ORDER_NO#* combined with *PRODUCT_NO#*.

In Figure 1.5 the combination of the keys *PRODUCT_NO#* and *ORDER_NO#* is required to identify the other logical record fields. Actually, the *ORDER_LINE* record is not a stand-alone record; it is rather the *derivation* of the logical integration of the *ORDER* and *PRODUCT*

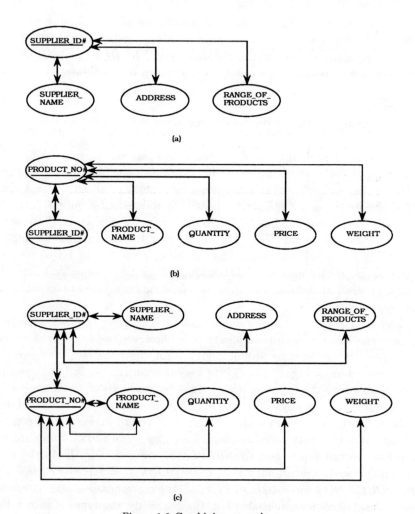

Figure 1.3 Combining user views.

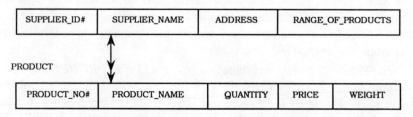

Figure 1.4 Association between two logical records.

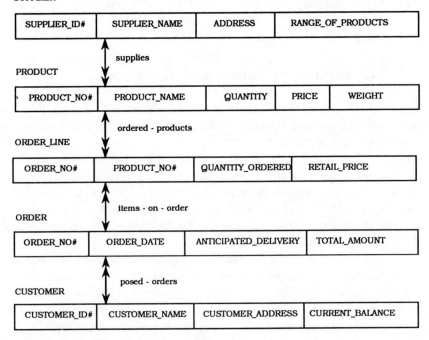

Figure 1.5 Graphical representation of the suppliers-and-products database.

records, including some additional data items such as *QUANTITY_ORDER* and *RETAIL_PRICE*. This means that the association between *ORDERS* and *PRODUCTS* could have been represented as a many-to-many association. Indeed, each customer order may request several products, while at the same time each product may have many pending orders.

In general, properly designed databases do not explicitly include many-to-many associations between logical records. Each many-to-many association is resolved into two one-to-many associations (e.g. the associations between *PRODUCT* and *ORDER_LINE*, and *ORDER* and *ORDER_LINE* in Figure 1.5) by the introduction of an intermediate record (e.g. the *ORDER_LINE* logical record) having as primary key the combination of the primary keys of the two many-to-many associated logical records.

It might be argued that resolving a many-to-many association into two one-to-many associations is achieved at the cost of additional redundancy as the data items *ORDER_NO#* and *PRODUCT_NO#* are repeated in *ORDER_LINE*. However, one must remember that we are dealing with logical record representations and not physical records. This implies that separate occurrences of the data items *ORDER_NO#* and *PRODUCT_NO#* may not be physically stored in the *ORDER_LINE* record occurrences.

1.4   Database schemas and instances

The overall design of the database is called the database schema. There are three different types of schemas in the database, and these are partitioned according to the levels of abstraction illustrated in Figure 1.1. At the highest level we have multiple *external schemas* which correspond to different perceptions of the data contained in the database. Sometimes in the literature an external schema is referred to as a *subschema*. At the intermediate level we have the conceptual level, sometimes referred to as the *conceptual schema* or simply *schema*, while at the lowest level of abstraction we have the *physical schema*.

The conceptual schema describes the logical relationship between data items, together with integrity constraints. A fundamental impact of a conceptual schema is that the concepts used harmonize – and to a certain extent make possible – human communication. In a way, a conceptual schema constitutes a general agreement concerning how to perceive the modeled entities in the real world and will certainly influence the methods of organizing the information needs of an organization. Finally, at a lower level the physical schema of the database provides the appropriate interface with its underlying hardware architecture. An internal interface is the interface between the implemented database system and the actual physical storage facilities. This latter kind of schema uses complex data structures to build complex architectures for organizing the data.

The DBMS software is responsible for mapping between these three types of schema. It must be in a position to check the schemas for consistency, i.e. that each external schema is really derived from the appropriate conceptual schema, and must use the information in the schemas to map between each external schema and the physical schema via the conceptual schema. The conceptual schema is related to the internal schema through a *conceptual/internal mapping*. This enables the DBMS to find the actual record or combination of records in physical storage that constitute a logical record in the conceptual schema, together with any constraints to be enforced on operations on that logical record. Finally, each external schema is related to the conceptual by an *external/conceptual mapping*. This enables the DBMS to map names in the user's view on the specified part of the conceptual schema description.

It is helpful to consider an example to clarify such issues as the conceptual and the external schemas. The representation of Figure 1.6 is intended to model a sample database for a hypothetical university.

As mentioned previously the most general logical view of the database description is called the conceptual schema or simply schema. Figure 1.6 shows an example of such a schema. The schema contains a number of logical database records, such as *STUDENT* and *STAFF_MEMBER*. The logical records are connected with arrows signifying interrecord relationships. As explained in the previous section the labels on the arrows specify the semantics of the relationship; for example the *enrolled* relationship specifies which students are enrolled in which courses. Furthermore, the data items shown in each logical record illustrate the kind of information that might be contained in such records. Obviously, a real database would certainly include more logical records, each record containing many more data items.

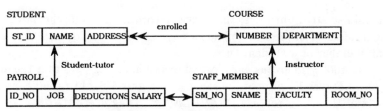

Figure 1.6 Schema for the university database.

Although the schema offers a complete description of the logical structure and content of the database most end users are concerned only with a small fraction of this information. A user would normally require a few types of records and relationships which would then constitute the user's desired view of the system. As explained, this description of data is known as an external schema or simply subschema. There may be many different subschemas corresponding to the same schema. For example, someone working in the finance office of the university might only require information contained in the *PAYROLL#* part of the database. This person is interested in viewing not the entire database schema as illustrated in Figure 1.6, but rather a smaller portion of it concerning financial and administrative data. Accordingly, Figure 1.7 depicts two possible subschemas which correspond to the schema of Figure 1.6.

Users viewing the subschema of Figure 1.7(a) are normally persons concerned with interdepartmental information. To those persons the database appears to consist only of courses, students, and staff-members. A record for each staff-member is linked to a set of records representing the courses that this specific staff member is currently teaching; and each of these course records is linked to a set of records representing the students enrolled in that course. On the other hand, the subschema of Figure 1.7(b) is used

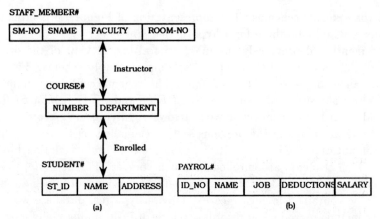

Figure 1.7 Two possible subschemas corresponding to the schema of Figure1.6.

for administrative purposes; the logical record in this subschema contains enough information needed to issue a pay bill to an employee, who is either a staff member or a student tutor.

The symbol # following each logical record name signifies that the logical records in Figure 1.7 are not the same as in Figure 1.6, but rather constitute subsets of these records, e.g. *STUDENT#, STAFF_MEMBER#*; or they may even be derived logical records, e.g. *PAY-ROLL#*.

To show how the above concepts are related to implementation issues we draw an analogy to the concepts of data types, variables, and values in the C programming language [12]. For example, if we try to define a conceptual schema for the university database we require several structure definitions. Thus, we may declare the relation *STUDENT* as follows:

```
struct student {
    char student_id[10];
    char student_name[20];
    char student_address[15];
};
```

This construct declares a structure called **student**. This structure declaration does not allocate storage space and can possibly be conceived as an external schema for the entity **student**. Now if we define the variable **student_1** of the type **student** as

```
struct student student_1;
```

we allocate space to the structure template of type **student** and we name this construct **student_ 1**.

Databases are dynamic in nature; this means that database contents are subject to change as data is inserted into the database or deleted from it.

As explained in section 1.1.1 the information content of the database at a particular point in time is called an instance of the database. To create a database instance we simply assign initial values to the members of the student structure in the following manner:

```
struct student student_1 = {"S605","Jones","London"};
```

In sum, as changes to the schema are infrequent, the purpose of a schema must be to capture the time-independent properties of data, i.e. properties that are true for all time. In general, we are not interested in properties that merely happen to apply by chance at some specific instant in time. For example, the property that each product has a price is true for all time; by contrast the property that every sofa is located in London is purely coincidental and is certainly not true for all time. Throughout the following chapters we will be equally concerned with the schema parts of tables as well as with their value parts.

1.5 High-level data oriented languages

Each user who wishes to interact with a DBMS has a special command language at his or her disposal. The command language of a DBMS is normally a high-level data language. Such a language provides a set of commands, each of which operates either on the entire contents of a file at once, or on the contents of multiple files. Elements of this high-level data language include operators to select logical records from a file according to specified criteria, sort selected logical records, calculate statistics, i.e. the sum or average, on certain fields of the entire file, etc.

A single statement of a high-level data language implies a series of underlying processing steps. Normally, the user view of the database would consist of the minimum necessary information – at the level of logical names and relationships – excluding physical storage considerations. By the use of such a high-level data language the processing specification is easier to write, clearer to comprehend, and relatively straightforward to modify.

In principle, any given high-level data language is really a combination of two subordinate data languages, a *data definition language* (DDL), which provides for the definition of data entities and elements, and a *data manipulation language* (DML) which provides for the manipulation of the defined data entities.

1.5.1   The data definition language

The database schema is specified by a set of definitions expressed by means of a special language called a data definition language. A DDL is a descriptive language which allows the user to describe and name the entities required for the application and the associations which may exist between the different entity descriptions (i.e. schemas). The DDL is used to develop a schema or even to modify an existing one. It cannot be used to manipulate data.

The result of the interpretation of the DDL statements is a set of tables stored in special files collectively called the *data catalogs*. Data catalogs are tables that contain *meta-data*; that is data which describes objects in the system. This integrates the catalogs in the underlying system and makes it easier for them to be accessed or manipulated. The data catalogs contain definitions of records, data items, and other objects that are of interest to users or are required by the DBMS. The DBMS normally consults the data catalogs before the actual data is modified in the database system.

1.5.2   The data manipulation language

A data manipulation language provides a set of operations that support the basic data manipulation operations on the contents of the database. Data manipulation operations usually include the following:

1. The insertion of new data into the database.
2. The modification (updating) of data stored in the database.
3. The retrieval of data contained in the database.
4. The deletion of data from the database.

Thus, one of the primary functions of the DBMS is to support a data manipulation language in which the user can formulate commands that will cause such data manipulation to occur. Data manipulation applies to the schema and subschema levels as well as to the physical level. However, on the physical level one must define rather complex low-level procedures that allow for efficient data access. Contrary to this, at higher levels emphasis is placed on the ease of utilization. The effort is put into providing efficient user interaction with the system.

DMLs are distinguished by their underlying retrieval sublanguages; we thus distinguish between two types of DML, the *procedural* and the *nonprocedural*. The prime difference between these two data manipulation languages is that in procedural languages the database statements treat records individually, while in non-procedural data manipulation languages the statements operate on sets of records. Consequently, procedural languages specify how the output of a DML statement must be obtained, while non-procedural DMLs describe only what the output has to be like.

Procedural DMLs

In a typical retrieval or update the required data may be located in more than one record in any file, and in more than one file. Thus, a retrieval that permits accessing of only one record (or part of a record) at a time will require the writing of a procedure for any given retrieval. With a procedural DML the user should specify what data is needed and how to obtain it. This means that in order to communicate with the database the user should express all the data access operations which are to be used by calling appropriate procedures to obtain the information required. Such a procedural DML retrieves a record, processes it, and based on the results obtained by this processing retrieves another record that would also be processed, and so on. This process of retrievals continues until the data requested from the retrieval has been gathered. Network and hierarchical DMLs are normally procedural.

Non-procedural DMLs

With non-procedural DMLs the required data may be specified in a single retrieval or update expression. Non-procedural DMLs require the user to specify what data is required without specifying how it is to be obtained. With non-procedural languages the DBMS translates a DML expression into a procedure (or sets of procedures) that manipulates the required sets of records. Relational database systems normally include some form of non-procedural language for data manipulation. Non-procedural DMLs are normally easier to learn and utilize than procedural DMLs because less work is done by the user and more by the DBMS.

The part of a DML that involves information retrieval is called a *query language*. A query language can be defined as a high-level special-purpose language used in the context of information retrieval to satisfy diverse requests for retrieval of data held in databases [13]. A query language is normally interactive, and is able to process a wide range of queries by employing an interactive query language processor. This enables the user to issue high-level retrieval statements to the DBMS. The term *query* is therefore reserved to denote a statement expressed in a query language. A query language frees the programmer from concern for how data structures are internally implemented and what algorithms are operating on stored data representations [14]. As such query languages provide the users with a considerable degree of data independence [15], the terms query language and data manipulation language are commonly used interchangeably, although this is technically incorrect.

1.5.3   Types of DBMS

According to the foregoing it seems plausible to classify database management systems on the basis of the type of data manipulation language they utilize. Consequently, we can distinguish between *navigational* and *non-navigational* (or *automatic navigation*) database management systems. Navigational database management systems normally select one data item at a time by following a logical path, i.e. navigating through the database structure. By contrast, in non-navigational database management systems the required data may be specified in a single retrieval expression which has a degree of complexity proportional to the complexity of the retrieval expression. The non-navigational system is capable of automatically translating retrieval expressions into procedural calls that fetch the required sets of records.

The navigational DBMS

The distinguishing feature of navigational DBMSs is the existence of physical links (i.e. chains of pointers) connecting various data records together. Navigational DBMSs are used to implement single record-at-time query methods; thus, they are used as the basis for the materialization of procedural query languages. It is exactly this process of retrieving a sequence of data records from a database that has been termed *navigation*, since the user's application program navigates through the data files of the database picking up the appropriate records one at a time.

As an example, we show in Figure 1.8 how a simplified view of the suppliers-and-products database could be represented in a navigational form. An organization like the one depicted in Figure 1.8 is called a *multilist file organization* [16], [17]. Actually, the multilist file organization is used as the basic building block for implementation of navigational systems such as for example the IDMS (Integrated Database Management System), which is a typical network DBMS, and the hierarchical database system IMS/VS.

A multilist file organization can be defined as a file organization in which different groups of records are chained together in such a way that an individual file may contain many different record lists. For example, in Figure 1.8 we chained together all products supplied by the same supplier; in other words for each supplier we have a list of corresponding products. In exactly the same fashion and by means of additional pointers we could, for example, have a list of products for each distinct product price category.

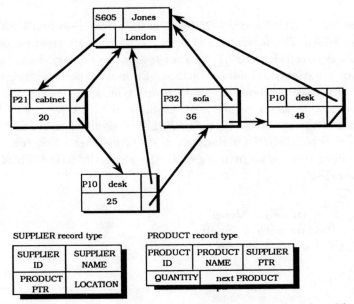

Figure 1.8 The suppliers-and-products database: navigational version with sample values.

What this implies is that multiple pointers are employed, one each for the different "paths" through the data. Normally, each such path links records with some common characteristic.

In the multilist data structure representing the "suppliers-and-products" of Figure 1.8 a physical link connects a *SUPPLIER* data record with a linked list of *PRODUCT* data records for the products supplied by that *SUPPLIER*. We often refer to such a structure as a *navigational-set*. Note that in the navigational-set of Figure 1.8 each *PRODUCT* record contains a physical link to its corresponding *SUPPLIER* record.

As previously stressed, navigational DBMSs permit the formulation of one-record-at-a-time queries. That is, if you wish to find out how many orders for desks the *SUPPLIER* Jones has already had, you are forced to write a small application program to retrieve the corresponding records. This program includes a loop of repeated commands to the database to retrieve a single record at a time. To illustrate how these commands execute, let us construct a sample application program that prints the total number of desks supplied by Jones. Note that in the following sample application program constructs such as *Supplier.name* or *Product.name* are called *qualified field* names. A qualified field name consists of the name of a data record, e.g. *SUPPLIER*, and a field part in that record separated by a period.

Note that the next sample program refers to a database that contains information about suppliers and products. This database contains two types of record, *SUPPLIER* and *PRODUCT*, each including several data fields (see Figure 1.8). The occurrences of these record types are grouped together into a set type called *SUPPLY*. The *set type* is the primary distinguishing feature of a navigational data structure. Each set type in a navigational schema is defined to have a certain record type as its *owner* and some other record type as its *member*. For example, the set type *SUPPLY* may be defined with the record type *SUPPLIER* designated as its owner and the record type *PRODUCT* designated as its member. Consequently, a set type occurrence is an instance of all the physically linked records in a navigational-set.

```
sum := 0;
find any Supplier using "Jones";
find first Product within Supply;
while not end of linked list do
begin
      get Product;
      if Product.name == "desk"
          sum := sum + 1;
      find next Product within Supply;
end
print(sum);
```

The set type SUPPLY for the above sample program may be defined as follows:

```
set name is Supply;
owner is Supplier;
member is Product;
```

A *set type occurrence* consists of precisely one occurrence of its owner record type together with zero or more than one occurrences of its member record type. The zero occurrence would arise if, for example, some supplier currently supplies no products. For example, in Figure 1.8 we have a *SUPPLY* set occurrence which includes only one owner (supplier Jones) and four members.

The non-navigational DBMS

The other broad category of DBMS is called non-navigational or automatic navigation DBMS. Relational DBMSs are typical examples of this latter category. Non-navigational DBMSs do not use multilist file organizations and do not store record pointers to related records. Rather, they rely on efficient methods for the processing of queries when fields in one data record have to be matched against fields in another data record.

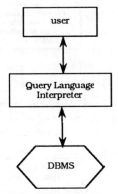

Figure 1.9 Interaction with the DBMS via the use of a query language.

In the following we show, for demonstration purposes only, how the previous navigational query can be expressed in terms of a relational (non-navigational) database product.

count (**join** supplier **on** prod_id **with** product **on** prod_id **where**
      supplier.name = "Jones" **and** product.name = "desk");

Note that this non-procedural query does not instruct the DBMS which data record to fetch first and which to fetch next. Therefore, such queries which manipulate a set of records are said to be non-procedural or non-navigational, because they do not explicitly give the DBMS a procedure to follow.

1.5.4   Query execution within the DBMS

In the preceding sections we introduced basic concepts and terminology related to database management systems. In this section we give a concrete picture of how the DBMS is related to other parts of system software.

The main method for user interaction with the DBMS, as adopted by the system developed in this book, is shown in Figure 1.9. The user can issue various query language statements supported by the DBMS. These statements are processed by the query language interpreter which calls the appropriate DBMS procedures to perform the requested operations. Actually, not all relational systems are interpretive, a small number of them are compiling systems, e.g. the products SQL/DL and DB2. Such compiling systems guarantee that all user statements are compiled prior to execution time into appropriate machine code instructions [18], [19]. However, they are much more difficult to implement than interpretive systems.

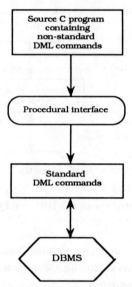

Figure 1.10 Interaction with the DBMS via nonstandard DML procedures.

In addition to providing a query language, REQUIEM (the relational database system whose design and implementation will be fully described throughout this book), like most modern DBMSs, offers to users the option to write application programs in a general purpose programming language. In the case of REQUIEM it is the C programming language. These application programs use predefined REQUIEM DML procedures which achieve communication with the DBMS and consequently with the database contents. To the user the DML procedures appear to be merely an extension of the standard system libraries. Most of these DML procedures are exactly the same as the ones supporting the query language; however, there are some additional DML procedures which eventually have to be mapped into C statements that call the standard DBMS procedures. The modified source program is then compiled in the conventional way, see Figure 1.10. Thus, REQUIEM does not support an *embedded sublanguage*, but provides the user with a full *programmable procedural interface*. Accordingly, all of the customized user interface is written by utilizing predefined C procedures. More information on this topic can be found in Chapter 14 which covers the REQUIEM programming interface.

Each of the above approaches has its merits. With a query language it is possible to obtain results much more quickly because there is no need to write and debug programs. However, the query language has built-in limitations, as it is quite difficult to perform functions for which the language was not defined, such as arithmetic manipulations. On the other hand, although a DML programming interface allows the user to utilize all the power and the flexibility offered by the general purpose programming language, it requires much more effort and understanding from the user. More details and examples of DMLs and their use can be found in [3], [19].

At this stage we would like to state that some systems do not support a procedural interface, but rather provide an embedded sublanguage which requires the services of a preprocessor. Thus, the label "procedural interface," depicted in Figure 1.10, should be replaced by that of a preprocessor. To clarify all these issues we append an example from a well-known system, INGRES [1], that supports an embedded sublanguage.

The query language supported by INGRES is called QUEL, while the customized user interface is provided by embedded QUEL (EQUEL). EQUEL consists of the QUEL embedded in the C programming language. Any EQUEL statements are preprocessed into an equivalent QUEL statement as long as they are prefixed by $\#\#$ signs. C program variables are also prefixed by $\#\#$ signs and can be used anywhere in QUEL statements (of course, they cannot stand in for command names). The following example was taken from [1] and performs one query: it reads in the name of an employee and prints out his name and his salary in the specified format.

```
main() {
  ##char EMPLOYEE_NAME[20];
  ##int PAYMENT;

  while (READ(EMPLOYEE_NAME)) {
    ## RANGE OF E IS EMPLOYEE
    ## RETRIEVE(PAYMENT = E.SALARY)
    ## WHERE E.NAME = EMPLOYEE_NAME
      ##{
      PRINT(''The salary of '' , EMPLOYEE_NAME, ''is'', PAYMENT);
      ##}
  }
}
```

In this example EMPLOYEE is a relation defined as

$$\text{EMPLOYEE (NAME, DEPT, SALARY, AGE)}$$

and E is a record variable that spans the table *EMPLOYEE*. The outcome of this query is the set of all records in the table that satisfy the qualification *E.NAME = EMPLOYEE_NAME* (a user-specified name).

The sequences of operations performed by the DBMS in processing a query and a DML request are essentially the same. The DBMS must be able to interpret the instruction statements in terms of the external schema, map these into equivalent statements in terms of the conceptual schema, and finally map the conceptual schema statements into physical database statements. This sequence of actions is shown in Figure 1.11 using three major building blocks:

1. The DBMS internals which guarantee efficient operating conditions on behalf of the database.
2. The operating system which supports the DBMS.
3. The different database schemas.

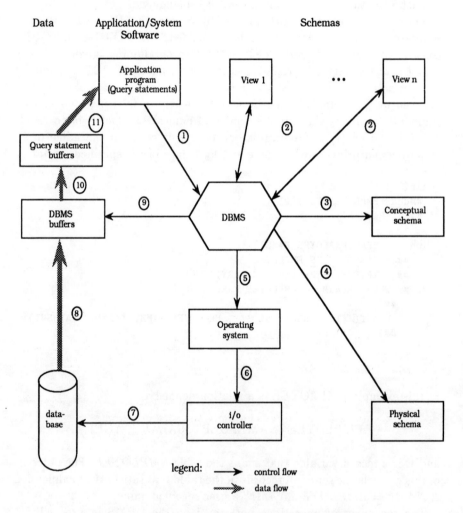

Figure 1.11 Sequence of actions performed by a DBMS.

Referring to Figure 1.11 we suppose that a query (or application program) has initiated a request to read data from the database. This **read** statement has to be forwarded to the DBMS (step 1). To process this statement, the DBMS must first associate it with an existent subschema and verify the validity of the statement (step 2), then the DBMS maps the subschema into its corresponding conceptual schema and determines the type of logical records to be fetched (step 3); subsequently the DBMS consults the physical schema to determine which physical records are required and marks the location of these records in the database files (step 4). At this stage the DBMS has transformed a logical request for a subschema record into physical requests to read data from one or more files. These requests are then forwarded to the operating system (step 5). The operating system examines the i/o requests by consulting the various parameters of the physical schema, e.g. record length and record location, and transmits the order to the i/o controller that manages the storage devices of the system (step 6). The i/o operations corresponding to the i/o requests transfer the required data into the DBMS buffer area (steps 7 and 8). Incidentally, here the thick gray arrows represent the flow of data, while all solid line arrows represent flow of control. Subsequently, the DBMS selects from its buffers the data required by the initial query, executes the necessary transformations using the conceptual-external schema mappings and then places the data into the query statement buffers (steps 8 and 9). Finally, if everything goes according to plan, the user receives the answer corresponding to his request, otherwise the DBMS informs the user what was wrong with his query in case of a syntactically or semantically ill-defined query.

1.5.5   Overall structure of the DBMS

The DBMS is partitioned into several software components (modules), each of which is assigned a specific operation. As stated previously, some of the functions of the DBMS are supported by its underlying operating system. However, the operating system provides only rudimentary services and the DBMS must be built on top of it. Thus, the design of a DBMS must take into account the interface between the DBMS and the operating system.

The major software components in a DBMS environment are depicted in Figure 1.12. This diagram shows how the DBMS interfaces with other software components such as user queries and access methods (file management techniques for storing and retrieving data records). For a detailed coverage of access methods and their performance see [20], [21].

1. *Query decomposer.* This is a major DBMS operating component which transforms queries into a series of low-level instructions directed to the database control manager.

2. *Database control manager (DCM)*. The DCM is a module that interfaces with user-submitted application programs and queries. The DCM accepts queries, or calls for data, and examines the external and conceptual schemas to determine what conceptual records are required to satisfy the request. The DCM then places a call to the file manager to fill the request.

3. *File manager*. The file manager manipulates the underlying storage files and manages the allocation of storage space on the disk. It establishes and maintains the list of structures and indices defined in the storage schema. If hashed files are used it calls on the hashing procedures to generate record addresses. However, the file manager does not directly manage the physical input and output of data. Rather it passes the requests on to the appropriate access methods, which either read data from or write data into the system buffer.

4. *DML preprocessor*. This module converts nonstandard DML statements embedded in an application program into standard procedure calls in the host language. The DML preprocessor must interact with the query decomposer in order to generate the appropriate code.

5. *DDL interpreter*. The DDL compiler converts DDL statements into a set of tables containing meta-data. These tables are then stored in the catalogs while vital information is also stored in data file headers.

In addition to the above modules several other data structures are required as part of the physical level implementation. These structures include data and index files and the data catalogs. Recently, an attempt has been made towards the standardization of database mangement systems and a reference model has been proposed by the Database Architecture Framework Task Group (DAFTG) [22]. The purpose of this reference model is to define a conceptual framework aiming to divide standardization attempts into manageable pieces and to show at a very broad level how these pieces could be interrelated.

1.6 The concept of data independence

As shown in Figure 1.1 there are mappings between each of the various levels of the data model. The DBMS provides the mappings between the user views and the conceptual schema. It also provides the mappings between the conceptual schema and the physical schema. These mappings guarantee the translation of a user request for logical data into corresponding requests for physical data. Consequently, we distinguish between two levels of data independence.

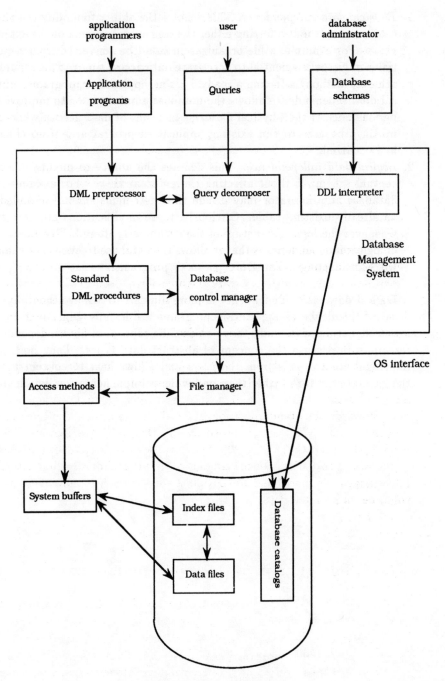

Figure 1.12 The DBMS environment.

1. *Physical data independence.* This denotes the ability to modify the physical schema without affecting either the conceptual schema or the external views. For example, a file organization could be converted from sequential into virtual sequential to accelerate data access times. This should be achieved without affecting already existing application programs. Physical data independence allows the database administrator to improve the performance of the physical database in terms of data access, while permitting the user to run existing application programs as if no changes had occurred.

2. *Logical data independence.* This denotes the ability to modify the conceptual schema without affecting the external views. For example, the database administrator may decide that new fields should be added to an already existing table. Obviously, these modifications are necessary whenever the logical structure of the database is altered. The advantage of logical independence is that it allows the database to evolve, or change, without affecting existing user views or programs.

Logical database independence is more difficult to achieve than physical data independence as application programs are heavily dependent on the logical structure of the data they access. The concept of data independence resembles in a sense the concept of abstract data types. They both hide implementation details from the users and allow them to concentrate on the general structure rather than on low-level implementation details [5].

2

The Relational Approach to Databases

The aim of this chapter is to present the reader with a brief and rather informal overview of the theory which underlies the relational data model and relational database systems. REQUIEM's query language, RQL, will be used throughout this chapter as a vehicle for illustrative purposes. RQL like most other current relational products, e.g. SQL/DL, EQUEL, and SQL Plus, does not provide full support for the complete range of the relational data model as proposed by E.F.Codd [23]. Nevertheless, REQUIEM could easily be regarded as a fairly representative example of relational systems as currently implemented.

2.1   The relational data model revisited

From a historical perspective, the relational model was first defined in 1970 when E.F.Codd introduced the idea of using the mathematical concept of relations (in set theory) as the means to model data. However, it took quite a while before the first fully supported relational database systems appeared on the market. Indicative is the fact that SQL/DS, IBM's first fully supported relational DBMS, was actually announced in January 1981 [24], although experimentation at IBM had been taking place since the early 1970s with the PRTV (Peterlee Relational Test Vehicle) system.

In the relational model, data is viewed as a collection of non-hierarchical time-varying relations. Under this perspective the relational database model enables the utilization of the powerful operations of an algebraic expression language, the relational algebra, or the extension of this formal language toward data querying and manipulation. In this data model relational algebra can be used to decompose a complex logical structure into a collection of simple relations so that complex requests can perform accessing and updating of data in a relatively simple, yet effective, manner. The relational model provides attractive features which are not supported by the conventional navigational models such as the hierarchical or the network data models. These features include the following:

1. High-level query languages: These languages are closer to natural languages and have been developed specifically to access the data held in relational databases. Such query languages are highly non-procedural, in contrast to the hierarchical (IMS DL/1) or network (CODASYL) navigational languages which are extremely procedural. Relational query languages operate in terms of sets of records, rather than on one record at a time.
2. Implementation independence: The aim of the relational model is to represent logically all relationships, and hence alleviate the user from physical implementation details. This means that the user does not have to concern himself with how the various inter-record relationships are implemented, and which access paths are employed in the internal level. Implementation independence is frequently referred to in the literature as *data independence.*
3. Simplicity: To a large extent, simplicity can be attributed to the relational model and may be considered as one of the prime reasons for the justification of the relational approach. This simplicity can be attributed to the fact that not only does this model support a highly abstract view of data but also major functional decisions are left to the DBMS and not to the user.

In the following we will concern ourselves with three aspects of the relational model, namely with its structural, its manipulative, and its integrity parts. All these aspects will be examined in turn by using RQL. Those who are interested in understanding the features and the internals of the hierarchical and/or network data models may refer to [3] or [19].

2.2   The structure of a relational database

A relational database can be perceived by the user as a collection of tables, each of which is assigned a unique name. Tables constitute the logical and certainly not the physical data structure part of a relational database. This implies that at the internal level the system is free to utilize any of the traditional techniques (sequential files, indexing, inverted files, etc.), provided that it is capable of mapping those structures into table constructs at the logical level. Each table consists of a *table header* and a *table body*. The table header consists of a fixed set of columns which are usually referred to as *attributes*. On the other hand, the body of a table consists of a time-varying set of rows called *tuples*. There is a close correspondence between the notion of a table and that of the mathematical concept of relation from which the relational database has taken its name. For reasons of convenience, in this book we shall treat the terms "table" and "relation" as if they were synonymous.

Example 2.2.1

To put the whole idea into perspective, consider the relation SUPPLIER of the suppliers-and-products database as depicted in Figure 2.1.

The header of the relation *SUPPLIER* consists of the three attributes *SUP_ID#*, *SUP_NAME*, and *LOCATION*. Similarly, the relation *PRODUCT* contains, for each product, a product number (*PROD_NO#*), a product name (*PROD_NAME*), a weight (*WEIGHT*), and the product finish (*FINISH*). At one point in time the body of the relation *SUPPLIER* consists of four rows or tuples.

Each of these tuples consists of the values of the three attributes in the table header. There corresponds exactly one such attribute value for each of the three attributes contained in the header of the relation *SUPPLIER*. For example, consider the *SUPPLIER* tuple with the identification number 605. This can be represented as follows:

$< 605, Jones, London >$

From what has been mentioned so far, one can certainly understand that the smallest unit of data supported by the relational data model is that of the individual data value. Such data values are *atomic* in the sense that they cannot be further decomposed as far as the model is concerned.

An attribute draws its eligible values from a reservoir of data values, which actually comprises its corresponding *domain*. It must be understood that domains are essentially conceptual in nature. This implies that domains are not stored in the database as actual sets of values. However, "they should be specified as an integral part of the database definition; and then each attribute definition should include a reference to the corresponding domain" [19].

Finally, the number of attributes in the relation header specifies the *degree* of the corresponding relation, while the number of the included tuples in the

SUPPLIER

SUP_ID#	SUP_NAME	LOCATION
605	Jones	London
612	Schmidt	Zurich
827	Dupont	Paris
855	Dick	Bonn

PRODUCT

PROD_NO#	PROD_NAME	WEIGHT	FINISH
10	desk	150	pine
12	bookcase	100	cherry
21	cabinet	80	oak
25	sofa	20	oak
33	dresser	90	pine

SUPPLY

SUP_ID#	PROD_NO#	QUANTITY
605	21	150
612	10	200
827	12	120
855	25	135
605	33	100

Figure 2.1 The suppliers-and-products database.

body specifies its *cardinality*. Consequently, in the suppliers-and-products database, relations *SUPPLIER* and *SUPPLY* are of degree three, while relation *PRODUCT* is of degree four. Thus, we sometimes refer to Codd's relational model as the *n-ary* relational model.

One important fact to notice is that the degree of a relation is normally of static nature, while its cardinality is of dynamic nature since the number of tuples included in a relation tends to vary gradually as a function of time.

In conclusion, we draw attention to some relation properties which are of vast importance to the material that follows:

1. Individual data values are atomic: All attribute values are non-decomposable, meaning that if any arbitrary numerical or character string value were to be decomposed into smaller fractions then it would certainly

change its substance, and hence lose its meaning.

2. Values corresponding to distinct attributes are homogeneous in nature: This property implies simply that all attribute values belonging to a specific domain are the same type. For example, this means that we cannot freely intermix character strings with numerical values and assign them as values to a specific attribute.

3. All tuples in a relation are distinct: A relation should never contain identical tuples.

4. The ordering of tuples in a relation body is immaterial; that is, tuples can be interchanged without affecting the information content of the relation.

5. The order of attribute names in a relation header is immaterial.

We close this section by defining what a relational system actually is. Briefly, a *relational system* is a system in which:

(a) The data is perceived by the users in a table format; and

(b) The operators at the users' disposal are operators which normally accept one or more relations as input and generate new tables from the old. Actually this is an attractive property known as the property of *closure* [19]. This means that given one or more correctly defined relations, applications of the various relational operations on them will always result in correctly defined relations.

For example, there will be an operator which will extract the subset of tuples in a given relation, and another to extract the subset of the attributes in a relation header. Obviously, a tuple and attribute subset of a relation are both contained in the relations themselves. Consequently, when we speak about a relational system in this context, we mean, loosely speaking, that the system in question has been developed in accordance with the major principles of the relational data model.

However, it must be noted that some systems claim to be relational by supporting table-like formats but not any of the relational operators **select**, **project**, and **join** (explicitly or implicitly) in any form. Such systems do not qualify as relational systems; nor does a system that allows the user to select (retrieve) records on the basis of some attribute only if that attribute is indexed [18]. This is common practice if the system requires predefinition of some particular structure to perform a select or retrieve operation. It is obvious that such systems completely lack the notion of data independence.

2.3   Data manipulation in relational databases

There are two classes of special purpose relational formal data manipulation languages which characterize most available methods for processing relational databases. These are the *relational algebra* and the *relational calculus*. Although some relational database mangement systems allow the use of programs written in procedural languages to access a relational database, the common practice is to utilize elements of one or even both of those high-level special purpose data manipulation languages. These languages are basically self-contained in the sense that they provide a wide variety of data retrieval and data maintenance operations. Furthermore, they comprise set-oriented languages in which all tuples, possibly emanating from several relations, are processed in a single language statement without the explicit use of iterational constructs. These two languages are "pure" in the sense that they lack the syntactic sugar of commercial query languages.

The term "relational algebra" is used to denote the manipulative part of the relational data model, and consists of a set of eight fundamental operators. Each of these operators takes either one or two relations as its operands and produces a new relation as its result. The relational algebra operators were originally defined by E.F.Codd and were first presented in [23]. The operators are classified into two groups, each of which contains four such operators:

1. The special relational operators **select**, **project**, **join**, and **divide**.
2. The traditional set operators **union**, **intersection**, **difference**, and **cartesian product** (cross-product).

Languages realized on the basis of relational calculus manipulate relations implicitly by specifying predicates that may involve attributes from several relations, which should be satisfied by a desired set of tuples. Relational calculus normally combines the special relational operations **select**, **project**, and **join** into one operation called **retrieve**. It also introduces the **where** predicate clause to specify the interrelation associations used for implicitly joining relations in the retrieve operation. There are currently two different but related forms of relational calculus, one in which the relational variables represent tuples [23], and one in which the relational variables represent values drawn from a particular domain [25]. These variants are called the *tuple relational calculus* and the *domain relational calculus* respectively. For example, QUEL, the query language for the INGRES database system, is based on the tuple relational calculus, while the QBE (query by example) database system offers a query language that is based on the domain relational calculus.

2.3.1 The relational operators

Retrieval statements in relational algebra are generally effected by the specification of a sequence of operations. In this sense the relational algebra is essentially a procedural or navigational retrieval language. However, operations in relational algebra are very high level, and much could be accomplished in a single operation. Furthermore, it is possible to nest a sequence of relational algebraic expressions into a single expression that gives the language a non-procedural substance, i.e. a *closed* algebra. As mentioned previously, in relational algebra we employ both the traditional mathematical set operations and the relational operations.

Four principal relational operations exist: **select, project, join,** and **divide.** The **select** and **project** operations take one operand and therefore are called *unary relational operations.* The other two operations require a pair of operands and are therefore called *binary relational operations.* We shall illustrate these operations in terms of relations from the suppliers-and-products database.

Select
The selection operation is the simplest operation on relations. It effectively reduces the numbers of tuples in a relation by deleting from it all the tuples that do not satisfy the selection condition. We denote the selection operation by

select from < *relation* > **where** < *predicate* > ;

Here the construct < *relation* > is the name of a given relation or even the result of another relational expression, as we shall see later in this book. In a selection operation the selection condition, also known as *predicate,* can contain comparisons between specific attribute values and other attribute values in the same tuple, or comparisons between specific attribute values and constants like numeric values or character strings. Only those rows (tuples) satisfying the predicate are kept. The selection conditions can include any of the comparison operators =, >, ≥, <, ≤, and ≠ and the logical operators **and** (&), **or** (|), and **not** (~). From that already mentioned, it follows that a selection expression yields a horizontal subset of a given relation.

Example 2.3.1

Select all those tuples from relation PRODUCT where the products have an oak finish.

This query can be formulated as follows:

select from product **where** finish = "oak";

Result:

PRODUCT_NO#	PROD_NAME	WEIGHT	FINISH
21	cabinet	80	oak
25	sofa	20	oak

Here, the relation *PRODUCT* is the operand, **select** is the operator, and the illustrated relation is the result of the query. Obviously *PRODUCT* is the name of the relation on which the selection operation will be applied. The value "oak" is enclosed by double quotes because it is a character string constant that represents the desired literal value for the attribute *FINISH*. The construct *FINISH* is not enclosed in quotes because it is an attribute name of the relation *PRODUCT*. In general, characters and character strings that are literal values must be enclosed in quotes to distinguish them from attribute names or numeric values (which must not be enclosed within quotes). A numeric value must not be enclosed between quotes, in general, unless it is being regarded as a string character.

We may enclose any valid logical expression in the predicate following the operand expression as previously explained; parentheses may also be used to indicate the desired order of evaluation. Consider the following example.

Example 2.3.2

Select all those tuples from the PRODUCT relation where the products have an oak finish and a weight heavier than 50.

select from product **where** finish = "oak" & weight > 50;

By specifying a logical operation in the predicate we restrict the output of the select command to just those tuples of the relation *PRODUCT* that satisfy the predicate that follows the **where** clause.

Incidentally, we could formulate the previous query by using *qualified attribute names* throughout, as follows:

select from product
    where product.finish = "oak" & product.weight > 50;

A qualified attribute name consists of a relation name separated by a period from an attribute name that is part of the specified relation. Although in the previous example it was not necessary to use qualified attribute names, it may sometimes be essential.

Project

The relational operation **project** allows columns in a relation to be masked. The projection operation yields a vertical subset of a given relation, that is, it yields that subset obtained by masking specified attributes and then eliminating any resulting redundant duplicate tuples within the selected attributes. The projection operation accepts a single relation name as operand that is denoted by the symbol *<relation>*. Actually, *<relation>* can be either the name of a given relation or the result of a relational expression. We shall denote the projection operation by:

project *<relation>* **over** *<attribute–list>* **where** *<predicate>* ;

All the names in the list of attributes that follows the keyword **over** must be attributes of the projected relation. The result of the projection operation can result in a decrease in the number of tuples and is obtained by the following:

1. Removing from the relation all attributes that are not included in the list of attribute names.
2. Removing from the result of (1) all duplicate tuples and, thus, effectively reducing the number of tuples in the resultant relation so that no two tuples are identical.

Example 2.3.3

Find product names and their corresponding weights from relation PRODUCT.

This query can be formulated as follows:

project product **over** product_name, weight;

Result:

PROD_NAME	WEIGHT
desk	150
bookcase	100
cabinet	80
sofa	20
dresser	90

The result of this query is a relation formulated by obtaining the subset of the relation *PRODUCT* by selecting the designated attributes *PRODUCT_NAME* and *WEIGHT* in the specified order. Obviously, a projection operation provides us with the means of reordering the attributes of a given relation when desired since with it we ascribe significance to the order of tuples within a relation.

By applying a projection operation to the result of a selection operation we can extract information from a relation to answer a very simple yet practical query, such as the one shown in the following example.

Example 2.3.4

Find the names and weights of these products which have an oak finish.

This query can be formulated as follows:

project (select from product **where** finish = "oak")
       over product_name, weight;

Result:

PROD_NAME	WEIGHT
cabinet	80
sofa	20

Actually the previous query consists of two parts: *select* and *project*. First we form a new relation by taking a horizontal subset of the relation *PRODUCT*, that is, we assemble all the tuples that satisfy the finish = "oak" predicate and then we form a vertical subset of this relation by extracting the specified attributes *PRODUCT_NAME* and *WEIGHT*.

Join

The relational operation **join** is a dyadic operation which accepts two relations as operands and forms a new, wider, relation by concatenating each tuple of the first relation with every tuple from the second relation that has the same value in a common attribute called the *join attribute*. Normally, the join attribute is shown only once in the result relation. If the relations have some attributes in common, the **join** operation produces as its result a relation with all the names of the first relation together with any extra attributes from the second. Tuples are selected from the first relation, and extra values are concatenated from these tuples in the second relation which have matching values in their common attributes. This form of **join** that forces all redundant (duplicate) attributes to be eliminated is called a *natural join*.

Example 2.3.5

Find for all suppliers the products that they supply and the quantities they have in stock.

This query can be formulated as follows:

join supplier **on** sup_id **with** supply **on** sup_id;

Result:

SUP_ID#	SUP_NAME	LOCATION	PROD_NO	QUANTITY
605	Jones	London	21	150
605	Jones	London	33	100
612	Schmidt	Zurich	10	200
827	Dupont	Paris	12	120
855	Dick	Bonn	25	135

Notice that this query implies that the tuples of the two relations *SUPPLIER* and *SUPPLY* should be compared on their common attribute *SUP_ID*. Actually, the condition which is implied here is *supplier.sup_id = supply.sup_id*. This condition is said to be a *join condition* or *join predicate*, and the attributes *supplier.sup_id*, and *product.sup_id* are said to be the *join condition attributes*. Since the comparison operation in the join predicate is equality, this kind of join is sometimes explicitly referred to as *equijoin*.

To understand how the previous query works, consider any two tuples from each of the relations *SUPPLIER* and *SUPPLY*, respectively, as depicted in Figure 2.1 – say the following two tuples:

SUP_ID#	SUP_NAME	LOCATION
605	Jones	London

SUP_ID#	PROD_NO#	QUANTITY
605	21	150

These two tuples can be concatenated as the value of their **join** attribute coincides. Therefore, they generate the following wider tuple:

SUP_ID#	SUP_NAME	LOCATION	PROD_NO	QUANTITY
605	Jones	London	21	150

since they satisfy the **join** predicate in the **join** statement. Actually, there is no requirement for the comparison operator in a **join** predicate to be equality, though it very often will be the case. Actually, we could as well define a *greater-than join*, or a *less-than join*. However, the relational data manipulation language that we will examine in the next chapter considers only equijoin operations. In any case, it must be noted that all valid **join** operations should draw the values for their **join** attributes from the same domain, in which case they are said to be *join compatible*.

In the previous example the relations *SUPPLIER* and *SUPPLY* are literally joined on their common attribute *SUP_ID*. Observe that one of the two common attributes has been eliminated in the final result: such a **join** operator is normally called the *natural join* [3] and is the only **join** operator supported in RQL.

Division

The division operator in its simplest form divides a relation of degree two (the dividend) by a relation of degree one (the divisor) and produces a result relation (the quotient) of degree one. The quotient consists of all values of an attribute of the dividend that match all the values in the divisor relation.

In the following example the dividend relation, say $R1$, has the two attributes *SUP_ID* and *PROD_NO*, while the divisor relation, say $R2$, has the attribute *PROD_NO*, where the attributes $R1.PROD\_NO$ and $R2.PROD\_NO$ are defined on the same domain. The division of $R1$ by $R2$ is a relation, say $R3$ (the quotient), with sole attribute *SUP_ID*, such that every value a (e.g. the value 605) of $R3.SUP\_ID$ appears as a value of $R1.SUP\_ID$, and the pair of values $< a, b >$ appears in $R1$ for *all* values b (e.g. the values 10 and 12) appearing in $R2$.

Example 2.3.6

Find the supplier identification number for all suppliers who supply the products 21 and 33.

Result:

SUP_ID#	PROD_NO
605	21
605	33
612	10
827	12
855	25

÷

PROD_NO
21
33

= 605

Division is the only *derived relational operation* that is not directly supported by REQUIEM. The other two derived operations are **join** and **intersection**. These derived operations can be expressed in terms of the five *primitive* operations **select, project, union, difference,** and **cartesian product.**

2.3.2   The set operators

Each of the traditional set operations takes two operands. For all except the **cartesian product** the operand relations must satisfy the following conditions:

1. The two operands (relations) must contain the same number of attributes, i.e. both relations have the same degree.
2. The domains of the *ith* attribute of each relation must be the same, although attribute names do not necessarily have to be the same.

Relations satisfying the above conditions are said to be *union-compatible* [3]. In the following we shall discuss only the set operations that are supported by RQL, namely **union, intersect,** and **difference.**

Union and intersection

The *union* of two union compatible relations R and S is a new relation consisting of the set of all tuples t belonging to either relation R or relation S or both. Any duplicate tuples appear only once in the resulting relation. On the other hand, the *intersection* of the former two relations R and S is a new relation consisting of the set of all tuples that are common to R and S. Evidently all tuples in the result of a union or intersection have exactly the same number of attributes, i.e. the resultant relation is of the same degree, with the relation from which they originate. Figure 2.3 depicts the union and the intersection of the two relations that are shown in Figure 2.2.

SUPPLIER	LOCATION
Jones	London
Schmidt	Bonn
Henry	Paris
Bradley	New York

SUPPLIER	LOCATION
Jones	London
Black	Edinburgh
Henry	Paris

Figure 2.2 Two SUPPLIER–LOCATION relations, R and S.

SUPPLIER	LOCATION
Jones	London
Schmidt	Bonn
Henry	Paris
Bradley	New York
Black	Edinburgh

SUPPLIER	LOCATION
Jones	London
Henry	Paris

Figure 2.3 Union and intersection of the relations R and S.

Difference

The difference between two union-compatible relations R and S is a new relation consisting of the set of all tuples t belonging to R but not to S. For example the difference between the above relations R and S of Figure 2.2 is depicted in Figure 2.4.

SUPPLIER	LOCATION
Schmidt	Bonn
Bradley	New York

Figure 2.4 The difference between the relations R and S.

2.4   Relational data integrity

To be of any use the information stored in the database must be consistent, meaning that it should conform to the real world entities that it is supposed to represent. Thus we require a collection of integrity rules which restrain the valid sets of database instances. Since a database relation stems directly from the mathematical notion of a set relation, and sets by definition contain no duplicate elements, it follows that no duplicate tuples should be permitted in a given relation. The fact that duplicate tuples are not permitted in a relation implies that a given relation should have a single key as its principal means of identification. This key is in fact called the primary key of that relation.

Primary keys are of great importance since they provide the sole means of identifying a given relation tuple. Characteristically C.J.Date mentions in [19] that primary keys provide the "sole tuple-level addressing mechanism within the database." Thus the combination of a relation's name and its primary key is sufficient to guarantee the accessing of some individual tuple within that relation. As primary keys have a special meaning for relations, they must differ from the other keys in the operations that can be performed on them; for example, they should never obtain a *null value* [26]. A null value is a special value that is used to represent an unknown or inapplicable value. It is certainly not the same as a numeric zero or blank string, which are often valid attribute values.

Besides relations which correspond to entities in the real world, a database normally contains *relationship relations* which are used to relate the former types of relations. Relationship relations contain tuples with attributes that are the primary keys of other relations; e.g. the relationship relation *SUPPLY* where the attribute *SUP_ID* occurs as the primary key of the relation *SUPPLIER*, as in Figure 2.1. A *foreign key* is an attribute in a relationship relation which at the same time is the primary key of another relation.

In general, a foreign key in a relation is an attribute serving as a reference mechanism to another relation. Thus, by making the foreign keys in a relation explicit we illustrate that this specific relation is associated with another relation via the contents of its foreign keys.

A relational DBMS must offer users the possibility of defining primary keys in terms of attributes that uniquely identify a relation. In SQL for example this is done via the statement **create unique index**, while in RQL it is accomplished during the definition phase of a relation (for more information refer to the next chapter). Consequently, during the creation phase of each additional tuple the DBMS must verify that the primary key does not already exist. Moreover, the DBMS must make sure that these primary keys never obtain undefined values, i.e. null values, since this would result in the violation of the primary key uniqueness property.

The foregoing discussion leads to the formulation of two general data integrity rules for the relational model. These rules are general in the sense that any database system that conforms to the relational model is required to obey them. Additionally, each individual database system may have a set of additional integrity rules that are specific to it alone. The two general relational integrity rules are as follows:

1. **Entity integrity:** No attribute participating in the primary key of a base relation (not a derived relation, such as a view) is allowed to accept null values.

2. **Referential integrity:** If a base relation R_1, e.g. *SUPPLY* in Figure 2.1, includes a foreign key F_k, e.g. *SUP_ID*, matching the primary key P_k, e.g. *SUP_ID*, of some other base relation R_2, e.g. *SUPPLIER*, then every value of F_k, e.g. 605, 612, 827 in R_1 must be equal to the value of the primary key P_k in some tuple of R_2. This means that any reference from a relationship relation to a tuple of another relation must be made in terms of an existing tuple of the referenced relation.

There are two important points to note as far as referential integrity is concerned. First, the fact that R_1 includes the foreign key F_k does not necessarily mean that F_k is part of R_1's primary key (if we consider R_1's primary key to be a multi-attribute key). In general, referential constraints arise whenever one relation includes references to another. Consider for example the university database as depicted in Figure 1.6. Here, we assume that each *STAFF_MEMBER* relation includes references via its *FACULTY#* attribute to some FACULTY relation. The referential constraint in this example would typically be that every value of the *FACULTY#* attribute appearing in the *STAFF_MEMBER* relation must occur as some value of the *FACULTY#* attribute appearing in some tuple of the FACULTY relation. Needless to say, the attribute *STAFF_MEMBER.FACULTY#* is not part of the primary key of the relation *STAFF_MEMBER*.

Second, the referential integrity rule as defined above is slightly different from the original rule defined by C.J.Date in [27]. In this reference C.J.Date allows foreign keys in some relations to obtain null values. However, this viewpoint does not apply to RQL, since it does not support null values.

We will not discuss the justification for entity integrity and referential integrity any further. It suffices to say that REQUIEM supports both of them; we rather direct any readers interested in more information to consider the two excellent articles [27] and [28].

3

An Overview of the
REQUIEM Data Language

The aim of this chapter is to provide an extended coverage to some of the major facilities of the REQUIEM data language. More specifically we will be concerned with the three aspects of the data language, namely the data definition, the data manipulation, and the data integrity facilities. We first discuss the general features of the data language as seen at the user level and then elaborate on several important implementation issues.

3.1 REQUIEM and the RQL framework

In principle, there are some fairly stringent requirements associated with the functionality of small or medium scale database systems. They must meet the diverse needs of the business community and at the same time offer user-friendly facilities. Database management systems should satisfy the needs of a large spectrum of users in such a way as to permit them to express their problems and queries in the most natural manner.

These points imply that database systems should offer the users a powerful, yet simple, data model to use as the basis for the specification of their conceptual requirements. In the previous chapters we have explained how such facilities are provided by database systems based on the relational model. The general idea is that the DBMS should make the user feel comfortable. This means that the users should ideally perceive the way the query language allows them to formulate requests both as adequate and satisfactory. In this sense, it would be highly desirable to have a choice of open-ended query interfaces and some means of easily providing some novel ones.

Obviously, DBMSs that offer a set of modules in the form of database function specifications that permit the development of customized query language interfaces to the system are highly desirable. Such DBMSs are termed *extensible DBMSs* [29]. An extensible DBMS hopefully offers a powerful and efficient system kernel that allows for extensions by customizing its basic functions on the uppermost level. This means that such an extensible DBMS should be designed to be "query language independent" in order to provide mechanisms for language designers to design experimental query languages without the need for the intricate file access and manipulation code that constitutes the file manager component of the DBMS. This chapter describes the query language of such an extensible relational database management system, called REQUIEM. It also describes how conceptual (user) level issues can be mapped to implementation level issues.

The name REQUIEM is an acronym standing for "RElational Query and Update Interactive SystEM". As it name suggests REQUIEM is an interactive system with facilities for querying and updating a database. REQUIEM is in fact a relational database system implemented on the Unix* operating system and currently runs on Sun computers under Sun-OS 3.4. REQUIEM is primarily a prototype developed as a single user system to demonstrate the feasibility of supporting a fullyfledged relational query language called RQL. However, the system provides an open-ended structure in that it can be easily extended to incorporate multi-user mechanisms.

REQUIEM offers a complete query language interpreter which consists of a set of special purpose modules written in C. The query language interpreter provides its own tools for lexicographical analysis and parsing. The REQUIEM parser employs incremental parsing techniques and is a complex module which consists of roughly 2,300 lines of C source code. The lexical analyzer is also a highly specialized tool as it performs, amongst others, view checking and expansion, and comprises 750 lines of C code. The entire REQUIEM implementation consists of just over 10,000 lines of code and occupies 140 kbytes on disk.

The fact that REQUIEM does not rely on the assistance of such language development tools as *yacc* or *lex* [30] implies, that REQUIEM and RQL can, with reasonable effort, be ported to non-Unix environments supporting C. For example, REQUIEM has been successfully ported to the Apple Macintosh (using the Lightspeed C compiler). In sum, our ambition is to provide users with a DBMS and a query language portable to a variety of small to medium scale systems.

In designing RQL our philosophy has always converged on two principal design issues:

---

*Unix is a trademark of AT&T Bell Laboratories.

1. Designers of query languages should always be parsimonious in the number and complexity of the constructs they embed into the language. A powerful language with many and complex constructs does not necessarily imply acceptance. The aim is introduce fewer constructs with general applicability and less complexity, which is probably easier to implement and at the same time guarantees that queries formulated in that particular language are easier to reason about.
2. Designers should provide clear user interfaces so that the syntax and the structure of the language could be altered or augmented at any time to reflect the potential needs of the users. Such interface facilities can be constructed as front-ends to an existing database management system and improve the process of identifying and retrieving the required information from the database. This means that the designer must make the right assumptions as to how these front-ends interface with the DBMS primitives in order to achieve versatility and adaptability. For example, one could provide a friendly user interface facility for the development of query languages for non-programmers. Furthermore, this implies that an extensible query language is possibly preferable, for practical purposes, to a more powerful language offering a rigid structure.

RQL has points in common with SQL (actually in some respects the RQL syntax resembles that of SQL [31]) in the sense that it comprises a complete stand-alone query language. Consequently, RQL (like SQL) frees the user from such major decisions and concerns as to how data structures are implemented in the internal level, and what kind of algorithms are operating on the data stored in the database. Moreover, RQL provides the user with the notions of physical and logical data independence, as well as relational data integrity.

In the following we present an outline of the RQL data definition and manipulation parts. We concentrate on the operational capabilities of RQL, and we provide several examples to clarify our points of view. Many issues that will be described are based along the lines of the theory presented in the previous chapter. RQL (like SQL) uses a combination of both relational algebra and relational calculus constructs. In the rest of this chapter we will elaborate on such issues as the following:

1. Relation creation, and refreshment.
2. Data insertion, update, and deletion.
3. Data retrieval from several relations satisfying the selection predicate criteria.
4. Nested retrieval.
5. The possibility of processing data via arithmetical and logical calcula-

tions.

6. Assigning results either for printing (on terminal or directing them to files), or as intermediate values corresponding to new relations.
7. View creation.
8. Catalog manipulation.

Our basic intention is not to give an exhaustive presentation of the RQL syntax, but rather to stress its main features and capabilities. Readers who wish to have a complete description of the language syntax can refer to Appendix A.

3.2   The user perspective

A REQUIEM database is organized as a collection of named relations. The named relations are normally created by the users and fall into two major categories: base relations and views.

A *base relation* is a "concrete" relation in the sense that it physically exists in terms of physically stored records and indices. In contrast to a base relation, a *view* is a virtual relation in the sense that it does not physically exist in storage, but is perceived as a real table. Loosely speaking, views correspond to what has been termed a subschema in Chapter 1. Views are defined by the user, as will be explained later, in terms of one or more underlying base relations.

3.2.1   Data definition functions

The data definition part of RQL allows the user to create base relations. In RQL relations are defined in terms of their attributes and the notion of domain appears only implicitly through the types (integer, real, or character) that the values of the attributes are assumed to take. In RQL each attribute can be declared with one of the following three data types:

1. integer (**num**).
2. real (**real**).
3. character string (**char**).

Each attribute in a relation has a distinct name, and attribute values are never allowed to be undefined, a fact which provides a minimum safeguard against certain inconsistencies, such as the introduction of null values.

Moreover, no keys are explicitly declared in the relation scheme, as the notions of primary, foreign, and secondary keys are inherent in RQL at the access path level.* Indices are defined by utilizing the **unique** statement during the process of relation creation. The option **unique** allows the user to specify that an attribute is a discriminating key (primary key) for a given relation. Furthermore, it indicates direct tuple access paths having a given key value. The support of key definitions in REQUIEM conforms to the relational data integrity rules as stated in section 2.4.

Notice that the option **unique** cannot normally be explicitly utilized by users when creating indices, as for example in SQL, since all unique indices must be created during the relation definition process. All other indices explicitly created by users via the **secondary** statement result in the introduction of secondary keys. The purpose of such secondary keys is to allow for quick and direct accessing of tuples in relation data files, in case that they are directly involved in the predicate selection clause.

To define a conceptual schema for the suppliers-and-products database as depicted in Figure 2.1, we use the **create** statement as follows:

```
create supplier (supid   (num (5), unique),
                 supname   (char (20), secondary),
                 location   (char (20))
                 );

create product (prodno (num (5), unique),
                prodname (char (20), secondary),
                weight   (real (10)),
                finish   (char (15))
                );

create supply (sid   (num (5)),
               prno (num (5)),
               quantity   (num (10)),
               foreign key sid references supid in supplier;
               foreign key prno references prodno in product;
               );
```

Each attribute definition in the **create** statement includes three items: an attribute name, a data type name for the attribute, and (optionally) a key specification. The attribute name must of course be unique within the base

---

*Access path mechanisms assist a relational system in establishing a starting point for the search of records within the file(s) underlying a relation.

relation. For example, consider the construct:

supid　(num (5), **unique**),

This construct defines the attribute *SUPID* as an integer where the constant 5 in the declaration represents the maximum length that the integer value of this specific attribute can attain. The keyword **unique** indicates that the attribute *SUPID* is a primary key for the relation *SUPPLIER*.

RQL requires every relation to have a single distinguishable primary key. Hence, a given **create** statement can include at most one **unique** key declaration as part of a relation definition. This comes in contrast to some proposals which suggest that relations should be permitted to include any number of effectively interchangeable unique keys. The primary key (i.e. the uniquely identified attribute) receives special treatment in any corresponding key specifications (see later in this section and also in section 3.2.3).

As illustrated in the previous example, foreign keys in RQL are introduced by the two **reference** clauses at the bottom of the last **create** statement, and act as intermediaries to represent references from one relation to another. In general, such reference clauses imply foreign to primary key matches, which in turn represent relationships between tuples. In a **create** statement the combination of any two foreign key attributes taken together is a primary key for the underlying relation. In fact in RQL, referential integrity constraints are explicitly specified by the user. Actually, the user specifies the referential constraints declaratively as part of the schema definition; these constraints are then imposed and maintained by the system itself.

As a result of the above three **create** statements, suitable entries will be made in the data catalogs, and space will be allocated for the base relations. Each new entry describes a new empty relation. Incidentally, such statements could be used at any moment during the life span of the database, unlike hierarchical and network systems where relations can be declared only during the initial creation phase.

There exist some interesting points in the foregoing example which require further elaboration:

1. Each of the relations *SUPPLIER* and *PRODUCT* has a single primary key as a result of the **unique** declarations. In particular, the primary key of relation *SUPPLIER* is *SUP_ID*, while the primary key of relation *PRODUCT* is *PROD_NO*.
2. The relation *SUPPLY* contains two foreign keys, namely *SID* and *PRNO*, whose combination actually forms the primary key of the relation. This

is a direct consequence of the **unique** declarations in the relations *SUP-PLIER* and *PRODUCT* and the **reference** clause that immediately follows the definition of relation *SUPPLY*. Notice the absence of a **unique** attribute declaration in the relation *SUPPLY*. It is important to realize that *SUPPLY* is not a stand-alone (independent) relation, but associates the two formerly defined relations with one another. Such relations that cannot exist independently are called *composite relations*. Obviously, composite relations require their referenced *target relations* to be defined prior to their own definition. Finally, one word of caution: REQUIEM requires a composite relation to contain only two foreign keys, whose combination is automatically interpreted as the primary key for this specific relation. For example, the primary key of relation *SUPPLY* is the combination of the keys *SID* and *PRNO*.

3. The relations *SUPPLIER* and *PRODUCT* declare their attributes *SUP-NAME* and *PRODNAME* to be indexed to speed up any retrieval operations based on these attributes.

4. Finally, notice the existence of the statement delimiter (;) following each **create** statement.

As previously explained, REQUIEM provides a general integrity support mechanism along the lines of the **create** statement for primary and foreign key support. During the process of relation creation and data (attribute) definition, REQUIEM converts the entire range of definitional information from the logical structure to storage structure. Any updates or deletes of primary or foreign key values are performed along the lines of the referential integrity rules specified in section 2.4.

The modify statement
The statement

modify < *relation–name*>

modifies the names and lengths of the attributes of a particular relation. All attribute names and lengths are modified except for those of primary keys. The **modify** statement actually commences a dialog with the DBMS as to which attribute names and/or lengths should be altered.

The purge statement
Finally, it is possible to delete an existing base relation at any time by utilizing the statement:

purge < *relation–name*>

All tuples in the specified relation are subsequently deleted, as well as all indices and all the views defined on that relation. Furthermore, all corresponding entries made in the database catalogs vanish as well.

3.2.2   Data manipulation functions

The data manipulation part of RQL is used to specify any operations made against the contents of the database. Such operations include database interrogation and update. The data manipulation operations in RQL fall into four major categories: data insertion, data retrieval, data modification, and data deletion. The RQL data manipulation statements can be invoked either interactively, as we shall see later in this section, or from within an application program written in C (refer to Chapter 14).

The data manipulation part of RQL operates on both base and derived relations (views). At this stage we will concern ourselves only with base relations. Furthermore we assume that queries are entered at, and results are displayed on, an on-line terminal.

The basic structure of an RQL retrieval expression consists of the following clauses:

1. The **select** clause which is the selection clause used to list the tuples desired in the result of a query.
2. The **project** clause which is used to list the attributes desired in the result of a query.
3. The **join, union, intersect,** and **difference** clauses which list sets of tuples according to the well-known relational algebra principles.
4. The **expose** clause which introduces subqueries.
5. The **display** clause which displays sets of tuples sequentially as they are physically ordered in the relation data file.
6. The **from** and **with** clauses which specify the relations to be scanned or included in the result of a query.
7. Finally, the **where** clause which corresponds to the selection predicate. This clause consists of a predicate involving attributes of relations that appear in **select, project,** and **join** clauses.

Data insertion

The statement **insert** <*relation−name*> inserts new tuples into a relation. The insert statement in REQUIEM is interactive. Here the user types in the name of the relation after the statement **insert** and REQUIEM answers with the name of the first attribute of that relation. Subsequently, the user is prompted for the values of all attributes to be inserted. After an entire tuple has been inserted REQUIEM will return with its insert prompt. A null response to an attribute insert prompt will terminate tuple entry. During the process of data insertion REQUIEM prescribes the format for input source data; this provides a minimum safeguard against data inconsistency.

Primary key values must be inserted in the target relations first, followed by any foreign key insertions that match their values in associated composite relations. For example, consider the instance of the suppliers-and-products database as illustrated in Figure 2.1. Here, the user must insert the primary key values, e.g. 605, 612, into the relation *SUPPLIER* prior to inserting them into the relation *SUPPLY*. However, if the user decides to insert the tuples in the composite relation first, the operation will simply be rejected. This provides a minimum safeguard against referential inconsistency problems.

Data retrieval

During the process of data retrieval the user writes a series of queries that generate an intermediate relation as output. The relation resulting from a retrieval statement can either be simply displayed on the terminal by issuing the command **print;**, which causes intermediate file flushing, or can be directly fed to another retrieval operation as operand.

The select statement The selection process identifies a subset of the tuples contained in a relation. The inputs to the selection operator are a named relation and a predicate expression which provides the criteria for selecting the tuples in the specified relation. The predicate selection expression should contain at least the name of one attribute derived from the header of the relation as a variable operand. The result of an RQL retrieval operation is, of course, a new relation. Let us consider some simple sample queries using the suppliers-and-products database of Figure 2.1.

Example 3.2.1

To find the information pertinent to suppliers who are located either in London or in Paris, one can issue the following query:

select from supplier
      where location = "London" | location = "Paris";

In RQL, a predicate selection formula is an expression involving a linear sequence of operands, operators, and delimiters (left or right parentheses), put together using a predefined set of construction rules. These rules are similar to the rules utilized in high-level languages such as Pascal or C, for creating analogous logical expressions. The predicate selection subexpression is in fact a logical expression which yields a boolean result indicating which tuples should be selected and which should be rejected. RQL uses the mathematical symbols "|," "&," and "~" to achieve logical connection of predicate subexpressions. The logical operator "|" stands for the logical **or**, the logical operator "&" stands for the logical **and**, and finally the logical operator "~" stands for the logical **not**. It must be mentioned that the operation **select** selects a number of tuples as specified by the **where** clause; the keyword **all** is optionally specified to indicate that complete tuples must be selected. It is possible in a select statement to omit the keyword **all**.

The output of a selection statement is a relation containing a subset of the tuples held in the original relation and some communication message to the user concerning the anticipated volume of output tuples. In fact, every retrieval statement produces analogous communication messages as output. The logic underlying this design issue is quite simple: in some cases it might be desirable that the system does not continue with the retrieval process if the execution of the predicate selection formula has resulted in a large number of retrieved tuples. Often the user is only looking for a few tuples that satisfy the predicate selection formula. Hence, if the user is informed that a large number of tuples have been selected for output, he may wish to apply more restrictive conditions in the selection predicate to reduce the anticipated output.

RQL uses the == partial comparison operator to determine whether it should select a tuple, or not. In fact, this is a practical requirement because the user may for example not remember the full name of a supplier, or a product. Consider the following query:

select from supplier **where** supname == "Ja"

This query will produce as a result all *SUPPLIER* tuples which include a *SUPNAME* attribute value that starts with the two letters "Ja".

The project statement The projection operator projects or extracts named attributes from the specified relation. The projected attribute names are exactly those which the user wishes to see. The output of the projection process is again a relation containing all named attributes. In RQL the attributes to be projected should be separated by commas and follow the **over** clause. Any duplicate tuples resulting from a project operation are eliminated.

Example 3.2.2

Find the names of the suppliers who are based in London.

project supplier **over** supname **where** location = "London";

The join statement and the transient relation variables To select data from multiple semantically related tables the user must utilize the **join** construct. The **join** statement requires the two relations to have one or more attributes in common over which the join can be made. We will give a description of the **join** operation by means of examples.

Example 3.2.3

Consider the query "Find for all suppliers the products that they supply and the quantities they have already supplied."

This query is expressed as follows:

join supplier **on** supid **with** supply **on** sid;

A **join** operation in RQL can be conditional if it is combined with a predicate.

Example 3.2.4

Find for all suppliers the products that they supply and the quantities they have already supplied provided that each supply they made included more than 130 items of any kind.

This query can be formulated as follows:

join supplier **on** supid
    with supply **on** sid **where** quantity > 130;

Result:

SUP_ID#	SUP_NAME	LOCATION	PROD_NO	QUANTITY
605	Jones	London	21	150
612	Schmidt	Zurich	10	200
855	Dick	Bonn	25	135

To achieve the formulation of complex queries RQL provides the notion of *temporary relation variables.* The output resulting from a given query could be assigned to a specific relation variable through the statement:

assign <*relation−variable*> **to** <*query*>;

Example 3.2.5

Consider the query "Find all the supids, products, and quantities corresponding to all the suppliers in the database."

This rather complex query could be formulated in two steps. First we can locate all the suppliers, the products that they supply, and the quantities they have in stock by means of the following query:

assign temp1 **to**
> **join** supplier **on** supid **with** supply **on** sid;

Then we use the the temporary (transient) relation variable $TEMP1$ as part of the final query which looks like:

project temp1 **over** supid, prodname, quantity;

These kinds of constructs give RQL queries a procedural look; however, they add a lot to the versatility and expressive power of the language. Actually, there are many examples in relational database programming where the user is forced to create an intermediate transient relation in order to simplify or even optimize some larger computation. Transient relations are purged automatically at the end of each session; alternatively they could be destroyed by the user explicitly like ordinary relations by utilizing the **purge** statement.

On the other hand the above query could have been written as:

project (**join** supplier **on** supid
> **with** supply **on** sid) **over** supid, prodname, quantity;

Such queries are called *nested queries* and are very common in RQL. Queries can be nested to any depth in RQL and new relations are produced as a result. These two last examples show that it is possible to formulate the same query in different ways which is appealing and quite beneficial to the user.

Retrieval involving subqueries In RQL the user can combine several **project** and **select** clauses together to form a query. We call the combination of any selection or projection applied to a relation file a *retrieval process*. The retrieval process could either be a *nested retrieval* (nested query), or a *qualified retrieval* in which case the connective **in** is used to connect two subclauses together. In all cases the product of a retrieval process is again a new relation which can be further manipulated, assigned to, or displayed as any other relation by using the normal REQUIEM facilities.

In RQL *subqueries* are used to represent the set of values searched by the existential qualifier connective **in**. A subquery is a **project** expression nested inside an **expose** expression. Note that the subquery expression must represent a single attribute relation, which explains why such subqueries consist solely of **project** expressions. The system evaluates the overall query by evaluating the subquery first. In the most recent version of RQL, subqueries can have only one level of nesting, which implies that a subquery cannot be nested inside another.

Example 3.2.6

To put the whole thing into perspective let us consider the query "Find all supplier names and locations of those suppliers who supply more than 150 items of any product."

In the following we construct this query stepwise; we begin first by finding all *SUPPLIER_ID*s of suppliers supplying more than 150 items of any product. Consequently, we formulate the subquery:

project supply **over** sid **where** quantity > 150;

We must then find all the names and locations of those suppliers who were selected by the previous subquery. We achieve this by embedding the above subquery in an outer **expose** statement. Thus, the resulting query is:

expose supplier **over** supname, location
      when supid **is in** **project** supply
          over sid **where** quantity > 150;

The **in** connective stands for the existential qualifier of the relational calculus, and it tests for set membership. Here, set membership is the collection of values which have been produced by the subquery clause. Note that in our example no enclosing parentheses are required to surround the subquery. By default the **where** predicate associated with an **expose** statement is considered to be part of the subquery.

The **in** connective is also used in RQL to search a set of values included in a *predicate list*. The predicate list must contain at least two elements separated by commas. Consider the following example of an **in** predicate list:

> **project** supplier **over** supname, location
> **where** supid **in** (604, 605, 720);

The **where** clause in this simple example evaluates to TRUE only if the attribute *SUPID* attains one of the values contained in the predicate list. Actually, you can formulate the previous **expose** query by means of a predicate list if you have an idea of what kind of output you are expecting. The **in** connective in RQL is defined to be semantically equivalent to a logical expression involving only disjunctions. Contrary to the **in** predicate the **not in** connective is used in RQL to test for the absence of set membership.

Retrieval involving set operations In the following we assume that the syntax and semantics of RQL retrieval expressions involving set operations are as specified in Chapter 2. Consider the following example.

Example 3.2.7

To find all the products which may not at present be supplied by any supplier, we could use the construct:

> **difference** (**project** product
>   **over** prodno),
>   (**project** supply
>   **over** prodno);

Similarly, to find all products that are currently supplied (assuming that at the moment there are some products which are not supplied by any supplier), we may use the following query:

> **intersect** (**project** product
>   **over** prodno),
>   (**project** supply
>   **over** prodno);

The group statement In addition to the above, RQL offers to users the ability to partition a base table into *groups*, such that within each group belong all the attributes that contain the same value for the **group by** attribute. RQL provides a set of special built-in functions to be used in conjunction with the **group** statements. Such built-in functions include the constructs average(**avg**), minimum(**min**), maximum(**max**), total(**sum**), and count(**count**). Functions used in conjunction with **group** statements are called *aggregate functions* because they operate on tuple aggregates. Consequently, the **group** statement is used to split a relation into groups so that any built-in function can by applied to each of these groups.

Example 3.2.8

Thus, to find the total quantity of products supplied by each supplier we can write:

project supply **over** supid, quantity
        group by supid **sum**(quantity);

Result:

SUP_ID	TOTAL
605	250
612	200
827	120
855	135

Sometimes it is useful to define a predicate that applies to groups rather than to tuples. The **where** clause of RQL used in conjunction with **group** statements facilitates the formulation of such queries. For example to find the suppliers supplying a total of more than 150 items we write:

project supply **over** supid, quantity
        group by supid **where sum**(quantity) > 150;

Result:

SUP_ID	SUM_QUANTITY
605	250
612	200

Predicates in the **where** clause are internally applied after the formation of groups, so that the aggregate functions may be applied in such clauses.

The display statement Finally, the **display** statement of RQL is used to display on the screen a set of adjacent tuples as they are physically stored in the relation data file. Furthermore, the **display** statement could be used to position the cursor of a table. Initially, the cursor identifies a position in the table, namely the position just before the first tuple included in the relation data file. For example, the statement

display +0, 3 **using** supplier;

displays the first three tuples from the relation SUPPLIER and positions the cursor exactly after the third tuple. Displacements used in conjunction with a **display** statement could also be negative, which means that the cursor could move backwards. To reset the cursor to its initial position at the beginning of the file we use the statement:

display using supplier;

Data modification and data deletion

To modify the values in a relation, the user specifies which relation and which attributes are to be the object of the update operation. The tuples to be updated are specified by using a predicate selection expression, exactly as in the process of retrieval. If a given selection predicate identifies a subset of tuples in the given relation, the user can step through the entire set of specified tuples changing values in one tuple at a time. REQUIEM displays on the terminal screen the attribute name and value of every attribute in each selected tuple. Subsequently, it prompts the user with the corresponding attribute names to insert a new value.

When the user enters a value for a specified attribute, REQUIEM checks it for conformance to its definition, by including any required validation-consistency checks. Errors can be corrected on the spot by an on-line user. Upon entering values for all the specified attributes, the user can scan the terminal screen for a final visual check before instructing REQUIEM to accept and store permanently the newly specified values. For example, to update the values of the attributes *SUP_NAME* and *LOCATION* for all suppliers currently residing in Zurich, we write:

update supname, location
      from supplier **where** location = "Zurich";

The system then prompts the user to decide whether he/she wishes to make the changes (stored meanwhile in a temporary buffer) permanent.

All database updates that are committed by means of a special **commit** statement are written on the disk and cannot be undone. If the user decides not to commit the changes then REQUIEM undoes all the changes/deletions made during an update/delete session and recovers the original contents of the tuple affected by such an operation. After the updating/deletion of a tuple the user will be given the option to update/delete more tuples of the same relation, or to escape.

Deletion follows exactly the same pattern as updating, the only difference being that the user deletes specified sets of tuples. This means that the user deletes an entire tuple at a time, and not only a part of a specified tuple.

Example 3.2.9

To delete all suppliers currently residing in London, we can write:

delete supplier **where** location = "London";

The previous RQL statement deletes a set of tuples from the relation *SUPPLIER* which includes the value "London" in its location part. As the deleted tuples stem from a target relation they must conform to the general REQUIEM referential integrity constraints as we shall see in the following section.

3.2.3 Referential integrity in RQL

The problem of ensuring that every foreign key does in fact match a value of the corresponding primary key is a composite one if we consider the implications of foreign key updates and deletions. In order to maintain the referential constraint between the primary key in a target relation and its associated foreign key in a composite relation, REQUIEM performs some compensating activities. A **delete** operation (or an **update** on the primary key) on a target relation tuple could leave *dangling references* in the associated composite relation.* Such references become incorrect in the sense that they no longer refer to the desired key. To circumvent this problem we require specific primary key update and delete rules.

Let us concentrate on the delete rule first. If we attempt to delete a relation which is the target of a foreign key reference, we must then trigger cascading deletes on composite relation tuples that match the value of the deleted primary key. Furthermore, if an entire target relation is purged then

---

*Dangling references are created when we update or delete a primary key to which a foreign key contains a reference.

SUPPLIER

SUP_ID#	SUP_NAME	LOCATION
612	Schmidt	Zurich
827	Dupont	Paris
855	Dick	Bonn

PRODUCT

PROD_NO#	PROD_NAME	WEIGHT	FINISH
10	desk	150	pine
12	bookcase	100	cherry
21	cabinet	80	oak
25	sofa	20	oak
33	dresser	90	pine

SUPPLY

SUP_ID#	PROD_NO#	QUANTITY
612	10	200
827	12	120
855	25	135

Figure 3.1 The suppliers-and-products database after deletion of the London supplier tuple.

all composite relations that are associated with it are also automatically purged.

Consider the consequences of the previous **delete** statement which at first glance seems to be a harmless statement. As usual we assume that prior to the execution of this statement the database instance is as depicted in Figure 2.1. After processing the **delete** statement the database would look like that in Figure 3.1. This implies that the deletion of the primary key *SUP_ID* = 605, associated with the London supplier, has been cascaded to its matching values in the composite relation *SUPPLY*. As a result all *SUPPLY* tuples related to the removed London supplier disappear without any user intervention. Such kinds of referential constraints concerning primary and foreign keys also affect **update** statements.

The interpretation of the update rule is analogous to the delete case. If we attempt to update the value of a primary key in some target relation tuple then all matching tuples in the associated composite relations are updated accordingly.

Note, incidentally, that the user issuing the original delete/update requests does not need to hold any explicit delete or update privilege on the referencing relation in order for the above compensating actions to be performed.

3.2.4   File manipulation functions

REQUIEM can read and process a series of valid RQL statements from a *command file*. This file usually contains view definitions, but it could also contain any other retrieval statement. The user can process the statements included in the command file in two ways:

1. The name of the file could be passed as a command-line argument (in the Unix sense) before the user enters REQUIEM.
2. Alternatively, the command file could also be processed from within RQL by typing a "@" character before the command file name.

There also exists another category of files which can be processed by REQUIEM; these files are called *format files* and specify a format template into which attribute values should be substituted during a display or print operation. A format definition file should be specified in the user's current directory and should always have the suffix ".form" following its name. The format template has the form:

Text: <attribute−reference>

This means that there are only two types of information that can be included in a format definition file: plain text and attribute references, where attribute references are indicated by placing the name of the desired attribute between a pair of angle brackets. Text is any character format provided that it is not enclosed in angle brackets.

COMMAND FILE = format_file
Name: < *supname* >
Location: < *location* >

Example 3.2.10

Consider the format definition file "format_file." This file specifies the format that the attributes should have when displayed on the screen, or when forwarded to the output file "out_file" as the following two **print** *statements indicate.*

print using formatfile
　　supname, location **from** supplier;

print using formatfile
　　supname, location **from** supplier **into** outfile;

In addition to the above, when an attribute name is specified in a **print** statement it is possible to provide an alternate name, called an *alias*, for that attribute. This is useful in cases where it is desired that the relation headers in an output table contain alternate names for the actual attribute names. Alternate attribute names can be used in references to that attribute in the predicate selection clause as well as in a format definition file. The syntax for specifying aliases is:

<*attribute–name*> <*alias*>

Consider the following example.

COMMAND FILE = format_file
Name: < *sn* >
Location: < *lc* >

print using format_file
　　supname sn, location lc **from** supplier;

The import and export statements　RQL provides two additional file manipulation statements: **import** and **export**. The **import** statement imports tuples from a file into a relation. **import** has the form:

import <*file–name*> [**into** <*relation–name*>];

where <*file–name*> is the name of the input file internally qualified by the suffix **.dat**. This input file must contain values of the tuple attributes, with each attribute on a separate line. Subsequently, the tuples are appended to the named relation.

　　The **export** statement exports tuples from a relation into a file. If the file name is omitted then output is forwarded to the terminal. **export** has the form:

export <*relation–name*> [**into** <*file–name*>];

3.2.5   View functions

Views are virtual relations – that is, relations that do not exist in their own right but appear to the user as if they did. Views are not supported by their own private (physically separate) data, but are derived from some already existing base relation(s). This definition of views in terms of other relations is also stored in the system catalogs in a catalog relation called *SYSVIEW*.

In REQUIEM, for example, the statement **define view** allows the user to define a view. To define a view called OAK-PRODUCT, the user would write:

define view oak-product **as**
      select from product
            where finish = "oak";

When this **define view** statement is executed the subquery following the keyword **as**, which is actually the definition of the view, is not executed; instead, it is simply saved into the views catalog, under its name *OAK-PRODUCT*. To the user, however, the view OAK-PRODUCT acts as a sort of dynamic window on the actual relation *PRODUCT*, thus allowing the user to visualize the database differently. Every invocation of the name *OAK-PRODUCT* results in a textual substitution of the view under question, and in its immediate execution.

Example 3.2.11

Consider the retrieval statement against the previous view as illustrated in the following query:

project oak-product **over** prodname;

Result:

PROD_NAME
cabinet
sofa

Such operations against a view are handled by the system internally by merging the **select** statement of the view definition with the **project** statement of the previous query to give a modified query. The modified query can now be executed in the normal way. In other words, the original **project** statement on the view is converted into an equivalent RQL statement in terms of the underlying relation.

Views are dynamic images of a certain part of the database. For example, changes to the relation *PRODUCT* will automatically and instantaneously be made visible through the *OAK-PRODUCT* view (provided of course that those changes have to do with the product names in relation *PRODUCT*); likewise, any changes to *OAK-PRODUCT* will be automatically and instantaneously applied to the base relation *PRODUCT*, and hence of course made visible to all users through that view.

The principal purpose of views, as our example has implied, is simply to facilitate the user's perception of the database and thereby to simplify the user's job. In fact, views combine several attractive features: they not only simplify database queries but at the same time allow data to be perceived by different users in different ways; moreover, they allow the users to be shielded from changes in the structure of the actual relations and provide an automatic measure of security for hidden data. However, there exist some inherent drawbacks as far as view manipulation is concerned. This stems from the dynamic nature of views.

As we have already explained in outline, through the previous example, retrieval operations such as **select**, **project**, etc. on a view work perfectly well. But when it comes to **update** operations the situation is quite different. It is not always possible to carry out updates* on the contents of a view. Updates on views in RQL are subject to a number of restrictions. RQL allows a view to be updated only if it represents a simple row-and-column subset of a single underlying base relation (for example it is not the product of a **join** operation). During this process it also made sure that this update propagates to the underlying base relation. In the case where there exists a one-to-one relationship between the tuples of a given view and those of a base relation, updates are feasible. However, as far as the case of projections is concerned, one must determine beforehand the implications that such an operation is going to have on the values of attributes that do not appear in the view. The details of view updating are beyond the scope of this section, and will be covered in detail in Chapter 12 which is specifically devoted to view manipulation. For the moment it suffices to say that views in REQUIEM are updatable if they conform to the following rules:

1. A view is built from exactly one base relation. Here views created on the basis of other views, as well as views resulting from joins, do not qualify.
2. A view represents a simple row-and-column subset of a single underlying table. Any modification such as insertion, deletion, or update on the contents of the view must result in an equivalent operation on the contents

---

*We are using the term "update" here to include insert and delete as well as update operations.

of its qualifying table.

The above rules amongst others guarantee that view modifications cannot be performed if a view is the outcome of the following:

1. Product statements.
2. **group by** statements.
3. Aggregate function statements.

From the foregoing discussion it should be clear that views can further simplify the user's perception of the contents of a database by concealing irrelevant information from a table, or by joining two distinct tables together so as to form a single table, etc. In fact, views can prohibit the inexperienced user from making radical changes in the logical structure of the database, and thus promote logical data independence [19].

3.2.6 Catalog functions

As far as REQUIEM is concerned a database is composed of both base and derived relations (views). Moreover, it is possible that each relation stored in the system has one or more access paths. It is also sometimes necessary to know which users are authorized to work on which data. REQUIEM keeps track of this kind of information by maintaining a set of special tables which constitute the *system* or *database catalogs*. System catalogs are themselves relations stored in the database, and REQUIEM allows the user to interrogate them and obtain information pertinent to the contents of the database. Catalog manipulation is affected via the use of the system's query language. Any viable RQL statement can operate on the system catalogs. It is however irrational to assume that the user could directly modify, insert, or delete the data contained in a catalog. The reason for this rule is quite clear; allowing such operations could prove to be extremely dangerous in the sense that it would be far too easy for information to be inadvertently destroyed in the catalogs, so that the system would no longer function properly. Data catalogs are updated automatically during the data definition phase or by data modification through the **create, update, delete,** and **purge** statements.

The REQUIEM system catalogs contain descriptions of all the objects in the system. Thus, catalogs contain entries for relations in the system (derived or non-derived), dependency links between different relations in the database, attribute descriptions, access paths, etc. For example there is a catalog relation in REQUIEM called *SYSTAB* that includes an entry, i.e. a row, for every relation defined in the system, giving amongst others such information as *RELNAME* (the name of the relation), *CREATOR* (identification of the creator of this relation), *NATRS* (the total number of attributes in that relation), and *DERIV* (an indication that this relation is a view and not a base relation). More information about system catalogs and their implementation and manipulation can be found in the special chapter devoted to the REQUIEM system catalogs; see Chapter 13. For the moment consider the following example which retrieves the names of all the relations containing an attribute *SUPID*.

project sysatrs **over** relname
      where atrname = "supid";

Result:

RELNAME
SUPPLIER
SUPPLY

Here, *SYSATRS*, like *SYSTAB*, is a catalog table containing entries for each attribute of every relation in the database (including the catalog tables themselves). *RELNAME* is the name of the containing relation and *ATR-NAME* is the name of the specific attribute required in that relation.

Furthermore, REQUIEM provides the **extract** statement which gives a tabular list of information pertaining to a relation, e.g. the attribute names, types, key definitions, and size of tuples in bytes. When a user wants to inquire about the definition of a relation, he/she can use the **extract** statement (rather than interrogate the catalogs) as this statement provides concise information which would otherwise require a number of catalog queries.

3.2.7   Authorization and security mechanisms

In REQUIEM *database security* implies the protection of the contents and the logical structure of the database against unauthorized disclosure, accidental modification, or destruction. It is therefore necessary to have a security mechanism to provide protection and thus to permit data to be manipulated only in an authorized manner. In a sense the view mechanism provides such a security mechanism by hiding sensitive data from unauthorized users, but this alone is insufficient. To perform any viable RQL operation the user must hold the appropriate *access privilege* for the operation and operands under question [19]. Examples of access privileges are the retrieval statements **select**, **project**, etc.; the **update** and **delete** statements; index statements (i.e. to open an index on the base relation concerned); and finally the unrestricted authority *DBA*. Furthermore, REQUIEM is in a position to utilize authorization mechanisms capable of reconsidering access privileges at any moment, thus according or rejecting access to several parts of the database as required. In RQL the security mechanisms are principally based on the SQL-like **grant** and **revoke** statements.

At system installation time a specific user is granted the *DBA* privileges, which means unrestricted control on the contents and the structure of the database. Any other user creating a relation is automatically granted all applicable privileges on that relation. This is accomplished internally via the **grant** statement. Any specific user holding a grant option can grant that privilege on a group of other users, or can revoke an already granted privilege through the **revoke** option. Consider the following examples:

grant update, delete on supplier **to group** db10;
grant select on product **to** James;
grant dba to Smith, James;
revoke dba from Smith;
revoke delete on supplier **from group** db10;

Authorization mechanisms are applied to base relations as well as to views. Access privileges imposed on relations and views are stored in a special catalog which can be manipulated by RQL constructs. Each time a **grant** or **revoke** statement is issued REQUIEM must first confirm that the user who issued the statement has the right to accord or refuse the privileges specified in the statement. If this is the case, the system combines the accorded or refused privileges with the ones already possessed.

3.3   Internal system organization

Each base relation in REQUIEM is represented as a combination of a stored data file and an index file. Thus, the principal elements of RQL are relations which are physically stored in secondary memory. Each data file comprises a file header and a file body. Records in the stored data file represent tuples of the base relation. Each record is stored as a byte-string of fixed length, corresponding to the maximum length of a tuple. The file header of a base relation includes information pertinent to the relation. Such information includes the names, types, and sizes of attributes, the total number of attributes contained in the base relation, key definitions, etc. Therefore, at any time you can locate any requested attribute value. Although the fixed length storage scheme described above consumes more space than normally required, it is faster than that of variable length records in the sense that updates in variable sized record storage schemes may require major file re-arrangements which are time consuming. On the other hand, fixed length records are certainly much simpler to implement and manipulate. Further-more, the file manager does not have to save tuple identifiers including indications of the tuple length, or even of individual field lengths. In the REQUIEM fixed record storage scheme the space freed by a deleted record is exactly that of the space required for a subsequent record insertion. The file header simply stores the address of the most recently deleted record. All the remaining records are chained together, that is the first available record on the list stores the address of the second available record, and so on. Now if a new record is deleted its address is copied in the file header, and simultaneously the previous current record joins the list of available records and in this way the whole list remains intact. Inserted records need simply to draw the address of the top record from the available record list, and occupy its space.

REQUIEM uses access paths which apply exclusively to relations. We will frequently use the term *index* or *index file* to designate this type of access. We can loosely say that an index is in reality a logical reorganization of tuples of a relation in terms of attribute values or of a group of attributes. Generally speaking we can say that the purpose of an index is to provide an *access path* to the data file that it is indexing. In other words, access path mechanisms are set up to establish a starting point for the search of records within an indexed file. This involves the definition of various forms of indices, key transformation algorithms, etc. Such access mechanisms are used to search within a given structure; they normally search over physically contiguous data elements. Whenever access paths are not used, tuples of a relation must be accessed absolutely sequentially (refer to Chapter 6 for more information).

REQUIEM supports multiple indices in an index file where the indexed attribute values may vary in length from one index to another. Indexing techniques handle internal duplicate keys of any data type, multiple entries pointing to the same record in a stored data file, multiple indices in use, variable length keys, and sequential advance through an index. Obviously, with such an implementation the same attribute value may occur in more than one data record. In general, we allow the same attribute value to be present in more than one entry, but we request that the combination of the indexed attribute and its offset in the data file be unique in any entry. Internal indices in REQUIEM are organized as B^+-trees, with each block of the index occupying one page in storage. Furthermore, to speed things up a *cache buffering* scheme is used to reduce the number of actual disk reads. In this context cache buffering denotes a collection of blocks that normally belong on disk, but are also being kept in memory space to improve performance. The algorithm used to manage the cache is simple and is based on LRU (least recently used) techniques [32], [33]. Blocks residing in the current index position are likely to be referenced again so they become candidates for caching. (By current index position we mean the index offsets within the blocks affected by the most recent insertion in the index file.) In this way read requests can be satisfied without a disk access. Again if the current index block is not in the cache, it is first read into the cache, and then any subsequent indexing operations can be performed on the contents of this cache buffer. Any updates or deletes are performed simultaneously on the contents of the cache blocks and on corresponding index file blocks held on disk. In this way information in the cache buffer is always consistent with the corresponding index blocks in the file. The cache method in REQUIEM is quite simple; it allocates space for one block at each index level and keeps the current block in the cache. Cache buffers are allocated in such a way that every open index file obtains its own set of cache buffers.

A critical issue that has to be accounted for as far as indices are concerned is the choice of the size of an index block. Blocks should correspond to units in which the operating system allocates disk space to files. The term *page* is thus reserved to indicate the unit of transfer between the database held in disk and memory storage. Index blocks should correspond exactly to page size, otherwise I/O performance degrades. For example, the choice of a size larger than that of a physical page results in fragmented files with obvious implications for performance. The optimal block size for index blocks for most Unix systems is 1 kbyte. The indexing structure of REQUIEM also stores some additional context information about the index file into the index file header. Such information includes the location of the root block, the levels of indexing, the current size of an index file, etc.

During the process of data insertion and update REQUIEM prescribes the format for input source data, and this provides a minimum safeguard against data inconsistency. The underlying data and index files are subsequently specially prepared to accept the data and store it in the database. When a base relation is created its name is encrypted and the index and data files of this relation appear simultaneously in the user's current directory. The data file name is the encrypted relation name followed by the suffix .db, while the index file name comprises the encrypted relation name followed by the suffix .indx. Indices are either created explicitly or implicitly as a result of statements issued by users. However, users are not responsible for stating where and how a certain index should be used. The decision as to whether a specific index is going to be used in response to a query is entirely dependent upon the system. Moreover, indices are never mentioned explicitly in RQL data manipulation statements.

The mapping technique used to transform the input data before storage in the database is quite simple. All input data should be first validated and then converted to byte-strings (character strings). During the conversion phase all converted data is placed in an intermediate tuple buffer, and subsequently follows the mapping phase where all transformed data is copied directly into the database. Input data is always stored in the database on a tuple basis. The validation criteria are applied to the data to be inserted in the database before transformation. Validation of the data to be input is made on the basis of information stored during the relation definition process, and of supplementary information provided by the system catalogs. Any data not conforming to the validation criteria is immediately rejected and the user is subsequently prompted to supply valid input data.

4

The REQUIEM
Architecture

One of the main objectives of REQUIEM is to facilitate the definition and organization of data in storage so that the users are in a position to retrieve, insert, or update any subset of the data in the database. This means that considerable attention must be given to the internal structure and organization of REQUIEM in order to accomplish the above objective in the best possible manner. The fundamental concerns of this chapter are the architectural components and the functionality of the REQUIEM modules that support data definition and manipulation. Additionally, we will also briefly examine the REQUIEM data structures that are involved in the overall process of data definition and manipulation. We will illustrate that locating a specific item in the database and presenting it to the user involves several tailor-made data structures whose prime purpose is to represent the retrieval context.

4.1   Description of the REQUIEM modules

In REQUIEM a database schema is specified by a set of definitions expressed by means of a special sublanguage called the REQUIEM data definition language. The REQUIEM DDL is a descriptive language which allows the user to describe and name the entities that are required for a given application. DDL statements can also be used to describe the associations which may exist between the different entity descriptions. Although DDL is used to develop a schema or even to modify an existing one, it cannot be used to manipulate data.

Execution of DDL statements does not simply create some empty relations:

at the same time a set of entries pertaining to the schema definition will
be stored in the system catalogs. Recall from Chapter 3 that the system
catalogs comprise a set of system-defined relations that contain useful meta-
data. Actually, the system catalogs contain definitions of relations, data
items, and other objects that are required by the DBMS (see Chapter 13).

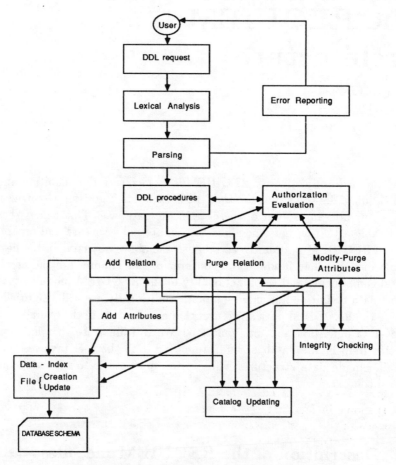

Figure 4.1 A functional description of the DDL processor.

We collectively refer to all the software modules of REQUIEM that deal
with the implementation of DDL operations as the *DDL processor*. A functional description of the DDL processor is depicted in Figure 4.1. This
figure shows how the various software components of the DDL processor
interact with each other in order to fulfill a user DDL request. Each DDL
request is first checked to ensure it conforms to the predefined lexical and
syntactical constructs of the DDL, then the appropriate DDL functions are
called. These functions either create a new database schema or update an

existing one. Consequently, base relations and attributes are included in the final database schema or deleted from it according to the user's wishes. Meanwhile, all user DDL requests have been checked to ensure they conform to the predefined user privileges and to the system integrity constraints as mentioned in Chapters 2 and 3.

As explained in the previous chapters a query in the context of information retrieval is a request for information from the database. This request can obviously be satisfied from information already contained in the database. Actually, the answer to the request would normally be obtained after manipulating the information obtained from the database. The data request is formulated in terms of a query language which conveys to the database management system the request of the user in an understandable form. Thus, one of the primary functions of REQUIEM is to support a query language in which the user can formulate commands that will cause such data manipulation to occur.* Data manipulation applies to the schema and subschema levels, while the particular way of choosing to implement the data manipulation statements has to do with the organization of the physical level. However, on the physical level one must define rather complex procedures that allow efficient data access as we shall see later in Chapter 6. On the other hand, at higher levels emphasis is placed on the ease of utilization; thus the effort is used in providing efficient user interaction with the system.

When a query is stated in a query language it is processed by a query processor. The prime task of the query processor is to analyze the query and determine the set of information to be retrieved or checked from the database and the types of manipulation that have to be performed on the information obtained from the database. Thus, we collectively refer to the part of REQUIEM that deals with the implementation of DML operations as the *query processor*. A functional description of REQUIEM's query processor is shown in Figure 4.2. This figure shows how the various software components of the query processor interact with each other in order to implement a user DML request. Each DML request (query) is first checked to ensure it conforms to the predefined lexical and syntactical constructs of the DML, then the appropriate DML functions are called. These functions decompose each query into its constituent parts. In the case that a predicate is involved in a query these functions first check the predicate for syntactic correctness and subsequently they generate the appropriate environment (i.e. abstract stack machine) for query evaluation. Each tuple is evaluated in turn and all the tuples satisfying the predicate are finally gathered in a transient relation file which is the outcome of the posed query. All tuples

---

*In this context we use the terms data manipulation and query language interchangeably for reasons of simplicity, although this is technically incorrect.

are also checked for semantic congruence at run-time; any resulting errors
are reported back to the user and evaluation is immediately aborted.

In this text we collectively refer to the REQUIEM DDL and DML as
RQL. Our purpose is to elaborate on the architectural constituents of each
individual module depicted in Figures 4.1 and 4.2, and explain its code
implementation in some detail. To achieve this, you need first to make
yourselves familiar with the data structures implementing REQUIEM.

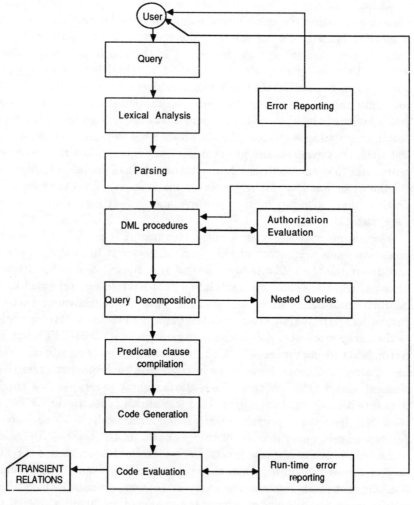

Figure 4.2 A functional description of the query processor.

4.2 The REQUIEM source file headers

Any program in C that makes use of the standard I/O library must contain at least one file header, usually **stdio.h**. Headers in C play an important role in the successful design and implementation of application programs. They are generally thought of as the usual repository for the definition of system library function types and macros [34]. In C, application programmers have the appropriate mechanisms for defining their own private file headers which can eventually be referenced by the preprocessor *#include* directive exactly as the system-defined headers. Note that by convention file headers in C end always in .h. To compile all the programs that collectively implement REQUIEM you will need the source file header named **requ.h**. This header, shown in Listing 1 at the end of this chapter, contains definitions of constants, macros, and data types that will be used throughout the system during compilation. You can change these definitions to suit your own taste and applications; however, you must be aware of such problems as structure and union alignment. Such alignment problems are compiler-specific; for example, some compilers insist that certain data types start at word boundaries. A bad design choice would most certainly lead to holes in structures and unions and make your programs inefficient with respect to storage usage, or in the worst case inoperative. We consider [34] as the best source available for learning about these and related problems.

To understand the RQL queries you must look at their sentence construction very carefully. You must think of RQL sentences as being composed of a series of components, and try to break each sentence down to its atomic elements, such as attribute names and reserved words. In the next chapter we shall see that these atomic elements are called tokens in the compiler terminology. The REQUIEM lexical analyzer returns an integer encoding when encountering each specific token. For example, the token for a particular character is its conventional ASCII representation. However, to distinguish reserved words, such as the keyword **where**, we normally encode them by an integer value that is less than any integer encoding a character. Therefore, we chose to represent all integer values encoding RQL tokens as negative integers. To enable the various REQUIEM functions to sense the presence of such tokens, we must make their definitions part of the REQUIEM programs. This can obviously be achieved only if token definitions are made part of the **requ.h** header. The **requ.h** header also defines several program constants such as the program limits, operand types, and attribute data types that are used throughout the modules implementing REQUIEM. It also defines the error codes that are returned to the user by the REQUIEM functions in the case of an error encountered during the parsing or execution of a query.

The most important part of **requ.h** is, however, the data type definitions
used throughout the REQUIEM modules. These data type definitions are
generic and used by all the data management functions. However, to implement the system storage structure a combination is required of the **requ.h**
file header and the **btree.h** file header which is used to define the data
structures and constants used solely by the B^+-tree implementation functions and the access path modules. For more information on the **btree.h**
file header and the system storage structure in general refer to Chapter 6
and Appendix B. We can divide the **requ.h** data structures in three broad
categories: the *data file specification*, the *query processing*, and the *utility*
data structures. The **requ.h** data structures used to implement relation
data files and the organization of data tuples within a data file are called
the data file specification structures. The data structures required to support the processing of queries are called query processing data structures.
Finally, the remaining data structures that are used throughout REQUIEM
are called utility data structures.

The data structures shown in Figure 4.3 belong to the first two categories,
that is they are data file specification and query processing data structures.
We sometimes refer to these structures collectively as the *retrieval context* of
a particular query. A retrieval context is always set up during the execution
of a query and its prime purpose is to store the information required to
assist the query processor in executing the query.

We start our discussion by considering the data file specification data
structures first. In REQUIEM a data file consists of a header record followed
by a series of fixed length data records; the data tuples. The header record
has the same length and the same format for all files, while the length of data
tuples is relative and depends on the attribute composition of a particular
file.

The **attribute**, **header**, and **relation** data structures are primarily used to
describe and implement data files pertaining to a specific relation. These
three structures are used for the representation of the actual relations in
a query statement. Actually, the structure **relation** is a nested structure
since it incorporates the data structure **header**. The structure **header** is in
turn also a nested structure as it contains an array of **attribute** structures.
There is exactly one **attribute** structure for each attribute contained in a
given relation. We can think of structure **relation** as a compound structure
which consists of a single **header** structure and a set of **attribute** structures.
As a matter of fact this layout parallels the structure of relation data files
in REQUIEM.

To read or assign a relation file we just need the name of its underlying
relation (**rl_name**) and its file descriptor (**rl_fd**) which is used by the basic
I/O routines to access the file on the disk. The element **rl_store** is a flag

indicating whether a store operation has happened. This store operation is normally the result of such database operations as **insert** or **update**. If this particular flag is set, the system knows that it needs to flush the contents of the tuple buffer, which comprise the normal means of communication between primary memory and storage, onto the disk before closing the corresponding relation file.

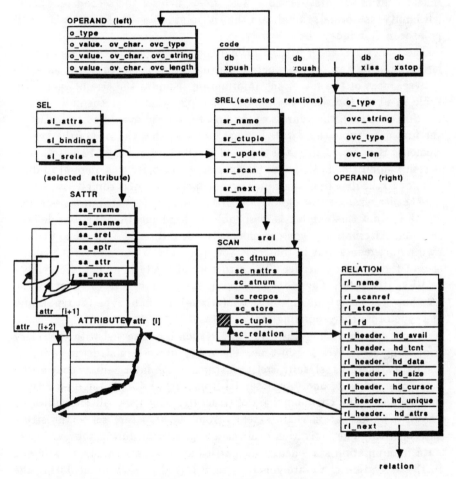

Figure 4.3 The REQUIEM data structures implementing the retrieval context.

The element **rl_scanref** indicates the number of scans used to reference a particular relation during run-time. Actually, rl_scanref is incremented each time that a reference to relation name is made and is decremented when the corresponding request is satisfied; both this and the previous element have to do with implementation of the REQUIEM file manager, described in Chapter 5. The system can close the file in question only after all references to it have been dealt with; this implies that rl_scanref must have already been set to zero. Finally, the relation element rl_next is used to point to the next relation in the list of relations referenced by a query. For example, consider a **join** statement which involves two relations and requires accessing of their corresponding data and index files. The relation structures for this query are set up at run-time and are connected to each other by means of the rl_next field of the first relation. The rl_next field of the second relation is left empty, as normal, to indicate that it points to nowhere, i.e. it is a null pointer in C language terminology.

The structure **header** is used primarily to describe the contents of a relation data file and contains permanent data that is stored in the data file between uses of the file. Such information includes the size of each data tuple in bytes (hd_size), the number of tuples that exist currently in the relation (hd_tcnt), the address of the first record (hd_avail) and the offset to the first data tuple (hd_data). It must be noted that the size of the header elements is adjusted to make the header structure exactly 512 bytes. The reason behind this is that most Unix systems transfer this amount of data from or to the disk in a single disk access operation. Accordingly, the structure **header** reserves space for 31, i.e. *NATTR*, slots for attribute structures. We think that this number is reasonable for implementing any user-defined relation. Alternatively, you can change the definition of *NATTR* to fit your own requirements, but in that case you will have to re-estimate the actual size of the structure **header**. The structure **attribute** is used to implement relation attributes. Therefore, it contains such members as the name of the attribute (at_name), its size in bytes (at_size), its data type (at_type), and the type of its corresponding index (at_key).

Figure 4.3 shows how the structure **relation** is connected with the query processing structures at run-time. The query processing structures include the data structures **sel, sattr, srel,** and **scan** and the intermediate code structures **operand** and **code**. As observed from Figure 4.3 all these structures are chained into a common chain of structures which we call the *activation chain*. The activation chain extends from the structure **sel** to the structure **relation**. The activation chain is always set up during the parsing of data manipulation statements. In particular, all the structures contained in the activation chain are generated and linked to each other during the process of query decomposition. The *intermediate code structures* which include the code array and the operand structures, at the top of Figure 4.3, are generated during the compilation of predicate expressions and are used by the predicate expression evaluator during query evaluation. This means that a query which does not involve any predicate expressions will be evaluated only in terms of the activation chain developed at the time of query decomposition.

We will take a closer look at the REQUIEM query processing structures now. The structure **sel** is an ancillary structure whose sole purpose is to link the selected relations (**srel**) and selected attribute (**sattr**) structures to one another by means of structure pointers. The pointer member of this structure, **sl_bindings**, is used to connect the activation chain with the appropriate binding structures in the case of user-defined application programs; see Chapter 14. The structure **srel** contains information pertaining to the contents of a relation involved in a query, while the linked list of **sattr** structures, pointed to by the **sel** structure element **sl_attrs**, is used to record information pertaining to each individual attribute of this relation. Finally, the structure **scan** is used to record information required during the process of file management. Such information includes the tuple buffer **sc_tuple** which is filled with the contents of the tuples satisfying a query, the actual location of the tuple in the data file **sc_recpos**, the number of attributes in a relation **sc_natrs**, etc. As the individual components of the query processing data structures are covered in detail in forthcoming chapters there is no need to describe them any further.

The utility data structures are special purpose data structures which are tailored to meet the particular requirements of specific REQUIEM tasks, such as indexing or view processing. We shall describe these structures in some detail in the chapters which cover the REQUIEM modules that utilize them.

4.3   Sample query processing in REQUIEM

To show how RQL queries are processed we will consider a sample RQL statement which we will use throughout this section as a vehicle to demonstrate query processing related issues. The **delete** statement is one of the most representative RQL statements as it involves predicate expression evaluation, tuple fetching, I/O operations, and possibly indexing. Consider the following sample query:

delete from *Supplier* **where** *location* = *"London"*;   (4.1)

If executed this query will result in multiple tuple deletion.

Let us consider how this query will be executed stepwise by the various REQUIEM modules. First the lexical analyzer part of REQUIEM will start assembling the input characters of the above query until it recognizes the keyword **delete**. Subsequently, the lexical analyzer will exit to the parser by indicating that it has recognized a valid RQL statement. Accordingly, it is the task of the REQUIEM parser to resume execution. The parser will first

make sure that the syntax of the above delete statement is as anticipated
by the RQL syntax rules. In doing so the parser calls the query decomposer
part of REQUIEM which assists the parser in recognizing the RQL symbols
in an input query. The query decomposer will call the predicate expression
compiler as soon as it encounters the symbol **where** which introduces RQL
predicates. Next, the query decomposer returns to the parser after having
made sure that the predicate compiler has correctly parsed the predicate
associated with query 4.1 and has generated intermediate code which is to
be evaluated by the predicate expression evaluator. It is during this stage
that the query decomposer and the predicate expression compiler build the
retrieval context for the **delete** statement. Actually, the query decomposer
builds the activation chain for the **delete** statement, while the predicate expression compiler constructs the intermediate code structure depicted at the
top of Figure 4.3. It must be noted that in this case the intermediate code
structure comprises a code array which includes two operand elements corresponding to the attribute *LOCATION* and the character constant *London*
which are involved in the predicate of the **delete** query.

Now the parser has to consider how the query will be further processed.
It must first decide whether the attributes involved in the predicate expression are indexed or not. Let us assume for the sake of the example that
the attribute location is not indexed, which is actually true if we consider
the definition of the suppliers-and-products database schema in Chapter 3.
Consequently, the parser calls the file manager part of REQUIEM which
will fetch the tuple(s) to be deleted from the appropriate file underlying
the *SUPPLIER* relation. During the process of tuple fetching the predicate
associated with **delete** statement is evaluated so that only the tuples which
satisfy the predicate are fetched from the appropriate file. The file manager
will then place the tuples(s) fetched from the file into a tuple buffer and
set appropriate control bits in each tuple to indicate that the tuples have
been deleted. Subsequently, the file manager will rewrite the contents of the
tuple buffer back to the appropriate file. When all the tuples have been processed the file manager returns to the parser. Finally, the parser will check
the existence of any interpretation errors and if everything went according
to plan it will report back to the user that it has deleted the appropriate
number of tuples; otherwise the deletion process will be abandoned with the
appropriate error message forwarded to the user.

4.4   Source listing 1

file: requ.h

```
1    /* REQUIEM - definition file */
2    #include <stdio.h>
3    #include <ctype.h>
4    #include <string.h>
5
6    /*-----------------------------------------------------------
7    |                       definitions                        |
8    ----------------------------------------------------------- */
9
10   #define BOOL        int
11   #define DQUOTE      '"'
12   #define EOL         '\n' /* define end of line */
13   #define EQUAL       0
14   #define FALSE       0
15   #define FAIL        -1
16   #define FIRSTGTR    1
17   #define FIRSTLSS    -1
18   #define HTSIZE      1009 /* must be prime to hash */
19   #define INDEX       0
20   #define IO_ERROR    -2   /* returned if user enters wrong data */
21   #define NEWLINE     '\n' /* define carriage return line feed */
22   #define NO_ERROR    0    /* error free computation */
23   #define NOINDEX     1
24   #define TERMINATOR  ';'  /* RQL sentence terminator */
25   #define SLASH       '/'
26   #define TRUE        1
27   #define VOID        int
28
29   /* -----------------------------------------------------------
30   |               external function  definitions            |
31   ----------------------------------------------------------- */
32
33   extern char *malloc();
34   extern char *rmalloc();
35   extern char *calloc();
36   extern char **dcalloc();
37   extern char *sprintf();
38   extern char *strcat();
39   extern char *strcpy();
40
41   /* -----------------------------------------------------------
42   |                   macro definitions                     |
43   ----------------------------------------------------------- */
44
45   #define is_alpha(ch) ((((ch) >= 'A' && (ch) <= 'Z') ||\
46                          ((ch) >= 'a' && (ch) <= 'z')) ? 1 : 0)
47   #define is_digit(x) ((x>='0' && x<='9') ? 1 : 0)
48   #define is_blank(x) ((x==' ') ? 1 : 0)
49   #define to_decimal(x) (x-'0')
50   #define to_upper(ch) (((ch) >= 'a' && (ch) <= 'z')?\
51                          (ch) - 'a' + 'A' : (ch))
52   #define put_back(ch)    (put_back_char = (ch))
53   #define to_lower(ch) (((ch) >= 'A' && (ch) <= 'Z') ?\
54                          (ch) - 'A' + 'a' : (ch))
55   #define BELL            putchar(7)
```

```
56    #define MAX(x, y)        (((x) >= (y)) ? (x) : (y))
57    #define MIN(x, y)        (((x) <= (y)) ? (x) : (y))
58    #define is_sign(x)       ((x == '-' || x == '+') ? 1 : 0)
59    #define MALLOC(x)        ((x *)malloc(sizeof(x)))
60    #define CALLOC(n, x)     ((x *)calloc((unsigned) n, sizeof(x)))
61
62    /* ---------------------------------------------------------
63       | The following macros simplify the inline code,        |
64       | they prevent having to type complex constructs like:  |
65       | slptr->sl_rels->sr_scan                               |
66       | this would be written as:   SEL_SCAN                  |
67       --------------------------------------------------------- */
68
69    #define ATTRIBUTE_KEY    saptr->sa_attr->at_key
70    #define ATTRIBUTE_SIZE   saptr->sa_attr->at_size
71    #define ATTRIBUTE_TYPE   saptr->sa_attr->at_type
72    #define OPERAND_LENGTH   c_operand->o_value.ov_char.ovc_length
73    #define OPERAND_STRING   c_operand->o_value.ov_char.ovc_string
74    #define OPERAND_TYPE     c_operand->o_value.ov_char.ovc_type
75    #define RELATION_HEADER  rptr->rl_header
76    #define SCAN_HEADER      sptr->sc_relation->rl_header
77    #define SCAN_RELATION    sptr->sc_relation
78    #define SCAN_TUPLE       sptr->sc_tuple
79    #define SEL_ATTRS        slptr->sl_attrs
80    #define SEL_HEADER slptr->sl_rels->sr_scan->sc_relation->rl_header
81    #define SEL_NATTRS       slptr->sl_rels->sr_scan->sc_nattrs
82    #define SEL_RELATION     slptr->sl_rels->sr_scan->sc_relation
83    #define SEL_RELS         slptr->sl_rels
84    #define SEL_SCAN         slptr->sl_rels->sr_scan
85    #define SEL_TUPLE        slptr->sl_rels->sr_scan->sc_tuple
86    #define SREL_HEADER      srptr->sr_scan->sc_relation->rl_header
87    #define SREL_NEXT        srptr->sr_next
88    #define SREL_RELATION    srptr->sr_scan->sc_relation
89
90    /* ---------------------------------------------------------
91       |                    program limits                     |
92       --------------------------------------------------------- */
93
94    #define CODEMAX     100    /* maximum length of code array */
95    #define KEYWORDMAX  12     /* maximum keyword length */
96    #define LINEMAX     132    /* maximum input line length */
97    #define NUMBERMAX   30     /* maximum number length */
98    #define STACKMAX    20     /* maximum interpreter stack size */
99    #define STRINGMAX   132    /* maximum string length */
100   #define TABLEMAX    132    /* maximum table output line */
101
102   /* ---------------------------------------------------------
103      |                    token definitions                  |
104      --------------------------------------------------------- */
105
106   #define EOS        '\0'
107   #define LSS        -1
108   #define LEQ        -2
109   #define EQL        -3
110   #define NEQ        -4
111   #define GEQ        -5
112   #define PART       -6
113   #define GTR        -7
114   #define ADD        -8
115   #define SUB        -9
116   #define MUL        -10
```

```
117     #define DIV             -11
118     #define MOD             -12
119     #define INSERT          -13
120     #define CHAR            -14
121     #define NUM             -15
122     #define ID              -16
123     #define STRING          -17
124     #define NUMBER          -18
125     #define UPDATE          -19
126     #define PRINT           -20
127     #define IMPORT          -21
128     #define EXPORT          -22
129     #define INTO            -23
130     #define VIEW            -24
131     #define FOREIGN         -25
132     #define EXTRACT         -26
133     #define DEFINE          -27
134     #define SHOW            -28
135     #define USING           -29
136     #define SORT            -30
137     #define BY              -31
138     #define KEY             -32
139     #define REFERENCES      -33
140     #define SET             -34
141     #define REAL            -35
142     #define REALNO          -36
143     #define ALL             -37
144     #define OVER            -38
145     #define PROJECT         -39
146     #define MODIFY          -40
147     #define DROP            -41
148     #define JOIN            -42
149     #define ON              -43
150     #define WITH            -44
151     #define SIGNEDNO        -45
152     #define UNION           -46
153     #define INTERSECT       -47
154     #define DIFFERENCE      -48
155     #define DISPLAY         -49
156     #define FOCUS           -50
157     #define AS              -51
158     #define HELP            -52
159     #define SELECT          -53
160     #define FROM            -54
161     #define WHERE           -55
162     #define CREATE          -56
163     #define DELETE          -57
164     #define ASGN            -58
165     #define IN              -59
166     #define UNIQUE          -60
167     #define SECONDARY       -61
168     #define BOOLEAN         -62
169     #define COUNT           -63
170     #define GROUP           -64
171     #define AVG             -65
172     #define MAXM            -66
173     #define MINM            -67
174     #define SUM             -68
175     #define ASSIGN          -69
176     #define TO              -70
177     #define PURGE           -71
```

```
178   #define EXIT           -72
179   #define QUIT           -73
180   #define IS             -74
181   #define WHEN           -75
182   #define EXPOSE         -76
183
184   /* ------------------------------------------------------------
185        |                operand type definitions                 |
186        ------------------------------------------------------- */
187
188   #define LITERAL    1
189   #define ATTR       2
190   #define TEMPBOOL   3
191   #define TEMPNUM    4
192   #define VAR        5
193
194   /* ------------------------------------------------------------
195        |              attribute type  definitions                !
196        ------------------------------------------------------- */
197
198   #define TCHAR    1
199   #define TNUM     2
200   #define TREAL    3
201
202   /* ------------------------------------------------------------
203        |             tuple status code definitions               |
204        ------------------------------------------------------- */
205
206   #define ACTIVE   1
207   #define DELETED  0
208
209   /* ------------------------------------------------------------
210        |      relation header & page format definitions          |
211        ------------------------------------------------------- */
212
213   #define ASIZE          16      /* size of an attribute entry */
214   #define ANSIZE         10      /* size of an attribute name */
215   #define HEADER_SIZE 512        /* size of relation header */
216   #define HDSIZE         16      /* size of a relation entry */
217   #define NATTRS         31      /* number of attrs in header */
218   #define QUATTRSIZE     21      /* qualified attribute size */
219   #define RNSIZE         10      /* size of a relation name */
220
221   /* ------------------------------------------------------------
222        |                error code definitions                   |
223        ------------------------------------------------------- */
224
225   #define END        0 /* end of retrieval set */
226   #define INSMEM     1 /* insufficient memory */
227   #define RELFNF     2 /* relation file not found */
228   #define BADHDR     3 /* bad relation file header */
229   #define TUPINP     4 /* tuple input error */
230   #define TUPOUT     5 /* tuple output error */
231   #define RELFUL     6 /* relation file full */
232   #define RELCRE     7 /* error creating relation file */
233   #define DUPATT     8 /* duplicate attribute on relation create */
234   #define MAXATT     9 /* too many attributes on relation create */
235   #define INSBLK    10 /* insufficient disk blocks */
236   #define SYNTAX    11 /* command syntax error */
237   #define ATUNDF    12 /* attribute name undefined */
238   #define ATAMBG    13 /* attribute name ambiguous */
```

```
239    #define RLUNDF      14 /* relation name undefined */
240    #define CDSIZE      15 /* boolean expression code too big */
241    #define INPFNF      16 /* input file not found */
242    #define OUTCRE      17 /* output file creation error */
243    #define INDFNF      18 /* indirect command file not found */
244    #define BADSET      19 /* bad set parameter */
245    #define HASHSIZ     20 /* hash table size exceeded */
246    #define UNOP        21 /* union operand not allowed */
247    #define UNLINK      22 /* error in removing files */
248    #define LINK        23 /* error in renaming files */
249    #define WRLEN       24 /* wrong length of identifier */
250    #define BADCURS     25 /* cursor mispositioned */
251    #define WRONGID     26 /* wrong identifier specified */
252    #define UNDEFVAR    27 /* undefined variable */
253    #define STACKOVRFL  28 /* stack overflow */
254    #define STACKUNDFL  29 /* stack underflow */
255    #define INCNST      30 /* inconsistent info. */
256    #define INDXCRE     31 /* index creation error */
257    #define NOKEY       32 /* key attribute not specified */
258    #define IXFLNF      33 /* index file not found */
259    #define IXFAIL      34 /* indexing failed */
260    #define DUPTUP      35 /* duplicate tuple */
261    #define NOEXSTUP    36 /* non-existent tuple */
262    #define IXATRNF     37 /* indexed attribute not found */
263    #define IXDELFAIL   38 /* index delete failed */
264    #define KEYEXCD     39 /* key length exceeded */
265    #define WRIXCOM     40 /* write index error */
266    #define WRPREDID    41 /* wrong predicate id */
267    #define AGGRPARAM   42 /* wrong aggregate function parameter */
268    #define FILEMV      43 /* error in file transfer */
269    #define WRNRELREM   44 /* non-existent relation file */
270    #define UNDEFTYPE   45 /* undefined attribute type */
271    #define LINELONG    46 /* command line too long */
272    #define UPDTERR     47 /* error in updating */
273    #define NOALIAS     48 /* no aliases allowed */
274    #define NJOIN       49 /* join operation failed */
275    #define QUATTR      50 /* define qualified attribute is needed */
276    #define UNATTR      51 /* inapplicable attribute name */
277    #define MAX5        52 /* maximum no. of attributes exceeded */
278    #define NESTED      53 /* error in nested command */
279    #define VIEWDEF     54 /* wrong view definition */
280    #define VIEWDEL     55 /* wrong view deletion */
281    #define UNIQEXCD    56 /* no. of unique keys exceeded */
282    #define TOOMANY     57 /* too many indexed attributes */
283    #define WRNGFGNKEY  58 /* wrong foreign key */
284    #define WRNGCOMB    59 /* wrong foreign key combination */
285    #define WRNGINS     60 /* wrong insertion operation */
286    #define ILLREL      61 /* illegal relation name */
287    /* ------------------------------------------------------------
288    |                   structure definitions                     |
289    ------------------------------------------------------------ */
290
291    /* -------------- command & query structures --------------- */
292
293    struct attribute { /* static boundary: cater for alignment */
294        short at_size;              /* attribute size in bytes */
295        char  at_name[ANSIZE];      /* attribute name */
296        char  at_type;              /* attribute type */
297        char  at_key;               /* attribute key */
298        char  at_semid;             /* semantically identical attribute */
299        char  at_unused[ASIZE-ANSIZE-5]; /* unused space */
```

```
300    };
301
302    /* in disk file descriptor */
303    struct header {  /* alignment: size must be 512 bytes */
304      long  hd_avail;      /* address of first free record */
305      short hd_cursor;     /* relative cursor position */
306      short hd_data;       /* offset to first data byte */
307      short hd_size;       /* size of each tuple in bytes */
308      short hd_tcnt;       /* no. of tuples in relation */
309      short hd_tmax;       /* relative pos. of last tuple */
310      char hd_unique;      /* unique attribute specifier */
311      char hd_unused[HDSIZE-15];        /* unused space */
312      struct attribute hd_attrs[NATTRS]; /* table of attributes */
313    };
314
315    struct relation {
316      char rl_name[RNSIZE]; /* relation name */
317      int rl_store;          /* flag indicating a store happened */
318      int rl_fd;             /* file descriptor for relation file */
319      int rl_scnref;         /* number of scans for this relation */
320      struct header rl_header;  /* relation file header block */
321      struct relation *rl_next; /* pointer to next relation */
322    };
323
324    struct scan {
325      struct relation *sc_relation; /* ptr to relation definition */
326      long sc_recpos;               /* tuple-pos. in data file */
327      unsigned int sc_nattrs;       /* no. of attrs in relation */
328      unsigned int sc_dtnum;        /* desired tuple number */
329      unsigned int sc_atnum;        /* actual tuple number */
330      int sc_store;                 /* flag indicating a store */
331      char *sc_tuple;               /* tuple buffer */
332    };
333
334    struct sattr {
335      char *sa_rname;           /* relation name */
336      char *sa_aname;           /* attribute name */
337      char *sa_name;            /* alternate attribute name */
338      char *sa_aptr;            /* ptr to attr in tuple buffer */
339      struct srel *sa_srel;     /* ptr to the selected relation */
340      struct attribute *sa_attr; /* attribute structure ptr */
341      struct sattr *sa_next;    /* next selected attr in list */
342    };
343
344    struct sel {
345      struct srel *sl_rels;       /* selected relations */
346      struct sattr *sl_attrs;     /* selected attributes */
347      struct binding *sl_bindings; /* user variable bindings */
348    };
349
350    struct srel {
351      char *sr_name;          /* alternate relation name */
352      struct scan *sr_scan;   /* relation scan structure ptr */
353      int sr_ctuple;          /* current fetched tuple flag */
354      int sr_update;          /* updated tuple flag */
355      struct srel *sr_next;   /* next selected relation in list */
356    };
357
358    struct unattrs {
359      char *name;    /* attr name participating in a union */
360      short size;    /* size of attribute in bytes */
```

```
361    };
362
363    /* --------------code evaluation structures ---------------- */
364
365    union code_cell {
366      int (*c_operator)();
367      struct operand *c_operand;
368    };
369
370    struct operand {
371      int o_type;              /* type ,i.e. ATTR, VAR, etc. */
372      union  {
373        struct {
374          int ovc_type;        /* type of attribute, i.e. char, int */
375          char *ovc_string;  /* attribute value */
376          int ovc_length;    /* length of attribute */
377        } ov_char;
378        int ov_boolean;        /* result of a logical operation */
379      } o_value;
380    };
381
382    struct symbol {
383      char varname[ANSIZE+1];
384      struct operand *varopd;
385    };
386
387    /* -------------- pgm interface structures ------------------ */
388
389    struct binding {
390      struct attribute *bd_attr;  /* bound attribute */
391      char *bd_vtuple;.            /* pointer to value in tuple */
392      char *bd_vuser;             /* pointer to user buffer */
393      struct binding *bd_next;    /* next binding */
394    };
395
396    /* ---------------- view & icf structures -------------------- */
397
398    struct cmd_file {
399      FILE *cf_fp;
400      struct text *cf_text;
401      int cf_savech;
402      char *cf_lptr;
403      struct cmd_file *cf_next;
404    };
405
406    struct text {
407      char *txt_text;
408      struct text *txt_next;
409    };
410
411
412    struct view {
413      char *view_name;
414      struct text *view_text;
415      struct view *view_next;
416    };
417
418    /* -------------- transient file structures ----------------- */
419
420    struct trans_file {
421      char t_file[RNSIZE+5];
```

```
422     struct trans_file *t_next;
423   };
424
425   /* -------------- hash & indexing structures -------------- */
426
427   struct hash {
428     char      *value;         /* token value to be hashed */
429     char      *relation;      /*  relation token  */
430     int       dup_tcnt;       /* no of duplicate entries */
431     double    aggr_param;     /* aggregate function parameter */
432   };
433
434   struct pred {
435     char *pr_rlname;          /* name of rel containing index */
436     char **pr_ixtype;         /* type of index */
437     char **pr_atname;         /* attr name of indexed attr */
438     struct operand **pr_opd;  /* operand struct of indexed attr */
439   };
440
441   struct skey {
442     int sk_type;
443     struct attribute *sk_aptr;
444     int sk_start;
445     struct skey *sk_next;
446   };
447
448   /* ------------------------------------------------------------ */
```

5

File Management

Before discussing the design and implementation of REQUIEM it is sensible to develop an understanding of the way in which data is organized in secondary storage. In this and the next chapter we focus our attention on the random access file organization scheme utilized by the REQUIEM file manager and the dense indexing scheme used by the REQUIEM access plan modules. These two chapters provide the necessary foundation for an understanding of how relational data is to be stored and show how the relational approach is mapped onto the well-known concepts of data files and indices. We begin by considering the functionality and implementation of the file management module.

The file manager part of REQUIEM uses the conventional disk management facilities of the underlying operating system in such a way as to permit REQUIEM to regard the disk space as a collection of stored files. The low-level operations performed by the file manager include the retrieval of stored records (tuples) for a given file, or the addition, replacement, and deletion of stored records. Using these low-level or primitive file management operations the DBMS is in a position to manipulate the storage structures underlying the conceptual level in a way that is tailored to the needs of particular queries.

5.1   File organization

The term "file organization" refers to the way in which records are stored in a data file. In other words it is reserved to refer to the data structures used for organizing data. The type of access to records available on a data file depends on the organization of the file and the storage media. An operating system features at least two types of file access: *sequential* and *random*.

When a file is arranged sequentially, programs read (or write) the file from beginning to end, accessing all records in succession. This means that, for example, the fifth record of the file can be read (or written) only after the first four records have been read (or written). Obviously, searching for a particular record requires the same process. Sequential files are generally opened in read or write mode, thus refusing to rewrite (update) any record in place. The user is forced to copy a file to another file during updating. The fact that sequential files are limited to sequential access implies that programmers can utilize records of varying length.

With *random access file organization* (often referred to as *direct file organization*) the program can read an individual record specified by its rank directly, without having to access any previous records first. This organization is, thus, described as random because it is possible to access a specific record within the data file without having to traverse sequentially through the entire file. Random files can be opened in read or write mode and generally offer only fixed length records. The logical ordering of the records in a randomly organized file need not bear any resemblance to their physical sequence. A common interpretation of random file organization that is available in most high-level programming languages is called *relative file organization* [16]. With this file organization the position of a record in the data file is specified as a record number relative to a prespecified position in the file, e.g. the beginning of the file or the current position in the file. Each record address can be computed according to the following formula:

$$record\_address = (relative\ record\ no.\ *\ record\ length) + origin \quad (5.1)$$

where *record length* must be a fixed length, and *origin* can specify any location in the file. Normally, the origin is taken to mean the beginning of the file. The limitation that records must be of fixed length imparts an advantage: namely, the data file can be updated in place. Relative files can be opened for sequential access and can be treated as sequential files, if this is required.

The above forms of file access are normally provided by most of the well-known operating systems. Nevertheless, the behavior of one operating system may significantly differ from another. In fact, one of the most successful operating systems is Unix which presents significant deviations from the classical description of operating systems [30]. Unix is a very flexible system to use with a DBMS, which will manage file records for each task, and a difficult system to use without a DBMS as its file structures are not easy to utilize with application programs.

The Unix operating system provides random access to files through programs written in such high-level languages as C and Fortran-77, so that the average user never needs to be concerned with how the internal operation is carried out. Effectively, it allows you to think about a file as a character array on disk and it provides a mechanism for setting or repositioning an internal file pointer. Explicit pointer positioning can be achieved by using the system call lseek(). The general form of this function is

$$lseek(fd, \; offset, \; origin) \tag{5.2}$$

Its effect is to force the current position in the file specified by the file descriptor *fd* to point to the position *offset*. This position is taken relative to the location specified by the integer *origin* which can assume one of the values 0, 1, or 2 to signify that *offset* is to be measured from the beginning, from the current position, or from the end of the file, respectively.

Generally speaking, an operating system does not offer all the file access capabilities that are required by database management. This implies that we shall have to rely on the DBMS to perform those file access operations that are not possible with the operating system alone. The most usual file access modes required by database management rely on retrieval of records ordered by record keys. This kind of retrieval is usually provided by some sort of index structure.

An index is normally stored in an index file and associates the value of some field or fields of a record (usually called an index or search key) with a pointer identifying the address of the record containing the value of the index key in a data file. Using an index a program can retrieve the records that have a field matching the given index key value. For example, by using an index built on the supplier identification number field, a program can access the supplier data file by means of this identification number. Accordingly, you can retrieve records matching the index key field, records whose index key field is greater than or equal to the given index key field, etc. We say that a file uses some kind of indexed organization if it contains at least one index that enables direct data record searches and accesses.

Indices can be of two types: *primary* and *secondary*. Primary indices guarantee the uniqueness of the searched key field; each record includes a unique index key field value, which does not exist in any other record of that file. For example, an index by *SUP_ID* on the supplier data file of the suppliers-and-products database must be a primary index as explained in Chapter 3. Secondary indices (0, 1, or several per file) do not guarantee such index key uniqueness. For example, an index on supplier name is secondary as two supplier records may contain the same name.

Indexed sequential file organization provides sequential and random access to the records in a file in terms of a single index key field. However, many applications in database management require access to records in a data file by more than one key field. The other key fields which may be used to identify the data records in a file are the secondary indices. Consequently, this file organization is known as *multiple-key file organization*.

Finally, another mode of file access which is particularly useful for database management, as we shall see later in this book, is hashing.

5.2   Record representation

In a first approximation a relation can be thought of as a file and its tuples as records of a single fixed length. In fact, this is an oversimplification of relational database storage. If such a database were to be functional, it would require access paths. For example, it would contain an index table stored in a file which is called an index file. Index keys in the index files point to storage locations of fixed length data records in the data file. Alternatively, files can be structured in such a way that each file can accommodate records of variable lengths. In general, files comprising fixed length records are easier to implement than variable length record files and in this text we will consider only files comprising fixed length records. Files of variable length record may use many of the techniques applied to the fixed length case; more information on variable length records can be found in [20].

Suppose that we want to search through a fixed length file, deleting all records satisfying some easily checked criterion. This operation involves reading through a file in no particular order and picking out the qualifying records. Let us look at this operation in some detail as an example. As a handy example of a fixed length record let us consider a data file consisting only of supplier records to represent the relation *SUPPLIER*. Each supplier record can be defined by using the RQL data definition facilities as explained in Chapter 3.

If we assume that each character occupies a single byte, our typical *SUPPLIER* record occupies 55 bytes (5 bytes for the attributes *SUP_NO* and *PROD_NO*, 20 bytes for the attribute *SUP_NAME* and finally 25 bytes for the attribute *SUP_ADDRESS*), see Figure 5.1. The normal approach is to use the first 55 bytes in total to store the first record, the next 55 bytes to store the next record, and so on. However, there is a serious problem associated with this kind of approach: it is quite difficult to delete a record from this structure. The memory space occupied by the deleted record must either be filled with some other record of the file, or the record must be marked as deleted and ignored.

When a record is deleted, say the one with *SUP_NO* value 135, we would move the record that succeeds it into the space occupied by the deleted record, and so on, until each record succeeding the deleted record has been displaced one position ahead, see Figure 5.2. This approachq is called *record compression* and can be time consuming as it may involve moving a

	SUP_NO	SUP_NAME	SUP_ADDRESS	PROD_NO
Record 1	125	Jones	London	21
Record 2	128	Black	New York	25
Record 3	135	Gray	Paris	17
Record 4	127	Smith	Zurich	12

Figure 5.1 The supplier data file.

substantial number of records. On the other hand, a simple delete mark on a deleted record is not sufficient since it implies a searching procedure to locate the available space when an insertion is required. This predicament can be remedied by the use of a special data structure known as the file header.

	SUP_NO	SUP_NAME	SUP_ADDRESS	PROD_NO
Record 1	125	Jones	London	21
Record 2	128	Black	New York	25
Record 3	127	Smith	Zurich	12

Figure 5.2 The supplier data file after deletion of the third record using record compression.

Normally, each data file in REQUIEM contains a file header or *file control block* which includes information about the nature of the file. This descriptive material includes the length of the records, the address of the first data record in the file, the number of records stored in the file, whether or not there are indices associated with the file and what kind of indices, and so on. When a file is opened for use, all of the information in the header is brought into memory and thus becomes available for inspection. In a data file deleted records (tuples) may be intermixed with the active, but usually have a delete character (tuple status code = DELETED) as their first character. As mentioned in Chapter 4 data file headers have a standard size of 512 bytes. Once you know the size of the data file header you can manipulate the records contained in this file fairly easily. What you need to do is to open the data file and call lseek() to get past the data file header. Subsequently, you can call the standard C function read() to read each record, using the size of the record. You should always check whether the record you have just read contains a delete or active tuple status character. Recall that each database record in REQUIEM is implemented using pure ASCII character set representations.

In REQUIEM there is a data file header as well as an index file header for each relation. Amongst other things, what we require from the data file header is to store the address of the first data record in the data file whose contents are deleted. Subsequently, we mark this data record as deleted and use it to store the address of the next available record. What this

implies is that the linking of a new free record to its successive free record
is realized by setting the pointer field of the former to a value that gives the
address of the latter. In this way we obtain a *linked list of available records*
whose list head is stored in the data file header (see Figure 5.3). If no list
space is available then the list head points to nothing and all insertions are
performed at the end of the file.

The use of pointers demands very careful programming on behalf of the
system programmers. If we change the contents of a record pointed to by
another record in the list, that pointer becomes invalid in the sense that it
no longer points to the intended record. Such pointers are called *dangling
pointers* and should be avoided at any cost.

The above file organization implies that each relation is stored as a combination of a data and an index file. This allows REQUIEM to take full
advantage of the facilities provided by the underlying operating system,
and assume that all data records are of fixed length. A large-scale and more
sophisticated DBMS, such as SQL/DS, does not rely directly on the underlying operating system for file management. Such a DBMS may choose to
store all relations in one large operating system file whose management is
left to the DBMS file manager.

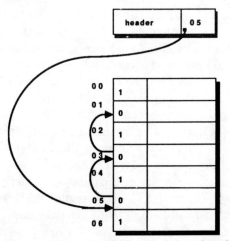

Figure 5.3 List of available records in a data file.

5.3   File management in REQUIEM

In the following section we shall describe the functions that REQUIEM provides for file management in more detail. The REQUIEM file management

functions can be divided into three broad categories:

1. File access: open and close a relation data file.
2. Tuple access: fetch, store, update, and delete a tuple.
3. Utility functions: position the file pointer, generate a file name, transform a tuple index into a file relative address, adjust a data tuple.

REQUIEM provides three functions that you can use to initialize and complete access to a relation data file, namely **rfind()**, **db_ropen()**, and **db_rclose()**. Once a file has been opened, information about the corresponding relation is stored in a structure of type **relation**. This structure holds indispensable information that is required to access the data contained in a relation, namely its tuples. In general, more than one relation can be involved in a query (consider for example a **join** statement). At some point each of these relations involves access to its corresponding data file. Hence, the information associated with this relation is assembled and stored into its respective **relation** structure, see Figure 4.3. The structures of all relations involved in a query statement are placed into a first-in-first-out *fifo* list. A pointer to the head of the list is stored in the variable **relations**. This variable can only be accessed by functions that are local to the file management module.

As explained in the previous chapter a retrieval context holds the information that is necessary to access an individual tuple of a relation on the disk. This information consists of the following items:

1. The relation name.
2. A flag indicating that a store has taken place.
3. The file descriptor by means of which the relation file can be accessed on the disk.
4. The header block containing relation-specific data.
5. Data that is used when a disk access must be performed to read or write a tuple.
6. The number of **scan** structures that are used to access an individual tuple.

The function **rfind()** is called in REQUIEM whenever a relation prepares itself for data access. This function returns a pointer to the relation structure that can be used to access the stored relation whose name is supplied as a parameter. When entering the function, the list of already loaded relations is checked to determine whether the requested relation has already been opened for data access. If a relation has been found in the list of already loaded relations, the function terminates by returning a pointer to the loaded relation's relation structure. Otherwise, the internal name of the

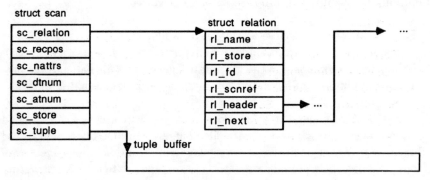

Figure 5.4 The scan structure.

relation file is appropriately generated, a new relation data file is physically created and a new relation structure is allocated and initialized. As a last activity, the relation name is copied into the relation structure and the new structure is linked into the list of already loaded relations. Finally, a pointer to the relation structure is returned and the function terminates.

Actually, the function **rfind()** is invoked within the function **db_ropen()**. This function is called whenever a relation should be accessed during query processing. The C structure that holds the information utilized when tuples are to be sequentially accessed is, as normal, the **scan** structure (see Figure 5.4). We will discuss the internals of this structure in more detail during the description of the fetching and storing of tuples, later in this chapter. Function **db_ropen()** commences execution by requesting a relation structure through a call to the function **rfind()**. Next, it allocates and initializes a **scan** structure. If the current call to the function **db_ropen()** is the first call involving a given relation, the corresponding relation file is opened for reading and writing by a call to the operating system routine **open** and the corresponding file descriptor is stored into the **relation** structure. All subsequent calls to the function **db_ropen()** assume that the relation file has already been opened by a prior call and that it has not been closed in the meantime. In order to guarantee the correctness of this mechanism the relation structure contains the element **rl_scnref** that serves as the reference counter for a specified relation. Each time a new access to the relation is established, by a call to the function **db_ropen()**, **rl_scnref** is incremented. This counter is decremented whenever an access to the relation concludes by a call to the function **db_rclose()** which attempts to close an already opened relation file whenever the file is not going to be used for any further access.

Function **db_rclose()** is called when a sequential access to a relation is about to terminate. Prior to closing the relation file, **db_rclose()** must determine by checking the scan element sc_store whether any tuples have been stored in, or deleted from, the relation file. If so, the relation header must be updated to reflect the modified contents of the stored relation file. This task is accomplished by invoking the function rc_done() and supplying it with the appropriate actual parameters. If the present reference represents the final reference to this specific relation, the relation data file must be closed thereafter. Subsequently, the relation's index file is closed as well and the global variable pixd (indicating the existence of an index file counterpart of the current data file) is cleared to indicate that currently no open index exists for this relation. Finally, the corresponding relation structure is removed from the list of the already loaded relation structures and the space occupied by the scan structure is freed.

Once a relation has been opened for access, after a call to the function db_ropen(), a set of functions is needed to implement access to specified tuples of this specific relation. There are several operations associated with working with tuples in a given relation: searching for a tuple in the relation, adding a tuple to the relation, and removing a tuple from the relation. For this purpose REQUIEM offers the following functions:

1. fetch_tuple() which fetches the next tuple from the disk and stores it in a tuple buffer for later use and manipulation.
2. store_tuple() which stores a tuple on the disk.
3. delete_tuple() which deletes a specified tuple from the relation file.
4. update_tuple() which updates entire tuples or portions of specified tuples.

In the following we elaborate on each of the above functions in turn.

5.3.1 Tuple fetching

Access to tuples of a relation is performed by means of the scan structure. This structure indicates whether a requested tuple has already been read from the disk and is already stored in its respective tuple buffer. If a tuple must be fetched from the disk, the scan structure holds the information required to locate the tuple in the corresponding relation data file. A scan structure is provided each time sequential access to the tuples of a relation is requested. The main members of the scan structure are depicted in Figure 5.4. The element sc_dtnum holds the relative number of the desired tuple whereas the element sc_atnum holds the relative number of the tuple that has currently been retrieved from the disk and has been stored in the tuple buffer of the scan structure. It must be noted that for identification purposes each tuple in the data file, whether active or not, has a unique

relative tuple number. Relative tuple numbers start from 1 and extend to
the relative number of the last tuple in the data file. This relative number of
the last tuple in the data file is always stored in the relation header element
hd_tmax.

In general, if a tuple has been successfully retrieved from the disk the
tuple buffer sc_tuple contains all the tuple data, i.e. the attribute values
contained in this tuple. The first byte of each tuple denotes the status of
the corresponding stored tuple. For a nondeleted tuple this first byte, also
referred to as the *status byte*, of the tuple buffer contains the value ACTIVE
indicating an active tuple. For a deleted tuple the status byte of the tuple
buffer is set to the value DELETED and the tuple buffer merely contains the
address (i.e. offset with respect to the beginning of the relation file) of the
next free tuple in the data file. This information is used to access the next
free tuple in the free list (see Figure 5.3).

Each stored relation file descriptor (rl_fd) has a *current position* in the
data file associated with it. System call routines such as **read()** and **write()**
maintain this; when either of these functions performs I/O, it is done at the
current file position, which is then incremented by the number of bytes actually read or written. As these reads or writes in REQUIEM are performed
in terms of fixed sized tuples we sometimes refer to the current file position as the *current tuple position* which is used to indicate the start address
of the current tuple in a data file. Actually, the scan structure contains a
specific member called the current tuple address identifier (sc_recpos) which
always preserves this address to facilitate I/O operations. Before embarking
on the description of the tuple I/O routines we will briefly describe how this
current tuple position can be set or reset during I/O operations.

Normally, when a file is first opened its current position is set at the
beginning of the file. Read or write operations cause the current position
to be incremented so that every byte is accessed in turn. However, I/O is
not always performed sequentially; random I/O is also possible. This capability is inherent in the operating system routine lseek(). By means of
this function it is possible to change the current tuple position in a file, and
either skip bytes or go back to ones previously read or written at will. Function lseek() takes a file descriptor as argument and seeks to a prespecified
position in a file. This prespecified position can be adjusted by means of a
specific flag which actually describes how the offset (size of a given tuple)
is applied. This *offset flag* in the REQUIEM file management operations
is always set in such a way that the current tuple position and the current
position always coincide.

Let us now revert to our previous topic, namely the search of tuples in a
given stored relation. Sequential access to the tuples of a relation is triggered
by a call to the query decomposer function **begin_scan()**. This function

simply sets the number of the desired tuple to 0 indicating that in the next tuple fetching operation the first tuple of the relation should be accessed. This information is used inside the function **fetch_tuple()** which is called by the query decomposer function **fetch()** whenever the next tuple of a relation is requested (see Figure 5.5). Actually, Figure 5.5 should be combined with Figure 10.3, which depicts the query decomposer function calls, to get a picture of how the query decomposer and the file manager function calls are intertwined. Next, the function loops sequentially through the tuples of a given relation until the next active tuple has been retrieved from the disk and stored in the tuple buffer of the **scan** structure, see Figure 5.4. For this purpose function **fetch_tuple()** invokes the function **get_tuple()** by passing to it the relative number of the next tuple in the sequence as an actual parameter (see Figure 5.5).

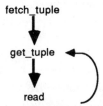

Figure 5.5 The function calls required for tuple fetching.

Two **scan** members are involved in the accessing of the next active tuple from the data file, namely **sc_dtnum**, which holds the number of the most recently fetched tuple, and **sc_atnum** which presents the relative number of the tuple that is currently stored in the tuple buffer. When fetching the next tuple, the function **get_tuple()** is called by passing to it the relative number of the next tuple in the data file, i.e. we increment the relative number of the last fetched tuple by one. When the function **get_tuple()** returns successfully, the scan element **sc_dtnum** is also incremented by one in the body of **fetch_tuple**, to indicate that the desired tuple has already been read and stored in the tuple buffer. Then, the status byte of the tuple just read is checked to determine whether the tuple is active or not. If an active tuple has been located, the function **fetch_tuple()** returns successfully; if not the function **get_tuple()** is called once again with the index of the next tuple.

Function **get_tuple()** performs the disk I/O operations required to read the desired tuple from disk and store it in the tuple buffer of the scan structure. First it confirms whether the requested tuple is already stored in the tuple buffer or not. This test is performed by comparing the number of the desired tuple (contained in the formal parameter **tnum**) with the relative number of the tuple stored in the buffer (the value of the **scan** element **sc_atnum**). If the relative number of the requested tuple is equal to the value of the header element **sc_atnum** then the requested tuple is already in the tuple buffer and the function **get_tuple()** returns immediately without having to read any data from the relation file. Alternatively, if a tuple must be read from the relation file it is first determined whether the index of the requested tuple refers to a valid tuple within the given stored relation. For this purpose the value of the header element **hd_tcnt**, which holds the relative number of the last tuple in the relation file, is compared with the relative number of the requested tuple. Next, the stored relative tuple pointer is adjusted to point to the beginning of the stored tuple by a call to the function **seek()**. In this function we compute the offset of the tuple within the relation file. Subsequently, the file pointer is adjusted accordingly by the system function **lseek()** so that the next read operation will start at the desired position. This position is eventually returned by **seek()** and stored in the **scan** element **sc_recpos**. Finally, the tuple data is read by a call to the system function **read()**.

5.3.2   Tuple storing

In REQUIEM we call the function **store_tuple()**, see Figure 5.6, whenever we wish to insert a new tuple into a given stored relation. First, we set the tuple status byte of the current tuple to **ACTIVE** and then decide whether there exists a free record in the list of free records. If not, the new tuple must be inserted at the end of the data file immediately after the current last tuple. The above distinction is made on the basis of the value of the header element **hd_avail**. This component either holds the address of the first record in the free list or is set to zero if no more free records exist. If no free records exist the address of the fictitious record which lies behind the physically last tuple in the corresponding relation file is calculated by a call to the function **seek()**. The call to this function forces the current position in the data file to point to this specific address. This address is stored as the address of the current tuple into the **sc_recpos** element of the **scan** structure. Alternatively, if a free record exists in the stored relation file then the tuple position identifier (**sc_recpos**) element of the **scan** structure must be updated to include the address of this free record. Hence, this free record is discarded as such and its address becomes the address of the current tuple which as previously mentioned is stored in the **hd_avail** element of the relation header. As stressed in the previous section free records point to their successor free record in the list of available records. This address must eventually be recorded in the relation header to denote the address of the next free record. For this reason the next free record is read from disk into the auxiliary tuple buffer **buf** by a call to the function **read_tuple()**.

Next, the file pointer of the relation file is repositioned to point to the beginning of the current tuple.

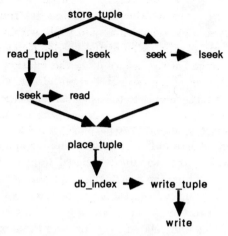

Figure 5.6 The function calls required to store a tuple.

At this point, the current tuple position has been adjusted and we are ready to write the current tuple onto the disk. For this purpose we call the function **place_tuple()**, see Figure 5.6. This function is mainly responsible for updating the index file (if indexing is required) for the relation in question. Whether indexing is required is determined by its key buffer argument. This key buffer contains for each indexed attribute its corresponding value. Obviously, the values that are stored in the key buffer are identical to the values that appear in its corresponding data tuple. If a call to the function **place_tuple()** is supplied with a non-empty key buffer argument then the flag parameter **updt** is checked to determine whether the key buffer values are to be inserted into the index file, or whether they should be updated or not. Depending on the value of the parameter **updt** the indexing functions **db_index()** or **update_ix()** are called with appropriate parameters to perform either a tuple insertion or a tuple update. Following that, the data tuple is written to the disk by a call to the function **write_tuple()**. The function **write_tuple()** simply writes the requested tuple onto the disk and increments the tuple counter.

5.3.3 Tuple deletion

Tuple deletion in REQUIEM can be triggered by invoking the query decomposer function **delete_attrs()**. The actual deletion of a tuple takes place only when the function **delete_attrs()** invokes the function **delete_tuple()** (see

Figure 5.7).

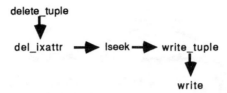

Figure 5.7 The function calls required for tuple deletion.

Function **delete_tuple()** accepts two parameters: a pointer to a scan structure and a so-called "delete buffer" **del_buf**. The delete buffer contains the indexed attribute values that should be deleted from the index file underlying a given relation. Thus, the first task of the function **delete_tuple()** is to remove any key attributes from the corresponding index file. This task is performed by a call to the indexing function **del_ixattr()** (for a more detailed discussion of this and related functions see the next chapter on the REQUIEM indexing mechanisms). Next, the tuple to be deleted is marked as such by storing in the status byte of its corresponding tuple buffer the value **DELETED**. The remaining bytes in this specific tuple buffer are used for storing the value of the current free tuple position held in the relation header element **hd_avail**. Then, the deleted tuple is linked into the free list of available records, see Figure 5.3, and the tuple position of this tuple becomes the new first free record in the data file and is stored in the header element **hd_avail**. This procedure is illustrated in Figure 5.2. Actually, Figure 5.1 shows the situation before, and Figure 5.2 shows the situation after, the specified tuple has been deleted and linked into the free list.

In order to preserve the new set of control data that has been recorded into the tuple buffer of the deleted tuple (namely the delete flag and the address of the next free tuple in the relation file) the tuple must be written onto the disk. This is achieved by a call to the function **write_tuple()**, exactly as explained in the case of tuple storing, immediately after the current tuple pointer has been adjusted by a call to the system function **lseek()**. Notice, however, that in the case of tuple deletion the tuple counter is not incremented.

5.3.4 Tuple updating

As a result of processing an **update** statement the query decomposer, through the function **update_attrs()**, will eventually evoke a call to the function **update_tuple()**, see Figure 5.8. This function guarantees that all modified tuples are written back to the disk. The fact that a tuple has been updated in the tuple buffer is indicated by setting the corresponding flag in the "selected relations" structure **srel** (see Figure 4.3). For this purpose the function **update_tuple()** inspects each selected relation structure to ensure whether the **sr_update** flag has been set or not. If an updated tuple is detected then function **db_rupdate()** is called. Function **db_rupdate()** first deletes all key values from the corresponding index file, then sets the status byte of the current tuple to ACTIVE and sets the current tuple position to point to the address of the current tuple. Finally, by a call to the function **place_tuple()**, which is the same function called by the tuple storing functions, see Figure 5.6, it sees that the tuple is written back to the disk at the specified address, guaranteeing thus that both the index and data files are updated simultaneously.

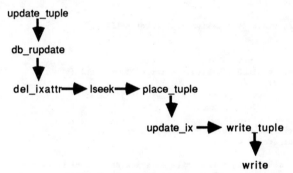

Figure 5.8 The function calls required for tuple updating.

5.4   Source listing 2

file: io.c

```
 1    /* REQUIEM -  File Manager low-level I/O routines */
 2
 3    #include <stdio.h>
 4    #include "requ.h"
 5    #include "btree.h"
 6    extern int sref_cntr;
 7    extern char errvar[];
 8    struct ix_header *pixd = NULL;
 9    char rel_fl[RNSIZE+5];
10    long seek();
11    static struct relation *relations = NULL; /* loaded rel defns */
12    struct ix_header *db_index();
13
14    /* -------------- find the specified relation --------------- */
```

```
15    struct relation *rfind(rname)
16         char *rname;
17    {
18      int fd;
19      char filename[RNSIZE+5];
20      struct relation *rptr;
21      char *pt_error();
22
23      /* look for relation in list currently loaded */
24      for (rptr = relations; rptr != NULL; rptr = rptr->rl_next)
25        if (strncmp(rname,rptr->rl_name,RNSIZE) == EQUAL)
26          return (rptr);
27
28      /* create a file name by appending .db */
29      make_fname(filename,rname);
30
31      /* lookup the relation file */
32      if ((fd = open(filename,0)) == -1) {
33        strcpy(errvar, rname);
34        errvar[strlen(rname)] = EOS;
35
36        return ((struct relation *)pt_error(RELFNF));
37      }
38
39      /* allocate a new relation structure */
40      if ((rptr = CALLOC(1, struct relation)) == NULL) {
41        close(fd);
42        return ((struct relation *)pt_error(INSMEM));
43      }
44
45      /* initialize the relation structure */
46      rptr->rl_scnref = 0;
47
48      /* read header block from file relation.db into rl_header*/
49      if ( read(fd, (char *) &RELATION_HEADER, HEADER_SIZE)
50                              != HEADER_SIZE) {
51        free((char *) rptr);
52        close(fd);
53        return ((struct relation *)pt_error(BADHDR));
54      }
55
56      /* close the relation file */
57      close(fd);
58
59      /* store the relation name */
60      strncpy(rptr->rl_name,rname,RNSIZE);
61
62      /* link new relation into relation list */
63      rptr->rl_next = relations;
64      relations = rptr;
65
66      /* return the new relation structure pointer */
67      return (rptr);
68    }/* rfind */
69
70    /* ------------------------------------------------------------ */
71
72    struct scan *db_ropen(rname)      /* open a relation file */
73         char *rname;
74    {
75      struct relation *rptr;
```

```
 76        struct scan *sptr;
 77        char *pt_error();
 78        char filename[RNSIZE+5];
 79        int i;
 80
 81        /* find the relation definition */
 82        if ((rptr = rfind(rname)) == NULL)
 83          return ((struct scan *)0);
 84
 85        /* allocate a new scan structure */
 86        if ((sptr = CALLOC(1, struct scan)) == NULL)
 87          return ((struct scan *)pt_error(INSMEM));
 88
 89        /* allocate a tuple buffer */
 90        if ((SCAN_TUPLE = rmalloc(RELATION_HEADER.hd_size)) == NULL) {
 91          free((char *) sptr);
 92          return ((struct scan *)pt_error(INSMEM));
 93        }
 94
 95        /* initialize the scan structure */
 96        SCAN_RELATION = rptr;        /* store relation struct addrs */
 97        sptr->sc_dtnum = 0;          /* desired tuple (non-existent) */
 98        sptr->sc_atnum = 0;          /* actual tuple (non-existent) */
 99        sptr->sc_store = FALSE;      /* no store done since open */
100        sptr->sc_nattrs = 0;         /* total no. of attributes */
101
102        for (i = 0; i < NATTRS; i++) {
103
104          /* check for the last attribute */
105          if (SCAN_HEADER.hd_attrs[i].at_name[0] == EOS)
106            break;
107
108          sptr->sc_nattrs++;
109        }
110
111        /* open relation file if necessary */
112        if (rptr->rl_scnref++ == 0) {
113
114          /* create the relation file name */
115          make_fname(filename,rname);
116
117          /* open the relation file */
118          if ((rptr->rl_fd = open(filename,2)) == -1) {
119            rptr->rl_scnref--;
120            free(SCAN_TUPLE);
121            free((char *) sptr);
122            strcpy(errvar, rname);
123            errvar[strlen(rname)] = EOS;
124
125            return ((struct scan *)pt_error(RELFNF));
126          }
127        }
128
129        /* return the new scan structure pointer */
130        return (sptr);
131     }/* db_ropen */
132
133     /* ------------------------------------------------------------ */
134
135     int db_rclose(sptr)       /* close the relation file */
136          struct scan *sptr;
```

```
137    {
138      /* close relation file if this is the last reference */
139      if (--SCAN_RELATION->rl_scnref == 0) {
140
141        /* rewrite header if any stores took place */
142        if (sptr->sc_store) {
143
144          /* write the header block */
145          if (!rc_done(SCAN_RELATION, TRUE)) {
146            free(SCAN_TUPLE);
147            free((char *) sptr);
148            return (error(BADHDR));
149          }
150        }                    /* close the relation and index file */
151        else
152          close(SCAN_RELATION->rl_fd);
153
154        dequeue_relations(SCAN_RELATION);
155      }
156
157      /* free the scan structure */
158      free(SCAN_TUPLE);
159      free((char *) SCAN_RELATION);
160      free((char *) sptr);
161
162      /* return successfully */
163      return (TRUE);
164    } /* db_rclose */
165
166    /* ------------------------------------------------------------ */
167
168    dequeue_relations(rel_ptr)
169        struct relation *rel_ptr;
170    {
171      struct relation *rptr, *lastrptr;
172
173      if (pixd) {
174        close_ix(pixd);
175        pixd = NULL;   /* reset index header pointer */
176      }
177
178      /* if the last relation in the list should be removed */
179      if (rel_ptr == relations && relations->rl_next == NULL) {
180        relations = NULL;
181        return;
182      }
183
184      /* remove  the relations from the relation list */
185      lastrptr = NULL;
186      for (rptr = relations; rptr != NULL; rptr = rptr->rl_next) {
187        if (rptr == rel_ptr) {
188          if (lastrptr == NULL)
189            relations = rptr->rl_next;
190          else
191            lastrptr->rl_next = rptr->rl_next;
192        }
193        lastrptr = rptr;
194      }
195    } /* dequeue_relations */
196
197    /* ------------------------------------------------------------ */
```

```
198
199    int fetch_tuple(sptr)   /* fetch next tuple from relation file */
200          struct scan *sptr;
201    {
202      /* look for an active tuple */
203      while (TRUE) {
204
205        /* check for this being the last tuple */
206        if (!get_tuple(sptr, (int) sptr->sc_dtnum + 1))
207          return (FALSE);
208
209        /* increment the tuple number */
210        sptr->sc_dtnum += 1;
211
212        /* return if the tuple found is active */
213        if (SCAN_TUPLE[0] == ACTIVE)
214          return (TRUE);
215
216      }
217    } /* fetch_tuple */
218
219    /* read data tuple at specified offset; put contents into buf */
220    read_tuple(rptr, data_offset, buf)
221          struct relation *rptr;
222          long    data_offset;
223          char    *buf;
224    {
225      long lseek();
226
227      /* seek the tuple in the data file */
228      lseek(rptr->rl_fd, data_offset, 0);
229
230      /* read tuple from data relation file */
231      if (read(rptr->rl_fd, buf, RELATION_HEADER.hd_size) !=
232          RELATION_HEADER.hd_size)
233        return(error(TUPIMP));
234
235      return(TRUE);
236    } /* read_tuple */
237
238    /* ----- update current tuple data and relation files ------- */
239    int db_rupdate(sptr, key_buf, del_buf)
240          struct scan *sptr;
241          char **key_buf;
242          char **del_buf;
243    {
244      long lseek();
245
246      /* check for foreign key consistency */
247      /* if attr is indexed remove its old value from index file */
248      if (key_buf) {
249        if (!updt_ixattr(&pixd, sptr, del_buf, key_buf))
250          return(error(IXDELFAIL));
251      }
252
253      /* make sure the status byte indicates an active tuple */
254      SCAN_TUPLE[0] = ACTIVE;
255
256      /* find the appropriate position for the tuple */
257      lseek(SCAN_RELATION->rl_fd, sptr->sc_recpos, 0);
258
```

```
259        /* write the tuple check for index */
260        if (!place_tuple(SCAN_RELATION, sptr->sc_recpos,
261                         key_buf, SCAN_TUPLE, UPDATES))
262          return(FALSE);
263
264        /* perform  foreign key modifications if necessary */
265        if (key_buf && del_buf)
266          change_fgnkey(pixd, sptr);
267
268        return(TRUE);
269
270      } /* db_rupdate */
271
272      /* ------------------------------------------------------------ */
273
274      int store_tuple(sptr, key_buf)       /* store a new tuple */
275          struct scan *sptr;
276          char **key_buf;
277      {
278        int tnum;
279        char *buf;
280        long next_free;
281        long lseek();
282
283        buf = (char *)calloc(1, (unsigned) SCAN_HEADER.hd_size+1);
284
285        /* make sure the status byte indicates an active tuple */
286        SCAN_TUPLE[0] = ACTIVE;
287
288        if (SCAN_HEADER.hd_avail != 0)  {
289            /* available space from previous deletions */
290          sptr->sc_recpos = SCAN_HEADER.hd_avail;
291
292          /* read tuple from first available position */
293          read_tuple(SCAN_RELATION, sptr->sc_recpos, buf);
294          sscanf(buf+1, "%ld", &next_free); /* find next free pos */
295          SCAN_HEADER.hd_avail = next_free; /* reset addr at header */
296
297          /* return to original tuple position */
298          lseek(SCAN_RELATION->rl_fd, sptr->sc_recpos, 0);
299
300          /* new current entry in data file */
301          tnum = (sptr->sc_recpos - HEADER_SIZE)/SCAN_HEADER.hd_size;
302        }
303        else {  /* no previous deletions */
304          /* estimate no. of current entries in data file */
305          tnum = SCAN_HEADER.hd_tcnt + 1;
306
307          /* find tuple disk position */
308          sptr->sc_recpos =
309            seek(SCAN_RELATION->rl_fd, SCAN_HEADER.hd_size, tnum);
310
311          /* preserve position of last tuple in data file */
312          SCAN_HEADER.hd_tmax = tnum;
313        }
314
315        /* write the tuple */
316        if (!place_tuple(SCAN_RELATION, sptr->sc_recpos,
317                              key_buf, SCAN_TUPLE, NO_UPDATE))
318          return (FALSE);
319
```

```
320         /* remember which tuple is in the buffer */
321         sptr->sc_atnum = tnum;
322
323         /* update the tuple count */
324         SCAN_HEADER.hd_tcnt += 1;
325
326         /* remember that a tuple was stored */
327         sptr->sc_store = TRUE;
328
329         /* free buffer and return successfully */
330         nfree(buf);
331         return (TRUE);
332    } /* store_tuple */
333
334    /* ---------------------------------------------------------- */
335
336    /* get a tuple from the relation file */
337    int get_tuple(sptr,tnum)
338         struct scan *sptr;
339         int tnum;
340    {
341      /* check to see if the tuple is already in the buffer */
342      if (tnum == sptr->sc_atnum)
343        return (TRUE);
344
345      /* check for this being beyond the last tuple in data file */
346      if (tnum > SCAN_HEADER.hd_tmax)
347        return (error(TUPINP));
348
349      /* read the tuple from its  disk position */
350      sptr->sc_recpos =
351        seek(SCAN_RELATION->rl_fd, SCAN_HEADER.hd_size, tnum);
352
353      if (read(SCAN_RELATION->rl_fd, SCAN_TUPLE,SCAN_HEADER.hd_size)
354                                    != SCAN_HEADER.hd_size)
355        return (error(TUPINP));
356
357      /* remember which tuple is in the buffer */
358      sptr->sc_atnum = tnum;
359
360      /* return successfully */
361      return (TRUE);
362    } /* get_tuple */
363
364    /* -------------- place tuple into data file ---------------- */
365    int place_tuple(rptr, recpos, key_buf, tuple_buf, updt)
366         struct relation *rptr;
367         long recpos;
368         char **key_buf, *tuple_buf;
369         BOOL updt;              /* update signal */
370    {
371      /* perform indexing */
372      if (key_buf != NULL && updt == FALSE) {
373        if ((pixd = db_index(rptr->rl_name, recpos, key_buf))
374                                            == NULL) {
375          buf_free(key_buf, 4);
376          return (FALSE);
377        }
378      }              /* if updating is required */
379      else if (key_buf != NULL && updt == TRUE)
380        if (!update_ix(recpos, key_buf, pixd)) {
```

```
381            buf_free(key_buf, 4);
382            return (FALSE);
383        }
384
385      if (!write_tuple(rptr, tuple_buf, FALSE))
386         return (error(TUPOUT));
387
388      /* return successfully */
389      return (TRUE);
390
391    } /* place_tuple */
392
393    /* ---------------- update modified tuples ------------------ */
394    int     update_tuple(srptr, key_buf, del_buf)
395         struct srel *srptr;
396         char      **key_buf, **del_buf;
397    {
398      /* check each selected relation for updates */
399      if (srptr->sr_update)
400         return(db_rupdate(srptr->sr_scan, key_buf, del_buf));
401
402      /* return successfully */
403      return(TRUE);
404    } /* update_tuple */
405
406    /* -------------- delete the specified tuple ---------------- */
407    int     delete_tuple(sptr, del_buf)
408         struct scan *sptr;
409         char      **del_buf;
410    {
411      long lseek();
412      BOOL  incr = FALSE; /* do not increment tuple counter */
413
414      if (del_buf) {
415        if (!del_ixattr(&pixd, sptr, del_buf))
416           return(error(IXDELFAIL));
417      }
418
419      /* make sure the status byte indicates a deleted tuple */
420      sptr->sc_tuple[0] = DELETED;
421
422      /*  get address of 1st free record */
423      sprintf(sptr->sc_tuple+1, "%ld", SCAN_HEADER.hd_avail);
424
425      SCAN_HEADER.hd_avail = sptr->sc_recpos; /* 1st free record */
426
427      /* find the position of the tuple in the data file */
428      lseek(SCAN_RELATION->rl_fd, sptr->sc_recpos, 0);
429
430      /* write the discarded tuple back */
431      if (!write_tuple(SCAN_RELATION, SCAN_TUPLE, incr))
432        return (error(TUPOUT));
433
434      /* decrement tuple counter */
435      SCAN_HEADER.hd_tcnt--;
436
437      /* perform  foreign key modifications if necessary */
438      if (del_buf)
439        change_fgnkey(pixd, sptr);
440
441      /* return successfully */
```

```
442       return (TRUE);
443
444    } /* delete_tuple */
445
446    /* ------------ transfer a file to another ------------------ */
447    int transfer(old_path, new_attrs)
448         char *old_path;                /* existing file */
449         struct attribute *new_attrs[]; /* attr val to be stored */
450    {
451      char old_file[RNSIZE + 5], new_file[RNSIZE + 5];
452      struct sel *retrieve(), *old_sel;
453      struct relation *rc_create(), *new_rel;
454      struct sattr *saptr;
455      struct attribute *aptr;
456      char *tbuf, *avalue, *stck(), *rem_blanks();
457      char    **key_buf = NULL;
458      /* tuple counter,  primary, and secondary key counters */
459      int     tcnt, p_cntr = 0, s_cntr = 2;
460      int  tup_offset, i, displ, size_diff;
461      long rec_pos;
462
463      /* create a new relation structure */
464      sref_cntr++;
465      if ((new_rel = rc_create(stck(rel_fl, sref_cntr))) == NULL) {
466        rc_done(new_rel, TRUE);
467        return (FALSE);
468      }
469
470      /* retrieve the relation file */
471      if ((old_sel = retrieve(old_path)) == NULL)
472        return(FALSE);
473
474      cmd_clear();   /* clears command line produced by retrieve */
475
476      /* create the selected attrs and decide about new rel  size */
477      for (saptr = old_sel->sl_attrs, i = 0;
478           saptr != NULL; i++,saptr = saptr->sa_next) {
479        /* add the attributes allowing enough space for
480           the longest common attribute */
481        if (!add_attr(new_rel,new_attrs[i]->at_name,
482                      new_attrs[i]->at_type,
483                      new_attrs[i]->at_size,
484                      new_attrs[i]->at_key)) {
485          nfree((char *) new_rel);
486          done(old_sel);
487          return (FALSE);
488        }
489      }
490
491      /* create the relation and index file headers */
492      if (!rc_header(new_rel, NOINDEX)) {
493        done(old_sel);
494        return (FALSE);
495      }
496
497      /* allocate and initialize a tuple buffer */
498      if ((tbuf =
499        (char *)calloc(1,(unsigned)(new_rel->rl_header.hd_size+1)))
500                                          == NULL ||(avalue =
501        (char *)calloc(1,(unsigned)(new_rel->rl_header.hd_size+1)))
502                                          == NULL) {
```

```
503        done(old_sel);
504        rc_done(new_rel, TRUE);
505        return (error(INSMEM));
506    }
507    *tbuf = ACTIVE;
508
509    /* loop through the tuples of the old rel, copy them to new */
510    for (tcnt = 0; fetch(old_sel, FALSE); tcnt++) {
511
512        /* create the tuple from the values of selected attrs */
513        tup_offset = 1;
514
515        for (saptr = old_sel->sl_attrs, i = 0; saptr != NULL;
516                                  saptr = saptr->sa_next, i++) {
517          aptr = saptr->sa_attr;
518          size_diff = new_attrs[i]->at_size - ATTRIBUTE_SIZE;
519
520          if (new_attrs[i]->at_name[0] != EOS)
521            if (!(displ =
522                  adjust(saptr, tbuf, size_diff, tup_offset))) {
523              done(old_sel);
524              rc_done(new_rel, TRUE);
525              return(FALSE);
526            }
527
528          /* check if indexing is required */
529          if (aptr->at_key != 'n') {
530            rem_blanks(avalue, saptr->sa_aptr, ATTRIBUTE_SIZE);
531            check_ix(&key_buf, aptr, &p_cntr, &s_cntr, avalue);
532          }
533          tup_offset += displ;
534        }
535
536        /* remove current index entries */
537        if (!del_ixattr(&pixd, old_sel->sl_rels->sr_scan, key_buf)) {
538          done(old_sel);
539          rc_done(new_rel, TRUE);
540          return(error(IXDELFAIL));
541        }
542
543        /* estimate record position of tuple to be stored */
544        rec_pos =
545          seek(new_rel->rl_fd, new_rel->rl_header.hd_size, tcnt+1);
546
547        /* update the  index file */
548        if (!update_ix(rec_pos, key_buf, pixd)) {
549          buf_free(key_buf, 4);
550          done(old_sel);
551          rc_done(new_rel, TRUE);
552          return (FALSE);
553        }
554
555        /* write the tuple into the new data file */
556        if (!write_tuple(new_rel, tbuf, FALSE)) {
557          done(old_sel);
558          rc_done(new_rel, TRUE);
559          nfree(tbuf);
560          return (error(INSBLK));
561        }
562
563        /* reset counters */
```

```
564        p_cntr = 0; s_cntr = 2;
565     }
566
567     /* cater for changes in size and name */
568     new_rel->rl_header.hd_tcnt =
569        old_sel->sl_rels->sr_scan->sc_relation->rl_header.hd_tcnt;
570     /* save auxiliary relation name */
571     sprintf(new_file, "%s.db", new_rel->rl_name);
572     strcpy(new_rel->rl_name,
573             old_sel->sl_rels->sr_scan->sc_relation->rl_name);
574     /* save original relation name */
575     sprintf(old_file, "%s.db", old_sel->sl_rels->sr_scan->
576             sc_relation->rl_name);
577
578     /* finish the selection */
579     done(old_sel);
580
581     /* finish relation creation */
582     if (!rc_done(new_rel, TRUE))
583       return (FALSE);
584
585     /* move contents of new-file to old-file */
586     if (!f_move(new_file, old_file))
587       return(error(FILEMV));
588
589     /* do housekeeping  and return successfully */
590     nfree(tbuf);
591     return (TRUE);
592 }/* transfer */
593
594 /* ---------- seek a tuple in a relation file --------------- */
595 static long seek(file_descr, tup_size, tnum)
596        int file_descr,     /* file descriptor */
597            tup_size,       /* size of tuple in bytes */
598            tnum;
599 {
600   long offset;
601   long lseek();
602
603   offset =
604      (long) HEADER_SIZE + ((long) (tnum - 1) * (long) tup_size);
605   return(lseek(file_descr, offset, 0));
606 }/* seek */
607
608 /* ------------------------------------------------------------ */
609
610 static make_fname(fname,rname)/* make rel name from file name */
611        char *fname,*rname;
612 {
613   strncpy(fname,rname,RNSIZE);
614   fname[RNSIZE] = EOS;
615   strcat(fname,".db");
616 }/* make_fname */
617
618 /* ------------ write current tuple into data file ---------- */
619 write_tuple(rptr, buff, incrs)
620        struct   relation *rptr;
621        char *buff;
622        BOOL incrs;
623 {
624    if (write(rptr->rl_fd, buff, RELATION_HEADER.hd_size)
```

```
625                                     != RELATION_HEADER.hd_size) {
626         rc_done(rptr, TRUE);
627         nfree(buff);
628         return (FALSE);
629       }
630
631       if (incrs) {  /* increment header counters */
632         RELATION_HEADER.hd_tcnt++;
633         RELATION_HEADER.hd_tmax++;
634       }
635
636       return(TRUE);
637
638     } /* write_tuple */
639
640     /* - get a record by its no. where it is known to be stored - */
641     cseek(sptr, tnum)
642         struct scan *sptr;
643         int    tnum;
644     {
645       long   offset, pos;
646       long   lseek();
647
648       offset = (long) SCAN_HEADER.hd_data +
649         ((long) tnum * (long) SCAN_HEADER.hd_size);
650
651       /* get to current position */
652       if ((pos = lseek(SCAN_RELATION->rl_fd, offset, 1)) == -1
653           || pos < (long) SCAN_HEADER.hd_data
654           || tnum >= SCAN_HEADER.hd_tcnt)
655         return (FALSE);
656       else
657         return (TRUE);
658     } /* cseek */
659
660     /* ------------------------------------------------------------- */
661
662     int adjust(saptr, tbuf, size_diff, offset)
663         struct sattr *saptr;
664         char *tbuf;
665         int size_diff, offset;
666     {
667       int i, attr_size, s_indx = 0;
668       char *size_buf;
669       char format[10];
670       struct relation *rel;
671
672       /* estimate size of new attribute */
673       attr_size = ATTRIBUTE_SIZE + size_diff;
674
675       /* get a relation pointer */
676       rel = saptr->sa_srel->sr_scan->sc_relation;
677
678       if ((size_buf =
679         calloc(1, (unsigned) rel->rl_header.hd_size+1)) == NULL) {
680         rc_done(rel, TRUE);
681         return (error(INSMEM));
682       }
683
684       for (i = 0; i < ATTRIBUTE_SIZE; i++) {
685         if ((ATTRIBUTE_TYPE == TNUM) || (ATTRIBUTE_TYPE == TREAL)) {
```

```
686            size_buf[s_indx++] = saptr->sa_aptr[i];
687            if ( i == ATTRIBUTE_SIZE-1){
688              if (size_diff < 0)    /* displace appropriately */
689                displace_num(size_buf, ATTRIBUTE_SIZE, size_diff);
690
691              /* right adjust number to fit length of
692               * widest common attribute */
693              sprintf(format, "%%%ds", attr_size);
694              sprintf(tbuf + offset, format, size_buf);
695
696              /* increment index to get past last character */
697              i++;
698              s_indx = 0;
699              break;
700            }
701          }
702          else {        /* only if character strings are involved */
703            if (i < attr_size)
704              tbuf[offset + i] = saptr->sa_aptr[i];
705            else if (size_diff < 0)
706              return(i);
707
708
709            if (i == ATTRIBUTE_SIZE - 1)
710              i += size_diff; /* new displacement */
711          }
712        }
713
714      nfree(size_buf);
715      return(i);      /* return displacement */
716    } /* adjust */
717
718    /* ----- displace if new field length < than initial -------- */
719
720    static displace_num(buf, len, diff)
721          char *buf;
722          int len, diff;
723    {
724      int i;
725
726      for (i= 0; i < len+diff; i++)
727        buf[i] = buf[i-diff];
728      buf[i] = EOS;
729
730    } /* displace_num */
731    /* ------------------------------------------------------------ */
```

6

The Physical Database Implementation

When an application or a user requests conceptual information the request is formulated in terms of the logical database structure. To a significant extent users conceive their needs and desires in terms of the structure of schemas or subschemas. As the purpose of the DBMS is to facilitate and simplify access to stored data, users need never concern themselves over the technicalities of the physical implementation of the system. Conceptual database requests are transparently transformed into equivalent requests expressed in terms of the stored database.

The actual storage location of the requested data is determined by means of a system-defined module known as the *logical/physical* database mapping module. The logical/physical mapping module typically contains a set of routines which access data sequentially, or by hashing, or by means of a particular kind of ordered primary indices called B-trees, or B^+-trees. The prime objective of these mapping routines is not only to conceal all device-dependent details from the DBMS but also to present it with a collection of stored files, each one consisting of a single type of stored record occurrences.

In the previous chapter we examined in some detail how the file management modules of a DBMS perform low-level data file accesses. In this chapter we discuss the representation of low-level REQUIEM indexing facilities along with algorithms that describe their manipulation.

6.1 Index structures

One of the objectives of a relational DBMS is to speed up data retrieval, which implies minimization of the number of disk accesses. For example, consider a relatively large data file and a DBMS which employs no special search accelerating technique. To locate a specific record in this data file we must scan the entire file sequentially. Accordingly, storage definition in a DBMS includes the specification of access paths to stored data. As explained, access paths are set up to establish a starting point for a search within a data file. There exist two types of access paths: those which apply to a single relation and those which link tuples of one relation to the tuples of another. We will use the terms *indexing* and *hashing* to designate the former type of access and *link* to designate the latter. In this book we will restrict our attention to indexing and hashing techniques.

Loosely speaking, we can say that indexing or hashing is in reality a logical reorganization of tuples of a relation in terms of certain attribute values or of a group of attribute values. Both techniques are used for providing fast direct access to a specific stored record on the basis of a given value for some attribute which normally is, but does not necessarily have to be, the primary key. In this chapter we deal only with indexing techniques.

The problem to be solved with indexing is as follows: given a constant (numeric, string, boolean, etc.), say C, find the data records that contain in their attribute A a value identical to that of C. Obviously, A must belong to the same existence domain as C, that is, if C is the name of a supplier, A must also be a supplier name. To understand this let us look at an example in some detail.

Example 6.1.1

Figure 6.1 represents an index file, called IX, on the SUP_NO attribute of the relation SUPPLIER. We assume that the length of each SUPPLIER tuple is 55 bytes, as explained in the previous chapter (see section 5.2), and that the first SUPPLIER data record is stored in decimal data file position 512.

The index file *IX*, like the data file corresponding to *SUPPLIER*, is stored on disk. The function of the index file is to indicate that for each value of the index key *SUP_NO* there exists a corresponding record in the data file *SUPPLIER* that contains that particular value in its *SUP_NO* field. The data file *SUPPLIER* is often said to be *indexed* by the index file *IX*. Since the index file is much smaller than the data file, the index lookup process will be much faster than a sequential scan of the data file as it involves fewer I/O operations. Obviously, it is not feasible to load the entire data file into main memory because of its physical size limitations. Incidentally, the type of index shown in Figure 6.1 is called a *dense index*. A dense index contains an index entry for every stored record in the indexed file. Conversely, *sparse*

SUP_NO	REC_ADDRESS
S125	622
S128	677
S135	512
S137	567
S142	732

	SUP_NO	SUP_NAME	SUP_ADDRESS	PROD_NO
512	S135	Jones	London	P21
567	S137	Black	New York	P25
622	S125	Gray	Paris	P17
677	S128	Smith	Zurich	P12
732	S732	Rogers	Sydney	P21

Index File IX   Data file Supplier

Figure 6.1 Principle of indexing.

indices are created only for a set of records. REQUIEM confines itself only to considering dense indices. For further information refer to [17] and [16].

In general, indices provide both direct and sequential access to the indexed data. This implies that, as already shown, we can locate data records having a specific value for the indexed attribute directly. Furthermore, we will be able to access all the records in the data file in the sequence defined by the index rather than by their physical sequence in the data record.

For example, to create a stored relation called *EMPLOYEE* comprising fixed length records, with an *EMP_NAME* field of 30 characters and a *SALARY* field of an 8-byte real in REQUIEM we must use the following statement:

```
create employee (emp_id   (num (5), unique),
                 emp_name   (char (30), secondary),
                 salary   (real (8)));
```

The option *UNIQUE* allows us to specify that the attribute *EMP_ID* is a discriminating key of the relation *EMPLOYEE*. It also indicates at the internal (physical) level direct tuple access paths having a specified key value. More specifically, this statement creates a particular form of index, called a B$^+$-tree, for the *EMPLOYEE* file on the attribute *EMP_ID*. That is, we need only specify that an attribute is either *UNIQUE* or *SECONDARY* to create B$^+$-tree indices; no program need be written.

For example, consider the relation *EMPLOYEE* as defined above. It is quite sensible to specify one primary index on the *EMP_ID* field and a secondary index on the *EMP_NAME* field. Furthermore, it is possible to construct an index over a combination of multiple fields. Such an index would include entries for every single combination in the relevant fields in the data file. REQUIEM requires that a relation contains at most two foreign key declarations. The combination of these two such foreign keys can then be used as a unique identifier for the records contained in the data file. In sum, this means that the DBMS itself cannot make the decision whether or not to create an index, but the database designer must make estimates for the operations anticipated in order to use the DBMS efficiently.

6.2   B$^+$-tree indexed files

The most notable disadvantage of the index file organization is that performance is degraded as the file grows. One of the most popular indexing methods, used by data management systems, that overcomes this predicament is the B$^+$-tree indexing organization. The B$^+$-tree file structure is the most widely used form of indexing that maintains its efficiency despite frequent insertions and deletions of data [5],[16], [35]. A B$^+$-tree is a particular type of multiway tree structured index. The original balanced multiway tree structured organization was devised by Bayer and McCreight [36] and was called B-tree. Since that time several variations have been proposed and called B$^+$-tree, B*-tree, etc. Here we describe a variation of the B$^+$-tree which was first suggested by Knuth [37].

In a B$^+$-tree structure all keys and associated data reside in the leaf nodes of the tree and are accessed via a multilevel index. In this tree organization branch nodes contain key values and pointers to lower levels. A B$^+$-tree index takes the form of a balanced tree in which every path leading from the root of the tree to a leaf of the tree has exactly the same length. The leaf nodes of a B$^+$-tree are the only nodes in the tree that contain record identifiers or addresses for records in the relation data file, and all keys appear in the leaf nodes. Nonleaf nodes (branch nodes) contain pointers to the next level of the index, thus forming a multilevel index on the leaf nodes. The structure of the branch nodes in the B$^+$-tree organization is exactly the same as for leaf nodes except that all pointers are pointers to other nodes and not pointers to records in the data file. Some keys are stored redundantly in this organization; but placing all keys and addresses in the leaf nodes allows for faster sequential processing. On the other hand, feasible branching is significantly increased.

When used on direct access devices (e.g. disks) information is transferred in blocks of fixed size (e.g. 1 kbyte) between the device and the system and the B$^+$-tree is implemented in such a way as to utilize one block per node. B$^+$-trees can, therefore, be used for fast random access via a specified key (index key). Basically, more than one such index key can be built for the same file, if more than one key exists for a given record. We call this kind of B^+-tree a *multivalued index* B^+-tree. For example, we may wish to have fast access to supplier records by both name and supplier identification. A B^+-tree can be built containing both these keys.

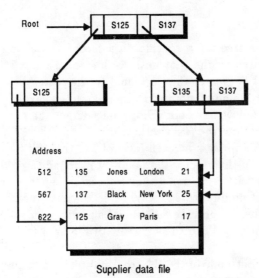

Figure 6.2 Diagram of a B^+-tree of order 2 as an index to the supplier data file.

Figure 6.2 shows a complete B^+-tree with primary indices for the *SUPPLIER* data file of Figure 6.1. The B^+-tree depicted in Figure 6.2 is of order 2. The *order* (m) of a tree, where m is an natural number, is the number of subtrees pointed to by an individual node. The requirement is that each branch node with the exception of the root node in the tree has between $m/2$ and m children. On the other hand, the root can have at least one and at most m children. We refer to the tree levels as *higher* in the direction of the root level and as *lower* in the direction of the leaf node level. To search the B^+-tree file for a particular entry in the data file requires establishing a search path from the root of the tree to some leaf node identifying the requested data record. To traverse the index of Figure 6.2 searching for a given key value we start at the root and label the pointers to the next level from 1 to n, and the keys from 1 to n. This means that in each level we have a maximum number of n pointers $(m/2 \leq n \leq m)$ to the next level, represented as $P_1, P_2, \ldots, P_n$ and a maximum number of n keys, represented as $K_1, K_2, \ldots, K_n$. The construct P_i is used to denote a pointer to the next level in the tree for those key entries that have a value greater than or equal to that of K_i. Consequently, a typical node of the B^+-tree can be represented as an ordered set of the form:

$$(P_1, K_1, P_2, K_2, \ldots, P_n, K_n)$$

Thus, we can perceive each node as consisting of entries of the form shown in Figure 6.3.

| Key value | Data reference/Node |

Figure 6.3 Typical node of a B$^+$-tree.

To search the tree for a specific data record containing a key value V we start by searching the root until we locate an index key, say K_i, with $1 \leq i \leq n$, that is greater than or equal to the search key value. We then extract the corresponding pointer P_i and search the next level node to which P_i points. We follow this pointer for values larger than or equal to the ith key and smaller than the $(i + 1)$th key.

We repeat this process at each level of the tree until we get to the appropriate leaf and then follow the pointer to the indicated data record. For reasons of simplicity we assume that the search key is a primary key and, thus, there exist no duplicate key values in the data records.

In the following we present the general algorithm for searching for a particular key value, say V, in the structure of Figure 6.4(c).

1. Start at the root node of the B$^+$-tree, and set an auxiliary node variable, say N, to the root node.

2. Let V be the value of the key of the data record we are currently searching for:

   (a) if $V \leq K_1$, follow the pointer P_1 to the next level of the B$^+$-tree and set N to the left lower node of the present node;

   (b) if $K_i \leq V \leq K_{i+1}$ (for some i where $1 \leq i \leq n$), follow P_{i+1} to the next level and then set V to the node pointed to by P_{i+1};

   (c) if $V \geq K_n$, follow P_n to the next level and set N to the right lower level node of N.

3. Repeat step 2 until the requested leaf is reached and the key is or is not found.

Figure 6.4 is a diagram of index block and data record structures and illustrates how a B$^+$-tree can evolve. The data records are labeled DR_i where the subscript i denotes the physical location where the data record is stored in the relative data file. To minimize the amount of index file I/O traffic, we organize the index pairs in blocks of fixed size. The address in the index pair in an upper entry then points to a single block on the lower level of the index. Index blocks are labeled IB_j, where the subscript j indicates that the index block is written to location j of the index file.

Figure 6.4 shows how the multilevel index splits when a new entry is inserted. It signifies that an insert may under certain circumstances cause adjustments to several levels of index blocks. In the worst case splitting will proliferate all the way up to the top of the B^+-tree, resulting, thus, in the introduction of a new root (parent to the old root, which has been split into two) and, thus, the tree will increase in height by an extra level. Note that in our example the tree always remains balanced: this property is a requirement for a B^+-tree.

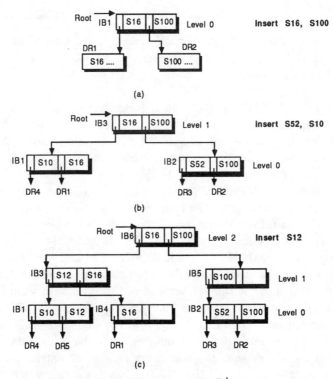

Figure 6.4 Insertion sequence of a B^+-tree.

The following algorithm caters for insertions into a B^+-tree and employs the previously presented tree-traversing algorithm:

1. Call the traversing algorithm to locate the leaf node, say N, in which V logically belongs. If there is enough room for a new entry, V is inserted into the node N and the insertion process terminates.
2. Otherwise, split the node N into two nodes, say N_1 and N_2. Move the lowest half of the values contained in N and place them in the left node N_1. Place the highest half of the values contained in N in the right node N_2. Promote the middle value, say V_1, to the parent node of N, say P, to serve as separator value for nodes N_1 and N_2. (Any future searches for value X, on reaching the node P, will have to be directed to node N_1

if $X \leq V_2$ and to node N_2 if $X > V_1$.)

3. Try to insert the value V_1 into P. As this insertion causes a split, proceed recursively until a new recursion does not cause a split. If the splitting propagates to the root, then create a new root.

Example 6.2.1

To understand how the previous algorithm functions, consider the B^+-tree structure of Figure 6.4(b) and assume that we wish to insert the key with value S12 in the tree.

As the value $S12$ is less than $S16$ it logically belongs to node IB1 which is, however, full. Therefore, a split must take place and the lower half of the IB1 entries, i.e. the values $S10$ and $S12$, remain in node IB1, while the higher entries, i.e. the value $S16$, are inserted into a new node, say IB4. Now, the middle value $S12$ must be inserted in the node IB3 (IB1's parent node). However, the node IB3 has not enough space to handle this entry forcing, thus, a new split. The lower half of the entries, i.e. the values $S12$ and $S16$, remain in the same node, the node IB3, while the higher half of the entries, i.e. the entry 100, is placed in the node IB4. A new node must be created now containing the middle value $S16$ and the value $S100$. The pointer field of the entry with value $S16$ points to the left subtree structure of Figure 6.4(c), while the pointer field of the entry with value $S100$ points to the right subtree structure of Figure 6.4(c). Obviously, all entries in the left subtree must be less than or equal to the value $S16$ while all entries in the right subtree must be less than or equal to the value $S100$.

Figure 6.4 shows that the maximum number of entries for each index block in the tree is two and that the tree can always grow only by one level upwards. As each data record is inserted into the data file the key of this record and its address (location) form the key–address pair for that entry. Each such key–address entry pair is eventually added to the multilevel index of the index file. Index keys stored in the leaf nodes and index keys stored in the branch nodes are actually duplicates. The index contains enough branch node index key low-level address pairs to ensure fast access to the leaf nodes. As index blocks keep filling, a split eventually occurs at the point where the last key lower level address was unsuccessfully attempted. A split indicates that the capacity of the underlying node was exceeded. In this case the middle key value is moved to the parent node and the sibling *level_0* index block is created.

In a B^+-tree deletion the key value in a leaf node needs to be deleted. Any copy of that key in the index must also be removed as our tree index does not

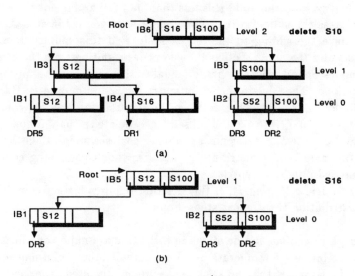

Figure 6.5 Deletion sequence for the B^+-tree of Figure 6.4(c).

allow any non-key values to be used as separators. If a leaf node becomes empty as a result of a deletion, it must be eliminated from the B^+-tree. To eliminate a leaf node we must delete the pointers to it from its parent node. On the other hand, if a deletion leaves a parent node, say P, less than half full, the node must be somehow combined with the node to its left or right. Next, its sibling node is examined to see if there is enough room to accommodate the information contained in P. If there is enough space these two nodes are coalesced so that the sibling contains all the useful entries, and then node P is deleted. When two nodes are combined, the entry at the higher level that points to the already eliminated node is also removed. In the converse case the entries must be redistributed so that each sibling has the appropriate number of key values and pointers. Deletions may leave only one entry in the root level node; in that case, the root level block is no longer required and the lower level node can now become the new root node. Examples of possible deletion scenarios are outlined in Figure 6.5.

The following algorithm implements B^+-tree deletion operations and is essentially the inverse of the version just described, but contains important exceptions.

1. Call the traversing algorithm to locate the leaf node, say N, to which V belongs. If the leaf node does not become empty V is removed from node N, and the deletion process terminates.
2. Otherwise, if the leaf node N is empty delete the node's entry at its parent

node, say P. If the node P is less than half full and is not the root node, compress the node P with sibling nodes as explained in step 3.

3. Retrieve the sibling to the left of node P if this sibling node, say S_l, exists and the number of combined entries resulting from the coalescence of nodes S_l and P is less than or equal to the number of permitted entries in a node. Then delete the parent entry for S_l and update P. If the above case does not apply, then retrieve the right sibling, say S_r, combine the nodes P and S_r into S_r, and subsequently delete the parent node entry for P and update S_r. If it is not possible to coalesce nodes, then the solution in this case is to redistribute pointers so that each sibling contains the approved number of entries.

4. Try to delete V from P. If this deletion requires further combination or redistribution then repeat steps 2 and 3.

Although insertions and deletions in a B^+-tree are quite complicated, they require relatively few operations. It is actually the performance of operations in B^+-trees that makes them a frequently used index structure in database implementations. Performance estimates of B^+-trees and in particular comparisons of B^+- and B-tree performance ratios can be found in [35].

6.3   Query optimization issues

The RQL language used throughout this book is a typical example of a high-level data language, which facilitates the retrieval of the precise set of data required, without requesting a description of how to perform the operations to obtain the data. Query statements specify which relations should be accessed; they also specify the relation predicates denoting which combinations of data from those relations are desired. They do not specify the access paths (e.g. indices) that are used to retrieve the data for each relation, or even the sequence in which relations should be accessed. However, effective access to the required data is always handled by the access mechanisms of the query language which depend on both the physical organization of the data as well as on the corresponding access paths defined by the database creator. The databases under consideration are composed of unsorted relations stored on a random access device such as a disk, and the access paths are materialized via indices (B^+-tree mechanisms) or hashing.

It is clear that the selection of indices for a database is an important aspect of the physical database design. Evaluation of RQL queries requires the choice of an efficient way of answering the user's query, by making use

of already defined indices, hashing and other aspects of the physical organization of the underlying database. It is the duty of a software module called
the *optimizer* to make these decisions based on an analysis of alternatives
for executing each statement and choose the execution plan that appears to
minimize the total processing cost. Accordingly, it is the overall purpose of
the optimizer to take into account the existence of specific access paths and
mechanisms in order to choose an efficient strategy for evaluating a given
relational expression.

In a relational system like REQUIEM the access paths must be explicitly
created by authorized users such as database administrators. The definition
of access paths is not a trivial task since an index designer must balance
the advantages of access paths for data retrieval against their drawbacks
in terms of maintenance costs. Such maintenance costs are incurred for
index inserts, deletes, and updates. It is not a good policy to create an
index for every attribute contained in a relation. Updates will be very
expensive in that design, and moreover, the indices will probably require
more total space than the stored relations themselves! This is the reason
why REQUIEM restricts the effective number of indices per relation. In
the current implementation only three indices per relation can be defined;
however, this is not a design policy, it was only decided for experimentation
purposes and can be adjusted to meet the requirements of your applications.
Recall that only one primary key index and two secondary key indices can
be specified. The system itself always generates an additional foreign key
index for composite relations as we have already explained. In retrospect,
a poor choice of physical design can undoubtedly result in poor system
performance, far below what the system would achieve if a better set of
access paths were available. To remedy this situation, design tools are
needed to aid users in selecting the appropriate access paths that support
system performance for a set of applications.

In this section, we briefly present an overview of the fundamental principles and techniques of optimization. This presentation is oriented towards the specific approach to optimization found in *REQUIEM*. Such optimization principles should be appropriately extended to meet the operational requirements of more sophisticated database management systems
used in mainframe environments. Although the optimization primitives in
REQUIEM are quite simple, they should give a flavor of how query optimization is performed. Those who require more information about query
optimization can refer to the comprehensive tutorial paper by M. Jarke and
J. Koch [38].

In the following we will explain why query optimizers for relational
database systems are necessary, consider simple and general principles for
query optimization, and show how a query optimizer generates an access

plan for a simple query. We start with a simple example which will be used throughout this section. This example also illustrates some of the potential of optimization.

Example 6.3.1

Consider the query "Get the names and addresses of suppliers who supply product 21" for which a possible RQL *formulation is:*

project (**join** supplier **on** sup_id **with** supply **on** sup_id
         where supply.prod_no = 21) **over** sup_name, location;

This query involves two different relations and two predicates. Somehow we must associate information across these two related relations. However, the query does not specify how to do this. Suppose now that the database contains 50 suppliers and 1,000 supply orders, of which only 20 are for part 21. If the system does not perform any optimization at all then it would try to create a transient relation that contains the information from both relations involved in the query. Subsequently, it would try to pick out those rows that satisfy all the aforementioned conditions. The sequence of events would then be as follows:

1. Compute the cross-product (cartesian product) of the relations *SUPPLIER* and *SUPPLY*. This step involves reading 1,050 tuples and constructing a relation containing 50 x 1,000 = 50,000 tuples.
2. Restrict the previous result according to the condition specified by the **where** clause. This step involves reading 50,000 entries and produces a relation consisting of only 20 tuples which is finally projected over *SUP_NAME* and *LOCATION* to generate the final result. Obviously, the final result would contain 20 tuples at most.

But the **where** clause, i.e. the relation predicate, can tell us that we do not have to use all these rows – what we can do is *restrict* the relation *SUPPLY* to just the tuples for part 21. This involves reading 1,000 tuples and produces a transient relation containing only 20 tuples. The resulting relation is joined with the relation *SUPPLIER* on *SUP_ID*. This step involves the retrieval of only 50 tuples and the result contains 20 tuples. These tuples are finally projected over *SUP_NAME* and *LOCATION* to produce the desired final result.

It is obvious that the above procedures are equivalent in the sense that they produce the same final answer, but it is clear that the second procedure is much more efficient than the first. The previous example, simple though it is, should give a preliminary idea of the kinds of problems encountered in practice.

Some of the most efficient improvements that can be achieved during query optimization are made simply by rearranging the order of operations. Thus, sometimes the DBMS moves selection operations so that they can be performed prior to instead of after join operations. This is mainly due to the fact that join operations produce large number of tuples. However, if the system can make some decisions earlier than performing the join it then reduces the number of generated tuples. This process, known as *restriction*, is an example of a general principle of data management computation. The DBMS should always use information from the system catalogs to control and reduce the output of a query at source level instead of waiting until later to test and reject a possibly large number of the generated tuples. More information on the topic of optimization of relational expressions and reordering of relational expressions can be found in [38] and [39].

The next section presents a brief explanation of some of the general principles that are used by query optimization when dealing with natural join queries, and outlines how the REQUIEM query optimizer generates an access path for our sample query.

6.3.1   Optimization of natural join queries

In relational database management systems files of records are stored without physical links between the individual records. Recall that a record from one file can be related with a record of another file only when the value in a field of the first record matches the value of a field in the second record. To combine information from this pair of files (that implement relations) a transient file is normally generated. Such transient files are called snapshots in the REQUIEM terminology. The transient file concatenates fields of records from the one file with those from the other file where the records happen to have identical values for some prespecified field. This process is known as the natural join of the two files.

There are normally two basic ways in which the database management system can join relations. The first is called the *nested loop join* and the second the *sort merge join* [17], [40]. The nested loop join assumes that there are no indices on the joined fields of the two relations that are going to be joined. In the implementation of the nested loop join the first relation is termed the *outer loop relation*, and the second the *inner loop relation*. You can parallel this join construct to a nested **for** loop construct in a conventional programming language, such as C or Pascal. Each record from the outer loop relation is successively compared with records in the inner loop relation. The qualifying records are then concatenated in the usual fashion and stored into a snapshot file. This method is quite impractical and certainly slow in terms of processing speed. However, you could improve this method and make it faster if you combined it with hashing (for more information see exercise 4 in Chapter 16). This method is then called *nested loop join with hashing* and is analyzed in depth in [17].

Natural joins can be made more efficient by sorting the underlying relation records first. This method is generally more efficient than a nested loops join and is called a *sort merge join*. The sort merge join algorithm sorts logically each relation file on the join field (attribute). After this is done, each relation file is scanned in order and each individual record of each relation is examined only once.* During this phase the relations are merged and the join result is created at the same time. Obviously, if one or both relation files are already sorted, there is no need to sort them before merging. Accordingly, an index will help the system to retrieve data in the desired order, thus significantly decreasing the processing time. This kind of sort merge join is called the *index join*. The index join involves reading in part of a single relation file, and then using an already existing index in this file to locate the matching records from a second relation file. In general, whenever we use sort merge or index joins to merge two relations we use the relation predicate to restrict the joined relations to those records that are worth preserving. The idea is to use as many restrictions as possible whenever relations are merged, and also to start with those merges that produce the smallest possible relations. Obviously, the sample query that we have used so far is much too simple to indicate the usefulness of this method; however, you may try to think of a realistic example along these lines and convince yourselves of the utility of the restriction method.

Next, let us examine how the REQUIEM optimizer may handle our sample query. The actual heuristics will vary from one optimizer to another; however, we will use methods that are quite typical. For practical reasons we will not make an exhaustive list of all possibilities, rather we assume that there exists an index on one or even both the attributes that will form the basis for the join operation. The information available to the optimization modules of REQUIEM is the structure of the query, the names and sizes of the relations involved, the available indices, the predicate involved, etc. For example, if a predicate is involved in the join query which includes indexed attributes, then the function join_in() is called to process the query.

Let us now redirect our attention to our sample query. If attribute *SUP_ID* is uniquely indexed (which is obviously the case), REQUIEM knows that all tuples in relation *SUPPLIER* are already sorted by means of their

---

*In this section we use the term relation file to denote the combination of a data and an index file.

corresponding index. Clearly, the next step will be to restrict the relation *SUPPLY* in terms of the predicate *SUPPLY.PROD_ID* = 21. However, before making this restriction REQUIEM checks whether the relation *SUPPLY* is already indexed on *SUP_ID*. In that case it invokes the function **join_two()** which performs both the restriction and the join at the same time by comparing the join field indices. Alternatively, if the *SUPPLY* relation is not indexed on *SUP_ID* then REQUIEM has first to read its data records and then to perform the restriction and the join operation.

We will not dwell any further on the implementation aspects of join queries in REQUIEM as the code implementation is quite straightforward and self explanatory. All that need be kept in mind is that the join functions are dispersed between three files, namely **parser.c**, **impl.c**, and **access.c**. In the next section we will present a systematic method for dealing with an optimization problem and show how the overall problem can be decomposed into a number of related yet independent subproblems.

6.3.2 Query processing strategies

The previous two sections have given us a rough idea as to why optimization is necessary. Clearly, optimization is an important issue in any relational system as the choice between a good and a poor strategy is a deciding factor which may have impact on the overall performance of the system. In relational systems the overall optimization process can be divided in a top-down fashion into four more or less independent implementation steps [38].

Before query processing can commence, the query optimizer must map a query specified in some relational query language into an internal query representation form by eliminating those parts which purely contribute to the syntactic sugar of the language in which the query was formulated. A suitable representation must be rich enough to express a large number of queries and should provide a well-defined basis for query transformation. Obviously, the most convenient internal forms of representation that a query can employ are the well-known formalisms of relational algebra and relational calculus. This translation process actually parallels that performed by the parser module of a compiling system.

Once the query has been mapped into a convenient internal representation form, the real optimization phase can begin. The purpose of this step is to convert this internal form of representation into some equivalent form which, however, is more efficient in terms of processing speed. The prime objectives of this transformation process are first the conversion of a query into a suitable equivalent form (sometimes referred to as its *canonical form*) so that all properties that apply to the original query also apply to its canonical form and, secondly, the elimination of redundancy. The latter objective involves the recognition of common subqueries which appear more than once in the same query expression.

After having transformed the formal (internal) representation of a given query into some canonical form, the optimizer must select a detailed strategy for the evaluation of the canonical query. At this stage such considerations as the existence and choice of specific indices, the order of tuple accessing and the distribution of data values, play a decisive role. The basic approach followed here is to regard the canonical query expression as specifying sequences of elementary operations such as selections, joins, or restrictions for which a good implementation (in terms of predefined low-level implementation procedures) and its associated processing cost are already known.

The previous step requires knowledge of a certain number of parameters, regarding the state of the database, from the system catalogs. Such parameters concern the existence of indices, the cardinality and degree of a relation, tuple lengths, etc. Hence, by using this kind of information the optimizer will be in a position to decide which procedure to use for implementing each single elementary operation in the query expression. The result of this step is a set of *access plans*. Each access plan is normally constructed by interweaving a set of candidate low-level implementation procedures, one such procedure for each of the primitive operations in the canonical query expression.

The final step involves the computation of processing costs for each individual access plan and the choice of the optimal access plan which will eventually be executed. The selection of the access plans is based on such factors as the estimate of the number of disk I/Os involved or CPU utilization. In general, the optimizer must generate a set of access plans rich enough to contain the optimal plan; however, it should try to keep this set within reasonable bounds to ensure a low optimization overhead.

As previously explained one of the most important factors for selecting a query processing strategy is to find a relational expression that is not only equivalent to the given query expression but at the same time also efficient to execute. There are a number of useful general principles that can be used as guidelines for query interpretation strategies in either algebraic or relational calculus languages. The most basic of those principles can be summarized as follows:

1. Perform selection as early as possible followed by projection operations, if any, to reduce the volume of data that must be operated upon.
2. Before carrying out a selection or projection operation, first make sure if you can use an index to reduce the amount of work involved instead of

performing a sequential search.

3. Group successive select and project operations into a single compound operation.
4. Try to perform any useful restrictions before performing a join operation.
5. Perform joins as late as possible.

As previously stressed, the structure of the REQUIEM optimizer is rather simple and provides many grounds for further improvement and extension by applying some of the concepts elaborated on in this section. We believe that this is quite a challenge for those who may wish to acquire practical experience on optimization techniques. For example, one important issue to be investigated is that of the optimization costs. There is no point in spending a long time optimizing relations that contain only a handful of tuples. A good optimizer must always know where to start from and, most important, when to stop.

6.4   Implementation of B+-tree structures

REQUIEM provides a collection of low-level functions for searching, inserting, and deleting key values in a B+-tree. These functions are a suitable adaptation (extension and modification) of the B-tree functions developed in [41]. The REQUIEM B+-tree functions assume that all keys stored in a B+-tree are character strings. Actually, REQUIEM accepts any types of data as key definitions; however, data held in an index or even a data file regardless of data type is internally transformed and stored as character strings. Moreover, REQUIEM allows keys to have variable length although it sets an upper limit for key lengths which should not be exceeded.

REQUIEM supports multiple keys and allows that the same value may occur in more than a single data record. This means that REQUIEM allows the same key (obviously, a secondary key) to appear in more than one B+-tree entry; however, it requires that the combination of a key and its associated address in the data file be unique. In addition to the above, REQUIEM uses a dummy entry (the hexadecimal constant 0xffffffff) which holds the highest possible key value in the B+-tree when it is created. This guarantees that searches can never go past the last key in a node. Obviously, the initial B+-tree structure comprises one leaf level block containing the dummy entry. Each higher level node contains one entry with the dummy key and a record pointer to the block of the succeeding lower level. In REQUIEM four index levels are allowed to represent the maximum tree capacity. These tree index levels contain index blocks (nodes) of 1 kbyte.

Such a B$^+$-tree implementation with four index levels can hold a substantially large number of records; for example, a four level B$^+$-tree with 1 kbyte blocks containing an average entry size of 50 bytes can store over 20,000 entries. Actually, the B$^+$-tree implementation limits can be altered in the B$^+$-tree definition file to suit the limits of a large commercial application where a relation may contain some tens of thousands of records.

In the following we shall direct our attention to the description of the REQUIEM functions that implement B$^+$-tree insertion, deletion, and searching for a specific key. These functions are used by the access path modules of REQUIEM which take full advantage of B$^+$-tree indices and hashing to find the fastest way to get the desired information. For further details concerning the implementation of the B$^+$-tree functions refer to the program listings in Appendix B.

6.4.1   B$^+$-tree management functions

Most of the functions managing the B$^+$-tree index files take two arguments: the address of an index file header (ixd) identifying the index file to be used, and a structure of the type **entry** which is used as a placeholder for a B$^+$-tree entry. This structure holds the address of the record in which this key is stored in the data file and the key value to be inserted into the B$^+$-tree. The index file header structure contains among other things a file descriptor to be used in conjunction with read and write calls, and pointers to functions which calculate or compare the addresses of specific entries. The current index block address and the offset location within this block are also stored in the index file header. Finally, the file descriptor holds enough space for the caching scheme of the B$^+$-tree implementation. The caching mechanisms allocate space to store the most recently used index blocks in the B$^+$-tree to speed up execution by reducing the number of actual disk reads. We will first explain the caching mechanisms of REQUIEM and then we will return to the description of entry structures in a B$^+$-tree.

In this context a *cache* is a set of buffers that logically belongs to the disk, but is being kept in main memory for performance reasons. To manage the cache we must intercept all read requests to see if the required buffer is already in the cache. If it is, the read request can be satisfied without a disk read access. Otherwise, the buffer is read into the cache, and all subsequent requests from this buffer can be made relative to the cache [33]. Cache buffers are allocated in the index file header so that each open index file contains its private set of caches.

The entry structure is used to store keys and addresses of index or data records in the B$^+$-tree module. The entry structure has a format similar to

that described in Figures 6.3 and 6.4. The character array **key** of the structure entry provides enough space (30 characters) to hold any user defined
key. The definition of structure **entry** looks as follows:

```
#define MAXKEY 30

struct indx_attrs {
    long lower_lvl;          /* pointer to lower level nodes */
    char key[MAXKEY];        /* key value part of an entry */
};
```

The group of functions listed in the source file **btree.c** in Appendix B manages the database B$^+$-tree index files. The functions are generic B$^+$-tree
management functions and the access path modules use them to implement
entry insertions, updates, deletions, etc. Consequently, they include functions to create and search B$^+$-trees, add and delete keys in B$^+$-trees, and
navigate B$^+$-trees in ascending or descending indexed attribute order.

The B$^+$-tree searching functions yield data record addresses that are used
to retrieve the data file records that match the indexed attribute values. The
functions **find_ix()**, **get_current()**, **get_next()**, and **get_previous()** are used
when searching for a particular key in the index file. Function **find_ix()** locates the first entry that contains a key value greater than or equal to that
specified by the function's **entry** argument. The function **get_current()** preserves the entry at the current position in the index and leaves it unchanged,
while functions **get_next()** and **get_previous()** advance the current position
or move the current position backward in the index file, respectively. The
last two functions copy the new current entry into a local entry structure
for subsequent processing.

To insert a new record into the B$^+$-tree we use the function call **find_ins()**.
This function calls the function **find_exact()** to verify that the current entry
(combination of key and its associated address in the data file) is not already
present in the index file and establishes the proper position in the index file
for performing the insertion. Function **insert_ix()** takes as arguments a
pointer to the index file header and an entry structure, and adds its entry
argument in front of the current position in the current index block. After
this insertion has occurred, the current position in the block is displaced
beyond the inserted entry. The function **find_del()** is the dual function to
find_ins() and is used to perform entry deletions. It also calls **find_exact()**
to locate the desired entry in the B$^+$-tree. Once the current entry has been
pinpointed, **find_del()** calls **del_ix()** to remove the current entry from the
index block. After the current entry has been deleted the current position in
this block is set in front of the entry that follows the deleted one. With this
basic set of functions, you should be able to perform most of the B$^+$-tree

management operations. These functions are the basic set of functions on top of which other more complex functions can be realized. The importance of the B^+-tree implementation routines will become more readily apparent when these routines are used to implement the complex programs of the next section.

6.5   Access path implementation in REQUIEM

The access path modules (APMs) in REQUIEM handle all actual data accessing in the stored relations. The APM interface is implemented as a set of functions whose calling conventions will be indicated later in this section. The APMs must provide linear ordering of tuples in a relation by means of an indexing mechanism so that the concept of the next (logical) tuple is well defined. Moreover, they must assign to each data record a unique tuple identifier (TID). This TID quantity in REQUIEM corresponds to the address of a specific tuple in the data file. One of the design goals of the APMs was to insulate the higher level software from the actual intricacies of the access methods, thereby making it easier to add new access modules. It is anticipated that the APMs could easily be tailored to the needs of users with special requirements.

In this section we will examine the functions implementing the access path code in REQUIEM. These functions provide the ability to perform insertions, look-ups, deletions, or updates in our B^+-tree implementation. You will most probably wish to tread lightly through the functions presented herein, devoting your time and attention only to those parts that may interest you. We will try to help by indicating what those points might be as we work our way through the access path functions.

For reasons of clarity the implementation of the B^+-tree accessing modules has to deal with the following main issues:

1. Creation of index files; this step involves special methods for associating foreign keys with their corresponding primary keys.
2. Searching of a given value in the B^+-tree.
3. Insertion of a new value in the B^+-tree; this step involves the correlation of foreign key values with their associated primary key values.
4. Deletion of specified key values in the B^+-tree; this step involves the deletion of the given key value in both index and data files. If the specific key to be deleted happens to be a primary key whose value matches that of a foreign key in some composite relation, then that value must be deleted correspondingly from all matching tuples in the composite relation.

5. Modification (updating) of a given key value; this step combines a deletion followed by an insertion step. That is, this step requires first the deletion of the given key value and then the insertion of the new key value which is used to replace it. Foreign keys are treated according to the last two steps.

6.5.1 Index creation routines

The REQUIEM index creation routines are contained in the file create.c and are used for creating the index part of a specific relation. REQUIEM provides some low-level tools for creating index files. It also offers generic low-level functions for adding indexed attribute instances to already created indexed files. Function b_index() provides a means of creating the index file associated with a created relation. This function accepts as argument a relation name and relies heavily on the use of the function create_ix() to physically realize the index file and to insert the properties of the indexed attributes into the appropriate index file header structure.

```
#define MAXKEYS 2
#define BNSIZE  10
struct indx_attrs {                       /* qualified foreign keys */
    char ix_refkey[MAXKEYS][24];    /* referenced attributes */
    char ix_prim[MAXKEYS][BNSIZE];  /* primary attributes */
    char ix_secnd[MAXKEYS][BNSIZE]; /* secondary attributes */
    char ix_rel[12];                /* relation name */
    char ix_foreign;                /* indicates a foreign key */
    int ix_datatype[2 * MAXKEYS];   /* data type of key attributes */
};
```

Figure 6.6 The indexed attributes structure.

The function ix_attr() is responsible for making an index entry for the attribute name it accepts as argument. The other arguments to ix_attr() are the name of the relation to which the attribute belongs, the type of the attribute, and an index counter indicating the relative number of this index type. Note that the structure indx_attrs (see Figure 6.6), which contains information pertaining to the indexed attributes, includes two (MAXKEYS) positions for primary index and another two for secondary index names. The two primary index positions in this structure are filled only when the underlying relation is a composite relation. In that case it contains the names of the two foreign keys. We use the boolean character variable ix_foreign in the structure indx_attrs (which is part of the index file descriptor) to keep track of whether the underlying relation is a composite relation or not. This flag is turned on (ix_foreign = 't') whenever an index file implements a composite relation.

6.5.2   Key searching functions

This subsection deals with the detailed strategy for processing a query that involves one or more indexed attributes in its predicate. This strategy is termed the access plan for this specific query and is in accordance with that mentioned in section 6.3. An access plan in REQUIEM includes not only the relational operations to be performed but also the indices to be used and the order in which data tuples are to be accessed.

This subsection explains how to use the access plan for processing certain types of queries that involve indexed predicate attributes, i.e. attributes that are indexed and happen to be part of the relational predicate. The access plan routines involve tracing the path from the root of the B⁺-tree to the data block in which the required record is supposedly stored. The REQUIEM function which is responsible for the access plan generation and the processing of the query containing indexed attributes in its predicate is called **access_plan()**. However, prior to embarking on a detailed discussion of this function we will explain how indexed predicate attributes are compiled by the predicate expression compiler.

As we shall see in Chapter 8, during the process of syntax analysis whenever the parser senses the presence of an indexed attribute by means of the predicate pointer **prptr** (allocated and assigned by the expression compiler during the compilation of such queries as **select, delete,** or **update**, etc.) it does not call the query decomposer to bring those data records satisfying the predicate from the data file. Instead, it leaves this decision to the function **access_plan()**.

In general, the indexing functions assume that all indexed predicate attributes are associated with a predicate structure containing an operand structure for each individual indexed attribute in the predicate.

Example 6.5.1

Consider the sample query, "Find all suppliers who have a supplier identification number between 120 and 200," which can be written as follows:

select all from supplier **where** sup_id > 120 & sup_id < 200;

Here, *SUP_ID* is the primary (**unique**) key of the relation *SUPPLIER*. To process this query the REQUIEM function which implements the **select** statements calls at some stage the predicate expression compiler to lay out an intermediate code array structure, as explained in Chapter 4. What normally happens is that the predicate expression compiler functions return the physical address of the *SUP_ID* attribute values. However, in the case of example 6.5.1 the predicate compiler functions will sense that the attribute *SUP_ID* is indexed and that it must contain a unique value as it constitutes a primary key. Therefore, these functions will no longer deal with the storing of the operand structure associated with the attribute *SUP_ID* into the intermediate code, rather they will leave this decision to the low-level function get_ixattr(). Predicate compilation functions, as you will see later in this book, do not handle the complication of indexed attributes; they simply deal with non-indexed ones.

The function get_ixattr() is responsible for allocating a predicate structure and for placing the values of the indexed attributes contained in this predicate structure. Function get_ixattr() accepts five parameters: a pointer to the relation structure associated with the indexed attribute (rlptr); the name (at_name); the type (at_type); and finally, the length (at_length) of the indexed predicate attribute and to the address of a pointer to the code array cell where the operand structure associated with this attribute is stored. The code array is laid out by the predicate expression compiler after compilation of the predicate expression of a given query has taken place. We use the variable prptr to point to a predicate structure that contains all information associated with an indexed predicate attribute. The variable prptr is a global variable that is used within the REQUIEM access path file to indicate the predicate structure associated with the query evaluation underway. This avoids the need to pass that pointer to the predicate structure as an argument in all functions that are used within this module. This predicate structure pointed to by prptr has the following format:

```
struct pred {
    char *pr_rlname;    /* name of relation containing the index */
    char **pr_ixtype;   /* type of index */
    char **pr_atname;   /* attribute name of indexed attribute */
    struct operand **pr_opd; /* indexed operand structure */
};
```

The variable pr_rlname denotes the name of the relation involved in the predicate, while the variables pr_ixtype and pr_atname are actually character arrays that are used to hold the type and name of all indexed attributes belonging to the relation pr_rlname. Finally, the array of operand structures pr_opd is used to hold information pertaining to each individual indexed predicate attribute.

If the predicate pointer prptr points to NULL, the function get_ixattr()

must allocate a new predicate structure and set **prptr** to point to it. Subsequently, **get_ixattr()** checks the key type of the indexed attribute to determine whether the index is a unique (primary) index (**at_key** = 'p') or a secondary key index (**at_key** = 's'). In both cases this function calls **check_pred()** to determine the type of the predicate attribute and to place appropriate information into corresponding character arrays within the predicate structure.

The function **check_pred()** steps through all the attributes contained in the relation structure pointed to by its argument **rlptr** and tries to locate the indexed attribute, e.g. the attribute (SUP_ID) in the sample query of example 6.5.1, within this structure. Once the function establishes that the given attribute already exists it makes certain that this attribute is not inserted in the B^{+}-tree once again. If the attribute is already inserted in the predicate structure, **check_pred()** simply ensures that both attribute instances point to the same operand structure in the **code** array. Finally, function **check_pred()** places all values pertaining to the predicate attribute into the appropriate location in the predicate structure.

Now, let us return to the function **access_plan()** which provides the only means of accessing the data record associated with the value of a given indexed predicate attribute. This function includes a number of interesting points worth noting. It combines the searching of an index value with the evaluation of all possible combinations of indexed and non-indexed attributes in the query predicate. It accepts as arguments a pointer **rel_ptr** to the transient relation structure where the results of this search will be stored (in other words **rel_ptr** is the pointer to a snapshot relation structure), a pointer (**slptr**) to the selection structure of the relation(s) involved in the query, the current tuple counter (**cntr**), and two booleans **hash** and **updt**.

We use the variable **hash** to keep trace of whether we actually require hashing of the tuples satisfying the predicate, or not. Hashing is always required after **project** or **group** queries. The flag **updt** is turned on whenever a call to the function **update()** of the parser results in a call to **access_plan()**; in all other cases this flag is turned off. The function **access_plan()** confirms whether a single indexed attribute or only identical attribute names, e.g. the predicate attributes in example 6.5.1, are involved in the query predicate.

If we consider our sample query in example 6.5.1, we can observe that the indexed attributes in the query have all the same type, e.g. SUP_ID, and that the upper value for them is 200 while the lower value is 120. This indicates that the index associated with the attribute SUP_ID has to be scanned from the value $P0*120$ to the value $P0*200$. The string $P0*$ always prefixes primary key values to distinguish them from secondary key values which are prefixed by $S0*$ and $S1*$. This means that only the key values in the index file within the appropriate range would satisfy the predicate.

Example 6.5.2

The index file IX of Figure 6.1 contains five entries satisfying the predicate of the sample query in example 6.5.1. These are (622, P0∗125), (677, P0∗128), (512, P0∗135), (567, P0∗137), and (732, P0∗142), where 622, 677, 512, etc., are record addresses in the data file.

Consequently, all data records associated with the primary key values of these entries are fetched from the data file.

After estimating the upper and lower attribute limits involved in the predicate, **access_plan()** forms the B$^+$-tree entry which matches the value of the key we are looking for. As the index is organized in ascending order we first form the entry corresponding to the lower primary key value (i.e. *P0∗120*). To locate the entry for the desired key in the B$^+$-tree we call the function **locate_ix()**. This function takes four arguments: the first is the address of the index header structure (**ixd**) which is local to **access_plan()**; the second is the entry (**e**) that we have currently formed; the third is another entry structure, called **e_2**, which contains the result of the scan after returning from **locate_ix()**; finally, the fourth argument (**data_level**) will receive the address of the data record associated with the key value we are currently searching for. The function **locate_ix()** calls the B$^+$-tree management functions **find_ix()** and **get_current()** to get the current entry in the B$^+$-tree that has a search value greater than or equal to that specified by the function's argument **e**.

After the function **locate_ix()** returns, function **access_plan()** continues execution by triggering the evaluation of the attribute values contained in the **code** array. The actual work is done by a call to function **xinterpret()**. If the evaluation was successful, **access_plan()** calls the low-level routine **set_path()** which performs the actual work of reading and writing tuples from and to the associated data files. Function **set_path()** first reads the data record associated with the search key. It then determines the kind of operation that the given query requires and writes the resulting tuple into the snapshot file. This function discriminates between queries requiring elimination of duplicate tuples and those simply requiring the display of all the resulting tuples. Eventually, function **access_plan()** gets the next entries in the B$^+$-tree by successive calls to the B$^+$-tree function **get_next()**. This interpretation and fetching process is repeated continuously until we either reach the bottom of the index file or the type of the index (key) prefix changes. A primary key prefix can change from a primary type to secondary, or from one secondary type to another (e.g. either from *P0∗* to

S0∗, or from *S0∗* to *S1∗*). Consider the following example:

Example 6.5.3

Assume that the index file of Figure 6.1 contains a primary index on the attribute SUP_ID as well as a secondary index on the attribute SUP_NAME. The entries in the index file then would look like:

622, P0∗125	677, P0∗128	. . .	732, P0∗142	622, S0∗Gray	. . .

With the above index organization the function **access_plan()** will stop execution immediately after it reaches the entry (622, S0∗Gray).

Finally, one word of caution. You may have observed that all the indexed predicate attributes contained in a predicate structure belong to a single relation, while all other attributes belonging to different relations are treated as non-indexed attributes. This is not a design flaw: this part of the implementation has been left for you to complete as an exercise.

6.5.3   Key insertion routines

The index module functions establish entry points for insertion or deletion of indexed attribute values and also determine the relative number of inserted or deleted indexed attributes. More importantly, the index module allows various approaches to be tried without having to change the calling functions. To insert a new entry into the B+-tree the file manager calls the function **db_index()**. This function accepts three arguments: the name of the relation where the insertion is to be performed (**name**); the address of the data record to which the indexed (primary or secondary) attribute belongs (**top_pos**), and finally, an index buffer (**ix_buf**). When a value, corresponding to an indexed attribute, is sent to an index file it is actually stored in an index buffer rather than being written immediately to the disk. If this index buffer is full then its contents are flushed to the disk in a single disk access operation.

This index buffering scheme is implemented by the function **check_ix()** which is called by the parser function **insert()** during insertion. This function allocates enough space for four indexed attribute entries. The first two indexed entries correspond to primary key entries (as explained in the following they are actually both occupied *only* when foreign keys are present) while the rest correspond to secondary key entries. Recall that in RE-QUIEM we can effectively have three indices per relation, i.e. one primary and two secondary indices at most. Function **check_ix()** decides about the type of the indexed entry, allocates space for the entry and stores each individual value into the appropriate position in the index buffer. For example, the value of the first secondary key will be inserted in the third position in the index buffer, as the two first slots in the buffer are reserved for primary keys.

We now return to the description of db_index(). This function first opens the index file corresponding to a given relation. Next, it calls index_attrs() to perform the actual attribute insertions in the B$^+$-tree and to write them back into the index file. The function index_attrs() first senses the insert-flag (insert) to determine whether a B$^+$-tree insertion or deletion is required. This flag is turned on whenever an insertion operation is required, and is turned off otherwise. After ascertaining the nature of the specific B$^+$-tree operation that is required, function index_attrs() forms the key prefix and then calls the low-level B$^+$-tree function associated with this operation.

One point about function index_attrs() which needs to be stressed right away is that during insertion the system must ascertain whether the relation underlying the insert operation is a composite relation. If this is the case then a primary key (composite key) must be formed for this relation by appropriately combining the values of the foreign keys involved in the insertion. The function combine_fkeys() is responsible for formatting a composite key whenever this is required. This function is invoked by index_attrs() and confirms that each foreign key value exists individually in the target relation referenced by that foreign key. If both foreign key values required to compose the primary key of a composite relation are present, then the composite key is formed and inserted together with both the foreign keys into the B$^+$-tree. Note that this composite key* contains always the prefix *P2** and its value is formed by coalescing the first two numerical values included in the index buffer in ascending order. Incidentally, the composite key is never itself inserted into the index buffer.

Example 6.5.4

---

*As explained in Chapter 3 the composite key in relation SUPPLY will be formed by combining the values of the foreign key attributes SID and PRNO which match the primary keys SUP_ID and PROD_NO, respectively. Let us assume now that SUP_ID contains the value 605 and that PROD_NO contains the value 21 as depicted in Figure 2.1. The composite key in SUPPLY will then have the internal value P2*60521, while the contents of three index buffers corresponding to relations SUPPLIER, PRODUCT, and SUPPLY would be as shown in Figure 6.7 (always assuming that the relation definitions of section 3.2.1 hold).*

---

*We use the term composite key to denote the primary key of a composite relation.

SUPPLIER IX_BUFFER	PRODUCT IX_BUFFER	SUPPLY IX_BUFFER
P0*605	P0*21	P0*605
		P1*21
S0*Jones	S0*cabinet	

Figure 6.7 The contents of the index buffers for the relations *SUPPLIER*, *PRODUCT*, and *SUPPLY*.

6.5.4   Key updating functions

Update of entries in the B$^+$-tree can be materialized through the following steps:

1. Find the entry to be updated in the B$^+$-tree and copy its indexed attributes to be deleted into the delete buffer.
2. Remove the original entry from the B$^+$-tree.
3. Update the entry by replacing the deleted values with the appropriate values as specified in the insert index buffer.
4. Finally insert the updated entry into the B$^+$-tree.

As each update operation necessarily involves a delete operation, we will not discuss key deletions separately, but will consider them in terms of updates.

When an RQL update operation involves indexed attribute updates (primary or secondary keys), the sequence of function calls required for tuple updating becomes quite complicated (contrast Figure 5.8 with Figure 6.8).

Updating a key value involves locating the B$^+$-tree entry containing the specific value to be updated by an appropriate call to the function access_plan(). By setting the updt-flag of this function to TRUE, function sel_path(), which receives the update flag as an actual parameter, comprehends that an update operation is in progress, and calls the function update_attrs(). Function update_attrs() stores a copy of the current data record in the tuple buffer sc_tuple of the REQUIEM scan structure, and updates the non-indexed attributes of the underlying relation by progressing through the tuple buffer contents. When update_attrs() encounters an indexed attribute it first invokes function update_keys(). The purpose of this function is to initialize the operations and data structures required to update an indexed entry in the index file. For this purpose it creates the

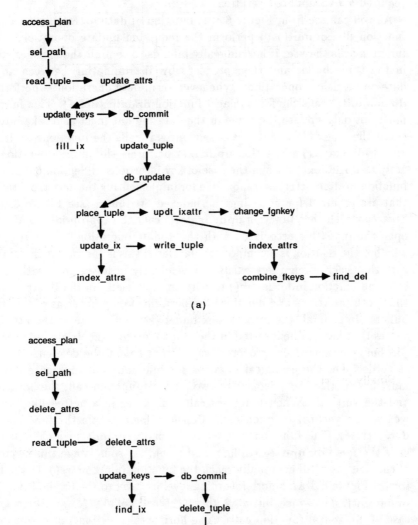

(a)

(b)

Figure 6.8 Updating and deletion index routines.

insert and delete index buffers and fills them with the appropriate key values required for an update operation.

As you can see from Figure 6.8(a) function **update_attrs()** next calls the function **db_commit()** to perform the requested update operations. This function asks the user if he/she really intends to commit the changes stored in the tuple buffer and then proceeds by discriminating between an update and a delete operation. Whenever an update operation is performed, **db_commit()** calls the file manager function **update_tuple()**. This function must not only update the tuple in the data file but must also take into account the index file updates. Consequently, it calls the functions **updt_ix()** and **updt_ixattr()**. Function **updt_ix()** performs the insert operation exactly as **db_index()** does in the case of key insertions in Section 6.5.3, while function **updt_ixattr()** is responsible for implementing the actual operations that are required for updating the indexed attributes (see Figure 6.8(a)). To accomplish this, function **updt_ixattr()** calls the appropriate function to open the index file associated with the update operation. Next, it checks whether the relation is a composite relation. If this is the case it then makes sure that each foreign key exists independently in its target relation, and calls the function **index_attrs()** to perform the deletes in the B$^+$-tree. Note that both insertions and deletions are performed only in terms of the index buffers. In general, the insert index buffer (**key_buf**) contains the attribute values that have to be inserted in the index file while the delete index buffer (**del_buf**) contains their associated values that have to be deleted.

To decipher the graphical notation for function calls in Figure 6.8 you must first notice the existence of two kinds of function call, the horizontal and the vertical. When functions call each other in a nested-like fashion we use the vertical function call. Consider for example the function **update_attrs()**. This function calls the function **db_commit()** which in its turn calls the function **update_tuple()**, and so on. At some stage this sequence of chained calls will eventually reach the function **index_attrs()**, at the bottom of Figure 6.8(a), before returning level by level to the original function **update_attrs()** (which initiated these chained calls). Now, consider the case of horizontal function calls. The horizontal function call corresponds to multiple function invocations from the body of a single function. The functions invoked always return to the function which called them. Take for example the function **place_tuple()**. This function calls the function **update_ixattr()** which after execution passes control to the function that called it, i.e. the function **place_tuple()**. Next, function **place_tuple()** calls function **change_fgnkey()**, which also returns to it, and so on.

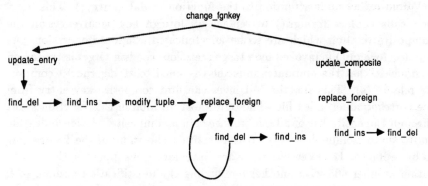

Figure 6.9 Updating and deletion of foreign keys.

Foreign key updating

Updating of foreign keys should be seen from two different perspectives: the perspective of the target relation, and that of the composite relation. To understand the semantics of foreign key updates consider the following example.

Example 6.5.5

Assume that we wish to update the supplier number of a SUPPLIER (target) relation entry for which there exists at least one matching SUPPLY (composite relation) entry. Moreover, assume that we are also interested in performing the reverse updating action, namely to update the supplier number of a SUPPLY entry for which there exists a target primary key in the relation SUPPLIER.

In REQUIEM the former update operation cascades to update the foreign keys in the matching *SUPPLY* tuples. On the other hand, to perform the latter operation we require that only the *SUPPLY* tuple in question is updated, thereby ensuring that the updated foreign key values exist in the corresponding target relation.

Let us now consider the first issue in some detail. Here, the function change_fgnkey() in Figure 6.8(a) is used to discriminate between composite and target relations. The next step will be to find those composite relation entries in the *SYSKEY* catalog that are associated with the given target relation. This investigation might turn out to be quite complicated as the primary key of a target relation might be a foreign key for more than one composite relation. We next open each composite data and index file associated with this target relation, and call the function update_entry() to update all the foreign key entries in the composite relation (see Figure 6.9).

We now direct our attention to the function **update_entry()**. This function calls **replace_foreign()** to replace all foreign key occurrences in the composite relation which are to be affected by the update operation. As **replace_foreign()** is invoked by a target relation, the flag **target** is turned on to indicate that these updates must be cascaded to all dependent composite relation(s). This function retrieves the first composite key entry from the corresponding index file. The outermost **for** loop in this function scans through the entire list of all primary keys in a composite relation index file and tries to isolate those entries that contain the value of the foreign key to be replaced. For example, if we are to replace the supplier with identification number 605 with another one having the identification number 622, then function **replace_foreign()** will try to isolate all index file entries in the relation *SUPPLY* which contain the value 605 in their composite keys. In this case it will identify the entries *P2∗60521* and *P2∗60533* (see Figure 2.1). This iteration loop continues until we either encounter the end of the index file or point past the primary composite key entries in the index file, exactly as shown in example 6.5.3. The innermost **for** loop then advances through the elements of the two index buffers (**del_buf, key_buf**) to locate those which need to be updated. Recall that in the case of a target update the index buffers contain exactly one foreign key entry prefixed by either *P∗0* or *P∗1*, and possibly one or more secondary key entries (see Figure 6.7). Next **replace_foreign()** forms the indexed value for the foreign key contained in the delete index buffer and deletes from the B^{+}-tree the foreign key entry to be updated. Subsequently, **replace_foreign()** forms the new foreign key value from the insert index buffer and then places it in the index file. This process is repeated continously until it exits from the outermost iteration loop.

We now focus our attention on the second issue that was mentioned earlier, namely the updating of composite relations. When dealing with composite entries which require updating of one or both foreign keys you must always make sure that the catenation of the inserted foreign keys is indeed a valid key combination. This implies that each foreign key must not only exist separately in its corresponding target relation but also that the combination of the two foreign keys is a unique combination, i.e. a primary key, for our composite relation. The function **f_consistency()** accomplishes the first requirement: it creates two key buffers for each foreign key and then calls function **chk_fgnkey()** to determine whether the updated foreign key values exist individually in their corresponding target relations.

Let us next see how update operations are performed in terms of composite relations in REQUIEM. We first call function **change_fgnkey()** once again to provide the means for managing the idiosyncrasies of foreign key updating (see Figure 6.8). As this time **change_fgnkey()** has to deal with composite relations it calls function **update_composite()** instead of **update_entry()** (see Figure 6.9). The purpose of **update_composite()** is to call function **check_replace()** which checks if the updated combination of foreign keys, i.e. the new composite key, already exists in the B$^+$-tree and returns the result of this test. Assuming that this check was successful, function **update_composite()** proceeds by invoking function **replace_foreign()** just as **update_entry()** did (see Figure 6.9). The sequence of actions in **replace_foreign()** are much the same as in the previous case, therefore there is no need to go through them.

Note that in the case of a composite key update we do not necessarily have to loop through all the separate occurrences of the foreign keys in the index file unless this is explicitly specified by the predicate in the update query. For example consider the following update queries:

update supno **from** supply;
update supno **from** supply **where** supno = 123;

The first query specifies that the user wishes to update database entries interactively while the second query specifies that the user wishes to update *all SUPPLY* entries having a *SUPNO* value equal to 123. In the first case REQUIEM lets the user decide which entries are going to be updated, while in the second it updates all associated entries.

As explained at the beginning of this section the pattern of actions required for the deletion of foreign keys from either a target or a composite relation is much the same as that required for foreign key updating. Actually, the same logic applies to both the updating and deleting of foreign key entries in an index file. The only difference is that in a delete operation both foreign keys and their associated composite keys are deleted from the index file and, thus, their corresponding entry is permanently removed from the index file rather than being replaced by a new entry.

6.6   Source listing 3

file: access.c

```
1    /* REQUIEM - access path module */
2    #include <stdio.h>
3    #include "btree.h"
4    #include "requ.h"
5
6    extern struct pred *prptr;
7    extern union code_cell code[];
8    extern char    **key_buf;
```

```
 9    extern char    **del_buf;
10    extern char    *join_on;
11
12            /* non-indexed attr flag set during compilation */
13    extern BOOL non_ixattr;
14    extern int xand(), xor(), xnot(), xlss(), xleq(), xeql(),
15            xgeq(), xgtr(), xneq(), xpart(), xstop(),
16            compf(), sizef();
17    BOOL stop_flag = FALSE;
18
19    /* ------------------------------------------------------------ *
20        |              index inserting routines                |
21        * ------------------------------------------------------------ */
22    struct ix_header *db_index(rname, tup_pos, ix_buf)
23        long tup_pos;
24        char *rname, **ix_buf;
25    {
26      struct ix_header ixd;
27      BOOL insert = TRUE;
28      char *pt_error();
29
30      /* open  index file and assign index header structure */
31      if (!assign_pixd(rname, &ixd))
32        return((struct ix_header *)pt_error(IXFLNF));
33
34      /* index the attributes according to their key specs */
35      if (!index_attrs(tup_pos, &ixd, ix_buf, insert))
36        return((struct ix_header *)pt_error(WRNGINS));
37
38      return(&ixd);   /* indexing was successful */
39    } /* db_index */
40
41    /* ------------------------------------------------------------ */
42
43    int    index_attrs(tup_pos, pixd, ix_buf, insert)
44        long tup_pos;
45        struct ix_header *pixd;
46        char    **ix_buf;
47        BOOL insert;
48    {
49      struct entry entr;
50      char    prefix[5];
51      int     i;
52
53      entr.lower_lvl = tup_pos; /* point to tuple pos in datafile */
54
55      /* form a primary key as combination of foreign keys,
56         if required */
57      if (insert)
58        if (!combine_fkeys(pixd, ix_buf, &entr))
59          return(FALSE);
60
61      for ( i = 0; i < 2 * MAXKEYS ; i++) {
62        /* index primary keys first */
63        if (i < 2 &&
64            *(pixd->dx.ixatts.ix_prim[i]) != EOS &&
65            ix_buf[i]) {
66          clear_mem(entr.key, 0, MAXKEY);
67          sprintf(prefix, "P%d*", i);
68          cat_strs(entr.key, prefix, ix_buf[i]);
69
```

```
70           if (insert) {
71             if (find_ins(&entr, pixd) == IX_FAIL)
72               return(error(DUPATT)); /* entry already there */
73           } else if (find_del(&entr, pixd) == IX_FAIL)
74             return(error(IXATRNF)); /* entry not there */
75         }
76
77         /* index secondary keys now */
78         if (i >= 2 &&
79             *(pixd->dx.ixatts.ix_secnd[i-2]) != EOS &&
80             ix_buf[i]) {
81           clear_mem(entr.key, 0, MAXKEY);
82           sprintf(prefix, "S%d*", i - 2);
83           cat_strs(entr.key, prefix, ix_buf[i]);
84
85           if (insert) {
86             if (find_ins(&entr, pixd) == IX_FAIL)
87               return(error(DUPATT)); /* entry already there */
88           } else if (find_del(&entr, pixd) == IX_FAIL)
89             return(error(IXATRNF)); /* entry not there */
90         }
91
92       }
93
94     return(TRUE);    /* return success */
95   } /* index_attrs */
96
97
98   /* -----------------------------------------------------------
99    |           index update, delete routines                  |
100   * ----------------------------------------------------------- */
101  int    update_ix(tup_pos, ix_buf, pixd)
102       long tup_pos;
103       char    **ix_buf;
104       struct ix_header *pixd;
105  {
106    /* index the attributes according to their key specs */
107    if (!index_attrs(tup_pos, pixd, ix_buf, TRUE)) {
108      close((pixd)->ixfile);
109      return(error(UPDTERR));
110    }
111
112    return(TRUE);    /* indexing was successful */
113  } /* update_ix */
114
115  /* -------------- update an indexed entry -------------------- */
116  update_keys(slptr, saptr, aptr, offset, old_value, new_value)
117       struct sel *slptr;
118       struct sattr *saptr;
119       struct attribute *aptr;
120       long    *offset;
121       char    *old_value, *new_value;
122  {
123
124    struct srel *srptr;
125    int p_cntr = 0, s_cntr = 2;      /* key counters */
126    struct relation *rptr;
127    struct ix_header ixd;
128    struct entry e, e1;
129    char    fname[RNSIZE+6];
130    int    i, scntr = 0;
```

```
131
132      rptr = SEL_RELATION;
133      srptr = SEL_RELS;
134
135      for (i = 0; i < srptr->sr_scan->sc_nattrs; i++) {
136        if (RELATION_HEADER.hd_attrs[i].at_key == 's')
137          scntr++;
138        else  if (RELATION_HEADER.hd_attrs[i].at_key == 'p')
139          p_cntr++;
140
141        /* locate the selected attribute and estimate its prefix */
142        if (strcmp(saptr->sa_aname,
143                   RELATION_HEADER.hd_attrs[i].at_name) == EQUAL)
144          break;
145
146      }
147      /* first two positions reserved for foreign keys */
148      s_cntr = 2 + scntr;
149
150      /* if predicate struct not available, form index key and
151       * locate key-attribute value in index file */
152      if (!prptr) {
153        /* if index file not open, open it */
154        if (!form_ix(fname, &ixd, SEL_RELATION))
155          return(FALSE);
156
157        /* form index-key to look for */
158        if (scntr > 0)
159          sprintf(e.key, "S%d*%s", scntr - 1, old_value);
160        else if (p_cntr > 0)
161          sprintf(e.key, "P%d*%s", p_cntr - 1, old_value);
162
163        /* position index file at an entry >= to search key */
164        find_ix(&e, &ixd);
165
166        /* get current entry */
167        get_current(&e1, &ixd);
168        rm_trailblks(e1.key);
169
170        /* compare entries */
171        if (strcmp(e.key, e1.key) == EQUAL)
172          *offset = e1.lower_lvl;
173        else
174          return(FALSE);
175      }
176
177      /* fill delete index buffer with attr values to be deleted */
178      fill_ix(&del_buf, aptr, p_cntr, s_cntr, old_value);
179
180      /* fill insert index buffer with attr values to be inserted */
181      fill_ix(&key_buf, aptr, p_cntr, s_cntr, new_value);
182
183      return(TRUE);
184
185  } /* update_keys */
186
187  /* ------------------------------------------------------------ */
188
189  BOOL del_ixattr(pixd, sptr, del_buf)
190       struct ix_header **pixd;
191       struct scan *sptr;
```

```
192            char    **del_buf;
193     {
194       BOOL insert = FALSE;
195
196       if (*pixd == NULL)
197         if ((*pixd = CALLOC(1, struct ix_header)) == NULL)
198           return(error(INSMEM));
199
200       /* open index file and assign index header structure */
201       if (!assign_pixd(sptr->sc_relation->rl_name, *pixd))
202         return(error(IXFLNF));
203
204       /* index the attributes according to their key specs */
205       if (!index_attrs(sptr->sc_recpos, *pixd, del_buf, insert)) {
206         close((*pixd)->ixfile);
207         return(error(IXDELFAIL));
208       }
209
210       return(TRUE);
211     } /* del_ixattr */
212
213     /* ------------------------------------------------------------ */
214
215     BOOL updt_ixattr(pixd, sptr, del_buf, key_buf)
216            struct ix_header **pixd;
217            struct scan *sptr;
218            char    **del_buf, **key_buf;
219     {
220       BOOL insert = FALSE;
221
222       if (*pixd == NULL)
223         if ((*pixd = CALLOC(1, struct ix_header)) == NULL)
224           return(error(INSMEM));
225
226       /* open index file and assign index header structure */
227       if (!assign_pixd(sptr->sc_relation->rl_name, *pixd))
228         return(error(IXFLNF));
229
230       /* check if new entry is a viable entry for foreign keys */
231       if (!f_consistency(*pixd, key_buf))
232         return(error(INCNST));
233
234       /* index the attributes according to their key specs */
235       if (!index_attrs(sptr->sc_recpos, *pixd, del_buf, insert)) {
236         close((*pixd)->ixfile);
237         return(error(IXDELFAIL));
238       }
239
240       return(TRUE);
241     } /* updt_ixattr */
242
243     /* ------------------------------------------------------------ */
244
245     /* fill in attribute to be updated, deleted */
246     fill_ix(key_buf, aptr, p_cntr, s_cntr, avalue)
247            char    ***key_buf;
248            struct attribute *aptr;
249            int     p_cntr, s_cntr;      /* primary and secondary keys */
250            char    *avalue;             /* value to be indexed */
251     {
252       char    key;     /* key type */
```

```
253
254        /* get key type */
255        key = aptr->at_key;
256
257        /* create a key buffer */
258        if (*key_buf == NULL)
259          if ((*key_buf = (char **)calloc(4, sizeof(char *))) == NULL)
260            return (error(INSMEM));
261
262        /* check for primary key */
263        if (key == 'p' && p_cntr - 1 < MAXKEYS) {
264          if (*avalue == EOS) { /* in case of deletion */
265            (*key_buf)[p_cntr-1] = (char *)NULL;
266            return(TRUE);
267          }
268
269          (*key_buf)[p_cntr-1] =
270            calloc(1, (unsigned) aptr->at_size + 1);
271          strcpy((*key_buf)[p_cntr-1], avalue);
272          return(TRUE);
273        }
274
275        /* check for secondary key */
276        if (key == 's' && s_cntr - 1 < 2 * MAXKEYS)  {
277          if (*avalue == EOS) {  /* in case of deletion */
278            (*key_buf)[s_cntr-1] = (char *)NULL;
279            return(TRUE);
280          }
281
282          (*key_buf)[s_cntr-1] =
283            calloc(1, (unsigned) aptr->at_size + 1);
284          strcpy((*key_buf)[s_cntr-1], avalue);
285          return(TRUE);
286        }
287
288        return(FALSE);
289      } /* fill_ix */
290
291      /* ------------------------------------------------------------- *
292         |                 foreign key support functions              |
293         * ------------------------------------------------------------- */
294
295      /* combine fgn keys to create a prim key for a composite rel */
296      combine_fkeys(pixd, keys, entr)
297          struct ix_header *pixd;
298          struct entry *entr;
299          char      **keys;
300      {
301        char *temp_1, *temp_2, *comb_key, prefix[5];
302        int len;
303        char *rem_blanks();
304
305        /* check whether this relation is a composite relation
306         * and both foreign key values are present */
307        if ((pixd->dx.ixatts.ix_foreign == 't') &&
308                              keys[0] && keys[1]) {
309          temp_1 = (char *)calloc(1, (unsigned) strlen(keys[0]));
310          temp_2 = (char *)calloc(1, (unsigned) strlen(keys[1]));
311
312          /* copy keys to temp buffers by discarding any
313           * trailing blanks in keys */
```

```
314        rem_blanks(temp_1, keys[0], strlen(keys[0]));
315        rem_blanks(temp_2, keys[1], strlen(keys[1]));
316
317        comb_key =  (char *)calloc(1, (unsigned) strlen(temp_1) +
318                                       (unsigned) strlen(temp_2));
319
320        /* see if combination of foreign keys already exists */
321        clear_mem(entr->key, 0, MAXKEY);
322        /* denotes primary key composed of two foreign keys */
323        sprintf(prefix, "P2*");
324
325        /* form the composite key for this entry */
326        if (strlen(temp_1) + strlen(temp_2) <= MAXKEY-3) {
327          cat_strs(comb_key, temp_1, temp_2);
328          cat_strs(entr->key, prefix, comb_key);
329        }
330        else {
331          /* compute how many chars will actually fit */
332          len = (MAXKEY-3) - strlen(temp_1);
333          strcat(comb_key, temp_1);
334          strncat(comb_key, temp_2, len);
335          cat_strs(entr->key, prefix, comb_key);
336          printf("The combination of your foreign keys is too ");
337          printf("long and this may lead into trouble!\n");
338        }
339
340        /* check if each foreign key exists individually,
341         * if not so report error */
342        if (!chk_keycat(pixd, temp_1, temp_2)) {
343          nfree(temp_1);
344          nfree(temp_2);
345          nfree(comb_key);
346          return(FALSE);
347        }
348
349        /* then insert the composite key formed by the merging
350         * of the  two foreign keys */
351        if (find_ins(entr, pixd) == IX_FAIL) { /* already there */
352          nfree(temp_1);
353          nfree(temp_2);
354          nfree(comb_key);
355          return(error(WRNGCOMB));
356        }
357        /* free buffers */
358        nfree(temp_1);
359        nfree(temp_2);
360        nfree(comb_key);
361      }
362
363    return(TRUE);
364  } /* combine_fkeys */
365
366  /* ------------------------------------------------------------ */
367
368  /*check for foreign key concistency */
369  f_consistency(pixd, keys)
370      struct ix_header *pixd;
371      char    **keys;
372  {
373    char *temp_1 = (char *)NULL, *temp_2 = (char *)NULL;
374
```

```
375        /* check whether this relation is a composite relation */
376        if (pixd->dx.ixatts.ix_foreign == 't') {
377          if (keys[0]) {
378            temp_1 = (char *)calloc(1, (unsigned) strlen(keys[0]));
379            /* copy key to temp buffer */
380            rem_blanks(temp_1, keys[0], strlen(keys[0]));
381          }
382
383          if (keys[1]) {
384            temp_2 = (char *)calloc(1, (unsigned) strlen(keys[1]));
385            rem_blanks(temp_2, keys[1], strlen(keys[1]));
386          }
387
388          /* check if each foreign key exists individually,
389           * if not report error */
390          if (!chk_keycat(pixd, temp_1, temp_2)) {
391            if (keys[0])
392              nfree(temp_1);
393
394            if (keys[1])
395              nfree(temp_2);
396
397            return(FALSE);
398          }
399
400          /* free buffers */
401          if (keys[0])
402            nfree(temp_1);
403
404          if (keys[1])
405            nfree(temp_2);
406        }
407
408      return(TRUE);
409      } /* f_consistency */
410
411      /* ------------------------------------------------------------ */
412
413      /* check whether foreign key values exist individually
414       * in its qualifying relation */
415      BOOL chk_keycat(pixd, f_key1, f_key2)
416          struct ix_header *pixd;
417          char *f_key1, *f_key2;
418      {
419        struct ix_header ixd;
420        struct entry entr;
421        char prefix[5], fname[RNSIZE+6], qua_rel[15];
422        int ret, tcnt;
423
424        /* loop through referenced key array in index file header */
425        for (tcnt = 0; tcnt < MAXKEYS; tcnt++) {
426
427          /* make sure that fgn key buffers contain non-null values */
428          if ((tcnt == 0) && !f_key1)
429            continue;
430
431          if ((tcnt == 1) && !f_key2)
432            continue;
433
434          /* find names of the qualifying rels and referenced keys */
435          l_substring(pixd->dx.ixatts.ix_refkey[tcnt], qua_rel);
```

```
436
437          /* form indexed value of primary key of the qualifier rel */
438          clear_mem(entr.key, 0, MAXKEY);
439          sprintf(prefix, "PO*");
440
441          /* form entry for the foreign keys */
442          if (tcnt == 0)
443            cat_strs(entr.key, prefix, f_key1);
444          else
445            cat_strs(entr.key, prefix, f_key2);
446
447          /* form the index file name for the qualifying relation */
448          cat_strs(fname, qua_rel, ".indx");
449
450          /* open the qualifier indexed file */
451          if (!make_ix(&ixd, fname)) {
452            finish_ix(&ixd);
453            return(FALSE);
454          }
455
456          /* find if value of primary key exists in qualifier */
457          ret = find_ix(&entr, &ixd);
458
459          /* close qualifier index */
460          close(ixd.ixfile);
461
462          if (ret != 0) {
463            printf("WRONG INSERTION:  ");
464            printf("value %s does not exist in relation # %s # !\n",
465                                          (entr.key)+3, qua_rel);
466            return(FALSE);
467          }
468        }
469
470      /* return successfully */
471      return(TRUE);
472
473    } /* chk_keycat */
474
475    /* ------------------------------------------------------------ */
476
477    BOOL change_fgnkey(pixd, sptr)
478         struct ix_header *pixd;
479         struct scan *sptr;
480    {
481      struct ix_header ixd;    /* composite index header */
482      struct sel *slptr, *db_select(), *retrieve();
483      struct sattr *saptr;
484      struct sel *slptr_comp;  /* composite rel select structure */
485      char fname[RNSIZE+6], fmt[100];
486      int tcnt, i;
487
488      fname[0] = EOS;
489
490      /* if this is a system catalog, return */
491      if (strncmp(SCAN_RELATION->rl_name, "sys", 3) == EQUAL)
492        return(TRUE);
493
494      /* if a target rel make changes in all composite rels */
495      if ( pixd->dx.ixatts.ix_foreign == 'f') {
496
```

```
497          /* project name of composite rel in the SYSKEY catalog */
498          sprintf(fmt, "syskey over relname where  qualifier \
499                             = \"%s\" & primary = \"%s\" ",
500             pixd->dx.ixatts.ix_rel, pixd->dx.ixatts.ix_prim[0]);
501
502          /* selection pointer to SYSKEY relation */
503          if ((slptr = retrieve(fmt)) == NULL)
504            return(FALSE);
505          else
506            cmd_kill();   /* clear command line */
507
508          /* loop through each relation name projected fom SYSKEY */
509          for (tcnt = 0; fetch(slptr, TRUE); tcnt++) {
510            saptr = SEL_ATTRS;
511
512            /* do not process same relation twice */
513            if (strncmp(fname, saptr->sa_aptr, strlen(saptr->sa_aptr))
514                                              == EQUAL)
515              break;
516
517            /* form the name of the composite index file */
518            cat_strs(fname, saptr->sa_aptr, ".indx");
519
520            /* open the composite indexed file */
521            if (!make_ix(&ixd, fname)) {
522              finish_ix(&ixd);
523              db_rclose(sptr);
524              return(FALSE);
525            }
526
527            /* open composite data file, return a select
528             * structure pointer */
529            sprintf(fmt, "from %s", saptr->sa_aptr);
530            if ((slptr_comp = db_select(fmt)) == (struct sel *)NULL)
531              return (FALSE);
532            else
533              cmd_kill();   /* clear command line */
534
535            /* check if displacement in index buffer is required */
536            displace_ixbufs(&ixd, SCAN_RELATION->rl_name);
537
538            /* delete all foreign key occurrences in composite rel */
539            if(!update_entry(&ixd,  slptr_comp)) {
540              done(slptr_comp);
541              db_rclose(sptr);
542              return(FALSE);
543            }
544
545            /* finish using index, write it in file and
546             * free selection structure */
547            close_ix(&ixd);
548            done(slptr_comp);
549          }
550
551  /*     db_rclose(slptr); */
552
553        /* current relation is not a target relation */
554        if (tcnt == 0)
555          return(TRUE);
556      }
557    else  /* relation is a composite relation */
```

```
558        return (update_composite(pixd));
559
560      /* return successfully */
561      for (i = 0; i < MAXKEYS; i++)
562        if (key_buf[i] || del_buf[i])
563          printf("Replaced #%s = %s# with #%s = %s# in %s !\n\n",
564                  ixd.dx.ixatts.ix_prim[i],
565                  del_buf[i],
566                  ixd.dx.ixatts.ix_prim[i],
567                  key_buf[i],ixd.dx.ixatts.ix_rel);
568      return(TRUE);
569
570    } /* change_fgnkey */
571
572    /* ---------------------------------------------------------- */
573
574    del_fgn(pixd, pentr, cntr)   /* delete foreign key entry */
575         struct ix_header *pixd;
576         struct entry *pentr;
577         int cntr;
578    {
579      char prefix[20];
580
581      /* form indexed value of each fgn key of the composite rel */
582      clear_mem(pentr->key, 0, MAXKEY);
583      sprintf(prefix, "P%d*", cntr);
584      cat_strs(pentr->key, prefix, del_buf[cntr]);
585
586      /* delete old foreign key entry in composite relation */
587      find_ix(pentr, pixd);  /* find pos of old key in B-tree */
588
589      if (find_del(pentr, pixd) == IX_FAIL)  /* then delete it */
590        return(FALSE);
591
592      /* if an update operation on foreign keys is required */
593      if (key_buf[cntr] && *key_buf[cntr])
594        /* form new key entry */
595        cat_strs(pentr->key, prefix, key_buf[cntr]);
596
597      return(TRUE);
598    } /* del_fgn */
599
600    /* ---------------------------------------------------------- */
601
602    BOOL update_composite(pixd)
603         struct ix_header *pixd;
604    {
605      if ( pixd->dx.ixatts.ix_foreign != 't')
606        return(FALSE);
607
608      /* curent relation is not a composite relation */
609      if (pixd->dx.ixatts.ix_refkey[0] == NULL)
610        return(TRUE);
611
612      /* check whether new composite key already exists */
613      if (!check_replace(pixd))
614        return(FALSE);
615      else
616        /* replace  old composite primary key entry with
617         * new key values */
618        replace_foreign(pixd, (struct sel *) NULL, FALSE);
```

```
619
620      /* finish using index write it in file and free
621       * selection structure */
622      close_ix(pixd);
623
624      /* return successfully */
625      return(TRUE);
626
627    } /* update_composite */
628
629    /* ------------------------------------------------------------ */
630
631    BOOL update_entry(pixd, slptr_comp)
632        struct ix_header *pixd;
633        struct sel *slptr_comp;
634    {
635      struct entry entr[2];
636      int i;                      /*  index counter of foreign key */
637      BOOL done = FALSE;
638
639      /* check whether new composite key already exists */
640      if (!check_replace(pixd))
641        return(FALSE);
642
643      /* loop through all keys in the index buffers */
644      for (i = 0; i < MAXKEYS; i++)
645        if ((key_buf[i] && *key_buf[i]) ||
646            (del_buf[i] && *del_buf[i])) {
647
648          /* if an update operation on foreign keys is required */
649          if (key_buf[i] && *key_buf[i]) {
650
651            /* update fgn key in data tuple only once per entry */
652            if (!done) {
653              /* replace composite primimary key entries
654               * with new key values */
655              replace_foreign(pixd, slptr_comp, TRUE);
656
657              done = TRUE;   /* tuple modified */
658            }
659          }
660          else {      /* a delete operation is required */
661            slptr_comp->sl_rels->sr_scan->sc_recpos =
662                                      entr[i].lower_lvl;
663
664            /* delete data file entry */
665            if (delete_tuple(slptr_comp->sl_rels->sr_scan,
666                             (char **) NULL) == FALSE)
667              return(FALSE);
668
669            /* delete foreign key occurrences */
670            if (replace_foreign(pixd, slptr_comp, TRUE) == FALSE)
671              return(FALSE);
672          }
673
674        }
675
676      return(TRUE);
677    } /* update_entry */
678
679    /* ------------------------------------------------------------ */
```

```
680
681     displace_ixbufs(pixd, r_name)
682         struct ix_header *pixd;
683         char *r_name;
684     {   int p_cntr;
685
686         /* find relative position of target relation in composite
687            indexed attributes structure */
688         for (p_cntr = 0; p_cntr < MAXKEYS; p_cntr++)
689           if (strncmp(pixd->dx.ixatts.ix_refkey[p_cntr],
690                       r_name, strlen(r_name)) == EQUAL)
691             break;
692
693         /* this is the second fgn key of the composite relation,
694            displace insert & delete index buffer contents one place
695            downwards */
696         if (p_cntr == 1) {
697           key_buf[p_cntr] =
698             calloc(1, (unsigned) strlen(key_buf[p_cntr-1]) + 1);
699           strcpy(key_buf[p_cntr], key_buf[p_cntr-1]);
700           del_buf[p_cntr] =
701             calloc(1, (unsigned) strlen(del_buf[p_cntr-1]) + 1);
702           strcpy(del_buf[p_cntr], del_buf[p_cntr-1]);
703
704           /* free index buffers */
705           nfree(key_buf[p_cntr-1]);
706           key_buf[p_cntr-1] = (char *)NULL;
707           nfree(del_buf[p_cntr-1]);
708           del_buf[p_cntr-1] = (char *)NULL;
709         }
710
711     } /* displace_ixbufs */
712
713     /* ------------------------------------------------------------
714        | replace the part of composite key holding the old        |
715        | value with its corresponding new value                   |
716        * ------------------------------------------------------------ */
717
718     BOOL check_replace(pixd)
719         struct ix_header *pixd;
720     { struct entry  entr;
721       int ret;
722       char temp[100];
723
724       if (key_buf) {
725         /* if both parts of composite key must be changed */
726         if ((key_buf[0] && *key_buf[0]) &&
727                     (key_buf[1] && *key_buf[1])) {
728
729           /* form composite key to be inserted */
730           cat_strs(temp, key_buf[0], key_buf[1]);
731           cat_strs(entr.key, "P2*", temp);
732
733           /* find entry >= than the 1st foreign entry key */
734           ret = find_ix(&entr, pixd);
735
736           if (ret == 0)  /* if entry found in record */
737             return(error(WRNGCOMB));
738         } /* only part of the composite key must be changed */
739         else if ((key_buf[0] && *key_buf[0]) ||
740                         (key_buf[1] && *key_buf[1]))
```

```
741           if (!check_part(pixd))
742               return(FALSE);
743      }
744
745      return(TRUE);
746 } /* check_replace */
747
748 /* ------------------------------------------------------------ */
749
750 check_part(pixd) /* check if composite key exists in B-tree */
751      struct ix_header *pixd;
752 {
753      struct entry  comp_entr, temp_entr;
754      int i, j, loc, ret;
755
756      clear_mem(comp_entr.key, 0, MAXKEY);
757      strcpy(comp_entr.key, "P2*");   /* set up composite prefix */
758
759      for (j = 0; ;j++) { /* if foreign key exists more than once */
760
761        for (i = 0; i < MAXKEYS && (key_buf[i]); i++) {
762
763          if (j == 0) { /* locate the first value of comp. key */
764             find_ix(&comp_entr, pixd);
765
766             /* get the current entry there */
767             get_current(&comp_entr, pixd);
768          }
769
770          /* stop if past composite key entries in B-tree  */
771          if (strncmp(comp_entr.key, "P2*", 3) != EQUAL)
772            break;
773
774          /* return location of old value in B-tree entry, make
775           * sure whether foreign key contained in left or right
776           * part of composite key */
777          if (i == 0)
778             /* left substring */
779             loc = lsubstring_index(comp_entr.key, del_buf[i]);
780          else
781             /* right substring */
782             loc = rsubstring_index(comp_entr.key, del_buf[i]);
783
784          /* replace old fgn key part with new fgn key in comp key */
785          if (loc != FAIL) {
786             /* copy value of composite entry */
787             structcpy((char *) &temp_entr,
788                       (char *)&comp_entr, sizeof(struct entry));
789
790             remove_substring(temp_entr.key, loc, strlen(del_buf[i]));
791             insert_string(temp_entr.key, key_buf[i], loc);
792
793             /* try to locate new composite key */
794             ret = find_ix(&temp_entr, pixd);
795
796             /* if entry already there report error */
797             if (ret == 0)
798                return(error(WRNGCOMB));
799          }
800        }
801
```

```
802            /* get further composite entries, unless at EOF */
803            find_ix(&comp_entr, pixd);
804            /* reset current pos in index file */
805            get_current(&comp_entr, pixd);
806            if (get_next(&comp_entr, pixd) == EOF_IX)
807              break;
808         }
809
810      return(TRUE);
811
812    } /* check_part */
813
814    /* ------------------------------------------------------------ */
815
816    replace_foreign(pixd, slptr, target)
817         struct ix_header *pixd;
818         struct sel *slptr; /* composite rel selection structure */
819         BOOL target;          /* on when we have a target rel */
820    {
821      struct entry  comp_entr, temp_entr, first_entr, sec_entr;
822      char sec_fkey[50];
823      int i, loc;
824      BOOL found = FALSE, done = FALSE; /* single iteration flag */
825
826      clear_mem(comp_entr.key, 0, MAXKEY);
827      strcpy(comp_entr.key, "P2*");
828
829      /* find entry >= the composite entry key (primary key ) */
830      find_ix(&comp_entr, pixd);
831      get_current(&comp_entr, pixd);  /* get the cur entry there */
832
833      /* replace old value in those entries in primary key
834       * that include the foreign key if foreign key exists
835       * more than once replace all their occurrences */
836      while(TRUE) {
837        for (i = 0; i < MAXKEYS; i++)  {
838          if ((key_buf[i] && *key_buf[i]) ||
839                            (del_buf[i] && *del_buf[i])) {
840
841            /* return location of old value in B-tree entry, make
842             * sure whether foreign key contained in left or right
843             * part of composite key */
844            if (i == 0)
845              loc = lsubstring_index(comp_entr.key,
846                             del_buf[i]); /* left substring */
847            else
848              loc = rsubstring_index(comp_entr.key,
849                             del_buf[i]); /* right substring */
850
851            /* old value cannot be found in remaining composite
852             * key entries */
853            if (found == TRUE && loc == FAIL && i == 0)
854              break;
855
856            found = FALSE;          /* reset found flag */
857
858            if (loc != FAIL) {    /* if entry located */
859
860                if (target && !done) {/* more than 1 key occurrence */
861
862                   /* del fgn key entry and form new key if required */
```

```
863              if (!del_fgn(pixd, &first_entr, i))
864                return(FALSE);
865
866              if (key_buf[i] && *key_buf[i]) {
867
868                /* insert new foreign key entry */
869                if(find_ins(&first_entr, pixd) == IX_FAIL)
870                  break;
871
872                if (!modify_tuple(slptr,
873                                  pixd->dx.ixatts.ix_prim[i],
874                                  key_buf[i],
875                                  first_entr.lower_lvl))
876                  return(error(UPDTERR));
877              }
878              else if (key_buf[i] == NULL) {/* delete data tuple*/
879                slptr->sl_rels->sr_scan->sc_recpos =
880                                  first_entr.lower_lvl;
881
882                /* delete data file entry */
883                if (delete_tuple(slptr->sl_rels->sr_scan,
884                                 (char **) NULL) == FALSE)
885                  return(FALSE);
886              }
887            }
888
889            /* if update is required */
890            if (key_buf[i] && *key_buf[i]) {
891
892              /* preserve old composite key entry */
893              structcpy((char *)&temp_entr,
894                        (char *)&comp_entr, sizeof(struct entry));
895
896              /* replace old substring with new substring in
897               * composite key */
898              remove_substring(temp_entr.key,
899                               loc,
900                               strlen(del_buf[i]));
901              insert_string(temp_entr.key, key_buf[i], loc);
902
903              /* insert new composite key */
904              if (find_ins(&temp_entr, pixd) == IX_FAIL)
905                return(error(IXFAIL));
906
907              /* if it is a composite relation return */
908              if (!target)
909                return(TRUE);
910            }
911
912            /* remove old composite key */
913            if (!done) {
914              if (find_del(&comp_entr, pixd) == IX_FAIL)
915                return(error(IXDELFAIL));
916
917              found = TRUE;   /* primary subkey found */
918            }
919
920            /* delete the second fgn key component in index file
921             * associated with the deleted composite key */
922            if (key_buf[i] == NULL && !done){
923
```

```
924                    /* preserve old composite key entry */
925                    structcpy((char *) &temp_entr,
926                            (char *) &comp_entr, sizeof(struct entry));
927
928                    /* remove from composite key its foreign part */
929                    remove_substring(temp_entr.key,
930                                  loc,
931                                      strlen(del_buf[i]));
932                    /* form the second foreign key */
933                    if (i == 0)
934                      cat_strs(sec_fkey, "P1*", (temp_entr.key)+3);
935                    else
936                      cat_strs(sec_fkey, "P0*", (temp_entr.key)+3);
937
938                    clear_mem(sec_entr.key, 0, MAXKEY);
939
940                    /* delete this key */
941                    strcpy(sec_entr.key, sec_fkey);
942
943                    /* find entry >= comp. entry key (primary key) */
944                    find_ix(&sec_entr, pixd);
945
946                    if (find_del(&sec_entr,pixd) == IX_FAIL)/* delete */
947                      return(error(IXFAIL));
948
949                    done = TRUE;
950
951                    /* if it is a composite relation return */
952                    if (!target)
953                      return(TRUE);
954
955                    /* get back where we were */
956                    find_ix(&comp_entr, pixd);
957                  }
958            } /* if loc */
959
960          } /* if key_buf */
961        } /* for i */
962
963
964        if (!found) {   /* get next entry in the index */
965          if (get_next(&comp_entr, pixd) == EOF_IX)
966            break;
967
968          /* stop if past composite key entries in B-tree  */
969          if (strncmp(comp_entr.key, "P2*", 3) != EQUAL)
970            break;
971        }
972        else { /* after a previous delete the index
973               * position is in front of current */
974          get_current(&comp_entr, pixd);
975
976          /* if past primary sub-key exit loop */
977          if (del_buf[0] &&
978              strncmp(del_buf[0],
979                    comp_entr.key + 3,
980                    strlen(del_buf[0])) != EQUAL)
981            break;
982
983          if (key_buf[0]) {   /* if first fgn key was replaced */
984          /* if first part of comp. key and inserted fgn key match */
```

```
985              if (strncmp((comp_entr.key)+3,
986                           del_buf[0],
987                           strlen(del_buf[0])) > 0)
988                break;   /* exit the loop */
989            }
990          else if (key_buf[1]) { /* if second fgn key was replaced */
991            if (strncmp((comp_entr.key)+3 + strlen(comp_entr.key+3)
992                        - strlen(key_buf[1]),
993                        key_buf[1], strlen(key_buf[1])) == EQUAL)
994              if (get_next(&comp_entr, pixd) == EOF_IX)
995                break;
996          }
997        }
998
999        /* stop if past composite key entries in B-tree  */
1000       if (strncmp(comp_entr.key, "P2*", 3) != EQUAL)
1001         break;
1002       else
1003         done = FALSE;
1004     }
1005
1006     return(TRUE);
1007
1008 } /* replace_foreign */
1009
1010 /* ------------------------------------------------------------ */
1011
1012 BOOL modify_tuple(slptr, fkey_name, new_value, data_level)
1013     struct sel *slptr; /* composite relation sel pointer */
1014     char *fkey_name;   /* name of fgn key in composite rel */
1015     char *new_value;   /* new value of foreign key */
1016     long data_level;   /* pos of fgn key in comp rel file */
1017 {
1018     struct relation *rptr;
1019     struct sattr *saptr;
1020
1021     rptr = SEL_RELATION;
1022
1023     /* read original relation from data file */
1024     if (read_tuple(rptr, data_level, SEL_TUPLE) == FALSE)
1025       return(FALSE);
1026
1027     /* look for fgn key within selected attributes structure */
1028     for (saptr = SEL_ATTRS; saptr != NULL; saptr = saptr->sa_next)
1029       if (strcmp(fkey_name, saptr->sa_aname) == EQUAL) {
1030         /* store its new value */
1031         store_attr(saptr->sa_attr, saptr->sa_aptr, new_value);
1032         saptr->sa_srel->sr_update = TRUE;
1033         /* data tuple address */
1034         saptr->sa_srel->sr_scan->sc_recpos = data_level;
1035         break;
1036       }
1037
1038     /* write changes back to file */
1039     if(!update_tuple(slptr->sl_rels,(char **)NULL,(char **)NULL))
1040       return(FALSE);
1041
1042     /* return successfully */
1043     return(TRUE);
1044
1045 } /* modify_tuple */
```

```
1046
1047    /* ----------------------------------------------------------
1048     |                   index searching routines              |
1049     * ---------------------------------------------------------- */
1050
1051    int access_plan(rel_ptr, slptr, cntr, hash, updt)
1052        struct relation *rel_ptr;
1053        struct sel *slptr;
1054        int    *cntr;
1055        BOOL hash, updt;
1056    {
1057      struct ix_header ixd;
1058      struct entry e, e2;
1059      struct relation *rptr;
1060      char    *buf;
1061      char    fname[RNSIZE+6];
1062      char    upper[35], lower[35];
1063      int     path_res, i = 0;
1064      long    data_level;
1065      BOOL opt = FALSE, temp_ixattr;
1066
1067      /* initialize local variables */
1068      *cntr = 0;
1069      clear_mem(lower, 0, 35);
1070      clear_mem(upper, 0, 35);
1071      upper[0] = lower[0] = EOS;
1072      rptr = SEL_RELATION;
1073
1074      /* form an index file name and open the corresponding file */
1075      if (!form_ix(fname, &ixd, rptr))
1076        return(FALSE);
1077
1078      /* allocate and initialize a tuple buffer */
1079      if ((buf = calloc(1, (unsigned) RELATION_HEADER.hd_size + 1))
1080                                     == NULL) {
1081        rc_done(rptr, TRUE);
1082        return (error(INSMEM));
1083      }
1084
1085      /* if only one, or the same, indexed attr in predicate */
1086      if (prptr->pr_ixtype[i] && prptr->pr_ixtype[i+1] == NULL &&
1087                                     !non_ixattr) {
1088        /* locate the indexed attribute */
1089        /* if two indexed predicates start from b.o.ix */
1090        if ((opt = gtr_equ(4, &e, lower, 0, upper)) == FALSE)
1091          opt = lss_equ(4, &e, lower, 0, upper);
1092
1093        if (opt == FALSE)  /* no optimization possible */
1094          lower[0] = upper[0] = EOS;
1095
1096        /* form the B-tree search entry */
1097        cat_strs(e.key, prptr->pr_ixtype[i], lower);
1098
1099        /* locate the lower search key entry in B-tree */
1100        if (!locate_ix(&ixd, &e, &e2, &data_level)) {
1101          finish_ix(&ixd);
1102          return(FALSE);
1103        }
1104      } else if (prptr->pr_ixtype[0] == NULL) {
1105        finish_ix(&ixd);
1106        return(error(WRIXCOM));
```

```
1107          }
1108
1109          /* if there is a 2nd  or a non-indexed attr in predicate */
1110          if (non_ixattr || prptr->pr_ixtype[i+1]) {
1111
1112             /*  find the start of associated indexed key */
1113             strncpy(e.key, prptr->pr_ixtype[i], 3);
1114             if (!locate_ix(&ixd, &e, &e2, &data_level)) {
1115                finish_ix(&ixd);
1116                return(FALSE);
1117             }
1118
1119             /* read curent index and get other attrs in predicate */
1120             read_get(rptr, slptr, buf, data_level);
1121          }
1122
1123          /* preserve value of global index flag in the case
1124           * of composite deletes, updates */
1125          temp_ixattr = non_ixattr;
1126          while (TRUE) {      /* interpret the results of the search */
1127             /* 1 indexed attr in predicate with prefix in ix_type[0] */
1128             if (temp_ixattr == FALSE && prptr->pr_ixtype[i+1] == NULL) {
1129
1130                /* if search limit has been exceeded exit */
1131                if (upper[0] != EOS) {
1132                   if (strcmp(e2.key + 3, upper) > 0)
1133                      break;
1134                }
1135
1136                /* in case of only one indexed attribute, if
1137                 * interpretation successful or new search  key value
1138                 * same with the old search key value, keep on searching */
1139
1140                if (xinterpret()) {
1141
1142                   if ((path_res = sel_path(&ixd, updt, hash, cntr,
1143                         buf, rptr, rel_ptr, slptr, data_level)) == FALSE)
1144                      return(FALSE);
1145                   else if (path_res == FAIL) {
1146                      finish_ix(&ixd);
1147                      return(path_res);
1148                   }
1149                } else if (opt  && strcmp(e.key, e2.key) != EQUAL)
1150                   break;
1151             }
1152             else {  /* inside 2nd indexed or non-indexed attr loop */
1153
1154                /* read current index and get other attrs in predicate */
1155                read_get(rptr, slptr, buf, data_level);
1156
1157                if (xinterpret()) {  /* evaluate the result */
1158
1159                   if ((path_res = sel_path(&ixd, updt, hash, cntr,
1160                         buf, rptr, rel_ptr, slptr, data_level)) == FALSE)
1161                      return(FALSE);
1162                   else if (path_res == FAIL) {
1163                      finish_ix(&ixd);
1164                      return(path_res);
1165                   }
1166                   /* restore code array after the fetch in comp rel */
1167                }
```

```
1168            }
1169
1170            if (get_next(&e2, &ixd) == EOF_IX)
1171               break;
1172            rm_trailblks(e2.key);  /* remove any trailing blanks */
1173
1174            if (strncmp(e2.key, prptr->pr_ixtype[i], 3) != EQUAL)
1175               break;
1176
1177            assign_pred(prptr->pr_opd[i], &e2, &data_level);
1178          }
1179
1180          nfree(buf);
1181          non_ixattr = FALSE;  /* reset non-indexed flag */
1182          finish_ix(&ixd);
1183
1184          return(TRUE);
1185       } /* acces_plan */
1186
1187       /* ------------------------------------------------------------ */
1188
1189       BOOL locate_ix(pixd, entr1, entr2, data_level)
1190            struct ix_header *pixd;
1191            struct entry *entr1, *entr2;
1192            long     *data_level;
1193       {
1194          /* find entry containing a key value >= to that of entr1 */
1195          find_ix(entr1, pixd);
1196
1197          /* get current entry from index file */
1198          get_current(entr2, pixd);
1199          rm_trailblks(entr2->key);  /* remove any trailing blanks */
1200
1201          /* if key prefixes are not identical */
1202          if (strncmp(entr2->key, prptr->pr_ixtype[0], 3) != EQUAL) {
1203             strncpy(entr1->key, prptr->pr_ixtype[0],  3);
1204             entr1->key[3] = EOS;
1205             find_ix(entr1, pixd);
1206             get_current(entr2, pixd);
1207             rm_trailblks(entr2->key);  /* remove any trailing blanks */
1208          }
1209
1210          /* assign new values to the 1st operand structure in the
1211           * predicate structure */
1212          assign_pred(prptr->pr_opd[0], entr2, data_level);
1213
1214          return(TRUE);
1215
1216       } /* locate_ix */
1217
1218
1219       /* ------------------------------------------------------------ */
1220
1221       sel_path(pixd, updt, hash, cntr, buf,
1222               rptr, rel_ptr, slptr, data_level)
1223            struct ix_header *pixd;
1224            struct sel *slptr;
1225            struct relation *rptr, /* original relation file */
1226               *rel_ptr;                /* transient relation files */
1227            BOOL updt, hash;
1228            char     *buf;
```

```
1229          long    data_level;
1230          int    *cntr;
1231  {
1232    int res;  /* obtains three values TRUE, FALSE, and FAIL */
1233
1234    /* read original relation from data file */
1235    if (read_tuple(rptr, data_level, SEL_TUPLE) == FALSE) {
1236      finish_ix(pixd);
1237      return(FALSE);
1238    }
1239
1240    if (rel_ptr == NULL) {  /* deletion must be performed */
1241      res = delete_attrs(slptr, cntr, data_level);
1242      return(res);  /* if res = FAIL, no futher deletions */
1243    }
1244
1245    if (updt) {     /* update must be performed */
1246      res = update_attrs(slptr, cntr, data_level);
1247      return(res);      /* if res = FAIL, no futher updates */
1248
1249    }
1250    else {
1251      if (hash == FALSE) {
1252        /* copy tuple in buffer */
1253        structcpy(buf, SEL_TUPLE,  RELATION_HEADER.hd_size);
1254        write_data(rel_ptr, buf, cntr); /* write data back */
1255      }
1256      else
1257        hash_data(rel_ptr, rptr, slptr, buf, cntr);
1258    }
1259    return(TRUE);
1260
1261  } /* sel_path */
1262
1263  /* ------------------------------------------------------------ */
1264
1265  /* check if attr to be inserted or updated requires indexing */
1266  check_ix(key_buf, aptr, p_cntr, s_cntr, avalue)
1267        char    ***key_buf;
1268        struct attribute *aptr;
1269        int    *p_cntr,            /* primary key pointer */
1270          *s_cntr;                 /* secondary key pointer */
1271        char    *avalue;           /* value to be indexed */
1272  {
1273    char    key;                   /* key type */
1274
1275    /* get key type */
1276    key = aptr->at_key;
1277
1278    /* create a key buffer */
1279    if (*key_buf == NULL)
1280      if ((*key_buf = (char **)calloc(4, sizeof(char *))) == NULL)
1281        return (error(INSMEM));
1282
1283    /* check for primary key */
1284    if (key == 'p' && *p_cntr < MAXKEYS)  {
1285      (*key_buf)[*p_cntr] = rmalloc(aptr->at_size + 1);
1286      strcpy((*key_buf)[(*p_cntr)++], avalue);
1287      return(TRUE);
1288    }
1289
```

```
1290        /* check for secondary key */
1291        if (key == 's' && *s_cntr < 2 * MAXKEYS)  {
1292          (*key_buf)[*s_cntr] = rmalloc(aptr->at_size + 1);
1293          strcpy((*key_buf)[(*s_cntr)++], avalue);
1294          return(TRUE);
1295        }
1296
1297        return(FALSE);
1298      } /* check_ix */
1299
1300      /* ------------------------------------------------------------ */
1301
1302      BOOL write_data(tmprel_ptr, buf, cntr)
1303          struct relation *tmprel_ptr;    /* snapshot rel pointer */
1304          char    *buf;
1305          int     *cntr;
1306      {
1307        (*cntr)++;  /* increment tuple counter */
1308
1309        /* write tuple in the temporary data file */
1310        if (!write_tuple(tmprel_ptr, buf, TRUE)) {
1311          rc_done(tmprel_ptr, TRUE);
1312          return(error(INSBLK));
1313        }
1314        return(TRUE);
1315      } /* write_data */
1316
1317      /* ------------------------------------------------------------ */
1318
1319      read_get(rptr, slptr, buf, data_level)
1320          struct relation *rptr;
1321          struct sel *slptr;
1322          char    *buf;
1323          long    data_level;
1324      {
1325        int    i;
1326        char    a_value[LINEMAX], *pr_value;
1327        struct sattr *saptr;
1328        char *rem_blanks();
1329
1330        /* fill the scan buffer with the data tuple */
1331        read_tuple(rptr, data_level, buf);
1332        structcpy(SEL_TUPLE, buf, RELATION_HEADER.hd_size);
1333
1334        /* get the other attributes in the predicate */
1335        for (i = 1; prptr->pr_ixtype[i]; i++)
1336          for (saptr = SEL_ATTRS; saptr != NULL;
1337                                  saptr = saptr->sa_next) {
1338            if (strcmp(prptr->pr_atname[i],saptr->sa_aname)== EQUAL) {
1339              pr_value = prptr->pr_opd[i]->o_value.ov_char.ovc_string;
1340              get_attr(saptr->sa_attr, saptr->sa_aptr, a_value);
1341              rem_blanks(pr_value, a_value, strlen(a_value));
1342              prptr->pr_opd[i]->o_value.ov_char.ovc_length =
1343                                  strlen(pr_value);
1344            }
1345          }
1346
1347      } /* read_get */
1348
1349      /* -------------------------------------------------------------
1350          |                    auxilliary index routines                    |
```

```
1351        - ---------------------------------------------------------- */
1352
1353    BOOL make_ix(pixd, fname)
1354        struct ix_header *pixd;
1355        char     *fname;
1356    {
1357
1358      if (open_ix(fname, pixd, compf, sizef) < 0)
1359        return(error(IXFLNF));
1360
1361      return(TRUE);
1362
1363    } /* make_ix */
1364
1365    /* ---------------------------------------------------------- */
1366
1367    /* form  index file and open associated file */
1368    form_ix(fname, pixd, rptr)
1369        struct relation *rptr;
1370        struct ix_header *pixd;
1371        char     *fname;
1372    {
1373      cat_strs(fname, rptr->rl_name, ".indx");
1374
1375      if (!make_ix(pixd, fname)) {
1376        finish_ix(pixd);
1377        return(FALSE);
1378        }
1379
1380      return(TRUE);
1381    } /* form_ix */
1382
1383    /* ---------------------------------------------------------- */
1384
1385    /* assign predicate structure memebers */
1386    assign_pred(p_opd, entr, d_level)
1387        struct operand *p_opd;
1388        struct entry *entr;
1389        long     *d_level;
1390    {
1391      strcpy(p_opd->o_value.ov_char.ovc_string, entr->key + 3);
1392      p_opd->o_value.ov_char.ovc_string[strlen( entr->key+3)] = EOS;
1393      p_opd->o_value.ov_char.ovc_length =
1394                    strlen(p_opd->o_value.ov_char.ovc_string);
1395      *d_level =  entr->lower_lvl;
1396
1397    } /* assign_pred */
1398
1399    /* ---------------------------------------------------------- */
1400
1401    BOOL    assign_pixd(rname, pixd)
1402        char *rname;
1403        struct ix_header *pixd;
1404    {
1405      char    fname[RNSIZE+6];
1406
1407      cat_strs(fname, rname, ".indx");
1408
1409      if (!open_ix(fname, pixd, compf, sizef))
1410        return(FALSE);
1411      else
```

```
1412            return(TRUE);
1413
1414    } /* assign_pixd */
1415
1416    /* --------------------- finish indexing --------------------- */
1417
1418    finish_ix(pixd)
1419            struct ix_header *pixd;
1420    {
1421        close_ix(pixd);
1422        if (prptr)
1423            free_pred(&prptr);
1424
1425    } /* finish_ix */
1426
1427    /* -----------------------------------------------------------
1428       |                predicate optimising routines            |
1429       ----------------------------------------------------------- */
1430
1431    gtr_equ(ix, e, lower, op, upper)
1432            struct entry *e;
1433            int     ix, op;
1434            char    *lower;
1435            char    *upper;
1436    {
1437        int     (*code_op)();
1438        int     disp = 6;
1439        int     ix1;
1440
1441        code_op = code[ix].c_operator;
1442        if (code_op == xgtr || code_op == xgeq
1443            || code_op == xeql || code_op == xpart) {
1444
1445            if (lower[0] != EOS) {
1446                if (strcmp(code[ix-1].OPERAND_STRING, lower) > 0) {
1447                    strcpy(lower, code[ix-1].OPERAND_STRING);
1448                    lower[strlen(code[ix-1].OPERAND_STRING)] = EOS;
1449                }
1450            } else {
1451                strcpy(lower, code[ix-1].OPERAND_STRING);
1452                lower[strlen(code[ix-1].OPERAND_STRING)] = EOS;
1453            }
1454
1455            if (code[ix+1+op].c_operator == xstop) {
1456                stop_flag = TRUE;
1457                return(TRUE);
1458            } else if (code[ix+disp+op].c_operator == xand) {
1459                ix1 = ix + disp + op - 1;
1460                if (lss_equ(ix1, e, lower, op = 1, upper)) {
1461
1462                    if (upper[0] != EOS) {
1463
1464                        if (stop_flag)
1465                            return(TRUE);
1466
1467                        if (strcmp(code[ix1+disp-2].OPERAND_STRING,
1468                                                   upper)< 0) {
1469                            strcpy(upper, code[ix1+disp-2].OPERAND_STRING);
1470                            upper[strlen(code[ix1+disp-2].OPERAND_STRING)] = EOS;
1471                        }
1472                    } else {
```

```
1473                    strcpy(upper, code[ix+disp-2].OPERAND_STRING);
1474                    upper[strlen(code[ix+disp-2].OPERAND_STRING)] = EOS;
1475                  }
1476
1477                return(TRUE);
1478              } else if (gtr_equ(ix1 + disp - 1, e, lower, op = 1, upper))
1479                return(TRUE);
1480          }
1481        }
1482
1483      return(FALSE);
1484    } /*gtr_equ */
1485
1486    /* ------------------------------------------------------------ */
1487
1488    lss_equ(ix, e, lower, op, upper)
1489          int    ix, op;
1490          struct entry *e;
1491          char   *lower, *upper;
1492    {
1493      int    (*code_op)();
1494      int    disp = 6;
1495      int    ix1;
1496
1497      code_op = code[ix].c_operator;
1498      if (code_op == xlss || code_op == xleq
1499          || code_op == xpart || code_op == xeql) {
1500
1501        if (code[ix+1+op].c_operator == xstop) {
1502          if (!op) {
1503            strcpy(upper,
1504                    code[ix-1].OPERAND_STRING);
1505            upper[strlen(code[ix-1].OPERAND_STRING)] = EOS;
1506          }
1507          stop_flag = TRUE;
1508          return(TRUE);
1509        } else if (code[ix+disp+op].c_operator == xand) {
1510
1511          if (upper[0] != EOS) {
1512
1513            if (stop_flag)
1514              return(TRUE);
1515
1516            if (strcmp(code[ix-1].OPERAND_STRING, upper) < 0) {
1517              strcpy(upper, code[ix-1].OPERAND_STRING);
1518              upper[strlen(code[ix-1].OPERAND_STRING)] = EOS;
1519            }
1520          } else {
1521            strcpy(upper, code[ix-1].OPERAND_STRING);
1522            upper[strlen(code[ix-1].OPERAND_STRING)] = EOS;
1523          }
1524
1525          ix1 = ix + disp + op - 1;
1526
1527          if (gtr_equ(ix1, e, lower, op = 1, upper)) {
1528            if (lower[0] != EOS) {
1529
1530              if (stop_flag)
1531                return(TRUE);
1532
1533              if (strcmp(code[ix1+disp-2].OPERAND_STRING, lower) > 0) {
```

```
1534                    strcpy(lower,
1535                            code[ix1+disp-2].OPERAND_STRING);
1536                       lower[strlen(code[ix1+disp-2].OPERAND_STRING)] = EOS;
1537                    }
1538              } else {
1539                strcpy(lower,
1540                        code[ix1+disp-2].OPERAND_STRING);
1541                lower[strlen(code[ix1+disp-2].OPERAND_STRING)] = EOS;
1542              }
1543
1544            return(TRUE);
1545          }
1546        }
1547      }
1548    return(FALSE);
1549  }
1550
1551  /* ------------------------------------------------------------
1552    |                  index predicate routines                |
1553     ------------------------------------------------------------ */
1554
1555  get_ixattr(rlptr, opr, atr_name, atr_key, atr_len)
1556        struct operand **opr;
1557        struct relation *rlptr;
1558        char    atr_key, *atr_name;
1559        int     atr_len;
1560  { int i;
1561
1562    if (prptr == NULL) {
1563      if (set_pred(&prptr) == FALSE)
1564        return (error(INSMEM));
1565    }
1566
1567    /* increment the key indexes */
1568    if (atr_key == 'p') /* place new value into operand struct */
1569      check_pred(rlptr, opr, atr_name, atr_key, atr_len);
1570    else if (atr_key == 's')
1571      check_pred(rlptr, opr, atr_name, atr_key, atr_len);
1572
1573    /* loop thro' the predicate attributes  */
1574    /* more than one different attributes exist */
1575    for (i = 0; prptr->pr_ixtype[i]; i++)
1576      if (strcmp(prptr->pr_atname[i], atr_name) != EQUAL)
1577        return(FAIL);
1578
1579    /* return successfully */
1580    return(TRUE);
1581  } /* get_ixattr */
1582
1583  /* ------------------------------------------------------------ */
1584
1585  check_pred(rlptr, opr, atr_name, atr_key, atr_len)
1586        struct relation *rlptr;
1587        struct operand **opr;
1588        char    *atr_name;
1589        char    atr_key;
1590        int     atr_len;
1591  {
1592    int    j = 0;  /* key type counter */
1593    int    ct, i, temp;
1594    BOOL   opr_set = FALSE; /* operand structure set flag */
```

```
1595
1596        if (prptr->pr_rlname == NULL) {
1597          prptr->pr_rlname = rmalloc(RNSIZE + 1);
1598          strcpy(prptr->pr_rlname, rlptr->rl_name);
1599          prptr->pr_rlname[strlen(rlptr->rl_name)] = EOS;
1600        }
1601
1602        /* loop thro' the atributes in the relation structure */
1603        for (i = 0; *(rlptr->rl_header.hd_attrs[i].at_name); i++) {
1604          if (rlptr->rl_header.hd_attrs[i].at_key == atr_key) {
1605            if (strcmp(atr_name,
1606                        rlptr->rl_header.hd_attrs[i].at_name) != EQUAL)
1607              j++;   /* same key type but different atribute names */
1608            else {
1609              /* go to next empty position in the predicate array */
1610              for (ct = 0; prptr->pr_ixtype[ct]; ct++)
1611                ;
1612
1613              /* preserve the relative location of next entry */
1614              temp = ct;
1615
1616              /* loop thro' the predicate attributes once again */
1617              /* if there is at least one entry */
1618              for (ct = 0; prptr->pr_ixtype[ct]; ct++)
1619                if (temp &&
1620                    strcmp(prptr->pr_atname[ct], atr_name) == EQUAL) {
1621                  *opr = prptr->pr_opd[temp] = prptr->pr_opd[ct];
1622                  opr_set = TRUE;
1623                }
1624
1625              /* discriminate between the entries requiring hashing
1626               * and those that do not */
1627              if (!opr_set) {
1628                if (rlptr->rl_header.hd_attrs[i].at_key == 'p')
1629                  put_pred(*opr, atr_name, atr_len, ct, j, TRUE);
1630                else
1631                  put_pred(*opr, atr_name, atr_len, ct, j, FALSE);
1632              }
1633            }
1634          }
1635        }
1636      } /* check_pred */
1637
1638      /* ----------------------------------------------------------- */
1639
1640      put_pred(opr, atr_name, len, ct, indx, flag)
1641          struct operand *opr;
1642          BOOL flag;
1643          int    len, ct, indx;
1644          char   *atr_name;
1645      {
1646        prptr->pr_ixtype[ct] = (char *) calloc(1, (unsigned) len + 5);
1647        prptr->pr_atname[ct] =
1648          (char *) calloc(1, (unsigned) strlen(atr_name) + 1);
1649
1650        /* initialize the indexed predicate attribute types */
1651        if (flag)  /* primary keys include the prefix P0* */
1652          sprintf(prptr->pr_ixtype[ct], "P%d*", indx);
1653        else       /* secondary keys include the prefix S(indx)* */
1654          sprintf(prptr->pr_ixtype[ct], "S%d*", indx);
1655
```

```
1656        strcpy(prptr->pr_atname[ct], atr_name);
1657
1658        if ((prptr->pr_opd[ct] =
1659            CALLOC(1, struct operand )) == NULL) {
1660          free_opr(prptr->pr_opd[ct]);
1661          return (error(INSMEM));
1662        }
1663
1664        if ((opr->o_value.ov_char.ovc_string =
1665            rmalloc(len + 1)) == NULL) {
1666          free_opr(opr);
1667          return (error(INSMEM));
1668        }
1669
1670        prptr->pr_opd[ct] = opr;
1671
1672        return(TRUE);
1673      } /* put_pred */
1674
1675      /* -------------------------------------------------------------
1676         |          join functions implementing B-tree conceptes    |
1677         ------------------------------------------------------------- */
1678
1679      /* with a join statement involving indexed prediacte(s) */
1680      join_ix(relptr, slptr, cntr, join_keys, ix_cntr,
1681                              duplc_attr, ref_attr, d_indx, tbuf)
1682          struct relation *relptr;
1683          struct sel *slptr;
1684          int    *cntr, ix_cntr, d_indx;
1685          char   *join_keys, **duplc_attr, **ref_attr, *tbuf;
1686      {
1687        struct ix_header ixd;
1688        struct entry e1, e2;
1689        struct relation *rptr;
1690        struct srel *srptr, *n_srptr;
1691        char    *name;
1692        char    fname[RNSIZE+6];
1693        BOOL first, proceed = TRUE;
1694        int     i = 0;
1695        long    data_level;
1696
1697        *cntr = 0;
1698
1699        /* preserve name of first relation */
1700        name = SEL_ATTRS->sa_rname;
1701
1702        if (ix_cntr > 1) /* both keys indexed on same attribute */
1703            return(join_two(relptr, slptr, cntr, join_keys,
1704                            duplc_attr, ref_attr, d_indx, tbuf));
1705
1706
1707        /* check if first relation contains index */
1708        if (strcmp(name, prptr->pr_rlname) == EQUAL)
1709          first = TRUE;
1710        else
1711          first = FALSE;
1712
1713        /* relation pointer points to first relation structure */
1714        rptr = SEL_RELATION;
1715
1716        /* else rel pointer points to second relation structure */
```

```
1717        if (first == FALSE)
1718          rptr = rptr->rl_next;
1719
1720        /* open the associated index file */
1721        if (!form_ix(fname, &ixd, rptr)) {
1722          finish_ix(&ixd);
1723          return(FALSE);
1724        }
1725
1726        /* copy index type, and locate attribute in index-file */
1727        strcpy(e1.key, *(prptr->pr_ixtype));
1728
1729        if (!locate_ix(&ixd, &e1, &e2, &data_level)) {
1730          finish_ix(&ixd);
1731          return(FALSE);
1732        }
1733
1734        if (first) {  /* scan second relation data file */
1735          srptr = SEL_RELS->sr_next;  /* non-indexed data file */
1736          n_srptr = SEL_RELS;          /* indexed data file */
1737        } else {
1738          srptr = SEL_RELS;
1739          n_srptr = SEL_RELS->sr_next;
1740        }
1741
1742        while (proceed) { /* open appropriate data file */
1743
1744          proceed = process(srptr, TRUE);
1745
1746          while (TRUE && proceed) {
1747            if (xinterpret()) {
1748
1749              if (!(read_tuple(rptr, data_level,
1750                               n_srptr->sr_scan->sc_tuple))) {
1751                finish_ix(&ixd);
1752                return(FALSE);
1753              }
1754
1755              if (!(join_write(slptr, relptr, tbuf,
1756                               duplc_attr, ref_attr, d_indx, cntr))) {
1757                finish_ix(&ixd);
1758                return(FALSE);
1759              }
1760            }
1761
1762            /* get subsequent entries in index file */
1763            if (get_next(&e2, &ixd) == EOF_IX)
1764              break;
1765            rm_trailblks(e2.key);  /* remove any trailing blanks */
1766
1767            if (strncmp(e2.key, prptr->pr_ixtype[i], 3) != EQUAL)
1768              break;
1769
1770            /* assign new values to predicate structure */
1771            assign_pred(prptr->pr_opd[i], &e2, &data_level);
1772
1773          }
1774
1775          /* copy index type, and locate attribute in index file */
1776          strcpy(e1.key, *(prptr->pr_ixtype));
1777
```

```
1778            if (!locate_ix(&ixd, &e1, &e2, &data_level)) {
1779              finish_ix(&ixd);
1780              return(FALSE);
1781            }
1782
1783        }
1784
1785      finish_ix(&ixd);
1786      return(TRUE);
1787
1788    } /* join_ix */
1789
1790    /* ------------------------------------------------------------ */
1791
1792    /* form join format and write resulting tuple */
1793    join_write(slptr, relptr, tbuf, duplc_attr, ref_attr, d_indx, cntr)
1794          struct sel *slptr;
1795          struct relation *relptr;
1796          char    *tbuf, **duplc_attr, **ref_attr;
1797          int     d_indx, *cntr;
1798    {
1799        /* form join format, remove any duplicate attribute names */
1800        if (do_join(slptr, duplc_attr, ref_attr, d_indx, tbuf) == FALSE)
1801          return(FALSE);
1802
1803        /* write tuple in new relation */
1804        if (!write_tuple(relptr, tbuf, TRUE)) {
1805          rc_done(relptr, TRUE);
1806          return(error(INSBLK));
1807        }
1808
1809        /* increment resulting relation tuple counter */
1810        (*cntr)++;
1811
1812        return(TRUE);
1813
1814    } /* join_write */
1815
1816    /* ------------------------------------------------------------ */
1817
1818    join_two(relptr, slptr, cntr, join_keys,
1819            duplc_attr, ref_attr, d_indx, tbuf)
1820          struct relation *relptr;
1821          struct sel *slptr;
1822          int     d_indx, *cntr;
1823          char    **duplc_attr, **ref_attr, *tbuf;
1824          char    *join_keys;
1825    {
1826      struct ix_header ixd1, ixd2;
1827      struct entry e1, e2, e3, e4;
1828      struct relation *rptr;
1829      struct scan *sc_ptr1, *sc_ptr2;
1830      struct sattr *saptr;
1831      char    *name, *ref_joinon = NULL;
1832      char    fname1[RNSIZE+6], buf1[5];
1833      char    fname2[RNSIZE+6], buf2[5], temp[LINEMAX+1];
1834      int     j, i = 0;
1835      long    data_level1, data_level2;
1836      BOOL    bottom;                  /* obtains three values */
1837      BOOL    proceed = TRUE;
1838      int     f_ix = 0, s_ix = 0;
```

```
1839
1840        /* loop through semantically indentical attrs in second rel */
1841        for (j = 0; j < d_indx; j++)
1842          if (duplc_attr[j] && strcmp(duplc_attr[j], join_on)) {
1843            ref_joinon = duplc_attr[j];
1844            break;
1845          }
1846
1847        /* relation pointer points to first relation structure */
1848        rptr = SEL_RELATION;
1849        sc_ptr1 = SEL_SCAN;
1850        sc_ptr2 = SEL_RELS->sr_next->sr_scan;
1851        temp[0] = EOS;
1852
1853        /* open index files */
1854        if (!form_ix(fname1, &ixd1, rptr) ||
1855            !form_ix(fname2, &ixd2, rptr->rl_next)) {
1856          finish_ix(&ixd1);
1857          finish_ix(&ixd2);
1858          return(FALSE);
1859        }
1860
1861        /* preserve name of first relation */
1862        name = SEL_ATTRS->sa_rname;
1863
1864        /* loop thro' the selected attributes */
1865        for (saptr = SEL_ATTRS; saptr != NULL;
1866                                saptr = saptr->sa_next) {
1867
1868          if (strcmp(saptr->sa_rname, name ) == EQUAL) {
1869            if (strcmp(saptr->sa_aname, join_on) == EQUAL)
1870              proceed = FALSE;
1871
1872            /* copy index type of first indexed attribute */
1873            if (proceed && ATTRIBUTE_TYPE == join_keys[0])
1874              f_ix++;
1875          } else { /* in second relation */
1876            if ((strcmp(saptr->sa_aname, join_on) == EQUAL) ||
1877                ref_joinon &&    /* semantically equiv. atrs. */
1878                strcmp(saptr->sa_aname, ref_joinon) == EQUAL)
1879              proceed = TRUE;
1880
1881            /* copy index type of second indexed attribute */
1882            if (!proceed  && ATTRIBUTE_TYPE == join_keys[1])
1883              s_ix++;
1884          }
1885        }
1886
1887        /* form the keys of both joined attributes */
1888        key_def(buf1, join_keys[0], f_ix);
1889        key_def(buf2, join_keys[1], s_ix);
1890
1891        /* locate the joined attributes in both index files,
1892           start with second file */
1893        strcpy(e3.key, buf2);
1894
1895        if (!locate_ix(&ixd2, &e3, &e4, &data_level2)) {
1896          finish_ix(&ixd1);
1897          finish_ix(&ixd2);
1898          return(FALSE);
1899        }
```

```
1900
1901     do {
1902         /* locate the joined attributes in first index files */
1903         strcpy(e1.key, buf1);
1904
1905
1906       if (!locate_ix(&ixd1, &e1, &e2, &data_level1)) {
1907           finish_ix(&ixd1);
1908           finish_ix(&ixd2);
1909           return(FALSE);
1910       }
1911
1912       assign_pred(prptr->pr_opd[i], &e2, &data_level1);
1913
1914       /* read first relation data */
1915       if (!(read_tuple(rptr, data_level1, sc_ptr1->sc_tuple))) {
1916           finish_ix(&ixd1);
1917           finish_ix(&ixd2);
1918           return(FALSE);
1919       }
1920       bottom = FALSE; /* start at top of 1st relation */
1921
1922       while (TRUE) {   /* loop thro' first relation entries */
1923
1924           /* read second relation data tuple */
1925           if (!(read_tuple(rptr->rl_next,
1926                             data_level2,
1927                             sc_ptr2->sc_tuple))) {
1928             finish_ix(&ixd1);
1929             finish_ix(&ixd2);
1930             return(FALSE);
1931           }
1932
1933           if (xinterpret()) {
1934             /* form join attrs and write result in relptr struct */
1935             if (!(join_write(slptr, relptr, tbuf,
1936                             duplc_attr, ref_attr, d_indx, cntr))) {
1937               finish_ix(&ixd1);
1938               finish_ix(&ixd2);
1939               return(FALSE);
1940             }
1941
1942             /* store value of joined attribute of second relation */
1943             strcpy(temp, e4.key);
1944             temp[strlen(e4.key)] = EOS;
1945             if (bottom)  /* already at bottom of first relation */
1946               bottom = FAIL;  /* stop scanning, result obtained */
1947
1948           }
1949
1950           /* get subsequent entries in first index file */
1951           if (get_next(&e2, &ixd1) == EOF_IX) {
1952             if (bottom != FAIL)
1953               bottom = TRUE; /* reached bottom of 1st rel index */
1954             break;
1955           }
1956           rm_trailblks(e2.key);  /* remove any trailing blanks */
1957
1958           if (strncmp(e2.key, prptr->pr_ixtype[i], 3) != EQUAL) {
1959             bottom = TRUE;  /* surpassed 1st relation index */
1960             break;
```

```
1961            }
1962
1963            /* read first relation data tuple */
1964            assign_pred(prptr->pr_opd[i], &e2, &data_level1);
1965            if (!(read_tuple(rptr, data_level1, sc_ptr1->sc_tuple))) {
1966              finish_ix(&ixd1);
1967              finish_ix(&ixd2);
1968              return(FALSE);
1969            }
1970
1971            /* compare attr values if they do not match exit loop */
1972            if (temp[0] != EOS && strcmp(temp, e2.key) != EQUAL) {
1973              temp[0] = EOS; /* reset temporary variable */
1974              break;
1975            }
1976
1977          }
1978
1979          /* get subsequent entries in second index file */
1980          if (get_next(&e4, &ixd2) == EOF_IX)
1981            break;
1982          rm_trailblks(e4.key);  /* remove any trailing blanks */
1983
1984          /* any subsequent entries do not match */
1985          if (bottom == FAIL && strcmp(e4.key, temp) != EQUAL)
1986            break;
1987
1988          data_level2 = e4.lower_lvl;
1989
1990          /* compare prefixes, determine if a different index
1991           * has been reached */
1992          if (strncmp(e4.key, buf2, 3) != EQUAL)
1993            break;
1994
1995        } while (TRUE);
1996
1997        finish_ix(&ixd1);
1998        finish_ix(&ixd2);
1999        return(TRUE);
2000
2001  } /* join_two */
2002
2003  /* ------------------------------------------------------------ */
2004
2005  /* form the appropriate key prefix to be scanned */
2006  key_def(def, key, ix_no)
2007          char    *def, key;
2008          int     ix_no;
2009  {
2010    if (key == 's')
2011      sprintf(def, "S%d*", ix_no);
2012    else if (key == 'p')
2013      sprintf(def, "P%d*", ix_no);
2014
2015    def[3] = EOS;
2016
2017  } /* key_def */
2018
2019  /* -------------------- EO access.c file --------------------- */
```

7

Lexical Analysis

One of the primary functions of REQUIEM is to support a query language in which the user can formulate statements that will enable him or her to access and manipulate data as organized by the relational data model. These statements are processed by the query language interpreter which calls the the appropriate REQUIEM routines to perform the requested operations. The query language interpreter is divided into four subcomponents:

1. The lexical analyzer.
2. The parser.
3. The query decomposer.
4. The predicate expression compiler and evaluator.

In this chapter we elaborate on the fundamental methods and operations that are necessary for interpreting typical query language statements. Note that we have no intention of covering the subject of compiler design and construction down to its most intimate details. As each subject is covered we suggest appropriate references for those readers who wish to investigate the subject matter in more detail. We shall use RQL statements as examples throughout this chapter; however, the concepts and techniques followed herein can be easily applied to the compilation of query statements in other languages.

7.1   An introduction to lexical analysis

For the purposes of compiler design and construction, a high-level programming language, as well as a query language, is normally designed in terms of a particular *grammar*. In broad terms, a grammar is a formal specification of the *syntax*, or form, of legal statements expressed in that language. For example, an assignment statement can be represented in terms of a grammar as the sequence of a variable name followed by an assignment symbol such as ":=," followed by a valid expression. The topic of compilation or interpretation then becomes one of matching the statements written by the user against the structures specified by the grammar; and finally generating the appropriate code, in a lower level language, for each statement. For further information on the grammar and syntax of RQL refer to the next chapter.

During the initial phase of the compilation process, the compiler views the source statements as a sequence of character symbols. This stream of character symbols constitutes the source statements of the language and is read from left to right by being grouped into logical units, called *tokens*. Tokens can be thought of as the fundamental building blocks of the source language being utilized. Consequently, tokens are sequences of characters having a collective meaning. The task of analyzing the source statements and recognizing and classifying the various tokens is commonly known as *lexical analysis* or *scanning*. The part of the compiler or interpreter that performs the task of the source program analysis is called the *lexical analyzer* or *scanner*.

Lexical analyzers are usually designed to recognize keywords and operators, as well as integers, real numbers, character strings, and other items that are written as part of the source statements. Naturally, the exact set of tokens to be recognized depends on the programming language to be compiled or interpreted and the grammar being used to describe it. In its simplest form the lexical analyzer locates these character strings and classifies each of them separately. Lexical analysis entails the discarding of *layout characters* such as blanks, and tabs, or newlines and comments. In general, layout characters may occur between any two tokens. Furthermore, it involves the recognition of *reserved symbols*, such as the keywords and operators used in the particular language to be translated. Some of the most common types of tokens encountered in this text are the following:

1. Identifiers.
2. Keywords, such as **select**, **where**, etc.
3. Sign symbols such as $+, -, *$, etc.

The sequence of input characters that makes up a concrete token is referred to as a *lexeme* [42]. It is the purpose of the lexical analyzer to forward the tokens to the parser and to insulate it from the lexeme representation of the tokens. To exemplify the previous statement consider the following sequence of characters:

salary > 1000 & **salary** <= 5000; (7.1)

In the process of lexical analysis the characters in the previous statement would be grouped into the following tokens:

1. The identifier **salary**.
2. The relational operator >.
3. The constant 1000.
4. The logical operator &.
5. The identifier **salary** (once more).
6. The logical operator <=.
7. The constant 5000.
8. The terminate symbol ";."

Any blanks separating the characters of the previous tokens would normally be eliminated during the process of lexical analysis. Normally, it is straightforward to group characters into tokens. However, sometimes the lexical analyzer may have to look beyond the token itself before it can group characters with assurance. For example, the character read may be the first character of more than one legal token; consider the character > which signals the start of both tokens > and >=. In such cases the lexical analyzer is so designed that it can distinguish between these two simple items, and can resolve any resulting ambiguities merely by reading the next character(s) and deciding what to do. This process is known as *lookahead*.

A grammar for a particular language normally treats an identifier as a token. Therefore, a parser based on such a grammar expects to see the same token of the type <u>id</u> every time an identifier appears in the input. Consequently, the logical expression (7.1) would be converted by the lexical analyzer into the following token stream:

<u>id</u> > <u>number</u> & <u>id</u> <= <u>number</u> <u>separator</u> (7.2)

At this point we should stress the fact that, normally, the grammar of a particular language describes in general only syntactic aspects of a language, not *semantic aspects*, i.e. it conveys no meanings of the various statements in the language. Such knowledge about the structure of the language can be supplied in the code generating functions of the compiler or interpreter.

To illustrate the difference between the syntax and semantics consider the following statements:

··· **where salary** < **basic_salary** + **benefits**;
··· **where salary** < **ground_salary** + **raise**;

where **salary**, **basic_salary**, and **benefits** are attributes with integer values and **ground_salary** and **raise** are attributes which assume real values. Although both statements have identical syntax their semantics are quite different. The first statement specifies that the attributes in the expression are to be added using integer arithmetic operations, with the result being compared with the value of the attribute **salary**. The second statement specifies a floating-point addition, with the result being converted to an integer before being compared with the attribute **salary**. Although the above two statements would be described in the same way by the underlying grammar, they would definitely result into different sequences of machine-code instructions. These differences between the two statements would be detected during the process of code generation by the code generation functions. For a more detailed discussion on the nature of grammars, as well as the topic of code generation, refer to Chapters 8 and 11. In particular, in Chapter 11 you will have the chance to observe how semantic analysis in REQUIEM is interweaved with expression evaluation.

7.2   Token specification

When considering statements like 7.2 it is useful to associate the token with type <u>id</u> with its lexeme **salary**, and distinguish between the token with type <u>number</u> (representing a constant) and the values 1,000 and 5,000 associated with instances of this token. What we would like to emphasize at this point is that the internal representation of an identifier, such as **salary**, is quite different from the physical sequence of characters that forms this identifier. For example, in REQUIEM the lexical analyzer uses the function **get_number()** to return the internal representation of numeric constants associated with the mnemonic **NUMBER**. This mnemonic is associated with a particular fixed length internal code number through the use of a C **define** directive (see Figure 7.1). A token, such as **ID**, is actually represented by a unique integer encoding a character in the ASCII character set. Actually all identifiers have the same mnemonic representation no matter what their lexemes. Obviously, the mnemonic representation of identifiers is not numeric. The definitions of all token representations in a given language are stored in a table called the *token definition table*. This technique is invaluable in programming as it makes programs readable while facilitating changes. In REQUIEM all token definitions are in the definition file **requ.h**.

As observed from the token definition table, all mnemonics are associated with encoded values. It is the job of the lexical analyzer to maintain and manipulate the token definition table where all possible reserved mnemonics

#define	ID	−16
#define	STRING	−17
#define	NUMBER	−18

Figure 7.1 The token definition table.

are kept. Tokens are normally encoded by negative integers to distinguish them from any other integers encoding a character.

KEYNAME	KEYTOKEN
"all"	ALL
"as"	AS
...	...
"select"	SELECT
"set"	SET
"show"	SHOW

Figure 7.2 The reserved keywords table.

Query languages use special character strings such as **select, project**, and **where** to identify specific language constructs. These character strings, known as keywords, must satisfy the rules for forming identifiers. The previous decision is facilitated if keywords are *reserved* words, that is they cannot be used as identifiers. Consequently, all lexemes that are not associated with keywords are treated as identifiers.

In REQUIEM, keyword tokens and their associated mnemonics are contained in a C-structure called **keywords**. This structure is maintained and manipulated by the lexical analyzer of REQUIEM. Each keyword entry comprises a pair containing a character string called **keyname**, to hold the name of a specific token and an integer called **keytoken** to represent the mnemonic associated with this token. For a sample listing of the association between token names and their mnemonics refer to Figure 7.2 which illustrates the REQUIEM *reserved keywords table*. In this figure all key tokens have an encoded value residing at the token definition table.

When the token being scanned is a keyword or an operator, such a coding scheme supplies the parser with sufficient information. In the case of an identifier, however, it is also necessary to specify the particular identifier name that was used during scanning. The same applies also for integers, reals, string constants, etc. This can be accomplished by associating a *token specifier* with the type code for such tokens. The token specifier provides the parser with the identifier name, value, type, etc. All these quantities are detected by the lexical analyzer. In some cases lexical analyzers are designed to enter identifier components directly into a *symbol table*; subsequently they associate this entry with the identifier by means of a pointer. In that case, the token specifier for a particular identifier is a pointer to the symbol table entry for that identifier.

7.3   The design of the lexical analyzer

As previously stated the lexical analyzer is that part of a compiler or interpreter that reads in the source program characters of a particular language and constructs the source program tokens. The purpose of separating the analysis of a given program into two distinct phases, namely lexical analysis and syntactic analysis, is to simplify the overall design of the compiler or interpreter. In general, it is easier to specify the structure of tokens than the syntactic structure of the source program, and by including certain constructs in the lexical rather than the syntactic structure, one simplifies the design of the parser. This means that by merely examining the contents of a token the parser eventually gets more information about which actions to perform at each step. Further reasons for separating lexical from syntactic analysis can be found in [42].

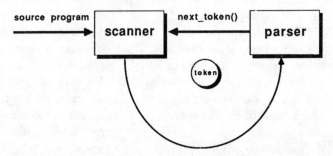

Figure 7.3 Collaboration of lexical analyzer and parser in REQUIEM.

A lexical analyzer may be programmed in two different ways. It may be implemented as a separate compiler pass which performs a complete lexical analysis of the source text. As the result of this pass a table containing the source program in some internal symbol (token) format is handed to the parser. Alternatively, it may be implemented as a special procedure called by the parser whenever it needs to consume a new token (see Figure 7.3). Thus, when called, the lexical analyzer recognizes the next token in the source program and forwards it to the parser. This latter method is undoubtedly simpler to implement. Any additional advantages of this method can be attributed to the fact that the entire source program need not be constructed and kept in volatile memory. Throughout this chapter and the next we will assume that the lexical analyzer is to be implemented in this manner.

Our intention is to outline the general guidelines of constructing a lexical analyzer that isolates a token either from a source string or from an input buffer and produces a pair consisting of the appropriate token and its associated value, i.e. its lexeme. An intermediate step in the design and construction of a complex program like a lexical analyzer is to describe its behavior by means of a specialized kind of flowchart [42],[43]. This approach is particularly useful in the case of a lexical analyzer because the pattern of actions to be taken is always dependent on what characters may have been consumed up to this time. The specialized flowchart for lexical analyzers is called a *transition diagram* and depicts the actions undertaken by the lexical analyzer when called by the parser to input the next token. A transition diagram consists of circles called *states* and of arrows interconnecting these circles, called *edges*. The labels on the various edges leaving one state indicate the input characters that can be assumed after the transition diagram has reached that state. One state is labeled the *start* state. This is the initial state of the transition diagram where control resides when the lexical analyzer begins to recognize a token.

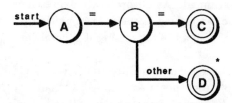

Figure 7.4 Transition diagram for "=" and "==."

The transition diagram for the patterns "=" and "==" is shown in 7.4. The starting state of the transition diagram is the state labeled "A." The edge from state A, labeled "=," indicates that the next input character to be read is "=." If this is the case then the state labeled "B" is reached. If the next character read is "=" then we reach state "C," and have recognized the token "==." If the next character is any other character, which signifies any character that is not indicated by any of the edges leaving "B," we have recognized the token "=" and reached state "D." Otherwise no legal state has been reached and we have failed to recognize either "=" or "==."

Observe that the character "=" and an additional character should be read as we follow the trail of edges from the start state to the end state

"D." As this additional character does not belong to the operator "=," the lookahead pointer must be retracted one character. We use the symbol "∗" to indicate situations where input retraction must take place in order to determine the source token.

On reaching state "B" we do not stop but continue by reading the next input character. Therefore, we end up either in state "C" or "D" depending on which pattern we wish to recognize. States "C" and "D" are called *terminal* or *accepting* states, and this is indicated by the double circles. Terminal states signify a state in which an acceptable token has been recognized. In general, there may be several transition diagrams, each of them specifying a different group of tokens. If failure occurs a lookahead symbol pointer must be retracted to its start, and another token is searched for, using another transition diagram (see Figures 7.4 and 7.5). If all transitions have been exhausted without success, then a syntax error has been detected and is reported to the user.

Example 7.3.1

Let us consider a significantly more complex transition diagram for predicate operators used in RQL query statements (see Figure 7.5). Notice that Figure 7.5 contains the simple transition diagram of Figure 7.4.

As can be seen from Figure 7.5 the transition diagram returns the type of the token just scanned. As all predicate expressions have similar translation patterns, we can express a concise recognition pattern for a predicate operator just once, instead of expressing it several times, i.e. once for each predicate operator met.

Obviously, the sequence of transition diagrams should be converted into a concise fragment of program code which will then detect the tokens specified by the transition diagrams. A systematic method should be adopted which considers all transition diagrams and constructs segments of code according to the number of states and edges in the diagrams. If the language in which we are coding the scanner provides a **case** statement, then this statement should be used to represent each edge leaving the starting state, with one return statement for each terminal state.

In case the input is buffered, a function **next_char()** is used to read the next character either from the standard input or from an input buffer. If there exists an edge labeled by the character just read or labeled by a group of characters containing the character just read, then control is transferred to the code materializing the state pointed to by that edge. If there exists no such edge the present character is compared successively with all the remaining edges and in case of failure the program enters a default state

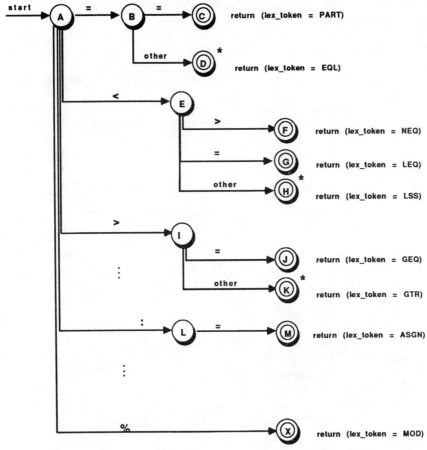

Figure 7.5 Transition diagram for the predicate expression operators.

where an error is reported. The program code that is generated for the function **get_predopd()**, which recognizes the structure of predicate operators, is outlined in the sample program fragment illustrated in Figure 7.6.

Transition diagrams belong to the category of tools known as *finite-state automata*. A finite-state automaton (FA) is a generalized transition diagram used for recognizing the lexical constituents of a particular language. A finite-state automaton contains a finite number of states, some of which are final states, and control passes from one state to another as each character of an input string is read according to the specified set of transitions. If, after reading the final character of a particular string, the automaton is in one of its final states the string is said to be accepted by the automaton. Otherwise, the string does not belong to the language that is accepted by the automaton, and is consequently rejected. A finite-state automaton can

```
/* get_rel - get a predicate operator */
static int get_predopd()
{
    int ch;

    switch (ch = skip_blanks()) { /* get 1st non-blank character */
    case '=':
            next_char();  ch = skip_blanks();
            if (ch == '=') { /* definition of partial comparison */
                next_char();
                lex_token = PART;
                return(TRUE);
            }
            else
              lex_token = EQL;   /* definition of equal  */
            return (TRUE);

    case '<':
            next_char(); ch = skip_blanks();
            if (ch == '>') {      /* non equal is <> */
                next_char();
                lex_token = NEQ;
            }
            else if (ch == '=') { /*  less equal is <= */
                next_char();
                lex_token = LEQ;
            }
            else
                lex_token = LSS;
            return (TRUE);


             . . .


    case '+':
            next_char();
            lex_token = ADD; /* definition of add  */
            return (TRUE);


             . . .


    default:
            return(FALSE);  /* no other relational ops */
    }

} /* get_predopd */
```

Figure 7.6 Code implementation for the function **get_predopd()**.

be *deterministic* or *non-deterministic* [43], [44]. A deterministic finite-state automaton (DFA) indicates that the same symbol cannot match the label of two edges leaving a specific state. By contrast, if the same symbol can match the labels of two or more edges leaving the same state the FA is termed a non-deterministic FA. All the transition diagrams used as examples in this chapter are deterministic. In fact REQUIEM confines itself to considering only DFAs.

7.4   Lexical analysis in REQUIEM

In REQUIEM the function **init_scan()** is used to initialize the process of lexical analysis and to make the first token of the source statement available. This function initializes the lexical analyzer environment by setting the variable **line_start** which signifies the beginning of the line, as well as the lookahead and indirect command file (external file) variables. The function **q_scan()** initiates the command line scanning by loading the global string variable **cmd_line** with the query specified in the formal parameter **qfmt**, and subsequently sets the pointer **lptr** to point to the beginning of the string contained in the command line buffer **cmd_line**. We will explain how this is accomplished later in this section.

The actual process of lexical analysis is carried out by the function **next_token()** called by the parser immediately after executing the function **q_scan()**. The function **next_token()** triggers a chain of function invocations. Functions called directly or indirectly by **next_token()** scan the next language token in the source stream and return a token specification for it in terms of the following global variables:

1. **lexeme** in all cases represents the lexeme of the token scanned. It normally contains the value of the keyname field of the reserved keywords table. This variable can also include the name of a view, or the string value of a constant.
2. **lex_token** represents the type of the token scanned. It can obtain values like **NUMBER** for integer constants, **REALNO** for constants of type real, and **STRING** for string constants, or **ID** for identifiers or **SIGNEDNO** in the case of signed numbers. It also contains the mnemonic representation of operators, e.g. **ADD** for +, **MINUS** for −, **ASSIGN** for :=. Finally, it assumes the value ";" in the case of the source statement terminator.
3. **lex_value** contains the value of numerical (integer or real) constants.
4. **saved_ch** saves the individual characters that make up a particular lexeme.

5. saved_tkn represents the type of the token which has already been scanned. It can obtain the same values as lex_token.

Example 7.4.1

Figure 7.7 illustrates the values that the above variables assume during the scanning of the RQL *query:*

select from *employee* **where** *salary* > *1000;*

7.4.1 System–user communication

Before we return to the description of the function **next_token()** we will first explain how the user and the system communicate with each other. We will return to the implementation of scanning functions in the next section. REQUIEM communicates with the user normally through the operating system facilities to read in the stream of characters which make up the source query. These characters are finally forwarded to the lexical analyzer which separates them into groups that lexically belong together, to make up the RQL tokens. Input stream characters in REQUIEM can emanate from diverse sources:

1. The simplest input mechanism (as seen from the REQUIEM standpoint) is to fetch characters on a one character at a time basis from the "standard input stream," normally the user's terminal. These characters are processed by the REQUIEM function **next_token()** which returns to the parser the type of the token it currently found.
2. It is possible to read and process RQL queries or subqueries from a command line by means of the function **q_scan()**. In this case input is buffered and can be read only from within REQUIEM. The function **q_scan()** can initiate line scan query parsing by forcing its formal parameter qfmt* to point to a string constant containing the query text. As a null qfmt argument indicates that the input may emanate from the user's on-line terminal, the function **next_token()** is again used to discriminate between standard input characters and the command line characters from the input buffer.
3. It is possible to read and process queries from an external command file whose name is passed as a command line argument to REQUIEM. This file is sometimes also referred to as an *indirect command file*. Indirect

---

*qfmt stands for query format.

token	lexeme	lex_tkn	saved_tkn	lex_val	svd_ch
select					s
					e
					l
					e
					c
select	select	−53 (SELECT)	−53		t
from					f
					r
					o
	from	−54 (FROM)	−54		m
employee					e
					m
					p
					l
					o
					y
					e
	employee	−16 (ID)	−16		e
where					w
					h
					e
					r
	where	−55 (WHERE)	−55		e
salary					s
					a
					l
					a
					r
	salary	−16 (ID)	−16		y
>	salary	−7 (GTR)	−7		>
1000					1
					0
					0
1000	"1000"	−18 (NUMBER)	−18	1000	0
;	"1000"	; (ascii)	;		;

Figure 7.7 Global variable values for the query "select from employee where salary > 1000;."

command files usually contain view definitions, but can also contain any valid RQL statement. Alternatively, it is possible to process indirect command files from within REQUIEM. This is accomplished only by typing an "@" symbol followed immediately by the name of the command file after the REQUIEM prompt. The lexical analyzer function **get_char()** is used to read the contents of the indirect command file only after **lptr** has been installed to point to the indirect command file text buffers.

Example 7.4.2

As the buffered input technique is used frequently throughout the remaining text we consider it worthwhile to illustrate in some detail how this technique operates. Buffered input is triggered when the parser issues a statement of the form:

$q\_scan(\ "select\ from\ employee\ where\ salary\ >\ 1000;\ ")$

Such statements as the one used in our previous example are used to indicate that during the execution of a user-specified query the parser for some reason requires the execution of a specific internal query. Execution of the function **q_scan()** results in the format specifier pointer **qfmt** pointing to the first character in the above select internal query, and is always triggered by the parser. Subsequently this entire character string will be stored in the command line buffer **cmdline** which is associated with buffered input, thus setting up the command line environment depicted in Figure 7.8. In REQUIEM we use the term *canned queries* to mean the internal queries executed by the system when it needs to perform a fairly complex task involving numerous accesses to the database. Here, the character string surrounded by the double quotes is the actual text of the canned query. REQUIEM will eventually use these canned queries to perform the necessary operations either on the contents of the system catalogs or on the database itself.

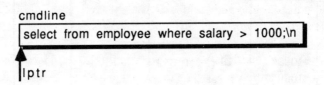

cmdline

| select from employee where salary > 1000;\n |

lptr

Figure 7.8 Command line scanning.

The contents of the character buffer **cmdline** are delimited by the *end-of-string* sentinel "\0" (EOS) or null character, which is the normal case when dealing with C strings. Additionally, the line pointer lptr points to the beginning of the input buffer cmdline, i.e. it points to the memory location holding the character "s" in our example. It is the responsibility of the lexical analyzer functions to advance the pointer lptr and consume the entire contents of the input buffer. The string of characters between the lptr pointer and the first blank character forms the current token. lptr scans ahead until a match for a valid pattern is found. Once the current lexeme is determined, see Figure 7.7, lptr is set to point to the character that follows the current lexeme. With this scheme, white space and escape sequences, such as newline or tab-characters, are treated as patterns that yield no token. When lptr points to the end-of-string sentinel the complete query contents have been recognized and consumed. Next, the input buffer is cleared and lptr is set to point to the null character. During the scanning of the input buffer of Figure 7.8 the lexical analyzer functions assign to the lexical analyzer's global variables the values indicated in Figure 7.7. The code in the lexical analyzer's functions, which is associated with the processing of buffered input, frequently performs tests to ascertain whether lptr points to the EOS character or not.

7.5   Dissection of the lexical analyzer functions

The actual process of scanning is incited only by the function next_token(). This function is called by the parser or the query decomposer functions whenever they require a new token from the input. Such functions examine only the type of the current token that is returned by the function next_token(). Accordingly, next_token() returns an integer value contained in the token definition table of Figure 7.1. This means that the function next_token() sets only the contents of the global variable lex_token. All the other lexical analyzer global variables are set by means of one of the lexical analyzer functions called directly or indirectly by next_token().

The function next_token() calls the function this_token(), which in turn calls the function token_type(), which calls the function skip_blanks() and so on. This sequence of function calls and returns is depicted in Figure 7.9. This also explains the reason why the above variables are global. They simply allow all the functions depicted in Figure 7.9 to access them and check or set their contents which will thus be made visible to all these functions.

Upon each call, the function next_token() invokes the function this_token() to get the current token in the input stream and also makes sure that the parser will get another token on its next call. Where a com-

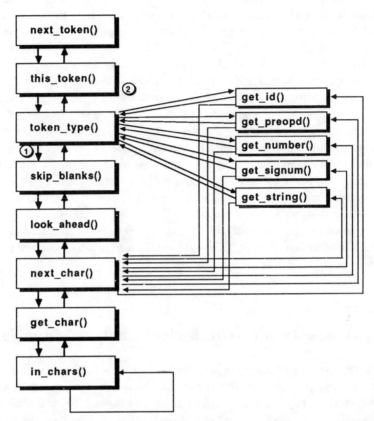

Figure 7.9 The chain of function calls to return the scanned token.

mand line internal query is present, it also ensures that the parser will exit successfully after the contents of the variable cmd_line have been properly consumed. The function this_token() first decides whether the token in the input statement constitutes a view call, and then returns the value of the variable lex_token to the function next_token() which called it. To decide whether the current token is a view call or not, function this_token() must certify that the type of the encountered token is an identifier. In doing so, function this_token() must examine the output returned by the function token_type(). The function token_type() confirms the presence of an already saved token and returns its type, or skips any blanks imposed between two characters and examines the next non-blank character.

The function token_type() discriminates between six cases; the next character in the source string may signify the beginning of any of the following token types:

1. Keyword.
2. Signed number.
3. Pure number.
4. String.
5. Predicate operator.
6. Individual character token.

To determine the type of the token the function **token_type()** calls one of the six following functions which are directly associated with the previously mentioned token types and which correspond to function calls depicted in Figure 7.9:

1. get_id().
2. get_signum().
3. get_number() .
4. get_string().
5. get_predopd().
6. next_char().

It is important to note that the presence of the symbol "−" in the source string does not necessarily imply the existence of a signed number. The "−" symbol can equally be a unary or binary operator in which case it is part of a logical expression (refer to the REQUIEM syntax in Appendix A). To discriminate between such cases the function **token_type()** consults the global variable **wh_signal**. This variable, when set, signifies the presence of a predicate expression which always starts with the keyword **where**. Finally, after determining the type of the current token, the function **token_type()** saves the type of the current token in the global variable **saved_tkn**. The idea is that if for some reason the parser requires the current token once more, after the input has been parsed, then it can recover its environment by a call to **this_token()**. By contrast, when the parser calls **next_token()** it clears the environment of the current token and prepares itself for receiving the next token in the source line.

In the material that follows we concentrate on the scanning algorithm. Language symbols such as :

$+, -, *, =, \%$

are easy to recognize. However, there are some cases where two or more symbols begin with the same character; for example:

$=, \quad ==, \quad or \quad <, \quad <=, \quad <>$

When the lexical analyzer has input the first character of a symbol and has recognized it, as for example the character "<," it must input the next character in the source statement to determine whether the character just read is juxtaposed with the symbol "=" or ">." If the lexical analyzer discovers that the next character is neither "=" nor ">," then it knows automatically that the first character simply denotes the token *LSS*. However, when the lexical analyzer finds this out, it has already input the first character of the next token in the source statement. This is quite normal in several cases when the lexical analyzer is asked to read a word symbol or a name.

When the next token in the input stream is to be scanned, the lexical analyzer must determine whether it should input the first character of this new token, or whether it has already done this during the scanning of the preceding token. In REQUIEM this task is done by means of the function **look_ahead()**. This function makes certain that the lexical analyzer is always one character ahead by inputting the next character from the source statement whenever it has recognized a character as being part of a valid token. The function **look_ahead()** calls the function **next_char()** to input the next character from the source string or from the input buffer (see Figure 7.9). The function **next_char()** gets the next character from input while stripping the source statement of any white space sequences appearing in the form of blank, tab, or newline characters. Furthermore, it determines whether the next character signifies input from an indirect command file. If so, it calls the function **cmd_fill()** which sets up the environment for an indirect command file. This function allocates space for the C structure **cmd_file** which will accommodate information about the indirect file and initializes its members. Finally, the function **next_char()** invokes the function **get_char()** which returns the current character in the input stream.

The function **get_char()** gets and returns the current input character. It must discriminate between these cases:

1. The input character stems from the command line. In this case the command line buffer **cmd_line** contains the statement, for example a canned query, which is going to be scanned and eventually parsed. The start of this buffer is as usual being pointed to by the command line pointer **lptr**. Normally, this pointer is set to NULL by the function **init_scan()**. However, if the buffer **cmd_line** contains a statement to be scanned then this pointer always points to its start. The command buffer is normally filled either by the contents of an indirect command file, or by the contents of a view that has to be processed. Sometimes the buffer is also used by the parser functions for storing and eventually processing complex canned queries. The command buffer stores indirect file contents, canned queries,

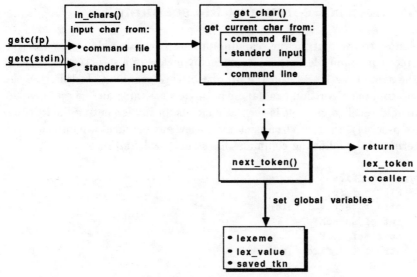

Figure 7.10 Implementation of function next_token().

or view statements on a line by line basis.

2. If the command line pointer **lptr** points to the NULL character, then input originates from the standard input (i.e. the terminal) or from an indirect command file. If the input comes from the standard input the function **in_chars()** is used to input the token characters.

3. If the input originates from an indirect command file, then characters from this file are read in and returned by the function **in_chars()**.

Finally, the function **get_char()** returns the next character in the input which is propagated and returned by the functions **next_char()**, **look_ahead()**, and **skip_blanks()**. The function **token_type()** consumes this specific character and by means of token type routines, which repeatedly call **next_char()** and **look_ahead()**, returns the type of the current token, i.e. the variable **lex_token**, to the functions **this_token()** and **next_token()** (see Figure 7.9). Figure 7.10 indicates how the function **next_token()** implements all the previously mentioned interactions. The function **getc(fp)** is the standard C library function for reading characters from the file pointed to by the file pointer **fp**. This function returns the value of the character just read as an integer value, therefore its output is assigned to an integer variable **ch** local to the function **in_char()**.

As observed from Figure 7.10 when function **get_char()** reaches the end of the source query it outputs the variable **lex_token** and terminates. During the process of scanning, all global variables obtain values pertinent to the token currently scanned.

7.6 Indirect command file scanning

It is most convenient for the scanning process if we are able to describe the indirect command file (icf) environment by means of a structure that could at the same time be used in the process of view scanning. In this case the same scanning algorithm can handle both view scanning and icf scanning. A C structure called cmd_file is the basic means for implementing the icf code. More precisely, an icf environment and a view environment are implemented in terms of the following command file structure definition:

```
struct cmd_file {
    FILE *cf_fp;
    struct text *cf_text;
    int cf_savech;
    char *cf_lptr;
    struct cmd_file *cf_next;
};
```

After the icf has been opened, all references pertinent to it are made only via the field cf_fp of the cmd_file structure which actually represents the icf file pointer. The currently saved token character should also be held in the cmd_file structure (see Figure 7.11). This is accomplished by means of the integer field cf_savech. The current icf line pointer cf_lptr is a character pointer pointing to the address of the command line pointer if one currently exists, otherwise it points to NULL (see Figure 7.11). For example, the cf_lptr can point to the beginning of textual definition of a canned query like that of Figure 7.8. The idea behind this technique is that the icf contents assume priority over any other command line arguments addressed by the pointer lptr. This actually means that the contents of a command file will be executed prior to the contents of the command line buffer.

As in REQUIEM where we may have multiple external files (or views) whose contents (definitions) must be executed (or loaded from the system catalogs, in the case of views), the icf environment may consist of more than one icf. In this case we demand that the icf structures are linked together into a linear list, the icf_list. The linear list organization is used here to create an icf array of unknown size. It is for exactly this reason that linked lists are used extensively in database-management software. Each cmd_file element is placed into a single linked list, and the list array elements can be accessed by following the cf_next links in the individual cmd_file structure (see Figure 7.11). The first successor element in the list is to be executed immediately after the current top element in the list. Note that the icf list members are executed on a last-in-first-out order.

The cmd_file field whose purpose is to differentiate between icfs and views

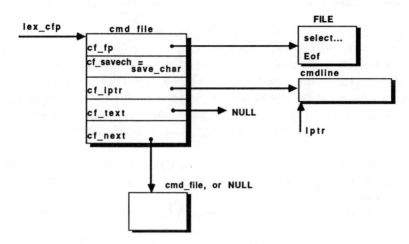

Figure 7.11 The command file structure.

is called **cf_text**. This field is also a structure pointer, just like **cf_next**; however, **cf_text** is used to point to the top element in the list of text structures which contain the view definition text. If the field **cf_text** points to NULL, as shown in Figure 7.11, then the **cmd_file** structure in question is associated with a particular command file. Alternatively, when **cf_next** points to a text structure then the current **cmd_file** structure is associated with a specific view. In this case the text associated with a given view definition is stored in the list of text structures pointed to by the **cf_text** field with each text member holding exactly one line of the view definition text (see Figure 7.12). In particular, what this implies is that while the text of a view definition can be read directly from its associated **cmd_file** structure, the statements contained in an **icf** should be read directly from the file by means of the function **in_char()**.

Let us now return momentarily to the function **next_char()** and see how it determines the presence of an **icf**. This function must obviously, upon entrance, check the first character of an identifier. If this specific character is the control symbol "@", then the name following this REQUIEM control symbol is the name of an **icf**. In this case, the function **com_file()** is called to generate the **icf** file context. This function opens the **icf**, and creates and initializes an **icf** structure. The program code which performs all the above tasks is as follows:

```
new_cfp->cf.text = NULL;
new_cfp->cf_savech = saved_ch;
...
```

```
lex_cfp = new_cfp;
...
```

Here, new_cfp is the address of a new icf structure. The variable lex_cfp is a global icf structure pointer called the *icf context pointer*. The function of the icf context pointer is to point to the very first icf element in the icf list (see Figure 7.11). Because an item may be inserted only at the top of the icf list, the function com_file() must establish a pointer to the first element in the list so that other parts of the lexical analyzer program will know where the list commences. This fact justifies the definition of lex_cfp as a global variable. The execution of the above program statements leads to the situation depicted in Figure 7.11.

Finally, function next_char() invokes the function get_char() which senses the existence of an icf and fetches its contents on a character at a time basis until the end-of-file (EOF) sentinel is met. This signifies that the icf contents have already been exhausted and that the data structure associated with this particular file has served its purpose and is no longer required. Therefore, the list element corresponding to the icf just read is removed from its position in the list, the links in the icf list are rearranged, and the space occupied by the deleted element is returned to the operating system to be made available for subsequent use. All the above activities are accomplished by the following program fragment:

```
old_cfp = lex_cfp;
ch = lex_cfp->cf_saved_ch;
. . .

fclose(old_cfp->cf_fp);
nfree(cfp);
```

The variable old_cfp is an auxiliary variable pointer which temporarily holds the address of the current cmd_file structure, so that lex_cfp could point to the next element in the linked list. Finally, prior to freeing the space occupied by the cmd_file structure, the connection between the file descriptor cf_fp and the icf is broken and the file is closed.

There are two additional points in the above code statements which require particular attention. First, the contents of the cd_savech field are assigned to the variable quantity ch, and the global variable save_ch is cleared. Subsequently, after the icf environment has been erased from memory the character value held by ch is returned by the function get_char(). Second, the global variable lptr is assigned the address of the icf structure field cf_lptr. Hence, the contents of the command line buffer are recovered and the lexical analyzer can resume control again by switching to the lexical analysis of the cmd_line contents, if there are any available.

The remainder of the lexical analyzer code implementation is straightforward, and thus does not deserve any further comment. The only program segments that are of importance and quite difficult to comprehend are those relating to view scanning. Therefore, the code implementation of view scanning will be analyzed in the next section. The complete listing of the C program implementing the REQUIEM scanner is given at the end of this chapter.

7.7   View scanning

As views are defined in terms of base relations and their textual definition is stored in the system catalogs, the concepts of view definition, loading, and manipulation are very important and need a detailed discussion: therefore views make up a chapter in their own right. However, issues relevant to view scanning will be covered in this section as they are closely related to their icf counterparts already discussed in the previous section. View scanning comprises a rather complex process; therefore we will focus our attention on several program segments implementing the various parts of the view scanning process. We defer detailed discussions of the RQL features for view management to Chapter 12; what follows is only a brief sketch.

In REQUIEM scanning of the view text and detection of the tokens comprising a view definition is accomplished by means of the lexical analyzer functions. Views are scanned during their definition and loading phases. Every time a view is defined or loaded a special environment called the *view_context* is set up to accommodate the new view. This process is quite similar to the process of creating an icf environment.

The intricacies of view scanning are administered by the function this_token(). The lexical analyzer uses this function to determine whether the identifier, just detected, coincides with the name of a view definition. To confirm this, the function this_token() must traverse the linear linked list of view definitions and compare the identifier in question with the names of the views currently loaded in the system. If it succeeds in locating the name of a view in the list of views, then the appropriate measures should be taken to fetch the textual definition of the view, parse it, and subsequently execute it.

To parse a view, a command file structure, like the one depicted in Figure 7.12, must be assigned to hold the contents of the scanned view. The following program segment sets up the necessary icf structure and initializes its fields appropriately:

```
new_cfp->cf_fp = NULL;
new_cfp->cf_text = view_ptr->view_text->text->next;
   . . .

lex_cfp = new_cfp;
```

Execution of the above program segment leads to the situation depicted in Figure 7.12.

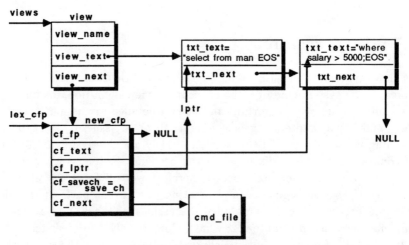

Figure 7.12 View scanning.

The variable **new_cfp** is the **cmd_file** structure used to accommodate the information pertinent to a view (see Figure 7.12). As the input tokens do not emanate from an **icf** the file descriptor associated with **new_ifp** is set to point to NULL and not to an **icf** as is the case in Figure 7.11. The line pointer **lptr** is set to point to the first character of the view text, while the text field, **cf_text**, of the **icf** structure is set to point to the continuation of the view text; see Figure 7.12. In this figure the list of text structures pointed to by the **view_text** field of the view structure is used to hold the view definition text. Each element of the list holds one view definition line as specified by the user during the view definition phase. It must be noted that each view definition line has been cleared from any extra blank or control characters, such as newline (\n) character, and has been delimited by the EOS sentinel. After the execution of the above statements the actual process of scanning the view tokens can commence. Thus, the function **this_token()** enters a while loop which invokes the function **token_type()** and checks to see whether the outcome of this call is an identifier. In this case the keyword that commences a query has been identified.

In trying to make sure that the returned token is of type id, the function token_type() enters the chain of lexical analyzer function calls as illustrated in Figure 7.9. The function succeeding token_type() in this linear hierarchy of calls will be subsequently entered. Finally, when function get_char() is invoked a check is performed to determine whether the line pointer lptr points to a non-empty text buffer. Since lptr points to the txt_text field of the first element in the text list structure, the first character of the view definition text held by the txt_text field, i.e. the character "s" in Figure 7.12, will be propagated to the function token_type(). This function automatically invokes the function get_id() to fetch the identifier contained in the txt_text buffer, i.e. the word "select." This identifier should match a keyword, thus it is checked against the keyword table contents to determine if it can initiate a valid query. If the check is successful, the parsing and query decomposing routines are entered and start consuming the successor tokens in the text buffer. Subsequently, the function get_char() will be repeatedly re-entered until the contents of the txt_text buffer are completely consumed and the lptr pointer points to the EOS delimiter in the first element of the text list. At this stage lptr will be set to point to the element pointed to by the text pointer field, cf_text, of the icf structure in Figure 7.12. This means that lptr now points to the continuation of the view text as contained in the second element of the text list pointed to by the members of the view definition structure view.

Now, the cf_text pointer in Figure 7.12 can be advanced to point to the third element in the text list, if one currently exists. The code for performing this sequence of actions is part of function get_char(). The sequence of control in the lexical analyzer program will eventually follow once again the same pattern of function invocations until the complete view definition text has been read. At this stage the view is already processed and the outcome of its execution can be seen on the user's terminal screen. Alternatively, the results of a view processing can be directed to a prespecified output file if this has been specified by the user.

This kind of lexical analyzer–parser interaction is some times referred to as *incremental parsing*. Incremental parsing is the parsing methodology used throughout REQUIEM; its semantics and functionality will be unveiled in the next chapter which is devoted to the parsing techniques used in REQUIEM.

View scanning concludes the discussion of the scanning program. The fact that this chapter describes a subtle program in terms of many small functions is in our judgement an art of cautious or defensive programming. There are several important reasons for coding programs as a set of small functions. It is much easier to write a sound function that performs one specific task and both writing and debugging are made simpler. It is also easier to maintain or modify a big program written in terms of small functions. You can readily adjust the set of functions that need to be rewritten expecting the rest of the code to function correctly. Furthermore, small functions tend to be self-documenting and highly readable. We should stress the fact that one cannot start with these routines right at the beginning of the coding process. Instead they tend to be "discovered" as the lexical analyzer is written. By observing at each stage what operations the scanner should perform, the systems programmer can come up with a handful of basic functions.

7.8   Source listing 4

file: lexan.c

```
 1    /* REQUIEM - lexical scanning functions */
 2
 3    #include <stdio.h>
 4    #include "requ.h"
 5
 6    extern BOOL view_operation;
 7    extern BOOL wh_signal;
 8    BOOL view_exists = FALSE;          /* view-existence flag */
 9    char lexeme[2*STRINGMAX+1];        /* string token value */
10    int lex_token;                     /* current token mnemonic */
11    char *lptr;                        /* current command line ptr */
12    float lex_value;                   /* current token value */
13    int saved_ch;                      /* saved character */
14    static int saved_tkn;              /* saved token type */
15    struct cmd_file *lex_cfp;          /* command file context ptr */
16    struct view *views;                /* view definitions */
17    static char *iprompt,*cprompt;     /* input prompts */
18    static char cmdline[2*LINEMAX+1];  /* current command line */
19    static int line_start;             /* flag indicates line start */
20    static struct {                    /* keyword table */
21        char *keyname;
22        int keytoken;
23    } keywords[] = {
24        "all", ALL,
25        "as", AS,
26        "assign", ASSIGN,
27        "avg", AVG,
28        "by", BY,
29        "char", CHAR,
30        "count", COUNT,
31        "create", CREATE,
32        "define", DEFINE,
33        "delete", DELETE,
34        "difference", DIFFERENCE,
35        "display", DISPLAY,
36        "drop", DROP,
```

```
37      "exit", EXIT,
38      "export", EXPORT,
39      "expose", EXPOSE,
40      "extract", EXTRACT,
41      "foreign", FOREIGN,
42      "focus", FOCUS,
43      "from", FROM,
44      "group", GROUP,
45      "help", HELP,
46      "insert", INSERT,
47      "intersect", INTERSECT,
48      "import", IMPORT,
49      "in", IN,
50      "into", INTO,
51      "is", IS,
52      "join", JOIN,
53      "key", KEY,
54      "minm", MINM,
55      "maxm", MAXM,
56      "modify", MODIFY,
57      "num", NUM,
58      "on", ON,
59      "over", OVER,
60      "print", PRINT,
61      "project", PROJECT,
62      "purge", PURGE,
63      "quit", QUIT,
64      "real", REAL,
65      "references", REFERENCES,
66      "secondary", SECONDARY,
67      "select", SELECT,
68      "set", SET,
69      "show", SHOW,
70      "sum", SUM,
71      "to", TO,
72      "union", UNION,
73      "unique", UNIQUE,
74      "update", UPDATE,
75      "using", USING,
76      "view", VIEW,
77      "with", WITH,
78      "when", WHEN,
79      "where", WHERE,
80      NULL, 0,
81    };
82
83   /* ------------------------------------------------------------ */
84
85   /* s_init - initialize the scanner */
86   s_init()
87   {
88      /* at beginning of line */
89      line_start = TRUE;
90
91      /* make the command line null */
92      lptr = NULL;
93
94      /* no lookahead yet */
95      saved_ch = EOS;
96      saved_tkn = 0;
97
```

```
 98      /* no indirect command files */
 99      lex_cfp = NULL;
100
101      /* no views defined */
102      views = NULL;
103    }
104
105    /* ------------------------------------------------------------ */
106
107    /* db_prompt(ip,cp) - initialize prompt strings */
108    db_prompt(ip,cp)
109         char *ip,*cp;
110    {
111      /* save initial and continuation prompt strings */
112      iprompt = ip; /* initial prompt */
113      cprompt = cp; /* continuation prompt */
114    }
115
116    /* ------------------------------------------------------------ */
117
118    /* q_scan(qfmt) - initiate line scan query parsing */
119    q_scan(qfmt)
120         char *qfmt;
121    {
122      /* set up the command line */
123      if (qfmt)
124        if (strlen(qfmt) < LINEMAX)
125          strcpy(cmdline, qfmt);
126        else
127          return(error(LINELONG));
128
129      /* start at the beginning of the command line */
130      lptr = cmdline;
131      iprompt = NULL;
132      lex_cfp = NULL;
133
134      /* no saved characters yet */
135      saved_ch = EOS;
136      saved_tkn = 0;
137
138      return(TRUE);
139    }
140
141    /* ------------------------------------------------------------ */
142
143    /* db_flush - flush the current input line */
144    int db_flush()
145    {
146      if (view_operation) {
147        cmd_clear();
148        return(TRUE);
149      }
150
151      while (saved_ch != '\n')
152        if (saved_ch > ' ') /* normal chars other than space exist */
153          return (error(SYNTAX));
154        else
155          saved_ch = get_char();
156
157      saved_ch = EOS;
158      line_start = TRUE;
```

```
159      return (TRUE);
160    } /* db_flush */
161
162    /* ------------------------------------------------------------ */
163
164    /* com_file - setup an indirect command file */
165    int com_file(fname)
166         char *fname;
167    {    struct cmd_file *new_cfp;
168         char *malloc();
169
170         if ((new_cfp = (struct cmd_file *)
171                  malloc(sizeof(struct cmd_file))) == NULL)
172           return (error(INSMEM));
173         else if ((new_cfp->cf_fp = fopen(fname,"r")) == NULL) {
174           nfree((char *) new_cfp);
175           return (error(INDFNF));
176         }
177         new_cfp->cf_text = NULL;
178         new_cfp->cf_savech = saved_ch;
179         new_cfp->cf_lptr = lptr;
180         new_cfp->cf_next = lex_cfp;
181         lex_cfp = new_cfp;
182
183         /* return successfully */
184         return (TRUE);
185    }
186
187    /* ------------------------------------------------------------ */
188
189    /* cmd_kill - kill indirect command file environment */
190    cmd_kill()
191    {
192      struct cmd_file *old_cfp;
193
194      while ((old_cfp = lex_cfp) != NULL) {
195        lex_cfp = old_cfp->cf_next;
196        if (old_cfp->cf_fp != NULL)
197          fclose(old_cfp->cf_fp);
198        saved_ch = old_cfp->cf_savech;
199        lptr = old_cfp->cf_lptr;
200        nfree((char *) old_cfp);
201      }
202
203      cmd_clear();          /* clear the command line environment */
204
205    } /* cmd_kill */
206
207    /* ------------------------------------------------------------ */
208
209    /* clear a command line and set saved characters */
210    cmd_clear()
211    {
212
213      if (lptr){
214        lptr = NULL;
215        lex_token = ';';
216        return(lex_token);
217      }
218      else
219        while (saved_ch != '\n')
```

```
220          saved_ch = get_char();
221
222     saved_ch = EOS;
223     saved_tkn = 0;
224     line_start = TRUE;
225
226     return(TRUE);
227 } /* cmd_clear */
228
229 /* ------------------------------------------------------------ */
230
231 /* next_token - get next token (after skipping the current) */
232 int next_token()
233 {
234     /* get the current token */
235     this_token();
236
237     /* make sure another is read on next call */
238     saved_tkn = 0;
239
240     /* make sure that you exit parser in case of command line
241      * arguments */
242     if (lex_token == NULL && lptr && *lptr == EOS) {
243       lex_token = ';';
244       lptr = NULL;
245
246       if (view_operation == TRUE) {
247         view_operation = FALSE;
248         this_token();      /* clear cmd-line terminator */
249         saved_tkn = 0;
250       }
251     }
252
253     /* return the current token */
254     return (lex_token);
255 } /* next_token */
256
257 /* ------------------------------------------------------------ */
258
259 /* this_token - return the current input token */
260 int this_token()
261 {
262   struct view *view_ptr;
263   struct cmd_file *new_cfp;
264   char *malloc();
265
266   /* find a token that's not a view call */
267   while (token_type() == ID) {
268
269     /* check for a view call */
270     for (view_ptr = views; view_ptr != NULL;
271          view_ptr = view_ptr->view_next)
272       if (strcmp(lexeme, view_ptr->view_name) == EQUAL) {
273         /* view name */
274         if ((new_cfp =
275             (struct cmd_file *)malloc(sizeof(struct cmd_file)))
276             == NULL)
277           printf("*** error expanding view: %s ***\n",lexeme);
278         else { /* load view environment to an icf structure */
279           new_cfp->cf_fp = NULL;
280           new_cfp->cf_text = view_ptr->view_text->txt_next;
```

```
281                new_cfp->cf_lptr = lptr;
282                lptr = view_ptr->view_text->txt_text;
283                /* point to view text */
284                new_cfp->cf_savech = saved_ch; saved_ch = EOS;
285                new_cfp->cf_next = lex_cfp;   /* link icf structure */
286                lex_cfp = new_cfp;
287                view_exists = TRUE;            /* view called */
288              }
289           saved_tkn = 0;
290           break;
291         }
292
293       if (view_ptr == NULL)
294         break;
295     }
296
297     return (lex_token);
298   } /* this_token */
299
300   /* ------------------------------------------------------------ */
301
302   /* token_type - return the current input token */
303   int token_type()
304   {
305     int ch;
306
307     /* check for a saved token */
308     if ((lex_token = saved_tkn))
309       return (lex_token);
310
311     /* get the next non-blank character */
312     ch = skip_blanks();
313
314     /* check type of character */
315     if (isalpha(ch))              /* identifier or keyword */
316       get_id();
317     else if (is_sign(ch)) {       /* sign */
318       if (!wh_signal)
319         get_signum();
320       else get_predopd();        /* part of a logical expression */
321     }
322     else if (isdigit(ch))         /* number */
323       get_number();
324     else if (ch == '"')           /* string */
325       get_string();
326     else if (get_predopd())       /* relational operator */
327       ;
328     else                          /* single character token */
329       lex_token = next_char();
330
331     /* save the type of the token */
332     saved_tkn = lex_token;
333
334     /* return the token */
335     return (lex_token);
336   } /* token_type*/
337
338   /* ------------------------------------------------------------ */
339
340   /* get_id - get a keyword or a user identifier */
341   static get_id()
```

```
342    {
343      int ch,nchars,i;
344      char *fold();
345
346      /* input letters and digits */
347      ch = skip_blanks();
348      nchars = 0;
349      while (isalpha(ch) || isdigit(ch)) {
350        if (nchars < KEYWORDMAX)
351          lexeme[nchars++] = ch;
352
353        next_char(); ch = look_ahead();
354      }
355
356      /* terminate the keyword */
357      lexeme[nchars] = EOS;
358
359      /* assume it's an identifier */
360      lex_token = ID;
361      if (isupper(*lexeme))
362        strcpy(lexeme, fold(lexeme));
363
364      /* check for keywords */
365      for (i = 0; keywords[i].keyname != NULL; i++)
366        if (strcmp(lexeme,keywords[i].keyname) == EQUAL)
367          lex_token = keywords[i].keytoken;
368
369    } /* get_id */
370
371    /* ------------------------------------------------------------ */
372
373    static get_signum()
374    {
375      int ch,nchars;
376
377      /* input letters and digits */
378      ch = skip_blanks();
379      nchars = 0;
380
381      while (is_sign(ch) || isdigit(ch)) {
382        if (nchars && is_sign(ch))
383          return(error(SYNTAX));
384
385        if (nchars < NUMBERMAX)
386          lexeme[nchars++] = ch;
387        /* clear previous character, and prepare to receive
388           the next one */
389        next_char(); ch = look_ahead();
390      }
391
392      /* terminate the keyword */
393      lexeme[nchars] = EOS;
394
395      /* assume it's an identifier */
396      lex_token = SIGNEDNO; /* token is a signed number */
397
398      return(TRUE);
399    } /* get_signum */
400
401    /* ------------------------------------------------------------ */
402
```

```
403    /* get_number - get an integer or a  float */
404    static get_number()
405    {
406      int ch, ndigits, no_real;
407
408      /* read digits and at most one decimal point */
409      ch = skip_blanks();
410      ndigits = 0; no_real = TRUE;
411      while (isdigit(ch) || (no_real && ch == '.')) {
412        if (ch == '.')
413          no_real = FALSE;
414        if (ndigits < NUMBERMAX)
415          lexeme[ndigits++] = ch;
416        next_char();            /* this combination clears character */
417        ch = look_ahead();      / * in savetch and reads next char */
418      }
419
420      /* terminate the number */
421      lexeme[ndigits] = EOS;
422
423      /* get the value of the number or real */
424      stf(lexeme, &lex_value);
425
426      if (no_real)
427        lex_token = NUMBER; /* token is an integer */
428      else
429        lex_token = REALNO;  /* token is real*/
430
431
432    } /* get_number */
433
434    /* ------------------------------------------------------------ */
435
436    /* get_string - get a string */
437    static get_string()
438    {
439      int ch,nchars;
440
441      /* skip the opening quote */
442      next_char();
443
444      /* read characters until a closing quote is found */
445      ch = look_ahead();
446      nchars = 0;
447      while (ch && ch != '"') {
448        if (nchars < STRINGMAX)
449          lexeme[nchars++] = ch;
450        next_char(); ch = look_ahead();
451      }
452
453      /* terminate the string */
454      lexeme[nchars] = EOS;
455
456      /* skip the closing quote */
457      next_char();
458
459      /* token is a string */
460      lex_token = STRING;
461    } /* get_string */
462
463    /* ------------------------------------------------------------ */
```

```
464
465     /* get_predopd - get a predicate operator */
466     static int get_predopd()
467     {
468       int ch;
469
470       switch (ch = skip_blanks()) { /* get first non-blank char */
471       case '=':
472         next_char();   ch = skip_blanks();
473         if (ch == '=') { /* definition of partial comparison */
474           next_char();
475           lex_token = PART;
476           return(TRUE);
477         }
478         else
479           lex_token = EQL; /* definition of equal  */
480         return (TRUE);
481       case '<':
482         next_char(); ch = skip_blanks();
483         if (ch == '>') { /* definition of non-equal is <> */
484           next_char();
485           lex_token = NEQ;
486         }
487         else if (ch == '=') { /* definition of less equal is <= */
488           next_char();
489           lex_token = LEQ;
490         }
491         else
492           lex_token = LSS;
493         return (TRUE);
494       case '>':
495         next_char(); ch = skip_blanks();
496         if (ch == '=') { /* definition of greater equal is >= */
497           next_char();
498           lex_token = GEQ;
499         }
500         else
501           lex_token = GTR; /* definition of greater */
502         return (TRUE);
503       case ':':
504         next_char(); ch = skip_blanks();
505         if (ch == '=') { /* definition of assignment */
506           next_char();
507           lex_token = ASGN;
508           return(TRUE);
509         }
510         else return(FALSE);
511
512       case '+':
513         next_char();
514         lex_token = ADD; /* definition of add  */
515         return (TRUE);
516       case '-':
517         next_char();
518         lex_token = SUB; /* definition of subtract  */
519         return (TRUE);
520       case '*':
521         next_char();
522         lex_token = MUL; /* definition of multiply  */
523         return (TRUE);
524       case '/':
```

```
525        next_char();
526        lex_token = DIV; /* definition of divide  */
527        return (TRUE);
528      case '%':
529        next_char();
530        lex_token = MOD; /* definition of modulus  */
531        return (TRUE);
532      default:
533        return(FALSE);   /* no other relational ops */
534      }
535    } /* get_predopd */
536
537    /* ------------------------------------------------------------ */
538
539    /* skip_blanks - get the next non-blank character */
540    static int skip_blanks()
541    {
542      int ch;
543
544      /* skip blank characters */
545      while ((ch = look_ahead()) <= ' ' && ch != EOS)
546        next_char();
547
548      /* return the first non-blank */
549      return (ch);
550    } /* skip_blanks */
551
552    /* ------------------------------------------------------------ */
553
554    /* look_ahead - get the current lookahead character */
555    static int look_ahead()
556    {
557      /* get a lookahead character */
558      if (saved_ch == EOS)
559        saved_ch = next_char();
560
561      /* if a character is already saved return it else
562       * return new lookahead character */
563      return (saved_ch);
564
565    } /* look_ahead */
566
567    /* ------------------------------------------------------------ */
568
569    /* next_char - get the next character */
570    static int next_char()
571    {
572      char fname[STRINGMAX+1];
573      int ch,i;
574
575      /* return the lookahead character if there is one */
576      if (saved_ch != EOS) {
577        ch = saved_ch;
578        saved_ch = EOS;
579        return (ch);
580      }
581
582      /* get a character */
583      ch = get_char();
584
585      /* skip spaces at the beginning of a command */
```

```
586     if (line_start && iprompt != NULL)
587       while (ch <= ' ')
588         ch = get_char();
589
590     /* use continuation prompt next time */
591     iprompt = NULL;
592
593     /* check for indirect command file */
594     while (ch == '@') {
595       for (i = 0; (saved_ch = get_char()) > ' '; )
596         if (i < STRINGMAX)
597           fname[i++] = saved_ch;
598       fname[i] = EOS;
599       if (com_file(fname) != TRUE)
600         printf("*** error opening command file: %s ***\n",fname);
601       ch = get_char();
602     }
603
604     /* return the character */
605     return (ch);
606   } /* next_char */
607
608   /* ------------------------------------------------------------ */
609
610   /* get_char - get the current character */
611   static int get_char()
612   {
613     struct cmd_file *old_cfp;
614     int ch;
615
616     /* check for input from command line */
617     if (lptr != NULL) {
618       while (*lptr == EOS && lex_cfp)    /* if there is an icf */
619         if (lex_cfp->cf_text == NULL) { /* consumed after lptr */
620           old_cfp = lex_cfp;
621           ch = lex_cfp->cf_savech; saved_ch = EOS;
622           lptr = lex_cfp->cf_lptr;    /* get value of icf lptr */
623
624           /* reset icf context pointer to point to next
625               cmd_file entry in list */
626           lex_cfp = lex_cfp->cf_next;
627           nfree((char *) old_cfp);
628           if (ch != EOS)
629             return (ch);
630           if (lptr == NULL)
631             break;
632         }
633         else {   /* view text processing */
634           lptr = lex_cfp->cf_text->txt_text; /* point to view text */
635           /* point to continuation of view text */
636           lex_cfp->cf_text = lex_cfp->cf_text->txt_next;
637         }
638
639       if (lptr != NULL && *lptr)
640         return (*lptr++);
641       else if (*lptr == EOS)
642         return(EOS);
643     }
644
645     /* print prompt if necessary */
646     if (line_start && lex_cfp == NULL) {
```

```
647        if (iprompt != NULL)
648          printf("%s",iprompt);
649        else if (cprompt != NULL)
650          printf("%s",cprompt);
651      }
652
653      if (lex_cfp == NULL)
654        if ((ch = in_chars(stdin)) == NEWLINE)
655          line_start = TRUE; /* signal beginning of newline */
656        else
657          line_start = FALSE;
658      else {  /* if indirect command file exists */
659        if ((ch = in_chars(lex_cfp->cf_fp)) == EOF) {
660          old_cfp = lex_cfp;
661          ch = lex_cfp->cf_savech; saved_ch = EOS;
662          lptr = lex_cfp->cf_lptr;
663          lex_cfp = lex_cfp->cf_next;
664          fclose(old_cfp->cf_fp);
665          nfree((char *) old_cfp);
666        }
667      }
668      /* return the character */
669      return (ch);
670    } /* get_char */
671
672    /* ------------------------------------------------------------ */
673
674    /* input characters from file or standard input */
675    int in_chars(fp)
676        FILE *fp;
677    {
678      static char buf[LINEMAX] = {0};
679      static char *pbuf = buf;
680      int ch, i;
681
682      if (fp!=stdin)
683        if ((ch = getc(fp)) == NEWLINE) /* place in char from file */
684          return getc(fp);    /* if NEWLINE get char in next line */
685        else
686          return ch;
687
688      if (*pbuf > 0)
689        return *pbuf++;
690
691      pbuf = buf;
692      for (i = 0; (ch = getc(fp)) != EOF; )
693        if (i < LINEMAX)  {
694          buf[i++] = ch;    /* fill buffer with on-line chars */
695          if (ch == NEWLINE)    break;
696        }
697        else {
698          printf("*** line too long ***\nRetype> ");
699          i = 0;
700        }
701      buf[i] = EOS;
702      return in_chars(fp);
703    } /* in_chars */
704
705    /* ------------------------------------------------------------ */
706
707    /* get_line - get a line from the current input;
```

```
708     *               to be used in conjunction with views */
709   char *get_line(buf)
710         char *buf;
711   {
712     int ch, i;
713
714     for (i= 0; (ch = next_char()) != '\n' && ch != EOF; )
715       if (i < LINEMAX)
716         buf[i++] = ch;
717       else {
718         printf("******* line too long ********\nRetype> ");
719         i = 0;
720       }
721     buf[i] = EOS;
722
723     return(buf);
724   }
725
726   /* ------------------------------------------------------------ */
727
728   /* this function is used with views, it simply checks for the
729    * existence of a view exactly as in the case of this_token */
730   int nxtoken_type()
731   {
732     /* get the current token */
733     token_type();
734
735     /* make sure another is read on next call */
736     saved_tkn = 0;
737
738     /* return the current token */
739     return (lex_token);
740   }
741
742   /* ------------------------------------------------------------ */
```

8

Syntax Analysis

In this chapter we will build on ideas developed in the previous one and discuss the relationship between the formal definition of the RQL syntax and the methods that can be used to parse RQL queries. We will explain how the method of parsing which is known as recursive descent imposes certain useful restrictions on the grammar of the query language.

8.1 Overview

In the previous chapter we showed how the lexical analyzer transforms a source statement into lexical units (tokens). The core of REQUIEM is the parser, the section of code that reads each RQL sentence on a word by word basis to decide its syntactic soundness. During this process the validity of syntactic keywords such as the correct spelling and proper use of the RQL commands is examined. In the case of an error, parsing is abandoned and the user is informed that an error has occurred by means of an error message.

In addition to the syntactic structure of the query, REQUIEM ascertains the validity of the involved database components, such as relations, attributes, and values. For example, if a component does not exist (e.g. if it has been misspelt) or a value is invalid, the user is informed via an error message. To perform this task, the parser calls the query decomposer. The query decomposer consults the contents of the system catalogs for definitions of the data, and accesses relation headers to assure itself of the existence of relation and attribute names. During the process of parsing and query decomposition, access paths are generated which are then used throughout the process of tuple fetching.

The processes of parsing and query decomposition are intertwined: in

certain situations the parser calls corresponding query decomposer routines
to check the validity of a given component. The query decomposition routines, in turn, continue parsing. As explained in the previous chapter the
approach described here can be called *incremental parsing*, as opposed to
the approach where the parser generates an intermediate form of the user
statement that is further transformed into a set of access programs that
actually access the data stored in database relations.

The aim of this chapter and the next is to present a brief but thorough
treatment of some of the major implementation aspects/mechanisms of
RQL, and thereby to pave the way for an understanding of the material
presented in subsequent chapters. Before embarking on any discussion of
the REQUIEM parser structure, we first briefly consider some elementary
concepts of language theory in order to provide the necessary background
for the later sections which focus on the more technical aspects of parsing.
Readers who are already familiar with such issues need only skim the next
section as a quick review to ensure a familiarity with all technical terms and
concepts introduced in later sections. Thereafter, we proceed by explaining
the general concepts and functionality underlying the parser.

8.2   Elementary concepts of language theory

In order to describe the parsing process of REQUIEM queries it is useful to
introduce some elementary concepts of formal language theory. Although
elaborating on this topic is far beyond the scope of this book we would like
to present some notation and terminology that are relevant to parsing and
translation. We will try to keep the following introduction as informal as
possible because we believe that in this way it is more easily and intuitively
understood by systems programmers and provides a high-level view of the
magnitude of problems encountered when implementing a language. We
start by defining some terms used throughout this chapter.

1. An *alphabet* is a non-empty finite set of *symbols*, where a symbol is an
   atomic entity such as a character or a keyword.
   Consider for example the alphabet of symbols to generate legal RQL
   statements. The elements of this alphabet, shown in Figure 8.1, are the
   legal tokens that can be identified by the REQUIEM lexical analyzer (see
   Chapter 7). These symbols are also referred to as the *terminal* symbols.

2. A *string* over an alphabet is any sequence of symbols of the alphabet. A
   string of length zero is called the *null string*.

ADD, ALL, AS, ASCENDING, ASGN, ASSIGN, AVG, BOOLEAN, BY, CHAR, COUNT, CREATE, DEFINE, DELETE, DIFFERENCE, DISPLAY, DIV, EOS, EQL, EXIT, EXPORT, EXPOSE, EXTRACT, FOCUS, FROM, GEQ, GROUP, GTR, HELP, ID, IMPORT, IN, INSERT, INTERSECT, INTO, IS, JOIN, LEQ, LSS, MAXM, MINM, MOD, MODIFY, MUL, NEQ, NUM, NUMBER, ON, OVER, PART, PRINT, PROJECT, PURGE, QUIT, REAL, REALNO, SECONDARY, SELECT, SET, SHOW, SIGNEDNO, SORT, STRING, SUB, SUM, TO, UNION, UNIQUE, UPDATE, USING, VIEW, WHERE, WITH

Figure 8.1 The RQL alphabet of token symbols.

Some examples of strings over the above-mentioned alphabet of legal RE-QUIEM tokens are:

(a) **create** employee **over project where join**;

(b) **select** salary **from** employee **where** salary > 4500;

(c) **select from** employee **where** sex **is** female;

It is obvious that the strings (a) and (c) are legal strings with respect to the set of tokens of REQUIEM, as they consist entirely of legal tokens, although they do not constitute legal REQUIEM statements. The set of valid REQUIEM statements is only a subset of the set of all possible strings. Actually, the set of legal strings is composed by obeying certain rules. Thus, we define the language.

3. A *language* over an alphabet is a specified set of strings formed according to the rules of this language. Hence, the set of all eligible strings is normally a subset of all possible strings.

The grammar for a specific language consists of a set of rules that describes how to generate the subset of strings that constitutes legal statements of a language. The grammar of REQUIEM would not allow the generation of the strings (a) and (c) in the previous example.

In order to describe the stepwise generation of a legal statement of a language, a set of intermediate symbols is needed. These symbols do not appear in any statement but are used as a kind of variable. They are defined in the set of *non-terminal* symbols. The desirable strings in a formal language are these strings which consist entirely of terminal symbols. This brings us to the following definition.

4. A *grammar* (G) is used to define a language, and can be defined to be a quadruple (N, T, S, P), where

(a) N is the alphabet of non-terminal symbols;

(b) T is the alphabet of terminal symbols;

(c) S is a special non-terminal symbol, called the *start symbol*; and

(d) P is a set of *productions* which describe how to generate the strings of the corresponding language. A production consists of two parts: the *left-hand side* and the *right-hand side*.

If each production of a grammar has the further property that all its left parts consist of a single non-terminal symbol then the grammar is said to be *context-free*.

5. A *sentence* of a language is a string that consists entirely of non-terminal symbols and is generated according to the rules defined in P. The sentences in RQL are the legal, that is syntactically correct, queries.

RQL is a context-free language; the grammar underlying RQL is outlined in Appendix A. To understand context-free parsers, you must look at the sentence construction of RQL queries very carefully. You must think of an RQL sentence as being composed of individual tokens.

8.3   The parsing problem

In the previous section we outlined how a grammar can be used to generate programs in a given programming language. However, the problem which the compiler or interpreter has to deal with is not how to generate programs but how to check the strings of symbols to see if they belong to the language and, if they do, to recognize the structure of the strings in terms of the productions of the grammar which underlies this specific language. This problem is called the parsing problem and will be investigated in this section and the next.

Rather than defining the syntax of RQL informally, we will give a precise definition using a context-free grammar. Consequently the RQL grammar will be described in terms of a context-free notation known as *Backus-Naur form*, or *BNF*. Context-free languages form an important subset of formal languages as they allow for efficient parsing. Informally, a context-free grammar, like RQL, is simply a set of productions. Productions in a context-free grammar are of the form:

$$A \rightarrow \alpha$$

where A is a non-terminal symbol, and α is a string consisting of terminal as well as non-terminal symbols. A is the left-hand side (lhs) of the production while the symbol α constitutes the right-hand side (rhs). We use the symbol $\rightarrow$ to denote a single step derivation. In a context-free grammar, every production has exactly one non-terminal symbol on its lhs, and can have any sequence of terminal and non-terminal symbols on its rhs. A production represents the syntactic rule that any occurrence of the lhs of a given production may be replaced by the symbols of its rhs.

BNF is a syntax *meta-language*. A meta-language is a language which is used to describe other languages. The symbols $<$, and $>$, and $\rightarrow$ or $::=$ are symbols of the meta-language and, consequently, not of the language being described. The symbol $\rightarrow$ or $::=$ stands for "is defined as." In BNF each production consists of a non-terminal symbol followed by the operator $::=$ and a right-hand production symbol. Non-terminals are delimited by $<$ and $>$ for ease of recognition. For example the production $<A> \rightarrow \beta$ or $<A>$ $::= \beta$ signifies that the non-terminal symbol A can be replaced by β in any string. If a non-terminal symbol has more than one alternate right-hand symbol, the alternatives are listed in one concise production separated by vertical bars $|$. A component of the right-hand part of a production that is surrounded by curly brackets { and } may appear any number of times (including zero) if this syntactic rule is applied. For example, by applying the rule $A \rightarrow \{b\}^*$ to the string cAc, any of the following string may be generated: cc, cbc, cbbc, etc.

Non-terminal symbols can also be recognized by the fact that they appear on lhs productions. A non-terminal is, in effect, a placeholder that must be replaced by a production having the appropriate non-terminal on its lhs. In contrast to that, terminals can never be changed or replaced as they stand for the tokens of the underlying language.

The overall purpose of a set of productions is to specify those sequences of tokens that are legal. To achieve this we start with a single non-terminal symbol, called the start symbol (S). The start symbol of the RQL grammar, as shown in Appendix A, is $<RQL-query>$. We then apply productions, replacing the non-terminals with other non-terminals or terminal symbols until only terminals remain. Any sequence of terminals that can be produced by this procedure is accepted as legal. Similarly, if a specific sequence of terminals cannot be produced by any sequence of non-terminal replacements the sequence is considered illegal. Thus, a string consisting of only terminal symbols is said to be a valid sentence in the language if it can be *derived* from the start symbol.

Query language statements often involve optional items or lists of items. To clearly represent such features we will introduce an extended BNF notation. In this notation optional items are enclosed in square brackets [and], while optional lists are enclosed by braces { and }. For example, in the following expression

---

*This construct stands for a short-hand notation for the rule "$A \rightarrow \varepsilon|b|Ab$," where ε denotes the empty string.

<select> ::= <sel-attrs> [<from-clause>[<predicate>]]

the select clause is defined to be a single *<sel–attrs>* non-terminal, optionally followed by a *<from–clause>* statement optionally followed by a *<predicate>*. This derivation process can be best modeled with a *syntax tree* or a *parse tree* where the root of the tree is the start symbol and the leaves are the terminals in the sentence. Now we can say that a string of symbols is valid in a particular language if we can build a parse tree for it. The process of parse tree derivation is referred to as *parsing*. The process of determining whether a sentence is valid or not is called *recognition*. As you might expect, recognition can only be achieved through parsing.

8.3.1   Recursive descent parsing

A well-known and easy to implement top-down parsing method which involves no backtracking, i.e. making repeated scans of the input, is known as the *recursive descent parsing* method [42]. Its name is taken from the recursive parsing procedures that descend through the parse tree to recognize the syntactic structure of the program. Recursive descent is one of the simplest parsing techniques used in practical compilers or interpreters.

The basic idea of recursive descent is that each non-terminal symbol has an associated parsing procedure that can recognize any sequence of tokens generated by that specific non-terminal. Obviously, within a parsing procedure, both terminals and non-terminals can be matched. For example, to match a non-terminal N, we call the parsing procedure associated with N. To match a terminal symbol, say T, we call an appropriate match procedure, say *match(T)*. This match procedure calls the scanner to bring the next token from the input string. If the next token is T, everything went according to the syntax rules and the token can thus be consumed. If, however, the next token is not T then a syntax error has been detected and an appropriate error message is produced. Some error repair is then necessary to restart the parser and continue the compilation process.

To see how this works, consider the very simple expressions of a hypothetical language:

<expression> ::= <term> <operator> <term>
<operator>   ::= '+' | '–'
<term>   ::= <number> | '(' <expression> ')'
<number>   ::= <digit> | <number> <digit>

A parser for these expressions would consist of two recursive procedures named **term()** and **expression()**, as illustrated in Figure 8.2. When the algorithm of Figure 8.2 recognizes an expression like

$$120 + (5 - 22) \tag{8.1}$$

it executes the following sequence of procedure calls:

Procedure called	Recognized symbol
Expression	120+(5–22)
Term	120
Term	(5–22)
Expression	5–22
Term	5
Term	22

Figure 8.3 shows the same sequence of actions as a tree structure. Each node of the tree corresponds to the recognition of a terminal or a non-terminal symbol of the above expression. The root of this ordered tree is labeled with the start symbol of the language, i.e. <*expression*>. The leaves are in turn labeled with the terminal symbols of the expression. A parse tree is a tree-structured diagram that has its nodes labeled with terminal and non-terminal symbols. Each intermediate node is labeled with a non-terminal symbol. If a production is applied to a non-terminal node, a successor for each symbol in the corresponding production is drawn and labeled with the respective symbol name.

This tree which shows the grammatical composition of an expression written in a given language, as for example expression 8.1, is called, as previously mentioned, a parse tree. Conceptually, the recursive descent parser builds the parse tree as soon as it has recognized the sentence or symbol that is associated with this branch. It should be clear at this point that a parser that uses recursive descent can be written from a suitable grammar with reasonable programming effort.

The advantages of writing a recursive descent parser are fairly obvious. The main advantage is, as explained, the easiness with which the parser can be written from the corresponding grammar. Another advantage is that, because of the close correspondence between the grammar and the parser, there is a high probability that the parser will be correct, or at least any errors will be of simple nature. The main disadvantage of this method is that the high incidence of procedure calls during syntax analysis is likely to make the parser relatively slow. Compared with some table-driven parsing methods, used for large and complex languages, the recursive descent parser is likely to be rather long. Recursive descent parsing, however, is perfectly adequate for query languages.

```
int expression()
{
  int tkn;

  if (!term())  /* left operand */
    return(FALSE);

  while(this_token() <= ADD && lex_token >= SUB) {
    tkn = next_token();

    if (!term())  /* right operand */
      return(FALSE);

    switch(tkn) {
    case ADD:
      if (!operator(xadd))
        return (FALSE);
      break;
    case SUB:
      if (!operator(xsub))
        return (FALSE);
      break;
    }
  }

  return(TRUE);
} /* expression */


int term()
{
  int tkn;

  if (this_token() == '('){
    next_token();

    if (!expression())
      return(FALSE);

    if (next_token() != ')')
      return(error(SYNTAX));
  }
  else if (this_token() == NUMBER) {
      return (get_number());
  }
  else
      return (error(SYNTAX));

  return(TRUE);
} /* term */
```

Figure 8.2 Simple algorithm for the recognition of expressions.

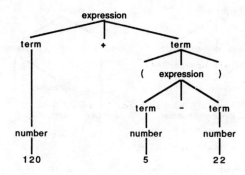

Figure 8.3 The parse tree for the expression 120+(5−22).

8.3.2 Ambiguous and suitable grammars

There are usually many ways to define a grammar describing a given language. As a result we must be careful when talking about the structure of a sentence according to a grammar. If, for example, any sentence generated by a grammar ends in more than one parse tree the grammar is said to be *ambiguous*. To show that a certain grammar is ambiguous, all we have to do is to find a sequence of tokens that produces more than one parse tree. Consider for example the following grammar for simple arithmetic expressions:

<expression> ::= <expression> + <expression>
            | <number>
<number>   ::= <digit> | <number> <digit>

When using this grammar to parse an expression like 10−5+1 we produce the two parse trees of Figure 8.4. These trees correspond to the two ways of parenthesizing this arithmetic expression, namely (10−5)+1 and 10−(5+1). The second assigns to the expression the value 4 instead of the customary value 6. Since a sentence like that with more than one parse tree usually has more than one meaning attached to it, we need to design unambiguous grammars for compiling and interpreting applications. Ambiguity is often a property of the grammar, not of the language. As the previous example indicates, there normally exist non-ambiguous grammars for the same language. We can thus make the language proposal unambiguous by insisting that the parse tree is built up by starting on the left.

Most of the methods for tackling this problem correspond to particular parsing methods. For example, parsing methods used with recursive descent parsing are top-down, i.e. they work from the sentence symbol towards the

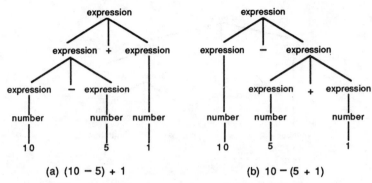

(a) (10 − 5) + 1   (b) 10 − (5 + 1)

Figure 8.4 The parse trees for an ambiguous grammar.

sentence. It is normal to read the sentence being parsed from left to right and never end up in a situation where the parser has to look back at the same symbols again to make another guess of the kind of sentence (if any) these symbols may form. A compilation method with this characteristic is known as *top-down parsing without backtracking*. In general, parsing methods are said to be *non-deterministic* or *deterministic* depending on whether backtracking is involved or not.

A suitable grammar for language recognition must not only be unambiguous, it must also be deterministic. What this means is that during parsing the sequence of the terminal symbols which remain to be parsed in a sentence, together with the present derived parse tree, must enable the parser to decide which production to use in order to complete the parse tree. Alternatively, the parser may discover that no tree can be constructed to accommodate the next input symbol.

Unfortunately ambiguity is not the only problem associated with the previous grammar. The grammar is inherently *left-recursive*, that is the non-terminal <*expression*> appears again at the beginning of its own derivation. This fact gives rise to an infinitely long sequence of grammatical phrases. The use of left recursion in the above expression can cause serious problems in a recursive descent parser. Suppose that in the parsing algorithm the procedure associated with the non-terminal <*expression*> decided to apply this production. As observed from the above expression the right-hand side begins with <*expression*> so that the procedure for <*expression*> is called recursively, and the recursive descent parser loops for ever. Remember from the previous chapter that the lookahead symbol changes only when a terminal in the right-hand side is matched. Since the production begins with the non-terminal <*expression*>, no changes to the input occur between these successive recursive calls causing, thus, an infinite loop. Left recursion can be eliminated by introducing additional terminals in the productions of a grammar: in other words by rewriting the offending production.

LL(1) grammars are a class of context-free grammars suitable for recursive descent parsing which cope with the problems of ambiguity and left recursion. The two L's in $LL(1)$ refer to the fact that strings are parsed from Left to right and Leftmost derivations are used. The symbol 1 denotes the fact that alternative productions are chosen by means of a single lookahead symbol. Here, we must note that even though the right-hand side of a production does not commence with a terminal, it may be possible to deduce that a given alternative for some non-terminal symbol may only give rise to strings that start with one out of a particular set of terminals. In the case of $LL(1)$ languages a parse tree can be built top-down with no backtracking. This implies that $LL(1)$ languages are tailor-made to meet the requirements of recursive descent parsers.

The $LL(1)$ property as you will probably find out by examining the body of the RQL grammar, as well as the REQUIEM predicate expression grammar, is quite straightforward. Actually, whenever there exists a question as to which production to use, the next symbol in the input sequence must enable the parser to determine what action to follow. The question arises only when the parser needs to choose between one of several derivations in a production. Here we may distinguish between two cases depending on whether each of the derivations starts with a terminal or a non-terminal symbol. In the first case the next input symbol can be only one of the terminal symbols. Alternatively, if we consider recursively all the derivations for all the non-terminal symbols we arrive at more terminal symbols which can replace these non-terminals. Obviously, the next input symbol must then be exactly one of the encountered terminals, which must therefore all be different. Once a grammar is $LL(1)$, a recursive descent-parser for its language can be built in a very straightforward manner. For more information on the topics of ambiguity, left recursion and $LL(1)$ grammars you can refer to [42], [44], and [45] .

8.4   The RQL predicate expression sublanguage

In Chapter 3 we mentioned that search conditions in RQL are introduced by the **where** clause which is normally used to qualify specific tuples, possibly for further processing. For a given tuple a search condition evaluates to TRUE or FALSE. The tuples that qualify are precisely those for which the condition evaluates to TRUE. The search condition is actually specified by the predicate that follows the keyword **where**. Recall that the predicate may combine many arithmetic expressions involving attributes, attribute names, and constants using comparison and/or logical operators. As a large number of RQL sentences can be characterized as predicate expressions, we can rightfully think of all predicate expressions as being derived from a specific language, called the *predicate expression sublanguage*. This sublanguage is actually part of RQL and contains its own set of productions which, of course, pertain to predicate expressions.

The RQL predicate expression sublanguage, exactly like RQL, is context-free, and its grammar is presented in Figure 8.5. In this figure the symbol N, as usual, denotes the set of non-terminal symbols while the symbol T denotes the set of terminal symbols in the RQL predicate expression sublanguage. Constructs like <*expression*>, <*factor*>, and <*term*> are examples of non-terminal symbols of the RQL predicate expression sublanguage. Similarly, the set of terminal symbols consists of the set of all printable characters and numbers including the special symbols &, |, <, >, =, $\cdots$, (see Figure 8.5). The start symbol of the grammar is the symbol <*expression*>. The productions are as usual described formally in the BNF meta-language.

The following example illustrates how a given predicate expression may be generated by the syntactic rules of the grammar that defines the RQL predicate expression sublanguage. The rules in this example are numbered in accordance with the productions in Figure 8.5.

Example 8.4.1

The predicate expression "weight > 100 & finish = "oak" " can be produced by applying the productions in the following sequence:

rule 1:	<primary> <logop> <primary>
rule 2:	<statement> <logop> <statement>
rule 3:	<simple−expression> <relop> <simple−expression> &
	<simple−expression> <relop> <simple−expression>
rule 5:	<term> <relop> <term>
	& <term> <relop> <term>
rule 6:	<factor> <relop> <factor>
	& <factor> <relop> <factor>
rule 7:	<operand> <relop> operand>
	& <operand> <relop> <operand>
rule 8:	<attribute> <relop> <number>
	& <attribute> <relop> <string>
rule 10:	<aname> <relop> <number>
	& <attribute> <relop> <string>

By applying the rules 11, 12, 13, 15, and 16 as illustrated in Figure 8.5, we get the resulting sentence in the RQL predicate expression sublanguage.

```
1  <expression>   ::= <primary> { <logop> <primary> }
2  <primary>      ::= <statement> |
                       <assgnt> <relop> <simple-expression>
3  <statement>    ::= <simple-expression>
                       { <relop> <simple-expression> }
4  <assignment>   ::= '(' <variable> ':=' <simple-expression> ')'
5  <simple-expr>  ::= <term> { <addop> <term> }
6  <term>         ::= <factor> { <mulop> <factor> }
7  <factor>       ::= <operand> | '(' <expression> ')' |
                       <nop> <factor>
8  <operand>      ::= <number> | <string> |
                       <attribute> | <variable>
9  <variable>     ::= '$' <chars>
10 <attribute>    ::= { <rname>.} <aname>
11 <number>       ::= <digit> | <number><digit>
12 <string>       ::= " <chars> "
13 <chars>        ::= nil | <chars> {<character>}
14 <nop>          ::= '~ '
15 <logop>        ::= '&' | '|'
16 <relop>        ::= '=' | '<>' | '<' | '>' | '<=' | '>='
17 <addop>        ::= '+' | '-'
18 <mulop>        ::= '*' | '/' | '
```

N = {'a', ⋯, 'z', 'A', ⋯, 'Z'}
 ∪ {'0', '1', '2', '3', '4', '5', '6', '7', '8', '9'}
 ∪ {'.', ';', ' '}
 ∪ { '|', '&'}
 ∪ {'$', '~ ', '(', ')'}
 ∪ {'=', '<>', '<', '>', '<=', '>=', '+', '-', '*', '%', '/' }

T = {<expression>, <primary>, <statement>, <assgnt>,
     <relop>, <simple-expression>, <variable>, <term>,
     <factor>, <mulop>, <operand>, <number>, <string>,
     <attribute>, <chars>, <rname>, <aname>,
     <digit>, <character>}

Figure 8.5 The grammar in BNF for the predicate expression sublanguage.

This sequence of steps can be alternatively illustrated by means of a parse tree. An example parse tree for the above expression is shown in Figure 8.6.

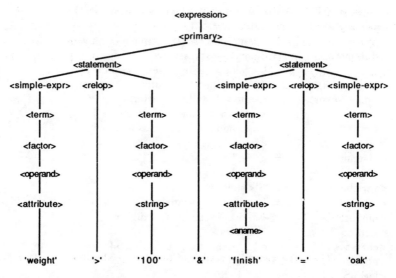

Figure 8.6 The parse tree for the expression: "weight > 100 & finish = "oak". "

8.4.1   An overview of expression compilation

In this section we will briefly discuss the general steps of the compiling process as related to the RQL predicate expression compiler. Predicate expression compilation normally consists of the following steps [42]:

1. Lexical analysis of predicate expressions.
2. Parsing of predicate expressions.
3. Code generation.
4. Code optimization.
5. Object code generation.

In the REQUIEM predicate expression compilation the last two steps are not performed. Compilation rather ends by generating and storing intermediate code in a code array. The predicate expression compilation steps will be presented analytically in Chapter 11. In the following we shall concentrate only on the parsing aspects of predicate expressions.

The purpose of parsing the predicate expressions is to determine whether a given string of tokens corresponds to the syntactic rules stated in the grammar of the language. Additionally, if inconsistencies or syntactic errors are detected, the user will be informed. RQL currently provides over 50 error messages forwarded to the user or implementor. In order to check the syntactic structure of a token string the parser generally examines only the type of each individual token. The result of the parsing step is an internal representation of the syntactic structure of the tokens that have been input. As already explained, this representation is usually in the form of a parse tree.

> *highest precedence :* ' ~ '
> ' * ', '/', '%'
> ' + ', ' – '
> ' := '
> ' = ', ' <> ', ' < ', ' > ', ' <= ', ' >= '
> *lowest precedence :* '|', '&'

Figure 8.7 The precedence of operators of the RQL predicate expression sublanguage.

The parse tree represents the information that is used during the phase of code generation to identify the appropriate sequence of actions required to perform the operations in a source statement. In RQL (as in most programming languages) each operator has a predefined precedence value. If more than one operator is specified in a source statement, the relative precedence value determines which operator should *take precedence* over the others. The precedence values associated with the operators are implicitly defined in the grammar. For the RQL predicate expression sublanguage the precedence of operators is depicted in Figure 8.7.

Example 8.4.2

Consider two simple expressions that are legal within the RQL predicate expression sublanguage:

1. *7 + 6 * 3*
2. *(7 + 6) * 3*

In fact it is a trivial task to decipher what the above expressions imply. In the first expression, the operator "*" takes precedence over the "+" operator and the result of the expression, as expected, is 25. By parenthesizing a part of the expression, the inherent precedence of the operators can be modified. Hence, in the second expression, the subexpression surrounded by parentheses takes a higher precedence yielding as a result the value 39.

If we take a closer look at the corresponding parse tree produced for the above expressions during parsing (cf. Figure 8.8), we can recognize how the precedence of the RQL operators is defined within its grammar. In the parse trees, each node either identifies a value (if the node is labeled with a corresponding token type) or an operator. All nodes that are not leaf nodes represent the intermediate value that can be obtained by evaluating the expression that is defined by their corresponding subtree. Thus, in the first parse tree depicted in Figure 8.8, the right operand of the "+" operator is the value that results from evaluating the product identified by the corresponding subtree. In the second case, the left operand of the "*" operator is defined by the subtree representing the sum.

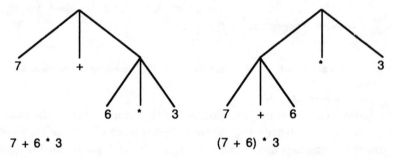

Figure 8.8 Two parse trees for the example expressions in the text.

By modifying the grammar of the language appropriately, the precedence of the operators can be adjusted. Precedence of "*" over "+" is achieved by stating in the grammar that <term> symbols can be connected by an <addop> operator. The <term> symbols can be subsequently transformed into a unique <factor> symbol or a pair of <factor> symbols connected by a <mulop> operator (see Figure 8.5). Thus, it is guaranteed that components of a sum can be products but components of a product can never be a sum. In the corresponding parse tree this manifests in the fact that the components of a sum can be subtrees representing products, thus guaranteeing that operations will be performed in the correct sequence.

Let us now consider how the parsing scheme for the sample predicate expression in example 8.4.1 is implemented in REQUIEM. Actual compilation commences by calling the function **expression()**. This function is implemented according to rule 1 of the grammar illustrated in Figure 8.5. Its implementation in the C programming language is as depicted in Figure 8.9.

```
/* compile an expression */
static int expression()
{
  int c;

  if (!primary())
    return (FALSE);

  while ((c = this_token()) == '|' || c == '&') {
    next_token();

    if (!primary())
      return (FALSE);

    switch(c) {
    case '|':        if (!operator(xor))
      return (FALSE);
      break;
    case '&':        if (!operator(xand))
      return (FALSE);
      break;
    default:         return(error(SYNTAX));

    }
  }

  /* return successfully */
  return (TRUE);
}
```

Figure 8.9 The C function to parse an expression.

Following this rule, the first component of an expression must be a
<primary>. Consequently, the first step in the function **expression()** is
to state that the next part of the source statement corresponds to a
<primary>. For this purpose the corresponding function, namely **primary()**
is called, which in turn calls other functions according to the rules of the
grammar. If a <primary> cannot be identified, then parsing is aborted and
the function **expression()** returns FALSE. If the parsing of the <primary>
was successful, the current token from the input stream is requested from
the lexical analyzer by a call to the function **this_token()**. If this token is the
terminal symbol "|" or "&", another <primary> must follow. The lexical
analyzer is then instructed to overwrite the current token and consume the
next token by calling the function **next_token()**. Finally, **primary()** is called
again to identify the corresponding <primary>. This process proceeds until
the token that follows a <primary> is not the terminal symbol "|" or "&".
In this case the function **expression()** ends and returns a TRUE signifying
that the phase of expression compilation has terminated successfully.

```
expression()
  primary()
    statement()
      simple()
        term()
          factor()
            get_operand()
              get_attr()
      simple()
        term()
          factor()
            get_operand()
              get_number()
    statement()
      simple()
        term()
          factor()
            get_operand()
              get_attr()
      simple()
        term()
          factor()
            get_operand()
              get_string()
```

Figure 8.10 The sequence of parse functions as executed during parsing the expression "weight > 100 & finish = "oak" ."

Figure 8.10 depicts the sequence of the functions associated with non-terminal symbols in the grammar as called during the phase of parsing. During the phase of parsing, the parse tree, illustrated in Figure 8.6, is constructed for the above sample expression.

8.5 The REQUIEM parser

There are many ways to implement a recursive descent parser that uses the RQL production rules. As seen from the previous section probably the easiest way is to create a recursive descent parser that uses a collection of mutually exclusive functions that descend through the productions of the grammar until they completely parse the entire sentence.

The syntax of RQL is stringently enforced and requires that every term in a query is defined explicitly. Consequently, before you start implementing an

$LL(1)$ parser you must first define a table to hold the language vocabulary (alphabet of terminal symbols) and the types of words that the parser can in general recognize. Recall that such a table is set up and processed by the lexical analyzer (see Figure 5.2). During parsing, an input sentence is checked for "correct" syntax. Its syntactic structure is determined on the basis of the sequence of permitted tokens. From a parser's standpoint tokens are perceived as the atomic components of a language. The RQL tokens are keywords or reserved words, constant expressions, names (identifiers) of relations, attributes files, views, etc.

The parser accepts a sentence as input and breaks it into a sequence of tokens produced by the lexical analyzer. As explained in the previous chapter, this is achieved by means of successive calls to the lexical analyzer functions **this_token()** and **next_token()**. By consulting the grammar rules the parser decides if the sequence of tokens forms a correct sentence of the language. If during this process an error is detected it is forwarded to the user, and parsing is abandoned. Seen from the user's perspective, this means that the user gets an error message that informs him/her about the type of error that has occurred. The user is then forced to input the corrected statement in order to get the desired results.

8.5.1   The parser implementation

The major concern of the function **parse()**, which is the central function of the REQUIEM parser, is to handle a number of different query statements and to process each of them by means of a query-specific function. The traditional way of programming this is by using a cumbersome **switch** statement to test the value of the switch index and to call the appropriate function. Instead, you might be tempted to set up a table of pointers to functions that can be indexed by a query type as is usual in assembly programming. In this way the calling function may be inattentive as far as the type of the query received is concerned, and the corresponding processing function will be invoked much quicker than if a **switch** or **if** / **else** construct were used. Such tables are commonly used in assembly language programming and are often called *dispatch* or *jump* tables.

Hence, to implement the function **parse()** we use the notion of pointers to functions. Pointers to functions are used primarily because they may save considerable coding and processing time, but there are two additional reasons. In C you cannot pass a function itself as an argument to another function, but you may pass a pointer to the corresponding function. Second, you cannot store a function in an array or structure, but once again, you may store a pointer to a function instead [46].

In function **parse()** the identifier **dispatch_table** is declared as an array of command structures. The data structure **command** contains two components. The first component is a pointer to the name of the query statement and the second is a pointer to the corresponding function which needs to be called:

```
struct command {
    char *name;
    int (* function)();
}
```

Because **dispatch_table** is an array its elements can be referenced by subscript, such as in **(*dispatch_table[i].function)()** which invokes the function pointed to by the pointer component of the ith element. Now, when a specific query statement is read from the terminal, e.g. a **select** statement, the dispatch table is searched until the appropriate command name is found. When found, the corresponding parsing function is called, e.g. the function that implements the select queries. In REQUIEM the function **evaluate()** fulfills this role by searching the dispatch table until it finds a match, which implies a call to the corresponding function. The function **evaluate()** accepts as arguments the parameter **cmd_type** which comprises a mnemonic representation of RQL statements that initiate a query, e.g. **select, project, group**; a pointer to the dispatch table array (**dispatch**); and the total number of entries in the table (**cmd_cnt**). The integer **cmd_type** contains the mnemonic representation of the token currently read from the terminal. The function **evaluate()** starts execution by searching the dispatch table to locate the parsing function which corresponds to the current token. Eventually, this function returns the output value produced by the invoked parsing function as its own return value as well. If no match is found, an error is reported. Function **evaluate()** performs a linear table search. However, if the table is larger a more sophisticated algorithm such as binary search can be used provided that the table is alphabetically sorted.

As already explained, the user communicates with REQUIEM interactively. During this interaction it is highly unlikely that the same query statement will be requested many times during a session. In general, different statements are entered so that it does not seem feasible to compile a query and produce machine code. Rather, an interpretative approach is adopted: no code is generated, instead a C function is executed as soon as its corresponding operation has been identified. This function is then responsible for parsing the remainder of the query.

The main parser routine **parse()** is usually invoked when a sequence of new tokens appears on the terminal. Then the first token of the input statement is requested via the lexical analyzer function **next_token()**.

Alternatively if the parser is called with a command-line argument it initializes the lexical analyzer environment by invoking the function **scan()** (for a more in-depth discussion of the various input sources of REQUIEM see Chapter 7). According to the type of the recognized token, the C function that implements the corresponding operation is called. This function is then responsible for parsing the remaining source statement whenever it requires additional information. In the case where a token does not correspond to any legal RQL operation a syntax error is reported to the user and parsing is abandoned. In any case the invoked parsing function returns a value indicating whether the operation was successful or not. This value is stored in the variable **status** and is returned as the result of the function **parse()**.

The general structure of the parsing functions that are called by the parser after isolating the token identifying a RQL operation is succinctly outlined in the following:

1. Get a token from the source statement via lexical analyzer functions, usually the function **next_token()**.
2. Check the syntax and the semantics of the requested RQL operation by determining the type and the validity of the token identified.
3. Check whether a nested query has occurred. In this case, the nested query is processed prior to parsing the outer query.
4. Whenever an error has occurred, stop processing and inform the user.
5. Perform the required operation and return a value indicating whether the operation has been performed successfully or not.

In this chapter we have shown how the parser examines the symbols returned from the lexical analyzer and translates sequences of tokens into calls to procedures. In the following chapter we will analytically describe how the query-specific functions (parsing functions) invoked by the REQUIEM syntax analyzer are used to implement the various RQL operations.

9

Implementation of Relational Operators

In the present chapter we will cover those aspects of REQUIEM dealing with the implementation of the conceptual level. This is the level where queries are posed. The function of this level is to ascertain what the user wishes retrieved and the conditions on which this retrieval is to be based. This level tries to map the user's initial query to low-level functions which will eventually fetch the actual data objects in the database and deliver them to the query decomposer functions. These functions then perform tests to decide which, if any, are the tuples to be retrieved.

9.1   The REQUIEM data language

As already explained, REQUIEM supports a single relational data language, RQL. The function of RQL is to support the definition, manipulation, and control of data in a relational database system. In fact, it is customary that relational data languages unify the functions of definition, manipulation, and control of the database into a single language. Remember from Chapter 3 that RQL operations that define and manipulate data in the form of tables can be arranged in terms of two separate sublanguages: the data definition language (DDL) and the data manipulation language (DML).

It is clearly desirable for architectural purposes to mix the processing of data description and data manipulation so as to make them indistinguishable. However, we believe that for educational purposes it is convenient to distinguish between the functions of the DDL and DML. And one word of caution: notice that in this text we normally do not distinguish between the terms "query language" and "DML". Rather, we use them interchangeably.

Although the term query language suggests retrieval only in the database field, query languages provide **insert, delete,** and **update** operations as well.

As previously explained, users of an already existing database interrogate, update, and manipulate the database objects by means of the data manipulation language. The DML provides operations which allow a user to pose queries to the contents of the database. Hence, the user is allowed to access the information stored in relations and to combine information of different relations. Additionally, the user can change the database content by inserting, deleting, or changing individual tuples belonging to a specific relation. The complete set of the RQL data manipulation functions is shown in Figure 9.1.

delete(), difference(), c_expose(), insert(), intersect(), join(), c_project(), c_select(), c_union(), update()

Figure 9.1 The REQUIEM DML.

The data manipulation language can be implemented as an independent dialog language. In this case the user can query the database by entering queries directly via a terminal. The query is then parsed by the DBMS and executed immediately. The result of the query can then be displayed on the terminal screen or can be used for posing further queries. Alternatively, DML statements can be embedded into a host language (for example C or Pascal). Programs written in that language are permitted to use specific DML commands (for example special DML procedures) to access or modify the database contents, as stated in Chapter 1.

assign(), count(), display(), exit(), export(), extract(), focus(), help(), import(), print(), quit(), view_show()

Figure 9.2 The REQUIEM auxiliary functions.

In RQL, we additionally provide a set of auxiliary functions. These functions are meant to display different kinds of information on the terminal screen. For example, **extract()** extracts a relation definition from a relation file and displays it on the terminal screen. The auxiliary function **help()** is provided to display on-line help information about all legal commands and their syntactic structure to the user. Finally, the functions **quit()** and **exit()** are provided to allow a user to leave REQUIEM. The complete listing of auxiliary functions is assembled in Figure 9.2.

9.2   The RQL data definition operators

REQUIEM incorporates certain instructions in its DDL portion which make
it possible to specify how this data is to be stored on disk storage devices, as
well as how this data is to be accessed and retrieved for processing purposes.
This correspondence between the conceptual and the physical scheme of a
database is more or less integrated into the DDL portion in most relational
DBMSs. Independently of the actual system being used, it will be necessary
at some point to specify these correspondences which are, of course, highly
system-specific. Moreover, the development of an external schema is carried
out using the same DDL functions as were used for the conceptual schema.
From REQUIEM's standpoint the principal DDL parsing functions are as
follows:

1. **create** creates a new relation and inserts its definition into the system
   catalogs.
2. **define** defines a view.
3. **modify** modifies an already existing relation definition.
4. **drop** drops a view definition.
5. **purge** purges a complete relation definition.

As the functions **view_define()** and **drop()** pertain to the external system
level we defer their description to Chapter 12 which deals with implementation of the external system level.

Function **create()** is the subject of the present section. Consider the
suppliers-and-products database definition as depicted in Figure 2.1. This
figure illustrates the structure of the database; in other words it indicates
how the relations in the database may be defined using the RQL data definition statements. It is not our purpose to describe the semantics of the
create statement in detail at this stage. A detailed description of this statement was given in Chapter 3. However, a point that needs to be stressed
right at the outset is that the RQL **create** statement is executed as soon as
it is encountered (actually this is the case with all the RQL statements as
you will see later in this book). If all three **create** statements in section 3.2.1
were entered at a user's terminal, REQUIEM would immediately build the
three relation headers depicted in that section. What actually happens is
that REQUIEM creates two files; a data and an index file for each relation.
Initially, these relations will be empty, which means that the file headers
of the corresponding files contain descriptions of the attribute constituents
of the relations as well as descriptions of the indexed attributes but they
contain no data tuples or index entries at all. However, corresponding entries are recorded in the system catalogs as a result of execution of these

consecutive **create** statements.

Consider the parsing function **create()** now. This parsing function is responsible for triggering the creation of a new relation and is called as soon as the parser encounters the token **CREATE**. Recall that relation definition is comprised of one or more *attribute definition* statements. Each such attribute definition row contains three items: an attribute name, a data type for the attribute, and (optionally) a key specification for this attribute. The attribute name must obviously be unique within the relation. The precise syntax of the **create** statement in BNF notation is as follows:

```
<create-stat> ::= create <relname>
                  (<attr-def>{,<attr-def>});
<attr-def>    ::= <attr_name> ( CHAR | NUM | REAL( <size> )
                  [ , <key-spec> ] )
```

The creation of a relation starts by recording the length of the relation name entered by the user. If this length is acceptable (not longer than that indicated by the value of the constant RNSIZE defined in file **requ.h**) the relation name is stored in the local variable **rname**. A call to the function **rc_create()** results in the creation and initialization of a new relation structure for the corresponding relation. Recall that in Chapter 4 we explained that a relation structure holds information concerning a relation that is utilized during tuple accessing. Remember that a relation structure incorporates a relation header structure which is used to describe the contents of a relation data file and contains permanent data that is stored on the disk between successive uses of this file. Such permanent data includes the attribute names, types, lengths, relation key types, etc. Actually, the function **rc_create()** returns the address of the created relation structure which is then pointed to by the variable **rptr** that is local to function **create()**.

Upon return from the function **rc_create()** parsing in the body of function **create()** continues according to the syntax of the above expression by assembling information concerning the attribute definition rows of the relation to be created. As you can probably see from the parser listing 5, the **create()** module is built around an endless iteration (**while(TRUE)**) loop which steps down from attribute definition to attribute definition until the entire list (array) of attribute definitions for a given relation has been consumed. The loop exits when we reach the rightmost parenthesis of the **create** statement, indicating, thus, that the parsing of this statement was successful.

Each attribute definition starts with specifying the name of its corresponding attribute. Subsequently, the length of the attribute name is checked against the constant ANSIZE and is stored in the local variable **aname**. Next, the attribute type is determined. The type specification must conform to one of the following predefined types: CHAR for a string type, NUM for an integer number, and REAL for a real number. After the type of the attribute has been stored in the local variable atype, the actual size of the attribute is estimated. Now that the size definition has been parsed an optional list of key specifications can follow. Initially, it is assumed that no key value is specified: the variable key which is local to create() is assigned the value "n" indicating that the present attribute represents no key attribute for the created relation.

To determine whether an index has been specified we call the indexing function chk_key_defs(). If the specified index is **unique**, this function turns on the header file flag hd_unique to indicate that a unique (primary) key for the underlying relation has been specified. Eventually, the function chk_key_defs() invokes the function ix_attr() to insert an indexed attribute entry in the B$^+$-tree associated with the created relation.

Each time that the parsing of an attribute definition row is syntactically correct we call function add_attr() to add a new attribute structure within the retrieval context associated with a given relation. This function also ascertains that no attribute having an identical name with the currently handled attribute has already been specified in the body of the created relation. It makes sure that the current total number of attributes for the present relation does not exceed the permitted REQUIEM limit. Recall that the attribute list for a particular relation is stored within its relation structure. After the attribute definition row has been parsed and its corresponding definition data has been inserted into the appropriate attribute list element, the total size of the tuple is augmented by the byte size of the newly created attribute.

Parsing continues until the attribute definition process concludes. This is indicated by a closing parenthesis and a semicolon. At this stage the process of relation creation must terminate. This is achieved by issuing a call to function cre_finish(). This function invokes the function rc_header() whose prime purpose is to materialize the relation file. Function rc_header() opens a new relation data file for the newly created relations. Along with the name of the relation to be created we must also specify some status flags that influence the mode of operation, i.e. whether the data file underlying a created relation is to be opened for reading, writing, or both reading and writing. An additional argument must also be provided specifying the type of file *access permissions*. Normally in REQUIEM all relation files are readable and writable only by the person who created them. You can, of course, alter the file access permissions to suit the application that you have in mind.

Function rc_header() also makes sure that the relation file of an already declared relation is not overwritten. After creating the data file underlying the defined relation this function next creates the index file corresponding to the created relation. It then writes the entire file header to the disk, and returns control to function cre_finish() which closes both relation files, terminating, thus, the process of relation creation.

As a final processing step in function create(), information pertaining to the newly created relation and its attributes must be made accessible to the DBMS. For this reason appropriate entries describing the created relation are made in the system catalogs. This task is accomplished by a call to the function cat_entry(). In an analogous manner function create() forwards a message to the user informing him about the successful creation of a new relation.

Notice that in our previous description we have deliberately avoided commenting on the parsing of a **reference** clause as its implementation was outlined in Chapter 6 which delineated concepts dealing with the materialization of the internal level of REQUIEM.

The fact that the RQL DDL statements can be executed at any time during the lifetime of a given database makes REQUIEM a very flexible system. Actually this part of REQUIEM follows the guidelines of such large systems as System R [2]. In more conventional medium scale systems the process of data definition is performed once and for all before commencing with the loading and the utilization of the database [3]. In such systems adding a new type of object into the database can be a very complicated issue involving the execution of some utility first to bring the entire system to a standstill and then to record the modified database definition. Obviously, this procedure requires the dumping and restoring of a substantial portion of the entire database, if not all of it. Contrary to this, in REQUIEM it is possible to create a few relations, insert the appropriate tuples, and then start using them immediately. It is also possible to add new relations or even new attributes in a piecemeal manner, without having to adjust any existing applications.

9.3   The RQL data manipulation operators

In this section we will proceed by describing three important DML parsing functions namely select(), join(), and project(). These operators were chosen because they illustrate some important points about implementing relational operators. In particular, the reasons for presenting these specific functions can be summarized in the following:

1. **select()** is one of the most basic DML parsing functions.
2. **join()** is an example of a rather complex parsing function involving several function calls to functions that are dispersed between three REQUIEM files, namely **parser.c**, **impl.c**, and **access.c**.
3. **project()** is an example of a parsing function that uses the REQUIEM hashing mechanism for generating a resulting relation.

9.3.1 Implementation of selection and join operations

The function **select()** offers the basic selection mechanism for REQUIEM. Its implementation is rather complex, because it mixes the implementation of two relational operators, namely **join** and **select**. These two related implementation algorithms interweave somehow throughout this section. The obvious and concrete topic is the way to implement **select** or **join** statements.

In REQUIEM only a single **join** operator is implemented, the natural join. The natural join in REQUIEM is specified in terms of two relations, called the *join relations*, and two semantically equivalent attributes belonging to respective join relations, the *join condition attributes*. The resulting relation consists of the total set of attributes in both relations, excluding any duplicate attributes. As the algorithm which implements **join** queries has a more general structure than the algorithm implementing query selection, we shall focus on the implementation aspects of the former algorithm.

The kind of **join** operation that we will describe in the present section assumes that no indices are involved in the join condition and is based on an algorithm called the nested loop join algorithm [17],[39]. The nested loop join is a value-based **join** operation that relies on using an iteration loop to call the first join relation data and fetch each of its tuples in turn; each time around the loop it calls the second join relation data file tuple with the key required to match the already fetched first relation tuple. Tuples having matching values in their join condition attributes are concatenated by eliminating one of the two identical attributes (preferably that of the second join relation as you will shortly see). As natural join is probably the single most useful form of join, in RQL we use the unqualified term join to refer to this particular operation.

The syntax of a **join** statement is as follows:

join $<rel_1>$ **on** $<attr_{1,i}>$
    with $<rel_2>$ **on** $<attr_{2,j}>$ [$<predicate>$];

where each **join** attribute can be represented by a pair $attr_{i,j}$ – i being the value that selects a relation and j being the value that selects an attribute within this relation. In REQUIEM we can internally implement a **join** operation in terms of a **select** operation. The former REQUIEM statement can, thus, be mapped to the following equivalent **select** construct:

select from $<rel_1>$, $<rel_2>$
    where $<rel_1.attr_{1,i}>$ = $<rel_2.attr_{2,j}>$;

In fact REQUIEM interprets each **join** statement by using the above-mentioned equivalent **select** construct. Actually, this operation is hidden from the users and the previous **select** clause is not a valid RQL statement for users!

Function **nat_join()** is primarily responsible for the parsing of **join** statements. As you will see later in this section, this function is designed to work in conjunction with the function **select()** which implements tuple selection. During the process of joining relations function **nat_join()** invokes the function **joined()**. This function is supplied with the appropriate arguments that convey information obtained during the process of parsing the **join** statement. The function simply consults its actual parameters and converts the **join** statement into a semantically equivalent **selection** statement. It then calls the parser once again to parse the resultant **select** statement, like the one described previously. Once the execution of this **select** statement has terminated, a transient relation, called *snapshot*, is generated. In REQUIEM snapshots convey the results of a successful query. Remember that operations in RQL obey the property of closure, meaning that the execution of normal DML operation will always result in a new snapshot relation.

A number of interesting points arise in connection with the parsing **select** and **join** clauses which eventually both have to be implemented by the same function, namely **select()**. We can distinguish between the following three cases during the implementation of **select** and **join** operators:

1. No indexing construct has been specified for the **select** clause predicate or the **join** condition attributes.
2. One or more indices have been specified for attributes involved in the predicate of the **select** clause; furthermore, this clause is a pure **select** clause, meaning that no **join** operation has been previously specified.
3. The join condition attributes are indexed.

As the function **select()** has to implement both **select** and **join** queries its internal structure is somewhat more complex than that of the functions that we have previously introduced. We will start by delineating the implementation concepts underlying the **join** operator which is far too complex when compared to the **select** operator.

Besides selecting given attributes from a set of relations, function **select()** must additionally ensure that in the case of a **join** statement the attributes of both **join** relations are collectively used in creating the resulting snapshot relation. Additionally, care must be taken that the snapshot includes no duplicate attributes and that only those tuples satisfying the **join** predicate are part of the snapshot relation. Furthermore, the **join** algorithm must also determine whether one or both the **join** condition attributes are indexed or not.

Before starting with the investigation of the **join** operations that include non-indexed join condition attributes, let us first see how the attributes which are eventually to be entered in the snapshot relation are retrieved from the two join relations. Initially, the function **select()** calls the routine **new_relation()** to create a new snapshot relation structure. The address of this new snapshot relation structure allocated by **new_relation()** is finally returned to function **select()**. Subsequently, to add the non-duplicate attributes to the attribute list of the snapshot, **select()** invokes the function **add_selattrs()**. This function is responsible for attribute insertion in a relation file and returns the number of indexed attributes involved in the **join** operation. Function **add_selattrs()** performs the following tasks:

1. It determines the key types of both **join** condition attributes; these key types are then stored in the character array **join_keys**. This array holds only two character elements specifying the type of the keys involved in the join predicate. Recall that a character "n" denotes a non-indexed attribute, a character "s" denotes an secondary index, and finally a character "p" denotes a primary index.
2. It confirms whether the resultant relation structure would accommodate any duplicate attributes, and if so it isolates them and stores them in the string array **duplc_attr** that is supplied by its calling function.

When entering this function the key array **join_keys** is initialized to "n" to indicate that none of the **join** condition attributes is indexed. Then the function loops repeatedly over the attribute structures of both **join** relations in the retrieval context. Next, **add_selattrs()** senses the character pointer **join_on** to decide whether any join condition attributes exist. This **join** specific pointer is set during parsing to indicate that a **join** operation is in progress. In this case, **join_on** points to the names of the indexed **join** condition attributes. Alternatively, if **join_on** points to NULL then no **join** condition attributes are present and this implies that the requested operation is actually a **select** and not a **join** operation.

As the snapshot file which will be the product of a **join** query contains the entire relation header part of the first **join** relation, care must be taken that the attribute names of this **join** relation are kept available for inspection. Consequently, these attribute names are stored in the buffer array joined_attr for later use. Subsequently, the function **add_selattrs()** determines if any entries in the string array joined_attr coincide with the names of the attributes of the second **join** relation. Next, all the duplicate attribute names, if any, are accumulated in a buffer called duplc_attr. Moreover, the types of the indexed **join** condition attributes are checked and inserted into the two dimensional character array join_keys. The array entry join_keys[0][0] contains the key type associated with the **join** condition attribute of the first **join** relation, while the array entry join_keys[1][0] contains the key type associated with the **join** condition attribute of the second **join** relation.

If no duplicate attribute names are encountered during the processing of the nested loop join then all snapshot tuples resulting from the concatenation of the tuples of the two joined relations must be inserted in the resulting snapshot file. This means that the flag **entry** which is local to **add_selattrs()** must be turned on to designate that only the appropriate attribute names must be inserted into the snapshot relation. If any duplicate attribute names are pinpointed in the second **join** relation then the **entry** flag must be turned off indicating, thus, that attribute names matching the ones held in duplc_attr are not to be reinserted into the snapshot relation. These attributes will have integrity tests performed on their values. By means of this method it is guaranteed that only non-duplicate attribute names from both **join** relations are inserted into the attribute structure array pointed to the snapshot relation structure.

After processing all the **join** relation attributes, the snapshot relation header is created by a call to function **rc_header()** exactly as explained in the case of the RQL **create** statement. Notice that the snapshot relation in REQUIEM comprises a pure data file and not a combination of an index and a data file. Finally, the function **add_selattrs()** returns the total number of the indexed joined condition attributes to its calling function, namely the parsing function **select()**.

If the requested **join** operation involves at least one indexed **join** condition attribute, function **join_ix()** is called as explained in Chapter 6. This function is responsible for making the appropriate B^+-tree entries and building the tuples of the snapshot relation. In the case of a **join** operation where none of the **join** condition attributes is indexed, function **select()** invokes the function **do_join()**. This function loops repeatedly over the selected attributes of both **join** relations and copies the values of their corresponding attributes into its tuple buffer (**tbuf**) argument. During this procedure, care must be taken when duplicate attributes are involved in the **join** query that their values are identical.

On entering the function do_join() we allocate a local buffer (buff) capable of storing the values of all existing duplicate attributes. Subsequently, we proceed by executing an iteration statement which fetches each individual attribute structure contained in the current retrieval context of both **join** relations. We term this kind of loop the *fetch loop*. If an attribute belonging to the first relation is accessed, it must be determined whether it matches one of the duplicate attributes that are already stored in the buffer duplc_attr or not. If this test is successful, the value of this specific attribute is stored in the appropriate position in the local buffer buff. In this way a duplicate attribute value can be compared with the value of its matching counterpart when the second **join** relation will be processed. All the attributes that pass this consistency test have their values copied into the appropriate location in the tuple buffer (tbuf) which is passed as argument to function do_join(). Note that REQUIEM assumes quite plausibly that when two attributes which belong to different **join** relations have identical names they must also have identical values in order to be included in the final snapshot relation.

If the comparison of duplicate attribute values fails to report identical values to the function do_join(), no snapshot tuple is constructed. By contrast, if the two compared values happen to be identical the value of the attribute of the second **join** relation should not be copied into the tuple buffer once again as the snapshot relation must contain only non-duplicate attribute values. When the entire list of selected attributes is exhausted the function terminates processing by returning the value TRUE to its calling function to indicate that a valid tuple has been generated. The function select() then continues execution by calling fetch() to retrieve the remaining tuples in both **join** relations and repeats the same procedure all over again until the entire tuple lists in both the joined relations have been exhausted. Finally, the function select() writes the snapshot tuples to the snapshot file on the disk and forwards an output message to the user reporting the total number of snapshot tuples generated.

In conclusion, what remains to be delineated is the processing of **select** statements. We shall outline only the implementation aspects of **select** clauses which involve no indexing operations as access_plan(), the main indexing function for **select** queries, was covered in Chapter 6. If a simple **select** operation is in progress, a fetch loop over the individual elements of the array of attribute structures of the retrieval context is performed, thereby accumulating all individual attribute values into the tuple buffer tbuf. Actually, individual attribute values are successively stored in the tuple buffer in the same sequence as they arrive from the array of attribute structures where they were originally stored. After the termination of this attribute value storing process the contents of the tuple buffer are written to the snapshot file by a call to the file manager function **write_tuple()**. Care must be taken when dimensioning the tuple buffer to ensure that enough space is reserved to hold the attribute values of the entire tuple.

In retrospect, function **select()** fully demonstrates the implementation features of **join** and **select** queries, and shows how they naturally fit into the overall structure of the REQUIEM data manipulation scheme.

9.3.2   Implementation of projection operations

In the following we will concentrate on the description of another important function, the function **project()**. This function is directly associated with projection operations; in fact its source code parallels that of the function **select()** when no indexing is utilized. In REQUIEM the **project** operator practically reduces the total number of attributes in a relation. The projection operation accepts as input a single relation whose name we shall denote by the placeholder *<relation_name>*. The construct *<relation_name>* can either represent a single relation or the result of a relational expression, in which case the relational expression must be delimited by parentheses. The operation **project** is denoted by:

project *<relation_name>*
     over *<list-of-attributes>* [*predicate*];

All the names encountered in the list of attribute names that follow the keyword **over** must be of attributes of *<relation_name>*. Such attributes are called the *projection attributes* in the REQUIEM terminology. The selection predicate that may be associated with the **project** operation, as in the case of **select**, can only pertain to individual tuples. The result of this **project** operation can be obtained by the following:

1. Disregarding all the *<relation_name>* attributes that are not included in the list of attribute names.
2. Eliminating from the previous result all redundant duplicate tuples so that in the final result no two tuples are identical.

At first glance a projection might seem to be a rather straightforward operation in comparison with a **join** operation. However, implementation of the projection algorithm deserves some commenting as it involves the removal of any duplicate tuples that may arise in the resultant relation. A projection in REQUIEM is performed by first creating a snapshot relation that consists solely of those attributes that are listed in the projection statement. In REQUIEM the projection operator corresponds closely to programs that extract a selected set of records (tuples) from an input table and prints particular fields (attributes) from each record. As previously stated, the projection operation can also be combined with a selection predicate, if this is requested. In this case both operations are processed in a single pass through the projected relation file. As the projection algorithm makes heavy use of hashing techniques we consider it more practical to start with the description of the hashing methodology in REQUIEM before embarking on the idiosyncrasies of the projection algorithm.

As previously stressed, one of the main reasons for choosing to describe the implementation of the **project** statement in the present chapter is that we can use it as a vehicle to illustrate the use of hashing techniques for handling duplicate tuple occurrences. We will not describe hashing in detail as this technique for random access is well known. Readers who are interested can obtain more information from [16], [48], [49]. In this section we will provide only a short overview of the hashing mechanism as used in REQUIEM.

```
struct hash {
    char      *value;        /* hash key value to be hashed */
    char      *relation;     /* relation token  */
    int       dup_tcnt;      /* number of duplicate entries */
    double    aggr_param;    /* aggregate function parameter */
};
```

Figure 9.3 A hash table entry.

The function of hashing is to simulate an associative memory without demanding that the hash table is actually sorted. In general, this technique is much faster and much more efficient than any other technique for doing so; for example, the binary search technique which assumes a sorted table. In REQUIEM the hash table is implemented as an array of fixed size. The size of the hash table must be a prime number to obtain better performance ratios. The entries in the hash table consist of four components (see Figure 9.3): the actual token value to be stored (the hash key), an occurrence counter that registers the number of occurrences of its associated hash key (**dup_tcnt**); the name of the relation from which the hash key emanates; and finally the value of the aggregate attribute computed so far for grouping operations. This particular arrangement suggests that hashing in REQUIEM is primarily used for the implementation of projection and grouping operations.

The REQUIEM hashing scheme converts the entire character string contents of a tuple by means of a *hashing function* into a *hash key*, or access key, for the entire tuple. The purpose of the hashing function is to give a good distribution to hash keys so that they can be uniformly scattered through the slots (entries in the sense of Figure 9.3) in the hash table. All slots in the hash table have room for a single hash key and all hash keys corresponding to the projected tuples must eventually be stored in one of these slots. When the hash keys of the projected tuples hash to the same value, a *collision* has occurred. If the contents of the colliding tuples are identical, a tuple has been duplicated, thus we increase the content duplicate tuple counter (**dup_tcnt**) associated with this specific entry, see Figure 9.3. If the collision happened because the hash keys of different tuples coincidentally collided in the hash table we use a *probe strategy* to resolve this situation. The probe strategy in the REQUIEM hashing scheme defines a sequence of probes that have to be made into the hash table until an empty slot is found into which the tuple entry is stored. Finally, the function **write_hash()** writes the contents of the hash table into a snapshot relation file after having appropriately processed the contents of each separate hash entry (slot) eliminating, thus, all duplicate projected tuples.

Now we will take a closer look at the main projection function, namely the function **project()**. In REQUIEM the function **project()** is called whenever the parser detects the presence of the token **project** in the input stream. This token signifies that the user requests the projection of a specified input relation over a set of given attributes. Parsing of **project** statements starts with the parser invoking the internal retrieval clause which, as we shall see in the next chapter, is normally associated with projection operations. This is accomplished by a call to the function **retrieve()** of the query decomposer which generates a snapshot relation and assigns the address of the selection (**sel**) structure associated with this snapshot to the local pointer **slptr**. More information on the implementation of this function can be found in the next chapter. What really matters at this stage is that the resultant snapshot relation contains the definition of the projected attributes assembled after a call to the function **create_attrs()**. Next, the selected tuples of the projected relation must be accessed and the values of the selected attributes must be stored in the snapshot relation. During this process, caution must be exercised so that no duplicate tuples are stored in the snapshot. Duplicate tuples can be generated if none of the projected attributes is a discriminating key attribute for the input relation. In this case, it might be possible that the collective values of the projection attributes appear more than once in the final relation.

If no indexing is involved in the predicate, a fetch loop over all the selected tuples must be performed. During each pass, a new tuple for the resultant relation is created from the values of the projection attributes by simply copying and concatenating them into the tuple buffer, exactly as in the case of the **select** and **join** operators. After this buffer has been filled, its corresponding tuple can be stored in the snapshot provided that it is a unique tuple for the resultant relation. The mechanism employed for this purpose is fairly simple and it naturally involves hashing. The central idea is to try to place the contents of the tuple buffer in the hash table. As previously explained, the hashing method informs us whether an element having a value identical to that of the tuple buffer has already been installed in the hash table. If so, the corresponding relation tuple is a duplicate tuple and must be discarded, otherwise the contents of the tuple buffer must be written to the snapshot file.

In general, the projection and grouping algorithms demand that the contents of the tuple buffer, which temporarily holds the resultant tuples on a one at a time basis, are hashed before any writing to the snapshot file takes place. By hashing the contents of the tuple buffer, measures are taken against entering the same tuple twice in the snapshot. Rather, the contents of the occurrence counter are incremented to indicate the presence of a duplicate tuple.

Duplicate tuple elimination is always associated with calls to function **db_hsplace()**. This function is called by the parsing function **project()**; **db_hsplace()** in turn invokes the hashing function **db_hash()** in order to attempt to insert the contents of the tuple buffer into the hash table. If the contents of the tuple buffer match those of an entry in the hash table, a successful termination is designated to the calling function. By interpreting this information the calling function (**db_hash()**) understands that a tuple having the same contents with those of the tuple buffer has already been written to the snapshot file. Consequently, this tuple is a duplicate tuple and its contents must be discarded. Conversely, when the actual tuple is unique, function **db_hash()** returns the value FALSE meaning that this tuple should be eventually written to the snapshot file.

Finally, if a project operator is associated with indexed predicate attributes the standard indexing function **access_plan()** is called to implement any further processing steps. Implementation then proceeds according to section 9.3.1 and Chapter 6.

9.3.3   Implementation of group operations

As you probably noticed in Chapter 3, the token PROJECT can also identify queries that require the rearrangement of the input relation into logical portions or *groups*. A group definition is introduced by the keywords **group by** and consists of a *grouping attribute* and an *aggregate attribute* that serves as a parameter of the *aggregate* function.

Example 9.3.1

Assume that we wish to interrogate the suppliers-and-products database to find out the total quantities of products that each supplier supplies. Here, the grouping attribute is clearly SUPID, while the aggregate attribute is QUAN-TITY. On the other hand, the aggregate function is obviously the system-defined function sum(). *A possible formulation for the above query is:*

project supply
          over supid, quantity
                    group by supid **sum**(quantity);

The aggregate function **sum**() is actually called, for all tuples in the input relation with two parameters, one explicit and one implicit. The explicit parameter of the aggregate function is the actual value of the aggregate parameter, e.g. *QUANTITY*, while the implicit value is the value calculated by any previous invocations of this aggregate function. It is assumed that the relation *SUPPLY* tuples have previously been grouped together as indicated by the value of the grouping attribute prior to the invocation of the aggregate function. Notice that each expression in the project statement must be double valued, that is, it must contain the grouping attribute name followed by the aggregate attribute name.

In general, the **group by** operation behaves very much like a **project** operation which allows us to define a new relation containing a single extra attribute, the aggregate attribute. The semantics of the **group by** operation are as follows:

1. It first partitions the values in the given grouping attributes into related subsets based on them all having the same value for the grouping attribute.
2. It then projects the relation over the grouping attribute. However, it computes a derived value by applying the aggregate function to the appropriate field of each tuple to be inserted in the resultant snapshot relation.
3. It finally places this value in an extra attribute, the aggregate attribute.

Obviously, the resulting snapshot relation contains only two attributes: the grouping attribute and the aggregate attribute (see Figure 9.4).

INVOICE_ID	CUSTOMER_ID	TERM_OF_PAYMENT	AMOUNT
I-628	C-2346	6/30/1989	2,689
I-835	C-9716	5/15/1989	7,500
I-883	C-1356	5/20/1989	2,000
I-924	C-2869	6/20/1989	5,000
I-926	C-1356	6/20/1989	1,500
I-930	C-1356	6/25/1989	3,000
I-935	C-2346	6/25/1989	2,000
I-936	C-1356	6/25/1989	2,500
I-937	C-9716	6/25/1989	3,500
I-938	C-9716	6/25/1989	6,000
I-939	C-2346	6/25/1989	2,500
I-940	C-1356	7/05/1989	1,000
I-946	C-1356	7/05/1989	4,000
I-956	C-9716	7/15/1989	4,500
I-958	C-9716	7/20/1989	7,000
I-960	C-2346	8/05/1989	6,500
I-966	C-9716	8/10/1989	1,500
I-988	C-1356	8/30/1989	1,000

CUSTOMER_ID	SUM_AMOUNT
C-1356	15,000
C-2346	13,689
C-2869	5,000
C-9716	30,000

Figure 9.4 The INVOICE relation, and the result of the group statement mentioned in the text.

Example 9.3.2

The next RQL statement partitions a relation called INVOICE into groups in terms of the grouping attribute CUSTOMER_ID.

project invoice
      over customer_id, amount
         group by customer_id **sum**(amount);

As is illustrated in Figure 9.4, each customer is represented by a unique *CUSTOMER_ID* and can have more than one pending invoice. Actually, both *CUSTOMER_ID* and *INVOICE_ID*, which is used to represent invoices, are foreign keys. The **group** statement allows the user to generate a relation which records the total amount of debts that each customer owes. Moreover, we can formulate a predicate so that only those customers whose sum of unpaid invoices exceeds a given amount may appear in the resultant group relation.

Let us now discuss the grouping mechanism of REQUIEM in some detail. The grouping mechanism is always introduced if the keyword **group** is encountered in a projection statement. As a result the function **group()** is called to implement the actual grouping operation. In this function parsing continues until the grouping attribute involved in the query is identified. Following that, a new snapshot relation is created together with its corresponding relation header, exactly as explained in a previous section. At this stage, the hash table is initialized by a call to the function **init_hash()**. Next, we proceed by checking if the first projection attribute matches the grouping attribute. Following this, a check is performed to detect the nature of the next token in the input sequence. Obviously, this token can only introduce either a predicate expression or an aggregate function.

If a predicate expression is identified the type of the aggregate function is preserved in the local variable tkn and parsing continues with the deciphering of the aggregate attribute that is delimited by parentheses. The name of this aggregate attribute is finally assigned to the variable **aggr_attr**. After that, we identify the aggregate function met in the input query by deciphering the token type stored in the variable tkn. Consequently, a pointer to the currently identified aggregate function is stored in the function pointer **funptr** which eventually invokes the appropriate built-in aggregate function. The previous description can be realized by means of the following program fragment:

```
/* determine the type of aggregate function &
                          set-up the appropriate function call */
  switch(tkn) {
   case AVG:
     funptr = average;
     strcpy(format, "avg_");
     break;

   case COUNT:
     funptr = count;
     strcpy(format, "cnt_");
     break;

      . . . . . . .

   case SUM:
     funptr = sum;
     strcpy(format, "sum_");
     break;
   default:
     return(error(SYNTAX));
  }
```

The selected tuples of the original relation are successively accessed by means of a fetch loop that retrieves the tuples from the relation data file. Next a syntactic test is made to determine whether the name of the specified aggregate function parameter, e.g. *AMOUNT* in example 9.3.2, and the name of the second projection attribute really correlate. Each time around the fetch loop a snapshot relation tuple is formed by combining the values of the projection attributes contained in the currently fetched data tuple. This is a two step process. First, the value of the first projection attribute, namely the value of grouping attribute *CUSTOMER_ID*, is copied into the buffer **partition**. Next, the value of the second projection attribute, namely the aggregate attribute *AMOUNT*, is copied into the auxiliary buffer **aux_tbuf**. This value must obviously be a numerical value; but like all REQUIEM data, regardless of data type, it is stored under its character representation. Then, the hash file function **db_hash()** is called to insert the value of the grouping attribute and the value of the aggregate attribute into the hash table. If a corresponding entry already exists there, the specified aggregate function (e.g. **sum()**) must be applied to the value of the aggregate attribute of this entry (e.g. *AMOUNT*). Subsequently, the aggregate component of the current hash entry, namely the component **aggr_param** (see Figure 9.3), is replaced by the value obtained after the application of the aggregate function.

Example 9.3.3

To understand the above implementation aspects more clearly consider the definition of the aggregate function **sum()** *that sums up the values of its two input parameters.*

The code implementation of this function looks as follows:

```
double sum(arg1, arg2)
  double arg1, arg2;
{
  return(arg1 + arg2);
} /* sum */
```

This function when called to group customer identification numbers and add up pending invoice sums will obtain the following values as actual parameters:

sum(amount, Hash_Table[HTIndex].aggr_param);

where amount is the numerical value of the sum due for the current invoice, while aggr_param stores the total amount of money that the current customer owes. Obviously, the contents of these two actual parameters must be added with the result forming the new value of the variable aggr_param.

When all tuples of the original relation have been processed, we store them in the snapshot relation file header. The entries in the hash table correspond to the tuples of the group snapshot file. Finally, function write_hash() is invoked to sort the hash table and eventually permanently transfer the resulting group tuples from the hash table to the snapshot file. Accordingly, a tuple is stored for each individual entry contained in the hash table.

If during the parsing of the present group clause a where subclause was encountered, the corresponding comparison operator must be determined and the appropriate operation must be applied before leaving the fetch loop. Consequently, the appropriate comparison operation associated with the aggregate attribute of the predicate is applied after a call to the function eval_tkn(). As a last step, the resulting tuples will be written to the snapshot file, exactly as previously explained, by invoking the function write_hash(). When all tuples have been stored on the disk, function write_hash() returns to its calling function, namely the function group(). To conclude with the process of grouping, group() frees the space occupied by the retrieval context data structures associated with the current grouping operation and forwards an appropriate message to the user.

9.4   Source listing 5

file: parser.c

```
1    /* REQUIEM - command parser */
2
3    #include <stdio.h>
4    #include "requ.h"
5    #include "btree.h"
6
7    extern int     lex_token;
8    extern char    lexeme[];
9    extern int     saved_ch;
10   extern float   lex_value;
11   extern int     xint_error;        /* interpretation error */
12   extern char    errvar[];          /* error  variable */
13   extern char    rel_fl[];
14   extern struct cmd_file *lex_cfp;   /* command file pointer */
15   extern struct ix_header *pixd;
16   extern struct hash **Hash_Table;
17   extern int     HTIndex;
18   extern BOOL    view_exists, restore_paren;
19   extern int     help(), db_import(), drop(), quit(),
```

```
20                    view_define(), view_show(), db_extract();
21    struct pred    *prptr = NULL;   /* predicate attribute bufr */
22    char           *join_on = NULL; /* name of join-attribute */
23    int            sref_cntr = 0;   /* snapshot reference counter */
24    int     assign(), s_count(), create(), difference(), delete(),
25            display(), export(), extract(), focus(), import(),
26            insert(), intersect(), modify(), print(), c_project(),
27            purge(), c_select(), terminator(), c_expose(), update(),
28            join(), c_union();
29    char    cformat[65];          /* print control format */
30    BOOL    no_print = FALSE;     /* print control flag */
31    BOOL    view_def = FALSE;     /* view definition control flag */
32
33    static struct command {    /* command parsing structure */
34      int  cmd_token;            /* token definition of command */
35      int  (*cmd_function)();    /* command function pointer */
36    } ;
37    static struct command despatch_table[] = {
38      { ASSIGN, assign },
39      { COUNT, s_count },
40      { CREATE, create },
41      { DEFINE, view_define },
42      { DELETE, delete },
43      { DIFFERENCE, difference },
44      { DISPLAY, display },
45      { DROP, drop},
46      { EXIT, quit },
47      { EXPORT, export },
48      { EXPOSE, c_expose },
49      { EXTRACT, extract },
50      { FOCUS, focus },
51      { HELP, help },
52      { IMPORT, import },
53      { INSERT, insert },
54      { INTERSECT, intersect },
55      { JOIN, join },
56      { MODIFY, modify },
57      { PRINT, print },
58      { PROJECT, c_project },
59      { PURGE, purge },
60      { QUIT, quit },
61      { SELECT, c_select },
62      { TERMINATOR, terminator },
63      { SHOW, view_show },
64      { UNION, c_union },
65      { UPDATE, update }
66    };
67
68    /* ------------------------------------------------------------ */
69
70    /* parse - parse a command */
71    int     parse(q_fmt, def_view)
72         char    *q_fmt;
73         BOOL    def_view;
74    {
75      BOOL    status;
76      int     c_type;
77
78      /* estimate the number of table entries */
79      int table_entries =
80        sizeof(despatch_table) / sizeof(struct command);
```

```
81
82        /* check for a command line */
83        if (q_fmt)
84          q_scan(q_fmt);
85
86        /* set view definition flag */
87        view_def = def_view;
88
89        /* determine the current statement type */
90        c_type = next_token();
91
92        /* find command and call the corresponding function */
93        status = evaluate(c_type, despatch_table, table_entries);
94
95        /* clear command line */
96        if (q_fmt)
97          cmd_kill();
98
99        /* free predicate attribute structure */
100       if (prptr)
101         free_pred(&prptr);
102
103       /* returns true or false from evaluation of parse routines */
104       return (status);
105     }
106
107     /* ------------------------------------------------------------ */
108
109     /* evaluate type of command and call parser function */
110     BOOL evaluate(cmd_type, despatch, cmd_cntr)
111         int cmd_type, cmd_cntr;
112         struct command despatch[];
113     {
114       struct command *cmd_ptr;
115       int func_res = FAIL;       /* result from a function call */
116
117       for (cmd_ptr = despatch;
118           cmd_ptr <= &despatch[cmd_cntr-1]; cmd_ptr++)
119
120         if (cmd_type == (*cmd_ptr).cmd_token) {
121           func_res = (*(*cmd_ptr).cmd_function)();
122           break;
123         }
124
125       if (func_res == FAIL)
126         return(error(SYNTAX));
127       else
128         return(func_res);
129
130     } /* evaluate */
131
132     /* ------------------------------------------------------------ */
133
134     static int difference()
135     {
136       return(db_union(FALSE, TRUE));
137     }
138
139     /* ------------------------------------------------------------ */
140
141     static int export()
```

```
142    {
143      return(db_export((char *) 0));
144    }
145
146    /* ------------------------------------------------------------ */
147
148    static int c_expose()
149    {
150      return(expose(no_print));
151    }
152
153    /* ------------------------------------------------------------ */
154
155    static int extract()
156    {
157      return(db_extract((char *) 0));
158    }
159
160    /* ------------------------------------------------------------ */
161
162    static int import()
163    {
164      return(db_import((char *) 0));
165    }
166
167    /* ------------------------------------------------------------ */
168
169    static int intersect()
170    {
171      return(db_union(FALSE, FALSE));
172    }
173
174    /* ------------------------------------------------------------ */
175
176    static int join()
177    {
178      return(nat_join(no_print));
179    }
180
181    /* ------------------------------------------------------------ */
182
183    static int c_project()
184    {
185      return(project(no_print));
186    }
187
188    /* ------------------------------------------------------------ */
189
190    static int c_select()
191    {
192      return(select(no_print));
193    }
194
195    /* ------------------------------------------------------------ */
196
197    static int c_union()
198    {
199      return(db_union(TRUE, FALSE));
200    }
201
202    /* ------------------------------------------------------------ */
```

```
203
204   static terminator()
205   {
206     if (cformat[0] != EOS) {
207       rprint(cformat);
208       clear_mem(cformat, 0, 65);
209       cformat[0] = EOS;    /* clear command format */
210     }
211
212     return(TRUE);
213   } /* terminator */
214
215   /* ----------------------------------------------------------- */
216
217   /* create - create a new relation */
218   static int     create()
219   {
220     struct relation *rc_create();
221     struct relation *rptr, *temp_rptr;
222     char   key, aname[2][ANSIZE+1], fgn_key[2][ANSIZE+1];
223     char   qualifier[2][RNSIZE+1], rname[RNSIZE+1],
224            **args, **dcalloc();
225     int    atype, i, arg_index, nattrs = 0, pc = 0, sc = 0;
226     BOOL   fgn_exists = FALSE;
227
228     /* get relation name and start relation creation */
229     if (next_token() != ID)
230       return (error(SYNTAX));
231
232     /* check size of relation id */
233     if (strlen(lexeme) >= RNSIZE)
234       return (error(WRLEN));
235     strcpy(rname, lexeme);
236
237     if ((rptr = rc_create(rname)) == NULL)
238       return (FALSE); /* create a new relation structure */
239
240     if (next_token() != '(')        /* check for attribute list */
241       return(rc_error(rptr));
242
243     /* parse the attributes */
244     while (TRUE) {
245       if (next_token() != ID) /* get the attribute name */
246         return(rc_error(rptr));
247
248       /* check size of attribute id */
249       if (strlen(lexeme) >= ANSIZE)
250         return (error(WRLEN));
251       strcpy(aname[0], lexeme);
252
253       if (next_token() != '(') /* line opening parenthesis */
254         return(rc_error(rptr));
255
256       /* get the attribute type */
257       next_token();
258       if (lex_token == CHAR) {
259         atype = TCHAR;
260       }
261       else if (lex_token == NUM) {
262         atype = TNUM;
263       }
```

```
264        else if (lex_token == REAL){
265          atype = TREAL;
266        }
267        else
268          return(error(UNDEFTYPE));
269
270        if (next_token() != '(')    /* size opening parenthesis */
271          return(rc_error(rptr));
272
273        if (next_token() != NUMBER) /* get the attribute size */
274          return(rc_error(rptr));
275
276        if (next_token() != ')')    /* size right parenthesis */
277          return(rc_error(rptr));
278
279        key = 'n'; /* non-key attribute */
280        if (this_token() == ',') {  /* check for key specs */
281          next_token();
282
283          if (!chk_key_defs(aname[0], &key, rptr,&pc, &sc))
284            return(rc_error(rptr));
285        }
286
287        if (next_token() != ')')    /* line right parenthesis */
288          return(rc_error(rptr));
289
290        /* add the attribute to created relation structure */
291        nattrs++;
292        if (!add_attr(rptr, aname[0], atype, (int)lex_value, key)) {
293          nfree((char *) rptr);
294          return(FALSE);
295        }
296
297        /* check for comma or final closing paren. */
298        switch (this_token()) {
299        case ',':
300          next_token();
301          break;
302        case ')':
303          break;
304
305        default:
306          next_token();
307          return(rc_error(rptr));
308        }
309
310        /* check for end of attributes */
311        if (this_token() != ID)
312          break;
313      }
314
315      /* if foreign keys exist */
316      for (i = 0; (this_token() == FOREIGN) && i < 2; i++) {
317        next_token();
318        fgn_exists = TRUE; /* foreign key exists */
319
320        /* get the neme of the foreign key */
321        if (next_token() != KEY)
322          return(rc_error(rptr));
323
324        if (next_token() != ID)
```

```
325          return(rc_error(rptr));
326        else
327          strcpy(fgn_key[i], lexeme);
328
329        if (next_token() != REFERENCES)
330          return(rc_error(rptr));
331
332        /* get the name of the primary key */
333        if (next_token() != ID)
334          return(rc_error(rptr));
335        strcpy(aname[i], lexeme);
336
337        if (next_token() != IN)
338          return(rc_error(rptr));
339
340        if (next_token() != ID)
341          return(rc_error(rptr));
342
343        /* preserve name of qualifying relation */
344        strcpy(qualifier[i], lexeme);
345
346        if (next_token() != ';')
347          return(rc_error(rptr));
348
349        if (!chk_fgn_key(rptr,fgn_key[i],qualifier[i],aname[i],&pc))
350          return(error(WRNGFGNKEY));
351        else                   /* change key specs to primary */
352          change_key(rptr, fgn_key[i], 'p');
353
354      }
355
356      if (next_token() != ')')    /* check for attribute list end */
357        return(rc_error(rptr));
358
359
360      /* retain a temporary copy of structure rptr */
361      if ((temp_rptr =
362          CALLOC(1, struct relation)) == (struct relation *) NULL)
363        return(FALSE);
364
365      structcpy((char *) temp_rptr,
366              (char *) rptr, sizeof(struct relation));
367
368      /* finish the relation creation and construct index */
369      if (!cre_finish(rptr)) {
370        free((char *) rptr);
371        return(FALSE);
372      }
373
374      /* make appropriate catalog entries */
375      if (!cat_entry(temp_rptr, nattrs, rname)) {
376        cre_finish(rptr);
377        free((char *) rptr); free((char *) temp_rptr);
378        return(FALSE);
379      }
380
381      if (fgn_exists) {
382
383        /* allocate argument array to hold catalog parameters */
384        arg_index = 4;
385        args = dcalloc(arg_index);
```

```
386
387         for (i = 0; i < 2; i++) {
388           /* insert key catalog arguments in argument array */
389           args[0] = fgn_key[i];
390           args[1] = rname;
391           args[2] = qualifier[i];
392           args[3] = aname[i];
393
394           if (!cat_insert("syskey", args, arg_index)) {
395             buf_free(args, 4);
396             return(FALSE);
397           }
398         }
399         /* decide about the semantically equivalent attributes */
400         if (! semid_attrs(rptr->rl_name, fgn_key, qualifier, aname))
401           return(FALSE);
402
403         buf_free(args, 4);
404       }
405
406     free((char *) rptr);
407     free((char *) temp_rptr);
408     sprintf(cformat, " Relation %s created  ", rname);
409     rprint(cformat);
410     cformat[0] = EOS;
411     return (TRUE);
412
413   }/* create */
414
415   /* ----------------------------------------------------------- */
416
417   /* insert - insert a tuple into a relation */
418   static int      insert()
419   {
420     struct scan *sptr, *db_ropen();
421     struct attribute *aptr;
422     char     avalue[STRINGMAX+1], base_name[ANSIZE];
423     char     **key_buf = NULL;
424     int      tcnt, astart, i;
425     int      p_cntr = 0, /* primary key counter */
426              s_cntr = 2; /* secondary key counter */
427     BOOL     insertion = TRUE;
428     char *prompt_input();
429
430     if (nxtoken_type() != ID)
431       return(error(SYNTAX));
432
433     /* preserve the relation-view name */
434     strcpy(base_name, lexeme);
435
436     /* make sure that the rest of the line is blank */
437     if (!db_flush())
438       return (FALSE);
439
440     if ((which_view(base_name)) == FAIL)
441       return(error(SYNTAX));
442
443     /* open the relation, return a scan structure pointer */
444     if ((sptr = db_ropen(base_name)) == NULL)
445       return (FALSE);
446
```

```
447        /* insert tuples */
448        for (tcnt = 0; ; tcnt++) { /* count inserted tuples */
449
450          if (tcnt != 0)     /* print separator if not first tuple */
451            printf("-------------------------------\n");
452
453          /* get attr values, astart points past tuple status code */
454          astart = 1;
455          for (i = 0; i < sptr->sc_nattrs; i++) {
456
457            /* get a pointer to the current attribute */
458            aptr = &SCAN_HEADER.hd_attrs[i];
459
460            /* check for the last attribute */
461            if (aptr->at_name[0] == EOS)
462              break;
463
464            /* prompt and input attribute values */
465            if (prompt_input(aptr, insertion, avalue) == NULL)
466              return(FALSE);
467
468            /* check for last insert */
469            if (avalue[0] == EOS)
470              break;
471
472            /* place the attribute value in sc_tuple */
473            store_attr(aptr, &SCAN_TUPLE[astart], avalue);
474
475            /* update the attribute start */
476            astart += aptr->at_size;
477
478            /* check if indexing is required */
479            if (aptr->at_key != 'n')
480              check_ix(&key_buf, aptr, &p_cntr, &s_cntr, avalue);
481          }
482
483          /* all attr values for this tuple have been processed */
484          if (avalue[0] == EOS)        /* check for last insert */
485            break;
486
487          /* store the new tuple */
488          if (!store_tuple(sptr, key_buf)) {
489            buf_free(key_buf, 4);
490            db_rclose(sptr); /* close relation file */
491            saved_ch = '\n';    /* force a newline */
492            return (FALSE);
493          }
494
495          /* reset  counters and free buffer */
496          p_cntr = 0;
497          s_cntr = 2;
498        }
499
500        /* close the relation and the index */
501        db_rclose(sptr);
502
503        /* check number of tuples inserted */
504        if (tcnt != 0)
505          sprintf(cformat, "# %d tuples inserted #", tcnt);
506        else
507          sprintf(cformat, "# no tuples inserted #");
```

```
508
509        /* return successfully */
510        buf_free(key_buf, 4);
511        key_buf = NULL;
512        rprint(cformat);
513        cformat[0] = EOS;        /* print result of insertion */
514        return (TRUE);
515
516    } /* insert */
517
518    /* ------------------------------------------------------------- */
519
520    static int      modify()
521    {
522
523        /* get relation name */
524        if (next_token() != ID)
525          return(error(SYNTAX));
526
527        /* make sure that the rest of the line is blank */
528        if (!db_flush())
529          return (FALSE);
530
531        if (!db_modify())
532          return(FALSE);
533
534        /* return successfully */
535        return(TRUE);
536
537    } /* modify */
538
539    /* ------------------------------------------------------------- */
540
541    static int assign()
542    {
543        char trans_file[RNSIZE+5];
544
545        if (next_token() != ID)
546          return (error(SYNTAX));
547
548        /* keep transient relation name */
549        strcpy(trans_file, lexeme);
550        strcat(trans_file, ".db");
551
552        if (next_token() != TO)
553          return (error(SYNTAX));
554
555        /* make sure that the rest of the line is blank */
556        if (!db_flush())
557          return (FALSE);
558
559        /* setup  prompt strings */
560        db_prompt((char *) 0, "TRANSIENT-RELATION-DEFINITION: ");
561
562        /* parse the assignment statement */
563        if (!parse((char *)NULL, FALSE))
564          return(FALSE);
565
566        if (!db_assign(trans_file))
567          return(FALSE);
568        else
```

```
569        return(TRUE);
570
571   } /* assign */
572
573   /* ---------- purge a base or transient relation ------------ */
574   static int purge()
575   {
576      char flat_file[RNSIZE+6];
577      char index_file[RNSIZE+6], response[5], prompt[65],
578          buf[70], fmt[70];
579      char rname[RNSIZE + 1];
580      struct sel *slptr, *db_select(), *retrieve();
581      struct sattr *saptr;
582      static BOOL ask = TRUE;
583      char *getfld();
584
585      if (nxtoken_type() != ID)
586        return (error(SYNTAX));
587
588      if (strncmp(lexeme, "sys", 3) == EQUAL ||
589                         fexists(lexeme) == FALSE)
590        return(error(WRNRELREM));
591
592      /* keep transient relation name */
593      strcpy(rname, lexeme);
594
595      strcpy(flat_file, lexeme);
596      strcat(flat_file, ".db");
597      strcpy(index_file, lexeme);
598      strcat(index_file, ".indx");
599
600      if (ask) {
601        sprintf(prompt,
602          "Irrecoverable relation deletion should I go ahead?\t: ");
603        getfld(prompt, response, 4);
604      }
605
606      if (! ask || strcmp(response, "yes") == EQUAL){
607        if (unlink(flat_file) == FAIL ||
608            unlink(index_file) == FAIL)
609          return(error(WRNRELREM));
610        else {
611        /* delete entries corresponding to catalog entries */
612        sprintf(buf,
613              "delete systab where relname = \"%s\";", rname);
614        if (!parse(buf, FALSE))
615          return(error(WRNRELREM));
616        saved_ch = '\n';
617
618        sprintf(buf,
619          "delete sysatrs where relname = \"%s\";", rname);
620        if (!parse(buf, FALSE))
621          return(error(WRNRELREM));
622        saved_ch = '\n';
623
624        sprintf(buf,
625          "delete sysview where base = \"%s\";", rname);
626        if (!parse(buf, FALSE))
627          return(error(WRNRELREM));
628        saved_ch = '\n';
629
```

```
630              /* project syskey over target relation */
631              sprintf(fmt,
632                "syskey over relname where qualifier = \"%s\";", rname);
633              if ((slptr = retrieve(fmt)) == NULL)
634                return(FALSE);
635              else
636                cmd_kill();   /* clear command line */
637
638              ask = FALSE;
639              /* loop through each relation name projected from SYSKEY */
640              while (fetch(slptr, TRUE)) {
641                saptr = SEL_ATTRS;
642
643                /* purge composite relation */
644                sprintf(buf, "purge %s;", saptr->sa_aptr);
645                if (!parse(buf, FALSE)) {
646                  ask = TRUE;
647                  return(error(WRNRELREM));
648                }
649
650                saved_ch = '\n';
651                cmd_clear();
652              }
653
654
655              sprintf(buf,
656                "delete syskey where relname = \"%s\"", rname);
657              if (!parse(buf, FALSE))
658                return(error(WRNRELREM));
659
660
661              sprintf(cformat, "#  relation %s deleted  #", lexeme);
662            }
663          }
664          db_rclose(slptr->sl_rels->sr_scan);
665          ask = TRUE;
666          return(TRUE);
667      } /* purge */
668
669      /* ------------ delete tuples from a relation --------------- */
670      static int    delete()
671      {
672          struct sel *retrieve(), *delete_view();
673          struct sel *slptr;
674          int     cntr = 0;  /* deleted tuple counter */
675          BOOL hash = FALSE, update = FALSE, del;
676
677          /* delete operation performed through a view ? */
678          if (token_type() != ID)
679            return(FALSE);
680
681          if (!fexists(lexeme)) {   /* it is a view call */
682            if ((slptr = delete_view()) == (struct sel *)NULL)
683              return (FALSE);
684          }
685          else {
686            /* parse the retrieval clause */
687            if ((slptr = retrieve((char *)NULL)) == (struct sel *)NULL)
688              return (FALSE);
689          }
690
```

```
691        if (!prptr) {   /* if predicate non-indexed */
692          /* loop through the selected tuples */
693          for ( ; fetch(slptr, TRUE); ) {
694            del = delete_attrs(slptr, &cntr, OL);
695            if (del == FALSE) {
696              done(slptr);
697              return(FALSE);
698              } else if (del == FAIL)
699              break;
700          }
701        } else { /* predicate attribute indexed */
702
703          /* implement deletion algorithm */
704          if (!access_plan((struct relation *)NULL,
705                             slptr, &cntr, hash, update)) {
706            done(slptr);
707            return(FALSE);
708          }
709        }
710
711        /* finish the selection, clear and reset buffers */
712        done(slptr);
713
714        /* detect existence of interpretation error */
715        if (xint_error) {
716          xint_error = FALSE;
717          return(FALSE);
718        }
719
720        /* check number of tuples deleted */
721        if (cntr > 0)
722          sprintf(cformat, "#       %d deleted      #", cntr);
723        else
724          sprintf(cformat, "#    no tuples deleted     #");
725
726        /* return successfully */
727        return (TRUE);
728
729      } /* delete */
730
731      /* ----------- update tuples from a relation -------------- */
732      static int     update()
733      {
734        struct sel *db_select(), *update_view(), *slptr;
735        struct relation *rptr;
736        BOOL    updt, updating = TRUE, hash = FALSE;
737        int     cntr = 0;
738
739        /* parse the select clause */
740        if ((slptr = db_select((char *) 0)) == (struct sel *) 0)
741          return (FALSE);
742
743        /* make sure that the rest of the line is blank */
744        if (!db_flush()) {
745          done(slptr);
746          return (FALSE);
747        }
748
749        if (!prptr) {   /* if predicate non-indexed */
750          /* loop through the selected tuples */
751          for ( ; fetch(slptr, TRUE); ) {
```

```
752              updt = update_attrs(slptr, &cntr, OL);
753              if (updt == FALSE) {
754                 done(slptr);
755                 return(FALSE);
756              } else if (updt == FAIL)
757                 break;
758            }
759          } else { /* predicate attribute indexed */
760            /* create a new relation */
761            if (!new_relation(&sref_cntr, &rptr, slptr, prptr, rel_fl)) {
762              done(slptr);
763              return(FALSE);
764            }
765
766            if (!access_plan(rptr, slptr, &cntr, hash, updating)) {
767              done(slptr);
768              return(FALSE);
769            }
770          }
771
772
773          /* finish the selection, clear and reset buffers */
774          done(slptr);
775
776          /* detect existence of interpretation error */
777          if (xint_error) {
778            xint_error = FALSE;
779            return(FALSE);
780          }
781
782          /* check number of tuples updated */
783          if (cntr > 0)
784            sprintf(cformat, "* %d  tuples updated   *", cntr);
785          else
786            sprintf(cformat, "* no tuples updated    *");
787
788          /* return successfully */
789          return (TRUE);
790
791        } /* update */
792
793        /* --------- print tuples from a set of relations ----------- */
794        static int     print()
795        {
796          struct sel *retrieve(), *db_select(), *slptr;
797          FILE *ffp = NULL, *ofp;
798
799          /* reset view existence flag */
800          view_exists = FALSE;
801
802          /* check for "using <fname>" */
803          if (this_token() == USING) {
804            next_token();
805
806            /* parse the using clause */
807            if (!using(&ffp, ".form"))
808              return (FALSE);
809
810            /* parse the select clause */
811            if ((slptr = db_select((char *) 0)) == (struct sel *) 0)
812              return (FALSE);
```

```
813         }
814         else if  /* parse the retrieval clause */
815           ((slptr = retrieve((char *) 0)) == (struct sel *) 0)
816             return (FALSE);
817
818         /* parse the into clause */
819         if (!redirect_to(&ofp, ".txt")) {
820           done(slptr);
821           return (FALSE);
822         }
823
824         /* check for normal or formatted output */
825         if (ffp == NULL)
826           table(ofp, slptr);
827         else
828           form(ofp, slptr, ffp);
829
830         /* finish the selection */
831         done(slptr);
832
833         /* close the form definition file */
834         if (ffp != NULL)
835           fclose(ffp);
836
837         /* close the output file */
838         if (ofp != stdout)
839           fclose(ofp);
840
841         /* free command line */
842         next_token();
843
844         /* return successfully */
845         db_remove();              /* remove all temporary files */
846         return (TRUE);
847
848       } /* print */
849
850       /* ------------------------------------------------------------ */
851
852       /* count the no. of tuples in a relation */
853       static int s_count()
854       {
855         struct relation *rlptr;
856         struct relation *rfind();
857         char relname[RNSIZE];
858
859         if (next_token() != ID)
860           return (error(SYNTAX));
861
862         strcpy(relname, lexeme);
863         if ((rlptr = rfind(relname)) == NULL)
864           return (FALSE);
865
866         if (this_token() != ';')
867           return(error(SYNTAX));
868
869         sprintf(cformat, "<   %d tuples counted    >",
870                                   rlptr->rl_header.hd_tcnt);
871
872         return(TRUE);
873
```

```
874    }
875
876    /* ------------------------------------------------------------ */
877
878    /* db_focus - focus on current tuple where focus lies */
879    static int    focus()
880    {
881
882      if (next_token() != ON)
883        return (error(SYNTAX));
884
885      /* parse the relation file clause */
886      if (next_token() != ID)
887        return (error(SYNTAX));
888
889      if (!db_focus()) /* implement focus */
890        return(FALSE);
891
892      /* return successfully */
893      return(TRUE);
894
895    } /* focus */
896
897    /* ------------------------------------------------------------ */
898
899    /* display the current tuple of a specified relation */
900    static int    display()
901    {
902      struct sel *retrieve();
903      struct sel *slptr;
904      int    c_width = 0, offset = 0;
905      int    reset = FALSE;
906
907      /* compute the displacement */
908      if (this_token() == SIGNEDNO) {
909        offset = atoi(lexeme); /* compute a signed number */
910        next_token();
911
912        if (this_token() == ',' ) {
913          next_token();
914          if (next_token() != NUMBER)
915            error(SYNTAX);
916          else
917            c_width = (int) lex_value;
918        }
919      } else
920        reset = TRUE;
921
922      /* parse the "using" clause */
923      if (next_token() != USING)
924        return (error(SYNTAX));
925
926      /* parse the select clause */
927      if ((slptr = retrieve((char *) 0)) == (struct sel *) 0)
928        return (FALSE);
929      if (reset)
930        SEL_HEADER.hd_cursor = 0;
931
932      if (!db_display(slptr, c_width, offset)) {
933        done(slptr);
934        return(FALSE);
```

```
935      }
936
937      done(slptr);
938      /* return successfully */
939      return(TRUE);
940
941    } /* display */
942
943    /* ------------------------------------------------------------ */
944
945    /* select - select tuples from a set of relations */
946    int      select(suppress)
947         BOOL      suppress;
948    {
949      struct sel *db_select();
950      struct sel *slptr;
951      struct relation *rptr;
952      struct sattr *saptr;
953      char     *tbuf;
954      char     rel_fl[12];
955      int      abase, i;
956      int tcnt, rc;         /* counter, result of do_join */
957      char     **duplc_attr, **ref_attr, join_keys[2];
958      BOOL     no_product = TRUE;
959      int      join_cntr = 0;
960      int      d_indx = 0;
961
962      /* parse the select clause */
963      if ((slptr = db_select((char *) 0)) == (struct sel *) 0) {
964
965        if (prptr)
966          free_pred(&prptr);
967
968        return (FALSE);
969      }
970
971      /* if view definition exit */
972      if (view_def) {
973        done(slptr);
974        return(TRUE);
975      }
976
977      /* create a new relation */
978      if (!new_relation(&sref_cntr, &rptr, slptr, prptr, rel_fl)) {
979        done(slptr);
980        return(FALSE);
981      }
982
983      /* create a joined attribute buffer if required */
984      if (join_on != (char *) 0) {
985        no_product = FALSE; /* x-product required */
986        if (!(duplc_attr = dcalloc(10)))  {
987          done(slptr);
988          return (error(INSMEM));
989        }
990
991        if (!(ref_attr = dcalloc(10))) {
992          done(slptr);
993          return (error(INSMEM));
994        }
995      }
```

```
996
997
998        /* add the selected attributes to the newly created relation,
999           in case of join eliminate attribute duplication */
1000       join_cntr = add_selattrs(slptr, rptr, join_keys,
1001                                   duplc_attr, ref_attr, &d_indx);
1002
1003       if (join_on != (char *) 0) {
1004         if (join_cntr == FAIL) {
1005           if (prptr)
1006             free_pred(&prptr);
1007           done(slptr);
1008           return(error(NJOIN));
1009         }
1010       }
1011
1012       /* allocate and initialize a tuple buffer */
1013       if ((tbuf = calloc(1, (unsigned)RELATION_HEADER.hd_size + 1))
1014                                            == (char *) 0) {
1015         rc_done(rptr, TRUE);
1016         return (error(INSMEM));
1017       }
1018       tbuf[0] = ACTIVE;
1019
1020       /* if no index for pred. attrs, or no index for joined - attrs
1021          loop through the selected tuples sequentially */
1022       if (prptr == (struct pred *) 0 || (join_on && join_cntr == 0)) {
1023         for (tcnt = 0; fetch(slptr, no_product); tcnt++) {
1024           /* create the tuple from the selected attributes */
1025           if (join_on) {
1026             if ((rc = do_join(slptr, duplc_attr,
1027                                 ref_attr, d_indx, tbuf)) == FALSE) {
1028               done(slptr);
1029               return(FALSE);
1030             }
1031             else if (rc == FAIL) /* tuple failed consistency test */
1032               continue;
1033           }
1034           else {
1035             abase = 1;
1036             for (saptr = SEL_ATTRS; saptr != (struct sattr *) 0;
1037                  saptr = saptr->sa_next) {
1038               for (i = 0; i < ATTRIBUTE_SIZE; i++)
1039                 tbuf[abase + i] = saptr->sa_aptr[i];
1040               abase += i;
1041             }
1042           }
1043
1044           /* in case of join write only one joined attribute */
1045           if (!write_tuple(rptr, tbuf, TRUE)) {
1046             rc_done(rptr, TRUE);
1047             return(error(INSBLK));
1048           }
1049         }
1050       }
1051       else if (prptr && join_on == (char *) 0) {
1052         if (!access_plan(rptr, slptr, &tcnt, FALSE, FALSE)) {
1053           done(slptr);
1054           return(FALSE);
1055         }
1056
```

```
1057       }      /* indexed predicate in join-query */
1058       else if (join_on && join_cntr >= 1) {
1059         if (!join_ix(rptr, slptr, &tcnt, join_keys,
1060                 join_cntr, duplc_attr, ref_attr, d_indx, tbuf)) {
1061           done(slptr);
1062           return(FALSE);
1063         }
1064       }
1065
1066
1067       /* finish the selection, clear and reset buffers */
1068       done(slptr);
1069
1070       /* finish relation creation */
1071       if (!rc_done(rptr, TRUE)) {
1072         buf_free(duplc_attr, d_indx);
1073         buf_free(ref_attr, d_indx);
1074         nfree(tbuf);
1075         nfree(join_on);
1076         join_on = (char *) 0;
1077         return (FALSE);
1078       }
1079
1080       if (join_on != (char *) 0)  { /* do house keeping */
1081         close(rptr->rl_fd);
1082         buf_free(duplc_attr, d_indx);
1083         nfree(tbuf);
1084         nfree(join_on);
1085         join_on = (char *) 0;
1086       }
1087
1088       /* detect existence of interpretation error */
1089       if (xint_error) {
1090         xint_error = FALSE;
1091         return(FALSE);
1092       }
1093
1094       if (!suppress)  /* check no. of tuples selected, print message */
1095         message(tcnt, cformat);
1096
1097       /* return successfully */
1098       return (TRUE);
1099
1100
1101     } /* select */
1102
1103     /* ------------------------------------------------------------ */
1104
1105     /* join - join selected tuples from a set of relations */
1106     int     nat_join(suppress)
1107         int     suppress;
1108     {
1109       char     **relat, **attrib;
1110       int      c, i,  r_indx = 0, a_indx = 0;
1111
1112       /* allocate and initialize pointers to relations and
1113          attributes */
1114       if (!(relat = dcalloc(2)
1115            || !(attrib = dcalloc(2))
1116            || ((join_on = calloc(1, ANSIZE+1)) == (char *) 0))
1117         return (error(INSMEM));
```

```
1118
1119        /* parse the expression */
1120        for( i= 0; i < 2; i++) {    /* if name a view do not expand */
1121          if (next_token() != ID)
1122            return (error(SYNTAX));
1123          else {
1124            relat[r_indx] = rmalloc(RNSIZE + 1);
1125            strcpy(relat[r_indx++], lexeme);
1126          }
1127
1128          if (next_token() != ON)
1129            return(error(SYNTAX));
1130
1131          if (next_token() != ID)
1132            return(error(SYNTAX));
1133          else {
1134            attrib[a_indx] = rmalloc(ANSIZE + 1);
1135            strcpy(attrib[a_indx++], lexeme);
1136          }
1137
1138          if (( c = this_token()) == ';' || c == WHERE || c == ')')
1139            break;
1140          else if (c == WITH)
1141            next_token();
1142          else
1143            return (error(SYNTAX));
1144        }
1145
1146        if (c == WHERE) {  /* join involves predicate */
1147          if (!joined(relat, attrib, r_indx, a_indx, TRUE))
1148            return(FALSE);
1149
1150        } else {
1151          if (c != ')') /* it is not a nested query */
1152            next_token(); /* clear the comma */
1153
1154          if (!joined(relat, attrib, r_indx, a_indx, FALSE))
1155            return(FALSE);
1156
1157        }
1158
1159        /* check for a join in a nested query */
1160        if (c == ')')
1161          saved_ch = ')';  /* push back a ")" character */
1162        else if (restore_paren) {
1163          saved_ch = ')';  /* push back a ")" character */
1164          restore_paren = FALSE;
1165        }
1166
1167        if (!suppress)
1168          terminator();
1169
1170        /* free buffers and return successfully */
1171        buf_free(relat, 2);
1172        buf_free(attrib, 2);
1173
1174        return(TRUE);
1175
1176      } /* join */
1177
1178      /* ------------------------------------------------------------- */
```

```
1179
1180    int      expose(suppress)
1181        BOOL       suppress;
1182    {
1183      struct sel *retrieve();
1184      struct sel *slptr;
1185      struct sattr *saptr;
1186      char   a_buffer[65], a_name[15], common[ANSIZE+1], relop[5];
1187      char   relation2[RNSIZE+1], qualifier[25], fmt[2*LINEMAX+1],
1188            constant[35];
1189      int      tkn, cntr = 0;
1190
1191      /* parse the retrieve clause */
1192      if ((slptr = retrieve((char *) 0)) == (struct sel *) 0)
1193        return (FALSE);
1194
1195      /* if view definition exit */
1196      if (view_def) {
1197        done(slptr);
1198        return(TRUE);
1199      }
1200
1201      if (next_token() != WHEN) {
1202        done(slptr);
1203        return(error(SYNTAX));
1204      }
1205
1206      a_buffer[0] = EOS;
1207
1208      /* get the exposed attribute names, fill attribute buffer */
1209      for (saptr = SEL_ATTRS;saptr != NULL;saptr = saptr->sa_next) {
1210        cntr++;
1211
1212        if (cntr > 5) {
1213          done(slptr);
1214          return(error(MAX5));
1215        }
1216
1217        if (a_buffer[0] != EOS) {
1218          sprintf(a_name, ", %s", saptr->sa_aname);
1219          strcat(a_buffer, a_name);
1220        } else
1221          strcpy(a_buffer, saptr->sa_aname);
1222      }
1223
1224      /* next token must be the common attribute name */
1225      if (next_token() != ID) {
1226        done(slptr);
1227        return(error(SYNTAX));
1228      }
1229
1230      /* preserve common attribute */
1231      strcpy(common, lexeme);
1232
1233      if (next_token() != IS) {
1234        done(slptr);
1235        return(error(SYNTAX));
1236      }
1237
1238      if (next_token() != IN) {
1239        done(slptr);
```

```
1240        return(error(SYNTAX));
1241      }
1242
1243      if (next_token() != PROJECT) {
1244        done(slptr);
1245        return(error(SYNTAX));
1246      }
1247
1248      /* next token must be the second relation name */
1249      if (next_token() != ID) {
1250        done(slptr);
1251        return(error(SYNTAX));
1252      }
1253
1254      /* preserve the relation name */
1255      strcpy(relation2, lexeme);
1256
1257      /* relations must be different */
1258      if (strcmp(SEL_ATTRS->sa_rname, relation2) == EQUAL) {
1259        done(slptr);
1260        return(error(SYNTAX));
1261      }
1262
1263      if (next_token() != OVER) {
1264        done(slptr);
1265        return(error(SYNTAX));
1266      }
1267
1268      /* common attribute */
1269      if (next_token() != ID) {
1270        done(slptr);
1271        return(error(SYNTAX));
1272      }
1273
1274      /* compare the current lexeme with the common attribute */
1275      if (strncmp(common, lexeme, strlen(lexeme)) != EQUAL) {
1276        done(slptr);
1277        return(error(UNATTR));
1278      }
1279
1280      if ((tkn = next_token()) == WHERE) {
1281
1282        if (next_token() != ID) {
1283          done(slptr);
1284          return(error(SYNTAX));
1285        }
1286
1287        /* create qualified attribute */
1288        strcpy(qualifier, relation2);
1289        make_quattr(qualifier, lexeme);
1290
1291        /* the next token must be a relational operator */
1292        tkn = next_token();
1293        if (relational_op(tkn, relop) == FALSE) {
1294          done(slptr);
1295          return(error(SYNTAX));
1296        }
1297
1298        /* the next token must be a numeric or string constant */
1299        tkn = next_token();
1300        if (ns_constant(tkn, constant) == FALSE) {
```

```
1301          done(slptr);
1302          return(error(SYNTAX));
1303        }
1304
1305        /* form the query to be processed */
1306        sprintf(fmt,
1307           "project (join %s on %s with %s on %s where %s %s %s) \
1308                   over %s", SEL_ATTRS->sa_rname, common, relation2,
1309                   common, qualifier, relop, constant, a_buffer);
1310      } else {
1311        /* form the query to be processed */
1312        sprintf(fmt,
1313           "project (join %s on %s with %s on %s) over %s",
1314               SEL_ATTRS->sa_rname, common, relation2,
1315               common, a_buffer);
1316      }
1317
1318      if (!parse(fmt, FALSE)) {
1319        done(slptr);
1320        return(FALSE);
1321      }
1322
1323      /* print the results */
1324      if (!suppress)
1325        terminator();
1326
1327      done(slptr);
1328      return(TRUE);
1329
1330    } /* expose */
1331
1332    /* ------------------------------------------------------------ */
1333
1334    /* project - project selected attributes from a relation */
1335    int     project(suppress)
1336        BOOL     suppress;
1337    {
1338      struct sel *retrieve();
1339      struct sel *slptr;
1340      struct relation *rptr;
1341      struct sattr *saptr;
1342      char     *tbuf, *aux_tbuf;
1343      char     rel_fl[12];
1344      int      cntr = 0, abase, i;
1345      BOOL     res;
1346
1347      /* parse the retrieve clause */
1348      if ((slptr = retrieve((char *) 0)) == NULL)
1349        return (FALSE);
1350
1351      /* if view definition exit */
1352      if (view_def) {
1353        done(slptr);
1354        return(TRUE);
1355      }
1356
1357      /* check for group clause */
1358      if (this_token() == GROUP) {
1359        next_token();
1360        res = group(slptr);
1361        done(slptr);
```

```
1362
1363        return(res);
1364    }
1365
1366    /* create a new relation */
1367    if (!new_relation(&sref_cntr, &rptr, slptr, prptr, rel_fl)) {
1368      done(slptr);
1369      return(FALSE);
1370    }
1371
1372    /* create the selected attributes */
1373    if (!create_attrs(rptr, slptr)) {
1374      done(slptr);
1375      return(FALSE);
1376    }
1377
1378    /* create the relation header and appropriate buffers */
1379    if (!header_buffs(rptr, slptr, &tbuf, &aux_tbuf)) {
1380      done(slptr);
1381      return(FALSE);
1382    }
1383
1384    /* if no indexed attrs, loop through the selected tuples */
1385    if (!prptr) {
1386
1387      for ( ; fetch(slptr, TRUE); ) {
1388        /* create the tuple from the selected attributes */
1389        abase = 1;
1390        aux_tbuf[0] = EOS; /* initialize indexes */
1391        for (saptr = SEL_ATTRS; saptr != NULL;
1392                                saptr = saptr->sa_next) {
1393          for (i = 0; i < ATTRIBUTE_SIZE; i++)
1394            tbuf[abase + i] = saptr->sa_aptr[i];
1395          /* strip-off blanks */
1396          strcat(aux_tbuf, tbuf + abase);
1397          /* reset */
1398          abase += i;
1399        }
1400
1401        /* eliminate redundant duplicate tuples if necessary
1402         * and write tuples into relation file */
1403        cntr += db_hsplace(aux_tbuf, rptr->rl_name, tbuf, rptr);
1404      }
1405    }
1406    else
1407      if (!access_plan(rptr, slptr, &cntr, TRUE, FALSE)) {
1408        done(slptr);
1409        return(FALSE);
1410      }
1411
1412    /* finish the selection, clear and reset buffers */
1413    done(slptr);
1414
1415    /* finish relation creation */
1416    if (!rc_done(rptr, TRUE))
1417      return (FALSE);
1418
1419    /* free hash table and buffers */
1420    nfree(aux_tbuf);
1421    nfree(tbuf);
1422    hash_done();
```

```
1423
1424      if (!suppress ) /* check no. of tuples selected, print message */
1425        message(cntr, cformat);
1426
1427      /* return successfully */
1428      return (TRUE);
1429
1430    } /* project */
1431
1432    /* ------------------------------------------------------------ */
1433
1434    /* group - group sets of attributes */
1435    int group(slptr)
1436        struct sel *slptr;
1437    {
1438      extern  double  atof(), count(), average(), minimum(),
1439              maximum(), sum();
1440      struct relation *rptr;
1441      struct sattr *saptr;
1442      char    *tbuf, *aux_tbuf, *name, *aggr_attr, format[20];
1443      char    partition[LINEMAX+1], rel_fl[12], *s_copy();
1444      int     cntr, i, tkn, length, type;
1445      double  num, (*funptr)();
1446      BOOL pred_flag = FALSE;
1447
1448      /* initialize static variables in functions avg and count */
1449      init_group();
1450
1451      /* check existence of "by" clause */
1452      if (next_token() != BY)
1453        return(error(SYNTAX));
1454
1455      /* check existence of qualifier attribute */
1456      if (next_token() != ID)
1457        return(error(SYNTAX));
1458
1459      /* create a new relation */
1460      if (!new_relation(&sref_cntr, &rptr, slptr, prptr, rel_fl))
1461        return(FALSE);
1462
1463      /* create the selected attributes */
1464      if (!create_attrs(rptr, slptr))
1465        return(FALSE);
1466
1467      /* create relation header */
1468      if (!rc_header(rptr, NOINDEX))
1469        return (FALSE);
1470
1471      /* initialize hash table */
1472      init_hash();
1473
1474      /* check coherence of 1st attribute with group field attr */
1475      if (strcmp(SEL_ATTRS->sa_attr->at_name, lexeme) != EQUAL)
1476        return(error(WRPREDID));
1477
1478      /* get the name of base relation */
1479      if (SEL_ATTRS->sa_rname == NULL && SEL_ATTRS->sa_name != NULL)
1480        return(error(NOALIAS));
1481      else
1482        name = s_copy(SEL_ATTRS->sa_rname);
1483
```

```
1484        tkn = next_token();
1485
1486        /* check for predicate expression */
1487        if (tkn == WHERE) {
1488          pred_flag = TRUE;
1489          tkn = next_token();
1490        }
1491
1492        /* check for aggregate function and its parameters */
1493        if (next_token() != '(')
1494          return(error(SYNTAX));
1495
1496        if (next_token() != ID)
1497          return(error(SYNTAX));
1498
1499        aggr_attr = s_copy(lexeme);
1500
1501        if (next_token() != ')')
1502          return(error(SYNTAX));
1503
1504
1505        /* determine type of aggregate function & define
1506         * appropriate function */
1507        switch(tkn) {
1508        case AVG:
1509          funptr = average;
1510          strcpy(format, "avg_");
1511          break;
1512        case COUNT:
1513          funptr = count;
1514          strcpy(format, "cnt_");
1515          break;
1516        case MAXM:
1517          funptr = maximum;
1518          strcpy(format, "max_");
1519          break;
1520        case MINM:
1521          funptr = minimum;
1522          strcpy(format, "min_");
1523          break;
1524        case SUM:
1525          funptr = sum;
1526          strcpy(format, "sum_");
1527          break;
1528        default:
1529          return(error(SYNTAX));
1530        }
1531
1532        /* increment size of second attribute */
1533        RELATION_HEADER.hd_size += 4;
1534
1535        /* length of first attribute in query */
1536        length = SEL_ATTRS->sa_attr->at_size;
1537
1538        /* allocate and initialize a tuple buffer */
1539        if ((tbuf=(char *)calloc(1,(unsigned)RELATION_HEADER.hd_size+1))
1540                                            == NULL) {
1541          rc_done(rptr, TRUE);
1542          return (error(INSMEM));
1543        }
1544        tbuf[0] = ACTIVE;
```

```
1545
1546      aux_tbuf =
1547        calloc(1, (unsigned) SEL_ATTRS->sa_next->sa_attr->at_size+4);
1548      /* check for name coherence between 2nd attribute and
1549       *  aggregate function parameter */
1550      if (strcmp(SEL_ATTRS->sa_next->sa_attr->at_name,
1551                                        aggr_attr) != EQUAL)
1552        return(error(WRPREDID));
1553
1554      if (((type = SEL_ATTRS->sa_next->sa_attr->at_type) != TNUM) &&
1555                                        (type != TREAL))
1556        return(error(AGGRPARAM));
1557
1558      /* fetch the values of the selected attributes,
1559         one tuple at a time */
1560      while (fetch(slptr, TRUE)) {
1561
1562        /* get the first attribute in the query */
1563        saptr = SEL_ATTRS;
1564
1565        /* create the tuple from the selected attributes
1566         * store first attribute value in buffer */
1567        for (i = 0; i < length; i++)
1568          partition[i] = saptr->sa_aptr[i];
1569        partition[length] = EOS;
1570
1571        /* get the next attribute in the query */
1572        saptr = saptr->sa_next;
1573
1574        /* store the second attribute's contents in buffer */
1575        for (i = 0; i < ATTRIBUTE_SIZE; i++)
1576          aux_tbuf[i] = saptr->sa_aptr[i];
1577        aux_tbuf[i] = EOS;
1578
1579        num = atof(aux_tbuf);
1580
1581        if (db_hash(partition, name, num)) {
1582
1583          /*  call built-in function */
1584          Hash_Table[HTIndex]->aggr_param =
1585            (*funptr)(num, Hash_Table[HTIndex]->aggr_param);
1586        } else {
1587          if (funptr == count)
1588            Hash_Table[HTIndex]->aggr_param = 1;
1589          else if (funptr == average)
1590            Hash_Table[HTIndex]->aggr_param = num;
1591        }
1592      }
1593
1594      /* adjust resulting relation parameters */
1595      strcat(format, SEL_ATTRS->sa_next->sa_attr->at_name);
1596      strncpy(RELATION_HEADER.hd_attrs[1].at_name,format, ANSIZE-1);
1597      RELATION_HEADER.hd_attrs[1].at_name[MIN(strlen(format),ANSIZE)] = EOS;
1598      RELATION_HEADER.hd_attrs[1].at_size += 4;
1599
1600      if (pred_flag) {
1601        tkn = next_token();
1602        switch (tkn) {
1603        case LSS:
1604          break;
1605        case LEQ:
```

```
1606            break;
1607         case EQL:
1608            break;
1609         case GEQ:
1610            break;
1611         case GTR:
1612            break;
1613         case NEQ:
1614            break;
1615         default:
1616            return(error(SYNTAX));
1617         }
1618
1619         if (next_token() != NUMBER)
1620            return(error(SYNTAX));
1621      }
1622
1623
1624      /* write resulting relation into file */
1625      if (pred_flag)  /* if predicate was encountered */
1626         cntr = write_hash(length, rptr, tkn, tbuf, aux_tbuf);
1627      else
1628         cntr = write_hash(length, rptr, FALSE, tbuf, aux_tbuf);
1629
1630      /* finish relation creation */
1631      if (!rc_done(rptr, TRUE))
1632         return (FALSE);
1633
1634      /* free hash table and buffers */
1635      nfree((char *) rptr);
1636      nfree(aux_tbuf);
1637      nfree(tbuf);
1638      nfree(name);
1639      nfree(aggr_attr);
1640      hash_done();
1641
1642      /* free predicate structure */
1643      if (prptr)
1644         free_pred(&prptr);
1645
1646      /* check number of tuples selected, print message */
1647      message(cntr, cformat);
1648
1649      /* return successfully */
1650      return(TRUE);
1651   } /* group */
1652
1653   /* ------------------------------------------------------------ */
1654
1655   /* union - unites all tuples from two relations */
1656   int      db_union(unite, diff)
1657         int      unite, diff;
1658   {
1659      struct sel *slptr;
1660      struct sel *retrieve(), *minus();
1661      struct relation *rptr;
1662      struct sattr *saptr, *aux_saptr, *next_saptr;
1663      struct unattrs f_rel[NATTRS];
1664      char      *tbuf, *aux_tbuf, *name;
1665      char      rel_fl[12];
1666      int      tcnt, lcnt, tup_offset, incr, i, k;
```

```
1667      int      size_diff, hs_cnt = 0;
1668      unsigned    hp_cnt = 0;
1669
1670      if (diff) {
1671        /* parse the difference clause */
1672        if ((slptr = minus()) == NULL)
1673          return(FALSE);
1674      }
1675      else {
1676        /* parse the retrieve clause */
1677        if ((slptr = retrieve((char *) 0)) == NULL)
1678          return (FALSE);
1679      }
1680
1681      /* create a new relation */
1682      if (!new_relation(&sref_cntr, &rptr, slptr, prptr, rel_fl)) {
1683        done(slptr);
1684        return(FALSE);
1685      }
1686
1687      /* check union relations for validity and
1688       * fill temporary relation */
1689      if (!check_union(rptr, slptr, f_rel, &name)) {
1690        done(slptr);
1691        return(FALSE);
1692      }
1693
1694      /* create the relation header and the required buffers */
1695      if (!header_buffs(rptr, slptr, &tbuf, &aux_tbuf)) {
1696        done(slptr);
1697        return(FALSE);
1698      }
1699
1700      aux_saptr = NULL;
1701      /* loop through the selected tuples */
1702      for (tcnt = 0; single_scan(SEL_RELS); tcnt++) {
1703        /* create the tuple from the selected attributes */
1704        tup_offset = 1;
1705        aux_tbuf[0] = EOS;
1706        k = 0;
1707
1708        for (saptr=SEL_ATTRS;saptr != NULL;saptr = saptr->sa_next) {
1709          /* first relation tuples should be first written,
1710           * discard momentarily tuples of second relation */
1711
1712          if (strcmp(saptr->sa_rname, name) != EQUAL) {
1713            /* reached 1st attribute of 2nd relation */
1714            if (tcnt == 0)
1715              aux_saptr = saptr;
1716
1717            /* exit loop and write the created tuple */
1718            break;
1719          } else  if (k < SEL_NATTRS) {
1720
1721            /* in first relation, f_rel contains the attribute lengths
1722               of the new relation; hence adjust displacements */
1723            size_diff = f_rel[k].size - ATTRIBUTE_SIZE;
1724
1725            if (!(incr = adjust(saptr, tbuf, size_diff, tup_offset))) {
1726              done(slptr);
1727              return(FALSE);
```

```
1728                    }
1729
1730               k++;  /* increment index for next attribute */
1731               strcat(aux_tbuf, tbuf + tup_offset);
1732               /* tbuf include spaces which cannot be used in hashing,
1733                * aux_tbuf catenates the strings and discards spaces
1734                resolving this problem */
1735
1736               tup_offset += incr;
1737            }
1738          }
1739          /* hash and write the tuples */
1740          if (unite)  /* union operation */
1741            hs_cnt +=
1742              db_hsplace(aux_tbuf, rptr->rl_name, tbuf, rptr);
1743          else
1744            db_hash(aux_tbuf, rptr->rl_name, (double) 0);
1745        }
1746
1747        /* insert the tuples of the second relation but in the order
1748         * as specified from their sequence in the first relation */
1749        lcnt = aux_saptr->sa_srel->sr_scan->sc_relation
1750           ->rl_header.hd_tcnt; /* no. of tuples in second relation */
1751        for (i = 0; i < lcnt && single_scan(SEL_RELS->sr_next); i++) {
1752          tup_offset = 1;
1753          aux_tbuf[0] = EOS;
1754          k = 0;
1755
1756          for (saptr = SEL_ATTRS; saptr != aux_saptr;
1757               saptr = saptr->sa_next, k++)
1758            for (next_saptr = aux_saptr; next_saptr != NULL;
1759                 next_saptr = next_saptr->sa_next)
1760              if ((strcmp(next_saptr->sa_aname,saptr->sa_aname)==EQUAL)
1761                 && k < SEL_NATTRS) {
1762                size_diff = f_rel[k].size - next_saptr->sa_attr->at_size;
1763                if (!(incr=adjust(next_saptr,tbuf,size_diff,tup_offset))) {
1764                  done(slptr);
1765                  return(FALSE);
1766                }
1767
1768                strcat(aux_tbuf, tbuf + tup_offset); /* reset */
1769                tup_offset += incr;
1770                break; /* match has been found */
1771              }
1772
1773          /* hash and write the tuples */
1774          if (unite || diff )  /* union or difference is required */
1775            hs_cnt +=
1776              db_hsplace(aux_tbuf, rptr->rl_name, tbuf, rptr);
1777          else /* intersection is required */
1778            hp_cnt +=
1779              db_hplace(aux_tbuf, rptr->rl_name, tbuf, rptr);
1780        }
1781
1782        /* finish the selection */
1783        done(slptr);
1784
1785        /* release auxiliary buffer storage */
1786        free_union(f_rel, (int) SEL_NATTRS);
1787
1788        /* finish relation creation */
```

```
1789     if (!rc_done(rptr, TRUE))
1790       return (FALSE);
1791
1792     /* free hash table and buffers */
1793     nfree(aux_tbuf);
1794     hash_done();
1795     hs_cnt += hp_cnt;
1796
1797     message(hs_cnt, cformat);
1798
1799     /* return successfully */
1800     return (TRUE);
1801   } /* db_union */
1802
1803   /* ------------------------------------------------------------ */
1804
1805   static struct sel *minus()
1806   {
1807     struct sel *slptr;
1808     struct sel *retrieve();
1809     char *pt_error();
1810     char **relat;
1811     int r_indx = 0;
1812     char fmt[30];
1813
1814     /* allocate and initialize pointers to relations */
1815     if (!(relat = dcalloc(2)))
1816       return ((struct sel *)pt_error(INSMEM));
1817
1818     /* parse the expression */
1819     if (next_token() != ID)
1820       return ((struct sel *)pt_error(SYNTAX));
1821     else {
1822       relat[r_indx] = rmalloc(RNSIZE + 1);
1823       strcpy(relat[r_indx++], lexeme);
1824     }
1825
1826     if (this_token() == ',')
1827       next_token();
1828     else
1829       return ((struct sel *)pt_error(SYNTAX));
1830
1831     if (next_token() != ID)
1832       return ((struct sel *)pt_error(SYNTAX));
1833     else {
1834       relat[r_indx] = rmalloc(RNSIZE + 1);
1835       strcpy(relat[r_indx], lexeme);
1836     }
1837
1838     next_token();
1839
1840     /* reverse the order of evaluation to cater for internal
1841      * representation, and to comply with semantics of difference */
1842     sprintf(fmt, "%s, %s", relat[1], relat[0]);
1843
1844     if ((slptr = retrieve(fmt)) == NULL)
1845       return ((struct sel *)NULL);
1846
1847     return(slptr);
1848
1849   } /* minus */
```

```
1850
1851    /* --------------------------------------------------------- */
```

file: create.c

```
1     /* REQUIEM - relation creation file */
2
3     #include "requ.h"
4     #include "btree.h"
5     #include <sys/file.h>
6     #include <stdio.h>
7
8     extern struct entry dummy_entry;
9     extern struct ix_header *pci;
10    struct indx_attrs *ix_atrs = NULL;
11    extern  char   errvar[];
12    extern  char   lexeme[];
13    extern  int    lex_token;
14    extern  float   lex_value;
15    BOOL sys_flag = FALSE;              /* true for system catalogs */
16
17    /* --------------------------------------------------------- */
18
19    /* rc_create(rname) - begin the creation of a new relation */
20    struct relation *rc_create(rname)
21         char *rname;
22    {
23      char *pt_error();
24      struct relation *rptr;
25
26      if (! sys_flag) {
27        if (strncmp(rname, "sys", 3) == EQUAL)
28          return((struct relation *) pt_error(ILLREL));
29      }
30
31      /* allocate the relation structure, with zeroed contents */
32      if ((rptr = (struct relation*)
33              calloc(1, sizeof(struct relation))) == NULL)
34        return ((struct relation *) pt_error(INSMEM));
35
36      /* initialize the relation structure */
37      strncpy(rptr->rl_name,rname,RNSIZE);
38      RELATION_HEADER.hd_tcnt = 0;
39      RELATION_HEADER.hd_data = HEADER_SIZE;
40      RELATION_HEADER.hd_size = 1;
41      RELATION_HEADER.hd_avail = 0;
42      RELATION_HEADER.hd_attrs[0].at_name[0] = EOS;
43      RELATION_HEADER.hd_cursor = 0;
44      RELATION_HEADER.hd_unique = 'f'; /* unique specifier: FALSE */
45
46      /* return the new relation structure pointer */
47      return (rptr);
48    } /* rc_create */
49
50    /* --------------------------------------------------------- */
51
52    /* rc_header - create the relation header */
53    int rc_header(rptr, no_ix)
54         struct relation *rptr;
55         BOOL no_ix;
```

```
56    {
57       char rname[RNSIZE+1],filename[RNSIZE+13];
58
59       /* create the relation file name */
60       strncpy(rname, rptr->rl_name,MIN(strlen(rptr->rl_name), RNSIZE));
61       rname[MIN(strlen(rptr->rl_name), RNSIZE)] = EOS;
62       sprintf(filename,"%s.db",rname);
63
64       /* create the relation file with read-write permissions
65          no overwriting is allowed if file exists */
66       if ((rptr->rl_fd = rc_exist(filename)) == -1) {
67         free((char *) rptr);
68         return (error(RELCRE));
69       }
70
71       /* create index file, if required */
72       if (no_ix == FALSE)
73         if (!b_index(rname))
74           return(error(INDXCRE));
75
76       /* write the header to the relation file */
77       if (write(rptr->rl_fd, (char *) &RELATION_HEADER,
78                                    HEADER_SIZE) != HEADER_SIZE) {
79         close(rptr->rl_fd);
80         free((char *) rptr);
81         return (error(BADHDR));
82       }
83
84       /* return successfully */
85       return (TRUE);
86    } /* rc_header */
87
88    /* -------- finish the creation of a new relation --------- */
89    int rc_done(rptr, r_free)
90         struct relation *rptr;
91         BOOL r_free;            /* free rptr flag */
92    {
93       long lseek();
94
95       /* write the header to the relation file */
96       lseek(rptr->rl_fd,0L,0);
97       if ((write(rptr->rl_fd, (char *) &RELATION_HEADER,
98                                    HEADER_SIZE)) != HEADER_SIZE) {
99         close(rptr->rl_fd);
100        free((char *) rptr);
101        return (error(BADHDR));
102      }
103
104      /* close the relation file */
105      close(rptr->rl_fd);
106
107      /* free the relation structure, if required */
108      if (r_free)
109        nfree((char *) rptr);
110
111      /* return successfully */
112      return (TRUE);
113    } /* rc_done */
114
115.   /* -------- add an attribute to relation being created ------ */
116    int add_attr(rptr,aname,type,size,key)
```

```
117            struct relation *rptr;
118            char *aname;
119            int type,size;
120            char key;
121    {
122      int i;
123
124      /* look for attribute name */
125      for (i = 0; i < NATTRS; i++)
126        if (RELATION_HEADER.hd_attrs[i].at_name[0] == EOS)
127          break;
128        else if (strncmp(aname,
129               RELATION_HEADER.hd_attrs[i].at_name,ANSIZE) == EQUAL)
130          return (error(DUPATT));
131
132
133      /* check for too many attributes */
134      if (i == NATTRS)
135        return (error(MAXATT));
136
137      /* store the new attribute */
138
139      strncpy(RELATION_HEADER.hd_attrs[i].at_name,aname,ANSIZE);
140      RELATION_HEADER.hd_attrs[i].at_type = type;
141      RELATION_HEADER.hd_attrs[i].at_size = size;
142      RELATION_HEADER.hd_attrs[i].at_key = key;
143      RELATION_HEADER.hd_attrs[i].at_semid = 'f';
144
145      /* terminate the attribute table */
146      if (++i != NATTRS)
147        RELATION_HEADER.hd_attrs[i].at_name[0] = EOS;
148
149      /* update the tuple size */
150      RELATION_HEADER.hd_size += size;
151
152      /* return successfully */
153      return (TRUE);
154    } /* add_attr */
155
156    /* --------------- check key definitions -------------------- */
157    BOOL chk_key_defs(aname, key, rptr, pc, sc)
158         char *aname, *key;
159         struct relation *rptr;
160         int *pc, *sc;        /* primary and secondary key indexes */
161    {
162      int tkn;
163
164      switch (tkn = next_token()) {
165      case UNIQUE:
166
167        *key = 'p';
168        /* key length + prefix must be less than max. key length */
169        if ((int) (lex_value + 3) >= MAXKEY) {
170          strcpy(errvar, aname);
171          return(error(KEYEXCD));
172        }
173
174        /* only one unique key per relation is allowed */
175        if (RELATION_HEADER.hd_unique == 't')
176          return(error(UNIQEXCD));
177        else
```

```
178              RELATION_HEADER.hd_unique = 't'; /* set to TRUE */
179
180          if (!ix_attr(rptr->rl_name, aname, tkn, ++(*pc)))
181            return(FALSE);
182
183          break;
184
185        case SECONDARY:
186
187          *key = 's';
188          if ((int) (lex_value + 3) >= MAXKEY) {
189            strcpy(errvar, aname);
190            return(error(KEYEXCD));
191          }
192
193          if (!ix_attr(rptr->rl_name, aname, tkn, ++(*sc)))
194            return(FALSE);
195
196          break;
197        default:
198          return(FALSE);
199        }
200
201        /* return successfully */
202        return(TRUE);
203      } /* chk_key_defs */
204
205      /* ------------check definition of foreign key -------------- */
206
207      int chk_fgn_key(rptr, fgn_key, qualif, ref_key, pc)
208          struct relation *rptr;
209          char *fgn_key, *qualif, *ref_key;
210          int *pc;
211      {
212        struct scan *sptr, *db_ropen();
213        int i;
214        BOOL found = FALSE;
215
216
217        /* open the relation, return a scan structure pointer */
218        if ((sptr = db_ropen(qualif)) == NULL)
219          return (FALSE);
220
221        /* look if referenced key exists and is a primary key */
222        for (i = 0; i < sptr->sc_nattrs; i++)
223          if (strcmp(ref_key,SCAN_HEADER.hd_attrs[i].at_name)==EQUAL) {
224            if (SCAN_HEADER.hd_attrs[i].at_key == 'p') {
225
226              /* make an index entry for this foreign key */
227              if (!ix_attr(rptr->rl_name, fgn_key, FOREIGN, ++(*pc))) {
228                db_rclose(sptr);
229                return(FALSE);
230              }
231
232              /* insert referenced key info. */
233              ix_refkeys(qualif, ref_key, *pc);
234
235              found = TRUE;      /* primary key in qualifier found */
236            }
237            break;
238          }
```

```
239
240      if (found == FALSE)
241        return(error(WRNGFGNKEY));
242
243      /* close the relation */
244      db_rclose(sptr);
245
246      /* correct foreign key definition */
247      return(TRUE);
248    } /* chk_fgn_key */
249
250    /* change key definition to primary (for foreign keys only) */
251    change_key(rptr, aname, key)
252        struct relation *rptr;
253        char *aname;
254        char key;
255    {
256      int i;
257
258      /* look for attribute name */
259      for (i = 0; i < NATTRS; i++)
260        if (strcmp(aname,RELATION_HEADER.hd_attrs[i].at_name)==EQUAL) {
261          /* store the new key definition */
262          RELATION_HEADER.hd_attrs[i].at_key = key;
263          break;
264        }
265
266    } /* change_key */
267
268    /* --------- verify existence of a file name -------------- */
269    static int rc_exist(filename)
270        char *filename;
271    {
272      int fd;
273      char *s = "snapshot";
274
275      if (!strncmp(filename, s, strlen(s))) { /* only for aux files */
276        fd = open(filename, O_CREAT | O_RDWR, 0600);
277        if (fd == -1)
278          printf("Warning: Auxiliary file is redeclared !!\n");
279      }
280      else { /* no file overwriting is allowed */
281        fd = open(filename, O_CREAT | O_RDWR | O_EXCL, 0600);
282        if (fd == -1)
283          printf("Warning: Relation file is redeclared !!\n");
284      }
285      return (fd);
286    } /* rc_exist */
287
288    /* --------- report syntax error during creation ------------ */
289
290    int rc_error(rptr)
291        struct relation *rptr;
292    {
293      nfree((char *) rptr);
294      return(error(SYNTAX));
295    } /* rc_error */
296
297    /* ------------- finish creation of a relation -------------- */
298
299    int cre_finish(rptr)
```

```
300        struct relation *rptr;
301    {
302      /* finish rel creation, construct index, do not free rptr */
303      if (!rc_header(rptr, INDEX))  /* create a relation header */
304        return (FALSE);
305
306      /* close the relation and index files */
307      close(rptr->rl_fd);
308      dequeue_relations(rptr);
309
310      /* return successfully */
311      nfree((char *) ix_atrs);
312      ix_atrs = NULL;
313      return(TRUE);
314
315    } /* cre_finish */
316
317
318    /* ------------------------------------------------------------
319     |              Index part of creation routines             |
320     ------------------------------------------------------------ */
321
322    int    b_index(fname)
323         char       *fname;
324    {
325      char  fn[16];
326
327      cat_strs(fn, fname, ".indx");
328
329      if (!create_ix(fn, &dummy_entry, sizeof(struct entry)))
330        return(FALSE);
331
332      /* return successfully */
333      return(TRUE);
334    }
335
336    /* ------------------------------------------------------------ */
337
338    int create_ix(f_name, pdum, ndum) /* create a new index file */
339         char       f_name[];         /* name of the file */
340         struct entry *pdum;          /* dummy enry for EOF */
341         int        ndum;             /* size of dummy entry */
342    {
343      struct block blk;
344      int   ret, i;
345      struct ix_header *pixhd;
346      long write_level();
347
348      if ((pixhd = (struct ix_header*)
349          calloc(1, sizeof(struct ix_header))) == NULL)
350        return (error(INSMEM));
351
352      pci = pixhd;
353      ret = create_ixf(f_name);
354      if (ret < 0)
355        return(FALSE);
356
357      pixhd->ixfile = ret;
358      pixhd->dx.nl = MAX_LEVELS;  /* all levels present */
359
360      strcpy(pixhd->dx.ixatts.ix_rel, ix_atrs->ix_rel);
```

```
361
362       for (i = 0; ix_atrs->ix_prim[i] && i < MAXKEYS; i++)
363         strcpy(pixhd->dx.ixatts.ix_prim[i], ix_atrs->ix_prim[i]);
364
365       for (i = 0; ix_atrs->ix_secnd[i] && i < MAXKEYS; i++)
366         strcpy(pixhd->dx.ixatts.ix_secnd[i], ix_atrs->ix_secnd[i]);
367
368       for (i = 0; ix_atrs->ix_refkey[i] && i < MAXKEYS; i++)
369         strcpy(pixhd->dx.ixatts.ix_refkey[i], ix_atrs->ix_refkey[i]);
370
371       pixhd->dx.ixatts.ix_foreign = ix_atrs->ix_foreign;
372
373       /* set up initial struct with a single entry using the
374        * dummy key as provided by the calling function */
375       move_struct((char *) &pixhd->dx.dum_entr, (char *) pdum, ndum);
376       clear_mem((char *)&blk,0,IXBLK_SIZE); /* make block of zeroes */
377       write_block(0L, &blk);   /* write at beginning of file */
378
379       /* set up index block for each level,
380        * record location of root block */
381       pixhd->dx.root_bk = write_level(pdum, ndum);
382
383       /* set up a free block list, start it after dummy blocks */
384       make_free(pixhd);
385       close_ix(pixhd);         /* close file updating header */
386
387       nfree((char *) pixhd);
388
389       return(TRUE);            /* successful creation */
390     } /* create_ix */
391
392     /* ----------------------------------------------------------- */
393
394     int close_ix(pix)            /* close an index file */
395         struct ix_header *pix;   /* index header */
396     {
397       write_ixf(0L, (char *) &pix->dx, sizeof(struct ix_disk));
398       close_ixf();             /* close the index file */
399     } /* close_ix */
400
401     /* ---- make an index entry for the specified attribute ----- */
402
403     int     ix_attr(rel_name, attr_name, type, tcnt)
404         char      *rel_name, *attr_name;
405         int       type;
406         int       tcnt;
407     {
408       if (tcnt > 2)
409         return(error(TOOMANY));
410
411       if (ix_atrs == NULL) {
412         if ((ix_atrs = CALLOC(1, struct indx_attrs)) == NULL)
413           return(error(INSMEM));
414
415         ix_atrs->ix_foreign = 'f'; /* set foreign keys to FALSE */
416       }
417       strcpy(ix_atrs->ix_rel, rel_name);
418
419       /* preserve names of primary, secondary and referenced keys */
420       if (type == UNIQUE || type == FOREIGN)
421         strcpy(ix_atrs->ix_prim[tcnt-1], attr_name);
```

```
422     else if (type == SECONDARY)
423       strcpy(ix_atrs->ix_secnd[tcnt-1], attr_name);
424
425     /* if two foreign keys exist they must be combined */
426     if (type == FOREIGN && tcnt == 2)
427       ix_atrs->ix_foreign = 't';
428
429     return(TRUE);
430   } /* ix_attr */
431
432   /* ------------------------------------------------------------ */
433
434   ix_refkeys(qualif, ref_key, tcnt)
435       char *qualif, *ref_key;
436       int       tcnt;
437   {
438     char q_ref[30];          /* qualified reference */
439
440     strcpy(q_ref, qualif);
441
442     /* primary keys in qualifying rel referenced by fgn keys */
443     make_quattr(q_ref, ref_key);
444     strcpy(ix_atrs->ix_refkey[tcnt-1], q_ref);
445
446   } /* ix_refkeys */
447
448   /* ------------------------------------------------------------ */
```

10

The REQUIEM Query Decomposer

The query decomposer is the module responsible for executing the data retrieval operations that have previously been identified during the parsing of queries. Query decomposer routines are called by the parser only at specific situations. The query decomposer routines normally accept as input the relations that are required for processing a user request and perform the necessary operations. One important task that the query decomposer performs is the manipulation of nested queries. Such nested queries consist of one or more inner subqueries and an outer subquery; an inner subquery provides its results for further use in its immediate outer subquery, thus enabling the user to formulate compact query statements.

10.1 The query decomposition routines

Query decomposition in REQUIEM is the process that breaks a query down into a series of function invocations. The prime objective of this process is the mapping of conceptual level statements to their equivalent physical level counterparts.

As previously explained, the task of the query decomposition module is to collect information that can be used throughout the process of tuple accessing. This information is used to access the required tuples of a relation during the invocation of a parsing function, such as **join** or **select**. Next, after the appropriate functions have been invoked the processed tuples are stored back on the disk. Again, at that point information about the best possible access path is used in order to increase efficiency.

Before we leave this brief introduction, it is also worth a brief digression on a problem related to fast tuple access methods in conjunction with query decomposition. In Chapter 6 we argued that indices are the only way to cope with the potential complexity of efficient tuple access. If a relation includes one or more indexed attributes, efficient access to the stored data is provided as the records can be uniquely and directly identified in the data file. In general, to achieve fast tuple access, indexed attributes must be contained in the query predicate. Obviously, users may be aware of the physical existence of such indices but cannot directly manipulate them in their data access requests. Whenever no indices are involved in the predicate, tuples are accessed sequentially – each access takes place at a position in the data file immediately after the previous one. Certainly this way of accessing relation tuples is less efficient in terms of processing speed when compared to indexing. The remainder of this chapter is devoted to concepts and techniques of conceptual to internal schema mapping and tuple accessing methods. In particular, the following sections describe some useful ideas and techniques that can be employed during tuple accessing.

10.1.1   Selection of a relation

Central to most DML operations in REQUIEM is a set of data structures that hold information concerning the relations that have been retrieved during the processing of a query. This information is used throughout most functions that manipulate one or more relations.

The selection structure **sel** is central to an understanding of the implementation of the query decomposer functions. Most of the functions that implement RQL operations have embedded parsing facilities. What actually happens is that the main parsing routine responsible for the syntactic analysis of a certain type of query, for example **project**, identifies only the requested operation and then invokes the corresponding query decomposer function to implement the necessary operations. In the current chapter we will focus our attention on the tuple accessing mechanisms of the query decomposer. Thereby, we will describe some of the more important functions of REQUIEM used to implement general purpose DML operations.

The core of the query decomposer comprises two *tuple selecting* functions, namely **retrieve()** and **db_select()**. These two functions are RQL syntax specific. Actually, **db_select()** is used during the parsing of queries where the set of selected attribute names or the keyword **all**, comes prior to specifying the selected relation. This is the case in **select**, or **update** queries where the names of the attributes to be updated precede a named relation. The function **db_select()** is called when the selection clause has the following syntax:

$\cdots$ <*selected attributes*> **from** <*relation*> **where** $\cdots$ (10.1)

Conversely, **retrieve()** is used when only the name of the selected relation precedes the set of selected attributes. This is the case in **project** statements (where the names of the attributes to be projected always follow a named relation) or in **delete** queries. **retrieve()** is called whenever the selection clause has the form:

$\cdots$ <*relation*> **over** <*selected-attributes*> $\cdots$ (10.2)

We will now concentrate on the relation and tuple accessing aspects of the two afore-mentioned query decomposition functions. Note that both these functions gradually create a retrieval environment and insert in it the information that is going to be later used to retrieve the tuples of the specified input relation(s). How individual tuples are really retrieved will be described in the following section.

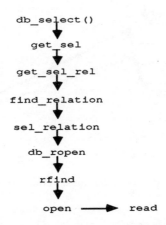

Figure 10.1 The nesting of functions for relation selection in **db_select()** or **retrieve()**.

Figure 10.1 depicts the series of function calls required to implement the functions **db_select()** or **retrieve()**. Actually, only the functions that affect the relation selection process are depicted in Figure 10.1. In fact, both tuple selecting routines **db_select()** and **retrieve()** invoke the same functions, they only differ in the sequence of function calls. In general, in both tuple selecting routines the selection of a relation is triggered by a call to function **get_sel()** (see Figure 10.1).

Let us defer the tuple accessing process for a moment and concentrate on how the retrieval context structures of Figure 10.2 are generated. Function

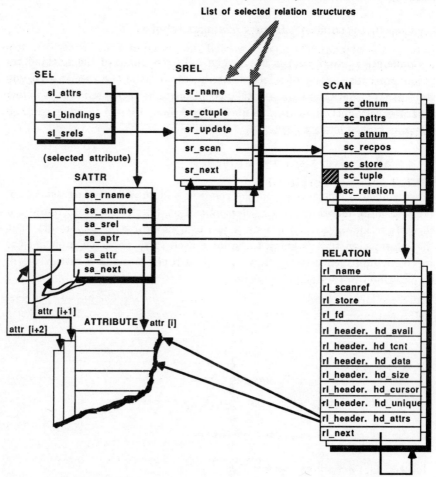

Figure 10.2 The structures generated during the selection of a relation.

retrieve() first allocates space for a selected relation structure (**srel**) to hold information about the relation in question (see Figure 10.2).

For each relation specified in a query a selected relation structure is generated and initialized and then placed through its **sr_next** pointer into a single linked list of selected relation structures. This list contains at its head the selection relation structure of the first named relation encountered in a query. Each **srel** structure also includes a pointer to a structure of type **scan**. Scan structures hold the kernel of information that is required during tuple fetching. The **scan** structure is generated through a call to the function **db_ropen()** which primarily opens the data file corresponding to an input relation and returns the scan structure associated with this specific relation file. The **sc_relation** pointer points to the relation structure of the relation associated with the returned scan structure.

Next, the header of the relation is read and placed into the header structure embodied in the relation structure of Figure 10.2. It is only when the file is closed by a call to the standard C system function **close()** that the newly allocated relation structure is placed in the linked list of loaded relations. At this stage, the selection process of a relation whose name was encountered in the input stream terminates.

10.1.2   Tuple retrieval

Once a given relation has been selected, we must be concerned with how its tuples can be retrieved. The only prerequisite for fetching tuples from a stored relation is that the selection structure corresponding to a given relation is generated within the retrieval context exactly as described in the previous section. To illustrate the process of tuple fetching in a practical way we shall use as an example throughout this section the parsing function **delete()** that is invoked each time a user decides to delete certain tuples from a relation.

Example 10.1.1

Consider the query "delete all London-based suppliers."

This query can be formulated as follows:

delete supplier **where** location = "London";

The above statement specifies that an entire set of tuples of the relation *SUPPLIER*, for which the predicate *location = "London"* is satisfied, must be deleted. Thus, after the parser has received and recognized the token DELETE it calls the parsing function **delete()**. As the syntax of the delete statement matches that of the construct 10.2 the query decomposer function **retrieve()** is called to further parse and subsequently decompose the **delete** query.

On entering the query decomposer function **retrieve()** we must first determine where its input originates from. Here, we normally distinguish between two cases. The input may originate from the user's terminal or it may be the product of a canned query. In the latter case we know that the format specifier argument **fmt** that preserves the entire query contents will eventually be copied to the command buffer associated with canned queries and that the command buffer contents will be parsed exactly as explained in Chapters 7 and 8. For the sake of simplicity we assume that the query in example 10.1.1 is not a canned query. Hence, the query decomposer asks the lexical analyzer to fetch the next token from the input stream of characters. Actually, function **retrieve()** expects to receive an identifier which designates the name of an already stored relation, namely the relation *SUPPLIER*. Consequently, the retrieval context of Figure 10.2 is gradually built up according to the previous section.

A function call to **get_sel_attrs()** ensures that the selection structure **sel**, the attribute array structure **attr[i]** and the selected attributes' structure **sattr** (see Figure 8.2) are set up and filled with the appropriate information which will subsequently be used to process the query. This function is responsible for fetching the attribute values from a given stored relation. Consequently, an element of type **sattr**, representing a selected attribute structure, is allocated and chained into the list of selected attributes for each attribute name encountered in a given query.

If all the attributes of a given relation are to be selected (indicated either by the token **ALL** or by a missing attribute list), no selected attribute list is generated and **sl_attrs** in the selection structure initially points to NULL. A pointer between the selection structure **sel** and the selected attributes' structure will be established after a call to the routine **all_attrs()**. As the **delete** query of example 10.1.1 demands the deletion of the entire set of attributes in the given relation, there will be three members in the attribute array **attr[i]**, each of them corresponding to one of the individual attributes in the relation *SUPPLIER*.

Next, **retrieve()** must confirm if a selected attribute clause is present in the input query. As known a selected attribute clause consists of a list of attribute names separated by commas. Alternatively, **retrieve()** may sense the presence of a nested subquery. As can be seen from the RQL syntax the presence of a nested query is always indicated by means of an opening parenthesis.

After performing the above sequences of actions and before exiting, function **retrieve()** checks whether a predicate expression is present in the input query. If a predicate expression is encountered, signified always by the existence of a **where** clause, the predicate expression compiler must be called to compile this predicate expression. A detailed analysis of the functionality and implementation of predicate compilation will appear in Chapter 11.

The next step that the parsing function **delete()** undertakes is to certify whether the attributes encountered in the predicate of the **delete** statement are indexed or not. Let us assume for the sake of the example that we are dealing with non-indexed attributes (which is obviously the case). As a result, the parsing function **delete()** must retrieve the tuples to be deleted, i.e. the ones that satisfy the given predicate. Accordingly, function **delete()**

enters a fetch loop, exactly like the parsing functions **select()** and **project()** did in the previous chapter. This fetch loop is triggered by repeatedly calling the query decomposer function **fetch()** to retrieve the qualifying tuples of the relation *SUPPLIER*. After fetching these qualifying tuples, function **delete()** initiates the actions necessary for their deletion. Actually, the parsing function **delete()** hands control over to the low-level function **delete_attrs()** whose prime responsibility is to delete attributes and tuples from the files underlying a given relation. In the following we will concentrate on the series of actions that the tuple fetching function performs. The sequence of low-level operations required to delete a given tuple has already been explained in Chapter 5.

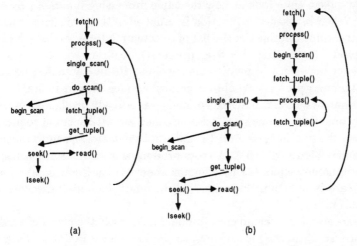

(a)   (b)

Figure 10.3 The sequence of function calls when accessing tuples of a non-indexed relation.

The sequence of function calls necessary to implement non-indexed tuple retrieval is depicted in Figure 10.3. As we can observe from this figure **fetch()** is the central function responsible for tuple accessing and processing. Besides being useful in its own right, the tuple fetching function illustrates some of the considerations involved in writing code for tuple accessing and also shows a real-life application of the REQUIEM query processing data structures. Function **fetch()** accepts two arguments: a pointer to the selection structure **sel** (see Figure 10.2), and a flag indicating whether the cross-product of two named relations should be formed. The tuple fetching function enters a loop which repeatedly calls the function **process()** to process all tuples fetched from the selected relation(s) in the current retrieval environment (see Figure 8.3).

When a tuple is retrieved the REQUIEM expression interpreter is called to check if the current tuple satisfies the predicate specified in the query (provided that one exists). When a given predicate is satisfied the expression interpreter returns the boolean value TRUE to signify that the tuple was successfully evaluated. This value is eventually returned to the function fetch(), which initiated the evaluation of the predicate, to indicate that the current tuple has been successfully processed. The individual attribute values contained in this tuple can then be accessed by means of the tuple buffer which is part of the scan structure of Figure 10.2.

10.1.3   Tuple processing

Let us now take a close look at how the tuple processing function process() operates. When invoked this function is supplied with a pointer to the first relation structure contained in the list of selected relations, and the boolean flag no_xprod. By testing this flag, process() confirms whether or not a cross-product between two relations is required. If this parameter no_xprod is TRUE no cross-product should be performed (see Figure 10.3(a)). This is the normal case. The only exception is, as already explained, when a join operation that involves no indexed condition attributes is requested. In this case the flag is turned off to indicate that a cross-product must be generated (see Figure 10.3(b)). A cross-product is always formed whenever two relation names separated by commas appear in an input query. Recall that this case is only possible when a join query has been specified (see section 9.3.1).

Things are simpler when no cross-product is formed: the result of a call to the function single_scan() is returned to the processing function. Function single_scan() uses the function do_scan() and assigns its return value to the current fetched tuple flag (sr_ctuple) element of the selected relation structure in the current retrieval context. The boolean sr_ctuple is turned on to denote that the present tuple has already been accessed and stored in the tuple buffer of the scan structure. By testing whether the flag sr_ctuple is turned on, function do_scan() determines if tuples have already been fetched. If none has, do_scan() calls begin_scan() to initiate a new scan process. Note that on the first call to fetch() the flag sr_ctuple is turned off and thus commences execution by fetching the first tuple in the data file. Once the scanning of tuples has been launched, function do_scan() invokes the low-level file manager function fetch_tuple() to fetch the actual data tuples from the disk and store them on a one by one basis in the tuple buffer for later use.

Suppose now that we wish to handle the more general problem of forming a cross-product of two or more relations. As already mentioned RE-QUIEM relies on the function process(), once again, for the implementation of the cross-product of two given relations. During the invocation of this function only the query processing data structures required for a pairwise concatenation of the original relation tuples are laid out in the current retrieval environment. It is worth mentioning at this stage that tuples from the distinct input relations are concatenated only if they include common values in their matching columns. This is a fact for the query evaluator to decide. Accordingly, the function **xinterpret()** is invoked by the fetching function immediately after **process()** returns.

```
int     process(srptr, no_xprod)
struct srel *srptr;
BOOL no_xprod;    /* signifies whether or not an x-product
                     between two relations should be formed */
{
    /* get a new tuple if this is the last relation in the list */
    if (SREL_NEXT == NULL || no_xprod)
        return(single_scan(srptr));

    /* check for the beginning of a new scan */
    if (srptr->sr_ctuple == FALSE) {
        begin_scan(srptr->sr_scan);

        /* get the first tuple */
        if (!fetch_tuple(srptr->sr_scan))
        return (FALSE);
    }

    /* look for a match with the inner relations in list */
    while (!process(SREL_NEXT, no_xprod))
        if (!fetch_tuple(srptr->sr_scan)) /* get the next tuple */
            return (srptr->sr_ctuple = FALSE);

    /* found a match at this level */
    return (srptr->sr_ctuple = TRUE);
} /* process */
```

Figure 10.4 The definition of the function **process()**.

Now let us focus on how the function **process()** implements the cross-product. As explained, a call to function **process()** must result in a pairwise concatenation of the tuples in the first two selected relation structures in the list of selected relations. To implement a cross-product operation, the parameter **no_xprod** of **process()** must be turned off. By finding the **no_xprod** turned off, **process()** understands that it must call itself recursively. During the first call to **process()** the scanning of the first (outer loop) relation in the list of selected relations is initialized as usual by a call to **begin_scan()**. Then, the first tuple of the outer relation is fetched by a call to **fetch_tuple()**. Next, the entire set of tuples belonging to the second element in the list of selected relations must be fetched. If this second (inner loop) relation structure is the last selected relation in the list this recursive call terminates by passing control to function **single_scan()** (see Figures 10.3 and 10.4). This function fetches the next tuple, if one exists; otherwise it returns FALSE. Thus, the recursive call to **process()** returns TRUE only if a tuple from the inner relation has been successfully fetched. Conversely, it returns FALSE to denote that no more tuples exist in the inner stored relation data file.

By testing the value returned by the function **process()** we can decide whether it is necessary to fetch the next tuple from the outer stored relation through a call to **fetch_tuple()**. This recursive call returns TRUE, to indicate that the next tuple of the inner stored relation has been retrieved. Consequently, the iteration loop in the body of function **process()** must not be entered (see Figure 10.4). Hence, the contents of the tuple buffer in the **scan** structure associated with the outer relation remain intact throughout this recursion phase. However, the tuple buffer scan structure associated with the inner relation is loaded with a new tuple from the inner stored relation as long as **process()** returns TRUE. The recursive call inside **process()** returns FALSE to indicate that all the tuples of the inner relation have been consumed. Now, the while loop in the body of function **process()** can be entered (see Figure 10.4). In this case the next outer relation tuple may be retrieved by a call to **fetch_tuple()**. This mode of operation continues up to the point when **fetch_tuple()** tries to read beyond the last tuple of the first stored relation. At this stage **process()** returns FALSE to its calling function which understands that the accessing of tuples has terminated.

10.2   Nested query processing

An alternative means of writing queries in REQUIEM is the use of nested queries which generate an unnamed intermediate relation. A nested query consists of a single outer subquery and one or more inner subqueries. Loosely speaking, a subquery is a normal RQL query which is nested inside another such query. A subquery denotes an unnamed relation which is dynamically created. Since this construct is unnamed it can only be used as a placeholder in the compound query; it cannot be referenced by name from some other part of the query.

In RQL the semantics of a subquery are identical to those of a normal query specification and subqueries can be nested to any depth. REQUIEM evaluates the overall query by evaluating the nested subqueries first. As the result of a nested DML operation, the system generates a new snapshot for each nested subquery.

Example 10.2.1

To find the names and departments of all employees who earn more than $40,000 per year, we must pose the following nested query:

project (**select from** employee **where** salary > 40000)
      over name, department;

The above query projects the snapshot relation that is generated by selecting all employees who earn more than $40,000, over the attributes *NAME* and *DEPARTMENT*. Alternatively, the same result could be obtained by posing the following two queries in succession:

assign tmp **to select from** employee **where** salary > 40000;
project tmp **over** name, department;

As you can see, the result of the **select** query is assigned to a transient relation, called *TMP*, and is then used in the **project** query. The nesting of queries, however, frees the user from the management of temporary relations. Moreover, a nested query is often more readable than a long sequence of elementary queries. This is of particular importance when views are defined. Even though a view can be defined as a complex query, it is always more easy to comprehend than the equivalent sequence of elementary statements linked by a set of temporary relations. However, in certain circumstances the use of transient relations can also be a very flexible facility. It must be clear that not all RQL statements can be used in a nested query. Only DML statements, i.e. statements that yield a snapshot relation as result, can be used as inner subqueries.

As you can see from the syntax of RQL in Appendix A nested queries are indicated by the presence of the non-terminal <*relation*>. This non-terminal can be expanded either to a relation name or to the name of one of the operations that are allowed to appear inside a query. Syntactically, a nested subquery is indicated to the parser by being enclosed in a pair of parentheses. In principle, the nesting of queries may be to any depth. In practice, however, the depth of nesting will seldom be more than three or four because such complex nested queries are very hard to comprehend and validate by a user.

The parsing of nested queries is initiated in the routines which perform a tuple selection. This seems reasonable, as a nested subquery can only appear inside a query exactly where a relation name can appear. Thus, we can confirm the existence of nested query statements within the two tuple selecting routines, namely **db_select()** and **retrieve()**, depending on the syntax structure of the nested query. These routines are called again to establish the retrieval environment which holds the necessary information for the query decomposer to implement tuple retrieval and to process the nested query statements successfully.

In general, a call to the function **nested_query()** initiates parsing of the nested query. Inside this function, the token following the opening parenthesis is examined to identify which kind of RQL operation is required. If an operation that introduces a legal nested subquery is encountered, its corresponding parsing function is called. Consequently, the parser is re-entered once more (in the case where only one subquery is present, refer to example 10.2.1 above) and the subquery is executed yielding a snapshot relation as a result. Finally, the internally generated snapshot name is processed as a normal relation name by the outer subquery, e.g. the **project** subquery in the sample nested expression in example 10.2.1.

The previous processing algorithm demonstrates quite clearly that nested queries in REQUIEM introduce multiple retrieval statements and require the use of multifile structures. The multifile structure in the implementation of nested queries is the outcome of the fact that a nested query must reference different relation files in its nested parts.

10.3   Source listing 6

file: quedcmp.c

```
1    /* REQUIEM - decompose queries and retrieve data */
2
3    #include "requ.h"
4    extern int      sref_cntr;
5    extern int      lex_token;
6    extern char     lexeme[];
7    extern char     rel_fl[];
8    extern char     *stck();
9    extern int      xint_error;
10   extern BOOL     view_exists;
11   char       errvar[ANSIZE];
12   BOOL wh_signal;                 /* selection predicate flag */
13   BOOL restore_paren = FALSE;  /* to be used with nested joins */
14
15   /* ----- select a set of tuples from a set of relations ----- */
16   struct sel *db_select(fmt)
17        char      *fmt;
18   {
19     struct sel *slptr;
```

```
20      char *pt_error();
21
22      /* check for a command line */
23      if (fmt != NULL)
24        q_scan(fmt);
25
26      /* allocate a sel structure */
27      if ((slptr =
28          (struct sel *)calloc(1, sizeof(struct sel ))) == NULL)
29        return ((struct sel *) pt_error(INSMEM));
30
31      /* initialize the structure */
32      SEL_RELS = NULL;
33      SEL_ATTRS = NULL;
34      slptr->sl_bindings = NULL;
35      wh_signal = FALSE;
36
37      /* parse the list of selected attributes */
38      if (!get_sel_attrs(slptr)) {
39        done(slptr);
40        return((struct sel *)NULL);
41      }
42
43      /* check for "from" clause */
44      if (this_token() != FROM) {
45        done(slptr);
46        return((struct sel *) pt_error(SYNTAX));
47      }
48
49      next_token();
50
51      /* expand view in case of view DML */
52      view_stat();
53
54      if (this_token() == ID) {
55        if (!get_sel(slptr)) {
56          done(slptr);
57          return((struct sel *)NULL);
58        }
59        /* if view name, it was simply a view definition */
60        view_exists = FALSE;
61      }
62      else {
63        /* check for nested clauses */
64        if (!nested_query())
65          return((struct sel *)NULL);
66
67        /* nested query processing */
68        if (!find_relation(slptr,stck(rel_fl,sref_cntr),(char *) 0)) {
69          done(slptr);
70          return((struct sel *)NULL);
71        }
72      }
73
74      /* check the list of selected attributes */
75      if (!check_attrs(slptr)) {
76        done(slptr);
77        return((struct sel *)NULL);
78      }
79
80      if (!predicate(slptr))
```

```
81         return((struct sel *)NULL);
82
83      /* return the new selection structure */
84      return (slptr);
85
86   } /* db_select */
87
88   /* --- retrieve a set of tuples from a set of relations ----- */
89   struct sel *retrieve(fmt)
90         char      *fmt;
91   {
92     char *pt_error();
93     struct sel *slptr;
94
95     /* check for a command line */
96     if (fmt != NULL)
97       q_scan(fmt);
98
99     /* allocate a sel structure */
100    if ((slptr =
101        (struct sel *)calloc(1, sizeof(struct sel ))) == NULL)
102      return ((struct sel *) pt_error(INSMEM));
103
104    /* initialize the structure */
105    SEL_RELS = NULL;
106    SEL_ATTRS = NULL;
107    slptr->sl_bindings = NULL;
108    wh_signal = FALSE;
109
110    /* check for selected relations clause */
111    if (this_token() == ID) {
112      if (!get_sel(slptr)) {
113        done(slptr);
114        return((struct sel *)NULL);
115      }
116      /* if view exists, it was simply a view definition  */
117      view_exists = FALSE;
118    } else {
119      /* check for nested clauses */
120      if (!nested_query())
121        return((struct sel *)NULL);
122
123      /* nested query processing */
124      if (!find_relation(slptr,
125                          stck(rel_fl, sref_cntr), (char *) 0)) {
126        done(slptr);
127        return((struct sel *)NULL);
128      }
129    }
130
131    /* check for "over" clause */
132    if (this_token() == OVER)
133      next_token();
134
135    /* parse the list of selected attributes */
136    if (!get_sel_attrs(slptr)) {
137      done(slptr);
138      return((struct sel *)NULL);
139    }
140
141    /* check the list of selected attributes */
```

```
142        if (!check_attrs(slptr)) {
143          done(slptr);
144          return((struct sel *)NULL);
145        }
146
147        /* check for "group" clause */
148        if (this_token() == GROUP)
149          return(slptr);
150
151        /* check for the existence of a "where" clause */
152        if (!predicate(slptr))
153          return((struct sel *)NULL);
154
155        /* return the new selection structure */
156        return (slptr);
157
158      } /* retrieve */
159
160      /* ------ check whether this query is a nested query -------- */
161      static int    nested_query()
162      {
163        int     status;
164
165        /* check first if this is a nested query
166           and then if it is a view call */
167        if (this_token() == '(' || view_exists) {
168
169          if (view_exists == FALSE)
170            next_token();
171
172          switch (next_token()) {
173          case DIFFERENCE:
174            status = db_union(FALSE, TRUE);
175            break;
176          case EXPOSE:
177            status = expose(TRUE);
178            break;
179          case INTERSECT:
180            status = db_union(FALSE, FALSE);
181            break;
182          case JOIN:
183            status = nat_join(TRUE);
184            break;
185          case PROJECT:
186            status = project(TRUE);
187            break;
188          case SELECT:
189            status = select(TRUE);
190            break;
191          case UNION:
192            status = db_union(TRUE, FALSE);
193            break;
194          default:
195            return(FALSE);
196          }
197
198          if (!status)
199            return(FALSE);
200
201          if (view_exists && this_token() == ';') { /* a view call */
202
```

```
203          /* clear query terminator  */
204          next_token();
205
206          view_exists = FALSE; /* reset flag */
207          return(TRUE);
208        }
209      else if (view_exists) {
210          view_exists = FALSE; /* reset flag */
211          return(TRUE);         /* exit */
212      } else
213          if (next_token() != ')') /* closing nested query paren. */
214          return(error(NESTED));
215      }
216    return(TRUE);
217  } /* nested_query */
218
219  /* ----------- check for existence of a predicate ----------- */
220  static int      predicate(slptr)
221        struct sel *slptr;
222  {
223    /* check for the existence of a "where" clause */
224    if (this_token() == WHERE) {
225      next_token();
226
227      wh_signal = TRUE;  /* predicate is present */
228
229      /* parse the boolean expression */
230      if (!xcompile(slptr)) {
231        done(slptr);
232        return (FALSE);
233      }
234    }
235
236    return(TRUE);
237
238  } /* predicate */
239
240  /* ------------- predicate in a join query ----------------- */
241  where_in_join(wh_attr, relop, constant)
242        char *wh_attr, *relop, *constant;
243  {
244    int tkn;
245
246    if (next_token() != WHERE)
247      return(error(SYNTAX));
248
249    /* get the relation name */
250    if (next_token() != ID)
251      return(error(SYNTAX));
252
253    strcpy(wh_attr, lexeme);
254
255    if (next_token() != '.')   /* must be a qualified attribute */
256      return(error(QUATTR));
257
258    /* get the attribute name */
259    if (next_token() != ID)
260      return(error(SYNTAX));
261
262    /* produce the qualified attribute */
263    make_quattr(wh_attr, lexeme);
```

```
264
265     /* the next token must be a relational operator */
266     tkn = next_token();
267     if (relational_op(tkn, relop) == FALSE)
268       return(error(SYNTAX));
269
270     /* the next token must be a numeric or string constant */
271     tkn = next_token();
272     if (ns_constant(tkn, constant) == FALSE)
273       return(error(SYNTAX));
274
275     /* in case of a nested call, check for closing parenth. */
276     if (this_token() == ')')
277       restore_paren = TRUE;
278
279     /* return successfully */
280     return(TRUE);
281
282   } /* where_in_join */
283
284   /* -- check if next token is a rel operator and return it -- */
285   BOOL relational_op(tkn, relop)
286        int tkn;   char *relop;
287   {
288     char *rel_op;
289
290     switch (tkn) {
291     case LSS:
292       rel_op = "<";
293       break;
294     case LEQ:
295       rel_op = "<=";
296       break;
297     case EQL:
298       rel_op = "=";
299       break;
300     case PART:
301       rel_op = "==";
302       break;
303     case NEQ:
304       rel_op = "<>";
305       break;
306     case GEQ:
307       rel_op = ">=";
308       break;
309     case GTR:
310       rel_op = ">";
311       break;
312
313     default: return(FALSE);
314     }
315     strcpy(relop, rel_op);
316     return(TRUE);
317
318   } /* relational_op */
319
320   /* ---------------- number or string constant ---------------- */
321   BOOL ns_constant(tkn, constant)
322        int tkn;   char *constant;
323   {
324     /* the next token must be a constant */
```

```
325      if (tkn != NUMBER && tkn != REALNO && tkn != STRING)
326        return(FALSE);
327
328      if (tkn == STRING)
329        sprintf(constant,"\"%s\"", lexeme);
330      else
331        strcpy(constant, lexeme);
332
333      return(TRUE);
334    } /* ns_constant */
335    /*----------------- finish a selection -------------------- */
337    int done(slptr)
338        struct sel *slptr;
339    {
340      struct sattr *saptr, *nxtsa;
341      struct srel *srptr, *nxtsr;
342      struct binding *bdptr, *nxtbd;
343
344      /* free the selected attribute blocks */
345      for (saptr = SEL_ATTRS; saptr != NULL; saptr = nxtsa) {
346        nxtsa = saptr->sa_next;
347        if (saptr->sa_rname != NULL)
348          free(saptr->sa_rname);
349        free(saptr->sa_aname);
350        if (saptr->sa_name != NULL)
351          free(saptr->sa_name);
352        free((char *) saptr);
353      }
354
355      /* close the scans and free the selected relation blocks */
356      for (srptr = SEL_RELS; srptr != NULL; srptr = nxtsr) {
357        nxtsr = SREL_NEXT;
358        if (srptr->sr_name != NULL)
359          free(srptr->sr_name);
360        db_rclose(srptr->sr_scan);
361        free((char *) srptr);
362      }
363      wh_signal = FALSE;
364      /* free the user bindings */
365      for (bdptr = slptr->sl_bindings;bdptr != NULL;bdptr = nxtbd) {
366        nxtbd = bdptr->bd_next;
367        free((char *) bdptr);
368      }
369
370      /* free the selection structure */
371      free((char *) slptr);
372
373    } /* done */
374
375    /* ------- fetch the next tuple requested by a query -------- */
376    int    fetch(slptr, no_xprod)
377        struct sel *slptr;
378        BOOL no_xprod;
379    {
380      struct srel *srptr;
381      struct binding *bdptr;
382
383      /* clear the update flags */
384      for (srptr = SEL_RELS; srptr != NULL; srptr = SREL_NEXT)
385        srptr->sr_update = FALSE;
```

```
386
387     /* find a matching tuple */
388     while (process(SEL_RELS, no_xprod)) {
389       if (xint_error) /* interpretation error detected */
390         break;
391       if (xinterpret()) {
392         for (bdptr = slptr->sl_bindings; bdptr != NULL;
393                                     bdptr = bdptr->bd_next)
394           get_attr(bdptr->bd_attr,bdptr->bd_vtuple,bdptr->bd_vuser);
395         return (TRUE);
396       }
397     }
398
399     /* no matches, failure return */
400     return (FALSE);
401   } /* fetch */
402
403   /* ---- get selected attribute type, pointer, and length ---- */
404   int     select_attr(slptr, rname, aname, ptype, val_ptr, plen)
405       struct sel *slptr;
406       char     *rname, *aname; /* rel and corresp. attr names */
407       int      *ptype, *plen;  /* attribute type and length */
408       char     **val_ptr;      /* buffer for attr value */
409   {
410     struct srel *srptr;
411     struct attribute *aptr;
412
413     if (!find_attr(slptr, rname, aname, val_ptr, &srptr, &aptr))
414       return (FALSE);
415     *ptype = aptr->at_type;
416     *plen = aptr->at_size;
417     return (TRUE);
418   } /* select_attr */
419
420   /* --------------- get selected attributes ----------------- */
421   static get_sel_attrs(slptr)
422       struct sel *slptr;
423   {
424     struct sattr *newsattr, *lastsattr;
425     int      error();
426
427     /* check for "all" or blank field meaning all attributes
428      * are selected */
429     if (this_token() == ALL) {
430       next_token();
431       return (TRUE);
432     } else if (this_token() != ID)
433       return (TRUE);
434
435     /* parse a list of attribute names */
436     lastsattr = NULL;
437     while (TRUE) {
438
439       /* get attribute name */
440       if (next_token() != ID)
441         return (error(SYNTAX));
442
443       /* allocate a selected attribute structure */
444       if ((newsattr =
445         (struct sattr *)calloc(1, sizeof(struct sattr ))) == NULL)
446         return (error(INSMEM));
```

```
447
448          /* initialize the selected attribute structure */
449          newsattr->sa_next = NULL;
450
451          /* save the attribute name */
452          if ((newsattr->sa_aname =
453                       rmalloc(strlen(lexeme) + 1)) == NULL) {
454            free((char *) newsattr);
455            return (error(INSMEM));
456          }
457          strcpy(newsattr->sa_aname, lexeme);
458
459          /* check for "." meaning "<rel-name>.<att-name>" */
460          if (this_token() == '.') {
461            next_token();
462
463            /* the previous ID was really the relation name */
464            newsattr->sa_rname = newsattr->sa_aname;
465
466            /* check for attribute name */
467            if (next_token() != ID) {
468              free(newsattr->sa_aname);
469              free((char *) newsattr);
470              return (error(SYNTAX));
471            }
472
473            /* save the attribute name */
474            if ((newsattr->sa_aname =
475                        rmalloc(strlen(lexeme) + 1)) == NULL) {
476              free(newsattr->sa_aname);
477              free((char *) newsattr);
478              return (error(INSMEM));
479            }
480            strcpy(newsattr->sa_aname, lexeme);
481          } else
482            newsattr->sa_rname = NULL;
483
484          /* check for secondary attribute name */
485          if (this_token() == ID) {
486            next_token();
487
488            /* allocate space for the secondary name */
489            if ((newsattr->sa_name =
490                        rmalloc(strlen(lexeme) + 1)) == NULL) {
491              if (newsattr->sa_rname != NULL)
492                free(newsattr->sa_rname);
493              free(newsattr->sa_aname);
494              free((char *) newsattr);
495              return (error(INSMEM));
496            }
497            strcpy(newsattr->sa_name, lexeme);
498          } else
499            newsattr->sa_name = NULL;
500
501          /* set rname in structure sattr */
502          if (SEL_RELS != NULL) {
503            if (!set_rname(slptr, SEL_RELATION->rl_name))
504              return(FALSE);
505          }
506
507          /* link the selected attribute structure into the list */
```

```
508         if (lastsattr == NULL)
509           SEL_ATTRS = newsattr;
510         else
511           lastsattr->sa_next = newsattr;
512         lastsattr = newsattr;
513
514         /* check for more attributes */
515         if (this_token() != ',')
516           break;
517         next_token();
518       }
519
520     /* return successfully */
521     return (TRUE);
522   } /* get_sel_attrs */
523
524   /* ------- insert a relation into sel structure ------------- */
525   static get_sel(slptr)
526         struct sel *slptr;
527   {
528     /* get the list of selected relations */
529     while (TRUE) {
530
531         /* get selected relation(s) */
532         if (!get_sel_rel(slptr))
533           return(FALSE);
534
535         /* check for more selected relations */
536         if (this_token() != ',')
537           break;
538         next_token();
539       }
540
541     /* return successfully */
542     return (TRUE);
543   } /* get_sel */
544
545   /* ------------------- get selected relations --------------- */
546   static get_sel_rel(slptr)
547         struct sel *slptr;
548   {
549     char     rname[KEYWORDMAX+1], *aname;
550
551     /* check for relation name */
552     if (next_token() != ID)
553       return (error(SYNTAX));
554     strcpy(rname, lexeme);
555
556     /* check for secondary relation name */
557     if (this_token() == ID) {
558       next_token();
559       aname = lexeme;
560     } else
561       aname = NULL;
562
563     /* set the relation name */
564     if (!set_rname(slptr, rname))
565       return(FALSE);
566
567     /* add the relation name to the relation list */
568     if (!find_relation(slptr, rname, aname))
```

```
569        return (FALSE);
570
571     /* return successfully */
572     return(TRUE);
573   } /* get_sel_rel */
574
575   /* -------------------- find a relation --------------------- */
576   static find_relation(slptr, rname, aname)
577        struct sel *slptr;
578        char      *rname, *aname;
579   {
580     struct scan *db_ropen();
581     struct srel *srptr, *newsrel;
582
583     /* allocate a new selected relation structure */
584     if ((newsrel =
585         (struct srel *)calloc(1, sizeof(struct srel ))) == NULL)
586       return (error(INSMEM));
587
588     /* initialize the new selected relation structure */
589     newsrel->sr_ctuple = FALSE;
590     newsrel->sr_update = FALSE;
591     newsrel->sr_next = NULL;
592
593     /* open the relation */
594     if ((newsrel->sr_scan = db_ropen(rname)) == NULL) {
595       free((char *) newsrel);
596       return (FALSE);
597     }
598
599     /* check for secondary relation name */
600     if (aname != NULL) {
601
602       /* allocate space for the secondary name */
603       if ((newsrel->sr_name =
604           malloc((unsigned) strlen(aname) + 1)) == NULL) {
605         free((char *) newsrel);
606         return (error(INSMEM));
607       }
608       strcpy(newsrel->sr_name, aname);
609     } else
610       newsrel->sr_name = NULL;
611
612     /* initialize record position */
613     newsrel->sr_scan->sc_recpos = 0;
614
615     /* find the end of the list of relation names */
616     for (srptr = SEL_RELS; srptr != NULL; srptr = SREL_NEXT)
617       if (SREL_NEXT == NULL)
618         break;
619
620     /* link the new selected relation structure into the list */
621     if (srptr == NULL)
622       SEL_RELS = newsrel;
623     else
624       SREL_NEXT = newsrel;
625
626     /* return successfully */
627     return (TRUE);
628   }
629
```

```
630     /* ------------------------------------------------------------ */
631
632     /* check the list of selected attributes */
633     static int     check_attrs(slptr)
634          struct sel *slptr;
635     {
636       struct sattr *saptr;
637
638       /* check for all attributes selected */
639       if (SEL_ATTRS == NULL)
640         return (all_attrs(slptr));
641
642       /* check each selected attribute */
643       for (saptr = SEL_ATTRS; saptr != NULL; saptr = saptr->sa_next)
644         if (!find_attr(slptr, saptr->sa_rname, saptr->sa_aname,
645                   &saptr->sa_aptr, &saptr->sa_srel, &saptr->sa_attr))
646           return (FALSE);
647
648       /* return successfully */
649       return (TRUE);
650     }
651
652     /* ------------------------------------------------------------ */
653
654     /* create a list of all attributes */
655     static int     all_attrs(slptr)
656          struct sel *slptr;
657     {
658       struct sattr *newsattr, *lastsattr;
659       struct srel *srptr;
660       struct attribute *aptr;
661       int     i, astart;
662
663       /* loop through each selected relation */
664       lastsattr = NULL;
665       for (srptr = SEL_RELS; srptr != NULL; srptr = SREL_NEXT) {
666
667         /* loop through each attribute within the relation */
668         astart = 1;
669         for (i = 0; i < NATTRS; i++) {
670
671           /* get a pointer to the current attribute */
672           aptr = &SREL_HEADER.hd_attrs[i];
673
674           /* check for last attribute */
675           if (aptr->at_name[0] == EOS)
676             break;
677
678           /* allocate a new selected attribute structure */
679           if ((newsattr =
680           (struct sattr *)calloc(1, sizeof(struct sattr ))) == NULL)
681             return (error(INSMEM));
682
683           /* initialize the new selected attribute structure */
684           newsattr->sa_name = NULL;
685           newsattr->sa_srel = srptr;
686           newsattr->sa_aptr = srptr->sr_scan->sc_tuple + astart;
687           newsattr->sa_attr = aptr;
688           newsattr->sa_next = NULL;
689
690           /* save the relation name */
```

```
691        if ((newsattr->sa_rname = rmalloc(RNSIZE + 1)) == NULL) {
692          free((char *) newsattr);
693          return (error(INSMEM));
694        }
695
696        strncpy(newsattr->sa_rname, SREL_RELATION->rl_name,
697                MIN(strlen(SREL_RELATION->rl_name), RNSIZE));
698        newsattr->sa_rname[MIN(strlen(SREL_RELATION->rl_name),
699                                          RNSIZE)] = EOS;
700
701        /* save the attribute name */
702        if ((newsattr->sa_aname = rmalloc(ANSIZE + 1)) == NULL) {
703          free(newsattr->sa_rname);
704          free((char *) newsattr);
705          return (error(INSMEM));
706        }
707        strncpy(newsattr->sa_aname,
708                SREL_HEADER.hd_attrs[i].at_name,
709                ANSIZE);
710        newsattr->sa_aname[ANSIZE] = EOS;
711
712        /* link the selected attribute into the list */
713        if (lastsattr == NULL)
714          SEL_ATTRS = newsattr;
715        else
716          lastsattr->sa_next = newsattr;
717        lastsattr = newsattr;
718
719        /* update the attribute start */
720        astart += aptr->at_size;
721      }
722    }
723
724    /* return successfully */
725    return (TRUE);
726  }
727
728  /* ------------------------------------------------------------ */
729
730  /* find a named attribute */
731  int     find_attr(slptr, rname, aname, val_ptr, psrel, pattr)
732      struct sel *slptr;
733      char       *rname, *aname;
734      char       **val_ptr;
735      struct attribute **pattr;
736      struct srel **psrel;
737  {
738    /* check for unqualified or qualified attribute names */
739    if (rname == NULL)
740      return (unqu_attr(slptr, aname, val_ptr, psrel, pattr));
741    else
742      return (qual_attr(slptr,rname,aname,val_ptr,psrel,pattr));
743  }
744
745  /* ------------------------------------------------------------ */
746
747  /* find an unqualified attribute name */
748  static int     unqu_attr(slptr, aname, val_ptr, psrel, pattr)
749      struct sel *slptr;
750      char       *aname;
751      char       **val_ptr;
```

```
752          struct srel **psrel;
753          struct attribute **pattr;
754   {
755      struct srel *srptr;
756      struct relation *relptr;
757      struct attribute *aptr;
758      int     i, astart;
759
760
761      /* loop through each selected relation */
762      *pattr = NULL;
763      for (srptr = SEL_RELS; srptr != NULL; srptr = SREL_NEXT) {
764        /* detect existence of multiple relations */
765        if (SREL_NEXT) {
766          relptr =   SREL_NEXT->sr_scan->sc_relation;
767
768          if (SEL_RELATION->rl_next == NULL)
769            SEL_RELATION->rl_next = relptr;
770
771          relptr->rl_next = NULL;
772        }
773        else {
774          relptr =   SREL_RELATION;
775          relptr->rl_next = NULL;
776        }
777
778        /* loop through each attribute within the relation */
779        astart = 1;
780        for (i = 0; i < NATTRS; i++) {
781
782          /* get a pointer to the current attribute */
783          aptr = &SREL_HEADER.hd_attrs[i];
784
785          /* check for last attribute */
786          if (aptr->at_name[0] == EOS)
787            break;
788
789          /* check for attribute name match */
790          if (strncmp(aname, aptr->at_name, ANSIZE) == EQUAL) {
791            if (*pattr != NULL)
792              return (error(ATAMBG));
793            *val_ptr = srptr->sr_scan->sc_tuple + astart;
794            *psrel = srptr;
795            *pattr = aptr;
796          }
797
798          /* update the attribute start */
799          astart += aptr->at_size;
800        }
801      }
802
803      /* check whether attribute was found */
804      if (*pattr == NULL) {
805        strcpy(errvar, aname);
806        errvar[strlen(aname)] = EOS;
807
808        return (error(ATUNDF));
809      }
810      /* return successfully */
811      return (TRUE);
812   }
```

```
813
814     /* ------------------------------------------------------------ */
815
816     /* find a qualified attribute name */
817     static int qual_attr(slptr, rname, aname, val_ptr, psrel, pattr)
818           struct sel *slptr;
819           char     *rname, *aname;
820           char     **val_ptr;
821           struct srel **psrel;
822           struct attribute **pattr;
823     {
824       struct srel *srptr;
825       struct relation *relptr;
826       struct attribute *aptr;
827       char     *crname;
828       int      i, astart;
829
830         /* loop through each selected relation */
831         for (srptr = SEL_RELS; srptr != NULL; srptr = SREL_NEXT) {
832
833           /* detect existence of multiple relations */
834           if (SREL_NEXT) {
835             relptr =   SREL_NEXT->sr_scan->sc_relation;
836
837             if (SEL_RELATION->rl_next == NULL)
838               SEL_RELATION->rl_next = relptr;
839
840             relptr->rl_next = NULL;
841           }
842           else {
843             relptr =   SREL_RELATION;
844             relptr->rl_next = NULL;
845           }
846
847           /* get relation name */
848           if ((crname = srptr->sr_name) == NULL)
849             crname = SREL_RELATION->rl_name;
850
851           /* check for relation name match */
852           if (strncmp(rname, crname, RNSIZE) == EQUAL) {
853
854             /* loop through each attribute within the relation */
855             astart = 1;
856             for (i = 0; i < NATTRS; i++) {
857
858               /* get a pointer to the current attribute */
859               aptr = &SREL_HEADER.hd_attrs[i];
860
861               /* check for last attribute */
862               if (aptr->at_name[0] == EOS)
863                 break;
864
865               /* check for attribute name match */
866               if (strncmp(aname, aptr->at_name, ANSIZE) == EQUAL) {
867                 *val_ptr = srptr->sr_scan->sc_tuple + astart;
868                 *psrel = srptr;
869                 *pattr = aptr;
870                 return (TRUE);
871               }
872
873               /* update the attribute start */
```

```
874              astart += aptr->at_size;
875          }
876          /* attribute name not found */
877          strcpy(errvar, aname);
878          errvar[strlen(aname)] = EOS;
879
880          return (error(ATUNDF));
881        }
882      }
883
884      /* relation name not found */
885      return (error(RLUNDF));
886  } /* qual_attr */
887
888  /* ------------------------------------------------------------ */
889
890  /* process each tuple in a relation cross-product */
891  int     process(srptr, no_xprod)
892      struct srel *srptr;
893      BOOL no_xprod; /* signifies whether or not an x-product
894                      * between two rels should be formed */
895  {
896    /* always get a new tuple if this is the last rel in list */
897    if (SREL_NEXT == NULL || no_xprod)
898      return(single_scan(srptr));
899
900    /* check for the beginning of a new scan */
901    if (srptr->sr_ctuple == FALSE) {
902      begin_scan(srptr->sr_scan);
903
904      /* get the first tuple */
905      if (!fetch_tuple(srptr->sr_scan))
906        return (FALSE);
907    }
908
909    /* look for a match with the remaining relations in list */
910    while (!process(SREL_NEXT, no_xprod))
911      /* get the next tuple in the scan */
912      if (!fetch_tuple(srptr->sr_scan))
913        return (srptr->sr_ctuple = FALSE);
914
915    /* found a match at this level */
916    return (srptr->sr_ctuple = TRUE);
917  }
918
919  /* ------------------------------------------------------------ */
920
921  int     do_scan(srptr)
922      struct srel *srptr;
923  {
924    /* check for beginning of new scan,
925       if no tuples have been fetched so far, begin scanning */
926    if (srptr->sr_ctuple == FALSE)
927      begin_scan(srptr->sr_scan);
928
929    /* get the first tuple */
930    if (!fetch_tuple(srptr->sr_scan))
931      return (FALSE);
932
933    /* return successfully */
934    return(TRUE);
```

```
935
936     } /* do_scan */
937
938     /* ------------------------------------------------------------ */
939
940     begin_scan(sptr)     /* begin scan at first tuple in relation */
941          struct scan *sptr;
942     {
943       /* begin with the first tuple in the file */
944       sptr->sc_dtnum = 0;
945
946     } /* begin_scan */
947
948     /* ------------------------------------------------------------ */
949
950     int  single_scan(srptr)
951          struct srel *srptr;
952     {
953       return (srptr->sr_ctuple = do_scan(srptr));
954
955     } /*scan_single */
956
957     /* ------------------------------------------------------------ */
958
959     /* get the value of an attribute */
960     get_attr(aptr, vptr, avalue)
961          struct attribute *aptr;
962          char      *vptr, *avalue;
963     {
964       int     i;
965
966       /* get the attribute value */
967       for (i = 0; i < aptr->at_size; i++)
968         *avalue++ = vptr[i];
969       *avalue = EOS;
970     }
971
972     /* ------------------------------------------------------------ */
973
974     /* put the value of an attribute */
975     store_attr(aptr, vptr, avalue)
976          struct attribute *aptr;
977          char      *vptr, *avalue;
978     {
979       int     i;
980
981       /* initialize counter */
982       i = 0;
983
984       /* right justify numbers */
985       if (aptr->at_type == TNUM || aptr->at_type == TREAL)
986         for (; i < aptr->at_size - strlen(avalue); i++)
987           vptr[i] = ' ';
988
989       /* put the attribute value */
990       for (; i < aptr->at_size; i++)
991         if (*avalue == EOS)
992           vptr[i] = EOS;
993         else
994           vptr[i] = *avalue++;
995
```

```
 996   }
 997
 998   /* ------------------------------------------------------------ */
 999
1000   set_rname(slptr, rname)
1001       struct sel *slptr;
1002       char     *rname;
1003   {
1004     if (SEL_ATTRS && SEL_ATTRS->sa_rname == NULL) {
1005
1006       /* save the relation name */
1007       if ((SEL_ATTRS->sa_rname = rmalloc(RNSIZE + 1)) == NULL)
1008         return (error(INSMEM));
1009
1010
1011       strncpy(SEL_ATTRS->sa_rname, rname,
1012               MIN(strlen(rname), RNSIZE));
1013       SEL_ATTRS->sa_rname[MIN(strlen(rname), RNSIZE)] = EOS;
1014     }
1015     return(TRUE);
1016   }
1017
1018   /* ------------------------------------------------------------ */
1019
```

11

Predicate Expression Evaluation

The selection clauses as defined in the relational database languages provide facilities for retrieving a set of tuples from a given relation on the basis of a selection predicate. The inputs to the selection process should be a specified relation name and a predicate expression which provides the selection criteria used in deriving the tuples from the specified stored relation. The predicate expression contains at least one named attribute from the given relation as a variable operand. The result of the selection process is a new relation having the same degree as its base relation and comprising all the tuples that satisfy the given predicate.

11.1 Predicate expressions in RQL

In RQL, the predicate expression of a query is introduced by the keyword **where**. A **where** clause consists of a set of atoms that can be connected by the logical operators &, |, and $\sim$. Each atom consists of relation attributes, constant expressions, or a simple attribute connected by one of the comparison operators $<$, $>$, $\leq$, $\geq$, $=$. Remember that predicate expressions in RQL also allow the use of parentheses nested to any depth, and assume a left-to-right order of infix operators with a predefined precedence.

Example 11.1.1

Consider the query *"select all products which have weight more than 100 lbs and have an oak finish."*

select all from product **where** weight > 100 & finish $=$ "oak";

The result of the former query is a snapshot relation that consists of all tuples of the relation *PRODUCT* that satisfy the predicate in example 11.1. During the selection of tuples the affected predicate expression has to be evaluated for each tuple in turn. This can be attributed to the fact that a predicate normally involves tuple-specific components, i.e. attribute variables. Therefore, each single attribute value must be retrieved from each tuple of the named relation and the predicate has to be evaluated by replacing all variable occurrences by their corresponding values. As an attribute may or may not be indexed, the corresponding access method must obviously be identified. The access methods are determined by the DBMS during predicate compilation, thus freeing the user from having to think in terms of physical data representation.

Consider the implications that the above example may have for each tuple of the *PRODUCT* relation. Here, the attribute names *WEIGHT* and *FINISH* in the predicate expression should be replaced by the values of their corresponding attributes in all the tuples currently included in the relation, much in the same way as normal variables in programming languages are. The predicate is then evaluated for each tuple in turn to yield a boolean value. On the basis of this boolean value an entire tuple can be included in the resulting snapshot relation, or discarded.

The main objective of the predicate expression subsystem is to transform an expression formulated in a specific expression sublanguage into a sequence of statements that can be executed efficiently by the underlying DBMS. From what has been mentioned so far it is obvious that the evaluation of predicate expressions must be performed in an effective manner in order not to degrade the overall throughput of the DBMS. In general, two approaches are feasible for predicate expression evaluation: *interpretation* and *compilation*. In the purely interpretative approach the mapping of high-level data language constructs to low-level access routines is done each time an evaluation of the expression is requested. On the other hand, if predicate expressions are to be compiled, then the expression under evaluation is transformed into an internal format as soon as the expression is first encountered. The compiled expression is then stored so that it may be accessed later when evaluation of the corresponding expression is requested. Each of the above approaches has its own merits which will be outlined briefly below.

11.1.1 Predicate expression interpretation

In the interpretative approach the operations involved in the expression are executed at source code level. The interpreter parses the expression and for each syntactic token met, such as an operator or an operand, takes the appropriate action. For example consider the predicate expression part of an RQL statement:

$$\cdots \textbf{where} \quad weight \; > \; 100 \; \& \; finish \; = \; \text{``}oak\text{''}; \tag{11.1}$$

During the process of parsing, after *WEIGHT* has been recognized as the name of an attribute, its value is fetched and subsequently stored. Then the > operator is recognized as a binary operator and the corresponding function is identified. Subsequently, the interpreter requests the right-hand side operand for the encountered operator, namely the constant 100. Finally, the function associated with the > operator is called with the value of the attribute *WEIGHT* and the constant 100 as parameters, yielding a boolean value that is used later during selection. Interpretation then proceeds in a similar fashion until the entire expression is consumed.

One attractive advantage of the interpretative approach is that it introduces no overhead for transforming a source code expression into an intermediate level for execution. If an expression is evaluated only once, or at least only a few times, this approach is feasible. On the other hand, interpretation of source code is much slower than execution of the equivalent compiled form. This is mainly due to the fact that each subsequent interpretation of an already executed expression involves lexical analysis and syntax analysis, although the expression is known to be syntactically correct when interpreted for the first time.

11.1.2 Predicate expression compilation

In order to increase execution speed, the process of compilation is used to transform an expression formulated in a query language into a format that can be executed by the underlying hardware. In a less rigid approach the compiler can even be used to transform source code into an intermediate form destined for some *abstract machine* (e.g. P-code in the case of UCSD-Pascal), instead of immediately computing the results. The advantage of this method is that execution speed can be substantially improved while reducing the compilation overhead.

11.1.3   The intermediate approach

The approach taken by REQUIEM is a combination of the interpretative and compilation approaches as mentioned above. A predicate expression is transformed by the expression compiler into an internal format suited for efficient evaluation at the phase of tuple selection. During tuple selection the compiled expression is processed by the *expression interpreter*, which evaluates the predicate expression for each tuple in turn. As explained, predicate expression evaluation is effected by substituting the attribute variables involved in the predicate expression with their actual values. The resulting boolean value is then used to determine whether this specific tuple is legitimate, or not.

Compilation of a predicate expression is performed once for each query during the process of query decomposition. During compilation, syntax errors are detected and reported to the user. If the expression is syntactically correct the operators are identified and the corresponding C functions are placed into a code array which stores the intermediate code for later evaluation. Additionally, the operands are identified and care is taken that their corresponding values can be accessed from the stored relation(s) during expression evaluation.

In the following section, the functions of the predicate expression compiler and interpreter of REQUIEM will be outlined together with the C code that actually implements them. To exemplify the functionality of the expression compiler and interpreter we introduce an example that shows how a predicate expression is compiled into an internal notation, and how that notation is utilized by the interpreter to evaluate the predicate expression in terms of the actual tuples stored in the database.

11.2   The predicate expression compiler

The predicate expression compiler of REQUIEM (PEC) parses an expression using recursive descent parsing. The first function that should be called during predicate expression compilation is the function corresponding to the (unique) start symbol of the grammar. Each reserved function is implemented according to the rules of the predicate expression grammar as applied to its corresponding non-terminal symbol. All legal sentences of the predicate expression sublanguage can be derived by starting with the special start symbol <expression> and recursively replacing non-terminal symbols with other non-terminal and/or terminal symbols, exactly as explained in Chapter 8. This manual process is directly reflected in the reserved C functions of the PEC. To give you an impression of how this parsing process is materialized, we consider the sample predicate expression 11.1.

The PEC starts by issuing a call to the compiling function **xcompile()**. The function **xcompile()** merely calls the function **expression()** that is associated with the start symbol of the predicate sublanguage grammar, namely <*expression*>, so that the compilation phase can commence. The parsing of predicate expressions then proceeds exactly as explained in section 8.4.

During the process of parsing a predicate expression, the corresponding intermediate code is generated and placed into the corresponding code array, which will subsequently be accessed by the predicate expression interpreter. If the parsing process is successful, the end of the generated code in the intermediate code array is marked as such and compilation stops. Conversely, if an error has occurred during the compilation phase, the space occupied by the code generated so far is released and compilation stops with **xcompile()**, returning the value FALSE to the query decomposer to indicate to the calling function that a compilation error has occurred. Subsequently, the appropriate error message is forwarded to the user. In the following section, we shall see how the PEC generates intermediate code for the evaluation of predicate expressions.

11.3   Intermediate code generation

During code generation the parse tree that has been constructed at the phase of parsing is used to transform the source statement into an intermediate language. In this task decisions are taken as to where data should be placed and how to access stored data and intermediate results. The choice of an intermediate language partly depends on the amount of code optimization that is requested from the compiler. If extensive code optimization is requested a *three address code** is preferred, whereas in the case of little or no optimization, assembly or machine code can be produced. In REQUIEM no particular code optimization is performed, so the code produced is in a form that can be directly executed by a *stack machine*. By stack machine we mean an abstract machine which has separate instruction and data memories and all arithmetic operations are performed on values on a stack.

Code generation in general is a complex and very specialized task. In REQUIEM, two facts simplify this job:

---

*Three address code is an intermediate code language in which each instruction consists of an operator and three addresses, two for the operands of the given operator and one for the result.

1. The syntax of the RQL predicate expression sublanguage is fairly simple.
2. The code produced directly reflects the syntax of the source code.

There are several approaches to code generation, but a method that is both elegant and efficient is that of the *syntax-directed translation* [42]. In this approach each node of the parse tree is associated with a piece of intermediate code. The actual code is generated by concatenating the code fragments associated with the nodes of the parse tree in a bottom-up manner, i.e. from the leaves up to the root. In REQUIEM, the parse tree is not actually produced. Parsing and code generation are not two separated steps but are carried out simultaneously. If a syntactic unit has been identified during parsing, the corresponding piece of code is placed in an intermediate code array. Thus, after a source statement has been successfully parsed, the corresponding code is produced and is stored in the code array for later execution.

Before we describe the actual code generation process in REQUIEM we will illustrate the main data structures that are used. The code array is an array that must be in a position to store the amount of intermediate code that is generated during the process of expression compilation. The generated code consists of two different types of elements, namely *operands* and *operators*. For that purpose the intermediate code array is declared as shown in Figure 11.1.

This C statement declares an array, namely **code**, that is able to store CODEMAX + 1 elements (cells) of type **code_cell**. An individual **code_cell** is defined as a union. In C, a union allows objects of different types to be stored in the same variable [12]. The programmer has to take care that during run-time the union objects are accessed properly. The union **code_cell** allows us to store an operator as a pointer to the corresponding C function in the component **int (*c_operator)()** as well as a pointer to an operand structure in the component **struct operand *c_operand**. In the case that an operator in the source statement is encountered, the variable **c_operator** holds a pointer to a reserved function. All tokens accompanying the current operator implementing function are stored as operands of different types, such as string constants, numerical constants, variables, or attributes of a relation. In order to be able to store these diverse types of operands in a uniform manner, the data structure **operand** is itself declared as a **union** construct, see Figure 11.1.

In Figure 11.1 we can recognize that the **operand** structure consists of two members, namely an integer (**o_type**), to indicate the type of the operand that is stored, and the union **o_value**. The **o_value** member of the **operand** structure consists of two components, the structure **ov_char** to hold the values which must accompany a given operand and the integer **ov_boolean** to store a boolean result value. The structure **ov_char** in its turn is used for storing strings; numerical values that are converted to a string format prior to being stored; variables as reserved empty operand structures (which receive their values as soon as the corresponding assignment statement is executed during code evaluation); and attributes. The component **ovc_string** holds a pointer to the character value of the operand. On the other hand **ovc_length** indicates the length of the operand value that has been stored. Finally, **ovc_type** is either **TNUM**, **TREAL**, or **TCHAR** depending on the type of the value that has been stored. If the operand in the predicate expression is an attribute name then **ovc_type** holds the type of the corresponding attribute (**TNUM**, **TREAL**, or **TCHAR**) while the integer component **ov_boolean** preserves the logical result of an intermediate evaluation step.

```
union code_cell code[CODEMAX + 1];

union code_cell {
  int (* c_operator)();
  struct operand *c_operand;
}

struct operand {
  int o_type;
  union {
    struct {
      int ovc_type;
      char *ovc_string;
      int ovc_length;
    } ov_char;
    int ov_boolean;
  } o_value;
}
```

Figure 11.1 The declaration of the code array and the corresponding structures.

Finally, the structure **operand** member **o_type** holds the type of the corresponding intermediate code operand function. Legal values are as follows:

1. **LITERAL** for numerical and string constants.
2. **ATTR** for attributes.
3. **TEMPBOOL** and **TEMPNUM** to hold intermediate results during interpretation.
4. **VAR** if the operand is a variable.

The two functions **operator()** and **operand()** are used to assist in placing an operator and operand, respectively, into the intermediate code array. If an operand is inserted the operator **xpush()** is stored prior to it in the code array, to allow the interpreter to push the operand value onto the run-time stack during predicate expression evaluation.

One function of the PEC that requires further attention and deciphering is the predicate expression function **get_operand()**, which fetches the operands of a predicate expression. Each time an operand is required, the parsing function **get_operand()** is called to determine the type of the next token. If an operand is identified, the function corresponding to that specific type of operator is called to allocate an operand structure and store it into the code array. We can distinguish between four types of operands:

1. NUMBER for integer constants, identified by function **get_number()**.
2. REALNO for real constants, also identified by function **get_number()**.
3. STRING for string constants, identified by function **get_string()**.
4. ID for variables and attributes, identified by function **xget_attr()**.

Let us consider the case of numerical operands. If an operand having one of the basic operand types NUMBER or REALNO is identified, the function **get_number()** is called. This function allocates a new operand structure and stores the type of the operand. Next, it converts the value of the numerical operand to its corresponding string format. Finally, the string representation of the numerical operand and its length are stored into their corresponding operand structure members.

The case where the token identified by the function **get_operand()** denotes an attribute identifier (operand type ID) is slightly more complicated. Firstly, it should be determined whether the attribute is qualified or non-qualified. To the extent that attribute names are not unique within the context of the database, the user or the system will have to qualify them to resolve any possible ambiguity of reference. Attributes are qualified by means of the name of their associated relation, as explained in Chapter 2. For example, consider the construct *PRODUCT.WEIGHT*; if a qualified attribute is encountered the relation name is stripped off and is stored in the variable **rname**, while the attribute name is stored in the variable **aname**. Next, REQUIEM should determine the storage location where the actual value of the attribute can be accessed for evaluation of the relevant predicate expression during the process of tuple selection. As explained in Chapter 5, for each relation involved in a query, a tuple buffer is allocated to hold its tuple contents during query processing. A call to the query decomposer function **select_attr()** determines the address of the tuple buffer; calculates the relative address (with respect to the start of the tuple buffer) where the specific attribute values will be held; and also estimates the number of

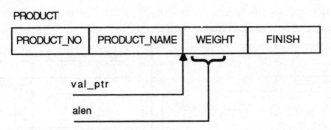

Figure 11.2 Determining the storage address of attribute values via a relation-specific tuple buffer.

bytes that will be occupied by each single attribute value in the tuple. Such information can be obtained from the relation header of the specific relation. As a result of a call to the function **select_attr()** the variables **atype**, **val_ptr**, and **alen** are assigned the type of the attribute, the relative address where the attribute values can be found, and the length of the attribute, respectively, for the relation *PRODUCT* (see Figure 11.2).

Figure 11.3 shows how the quantities residing in the tuple buffer are associated with their corresponding operand structure. Finally, the function **xget_attr()** sets the type of the operand to **ATTR** and assigns the value of the construct **atype** to the actual attribute type.

The addresses and lengths of indexed attributes participating in the predicate expression require special treatment. Whether an attribute is indexed or not can easily be determined by examining a special flag, called the *key flag*, in the relation header. If the key flag is set to "n", the corresponding attribute is non-indexed and the values of the previously set variables **val_ptr** and **alen** can be assigned to the corresponding components of the operand structure, namely **ovc_string** and **ovc_length**, respectively, as illustrated in Figure 11.3. Actually, the key flag indicates not only whether the corresponding attribute is indexed or not, but also what type of key this attribute is. Recall that key types can obtain the values "p" for a primary key, "s" for a secondary key, and "n" only in the case that the corresponding attribute is not indexed.

A case which demands particular attention is that of encountering indexed attributes during the fetching of operands. If an attribute specified in the predicate expression is indexed then the value and type of the operand associated with this specific attribute are passed to the indexing mechanism of REQUIEM by a call to the function **get_ixattr()**. This function inserts the value into a predicate operand structure and positions it in the appropriate location in the code array structure for later access by the low-level access path functions. At run-time the components of the operand structure of

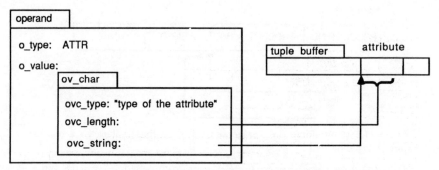

Figure 11.3 The operand structure in the case of a non-indexed attribute.

the function **get_ixattr()**, namely **ovc_string** and **ovc_length**, are set in such a way that during tuple selection, when the corresponding index file is opened, the component values of the operand structure can be directly accessed by means of the index mechanism.

After having discussed the main concepts of parsing and code generation in relation to the RQL predicate expression sublanguage, we would like to present an example of how an expression is parsed, and what actual intermediate code is generated.

As an example expression consider the same sample expression 11.1 used in the previous sections. Compilation is effected in the function **xcompile()** by setting the subscript of the code array to point to the first code array location. This subscript, namely **cndx**, is used throughout the whole compilation phase to indicate the current location in the code array where operands and operators will be inserted. Proper predicate expression compilation commences by calling the function that is associated with the start symbol of the underlying grammar, namely the function **expression()**, and parsing proceeds exactly as explained in Chapter 8.

It is during the parsing of predicate expressions that the intermediate code is generated and stored in the code array. Figure 11.4 depicts the code generated for expression 11.1 from which we can see that if an operator has been placed in the intermediate code array, the name of the implementing function that is associated with it appears inside a code cell. In the actual implementation, a pointer to this specific function is stored in the code array. Conversely, if an operand has been stored, then the address of the corresponding operand structure appears inside a code cell.

Operands stored in code array are always preceded by the function name **xpush**. Notice that in this intermediate code form an operator is inserted in the code array only after its two associated operands have been installed in the array. This kind of intermediate code is called postfix notation as

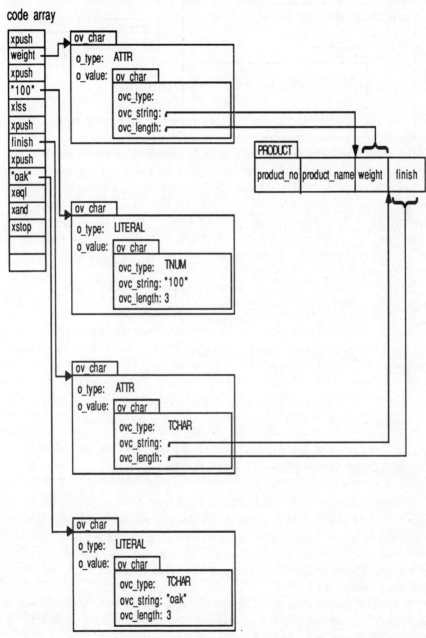

Figure 11.4 The code produced for the expression "weight > 100 & finish = "oak" ."

we will see later in the next section. For example the operand & will be installed in the code array only after its left operand, i.e. the expression *weight* > 100, is installed (in postfix notation) followed by its right operand, namely the expression *finish* = *"oak"*.

11.4   Intermediate code evaluation

During the process of translation, the compiler may need to acquire additional information concerning user-defined quantities. For example, the interpreter may need to know the type or length of an identifier. The code stored in the code array is, thus, generated by means of a syntax-directed translation scheme which specifies the translation of a given expression in terms of its syntactic properties. This translation scheme is also used to translate the conventional *infix* notation used in describing expressions into a *postfix* or *reverse polish* equivalent, which is easily handled with the aid of an evaluation stack. The elements of this stack are either addresses of storage locations or the values found at such addresses.

In the infix notation monadic operators appear before the operand, while dyadic operators appear between their operators [45]. For example, in RQL a term is written in the infix notation:

```
<term>    ::= <factor> <mulop> <factor>
<mulop>   ::= '*' | '/' | '%'
```

In the intermediate code language, the corresponding instructions appear in postfix order, i.e. each operator appears after its operand:

```
<term>    ::= <factor> <factor> <mulop>
<mulop> ::= '*' | '/' | '%'
```

Postfix notation is very useful for stack-oriented evaluation. This can be attributed to the fact that parentheses are not needed in postfix notation since there is never any doubt as to which operands belong to a particular operator. Furthermore, there is no such thing as operator precedence in this notation, though undoubtedly this must be taken into account in translating infix expressions to postfix.

A certain rearrangement of operators and operands is always involved in translating an infix notation into postfix. The postfix notation for an expression *Exp* can be defined inductively as follows [42]:

1. If Exp is a variable, or a constant, then the postfix notation for Exp is Exp itself.
2. If $Exp = Exp1$ **op** $Exp2$, where **op** is a binary operator, then its postfix equivalent is $Exp1$ $Exp2$ **op**, where $Exp1$, $Exp2$ are the postfix equivalents of $Exp1$ and $Exp2$, respectively.
3. If $Exp = (Exp1)$, the postfix notation for $Exp1$ is also the postfix notation for Exp.

For example, the infix expression $(a * b)/c$ would be equivalent to $ab * c/$. In postfix notation the operator is executed as soon it is encountered left to right. Thus, the expression

5 12 2 * +

is equivalent to the infix notation

$5 + (12 * 2)$.

As previously explained, postfix notation is ideal for a stack machine. When the stack machine scans a compiled expression from left to right the following actions are performed:

1. When an operand is encountered, its value is immediately pushed on top of the stack.
2. When a variable is encountered, code is generated to push its value on top of the stack.
3. When a dyadic operator is encountered, code is generated to apply the operator to the top two values held on the stack, replacing them with the result.
4. When a monadic operator is encountered, the stack machine applies it to the top value, replacing it with the result of applying the operator (step 3).

The above actions assume clearly that the stack machine can distinguish between monadic and dyadic operators. To put the whole thing into perspective it may be helpful to look at the following example:

$(3 * x)/2$

In postfix notation this would be translated into

$3x * 2/$

The corresponding sequence of actions is performed:

1. Push operand, constant 3.
2. Push the value of the variable x, assume $x = 4$.
3. Multiply (1) and (2), replace (1) and (2) by product.
4. Push operand, constant 2.
5. Divide (3) and (4), replace them with the result.
6. Leave the final result in the stack.

Figure 11.5 shows the stack at various stages during the execution of the above instructions. As the stack uses last-in first-out accessing it grows from the bottom of the figure towards the top. In each case the stack pointer sptr is shown to point to the current top of the stack.

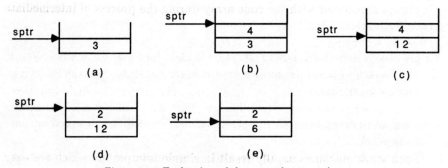

Figure 11.5 Evaluation of the example expression.

As illustrated in Figure 11.5(a), action 1 pushes the constant 3 onto the stack. Action 2 replaces the variable x with its value, namely 4, and pushes it on top of the previous value, Figure 11.5(b). In Figure 11.5(c) action 3 pops the first two operands from the top of the stack and replaces them with their product. Note that sptr has been decremented and now points to the new top of the stack, while the quantity 2 remains intact expecting to be overwritten at some future stage. In a similar fashion actions 4 and 5 produce the result depicted in Figure 11.5(d) and (e). Finally, the evaluation leaves only the end result in the stack with the stack pointer sptr pointing to its corresponding address.

The REQUIEM code contains instructions to load an address or value on to the top of the stack, to apply an operator to the top two elements on the stack, to store the value on top of the stack into a prespecified address and so on. These issues will be elaborated and explained in great detail through the next section which is devoted to intermediate code evaluation.

11.5   The predicate expression interpreter

The *predicate expression interpreter* (PEI) progresses through the code cell components of the intermediate code array and interprets the code that is stored there. Actually, this interpreter implements a stack machine when evaluating the operators that are stored in the code array. The result of this interpretation is a boolean value that is used to determine whether a tuple is to be accepted or rejected during the process of tuple selection. If during the evaluation process the operator xpush() is encountered the next element of the code array must be of type operand and should be pushed on to the run-time stack. If another kind of operator is encountered, its corresponding C function is invoked. This function normally pops the required number of operands from the top of the stack, and then accesses their associated values and calculates the result of the operation. Such intermediate results are always placed on top of the stack. Note that a run-time stack is always associated with the code array during the process of intermediate code evaluation. Finally, if the operator xstop() is encountered, execution stops by returning (as the result of the interpretation) the value of the topmost operand in the stack. This final pop operation empties the contents of the stack as the result operand is no longer required.

During interpretation it should be made certain that for each popoperation the stack is not empty (*stack-underflow*), and for each push-operation the stack is not already full (*stack-overflow*). If either of these cases occurs then interpretation should be immediately aborted.

Such stack machines usually result in simple interpreters which are easy to trace and debug. Our stack machine is actually nothing but an array of intermediate code containing a sequence of operators and operands. The operators make up the stack machine instructions (intermediate language instructions); each of them is implemented by an appropriate function call requesting its arguments, if any. The requested arguments immediately follow the instruction in the code array.

In REQUIEM the run-time stack holds the arguments of the operators, and any temporary results produced by them during predicate expression evaluation. The stack is declared as an array of a fixed number of elements of type operand (cf. Figure 11.1), as follows:

```
struct operand *stack[STACKMAX];
struct operand **stack_ptr;
```

The stack pointer variable stack_ptr always points to the top element in the run-time stack during interpretation. Its value can be adjusted inside the functions that store operands on the stack or remove operands from the stack, namely the functions **push()** and **pop()**. The function **push()** takes an operand as argument and stores it in the run-time stack at the position to where the **stack_ptr** points. Then, the **stack_ptr** is incremented to point to the next free cell. Conversely, the function **pop()** checks whether the stack is non-empty, decrements the **stack_ptr**, and returns the corresponding operand.

In a similar manner, the code array holds the intermediate code to be processed by the interpreter. This code is inserted in the code array during compilation by the PEC (refer to the previous section). Furthermore, the global variable **pc**, which is a pointer to code array cells, serves as the program counter. This variable always points to the current code cell during interpretation. Its value can be changed in one of the following two ways:

1. If an operand is pushed from the code array on to the run-time stack by means of the function **xpush()**, the program counter (**pc**) should be incremented to reflect this situation.
2. If an operator is fetched for execution inside the evaluation function **execute()**, which fetches and processes the intermediate code operators, the program counter should also be incremented to point to the next code cell.

When interpretation first starts, these two code evaluation pointers (**stack_ptr** and **pc**) are initialized to point to the first element of their corresponding arrays.

Execution of the intermediate code is quite simple and is effected by calling the function **execute()**. It is rather surprising how small and concise that function is, when one realizes that it runs the abstract machine once it is set up. This function steps through the code array and executes the corresponding operators. Actually, each cycle executes the function pointed to by the program counter **pc**. Execution continues until an operator returns **FALSE** to the execution function. This can happen in one of the following two ways:

1. If an error occurs during interpretation.
2. If the operator **xstop()** is encountered at the bottom of the code array. Subsequently, the constant **FALSE** is returned to indicate that a normal termination condition has occurred.

The operator **xstop()** is placed as the last instruction into the code array by the predicate expression compiler (refer to section 11.1.2). The critical point to realize here is that **execute()** marches through a sequence of code instructions until it encounters **xstop**, whereupon it returns.

Note that although the grammar of the predicate expression sublanguage allows for constructs such as *<digit>* *<addop>* | *<mulop>* *<character>*, the run-time system realizes by performing a type-checking that they have no meaning for the computation of a query, and complains to the user. Furthermore, all arithmetic constants are represented as doubles in C, as we are actually processing floating-point numbers in RQL which allows maximum width of number representation. Thus, the structure of all arithmetic operations is basically the same.

The general frame for the execution of an intermediate code operator can be described as follows: the operator fetches the required number of operands from the run-time stack, and evaluation is carried out by a call to the appropriate function. The result of the operation is then placed as an intermediate result on the run-time stack so that it can be easily accessed by any subsequent operators. Intermediate results are stored as operands of type **TEMPBOOL** or **TEMPNUM** depending on whether the resulting value is boolean or numerical.

As an example we consider the execution of a code fragment as depicted in Figure 11.4. We also assume that the program counter points to the code cell that contains the operator **xlss()**. When this operator is called inside the function **execute()** the run-time stack is in the state shown in Figure 11.6(a). The function **xlss()**, whose address is stored in its corresponding operator structure is then called and executed. As a result this function calls in turn the function **compare()** with the argument **LSS**. For the sake of code simplicity all comparison functions, such as **xlss()**, **xleq()**, **xeql()**, . . ., are implemented as calls to the generic comparison function **compare()**. This function performs comparisons as indicated by its argument. Next, the function **compare()** fetches the two operands from the run-time stack (cf. Figure 11.6(a)) by calls to the function **pop()**. Subsequently, the type of each operand is checked to see if it conforms to the operand type assigned to it by definition. Notice that only operands that have identical types can be compared. If the operand types are incompatible an error is indicated and interpretation is aborted. This is a minimum safeguard against semantic errors.

Depending on the type of the operands, we either call function **comp()** or function **ncomp()**. Function **comp()** is called to compare string operands, while function **ncomp()** is called to compare numerical operands. The value returned by these two functions is negative, zero, or positive depending on whether the value of the first operand is less than, equal to, or greater than the value of the second operand.

In the case of the operator **LSS**, in our previous example, the result is **TRUE** if the function **compare()** returned a value that was less than 0 indicating thus that the first operand (i.e. the attribute *WEIGHT*) has a

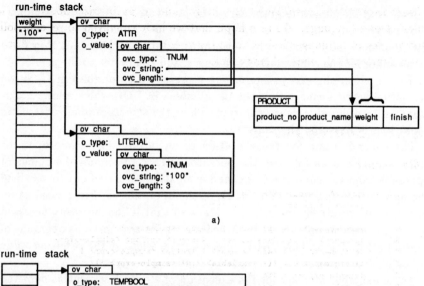

a)

b)

Figure 11.6 The run-time stack.

value less than that of the numeric constant 100. Once the result has been evaluated, a new operand structure of type **TEMPBOOL** is allocated and the result is stored. The operand is then pushed on to the run-time stack by a call to **push()**. The resulting stack is depicted in Figure 11.6(b). If the operands previously popped off the stack are classified as temporary they can be discarded and the space occupied by them can be released by a call to the function **free_opr()**. Subsequently, the execution of the current operator terminates and the next operator in the code array is fetched and processed, and so on. Finally, it must be mentioned that the outcome of the evaluated predicate expression is always a logic result contained in the variable **ov_boolean** of the last operand in the operand structure. This result is forwarded to the query decomposer which decides if the corresponding tuple is legitimate and can, thus, be placed in the snapshot file.

In the above discussion we have presented the concepts and a complete implementation of the RQL predicate sublanguage. This kind of language is fairly representative of related predicate expression sublanguages found in most current DBMSs. We believe that this chapter has provided enough background and adequate material to help advanced students and future implementors to comprehend the magnitude of problems underlying the design of a language. We also hope that we have conveyed to readers solid principles of language design and implementation so that they can design and develop their own sublanguages.

11.6   Source listing 7

file: *xcom.c*

```
1    /* REQUIEM - expression compiler
2       syntax: eliminates left recursion.
3
4       <expression> ::= <primary> { <logop> <primary> }
5       <primary>    ::= <statement> | <assgnt> <relop> <simple-expr>
6       <statement>  ::= <simple-expr> { <relop> <simple-expr> }
7       <assignment> ::= '(' <variable> ':=' <simple-expr> ')'
8       <simple-expr>::= <term> { <addop> <term> }
9       <term>       ::= <factor> { <mulop> <factor> }
10      <factor>     ::= <operand>|'('<expression>')'|<nop> <factor>
11      <operand>    ::= <number>|<string>|<attribute>|<variable>
12      <variable>   ::= '$'<chars>
13      <attribute>  ::= [<rname>.] <aname>
14      <number>     ::= <digit> | <number> <digit>
15      <string>     ::= '"' <chars> '"'
16      <chars>      ::= nil | <chars> { <character> }
17      <nop>        ::= '~'
18      <logop>      ::= '&' | '|'
19      <relop>      ::= '=' | '<>' | '<' | '>' | '<=' | '>=' | '=='
20      <addop>      ::= '+' | '-'
21      <mulop>      ::= '*' | '/' | '%'
22    */
23
24    #include "requ.h"
25
26    extern int lex_token;           /* current token value */
27    extern char lexeme[];           /* string token value */
28    extern BOOL xint_error;         /* variable to report
29                                     * interpretation errors */
30    extern struct symbol *symb;     /* symbol table for vars */
31    struct operand *get_opdstr();
32    union code_cell code[CODEMAX+1]; /* code array */
33    static struct sel *selptr;      /* saves sel-struct ptr */
34    static int cndx;                /* code array index */
35    static char varname[NUMBERMAX+1];/* stores temp var name */
36    BOOL non_ixattr = FALSE;        /* non-indexed attr in pred */
37
38    /* interpretation operators */
39    extern int xand();
40    extern int xor();
41    extern int xnot();
42    extern int xlss();
43    extern int xleq();
44    extern int xeql();
45    extern int xgeq();
```

```
46    extern int xgtr();
47    extern int xneq();
48    extern int xpart();
49    extern int xadd();
50    extern int xsub();
51    extern int xmul();
52    extern int xdiv();
53    extern int xmod();
54    extern int xpush();
55    extern int xstop();
56    extern int xassign();
57
58    /* ------------------------------------------------------------ */
59
60    /* xcompile - compile a boolean expression */
61    int xcompile(slptr)
62        struct sel *slptr;
63    {
64      /* save selection struc. ptr, initialize code array index */
65      selptr = slptr;
66      cndx = 0;
67
68      /* parse the boolean expression */
69      if (!expression()) {
70        code[cndx++].c_operator = xstop;
71        free_lits(code);
72        return (FALSE);
73      }
74
75      /* stop code execution by placing xstop as last instruction */
76      code[cndx++].c_operator = xstop;
77
78      /* return successfully */
79      return (TRUE);
80    } /* xcompile */
81
82    /* ------------------------------------------------------------ */
83
84    /* operator - insert an operator into the code array */
85    static int operator(opr)
86        int (*opr)(); /* pointer to opr function */
87    {
88      /* insert the operator */
89      if (cndx < CODEMAX)
90        code[cndx++].c_operator = opr; /* called thro' code array */
91      else
92        return (error(CDSIZE));
93
94      /* return successfully */
95      return (TRUE);
96    } /* operator */
97
98    /* ------------------------------------------------------------ */
99
100   /* operand - insert an operand into the code array */
101   static int operand(opr)
102       struct operand *opr;
103   {
104     /* insert the push operator */
105     if (!operator(xpush))
106       return (FALSE);
```

```
107
108      /* insert the operand */
109      if (cndx < CODEMAX)
110        code[cndx++].c_operand = opr;
111      else
112        return (error(CDSIZE));
113
114      /* return successfully */
115      return (TRUE);
116    } /* operand */
117
118    /* ------------------------------------------------------------ */
119
120    /* expr - compile an expression */
121    static int expression()
122    {       int c;
123
124            if (!primary())
125              return (FALSE);
126
127            while ((c = this_token()) == '|' || c == '&') {
128              next_token();
129              if (!primary())
130                return (FALSE);
131              switch(c) {
132              case '|':        if (!operator(xor))
133                return (FALSE);
134                break;
135              case '&':        if (!operator(xand))
136                return (FALSE);
137                break;
138              default:         return(error(SYNTAX));
139              }
140            }
141
142            return (TRUE);
143    } /* expression */
144
145    /* ------------------------------------------------------------ */
146
147    static int primary()
148    {
149      int tkn;
150
151      if (this_token() == '(') {
152        next_token();
153        if (this_token() != '$') {
154          if (!expression())
155            return(error(SYNTAX));
156          else {
157            if (next_token() != ')')
158              return (error(SYNTAX));
159          }
160          return(TRUE);
161        }
162
163        next_token();  /* strip off the $ */
164
165        if (!assign())  /* left operand */
166          return(FALSE);
167
```

```
168        if (next_token() != ')')
169          return (error(SYNTAX));
170
171        /* check for relational operation */
172        if (this_token() <= LSS && lex_token >= GTR) {
173          tkn = next_token();
174          if (!simple())    /* right operand */
175            return (FALSE);
176
177          if (!relop(tkn))  /* comparison operator */
178            return(FALSE);
179
180        } else return(error(SYNTAX));
181
182      }
183      else {
184        if (!statement())  /* left operand */
185          return (FALSE);
186
187      }
188      return (TRUE);
189    } /* primary */
190
191    /* ------------------------------------------------------------ */
192
193    static int statement()
194    {
195      int tkn;  BOOL rel_opr = FALSE;
196
197      if (!simple())  /* left operand */
198        return (FALSE);
199      while (this_token() <= LSS && lex_token >= GTR) {
200        tkn = next_token();
201        if (!simple())  /* right operand */
202          return (FALSE);
203
204        if (!relop(tkn)) /* comparison operator */
205          return(FALSE);
206
207        rel_opr = TRUE;
208      }
209
210      if (rel_opr == FALSE)
211        if (!in_list())
212          return(FALSE);
213
214      return (TRUE);
215    } /* statement */
216
217    /* ------------------------------------------------------------ */
218
219    static int relop(tkn)
220        int tkn;
221    {
222      switch (tkn) {
223      case LSS:
224        if (!operator(xlss))
225          return (FALSE);
226        break;
227      case LEQ:
228        if (!operator(xleq))
```

```
229        return (FALSE);
230      break;
231      case EQL:
232        if (!operator(xeql))
233          return (FALSE);
234        break;
235      case PART:
236        if (!operator(xpart))
237          return (FALSE);
238        break;
239      case NEQ:
240        if (!operator(xneq))
241          return (FALSE);
242        break;
243      case GEQ:
244        if (!operator(xgeq))
245          return (FALSE);
246        break;
247      case GTR:
248        if (!operator(xgtr))
249          return (FALSE);
250        break;
251      }
252
253      return(TRUE);
254
255    } /* relop */
256
257    /* ------------------------------------------------------------ */
258
259    static int factor()
260    {
261      if (this_token() == '('){
262        next_token();
263        if (!expression())
264          return(FALSE);
265        if (next_token() != ')')
266          return(error(SYNTAX));
267      }
268      else if (this_token() == '~') {
269        next_token(); /* same as this_token, clears lookahead char */
270        if (!factor())
271          return (FALSE);
272        if (!operator(xnot))
273          return (FALSE);
274      }
275      else if (!get_operand())
276        return (FALSE);
277
278      return (TRUE);
279    } /* factor */
280
281    /* ------------------------------------------------------------ */
282
283    static int assign()
284    {
285      struct operand *opr;
286      char *s_copy();
287
288      if (next_token() != ID)
289        return(error(SYNTAX));
```

```
290
291       /* save the variable name */
292       strncpy(varname,lexeme,MIN(strlen(lexeme), NUMBERMAX));
293       varname[MIN(strlen(lexeme), NUMBERMAX)] = EOS;
294
295       /* get a new operand structure */
296       if (!(opr = get_opdstr()))
297         return(error(INSMEM));
298
299       /* initialize the new operand structure */
300       opr->o_type = VAR;
301       opr->o_value.ov_char.ovc_type = TREAL;
302       opr->o_value.ov_char.ovc_string = s_copy(varname);
303
304       /* insert the operand into the code array */
305       if (!operand(opr)) {
306         free_opr(opr);
307         return (FALSE);
308       }
309
310       if (next_token() != ASGN)
311         return(FALSE);
312
313       if (!simple())
314         return(FALSE);
315
316       if (!operator(xassign))
317         return(FALSE);
318
319       return (TRUE);
320     } /* assign */
321
322     /* ------------------------------------------------------------ */
323
324     static int simple()
325     {
326       int tkn;
327
328       if (!term())   /* left operand */
329         return(FALSE);
330
331       while(this_token() <= ADD && lex_token >= SUB) {
332         tkn = next_token();
333         if (!term())   /* right operand */
334           return(FALSE);
335         switch(tkn) {
336         case ADD:
337           if (!operator(xadd))
338             return (FALSE);
339           break;
340         case SUB:
341           if (!operator(xsub))
342             return (FALSE);
343           break;
344         }
345       }
346
347       return(TRUE);
348     } /* simple */
349
350     /* ------------------------------------------------------------ */
```

```
351
352    static int term()
353    {
354      int tkn;
355
356      if (!factor())  /* left operand */
357        return(FALSE);
358
359      while(this_token() <= MUL && lex_token >= MOD) {
360        tkn = next_token();
361        if (!factor())  /* right operand */
362          return(FALSE);
363        switch(tkn) {
364        case MUL:
365          if (!operator(xmul))
366            return (FALSE);
367          break;
368        case DIV:
369          if (!operator(xdiv))
370            return (FALSE);
371          break;
372        case MOD:
373          if (!operator(xmod))
374            return (FALSE);
375          break;
376
377        }
378      }
379
380      return (TRUE);
381    } /* term */
382
383    /* ------------------------------------------------------------ */
384
385    /* get_operand - get operand (number, string, or attribute) */
386    static int get_operand()
387    {
388      /* determine operand type */
389      if (next_token() == NUMBER)
390        return (get_number(NUMBER)); /* result gets value TNUM */
391      else if (lex_token == REALNO)
392        return (get_number(REALNO)); /* result gets value TREAL */
393      else if (lex_token == ID)
394        return (xget_attr());              /* result gets value atype */
395      else if (lex_token == STRING)
396        return (get_string());             /* result gets value TCHAR */
397      else if (lex_token == '$')
398        return (get_variable());
399      else
400        return (error(SYNTAX));
401    } /* get_operand */
402
403    /* ------------------------------------------------------------ */
404
405    /* xget_attr - get an attribute argument */
406    static int xget_attr()
407    {
408      struct operand *opr;
409      struct relation *rlptr;
410      char rname[RNSIZE+1], aname[ANSIZE+1];
411      char *val_ptr;
```

```
412     int atype,alen;
413     int i, fail_ix = 0;
414     short n_attrs;
415
416     /* save the attribute name */
417     strncpy(aname,lexeme,MIN(strlen(lexeme), ANSIZE));
418     aname[MIN(strlen(lexeme), ANSIZE)] = EOS;
419
420     /* get a new operand structure */
421     if (!(opr = get_opdstr()))
422       return(error(INSMEM));
423
424     /* not a var, check for "." indicating a qual. attr name */
425     if (this_token() == '.') {
426       next_token();
427
428       /* the previous ID was really a relation name */
429       strcpy(rname,aname);
430
431       /* check for the real attribute name */
432       if (next_token() != ID)
433         return (error(SYNTAX));
434
435       /* save the attribute name */
436       strncpy(aname,lexeme,MIN(strlen(lexeme), ANSIZE));
437       aname[MIN(strlen(lexeme), ANSIZE)] = EOS;
438
439       /* lookup the attribute name */
440       if (!select_attr(selptr,rname,aname,&atype,&val_ptr,&alen))
441         return (FALSE);
442     }
443     else
444       if (!select_attr(selptr, (char *) 0, aname, &atype,
445                                           &val_ptr,&alen))
446         return (FALSE);
447
448     /* initialize the new operand structure */
449     opr->o_type = ATTR;
450     opr->o_value.ov_char.ovc_type = atype;
451     rlptr = selptr->sl_rels->sr_scan->sc_relation;
452     n_attrs = selptr->sl_rels->sr_scan->sc_nattrs;
453
454     /* in case of join we must make sure that the second relation
455      * structure is also accessed */
456     if (rlptr->rl_next && strcmp(rname,rlptr->rl_name) != EQUAL) {
457       rlptr = rlptr->rl_next;
458       n_attrs =  selptr->sl_rels->sr_next->sr_scan->sc_nattrs;
459     }
460
461     /* loop through the attributes of the sel structure */
462     for (i = 0; i < n_attrs ;  i++) {
463
464       /* compare the predicate name with the  attribute names */
465       if (strcmp(aname, rlptr->rl_header.hd_attrs[i].at_name)
466                                             == EQUAL)
467         break;
468
469     }
470
471     /* set up environment for indexed attributes */
472     if (rlptr->rl_header.hd_attrs[i].at_key != 'n')
```

```
473        fail_ix = get_ixattr(rlptr, &opr,
474                        rlptr->rl_header.hd_attrs[i].at_name,
475                        rlptr->rl_header.hd_attrs[i].at_key,
476                        alen);
477
478      /* if indexed environment set-up, or non-indexed attrs */
479      if (fail_ix == FAIL ||
480          rlptr->rl_header.hd_attrs[i].at_key == 'n') {
481        opr->o_value.ov_char.ovc_string = val_ptr;
482        opr->o_value.ov_char.ovc_length = alen;
483        non_ixattr = TRUE;    /* non-indexed attribute in predicate */
484      }
485
486      /* insert the operand into the code array */
487      if (!operand(opr)) {
488        free_opr(opr);
489        return (FALSE);
490      }
491
492      /* return successfully */
493      return (TRUE);
494  } /* xget_attr */
495
496  /* ------------------------------------------------------------ */
497
498  /* get_variable - get a variable argument */
499  static int get_variable()
500  {
501    struct operand *opr;
502    char name[ANSIZE+1];
503
504    if (next_token() != ID)
505      return(error(SYNTAX));
506
507    /* save the attribute name */
508    strncpy(name,lexeme,MIN(strlen(lexeme), ANSIZE));
509    name[MIN(strlen(lexeme), ANSIZE)] = EOS;
510
511    if ((strcmp(name, varname)) == EQUAL) {
512      if (symb == NULL) {
513        if (!(symb = MALLOC(struct symbol)))
514          return(error(INSMEM));
515        if (!(symb->varopd = MALLOC(struct operand)))
516          return(error(INSMEM));
517      }
518      opr = symb->varopd;
519      /* insert the operand into the code array */
520      if (!operand(opr)) {
521        free_opr(opr);
522        return (FALSE);
523      }
524
525      return(TRUE);
526    } else
527      return(error(UNDEFVAR));
528  } /* get_variable */
529
530  /* ------------------------------------------------------------ */
531
532  /* get_number - get a numeric operand */
533  static int get_number(num)
```

```
534          int num; /* discriminates between integers and reals */
535   {
536     struct operand *opr;
537
538     /* get a new operand structure */
539     if (!(opr = get_opdstr()))
540       return(error(INSMEM));
541
542     /* initialize the new operand structure */
543     opr->o_type = LITERAL;
544     if ((opr->o_value.ov_char.ovc_string =
545         rmalloc(strlen(lexeme)+1)) == NULL) {
546       free_opr(opr);
547       return (error(INSMEM));
548     }
549
550     /* operand type is either number or real */
551     if (num == NUMBER)
552       opr->o_value.ov_char.ovc_type = TNUM;
553     else
554       opr->o_value.ov_char.ovc_type = TREAL;
555
556     strcpy(opr->o_value.ov_char.ovc_string,lexeme);
557     opr->o_value.ov_char.ovc_length = strlen(lexeme);
558
559     /* insert the operand into the code array */
560     if (!operand(opr)) {
561       free_opr(opr);
562       return (FALSE);
563     }
564
565     /* return successfully */
566     return (TRUE);
567   } /* get_number */
568
569   /* ------------------------------------------------------------- */
570
571   /* get_string - get a string operand */
572   static int get_string()
573   {
574     struct operand *opr;
575
576     /* get a new operand structure */
577     if (!(opr = get_opdstr()))
578       return(error(INSMEM));
579
580     /* initialize the new operand structure */
581     opr->o_type = LITERAL;
582     if ((opr->o_value.ov_char.ovc_string =
583         rmalloc(strlen(lexeme)+1)) == NULL) {
584       free_opr(opr);
585       return (error(INSMEM));
586     }
587
588     /* operand type is character */
589     opr->o_value.ov_char.ovc_type = TCHAR;
590     strcpy(opr->o_value.ov_char.ovc_string,lexeme);
591     opr->o_value.ov_char.ovc_length = strlen(lexeme);
592
593     /* insert the operand into the code array */
594     if (!operand(opr)) {
```

```
595      free_opr(opr);
596      return (FALSE);
597    }
598
599    /* return successfully */
600    return (TRUE);
601  } /* get_string */
602
603  /* ------------------------------------------------------------ */
604
605  static int in_list()
606  {
607    int num, tkn, cntr = 0;
608    struct operand *opr;
609
610    if (next_token() != IN)
611      return(error(SYNTAX));
612
613    if (next_token() == '(') {
614      while ((num = next_token()) == NUMBER || num == REALNO) {
615
616        cntr++;    /* increment loop counter, and get number */
617        get_number(num);
618
619        if ((tkn = next_token()) == ',' || tkn == ')') {
620
621          /* test for equality */
622          if (!operator(xeql))
623            return(FALSE);
624
625          /* wait until both arguments of xor are present */
626          if (cntr > 1) {
627            if (!operator(xor))
628              return(FALSE);
629          }
630
631          if (tkn == ')')
632            break;
633        } else
634          return(error(SYNTAX));
635
636        /* if more numbers to come insert operand in code array*/
637        if ((num = this_token()) == NUMBER || num == REALNO) {
638
639          /* get a new operand structure */
640          if (!(opr = get_opdstr()))
641            return(error(INSMEM));
642
643          /* new operand is the attr met before the "in" clause */
644          opr = code[1].c_operand;
645
646          /* insert the operand into the code array */
647          if (!operand(opr)) {
648            free_opr(opr);
649            return (FALSE);
650          }
651        } else
652          return(error(SYNTAX));
653      }
654    }
655    else
```

```
656        return(error(SYNTAX));
657
658     if (cntr == 1)  /* need more than one argument in in_list */
659        return(error(SYNTAX));
660     else
661        return(TRUE);
662
663   } /* in_list */
664
665   /* ------------------------------------------------------------ */
666
667   /* free_lits - free the literals in a code array */
668   free_lits(cptr)
669        union code_cell *cptr;
670   {
671     for (; (*cptr).c_operator != xstop; cptr++)
672       if ((*cptr).c_operator == xpush )
673         if ((*++cptr).c_operand->o_type == LITERAL)
674           free((*cptr).OPERAND_STRING);
675   } /* free_lists */
676
677   /* ------------------------------------------------------------ */
678
679   /* assign a new operand structure */
680   struct operand *get_opdstr()
681   {
682     struct operand *opr;
683
684     if (!(opr = MALLOC(struct operand)))
685       return (NULL);
686     else
687       return(opr);
688   } /* get_opdstr */
689
690   /* ------------------------------------------------------------ */
691
692   /* free an operand structure */
693   free_opr(opr)
694        struct operand *opr;
695   {
696     if (opr->o_type == LITERAL || opr->o_type == VAR)
697       free(opr->o_value.ov_char.ovc_string);
698     free((char *) opr);
699   } /* free_opr */
700
701   /* ------------------------------------------------------------ */
702
```

file: xinterp.c

```
 1   /* REQUIEM - boolean expression evaluator, instruction code
 2    * is transformed into postfix notation and is placed on stack */
 3
 4   #include "requ.h"
 5
 6   extern union code_cell code[];  /* instruction code array */
 7
 8   extern int wh_signal;           /* selection predicate signal */
 9   struct operand *setup_res();
10   double atof();
```

```
11    static struct operand *stack[STACKMAX], /* stack */
12                           **stack_ptr;      /* stack pointer */
13    static union code_cell *pc;  /* program cntr during execution */
14    struct symbol *symb = NULL;  /* rudimentary symbol table */
15    BOOL xint_error = FALSE;      /* interpretation error variable */
16    char *s_copy();
17
18    /*------------------------------------------------------------ */
19
20    /* interpret a boolean expression */
21    int xinterpret()
22    {
23      struct operand *result;
24      BOOL res;
25
26      /* check for empty code clause */
27      if (wh_signal == FALSE)
28        return (TRUE);
29
30      /* set up stack with stack pointer stack_ptr */
31      stack_ptr = stack;
32      /* start executing */
33      execute();
34      /* get the result from the top of stack */
35      if (!xint_error) { /* if no errors, temporary asgs exist */
36        result = *--stack_ptr;
37        res = result->o_value.ov_boolean;
38
39        if ((result->o_type == TEMPBOOL) ||
40                          (result->o_type == TEMPNUM))
41          free_opr(result);
42      }
43      else res = FALSE;
44
45      /* make sure the stack is empty */
46      while (stack_ptr != stack) {
47        if (((*stack_ptr)->o_type == TEMPBOOL) ||
48                        ((*stack_ptr)->o_type == TEMPNUM))
49          free((char *) *stack_ptr);
50        stack_ptr--;
51      }
52
53      /* return result */
54      return (res);
55    }
56
57    static int execute()  /* execute the code operators */
58    {
59      for (pc = code; (*(*pc++).c_operator)(); )
60        ;
61    } /* xinterpret */
62
63    /*------------------------------------------------------------ */
64
65    int xstop()
66    {
67      return (FALSE);
68    } /* xstop */
69
70    static push(oprnd)
71        struct operand *oprnd;
```

```
72   {
73     if (stack_ptr+1 >= &stack[STACKMAX]) {
74       xint_error = TRUE;
75       return(error(STACKOVRFL));
76     }
77     *stack_ptr++ = oprnd;
78     return(TRUE);
79   } /* push */
80
81   int xpush()
82   {
83     push(((*pc++).c_operand));
84   } /* xpush */
85
86   static struct operand *pop()
87   {
88     if (stack_ptr-1 < stack) {
89       xint_error = TRUE;
90       return(NULL);
91     } else
92       return(*--stack_ptr);
93   } /* pop */
94
95   int xand()
96   {
97     return (boolean('&'));
98   } /* xand */
99
100  int xor()
101  {
102    return (boolean('|'));
103  } /* xor */
104
105  /*------------------------------------------------------------ */
106
107  static int boolean(opr)
108  {
109    struct operand *lval,*rval,*result;
110    int lv,rv,r;
111
112    if ((rval = pop()) == NULL)
113      return(error(STACKUNDFL));
114    if ((lval = pop()) == NULL)
115      return(error(STACKUNDFL));
116    lv = lval->o_value.ov_boolean;
117    rv = rval->o_value.ov_boolean;
118
119    if (!(result = setup_res(BOOLEAN))){
120      xint_error = TRUE;
121      return(error(INSMEM));
122    }
123
124    switch (opr) {
125    case '&':
126      r = (lv && rv);
127      break;
128    case '|':
129      r = (lv || rv);
130      break;
131    }
132    result->o_value.ov_boolean = r;
```

```
133     push(result); /* push result onto stack */
134     if ((lval->o_type == TEMPBOOL) || (lval->o_type == TEMPNUM))
135       free_opr(lval);
136     if ((rval->o_type == TEMPBOOL) || (rval->o_type == TEMPNUM))
137       free_opr(rval);
138     return (TRUE);
139   } /* boolean */
140
141   /*------------------------------------------------------------- */
142
143   int xnot()
144   {
145     struct operand *val,*result;
146
147     if ((val = pop()) == NULL)
148       return(error(STACKUNDFL));
149
150     if (!(result = setup_res(BOOLEAN))) {
151       xint_error = TRUE;
152       return(error(INSMEM));
153     }
154     result->o_value.ov_boolean = !val->o_value.ov_boolean;
155     push(result); /* push result onto stack */
156
157     /* if temporary result free operand structures */
158     if ((val->o_type == TEMPBOOL) || (val->o_type == TEMPNUM))
159       free_opr(val);
160     return (TRUE);
161   } /* xnot */
162
163   /*------------------------------------------------------------- */
164
165   int xlss()
166   {
167     return (compare(LSS));
168   } /* xlss */
169
170   int xleq()
171   {
172     return (compare(LEQ));
173   } /* xleq */
174
175   int xpart()
176   {
177     return (compare(PART));
178   } /* xpart */
179
180   int xeql()
181   {
182     return (compare(EQL));
183   } /* xeql */
184
185   int xgeq()
186   {
187     return (compare(GEQ));
188   } /* xgeq */
189
190   int xgtr()
191   {
192     return (compare(GTR));
193   } /* xgtr */
```

```
194
195    int xneq()
196    {
197      return (compare(NEQ));
198    } /* xneq */
199
200    /*------------------------------------------------------------ */
201
202    static int compare(cmp)
203          int cmp;
204    {
205      struct operand *lval,*rval,*result;
206      int comp_res;  /* result of comparison */
207
208      if (((rval = pop()) == NULL) || ((lval = pop()) == NULL)) {
209        xint_error = TRUE;
210        return(error(STACKUNDFL));
211      }
212
213      if (!(result = setup_res(BOOLEAN))){
214        xint_error = TRUE;
215        return(error(INSMEM));
216      }
217
218      if (cmp == PART) /* left oprnd must be same length as right */
219        lval->o_value.ov_char.ovc_length =
220                        rval->o_value.ov_char.ovc_length;
221
222      if (lval->o_value.ov_char.ovc_type == TCHAR) {
223        if (rval->o_value.ov_char.ovc_type != TCHAR) {
224          xint_error = TRUE;
225          return(error(WRONGID));
226        }
227        comp_res = comp(lval,rval);
228      }
229      else {
230        if (rval->o_value.ov_char.ovc_type == TCHAR) {
231          xint_error = TRUE;
232          return(error(WRONGID));
233        }
234
235        comp_res = ncomp(lval,rval);
236      }
237
238      switch (cmp) {
239      case LSS:
240        comp_res = (comp_res < 0);
241        break;
242      case LEQ:
243        comp_res = (comp_res <= 0);
244        break;
245      case EQL:
246        comp_res = (comp_res == 0);
247        break;
248      case PART:
249        comp_res = (comp_res == 0);
250        break;
251      case GEQ:
252        comp_res = (comp_res >= 0);
253        break;
254      case GTR:
```

```
255        comp_res = (comp_res > 0);
256        break;
257      case NEQ:
258        comp_res = (comp_res != 0);
259        break;
260      }
261
262      result->o_value.ov_boolean = comp_res;
263      push(result); /* push result onto stack */
264
265      /* if temporary results free operand structures */
266      if ((lval->o_type == TEMPBOOL) || (lval->o_type == TEMPNUM))
267        free_opr(lval);
268      if ((rval->o_type == TEMPBOOL) || (rval->o_type == TEMPNUM))
269        free_opr(rval);
270
271      return (TRUE);
272    } /* compare */
273
274    /*------------------------------------------------------------ */
275
276    static int comp(lval,rval)     /* compare two string operands */
277         struct operand *lval,*rval;
278    {
279      char *l_string,*r_string;   /* char strings to be compared */
280      int lcn, rcn;               /* length counters */
281      int min_len;                /* minimum length */
282
283      l_string = lval->o_value.ov_char.ovc_string;
284      r_string = rval->o_value.ov_char.ovc_string;
285
286      lcn = lval->o_value.ov_char.ovc_length;
287      rcn = rval->o_value.ov_char.ovc_length;
288
289      /* strip off blanks */
290      while (lcn > 0 && (l_string[lcn-1] == EOS ||
291                                   l_string[lcn-1] == 0))
292        lcn--;
293      while (rcn > 0 && (r_string[rcn-1] == EOS ||
294                                   r_string[rcn-1] == 0))
295        rcn--;
296
297      /* estimate minimum string length */
298      min_len = MIN(lcn, rcn);
299
300      while ((min_len--) > 0) {
301        if (*l_string != *r_string)
302          return((*l_string < *r_string) ? FIRSTLSS : FIRSTGTR);
303        l_string++;
304        r_string++;
305      }
306
307      return((lcn == rcn) ? EQUAL :
308                      ((lcn < rcn) ? FIRSTLSS : FIRSTGTR));
309    } /* comp */
310
311    /*------------------------------------------------------------ */
312
313    static int ncomp(lval,rval)
314         struct operand *lval,*rval;
315    {
```

```
316    char lstr[NUMBERMAX+1],rstr[NUMBERMAX+1];
317    int len;
318    double a1, a2;
319
320    strncpy(lstr,lval->o_value.ov_char.ovc_string,
321            (len = lval->o_value.ov_char.ovc_length));
322    lstr[len] = EOS;
323    strncpy(rstr,rval->o_value.ov_char.ovc_string,
324            (len = rval->o_value.ov_char.ovc_length));
325    rstr[len] = EOS;
326
327    a1 = atof(lstr);
328    a2 = atof(rstr);
329
330    return((a1 == a2) ? EQUAL : ((a1 < a2) ? FIRSTLSS : FIRSTGTR));
331
332  } /* ncomp */
333
334  /*------------------------------------------------------------ */
335
336  int xadd()
337  {
338     xdb_add(TRUE);
339  }
340
341  int xsub()
342  {
343     xdb_add(FALSE);
344  } /* xadd */
345
346  /*------------------------------------------------------------ */
347
348  static xdb_add(op_add)
349       BOOL op_add;
350  {
351    struct operand *lval, *rval;
352    double op1, op2, res;
353    struct operand *result;
354    char res_string[NUMBERMAX+1];
355
356    /* get operands, check for type mismatch */
357    if (((rval = pop()) == NULL) || ((lval = pop()) == NULL)) {
358      xint_error = TRUE;
359      return(error(STACKUNDFL));
360    }
361
362    if ((rval->o_value.ov_char.ovc_type == TCHAR)
363        || (lval->o_value.ov_char.ovc_type == TCHAR)
364        || (rval->o_type == TEMPBOOL)
365        || (lval->o_type == TEMPBOOL)) {
366      xint_error = TRUE;
367      return(error(WRONGID));
368    }
369
370    if (!(result = setup_res(NUMBER))){
371      xint_error = TRUE;
372      return(error(INSMEM));
373    }
374
375    op1 = atof(lval->o_value.ov_char.ovc_string);
376    op2 = atof(rval->o_value.ov_char.ovc_string);
```

```
377      if (op_add)  /* overflow is detected in main() - loop */
378        res = op1 + op2;
379      else
380        res = op1 - op2;
381
382      sprintf(res_string, "%.4lf", res);
383      result->o_value.ov_char.ovc_string = s_copy(res_string);
384      result->o_value.ov_char.ovc_type = TREAL;
385      result->o_value.ov_char.ovc_length = strlen(res_string);
386
387      push(result); /* push result onto stack */
388
389      /* free space in case of intermediate results */
390      if ((lval->o_type == TEMPBOOL) || (lval->o_type == TEMPNUM))
391        free_opr(lval);
392      if ((rval->o_type == TEMPBOOL) || (rval->o_type == TEMPNUM))
393        free_opr(rval);
394
395      return (TRUE);
396    } /* xdb_add */
397
398    /*------------------------------------------------------------ */
399
400    int xmul()
401    {
402      printf("multiply\n");
403    } /* mul */
404
405    int xdiv()
406    {
407      printf("divide\n");
408    } /* xdiv */
409
410    int xmod()
411    {
412      printf("modulus\n");
413    } /* xmod */
414
415    /*------------------------------------------------------------ */
416
417    int xassign()
418    {
419
420      struct operand *lval, *rval;
421
422      /* get operands, check for type mismatch */
423      if ((rval = pop()) == NULL)
424        return(error(STACKUNDFL));
425      if ((lval = pop()) == NULL)
426        return(error(STACKUNDFL));
427      if ((rval->o_value.ov_char.ovc_type == TCHAR)
428          || (lval->o_value.ov_char.ovc_type == TCHAR)
429          || (lval->o_type == TEMPBOOL)) {
430        xint_error = TRUE;
431        return(error(WRONGID));
432      }
433
434      if (symb == NULL) { /* if a var has not been encountered */
435        if (!(symb = MALLOC(struct symbol)))
436          return(error(INSMEM));
437      }
```

```
438
439        /* name of variable was contained in ovc_string */
440        symb->varopd->o_value.ov_char.ovc_string =
441          s_copy(lval->o_value.ov_char.ovc_string);
442
443        /* type of variable is always real */
444        lval->o_value.ov_char.ovc_type = TREAL;
445        lval->o_value.ov_char.ovc_string =
446          rval->o_value.ov_char.ovc_string;
447        lval->o_value.ov_char.ovc_length =
448          rval->o_value.ov_char.ovc_length;
449        structcpy((char *) symb->varopd,
450                  (char *) lval,
451                  sizeof(struct operand));
452      push(lval);
453      return(TRUE);
454    } /* assign */
455
456    /*------------------------------------------------------------- */
457
458    struct operand *setup_res(num) /* set up a result oprnd struct. */
459        int num;
460    {
461      register struct operand *result;
462
463      if (!(result = MALLOC(struct operand)))
464        return(NULL);
465
466      if (num == NUMBER)
467        result->o_type = TEMPNUM;
468      else
469        result->o_type = TEMPBOOL;
470
471      return(result);
472    } /* setup_res */
473
474    /*------------------------------------------------------------- */
475
```

12

View Processing

The concept of an external level is available to relational DBMS users through the provision of derived relations. This facility is very important for the practical use of query languages and provides a perspective of the data to certain users. These are users who are not allowed to see the whole database, and who must view it as though it just contained certain derived relations rather than the basic ones. However, as we shall see in the present chapter this idea of a derived relation goes further than facilitating the formation of a subschema.

12.1 Views

The notion of a derived relation is based on the idea that all relational expressions accept relations as arguments and furnish another relation as a result. If the expression appears in a query, the resulting relation may either be simply displayed on the user's terminal, in which case it is called a snapshot in the RQL terminology, or be stored temporarily in the database where it becomes a new relation called a transient relation. For certain kinds of query instead of evaluating the corresponding relational expression every time, it is convenient to consider the expression as defining a new virtual relation, called a *view*.

A view is a virtual relation that can be used to simplify access to a specific database, to protect parts of it, and to enhance data independence [47]. A view is defined as the declaration of the virtual relation which the view simulates, and the specification of how a view tuple is derived from the tuples of the underlying base relations. These parts are called the *view declaration* and the *view mapping specification*, respectively. The user of a view can only see the view declaration, as the mapping specification is part

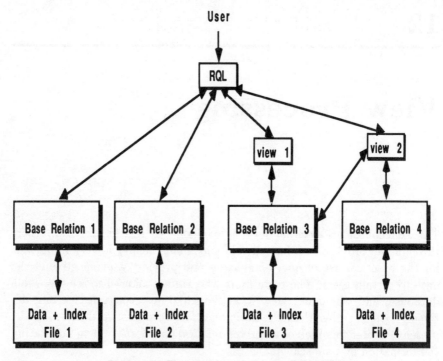

Figure 12.1 The mapping of views in REQUIEM.

of the view implementation. In retrospect, a view is a relation that does not directly exist in physical storage, but looks to the user as if it does. Just like base relations it can be created at any time. The prime difference between a base relation and a view is that the base relation is a physically existent relation in the sense that for each tuple of the base relation there exists a counterpart in the physical storage, and possibly physical access paths such as indices which directly support this specific relation. By contrast, a view is, as previously stated, a virtual relation, that is, a relation that does not exist in physical storage but is rather derived in terms of one or more base relations.

The term *view* must not be confused with the term *external view* as defined in Chapter 1. At the external level, the database is perceived as a set of *external views*, each defined by a corresponding external schema (see Figure 1.1). This is the outcome of the fact that it may be necessary for different users to acquire different external views. Broadly speaking, the term external view in RQL is taken to mean a collection of several relations, some of which comprise views and some of which are base relations. The external schema consists of the combination of the named definitions of these

Sup_id	Sup_name	Location
611	Jones	London
615	Henry	Paris
618	Rogers	New York
625	Smith	Dublin
633	Bates	London
638	Longfellow	London

Figure 12.2 An instance of the relation *SUPPLIER*.

views and relations, and is finally mapped on to the conceptual schema.*
Figure 12.1 illustrates how views and relations are associated with each
other and how they are mapped on to the physical structure of index and
data files. Actually, Figure 12.1 shows how REQUIEM is perceived by its
users.†

Let us now examine views in the RQL sense in some detail. In RQL, the
statement **define view** allows the user to define a view. Its general format
is as follows:

define view < *view_identifier* > **as** < *qualifying_query* >

The qualifying query may begin with a **select** or **project** statement or it
may encompass all the query options described in Appendix A. Actually
what happens when a view is defined is that the definition of this particular
view (in terms of its base relation) is stored in an appropriate system catalog,
called *SYSVIEWS*, and is remembered only under its specified view name.
A view is therefore implemented by using the view definition as a kind of
macro; the query contents of the view are macro-expanded so that the view
just refers to its base relations. Consider the following view definition in
RQL:

define view London_Suppliers **as**
    select from supplier **where** location = "London";

This view is defined in terms of the base relation *SUPPLIER* as depicted
in Figure 12.2. When the view *LONDON_SUPPLIERS* is defined the select

---

*An external/conceptual schema mapping defines the correspondence between the ex-
ternal or logical records of the external schema and the tuples of the conceptual schema.
An external record is, as you may have guessed, not necessarily the same as a physical
record.

†By the term user we mean here the end-users at on-line terminals or the application
programmers. Both these kinds of user will be using RQL statements to operate on base
relations or views.

expression is not evaluated. The view is simply expanded whenever its name is encountered in a legal RQL statement. Except for the fact that it is impossible to define access paths, the above view behaves as if it were a true relation. In particular, you can interrogate the view or even update and delete attributes or tuples from it if this is permitted.

Example 12.1.1

Consider the statement:

project London_Suppliers **over** sup_id, sup_name;

Result:

Sup_id	Sup_name
611	Jones
633	Bates
638	Longfellow

For performance and consistency reasons such queries on a view are translated into queries on the base relation rather than being executed on a materialization of the view itself [51]. REQUIEM will merge the **project** statement, issued by the user, with the **select** statement that was saved in the *SYSVIEW* catalog during the process of view definition. From this catalog the system recognizes that the **over** statement actually refers to the *SUPPLIER* relation, and hence it executes the **select** statement of the view definition first. Subsequently, the result of this query is used as an input relation in the **project** query statement. What actually happens is that the result of the view is first stored in a snapshot file and is then used as an input argument by the **project** statement in the place of the view identifier *LONDON_SUPPLIERS*. In the previous example the **project** statement behaves just like any normal **project** statement in a nested RQL query. As a matter of fact the equivalent operation is:

project (**select all from** supplier
        where location = "London") **over** sup_id, sup_name;

To the user, however, it is as if there actually existed a relation in the database called *LONDON_SUPPLIERS*, with the attributes and tuples as illustrated in Figure 12.3.

Actually, in RQL the table depicted in Figure 12.3 is the relation which is furnished as a result when the user calls the previously defined view by

Sup_id	Sup_name	Location
611	Jones	London
633	Bates	London
638	Longfellow	London

Figure 12.3 The view *LONDON_SUPPLIERS*.

its name, followed by the query terminator symbol (;), just like:

London_Suppliers;

Views are characterized by their dynamic nature. A view which results in a retrieval operation will only pass on the data it has received, or store the resulting file as a temporary file which does not belong to the database. In general, views provide subsets of databases that exist only after a view is executed. For example, *LONDON_SUPPLIERS* is in effect a "dynamic image" allowing users to visualize the underlying base relation differently. Any changes to the base relations supplier will become automatically visible at the view level. Furthermore, any permitted changes to the *LONDON_SUPPLIERS* view will be automatically registered in the base relation. This implies that users can also perform update or delete operations, not just search operations. In that case, all attributes located in the tuples that satisfy the search criteria, specified by the view, are updated or deleted from the database.

In general, a view completely defines a single file or multiple file access to a database. Moreover, a view always involves a retrieval operation. For example, consider the following broad categories of operations on views:

1. A DML selection operation on a view implies that a subset of the base relation tuples must be retrieved.
2. A delete operation on a view requires that a subset of the base relation tuples must be first located and subsequently deleted.
3. An update operation implies that the values of appropriate attributes must be altered only after the corresponding tuples have been retrieved.

The retrieval operation must preserve the uniqueness of the retrieved records, that is the DBMS must guarantee that records are retrieved in terms of the primary key of their underlying base relation. To understand this statement, you must understand the examples that are presented in the following section.

12.2   Operations on views

So far we have argued that views allow queries to be formulated by transforming the required operations into equivalent operations in terms of their underlying base relations. Thus, views allow queries to be expressed more simply as they tailor a database to the needs of its particular user. For retrieval operations the transformation process is quite straightforward and functions perfectly in all cases. However, a number of significant problems arise when users are able to interact with views as if they were "real" relations in the database. The difficulty concerns updates, deletions, or insertions expressed using views, and arises from the fact that a modification to the database expressed in terms of a specific view must be propagated to its base relations [50]. In the following we illustrate the problem of database modifications through views by means of simple examples. Moreover, the following discussion represents a sketch of the reasoning behind restrictions on certain view operations.

Consider the following two views, namely *LONDON_SUPPLIERS* and *SUPNAME_LOCATION*, both of which are views of the same base relation, namely *SUPPLIER*:

define view London_Supplier **as**
        select from supplier **where** location = "London";
define view Supname_Location **as**
        project supplier **over** sup_name, location;

Since a view name may theoretically appear wherever a relation name is allowed to appear, the following query may be posed:

update Supname_Location **where** location = "London";

Assume now that the view *SUPNAME_LOCATION* contains two suppliers having identical names, e.g. Smith, both located in London. These two virtual *SUPPLIER* tuples can be distinguished only by means of their primary key *SUP_ID* which is obviously missing. Accordingly, the above view update operation imposes a serious problem:

> If we try to update the record <Smith, London> to say <Smith, Paris>, the system will have to try to update some corresponding record in the underlying base relation *SUPPLIER* – but the question is, which one?

Things are equally complicated in the case of deletion. The system will not be able to distinguish which record to delete as the primary key *SUP_ID* has not been specified. Obviously, this attribute cannot be specified as the *SUP_ID* field is not part of the view. Inserting a new tuple into the view *SUPNAME_LOCATION*, say the record <Jones, Sidney>, is an equally interesting case. There are two reasonable approaches to dealing with this insertion operation:

1. Try to insert a corresponding record into the underlying base relation. This tuple must have the format <NULL, Jones, Sidney> which will obviously fail because the supplier identification field must be a non-null value as it comprises the primary key of the basic relation *SUPPLIER*. For further information refer to section 2.4.
2. Reject the insertion and return an error message to the user who issued the query.

The symbol **null** represents a null value [19]. It signifies that the value of a specific attribute is unknown or does not exist. Some relational systems take one of these approaches and create null values [19]. The presence of null values in base relations adds a substantial degree of complexity to the database management system, and to the database queries. For those who are interested, a very interesting treatment of null values in the relational database context is analyzed in [19]. Consequently, we can postulate that some views are inherently updatable, deletable, etc., whereas others are not. For example, not all the above problems exist in the case of the view *LONDON_SUPPLIERS*, and this is simply because this view perceives a horizontal subset of a single base table.

In such views there is a simple one-to-one correspondence between the tuples of the view and those of the base relation. Consequently, updates, deletions, and inserts pose no problems and can be handled relatively easy.

Consequently, RQL allows the definition of two types of view, those which are modifiable, and those which are not. In RQL, a view *V* is modifiable, that is one can perform updates, deletions, or insertions in its context, if and only if all the following conditions apply to the view context:

1. *V* is made up from only one base relation, say *R*.
2. There exists a one-to-one correspondence between the tuples of *V* and those of *R*, such that any modification on *V* results into an equivalent operation on *R*.

12.3   View implementation in REQUIEM

REQUIEM treats views in much the same way as base relations, as far as their implementation is concerned. It distinguishes between two function categories: the view definition and the view manipulation routines. Moreover, views in REQUIEM are subjected to loading, which means that the view context of an already defined view contained in the *SYSVIEW* catalog must be loaded at the beginning of each new session. In the following we will elaborate on the above issues. We assume that you are familiar with the concepts of the view context creation and view scanning. If you run into trouble during the following subsection, then refer to Chapter 7 and try to understand how views are created and scanned. In any case, it might be helpful to read the material that follows in conjunction with sections 7.5 and 7.6 to obtain an overall picture of how views are created, scanned, and manipulated.

12.3.1   View definition

We have already explained in outline by means of examples how a view is defined. What we did not mention is that since no attribute names can be specified explicitly in the **define view** statement, RQL assumes quite rightly that attribute names in a view are directly inherited from its source relations. In RQL every time a user defines a view the parser calls the function **view_define()** to manage the intricacies of view definition.

Although the code implementation of **view_define()** is rather long, it is straightforward to understand. First, the function **view_define()** must make sure that the token following the keyword **define** in the input statement is nothing other than **view**. Hence, it calls the function **nxtoken_type()** to fetch the next token from the input stream. The function of this routine is identical to that of **next_token()**, but **nxtoken_type()** does not allow view expansion whenever the name of a view is encountered. This means that if we encounter in an input statement the name of an already defined view function, **next_token()** and **this_token()** would expand this view and replace it by its view definition text, whereas **nxtoken_type()** and **token_type()** would preserve only the name of the view. Next, **view_define()** must ensure that the next token in the input is a valid name for a view which is going to be defined. Consequently the function **view_define()** ensures that the name of the view does not already exist as the name of a base table or of an already defined view. If these checks are successful it then allocates and initializes a view structure. After **view_define()** has consumed the token **AS** it has to make sure that the rest of the input line is blank. This is due to the fact that the **define** statement is an interactive statement which prompts the user to define a view. Subsequently, **view_define()** prompts the user for the view definition text which is stored in the corresponding view structure.

You must not forget that the text definition of a specific view might occupy more than one input line on your terminal. Accordingly, new text structures might be allocated to store the successive lines of a view definition text. Finally, you will be prompted to press a <return> character when your view definition has been completed.

As the view definition text is going to be stored in the view context, and more importantly in the system catalogs, the view definition must first be checked to ensure that it is syntactically sound. Therefore, the complete definition of a view is stored in a special buffer called **tex_buf**. The contents of this buffer are subsequently parsed, by calling the function **parse()**. At this stage the parser must understand that it should not execute the contents of **tex_buf** and that it should only report on their syntactic structure. The parser can only sense a view definition whenever the global flag **view_def** is turned on. If the view is syntactically correct, it is a valid view, and its corresponding view structure is linked into the view list. Finally, all information pertaining to a specific view is assembled and inserted into the system catalogs *SYSVIEW* and *SYSTAB*. Such information includes the base relation of a view, the creator of a view, the name of a view, its textual definition, etc. Recall at this point that REQUIEM assumes that modifiable views stem from a single base relation. Consequently, it is not strange that **view_define()** stores the name of the base relation in the system catalog only when the view is the product of either a **select** or **project** statement. RQL provides the user with two possibilities to examine the definition text of a specific view:

1. The user can either inspect the *SYSVIEW* catalog contents if he is allowed to.
2. The user can alternatively utilize the **show view** statement. However, in this case the user must specify the name of the view whose text must be inspected.

12.3.2   View loading

Each time a new session begins, all predefined views must be loaded into the view list afresh. To load a set of defined views REQUIEM must first open the view catalog *SYSVIEW* and project its contents over the attributes **view_name** and **text**. In the function **view_load()** we use two buffers to hold this information. The buffer **name_buf** preserves the name of a view while the buffer **texbuf** preserves its text definition. Subsequently, a new view structure must be allocated and initialized to hold the properties of the defined view. This view structure is finally linked into the view list. Before exiting, function **view_load()** closes all associated files and then forwards to the user a message stating the number of views that have already been loaded.

12.3.3 View manipulation

REQUIEM contains a handful of view manipulation functions, such as **delete_view()**, **drop_view()**, **find_view()**, and **which_view()**. All of them, except **drop_view()**, are called indirectly by means of some of the parser functions **select**, **project**, etc. The function **drop_view()** is called only when the user wishes to drop or delete an already defined view. The user is prompted to answer if he/she really means to delete the view in question. If this answer is affirmative, the view list is scanned until the view in question is located and its associated view structure space is deallocated by means of the function **delete_view()**. This space can, thus, be reused by any subsequent allocation calls. You must keep in mind that if you are doing a lot of allocation in your program, returning storage when you have finished with it can prevent your program from growing larger all the time. Before exiting, function **drop_view()** deletes all entries pertinent to the deleted view from the system catalogs *SYSVIEW* and *SYSTAB*. This can be achieved by means of the following two canned queries:

delete sysview **where**
>   viewname = string value of the variable lexeme;

delete systab **where**
>   viewname = string value of the variable lexeme;

These canned queries can only be executed when the parser is entered by means of a call to the function **parse()**.

The function **delete_view()** is a useful function which is invoked whenever the user wishes to perform view deletions or updates.

Example 12.3.1

Consider the following query:

delete *London_Suppliers* **where** *Sup_id = 122;*

where LONDON_SUPPLIERS is defined as on page 373.

The function **delete()** hands control over to function **delete_view()** once it has determined that the argument following the keyword **delete** is an already defined view. Function **delete_view()** must now determine which base table is associated with the view in question. To determine that, it must call the function **view_specs()** which returns amongst other things the name of the base relation (held in the character array **base**), and the predicate associated with this view (held in the character array **predicate**). For example, in the above definition the predicate is *location = "London"*. In that case the function **delete_view()** will associate that predicate with the predicate (if one exists) of the original query, namely, *sup_id = 122*. This is accomplished by means of the logical construct "&" which logically combines both predicates. Next, function **delete_view()** will pass control to the function **retrieve()** which will commence parsing the combined predicate associated with the ground query. Accordingly, the deletion will be performed in terms of the base relation. Finally, the utility function **which_view()** finds out if a view name exists within the view list and returns its name. In doing so, it calls first the function **find_view()** which determines if the view is really a member of the view list.

12.4   Source listing 8

file: view.c

```
1     /* REQUIEM - view manipulation file */
2
3     #include <stdio.h>
4     #include "requ.h"
5
6     extern char lexeme[];
7     extern char cformat[];
8     extern struct view *views;
9     extern int saved_ch;
10    extern char *strip_blank(), *strip_semicol();
11    BOOL  view_operation = FALSE;
12
13    /* --------------------- define a view ---------------------- */
14    int     view_define()
15    {
16      struct view *view_ptr = NULL;
17      struct text *texts, *txt_ptr, *txt_last, *tex_def;
18      char    textline[LINEMAX+1], creator[20], perms[10];
19      char base[RNSIZE+1], *tex_buf, **args, **dcalloc();
20      char *path(), *status();
21      int arg_index, loc, length = 0, tbase = 0, toffset = 0;
22      char *get_line();
```

```
23
24      if (nxtoken_type() != VIEW)
25        return (error(SYNTAX));
26
27      /* get view name */
28      if (nxtoken_type() != ID)
29        return (error(SYNTAX));
30
31      /* if view name exists as relation exit */
32      if (fexists(lexeme))
33        return (error(VIEWDEF));
34
35      /* find the view in the view table */
36      for (view_ptr = views; view_ptr != NULL;
37                      view_ptr = view_ptr->view_next)
38        if (strcmp(view_ptr->view_name, lexeme) == EQUAL) {
39          printf("\t Drop view to redefine it !\n");
40          cmd_clear();
41          return(TRUE);
42        }
43
44      /* allocate and initialize a view structure */
45      if ((view_ptr =
46          (struct view *) malloc(sizeof(struct view ))) == NULL)
47        return (error(INSMEM));
48      if ((view_ptr->view_name =
49                      rmalloc(strlen(lexeme) + 1)) == NULL) {
50        nfree((char *) view_ptr);
51        return (error(INSMEM));
52      }
53      strcpy(view_ptr->view_name, lexeme);
54      view_ptr->view_text = NULL;
55
56      if (nxtoken_type() != AS)
57        return (error(SYNTAX));
58
59      /* make sure that the rest of the line is blank */
60      if (!db_flush())
61        return (FALSE);
62
63      /* setup  prompt strings */
64      db_prompt((char *) 0, "VIEW-DEFINITION: ");
65
66      /* get definition text */
67      for (txt_last = NULL; ; txt_last = txt_ptr) {
68
69        if (txt_last != NULL)
70          printf("If view definition complete press <return> to exit\n");
71        /* get a line */
72        get_line(textline);
73
74        if (textline[0] == EOS || textline[0] == '\n')
75          break;
76
77        /* allocate a view text structure */
78        if ((txt_ptr =
79            (struct text *)malloc(sizeof(struct text ))) == NULL) {
80          view_free(view_ptr);
81          return (error(INSMEM));
82        }
83
```

```
84          if ((txt_ptr->txt_text =
85              rmalloc(strlen(textline) + 1)) == NULL) {
86          view_free(view_ptr);
87          return (error(INSMEM));
88          }
89
90          if (txt_last == NULL)
91          strcpy(txt_ptr->txt_text, textline);
92          else
93          sprintf(txt_ptr->txt_text, " %s", textline);
94
95          txt_ptr->txt_next = NULL;
96
97          /* link it into the view list */
98          if (txt_last == NULL)
99          view_ptr->view_text = txt_ptr;
100         else /* catenate continuation of view text */
101         txt_last->txt_next = txt_ptr;
102         }
103
104         /* check syntactic correctness of view */
105         for (tex_def = view_ptr->view_text; tex_def != NULL;
106             tex_def = tex_def->txt_next)
107         length += strlen(tex_def->txt_text)+1;
108
109         if ((tex_buf =
110             (char *) calloc(1, (unsigned) length + 2)) == NULL) {
111         view_free(view_ptr);
112         return (error(INSMEM));
113         }
114
115         if (strlen(tex_buf) > LINEMAX) {
116         view_free(view_ptr);
117         cmd_clear();
118         return (error(LINELONG));
119         }
120
121         for (tex_def = view_ptr->view_text; tex_def != NULL;
122             tex_def = tex_def->txt_next) {
123         strcat(tex_buf, " ");
124         strcat(tex_buf, tex_def->txt_text);
125         }
126
127         if (!parse(tex_buf, TRUE)) {
128         printf("syntactically wrong view definition\n");
129         nfree(tex_buf);
130         view_free(view_ptr);
131         saved_ch = NEWLINE;    /* force a newline */
132         return(FALSE);
133         }
134         else {
135         printf("View definition syntactically O.K\n");
136         saved_ch = NEWLINE;    /* force a newline */
137         }
138
139         /* link the new view into the view list */
140         if (txt_last == NULL) {
141         view_free(view_ptr);
142         return(TRUE);
143         }
144         else {
```

```
145         view_ptr->view_next = views;
146         views = view_ptr;
147       }
148
149       /* insert catalog arguments in argument array */
150       arg_index = 5;
151       args = dcalloc(arg_index);
152       args[0] = view_ptr->view_name;
153       args[1] = base;
154       args[2] = rmalloc(LINEMAX+1);
155
156       /* if long text expected */
157       if (view_ptr->view_text->txt_next != NULL) {
158         for (texts = view_ptr->view_text; texts != NULL;
159                             texts = texts->txt_next) {
160           toffset += tbase;
161           strip_blank(args[2] + toffset,
162                       texts->txt_text,
163                       strlen(texts->txt_text), &tbase);
164         }
165         *(args[2]+strlen(args[2])) = EOS;
166       }
167       else
168         strcpy(args[2],  view_ptr->view_text->txt_text);
169
170       /* find base name of a view */
171       if (strncmp("project", args[2], 7) == EQUAL) {
172         loc = 7;
173         get_base(base, &loc, args[2]);
174       }
175       else if (strncmp("select", args[2], 6) == EQUAL) {
176         loc = right_index(args[2], "from");  /* find "from" */
177         get_base(base, &loc, args[2]);
178       }
179       else /* more than one base names are involved */
180         strcpy(base, "none");
181
182       /* insert sysview catalog entry, three args */
183       if (!cat_insert("sysview", args, 3)) {
184         nfree(args[2]);
185         nfree((char *) args);
186         return(FALSE);
187       }
188
189       status(base, perms);
190       path(creator);
191
192       args[1] = creator;
193       args[2] = perms;
194       args[3] = base;
195       args[4] =  (char *) calloc(1, 2);
196       *(args[4]) = '0';
197       *(args[4]+1) = EOS;
198
199       /* insert sysview catalog entry, five args */
200       if (!cat_insert("systab", args, arg_index)) {
201         buf_free(args, 5);
202         return(FALSE);
203       }
204
205       nfree(tex_buf);
```

```
206        buf_free(args, 5);
207        cmd_clear(); /*  clear command line */
208
209        /* return successfully */
210        return (TRUE);
211
212    } /* view_define */
213
214    /* ------------------------------------------------------------ */
215
216    /* show a view */
217    int    view_show()
218    {
219      struct view *view_ptr;
220      struct text *txt_ptr;
221
222      if (nxtoken_type() != VIEW)
223        return (error(SYNTAX));
224
225      /* get view name */
226      if (nxtoken_type() != ID)
227        return (error(SYNTAX));
228
229      /* find the view in the view table */
230      for (view_ptr = views; view_ptr != NULL;
231                             view_ptr = view_ptr->view_next)
232        if (strcmp(view_ptr->view_name, lexeme) == EQUAL) {
233          printf("VIEW-EXPANSION: ");
234          for (txt_ptr = view_ptr->view_text; txt_ptr != NULL;
235               txt_ptr = txt_ptr->txt_next)
236            printf("\t%s\n", txt_ptr->txt_text);
237          break;
238        }
239
240      /* check for successful search */
241      if (view_ptr == NULL)
242        printf("*** no view named: %s ***\n", lexeme);
243
244      /* return successfully */
245      return (TRUE);
246
247    } /* view_show */
248
249    /* ------------------------------------------------------------ */
250
251    /* free a view definition */
252    view_free(view_ptr)
253        struct view *view_ptr;
254    {
255      struct text *txt_ptr;
256
257      while ((txt_ptr = view_ptr->view_text) != NULL) {
258        view_ptr->view_text = txt_ptr->txt_next;
259        nfree(txt_ptr->txt_text);
260        nfree((char *) txt_ptr);
261      }
262      nfree(view_ptr->view_name);
263      nfree((char *) view_ptr);
264    } /* view_free */
265
266    /* ------------------------------------------------------------ */
```

```
267
268    int load_views()
269    {
270      struct sel *retrieve();
271      struct sel *slptr;
272      struct sattr *saptr;
273      struct view *view_ptr = NULL;
274      struct text *txt_ptr = NULL;
275      char    texbuf[LINEMAX+1], nbuf[15];
276      int     tcnt, i;
277
278      if ((slptr = retrieve("sysview over viewname, text")) == NULL)
279        return(FALSE);
280      else
281        cmd_kill(); /* to clear command line */
282
283      for (tcnt = 0; fetch(slptr, TRUE); tcnt++) {
284        /* create the tuple from the selected attributes */
285        for (saptr = SEL_ATTRS; saptr != NULL; saptr = saptr->sa_next) {
286          for (i = 0; i < ATTRIBUTE_SIZE; i++) {
287            if (strcmp(saptr->sa_aname, "viewname") == EQUAL)
288              nbuf[i] = saptr->sa_aptr[i];
289            else
290              texbuf[i] = saptr->sa_aptr[i];
291          }
292        }
293
294        /* allocate and initialize a view structure */
295        if ((view_ptr =
296             (struct view *) malloc(sizeof(struct view ))) == NULL) {
297          done(slptr);
298          return (error(INSMEM));
299        }
300
301        if ((view_ptr->view_name =
302             calloc(1, (unsigned) strlen(nbuf) + 1)) == NULL) {
303          nfree((char *) view_ptr);
304          done(slptr);
305          return (error(INSMEM));
306        }
307
308        strcpy(view_ptr->view_name, nbuf);
309        view_ptr->view_text = NULL;
310
311        /* get definition text, allocate a view text structure */
312        if ((txt_ptr =
313             (struct text *)malloc(sizeof(struct text ))) == NULL) {
314          view_free(view_ptr);
315          done(slptr);
316          return (error(INSMEM));
317        }
318
319        if ((txt_ptr->txt_text =
320             rmalloc(strlen(texbuf) + 1)) == NULL) {
321          view_free(view_ptr);
322          done(slptr);
323          return (error(INSMEM));
324        }
325        strcpy(txt_ptr->txt_text, texbuf);
326        txt_ptr->txt_next = NULL;
327
```

```
328        /* link it into the view list */
329        view_ptr->view_text = txt_ptr;
330
331        /* link the new view into the view list */
332        view_ptr->view_next = views;
333        views = view_ptr;
334      }
335
336      db_rclose(SEL_SCAN);   /* close file */
337
338      if (tcnt)
339        printf("LOADING: %d views loaded\n", tcnt);
340
341      return(TRUE);
342    } /* load_view */
343
344    /* --------------- drop a defined view -------------------- */
345    int drop()
346    {
347      char buf[65], prompt[65], response[5];
348      struct view *view_ptr, *view_last;
349      char *getfld();
350
351      if (nxtoken_type() != VIEW)
352        return(error(SYNTAX));
353
354      if (nxtoken_type() != ID)
355        return(error(SYNTAX));
356
357      sprintf(buf, "delete sysview where viewname = \"%s\"",lexeme);
358      sprintf(prompt, "Commit changes ? (<yes> or <no>)\t: ");
359      getfld(prompt, response, 4);
360
361      if (strcmp(response, "yes") == EQUAL) {
362
363        /* find the view in the view table and free it */
364        for (view_ptr = views, view_last = NULL; view_ptr != NULL;
365            view_last = view_ptr, view_ptr = view_ptr->view_next)
366          if (strcmp(view_ptr->view_name, lexeme) == EQUAL) {
367            if (view_last == NULL)
368              views = view_ptr->view_next;
369            else
370              view_last->view_next = view_ptr->view_next;
371
372            view_free(view_ptr);
373            break;
374          }
375
376        /* delete the sysview entry first, then the systab entry */
377        if (!parse(buf, FALSE))
378          return(error(VIEWDEL));
379
380        sprintf(buf, "delete systab where relname = \"%s\"",lexeme);
381
382        if (!parse(buf, FALSE))
383          return(error(VIEWDEL));
384
385        sprintf(cformat, "# view %s definition deleted #", lexeme);
386      }
387      return(TRUE);
388    } /* drop */
```

```
389
390    /* ------------------------------------------------------------ */
391    struct sel *delete_view()
392    {
393      char *pt_error();
394      struct view *view_ptr;
395      struct sel *slptr, *retrieve();
396      char base[15], predicate[LINEMAX+1], fmt[2*LINEMAX+1];
397      int loc;        /* location where predicate lies */
398      BOOL found = FALSE;
399
400      /* get the  view name */
401      if (nxtoken_type() != ID)
402        return((struct sel *)pt_error(SYNTAX));
403
404      for (view_ptr = views; view_ptr != (struct view *)NULL;
405                             view_ptr = view_ptr->view_next)
406        if (strcmp(view_ptr->view_name, lexeme) == EQUAL) {
407          if (!view_specs(view_ptr, base, predicate, &loc))
408            return((struct sel *)NULL);
409          found = TRUE;
410          break;
411        }
412
413      if (found == FALSE)
414        return((struct sel *)pt_error(SYNTAX));
415
416      if (next_token() != WHERE)
417        return((struct sel *)pt_error(SYNTAX));
418
419      /* signify a view operation */
420      view_operation = TRUE;
421
422      if (loc != -1) /* there exists a "where" clause in view */
423        sprintf(fmt, " %s where %s & ", base, predicate + loc);
424      else
425        sprintf(fmt, "%s where", base);
426
427      if ((slptr = retrieve(fmt)) == (struct sel *) NULL)
428        return((struct sel *)pt_error(VIEWDEL));
429
430      return(slptr);
431    } /* delete_view */
432
433    /* ----------- find view and base relation name ------------- */
434    which_view(vname)
435         char *vname;
436    {
437      char fmt[STRINGMAX];
438      struct sel *slptr, *retrieve();
439      struct sattr *saptr;
440
441      if (find_view(vname)) {
442        sprintf(fmt, "systab over relname, deriv");
443
444        if ((slptr = retrieve(fmt)) == NULL)
445          return(FAIL);
446        else
447          cmd_kill();    /* clear command line */
448
449        while (fetch(slptr, TRUE)) {
```

```
450              saptr = SEL_ATTRS;
451              if (strcmp(saptr->sa_aptr, vname) == EQUAL)
452                  break;
453          }
454
455          /* copy the base relation name */
456          strcpy(vname, saptr->sa_next->sa_aptr);
457
458          done(slptr);
459
460          if (strcmp(vname, "base") != EQUAL)
461              return(TRUE);
462      }
463
464      return(FALSE);
465
466  } /* which_view */
467  /* ------------------------------------------------------------ */
468
469  BOOL find_view(view_name)
470      char *view_name;
471  {   struct view *view_ptr;
472      BOOL view_found = FALSE;
473
474      for (view_ptr = views; view_ptr != (struct view *)NULL;
475                          view_ptr = view_ptr->view_next)
476          if (strcmp(view_ptr->view_name, view_name) == EQUAL) {
477              view_found = TRUE;
478              break;
479          }
480      return(view_found);
481  } /* find_view */
482  /* --------------- get view specifications ------------------- */
483  static int  view_specs(view_ptr, base, predicate, loc)
484      struct view *view_ptr;
485      char *base, *predicate;
486      int *loc;
487  {
488      int  toffset = 0, tbase = 0;
489
490      struct text *texts;
491
492      /* if long text expected */
493      if (view_ptr->view_text->txt_next != NULL) {
494
495          for (texts = view_ptr->view_text; texts != NULL;
496                          texts = texts->txt_next) {
497              toffset += tbase;
498              strip_semicol(predicate + toffset, texts->txt_text,
499                          strlen(texts->txt_text), &tbase);
500          }
501          *(predicate+strlen(predicate)) = EOS;
502      }
503      else
504          cpy_nosemi(predicate,  view_ptr->view_text->txt_text);
505
506      /* find base name of a view */
507      if (strncmp("select", predicate, 6) == EQUAL) {
508
509          *loc = right_index(predicate, "from");  /* find "from" */
510
```

```
511        /* get the base name */
512        get_base(base, loc, predicate);
513        *loc = right_index(predicate, "where");  /* find "where" */
514
515        /* skip blanks after "where" */
516        if (*loc != -1)
517          while (is_blank(*(predicate + *loc)))
518            (*loc)++;
519
520      }
521      else { /* more than one base names are involved */
522        printf("Unaccepted operation on view specified\n");
523        return(FALSE);
524      }
525
526      return(TRUE);
527
528    } /* view_specifics */
529
530    /* ------------------------------------------------------------- */
531    int view_stat()
532    {
533      struct view *view_ptr;
534      char predicate[LINEMAX+1], fmt[2*LINEMAX+1], base[ANSIZE+1];
535      int tkn, loc;          /* location where predicate lies */
536      BOOL found = FALSE;
537      BOOL where_flag = FALSE;
538
539      /* get the  view name */
540      if (token_type() != ID)
541        return(FALSE);
542
543      for (view_ptr = views; view_ptr != (struct view *)NULL;
544           view_ptr = view_ptr->view_next)
545        if (strcmp(view_ptr->view_name, lexeme) == EQUAL) {
546          if (!view_specs(view_ptr, base, predicate, &loc))
547            return(FAIL);
548          found = TRUE;
549          break;
550        }
551
552      if (found == FALSE)
553        return(FALSE);
554      else
555        nxtoken_type();        /* clear view name */
556
557      /* get next standard input token */
558      tkn = this_token();
559
560      if (tkn == WHERE)
561        where_flag = TRUE;
562      else if (tkn != ';')
563        return(FAIL);
564
565      /* signify a view operation */
566      view_operation = TRUE;
567
568      if (loc != -1 && where_flag) /* there is a "where" clause */
569        sprintf(fmt, " %s where %s & ", base, predicate + loc);
570      else if (loc != -1 && where_flag == FALSE)
571        sprintf(fmt, "%s where %s", base, predicate + loc);
```

```
572      else
573        sprintf(fmt, "%s;", base);
574
575      q_scan(fmt);
576
577      return(TRUE);
578
579   } /* view_stat */
580
581   /* ------------------------------------------------------------ */
582
583   get_base(base, loc, predicate)
584        char *base, *predicate;
585        int *loc;
586   {
587      int i;
588
589      /* skip blanks after "from" */
590      while (is_blank(*(predicate + *loc)))
591        (*loc)++;
592
593      /* find base name */
594      for (i = 0; isalnum(*(predicate + *loc)) && i < ANSIZE; (*loc)++, i++)
595        base[i] = *(predicate + *loc);   /* copy base name */
596      base[i] = EOS;
597
598   } /* get_base */
599
600   /* ------------------------------------------------------------ */
```

13

The Database System Catalogs

We have used the system catalogs several times throughout this book already (especially in Chapter 3). As already explained, the REQUIEM catalogs effectively comprise a system-defined database in their own right and contain entries which concern diverse entities that are of particular interest to the database system itself. Examples of such entities are base relations, views, indices, access rights, and so on. In the present chapter we shall review the basic catalog types and facilities before concentrating on more concrete issues concerning system catalog implementation.

13.1   The use of system catalogs

In a practical database system the overall burden of attribute names, records, views, files, etc. may be so massive that it cannot be easily managed by the user. In fact, any practical database system should contain not only user-created relations, but also certain system relations, whose function is to hold the data that the system requires to monitor the behavior of the database. These system-defined relations are collectively referred to as the *database system catalogs*, or the *database dictionary* or *directory* (DB/D). Catalogs assist the user, or the database administrator, in his/her mental effort to cope with a huge amount of data concerning the structure of the database. Catalogs store all the definitions of data used by the database. They contain both machine readable and user-visible specifications including functional information on the database, the information entities, and their attributes, interrelationships, and meaning.

From the viewpoint of a relational DBMS a database is considered to be a collection of both base and derived relations with certain interrelationships among them. It is therefore necessary to distinguish between the base relations and the derived ones, and furthermore to confirm whether a certain relation contains one or more access paths. The data catalogs contain definitions of records, data items, relations, views, and other data objects that are of interest to the users or required by the data management software. In general, these definitions are accessed by the users when information about the characteristics of data contained in a database are required. The topic of this chapter is the use and implementation of such a database directory.

It is nearly impossible to separate the concepts of the DB/D from the use of database management systems, data administration concepts, and notions about information and its uses in organizations or enterprises. From a broader perspective, not only the DBMS but also the database administrator, the users, and any software tools dealing with diverse functions of database administration require information about the database content. Therefore, the database catalogs are thought of as the central repository of information about the database itself. As explained in Chapter 1 it is customary to use the word meta-data to indicate that a higher level of abstraction is involved in this organization of data. This means that reference is not made towards plain typical data; meta-data is rather data about data. Furthermore, data catalogs may include information about programs, processes, and authorities. For example, data inventory management requires pertinent facts and relationships about the various data entities, processes, users and even equipment in the data processing environment [52]. This has the effect that diverse directory systems are commercially available, and differ substantially in the given functionality, facilities, aspirations, and even terminology. These are side issues which will not be considered in this text. Readers who wish to acquire additional background on aspects not included herein, such as for example the selection or evaluation criteria of database dictionary/directory systems, can refer to interesting surveys presented in [52], [53], and [54]. This section explains the concepts underlying directory systems, and provides background information about database directory systems, including structure, contents, and functionality of a simple data directory system.

13.2   Integrated versus segregated directories

The information held in the system catalogs presents complex functional interrelationships. This kind of complexity points decisively towards having the contents of the system catalogs organized as a database within the database. If the information held in the system catalogs is timely, accurate, consistent, and above all usable and evolvable, then the DB/D is a valuable resource. However, if the information content of the DB/D is used ineffectively then the DB/D is quite likely to become a source of impediment to the DBMS or the needs of a user. There are two approaches to the implementation of this *meta-database* which influence the implementational structure of the database directory. Accordingly, system catalogs can be classified as being either *integrated* or *segregated*.

1. *Integrated Directory System (IDS):* An IDS depends upon an existing DBMS's facilities for managing its meta-data. The directory may be integrated as one of the features of the DBMS or it may be implemented as an additional system-defined database which is treated just like any other database within the DBMS environment. The advantage of this method is that the system catalogs have access to all corresponding DBMS features such as a query processor or integrity/recovery procedures. With this configuration the DBMS, and its related components, rely completely upon the database directory for the provision of meta-data. For example, a query processor can extract the definition/description of views from the DB/D, and the DBMS may apply integrity constraints as specified in the DB/D before storing a data element. The sole disadvantage of this method is its total incompatibility with other DBMSs.

2. *Segregated Directory System (SDS):* This kind of system is a completely self-contained system which does not rely upon any specific DBMS. Thus, it must supply the user with all the facilities and functionality which otherwise would be furnished only by an underlying DBMS. An SDS does not necessarily imply a centralized implementation as it is not tied to any specific DBMS, and can be used to describe information resources pertaining to diverse DBMS environments. This suggests that SDSs are particularly mature and advantageous for use in distributed database situations.

Consequently, SDSs are used in large installations and come endowed with a complex pattern of facilities. An SDS is considered to be a large database or perhaps a set of several databases, which include not just DBMS information such as relation descriptions but also for example the following:

1. Version facilities which allow multiple copies of any directory entry to be maintained.
2. Updating histories, this facility allows the history of updates to be recorded and provides an audit of changes to the database directory.
3. Reporting facilities.

4. Language interfaces, and so forth.

Most of these systems employ a command language which incorporates
its own syntax and semantics.

The trend in data management systems is towards fully integrated, *active
directory systems* which provide the sole source of meta-data in the system.
An active database directory is one in which the DB/D is the single source of
control over all references to meta-data. This ensures amongst other things
that data definitions are kept under close surveillance, providing, thus, an
accurate and complete basis of data descriptions for any future reference.
Most of the earlier DB/D systems have not reached the desired degree of
integration with their underlying environment. These systems tend to be
rather *passive directory systems* in the sense that they are free-standing or
independent of their underlying DBMS. Many software components of the
data management system – such as the DBMS, or application programs –
use their own internally generated meta-data, where definitions are normally
provided and maintained only for human users. Each such software package
is allowed to access a common DB/D and convert its meta-data into a
format required by this DB/D. Passive DB/Ds result in multiple sources
of data descriptions within the overall system, while failing to guarantee
that identical definitions identifying the same data are used throughout the
system.

It is obvious that an active DB/D is more attractive for a number of reasons. With active DB/Ds there is only a single definition of a database to
store and maintain. Hence, it is clearly not possible to have one such definition in one place and another definition in another. If, on the other hand,
the DB/D is passive or relatively passive, more storage space is required.
Furthermore, there is always some duplication of effort in maintaining two
or more copies of the same data, and above all great care must be taken
to ensure that the multiple definitions are actually identical [55]. Further
information about the use of passive DB/Ds and their implementation can
be found in [53] and [55].

The REQUIEM system catalogs make up an additional database in the
system which requires standard query language features and specially developed software for its manipulation. The REQUIEM DB/D is an active
integrated DB/D which depends upon standard REQUIEM functions for
its realization. These system catalogs assist the system in implementing
changes such as modifying existing attributes or adding new relation types
into an already existing schema and evaluating the impact of the proposed
changes. Obviously, any such changes to the DB/D are automatically registered in the system catalogs and will be reflected during the next invocation of REQUIEM. This kind of DB/D facilitates the system when taking

decisions relating to data consistency or uniformity issues, or when loading user-defined views. Furthermore, the REQUIEM directory helps the users to cope with what might under other circumstances be an overwhelming proliferation of relation and attribute names.

13.3 The functionality of a relational directory

In order to obtain the full benefits from a directory subsystem, its information should be complete, accurate, and certainly up to date. This implies that a directory subsystem should necessarily include some means of on-line access. The meta-data in the system catalogs is used as a point of reference so that all potential users may obtain a common understanding of the meaning of data. In order to ensure consistency, only authorized users such as database administrators should be allowed to maintain the directory if this is required. Note that statements like **insert**, **update**, and **delete** are not explicitly available to users for updating the information held in the DB/D. The reasons for controlling such update operations are obvious: it would be far too easy to destroy indispensable information contained in the system catalogs so that the DBMS environment would no longer function properly. In fact, in REQUIEM such operations are performed invisibly by the system itself, when necessary. However, it is actually the user who with his data definition or data updating statements triggers the catalog insertion or updating operations.

In a practical relational database system the catalogs consist of a handful of system-defined relations. It is not, however, our purpose here to give an exhaustive description of the system catalogs. Rather, we provide a somehow basic and simplified introduction to their structure and content. Our basic purpose is to show you how the information contained in the system catalogs can be helpful to the user as well as to the system. In sum, the principal system catalogs, which are required to describe a relational database and to assist the corresponding DBMS in implementing its operational tasks, are the following:

1. **Relations catalog**: This catalog maintains a tuple corresponding to each relation, or view of the database, including the database itself as well as the other system catalogs. For example, the relation name, its creator, its degree, and possibly certain statistical information regarding the contents and information on how tuple attributes can be accessed and stated.

2. **Attributes catalog**: For each relation described in the relations catalog,

a corresponding number of entries is recorded in the attributes catalog. This number of entries is equal to the number of attributes making up a specific relation. Each entry in this catalog specifies the name, type, and maximum length of its associated attribute.

3. **Views catalog:** This catalog confines itself to the description of views derived in terms of base relations. In addition to any information in the relations and attributes catalogs you can find supplementary information concerning the view, e.g. the text definition of the view.

4. **Access path catalog:** In this catalog one can find the access paths defined on base relations. For example, for each index one can find the relation, the associated attributes, and an indication whether the corresponding index is a primary key, a foreign key, and so on.

5. **Authorization and privileges catalog:** This catalog contains a list of users together with their associated privileges. The privileges can be associated with a given object and the corresponding operations that can be performed on these objects. The objects to which such privileges apply are base relations as well as normal query language statements such as **insert**, **update**, or **delete**.

Example 13.3.1

The catalog structure for a sample relation, called EMPLOYEE, might be as illustrated in Figure 13.1. This catalog structure is created automatically after executing the following data definition statements concerning the relation EMPLOYEE.

```
create employee (emp_id   (num (5), unique),
                 name     (char (20), secondary),
                 address  (char(30)),
                 salary   (real (10)));
```

As seen from Figure 13.1 the above definition statements have the following consequences:

1. An entry is made for the employee definition in the *SYSTAB* relation.
2. A set of four entries, each one corresponding to a specific attribute of the *EMPLOYEE* relation, are made into the *SYSATRS* relation.

This means that the definition–creation of a relation inserts a description of the relation being created into the DB/D. This description comprises multiple tuples in multiple catalog relations. These relation and attribute

SYSTAB				
RELNAME	CREATOR	PERMS	DERIV	NATRS
systab	sys	600	base	5
sysatrs	sys	600	base	5
sysview	sys	600	base	3
syskey	sys	600	base	4
employee	Jones	600	base	4

SYSATRS				
RELNAME	ATRNAME	TYPE	LENGTH	INDEX
systab	relname	char	12	yes
systab	creator	char	20	yes
systab	perms	num	5	no
systab	deriv	char	5	no
systab	natrs	num	8	no
sysatrs	atrname	char	20	yes
sysatrs	relname	char	12	yes
sysatrs	type	char	5	no
sysatrs	length	num	6	no
sysatrs	index	char	5	no
sysview	viewname	char	12	yes
sysview	base	char	12	no
sysview	text	char	123	no
syskey	fgnkey	char	12	yes
syskey	relname	char	12	no
syskey	target	char	12	no
syskey	primary	char	12	no
employee	empl_id	char	5	yes
employee	name	char	20	yes
employee	address	char	30	no
employee	salary	real	10	no

Figure 13.1 The system catalog contents after the creation of the relation *EM-PLOYEE*.

descriptions are an essential component of the DB/D. All the above information is required by the DBMS to perform its activities properly and is, therefore, maintained by the DBMS itself. The catalog for the *SYSTAB* and *SYSATRS* relations themselves are created automatically by the system during the phase of system installation/initialization.

As far as the retrieval of meta-data is concerned, the relational directory subsystem provides similar functional capabilities to those of a standard DBMS. Additionally, the data control features of the system catalogs include standard database functions such as security, integrity, recovery, and concurrency. Ideally, access rights should be selectively granted to the users as the description of the data content provides valuable information to the potential system intruders. This means that access privileges need to be built into the directory subsystem. The system catalogs themselves can be used to hold information about their potential users and to record details of the meta-data they may access. The access privileges should be flexible enough to allow any specific user to be authorized to use a specified subset of the directory database. This is usually accomplished by maintaining an access profile for each individual user. This access profile simply identifies the data content that is allowed to be retrieved by this particular user.

There are many interesting reasons for using relational DBMSs to implement an integrated system directory. In the following, we present succinctly the most important reasons for considering relational DBMSs as the natural candidate for implementing directory subsystems:

1. All facilities of the host DBMS are available for the DB/D as well. By furnishing catalogs which are themselves relations stored in the database, the DBMS allows the user to consult information relative to the database via the query language. Thus, the DB/D can be interrogated by means of the standard query language constructs, just like any other data in the system. Users do not have to learn two different languages, one for querying the DB/D, and one for querying the database. Furthermore, functions such as database recovery and transaction processing do not have to be implemented explicitly.

2. The relational environment is particularly well suited for supporting DB/D extensibility because of the provided notions of logical and physical independence. Consider for example the ability to modify the logical database descriptions without having to deal with the underlying physical database structure.

3. The adaptation of the DB/D as the only source of meta-data for a relational environment means that the system would get the adequate meta-data to carry its internal operations while promoting the integrity and consistency of data. This implies that the incorporation of a DB/D within a relational DBMS improves the functionality and the semantic cohesiveness of both these systems.

The above reasons clearly dictate the need for an automated DB/D realized in terms of the relational model. It is not surprising that a number of software products have been developed for the purpose of creating and maintaining a DB/D. It is also not unusual that the term DB/D is used to refer to the repository of meta-data, or to the combination of the DB/D software and the system catalogs. Hence, a DB/D comprises a database of meta-data, together with the software routines used to create and maintain the DB/D database.

13.4   The REQUIEM directory subsystem

The REQUIEM DB/D is thought of as the collection of information contained in the system catalogs as well as in the file headers of the data files required to implement a certain relation. The REQUIEM DB/D tends to require a complex conglomeration of data structures that can easily be manipulated via the DBMS. To the DBMS system, catalogs are fullyfledged relations which are interrogated and updated internally by means of the conventional DML statements, i.e. canned queries. In this way the system provides uniform access to both data and meta-data. In some cases, the DBMS also makes use of the data held in the DB/D, which implies that neither of these systems can function without the aid of the other. The reasoning is that since the DBMS must have access to the description of the database, there might as well be only one shared copy. The REQUIEM DB/D is often used by the DBMS to obtain the sizes and formats, as well as locations, of data records and fields.

The file implementing the REQUIEM catalog facilities (see listing 9) comprises two basic routines that allow the REQUIEM directory to be implemented. It is amazing how much can be achieved by means of these two routines. There exists, however, an important point which must be taken into account before the system catalogs are implemented. It is handy to devise the implementation algorithm in terms of two distinct phases: the *system initialization phase* and the *system operation phase*. This separation is mandatory because the user must not be in a position to define relations prior to generating the system catalogs. As the system catalogs are relations themselves it is undesirable for them to be explicitly created by normal interactive DDL statements. Rather, their definition statements must exist in a predefined external definition file. This policy was adopted mainly for consistency reasons as the system guarantees the automatic generation of the catalogs at its initialization phase before any user interaction. After this short phase has run to completion the system operation phase can follow. It is during this latter phase that the user can define relations and interact with the system in the usual manner.

Recall that during the system initialization phase the system catalogs are created and views are loaded from external files. At the termination of this phase the system catalogs must contain information pertinent to the organization of the DB/D. For example the system catalog *SYSTAB* must contain entries pertinent to itself as well as to other system tables such as the *SYSATRS* table, the *SYSVIEW* table, etc. The definitions of the system catalogs can be found in external files.

The function **main()**, which initializes REQUIEM, assumes that these definitions exist in a separate definition file. Actually, a user-specified external file fulfills this purpose by containing the definition of all the system catalogs (refer to Appendix C). The system becomes operational after the initialization phase has run to completion. Function **main()** is the actual place where REQUIEM begins execution. This start-up module has several responsibilities. It initializes the scanner through a call to the routine **s_init()**, it then sets up the system catalogs, and eventually transfers control to function **parse()** to initiate parsing. To create and load the system catalogs REQUIEM must first make certain that the system catalogs do exist. Accordingly, it directs control to function **fexists()**, by passing to it the argument "systab". This function performs a simple test to determine if the system relation *SYSTAB* really exists; if so, control is passed back to **main()** which proceeds by parsing the pending input statements. It is now that the user can first define relations; and tuples start automatically entering the system catalogs to describe these newly created relations as well as their attribute formation. By contrast if the system catalogs do not exist then function **main()** calls the scanner function **com_file()** to set-up the appropriate indirect command file **icf** environment (see Chapter 7) which will eventually handle the processing of the system catalog definition statements contained in the external catalog definition file. In the following, we will illustrate the mechanisms involved in creating the system catalogs during the system initialization phase. We feel that understanding this example is critical to understanding how the system catalogs are implemented and generally function.

Two basic functions exist that are called by all programs which use the system catalogs, namely **cat_entry()** and **cat_insert()**. The function **cat_entry()** accumulates the various data elements that should be inserted into the system catalogs, and decides when to enter these elements in the *SYSTAB* or *SYSATRS* catalogs. The function **cat_insert()** is a recursive function that actually inserts the appropriate data elements into the appropriate system catalogs after being instructed to do so. Recall that the *SYSTAB* relation contains a tuple for each system catalog including *SYSTAB* itself, and that the *SYSATRS* relation holds a tuple for each attribute in every system catalog including *SYSATRS* itself. This means that *SYSTAB* enters one tuple for every newly created relation while *SYSATRS* enters multiple tuples for the same relation.

The function **cat_entry()** accepts three arguments: the first argument serves a pointer to the relation structure associated with a created relation (rptr); the second is the degree of the relation; and, finally, the third is the name of the relation (rname). This function is used to obtain from the parser all information pertinent to a newly created relation. This explains why cat_entry() is invoked by the parser function create() each time a new relation is created. Initially, the function tests to see whether the relation in question is a system- or a user-created relation. When the relation is user-created, the function path() is called. This function assigns to the variable creator the name of the relation creator. Furthermore, additional information such as the access permissions and the degree of the relation is also assigned to the variables perms and degree, respectively. The variable deriv denotes whether a relation is a base relation ("base"), or view ("view"). These variables are pointed to by the members of the pointer array args. This pointer array is passed as an argument to the function cat_insert(), once all the information pertinent to the newly created relation has been accumulated. This function also accepts as argument the name of the system catalog (fname) into which tuple entries should be made. Consequently, the purpose of the function cat_entry() is to aid in organizing the appropriate volume of meta-data for the two system catalogs *SYSTAB* and *SYSATRS*.

As explained earlier we shall assume that the system has just entered its initialization phase. At this stage the system catalog *SYSTAB* must be first created and a tuple describing the table itself should be inserted in the *SYSTAB* relation. The function cat_insert() creates the data and index files associated with *SYSTAB* and returns a scan structure pointer (sptr) associated with this system catalog. Next the function must ensure that *SYSTAB* entries are inserted both into the *SYSTAB* and the *SYSATRS* catalog. This is accomplished by means of the following conditional statement contained in the function cat_insert():

$$\text{if } (strcmp(fname, \text{ "} systab \text{ "}) == EQUAL \ \&\&$$
$$(strcmp(args[0], \text{ "} sysatrs \text{ "}) == EQUAL)) \qquad (13.1)$$

This statement will first examine whether the name of the catalog relation into which a tuple entry will be made is identical to character string "systab". Then it will compare the first member of the args array, which includes the name of the relation whose description must be inserted in the system catalogs, with the string constant "sysatrs". In other words, the previous statement ensures that the currently created file is indeed *SYSTAB* and that the function cat_entry() has specified that a tuple pertinent to file *SYSTAB* should be inserted into the *SYSATRS* catalog – hence, the comparison with the character string "sysatrs". However, at this stage the compound statement following the previous conditional statement is skipped as the file *SYSATRS* does not even exist! Incidentally, the value of args[0] is at this point "**systab**". Therefore, the function **cat_insert()** directs control to the following iteration construct which enters a meta-data tuple for the relation *SYSTAB* into the file *SYSTAB*:

$$\text{for } (i = 0; i < \ arg\_indx; i{+}{+}) \qquad\qquad (13.2)$$

This loop initiates a scheme for performing buffered operations. A stream of characters representing the value of each individual attribute of *SYSTAB* is placed in the appropriate position in the buffer **sc_tuple**.

Recall that the structure **rl_header** is the relation header whose contents describe a relation data file (refer to Chapters 4 and 6). The DBMS often requires the data to make sense of the corresponding relation. The function **store_attr()** stores consecutive values of the *SYSTAB* attributes in the scan structure buffer **sc_tuple**. After control has left the above iteration construct the tuple buffer **sc_tuple** contains an entire tuple of meta-data for the relation *SYSTAB*. Subsequently, this tuple will be stored into the corresponding data via the function **db_rstore()**, and the function **cat_insert()** terminates. Function **cat_entry()** checks to see whether the table *SYSATRS* already exists. As the system catalogs have not yet been created, function **cat_insert()** knows that after it returns, control will be directed to the context of the indirect command file which is pending for execution. Execution of these special system-defined structures will result in the creation of the remaining system catalogs. Moreover, the function knows that the *SYSATRS* entries pertaining to the *SYSTAB* system catalog have not been recorded yet and that they will be handled immediately after the former catalog is created. Hence, the function **cat_insert()** terminates by passing control back to its calling module. After termination of the **create()** routine the user receives on his/her screen the message *"Relation SYSTAB created."*

The DBMS will now proceed with the creation of the remaining system catalogs. We shall elaborate only on implementation issues pertaining to the *SYSATRS* table. The implementation algorithm and the flow of control for the remaining system catalogs are exactly the same as for the *SYSVIEW* table or any user-defined relations. You may have noticed that the tuples which are pertinent to the *SYSTAB* attributes have not been inserted into the *SYSATRS* system catalog yet. And this is exactly what the combination of functions **cat_entry()** and **cat_insert()** must accomplish at this stage. It is worth mentioning that the entire process of system catalog creation is performed automatically without any intervention on the part of the user.

The function **cat_entry()** invokes the function **cat_insert()** to insert a tuple for the *SYSATRS* table into the system catalog *SYSTAB*. This means that at this instance the argument **arg[0]** points to the string constant "**sysatrs**". Consequently, the compound statement following the conditional statement 13.1 is entered. Prior to that a scan structure pointed to by the pointer **sptr** has been loaded with information concerning the relation *SYSTAB*. The compound statement accumulates information pertinent to the attributes of *SYSTAB* and initiates a series of recursive calls to insert appropriate attribute descriptions into the *SYSATRS* table. Actually, **cat_insert()** recurses five times, once for each *SYSTAB* attribute. During these recursive calls the conditional statement 13.1 is not entered, and control is rather directed to the iterative statement 13.2. This has the result that at termination of the recursive process five tuples containing meta-data about the system catalog *SYSTAB* are stored in the *SYSATRS* table, see Figure 13.1. Once the recursion has terminated, control returns to the function **cat_entry()** which inserts the meta-data tuples pertinent to the attributes of the relation *SYSATRS* into the same relation by initiating successive invocations of the function **cat_insert()**. The only part of this program example that seems to be tricky is the part associated with the conditional statement 13.1. We believe that once you have understood how this segment of code functions it is easy to comprehend how the system catalogs are implemented.

13.5   Source listing 9

file: cat.c

```
1     /* REQUIEM - catalog manipulation routines */
2     #include <stdio.h>
3     #include "requ.h"
4
5     extern int saved_ch;
6
7     /* ------------------------------------------------------------ */
8
9     /* prepare a catalog entry */
10    BOOL cat_entry(rptr, nattrs, rname)
11        struct relation *rptr;
12        int  nattrs;
13        char *rname;
14    {
15      char    creator[20];
16      char    deriv[10], index[10];
17      char    type[10], length[10];
18      char    perms[10], degree[10];
19      char    *path(), *status();
20      char    **args;
21      int     i, arg_index;
22
23      /* relation name catalog entry */
24      if (strncmp(rname, "sys", 3) == EQUAL) {
25        strcpy(creator, "sys");
```

```
26          creator[3] = EOS;
27     } else
28       path(creator);
29
30     /* get status information from file descriptor */
31     status(rname, perms);
32
33     /* evaluate catalog entries */
34     sprintf(degree, "%d", nattrs);
35     strcpy(deriv, "base");
36
37     /* insert catalog arguments in argument array */
38     arg_index = 5;  /* no. of attributes for systab */
39     args = dcalloc(arg_index);
40     args[0] = rname;
41     args[1] = creator;
42     args[2] = perms;
43     args[3] = deriv;
44     args[4] = degree;
45
46     /* insert systab catalog tuple */
47     if (!cat_insert("systab", args, arg_index))
48       return(FALSE);
49
50     /* insert sysatrs catalog tuple */
51     if (fexists("sysatrs")) {
52       args[0] = rptr->rl_name;
53
54       for (i = 0; ; i++) {
55
56         if (RELATION_HEADER.hd_attrs[i].at_name[0] == EOS)
57           break;
58
59         args[1] = RELATION_HEADER.hd_attrs[i].at_name;
60
61         if (RELATION_HEADER.hd_attrs[i].at_type == TCHAR)
62           strcpy(type, "char");
63         else if  (RELATION_HEADER.hd_attrs[i].at_type == TNUM)
64           strcpy(type, "num");
65         else if  (RELATION_HEADER.hd_attrs[i].at_type == TREAL)
66           strcpy(type, "real");
67         else
68           return(error(UNDEFTYPE));
69         args[2] = type;
70
71         sprintf(length, "%d",RELATION_HEADER.hd_attrs[i].at_size);
72         args[3] = length;
73
74         clear_mem(index, 0, 10);
75         if (RELATION_HEADER.hd_attrs[i].at_key != 'n')
76           strcpy(index, "yes");
77         else
78           strcpy(index, "no");
79         index[strlen(index)] = EOS;
80
81         args[4] = index;
82
83         if (!cat_insert("sysatrs", args, arg_index))
84           return(FALSE);
85       }
86     }
```

```
87
88     nfree((char *) args);
89
90     return(TRUE);
91   } /* cat_entry */
92
93   /* ------------------------------------------------------------ */
94
95   /* insert an entry into the catalog */
96   BOOL cat_insert(fname, args, arg_indx)
97        char *fname;
98        char **args;
99        int  arg_indx;
100  {
101    struct scan *sptr, *db_ropen();
102    struct attribute *aptr, *taptr;
103    char  **targs = NULL, **key_buf = NULL;
104    char length[10], type[10], index[10], avalue[LINEMAX+1];
105    int targ_index;
106    int i, j, astart, p_cntr = 0, s_cntr = 2;
107
108    /* open the relation, return a scan structure pointer */
109    if ((sptr = db_ropen(fname)) == NULL)
110      return (FALSE);
111
112
113    /* systab entries in sysatrs catalog should be made first */
114    if (strcmp(fname, "systab") == EQUAL &&
115                  strcmp(args[0], "sysatrs") == EQUAL) {
116      targ_index = 5;
117      targs = dcalloc(targ_index);
118      targs[0] = SCAN_RELATION->rl_name;
119
120      for (j = 0; j < targ_index; j++) {
121        taptr = &SCAN_HEADER.hd_attrs[j];
122        targs[1] = taptr->at_name;
123        if (taptr->at_type == TCHAR)
124          strcpy(type, "char");
125        else if (taptr->at_type == TNUM)
126          strcpy(type, "num");
127        else
128          return(error(INCNST));
129
130        targs[2] = type;
131        sprintf(length, "%d", taptr->at_size);
132        targs[3] = length;
133
134        if (taptr->at_key != 'n')
135          strcpy(index, "yes");
136        else
137          strcpy(index, "no");
138        index[strlen(index)] = EOS;
139
140        targs[4] = index;
141
142        /* recurse */
143        if (!cat_insert("sysatrs", targs, targ_index))
144          return(FALSE);
145      }
146    }
147
```

```
148      /* get attr values, astart points past tuple status code */
149      astart = 1;
150      for (i = 0; i < arg_indx; i++) {
151
152        /* get a pointer to the current attribute */
153        aptr = &SCAN_HEADER.hd_attrs[i];
154
155        /* check for the last attribute */
156        if (aptr->at_name[0] == EOS)
157          break;
158
159        strcpy(avalue, args[i]);
160        avalue[strlen(avalue)] = EOS;
161
162        /* place the attribute value in sc_tuple */
163        store_attr(aptr, &sptr->sc_tuple[astart], avalue);
164
165        /* update the attribute start */
166        astart += aptr->at_size;
167
168        /* check if indexing is required */
169        if (aptr->at_key != 'n')
170          check_ix(&key_buf, aptr, &p_cntr, &s_cntr, avalue);
171
172      }
173
174      if (targs != NULL)
175        nfree((char *) targs);
176
177      /* store the new tuple */
178      if (!store_tuple(sptr, key_buf)) {
179        buf_free(key_buf, 4);
180        db_rclose(sptr); /* close relation file */
181        saved_ch = NEWLINE;   /* force a newline */
182        return (FALSE);
183      }
184
185      /* close relation and index files */
186      db_rclose(sptr);
187      buf_free(key_buf, 4);
188      return(TRUE);
189
190   } /* cat_insert */
191
192   /* ------------------------------------------------------------ */
193
```

14

The REQUIEM Program
Interface

In Chapter 1 we hinted at the fact that RQL is used both as an interactive query language and as a callable program interface facility. Up to this point, however, we have inadvertently ignored the programming aspects of RQL and have assumed that RQL is used more or less only interactively. In the present chapter we focus our attention on the programming aspects of RQL. In particular, we shall explain how REQUIEM offers its users an explicit means of accessing stored data through application programs. Furthermore, we shall elaborate on some special DBMS functions which are provided for assisting application programs in accessing and manipulating the desired data. Finally, we shall explain how these programming interface functions maintain the integrity of the stored database.

14.1   Interfacing programs to databases

In the previous chapters we often stressed the fact that the purpose of a database system is to service the diverse needs of a wide community of users. Even though a DBMS consists of relatively generalized functions, the evolution of a DBMS (i.e. its ability to change in response to the growing user needs) will be very limited without providing generic facilities with which to extend the capabilities of the database system. There are many real life applications which require normal retrieval or even update tasks in a different way from that provided by the conventional DML facilities. For example, commercial firms rely very often on the existence of application programs that deal with important issues such as product accounting, financial accounting, or producing report charts. Such applications need the numeric processing or graphics facilities which are offered by most conventional high-level programming languages and which are clearly not offered by conventional DMLs. Moreover, there increasingly exists the need for developing programs for situations where the same database access steps are to be used frequently in the future. It is quite plausible to assume that a user, after performing the same command sequence over and over again, soon desires the ability to store that sequence of commands. Moreover, the user may require for practical purposes to modify slightly this long sequence of commands to satisfy the particular or general needs of an application. There exist several such situations where programming facilities are highly desirable for directly accessing and modifying the data stored in the database.

In sum, if the database resources are to be shared by diverse classes of users, and if the DBMS is to evolve to satisfy the needs of these users and applications, appropriate mechanisms must be provided to enable application programmers to use the database.

Generally speaking, application programs may access the stored data either by bypassing the DBMS facilities, or through the DBMS. Let us now concentrate on the implications of the first issue. Bypassing the DBMS means accessing the data directly from the stored database files. Some DBMSs do not provide the facilities to access the data items in a database through user-developed programs. This is particularly true for most database systems available on microcomputers. Nevertheless, it is possible for users to write programs which operate on the contents of the database by relying on the conventional data access methods available in high-level programming languages. There are two inherent problems associated with this approach. The first is that the programmer must have to know the stored form of the database. The second problem is far more complex and particularly important as it may affect other database users. If the developed application program only reads the database contents there is no real threat to the integrity of the data. However, if this program changes the stored data, it then poses a real danger to the integrity of the data as the data would no longer conform to its intended definition or validation criteria. Moreover, as the DBMS is unaware of these changes it may no longer be in a position to process the stored database files properly.

The preferred mode of interface to the database for application programmers is always through the DBMS. Technically speaking, a DBMS must provide a program interface to allow applications to be developed that could directly access and modify data stored in the database. A program interface module comprises the data-type definitions, data structures, and functions offered to an application programmer.

When the application programmers write a program to process the database, they must know its logical structure and definition (at least the required part of the database). They can then define the content and size of a working buffer and name specific files and data items in their program. By providing such mechanisms to the application programmers it is possible to extend and modify the capabilities of the system to perform certain useful processing tasks in a more general, more specialized, or even more effective way than by using the conventional DML facilities.

REQUIEM provides a callable program interface to allow application programs written in the C language to access stored relation files directly. The data structures required by application programs are contained in the file **interface.h**. To make this file available to application programmers it must be included in the source file of the application program in question. In the following we shall explain how REQUIEM accesses the stored data items by means of re-examining the customer–invoice database used in Chapter 9 to explain the implementation of the **group** statement.

CUSTOMER

CUSTOMER_ID#	NAME	STREET	LOCATION
C2346	Jonson	Wall Str.	New York
C3157	James	King's Rd.	London
C8275	Dupont	Rue de Paix	Paris
C9143	Walters	River Lane	Boston
C9716	Smith	Hill Rd.	Sydney

INVOICE

INVOICE_NO#	CUSTOMER_ID#	TERM_OF_PAYMENT	AMOUNT
I628	C9716	6/30/1989	2750.54
I712	C8275	12/23/1989	3568.98
I821	C3157	7/20/1989	7560.14

Figure 14.1 The customer–invoice database revisited.

Example 14.1.1

Consider the customer–invoice database structure as depicted in Figure 14.1. A realistic application developed around this database may require that information about unpaid invoices is combined with customer data in order to send a reminder to the customers concerned.

An application program named "reminder" may be designed to do the job. To be of real use this application program must have the capability to access data stored in the database directly, of course under the assumption that the database management system would allow an application program to access relations stored in the database. The reminder application program may be designed in such a way so as to loop through the entire list of invoices stored in the relation *INVOICE*, see Figure 14.1. For each invoice that has not been paid in the interval agreed upon, the program should access the customer data contained in the relation *CUSTOMER* and automatically print a reminder.

To give you a better insight and understanding we will elaborate on a sample application program written in C that implements the automatic reminder service described above. The two relations under consideration are depicted in Figure 14.1. The "reminder" program loops through the relation *INVOICE* which contains the pending invoices. Once the time limit for a particular invoice expires, the data for the corresponding customer is extracted from the *CUSTOMER* relation. After the required data has been accumulated a reminder is generated and printed. The source code for this sample program is outlined in Figure 14.2.

In order to get an executable version of the above application program, the program must be first compiled and then linked with the library containing the definitions of the appropriate functions. This library can be generated with help of the *makefile* facility as explained in Appendix C.

In order to generate the REQUIEM library we simply type:

makelib

This command compiles the modules that define the necessary REQUIEM functions and places them in a library called **requ.a**.* In order to link the reminder application program with the REQUIEM library the following command should be issued:

cc reminder.c -o reminder requ.a

This statement compiles the sample program and links it with the RE-QUIEM library, producing, thus, the object code for a program called **reminder**.

14.2   Implementing the program interface

The main purpose of the REQUIEM program interface is to enable the development of application programs that directly access data stored in

---

*We follow the normal Unix convention that a suffix **.a** denotes a library.

```
#include<stdio.h>
#include<interface.h>

main()
{
    struct sel *invoice;        /* selection pointer */
    char term_of_payment[20];   /* buffer for attribute value*/
    char cust_name[10];         /* holds the customer name */
    char invoice_no[10];        /* the id of the invoice in question */
    char today[20];             /* holds the current date */
    char *getDate();

    /* initialize requiem */
    requ_init(0, (char **) 0);

    /* generate a selection structure for the INVOICE relation */
    if ((invoice = retrieve("invoice where amount <> 0")) == NULL) {
      printf("Cannot retrieve invoices\n");
        exit();
    }

    /* put the current date into the variable "today"; the current
       date is provided by the function "getDate()", implemented in
       terms of standard functions of the underlying operating system.
     */

    strcpy(today, getDate());

    /* bind the user variables to attributes */
    bind(invoice, "invoice", "termofpay", term_of_payment);
    bind(invoice, "invoice", "name", cust_name);
    bind(invoice, "invoice", "invoiceid", invoice_id);

    /* loop through all selected tuples,
       check whether the term of payment has been exceeded.
       If so, call print_reminder to print a reminder.
     */

    while (fetch(invoice, FALSE)) {
      if (datecmp(today, term_of_payment) >= 0) {
        print_reminder(cust_name, invoice_id, term_of_payment);
      }
    }

    /* finish the selection */
    done(invoice);

} /* main loop */
```

(continued)

```
print_reminder(name, invoice_id, term_of_payment)
    char *name;            /* the customer name */
    char *invoice_id;      /* the invoice number */
    char *term_of_payment; /* term of payment for the given invoice */
{
    struct sel *customer;     /* selection pointer */
    char street[30];          /* street */
    char location[30];        /* location */
    char retrieve_sentence[40]; /* holds the retrieve sentence */

    /* generate a selection structure for the CUSTOMER relation */
    sprintf(retrieve_sentence, "customer where name = \"%s\"", name);

    if ((customer = retrieve(retrieve_sentence)) == NULL) {
       printf("Cannot retrieve customer\n");
          exit();
    }

    /* bind the user variables to attributes */
    bind(customer, "customer", "street", street);
    bind(customer, "customer", "location", location);

    while (fetch(customer, FALSE)) { /* loop thro' the selected customers */
       do_print(name, location, street, invoice_id, term_of_payment);
    }

    /* finish the selection */
    done(customer);

}/* print_remainder */
```

Figure 14.2 A sample application program showing the use of the REQUIEM program interface functions.

the REQUIEM database. Typical administration tasks such as modification, creation, or deletion of relations are not supported by the current implementation. These functions can only be executed by an on-line user utilizing the current user interface to enter the appropriate RQL statements. However, it must be mentioned that the present limitation of the current REQUIEM program interface, namely the support of data retrieval only, is not inherent in the overall design. The program interface can easily be extended to support all potential functions of the RQL query language.

Data retrieval in REQUIEM is generally performed via the function **retrieve()**. This function, when called with an appropriate string argument initializes a retrieval context that can be used to access individual tuples sequentially (for further details refer to Chapters 4 and 5). The argument of the function **retrieve()** is a character string that forms a legal RQL retrieve statement. The result of executing this function is a pointer to a selection structure that describes the current retrieval context.

This pointer can then be used in subsequent calls to the function **fetch()** to access the selected tuples on a one at a time basis.

Example 14.2.1

Given the two relations of Figure 14.1 consider the problem of retrieving all customers that are located in London.

In RQL we may formulate the following query to obtain the required information:

select all from customer **where** location = "London";

From this RQL statement we can easily derive the corresponding retrieve format specifier which, when used as an argument to the function **retrieve()**, will select the same set of data tuples. Consider the following expression:

sel_customer = retrieve("customer where location = \ " London \ ";");

After execution of the above function the variable **sel_customer** holds a pointer to the retrieval context that is used in subsequent calls to the function **fetch()** to access the individual data tuples for the relation *CUSTOMER*. The function **fetch()** does not allow the application program to directly access the tuple buffer which holds the attribute values of the current data tuple. This approach would require the application programmer to have a detailed knowledge about the record and field structure of the relation in question. For example, the sequence of attributes as well as the number of bytes that each attribute value can occupy in the tuple buffer must be known in order to compute the offset that an individual attribute has within the tuple buffer. It is only by means of this offset that the corresponding data can be accessed. Nevertheless, if we had used this approach we would have violated one important design requirement of relational systems, namely the requirement for data independence. The user of a DBMS must be able to access data stored in the database without being concerned with the physical structure of the stored relations.

The approach taken in REQUIEM frees the application programmer from taking care of the tuple structure when deciding to access the attribute values contained in a relation tuple. The REQUIEM program interface offers a mechanism that allows an application programmer to establish a means of connection between a given attribute and a user-supplied buffer. This mechanism that is responsible for this problem-dependent access to attribute values depends heavily on the so-called *binding mechanism*.

A special-purpose data structure called the binding structure is central to the implementation of the REQUIEM program interface. This structure has the inherent ability to bind a user-defined buffer within a given retrieval context, for example invoice_id, to an attribute so that during tuple fetching the value of the corresponding attribute is stored into this user-specified variable. As we shall see in the next section the REQUIEM program interface provides functions to establish a binding between an application-defined buffer and an attribute of the relation in question. Additionally, functions to read and store values of an individual attribute without using the REQUIEM binding mechanism are also provided.

14.3   The program interface functions

The functions that are provided by the REQUIEM program interface and may be used in any application program fall into two broad categories: the program utility functions and the attribute accessing functions. The main purpose of the program utility functions is to establish the REQUIEM program interface. On the other hand, the attribute accessing functions are used, as their name suggests, to access individual tuple attributes. It must be mentioned that the functions of the REQUIEM program interface can be used only in application programs that are linked with the corresponding program interface library, namely the file **requ.h**. We shall start by examining the structure and the operation of the program utility functions first.

14.3.1   The program utility functions

The program interface utility functions include the following general and special purpose functions:

requ_init()
The function **requ_init()** must be called prior to any other interface functions. This function first checks to see if the system catalogs exist. In the case that they do not, an argument may be provided with this function to hold the name of a user-provided command file that can be used to materialize the corresponding relations. The definition of the function **requ_init()** is contained in Appendix B.

retrieve()
The function **retrieve()** returns a pointer to the selection structure that is used by the function **fetch()** to iterate through the sequence of selected tuples. Its detailed description can be found in Chapter 10.

bind()
The function **bind()** is called to establish a binding between a user-supplied buffer and an attribute. The function creates an element of type **binding** that is linked to an internal binding list. This binding list holds an element of type **binding** for each attribute that has been bound to a user-supplied buffer and is always chained to the selection structure **sel**, see Figure 14.3. Figure 14.3 shows the binding structure that is associated with the "reminder" program of Figure 14.2 during run-time. In particular, we can observe from this figure that the **binding** structure stores the address of the user-supplied buffer, e.g. invoice_id,* in the component **bd_vuser**. Moreover, the **bd_attr** member of the binding structure is used to provide a pointer to the attribute structure, which is used to store this bound attribute (e.g. *INVOICE_ID*), in the current retrieval context. Finally, the component **bd_vtuple** provides the relative address of a given attribute within the tuple buffer. This address can be later used to copy successive attribute values into the user-supplied buffer.

The function **bind()** is primarily used to bind the value of a tuple attribute within a retrieval context. The function accepts four arguments: a database selection or context pointer (**customer**); a character string containing the relation name ("**customer**"); a character string containing the attribute name ("**invoice_id**"); and finally a user-defined bind-buffer (**invoice_id**) to receive the attribute value. It is actually the duty of the function **bind()** to create a new binding structure by first allocating space and then attaching the generated structure to the binding list, see Figure 14.3. The situation after execution of the three **bind()** statements in the sample reminder program is illustrated in Figure 14.3.

The application programmer may rely on the fact that after a tuple has been fetched for processing, by a call to the function **fetch()**, the value of each bound attribute will be stored in the address-space of its associated bind-buffer. Thus, this attribute value may be subsequently dealt with exactly like any value of an ordinary program variable. More specifically, in our sample "reminder" program this mechanism is used to retrieve the identification number of the current invoice, the customer's identifier (**customer_id**), and the term of payment that has been agreed upon (**term_of_payment**) for

---

*Notice that we normally use the name of an attribute to christen the user-defined variable that is associated with it. For example, the user-defined variable invoice_id is tied to the attribute *INVOICE_ID* in relation *INVOICE*.

each invoice stored in relation *INVOICE*. These fetched values are stored in the corresponding user-defined bind-buffers. The bind-buffer values are then used in the application program to determine if a reminder has to be forwarded to the given customer. In the case that a reminder has to be generated, the customer name is used to formulate a query to retrieve the customer's record from the relation *CUSTOMER*. Again, the binding mechanism is used to integrate the values of various attributes of the customer relation into the reminder form.

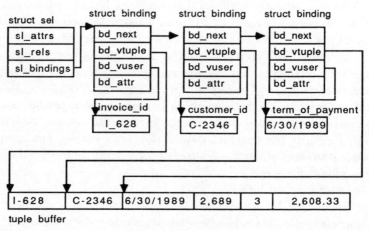

Figure 14.3 The list of binding structures corresponding to the sample reminder program.

fetch()

The function **fetch()** retrieves one tuple at a time from the given selection structure. A detailed description of this function can be found in Chapter 10. Once a binding has been established, REQUIEM guarantees that the user-provided variable receives the value of the bound attribute for each tuple fetched from the specified relation. This ability is inherent in the function **fetch()** which is called to fetch the next tuple from a stored relation in sequence. Recall that this function calls the function **process()** to process the contents of the currently fetched tuple. If the current tuple satisfies the predicate expression, if any, the list of bindings is then worked through. For each binding structure in the list of bindings the function **get_attr()** is called with the appropriate parameters. In this function the value of the requested attribute is literally copied into the user-supplied structure contained in the binding list, see Figure 14.3. This mechanism guarantees that after a tuple has been fetched the value of the bound attributes is automatically stored in the corresponding user variables.

done()

When all selected tuples have been accessed and processed the function **done()** is called to terminate access to the selected tuples. For this purpose the corresponding relation and index files are closed and the selection structure is freed. After execution of this function no further access to the database is possible by means of the retrieval context. Additionally, we unbind all bound attributes. This function should therefore only be called when all the desired tuples have been accessed and processed.

14.3.2 Access to individual attributes

Three additional functions are provided for accessing individual tuple attributes in a relation, namely **get()**, **put()**, and **store()**. These functions allow access to an attribute without having to bind it to a user-defined variable. Recall that the binding mechanism implemented by **bind()** allows automatic access to the attributes bound during tuple fetching. In contrast, consider the situation where you wish to access the value of an unbound attribute. For this purpose the REQUIEM program interface offers the following functions.

get()

Function **get()** does not rely on the automatic binding mechanism, rather it is expected that this function is invoked each time the value of a specific tuple attribute is required. This function is called with a data context pointer, a relation name, the name of the attribute in question, and a pointer to a buffer where the retrieved attribute values should be stored. By a call to **get_attr()** the attribute definition of the attribute can be found. This information can then be used to access the value of the attribute from the current tuple of the specified relation after a call to the function **get_attr()** has been made.

put()

The function **put()** is the dual of function **get()** and is used when the programmer decides to store a new value in a tuple attribute of a given relation. The function **put()** is called with exactly the same number and types of argument as function **get()**. However, instead of retrieving the value of the attribute in question, now the value supplied by an appropriate function parameter is stored as the new value of the tuple attribute after a call to the function **add_attr()**. Moreover, in function **get()** the **sr_update** flag of the selected relation structure **s_rel** is turned on, thus indicating that the corresponding tuple has been modified. This approach is similar to the standard approach to text editors: when editing a piece of text the user modifies only the data in the editor's text buffer. Only after the user has executed a **save** command is the text buffer stored into the corresponding text file, thus enforcing the changes.

store()
To store modified tuples back on the disk, function **store()** must be invoked. When called with a pointer to a list of selected relations this function checks the sr_update flag for each specified relation. If this flag is set then function db_update() is called to store the tuples of the specified relation on the disk. When modifying tuples of a relation you must make sure that before fetching the next relation tuple from storage you first call the function **store()** to make the changes permanent.

14.4   General remarks

Finally, one word of caution. You have probably guessed that the above-mentioned functions, namely **get()**, **store()**, and **put()**, do not rely on the indexing mechanism provided by REQUIEM. Actually, these functions are experimental functions used with a previous version of REQUIEM that did not include any indexing facilities, and obviously require appropriate extensions. Our prime purpose in this chapter was to demonstrate the feasibility of supporting application programs in REQUIEM through a handful of simple system functions.

As can be observed from the sample application program in Figure 14.2 the functions **bind()** and **get()** can only, safely, be used in conjunction with the function **fetch()** in a fetch loop that accesses the tuples of a stored relation in sequence. However, the real danger lies in the use of function **put()**. When using this function (as implemented so far) care must be taken that the attribute to be assigned the new value is not a key attribute. Otherwise, the index file of the relation would be corrupted as the function **put()** is used to store a new tuple attribute value directly in the tuple buffer without updating the corresponding attribute value in the index file. Consequently, the index file will not reflect the actual situation regarding the contents of the database. The next attempt to access the data by means of a query would most certainly launch your database organization into an arena of data anarchy! Therefore, we suggest that you appropriately extend these functions by appropriate calls to the REQUIEM indexing functions before you try using them. Some hints as to how to design the extended program interface functions are given in the list of exercises in Chapter 16.

14.5   Source listing 10

file: interface.h

```
 1    /* -----------------------------------------------------------
 2         | this file contains the definitions and data structures |
 3         | used by application programs                            |
 4         ----------------------------------------------------------- */
 5
 6    #define FALSE   0
 7    #define TRUE    1
 8
 9    #define ASIZE   16  /* size of a attribute entry */
10    #define ANSIZE  10  /* size of a attribute name */
11    #define HDSIZE  16  /* size of a relation entry */
12    #define NATTRS  31  /* number of attributes in header block */
13    #define RNSIZE  10  /* size of a relation name */
14
15
16    /* -------------- pgm interface structures ------------------ */
17
18    struct binding {
19       struct attribute *bd_attr;  /* bound attribute */
20       char *bd_vtuple;            /* pointer to value in tuple */
21       char *bd_vuser;             /* pointer to user buffer */
22       struct binding *bd_next;    /* next binding */
23    };
24
25    /* ------------- command and query structures --------------- */
26
27    struct attribute { /* static boundary: cater for alignment */
28       short at_size;              /* attribute size in bytes */
29       char  at_name[ANSIZE];      /* attribute name */
30       char  at_type;              /* attribute type */
31       char  at_key;               /* attribute key */
32       char  at_semid;          /* semantically identical attribute */
33       char  at_unused[ASIZE-ANSIZE-5]; /* unused space */
34    };
35
36    /* in disk file descriptor */
37    struct header { /* alignment: size must be 512 bytes */
38       long  hd_avail;          /* address of first free record */
39       short hd_cursor;         /* relative cursor position */
40       short hd_data;           /* offset to first data byte */
41       short hd_size;           /* size of each tuple in bytes */
42       short hd_tcnt;           /* no. of tuples in relation */
43       short hd_tmax;           /* relative pos. of last tuple */
44       char hd_unique;          /* unique attribute specifier */
45       char hd_unused[HDSIZE-15];            /* unused space */
46       struct attribute hd_attrs[NATTRS]; /* table of attributes */
47    };
48
49    struct relation {
50       char rl_name[RNSIZE]; /* relation name */
51       int rl_store;            /* flag indicating a store happened */
52       int rl_fd;               /* file descriptor for relation file */
53       int rl_scnref;           /* number of scans for this relation */
54       struct header rl_header; /* relation file header block */
55       struct relation *rl_next; /* pointer to next relation */
```

```
56    };
57
58    struct scan {
59      struct relation *sc_relation; /* ptr to relation definition */
60      long sc_recpos;               /* tuple position in data file */
61      unsigned int sc_nattrs;       /* no. of attrs in relation */
62      unsigned int sc_dtnum;        /* desired tuple number */
63      unsigned int sc_atnum;        /* actual tuple number */
64      int sc_store;                 /* flag indicating a store */
65      char *sc_tuple;               /* tuple buffer */
66    };
67
68    struct sattr {
69      char *sa_rname;             /* relation name */
70      char *sa_aname;             /* attribute name */
71      char *sa_name;              /* alternate attribute name */
72      char *sa_aptr;              /* ptr to attr in tuple buffer */
73      struct srel *sa_srel;       /* ptr to the selected relation */
74      struct attribute *sa_attr;  /* attribute structure ptr */
75      struct sattr *sa_next;      /* next selected attr in list */
76    };
77
78    struct sel {
79      struct srel *sl_rels;       /* selected relations */
80      struct sattr *sl_attrs;     /* selected attributes */
81      struct binding *sl_bindings;  /* user variable bindings */
82    };
83
84    struct srel {
85      char *sr_name;            /* alternate relation name */
86      struct scan *sr_scan;     /* relation scan structure ptr */
87      int sr_ctuple;            /* current fetched tuple flag */
88      int sr_update;            /* updated tuple flag */
89      struct srel *sr_next;     /* next selected relation in list */
90    };
91
92    struct unattrs {
93      char *name;   /* attr name participating in a union  */
94      short size;   /* size of attribute in bytes */
95    };
96
97    /* ------------------- forward declarations ----------------- */
98
99    extern struct sel *retrieve();
```

file: *pgm_int.c*

```
1    #include "requ.h"
2
3    /* store - store tuples */
4    int store(slptr, key_buf)
5        struct sel *slptr;
6        char **key_buf;
7    {
8      struct srel *srptr;
9
10     /* check each selected relation for stores */
11     for (srptr = slptr->sl_rels; srptr != NULL; srptr = SREL_NEXT)
12       if (srptr->sr_update) /* with indexing, if required */
13         if (!store_tuple(srptr->sr_scan, key_buf))
```

```
14              return (FALSE);
15
16      /* return successfully */
17      return (TRUE);
18    }
19
20    /* ------------------------------------------------------------ */
21    /* bind - bind a user buffer to the value of an attribute */
22    int bind(slptr,rname,aname,avalue)
23          struct sel *slptr; char *rname,*aname,*avalue;
24    {
25      struct binding *newbd;
26      struct srel *srptr;
27      char *malloc();
28
29      /* allocate and initialize a binding structure */
30      if ((newbd =
31          (struct binding *)malloc(sizeof(struct binding))) == NULL)
32        return (error(INSMEM));
33      newbd->bd_vuser = avalue;
34
35      /* find the attribute */
36      if (!find_attr(slptr,rname,aname,
37                     &newbd->bd_vtuple,&srptr,&newbd->bd_attr))
38        return (FALSE);
39
40      /* link the new binding into the binding list */
41      newbd->bd_next = slptr->sl_bindings;
42      slptr->sl_bindings = newbd;
43
44      /* return successfully */
45      return (TRUE);
46    }
47
48    /* ------------------------------------------------------------ */
49    /* get - get the value of an attribute */
50    int get(slptr,rname,aname,avalue)
51          struct sel *slptr; char *rname,*aname,*avalue;
52    {
53      struct srel *srptr;
54      struct attribute *aptr;
55      char *vptr;
56
57      /* find the attribute */
58      if (!find_attr(slptr,rname,aname,&vptr,&srptr,&aptr))
59        return (FALSE);
60
61      /* get the attribute value */
62      get_attr(aptr,vptr,avalue);
63
64      /* return successfully */
65      return (TRUE);
66    }
67
68    /* ------------------------------------------------------------ */
69    /* put - put the value of an attribute */
70    int put(slptr,rname,aname,avalue)
71          struct sel *slptr; char *rname,*aname,*avalue;
72    {
73      struct srel *srptr;
74      struct attribute *aptr;
```

```
75    char *vptr;
76
77    /* find the attribute */
78    if (!find_attr(slptr,rname,aname,&vptr,&srptr,&aptr))
79      return (FALSE);
80
81    /* put the attribute value */
82    store_attr(aptr,vptr,avalue);
83
84    /* mark the tuple as updated */
85    srptr->sr_update = TRUE;
86
87    /* return successfully */
88    return (TRUE);
89  }
90  /* ------------------------------------------------------------ */
```

15

Human–Computer Interaction

Even though a large number of users prefer the flexibility offered by conventional command interfaces of databases systems, many users require system assistance in formulating their queries. This is particularly true for the class of users known as end-users. These people normally feel much more confortable with the added structure and direction provided by special-purpose user interfaces which are tailored to meet the needs and requirements of the casual and non-data processing professional users. In the following we shall see that a good user interface system is more than just a concession to the unsophisticated user or fallible human memory; it actually fills the same function in an interactive environment as a job control language. We shall also explain why the user interface is an important tool for database users and shall give some implementation hints as how to improve the present user interface of REQUIEM.

15.1   User interface systems

As a diverse selection of casual users and non-data processing professionals utilize computers, the quality of the user interface * becomes an important aspect for the success of a software product. For an expert user a command oriented style of interaction may be adequate, as it allows a precise formulation of complex commands. In this sense, RQL for example provides a flexible and easy to use tool for an expert database user, once he/she has

---

*By definition the user interface is the uppermost layer in the system, thus it resides in the external level of a database system and its prime concern is to place the entire functionality of the database system at the disposal of users.

learned the precise syntax and semantics of the query language. For casual users, however, this may not be an easy task to accomplish. Consider for example a database system that is installed in a public library to enable visitors to search for appropriate books corresponding to a given topic or author. Most visitors come to the library only a few times per year to search for interesting titles and are obviously not inclined to learn a complex query language before they are able to search for a book; therefore, they look for the appropriate tool to support them in performing their task.

Such problems are particularly acute in the area of small computers, the so-called personal computers, as these systems are mainly used by non-data processing professionals. This is the main reason why most personal computer software developers have paid much more attention to the screen interface, providing menus and help screens, and letting the user control the processing steps. To be of real practical value, a user interface for a database must serve a wide variety of users with different training, knowledge, and background. In the present chapter we will concentrate on the description of two types of user interfaces: the *menu-driven interface* and the *direct manipulation interface* (see [56]). In a menu-driven user interface the user is presented with a list of possible alternatives from which he may select the appropriate one. A direct manipulation interface, on the other hand, presents a visual snapshot of the working environment together with the current objects in a symbolic, usually pictorial, form. Generally, a raster screen and some sort of pointing device such as a mouse are required for implementing such interfaces. Both systems are easy to use and require a minimal learning effort. For more experienced users, however, they soon become tedious and inefficient. A very important fact to remember about such systems is that they do not usually offer the functionality of a full DBMS query language.

In the forthcoming sections we will describe the user interfaces of two commercially available DBMSs which follow the above approaches. The systems described in the following represent two diametrically different approaches that may be studied together with the current user interface of REQUIEM to give you a feeling of the wide spectrum of existing user interfaces. Although the systems described herein provide interesting solutions to the problem of designing an acceptable user interface for a database system it must be stated that up to the present moment no general design principles have been elaborated for developing a "good" user interface.

All examples introduced in this chapter may be regarded as interesting alternatives – each one presenting its own strengths and weaknesses. Thereafter, we will focus on REQUIEM and propose some ideas for further improvement of its current line-oriented user interface.

15.2 Menu-driven systems

One of the more successful personal computer database management systems is the dBase III Plus* product available from Ashton-Tate. dBase III Plus comprises a fullyfledged relational DBMS that runs on a variety of personal computers. This DBMS provides an interactive menu-driven interface that is easy for non-programmers to use. The user is able to interact with the program during execution, monitoring its operation, and conditionally following different paths through its processing logic. From the user's perspective, dBase III Plus offers a rather interesting feature: it allows a user to select one of two interaction styles.

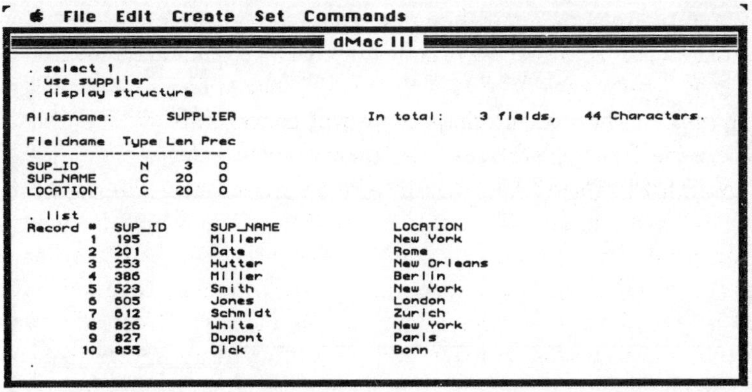

Figure 15.1 A dBase III Plus dialog fragment for displaying the structure and the contents of the *SUPPLIER* relation.

The "normal" dialog with dBase III Plus is available by means of a command language that allows a user to state both DDL and DML requests. This dialog is line-oriented, i.e. the system displays a prompt (the so-called *dot* prompt as it consists of a ".") and waits for the user to enter a command. A command is submitted to the system by pressing the <enter> key. After the current entry has been processed, the result or an error message is displayed on the terminal screen. Next, the system displays the dot again, indicating that it is ready to accept the next command. A complete overview of dBase III Plus can be found in [57]. For a sample dialog see Figure 15.1. All examples throughout this section are taken from the dMac III[†] application, an implementation of dBase III Plus for the Apple Macintosh.

At any point during the dialog the user may leave the command-oriented dialog and switch to a menu-driven mode of interaction. This menu system

---

*dBase III Plus is a registered trademark of Ashton-Tate.

[†]dMac III is a registered trademark of Format Software Ltd.

displays all current options available to the user and prompts the user to enter required parameters or to specify suboptions. This mode of operation is called *The Assistant Menu* or *Assistant* for short. When the user enters the Assist command the screen changes to that shown in Figure 15.2. A menu bar is displayed at the top of the screen which holds several menus for all functions that can be executed in the Assistant-mode. The Assistant helps the user to formulate syntactically correct commands by allowing him/her to select options specified in the menus. Such options are reasonable to a user who is used to utilizing available query language commands to develop database-oriented applications.

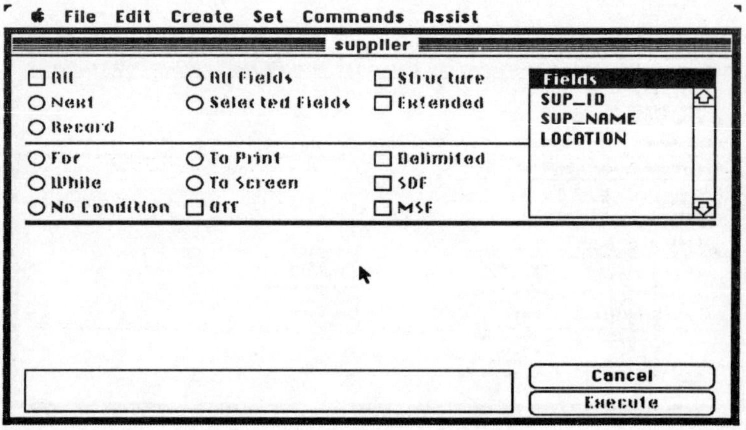

Figure 15.2 The initial *Assist* screen displaying the relation SUPPLIER.

Before embarking on the description of the Assistant in greater detail, let us present the basic interaction techniques required to use a Macintosh-like user interface. The Macintosh user interface has been designed in a so-called object-oriented way.* All objects are presented graphically on a high-resolution screen. A pointing device, generally a mouse, is used to select objects by clicking on the corresponding representation (the object's icon). A function is executed by selecting one operation out of a set of possible operations by means of menu selection. Generally speaking, the activity of directing attention to a particular piece of information is called *selection*. The system responds by giving visual feedback to indicate the current selection. Working with such a system is straightforward: no complex command syntax need be learned or memorized. In order to describe the kind of features available in menu-driven systems, we will use the Assistant to illustrate the style of such user interfaces.

---

*This is the way that entries in the dBase III Plus system are logically perceived and should not be confused with the actual implementation.

To begin using the system, one of the options in the menu must be selected. Figure 15.2 shows the screen displayed by the Assistant module. The cursor can be used to select different menus or to move up and down to select different options in the highlighted menu. If a menu item is not active it is drawn with a light grey pattern surrounding it. Moreover, if the user moves the cursor over an item that is not active, it will not be highlighted. For example to select the List operation in the Assistant, which roughly corresponds to the SQL **select** construct, we move the cursor into the menu title Commands (top line in Figure 15.2) and press the mouse button. The menu pulls down immediately and lets us select one of the active items. We move the cursor down over the list of items while holding the mouse button down until we reach the desired item. We then release the button, thus selecting the currently highlighted item. In our example, we release the mouse when the List item is highlighted.

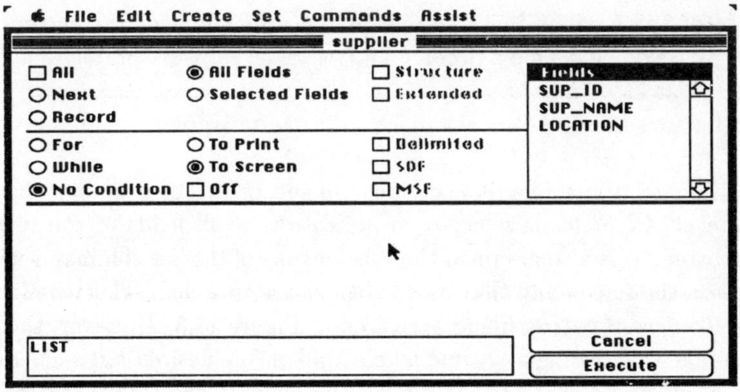

Figure 15.3 The screen after the *List* operation has been selected.

In the following we will explain how you can formulate a query with the help of the Assistant. The Assist-mode integrates two different dialog techniques:

1. Menu selection to select commands.
2. Free form text entry, e.g. for the formulation of predicate expressions.

In general, the dBase III Plus system displays the command that the user has currently issued in a fixed region of the screen. Thus, if you select a specific menu item you can immediately see the effect of your selection in the command area. This approach presents two apparent benefits: first you can get feedback from the system which then helps you to construct even more complex commands. On the other hand, by looking at the syntax of the generated command, you become more familiar with the underlying query language.

We will now illustrate in some detail how a user may actually pose a query with the help of the Assistant. As usual, all examples will be based on the suppliers-and-products database. The sample query that we would like to generate with the help of the Assistant can be stated in RQL as follows:

project supplier over sup_name, sup_id
          where location = "New York";

To formulate this query, we start by first selecting the requested operation, namely List, in the Commands menu. The effect of this selection is shown in Figure 15.3. Three changes on the screen image may be recognized:

1. The dBase III Plus keyword associated with our selection appears in the command area at the lower left of the screen ("List").
2. Some of the buttons in the panel in the upper half of the screen, e.g. "All", "Next", etc., have become active which implies that they may be selected at any time.
3. The buttons labeled *Cancel* and *Execute* are activated.

Additionally, some default selections are specified. For example, the button labeled *All Fields* is selected to indicate that all fields of the relation will be listed. It is also assumed that the output of the list command will be printed on the screen and that no conditions are specified. This is indicated by the *To Screen* button being activated in Figure 15.3. However, the user may change this setting any time by clicking on the desired buttons. In our example, we do not wish to include all the fields in the result; instead, we require a projection over two already specified fields. In order to achieve this, we activate the button labeled *Selected Fields*. As a visible result, we recognize that the button labeled *All Fields* is no longer selected; in fact, there is a strong connection between these two labels: only one of them may be selected at any time.

The next step will be to specify what fields (or attributes in the RE-QUIEM terminology) should be projected. This task is achieved by double-clicking on their corresponding field names in the area titled *Fields* in the upper right corner of the menu. This window holds all the fields that are contained in the current relation. A double-click on one of the field names will cause the corresponding name to be copied into the command area at the appropriate position in the query generated thus far. Figure 15.4 demonstrates this point. Alternatively, if you double-click on a field that has already been specified in the command area, the corresponding name is removed from the command. After having specified the fields *SUP_NAME* and *SUP_ID* we obtain the screen shown in Figure 15.4.

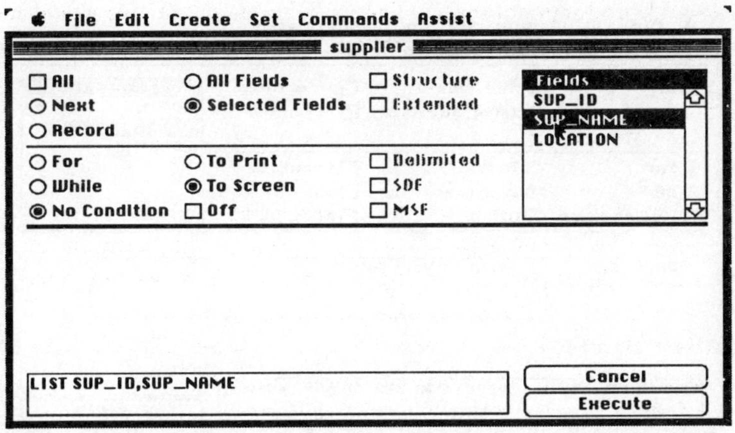

```
 ┌──────────────────────────────────────────────────────────────────┐
 │ ⬆ File  Edit  Create  Set  Commands  Assist                        │
 │ ┌──────────────────────────── supplier ─────────────────────────┐ │
 │ │ ☐ All          ○ All Fields       ☐ Structure    ┌─Fields──┐   │ │
 │ │ ○ Next         ◉ Selected Fields  ☐ Extended     │SUP_ID   │⬆  │ │
 │ │ ○ Record                                         │SUP_NAME │   │ │
 │ │                                                  │LOCATION │   │ │
 │ │ ○ For          ○ To Print         ☐ Delimited    │         │   │ │
 │ │ ○ While        ◉ To Screen        ☐ SDF          │         │   │ │
 │ │ ◉ No Condition ☐ Off              ☐ MSF          └─────────┘⬇  │ │
 │ │                                                                │ │
 │ │ ┌───────────────────────────────────┐    ┌── Cancel ──┐        │ │
 │ │ │LIST SUP_ID,SUP_NAME               │    └── Execute ──┘        │ │
 │ │ └───────────────────────────────────┘                          │ │
 │ └────────────────────────────────────────────────────────────────┘ │
 └──────────────────────────────────────────────────────────────────┘
```

Figure 15.4 The screen after the fields *SUP_ID* and *SUP_NAME* have been specified.

We next proceed by specifying the required predicate expression, namely to select only those suppliers with a prespecified location. For this purpose we select the keyword *For* from the lower panel on the screen. This causes a window labeled with this keyword to appear near the center of the screen. Next, a vertical bar at the upper left corner of this window starts blinking, indicating that this window is ready to receive your input text from the keyboard. If the cursor moves into this window it changes to the type of cursor known as the *text-entry cursor*. This indicates that you may now start typing text. More precisely in our example it means that you should try to enter the exact conditional expression required to complete the query. The visible effect of this interaction is shown in Figure 15.5.

Now that the desired query has been formulated we can select the option Execute in the lower right region of the screen. The resultant query is then executed in "normal" command mode and the result is displayed on the terminal screen as illustrated in Figure 15.6. Finally, the system prompts you to answer whether you would like to return to the Assist-menu or whether working with the command-oriented dialog is preferred.

In sum, this dynamic construction of structured commands helps the user to learn the query language, which obviously is a much more direct way to accomplish the same result. Users who work with the system casually, or users who cannot remember the commands of the underlying query language, may only infrequently do anything outside the menu system.

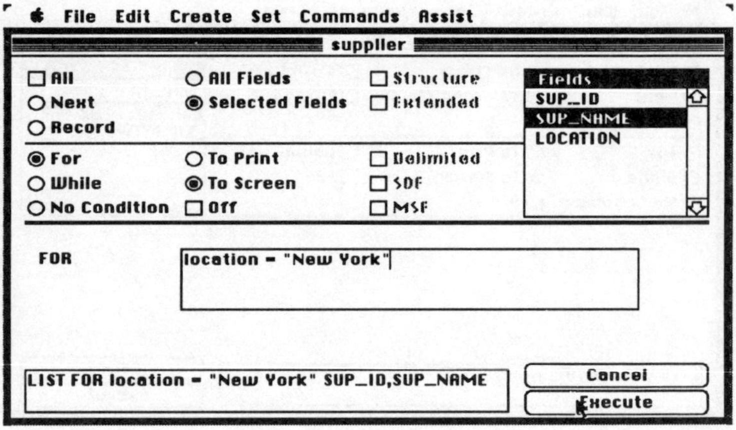

** File Edit Create Set Commands Assist**

supplier

☐ All	○ All Fields	☐ Structure	**Fields**
○ Next	◉ Selected Fields	☐ Extended	**SUP_ID**
○ Record			**SUP_NAME**
			LOCATION
◉ For	○ To Print	☐ Delimited	
○ While	◉ To Screen	☐ SDF	
○ No Condition	☐ Off	☐ MSF	

FOR   location = "New York"

LIST FOR location = "New York" SUP_ID,SUP_NAME

Cancel

Execute

Figure 15.5 The screen after the *List for* statement as been posed.

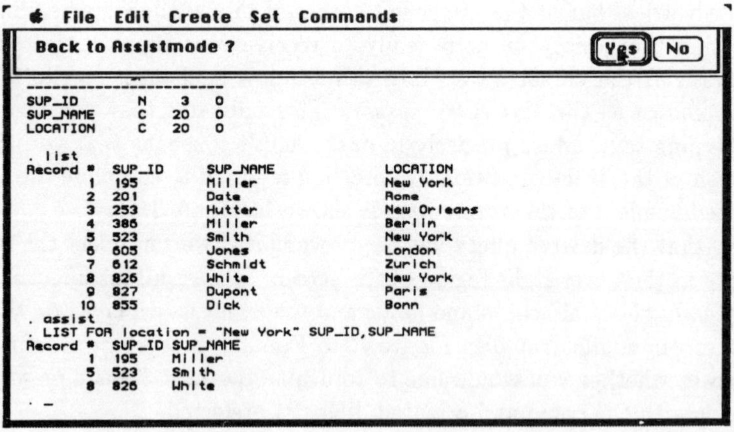

** File Edit Create Set Commands**

Back to Assistmode ?   Yes No

```
------------------------
SUP_ID      N    3    0
SUP_NAME    C   20    0
LOCATION    C   20    0

. list
Record #   SUP_ID    SUP_NAME          LOCATION
       1   195       Miller            New York
       2   201       Data              Rome
       3   253       Hutter            New Orleans
       4   386       Miller            Berlin
       5   523       Smith             New York
       6   605       Jones             London
       7   612       Schmidt           Zurich
       8   826       White             New York
       9   827       Dupont            Paris
      10   855       Dick              Bonn
. assist
. LIST FOR location = "New York" SUP_ID,SUP_NAME
Record #   SUP_ID SUP_NAME
       1   195    Miller
       5   523    Smith
       8   826    White
. _
```

Figure 15.6 The result of executing the sample query of Figure 15.6.

15.3   The direct manipulation approach

In this section, we will take a look at another system, called Helix, to illustrate some further possibilities with regard to the style of a user interface. Helix* is a system that has adopted the direct manipulation approach for its user interface [58]. With this system some representation of the object that the user is currently viewing or manipulating is visible on the screen. Thus, the user can see immediately the effect of any operations or modifications on the object of interest.

The basic objects of this direct manipulation system are represented as icons. These icons are used to represent basic entities in the database. The icons are hierarchical, that is an icon may consist of a set of more elementary entries represented by their corresponding icons. To manipulate an icon and its underlying elements you must first *open* it. In order to explain the above issues we briefly present the main features of the Helix system.

Field   Abacus   Template   Selection   Query   Index

Figure 15.7 The basic Helix icons.

A Helix database is represented as an object called *collection*. A collection represents both the structure and the information content of a database. A database, or collection in the Helix sense, consists of *relations* which in turn are composed of a set of *fields* that constitute the attributes of a relation. Additional objects that are the building blocks of a relation object (see Figure 15.7) are as follows:

1. The *abacus* for formulating algebraic functions or relations.
2. The *template* for defining input and output forms.
3. A *selection* that is used to define what template should be used to enter or display data.

Additionally, a *query* may be specified to delimit the number of records

---

*Helix is a registered trademark of Odesta Corporation Ltd.

to be displayed and an *index** may be used to specify the order in which the individual records of a relation must be displayed (sorted for example in descending order with respect to a given field).

In order to give you an idea of how to create a database using a direct manipulation user interface, we will try to create the *SUPPLIER* and *PRODUCTS* relations from the suppliers-and-products database.

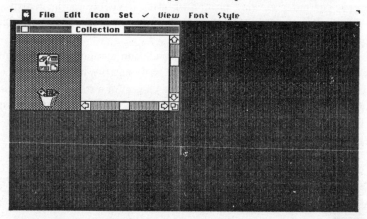

Figure 15.8 An empty collection.

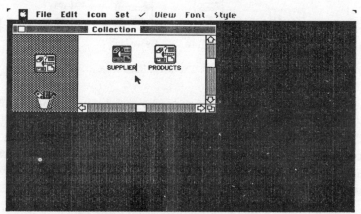

Figure 15.9 Collection with two relations.

When the system is ready to accept a command it displays an empty collection on the screen (see Figure 15.8). This empty collection indicates that no database has been created yet. A database can be defined by specifying

---

*The index in Helix should not be confused with the indexing mechanism in RE-QUIEM. The Helix index defines only the ordering in which the records of a relation are accessed.

its constituent relations. A relation is created by dragging a relation icon
shown in the left part of the collection window into the work area on the
right side and giving it an appropriate name.

Figure 15.9 shows the situation after the two empty relations *SUPPLIER*
and *PRODUCTS* have been created and named. In order to define a relation, we must first open the relation icon and then define the appropriate
attributes by dragging field icons into the work area of the relation window. Fields can be given appropriate names and types, for example Text,
Number, Date, etc. Figure 15.10 shows the result of the definition of the
SUP_NO field as numeric.

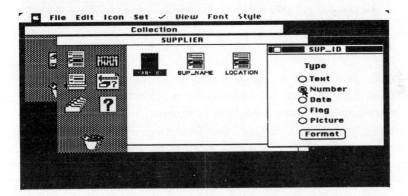

Figure 15.10 The supplier relation attributes defined.

The next step will be to define one or more *templates*. A template describes a form (display mask) that can be used for data entry and for displaying the contents of a relation to the user. A display mask defines the
field width and controls the character positions that the user can enter or
modify.

In Helix a template can be thought of as the basis for the definition of data
forms. A template is built up from a set of predefined component pairs: *label
rectangles* and *data rectangles*. A label rectangle is normally used to display
a label, or message, on its corresponding display mask. The actual field for
displaying and entering data is created by dragging a data rectangle icon
to the desired position on the work area. Once a data rectangle has been
created it must be associated with a field of the underlying relation. When a
data entry form (supplier entry form in Figure 15.11) of the current template
is displayed on the screen, each data rectangle can be used as a "window"
for its associated attribute. In the case of a data entry form, the user must
type a value for the attribute into its corresponding data rectangle. On the
other hand, in the case of an output display form, the value of the attribute
is displayed on the same data rectangle. A possible template definition for

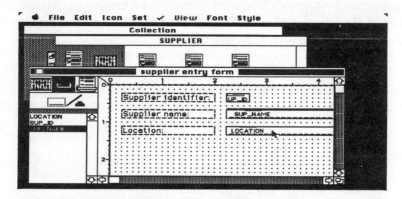

Figure 15.11 A template for data entry.

our example is shown in Figure 15.11. In this figure, the left row displays label rectangles that are used to indicate which attribute is associated with the corresponding data rectangle at its right.

In order to define and access forms for data entry and display, a *selection* must be defined. Once a selection icon has been brought into the working area of a relation it can be opened for specifying an appropriate selection (see Figure 15.12). A template that is used to define a form for entering and displaying data may then be selected. Optionally, *index* objects and *query* objects can be defined. An index in Helix is used to alter the order in which records of a relation are accessed; queries on the other hand are required to control the number of records to be accessed.

After having selected the menu item *show form* the corresponding form appears on the screen and you may begin to enter data into the relation just created (see Figure 15.13). Information stored in a relation can be displayed

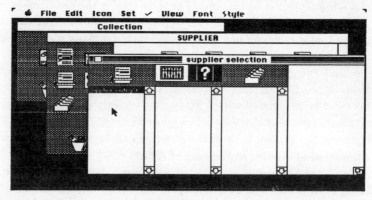

Figure 15.12 A selection object for entering supplier records.

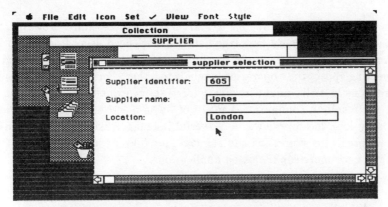

Figure 15.13 Entering data using a predefined template.

by selecting the appropriate function, i.e. *first, last, next, previous,* from the *show* menu. By selecting the previous or next entry you may step through the records of a relation.

To select a specified set of records, you must formulate a so-called *quick query* (see Figure 15.14). A quick query corresponds to a field that has been selected prior to opening the short query window. In this window you may restrict the accessible records by, for example, specifying that only supplier records having as location the value "New York" should be displayed. When you now step through the records of the relation, you will only see the appropriate entries.

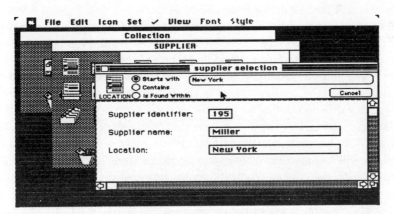

Figure 15.14 Defining a quick query.

The above examples can only give a flavor of working with Helix. As you may have noticed, in this system most operations are performed by direct manipulation and menu selection. The user need not learn a query language for manipulating a database. Instead, by learning the concepts of a few icons the user will be able to start working successfully. However, the lack of a powerful query language deters experienced users from accepting such an approach. For example, algebraic expressions must be formulated by connecting appropriate operation symbols together. Formulation of complex expressions in Helix might involve a large set of icons to be connected, so that the resulting configuration may not fit on a screen, so the user would probably lose the overview. A powerful language, like for example RQL and its predicate expression sublanguage, provides a more convenient tool, especially for more sophisticated applications.

15.4   The user interface of REQUIEM

We now continue our discussion of user interfaces by taking a closer look at the current user interface of REQUIEM. As previously explained, RE-QUIEM offers a command language (query language) for interacting with the database. A careful evaluation of the two approaches described in the previous sections reveals the fact that a powerful command language such as RQL seems to be the most natural vehicle for advanced users. A direct manipulation interface is easy for novices to use but quickly becomes tedious once you are familiar with the system. The same argument holds for a menu-driven user interface that confines the user to select only from a set of predefined alternatives: menu-driven interfaces tend to be rather inflexible and inefficient for experienced users.

Now that we understand the inherent limitations of using both the afore-mentioned approaches, and have been introduced to the fundamental concepts of the user interface methodology, we will take a look ahead at how easy it will be to adjust some advanced features of these approaches to the current REQUIEM configuration. In the following we will argue in favor of integrating different dialog techniques into a concise system. Such systems allow the user to select the dialog style that seems more natural for the task at hand. As we consider REQUIEM to be mainly dedicated to advanced users we will assume that a command language forms the basis for commu-nicating with the system. We will demonstrate how the command language approach can be extended by providing menu facilities. Furthermore, we will postulate a basic set of requirements which must be met by the menu systems that are to be integrated with command-oriented user interfaces. The use of such menus can complement the facilities of a command language by offering structural information about the application at hand. This can help the user form a better picture of his/her request.

We begin with a brief discussion on how the above features can be incorporated in REQUIEM. Note, however, that we will not present an implementation strategy as we used in the previous chapters. We will simply make useful suggestions and demonstrate several solutions to help you cope with the kind of predicament that you might be confronted with when trying to design a useful user interface module. Recall that the main purpose of the current implementation of REQUIEM is to provide a solid foundation for further development and experimentation with new ideas and features.

15.5   Implementation hints

During the design process of the present database management system one of our basic requirements was that REQUIEM should be easily portable to a variety of Unix systems. We made no restrictive assumptions as far as the underlying graphics software or hardware configurations were concerned: REQUIEM should be able to run, and as a matter of fact does run, on any character-oriented display. Thus, we recommend as a basis for further implementation the *Curses* screen-handling package [59], that is available for most Unix systems. This package provides the programmer with a set of routines for screen updating, getting input from the terminal, and cursor movement. The basic concept of Curses is the **window**. A window in the Curses terminology is an internal data structure that is used to describe how a certain part of the physical terminal screen should look. A **window** structure can be manipulated by means of Curses routines, and at any given time the programmer may decide to make the actual terminal screen (or a part of the screen) look like the image stored in a corresponding **window** structure by calling the appropriate Curses screen function.

Applications that use the Curses library for screen manipulation are fairly terminal-independent. The reason behind this is that the Curses implementation is based on the *termcap* database. The termcap database describes hardware terminals. It contains entries that describe the capabilities of a given terminal, such as "terminal has hardware tabs" or "terminal can underline," and indicates how certain operations are performed; for example, what escape sequence must be sent to the terminal to move the hardware cursor to a given location. An application that uses termcap usually starts by opening the termcap database and reading the entry that corresponds to the given terminal type. If a certain terminal operation is required, for example "clear the terminal screen," the application uses the name of the corresponding termcap variable (e.g. "cd") to get the escape sequence that is required by the terminal to perform the requested operation. By performing terminal operations on the basis of these symbolic names, a programmer

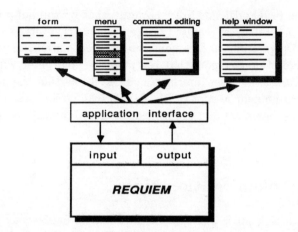

Figure 15.15 Architecture of REQUIEM: the user interface standpoint.

can be sure that his/her program will run on a variety of different terminals (assuming that an entry for the specific terminal used has been added to the corresponding termcap database). For a more detailed discussion of the Curses library and the termcap database we direct you to the appropriate Unix documentation [59], [60].

In the following we will present a list of helpful hints as to how the above features can be incorporated in the present REQUIEM user interface. As you may have noticed REQUIEM allows you easily to modify its user interface; in fact the entire pattern of communication between user and system is handled by a handful of functions. Thus, it is possible to replace the current user interface that uses line-oriented command-I/O with a more sophisticated one which provides some or even all of the above features.

Such a strict separation of an application from its user interface leads to the concept of an *application-independent user interface*. This approach reflects the fact that the development of a sophisticated user interface is a complex task that requires a large amount of time and money. By interposing a layer of abstraction between an application and the user interface it should become possible to develop an application without having to worry about the user interface, and to develop user interfaces that can be used for diverse needs and applications. This approach is further discussed in the area of *user interface management systems* (UIMSs).

The idea behind a UIMS is that it should be possible to localize all aspects of the user interface in a single module, namely the UIMS. The UIMS is then responsible for managing the entire communication set-up between user and application. It mainly undertakes two tasks:

1. It translates low-level input events into application-level concepts (for example a mouse click inside the area of an icon on the screen is transformed into an identifier for the corresponding object).
2. It translates output requests for an application into the low-level output routines required for satisfying the request in terms of the underlying hardware configuration. For example, the application request "display this object" is transformed into a sequence of drawing operations so that the picture of the corresponding object is displayed on the screen.

Moreover, a UIMS offers a text editor for defining the dialog between the user and an application. As this feature goes far behind the scope of this book it will not be pursued any further. The best source for those who wish to delve more deeply into the subject is [61], which also presents an overview of current research in UIMSs.

Figure 15.15 depicts the architecture of REQUIEM as seen from the user interface and as we would like to see it sometime in the future. As you can see, REQUIEM consists of two principal parts: the user interface module implementing forms, menus, command-line editing, help facilities, etc.; and the part implementing the main database operations. The application interface module depicted in Figure 15.15 is used to couple these two parts together. Its name stems from the fact that REQUIEM is seen as a concise application from the user interface perspective. All terminal I/O is implemented by the user interface (UI) module. Requests for input from the user are directed to the UI module where they are actually handled. Requests for displaying data are satisfied in a similar fashion. In general, REQUIEM applications need not be concerned with writing to the screen or about the format used to display the records of a relation since all this will be handled by the UI module.

In order to perform the requested tasks, the UI module must have some means of acquiring valuable information. For example, it may have to know how to display the contents of a given relation, i.e. whether to use a display form or not, and if such a form is requested, the kind of layout that should be used. This information could be stored with the system meta-data in the system catalogs. An alternative approach could be to change the output routines in such a way that the user is prompted, every time that the printing of data is requested, to specify the actual output format. For this purpose, a menu providing all available formats should be made available to the user for selection.

In the following we will try to provide you with more insight into how editing and menu facilities can be implemented in REQUIEM along the lines of the architecture depicted in Figure 15.15. Our aim is to provide a

brief but comprehensive view of the implementation aspects of such typical
system components in the REQUIEM environment.

15.5.1   Implementing command line editing

In general, RQL statements can be entered through a command line on the
user's terminal. When the current command has been formulated, the entire
command sequence is forwarded to the parser by pressing the <return> key.
As the REQUIEM parser works incrementally, it can confirm whether the
user input designates a syntactically complete RQL statement which can be
handed over to the query decomposer for further processing. In the event of
a partially stated command, the user is prompted to complete the current
statement. For this purpose, the continuation prompt "#" is displayed on
the command line to indicate that further input is expected from the part
of the user.

The "#" prompt is extensively used in the formulation of complex queries.
Whenever you press the <return> key the parser starts checking your input.
If your input constitutes a portion of a syntactically correct query the parser
displays the "#" prompt to inform you that you may continue typing (see
Figure 15.16).

```
REQUIEM: select from (
         # project supplier over
         # supname, location)
         # where location = "London"
         # ;

+++++++++++++++++++++++++++++++
+   <    2 tuples found    >  +
+                             +
/////////////////////////////

REQUIEM:
```

Figure 15.16 A dialog fragment while entering a complex query.

This line-oriented approach presents some inherent drawbacks which can
be very annoying. First of all, it is not possible to reuse information that has
previously been entered into the system. This feature would be very helpful,
in the case of error correction, or whenever the user decides to re-enter
the same query (or a slightly modified version of a previously formulated
query). In all the above cases, it would be very helpful to have some basic
editing facilities like those offered by simple text editors. These facilities
may include the following:

1. Movement of the cursor in a non-destructive manner over a command line.
2. Insertion of characters at the current cursor position.
3. Deletion of characters at the current cursor position.

As previously explained, it is beyond the scope of this chapter to give a detailed implementation of a text editor. We will rather concentrate on some general design principles which show you how to integrate the command-oriented interface of REQUIEM with an editor. The editor that we present here consists of at least three modules:

1. A main module, that interprets the user input and executes the corresponding commands or simply inserts the characters into the text buffer.
2. A structural module, that handles the internal structures for storing and manipulating the text.
3. An input/output module, that is responsible for displaying the corresponding portion of the stored text on the terminal screen.

The full implementation of a text editor along the above design principles is described in [62]. Here, the author discusses in depth the structure of a text editor and each of its functional modules with respect to the above points. If such an editor were to be integrated with the present REQUIEM user interface, some adaptations would have to take place. For example in normal text editors, only the user may insert characters by means of keystrokes; however, in the envisaged implementation the command editor must be able to receive input from diverse sources. For instance, the selection of a relation name by means of a menu may result in inserting a string (namely the relation name) into the command editor buffer. Moreover, all system messages must be directed to this command buffer so that the user can get a complete picture of its dialog with the system at a future stage.

The primary task of the command editor is to support the formulation of a command by providing powerful editing functions. In general, it allows the user to submit a command and finds the current binding between the command and its underlying editing functions. In this sense the main module interprets the command keystrokes as characters to be inserted into the text buffer. A special editor directive must be provided to allow the users to submit their "current command". This obviously implies that the command editor must be able to do some rudimentary parsing so that the "current command" can be located in its text buffer. A possible solution would be to interpret all data beyond the last system prompt as constituting a new command that is forwarded to the application interface, depicted in Figure 15.15, on user request. This application interface is interposed between REQUIEM and the user interface facilities and is used to map user requests from the user interface to the appropriate REQUIEM functions.

Additional features, such as command completion (cf. exercise 17 in Chapter 16), or identifying objects by menu selection, can be easily integrated into the command editor. For example command completion can be realized by sending an appropriate request to the application interface together with the partial command string. For this purpose the editor must be able to identify a partial command on the command line and forward it to the application interface. The application interface then decides how to execute the request for completion (for example call an appropriate parser routine) and sends the result back to the editor. The editor then automatically replaces the partial command with its expanded version as constructed by the REQUIEM parser. In that way a syntactically correct command is generated in a stepwise manner.

15.5.2   Implementing menus

We now focus on the implementation aspects of a menu system on top of the present REQUIEM interface. Since the main dialog technique used within REQUIEM is a command language, a menu system should be considered as an auxiliary dialog technique integrated with the underlying command language. That is, we do not wish to have an interface implemented solely in terms of menu interaction as in, for example, the ASSIST-mode in the dBase III Plus application. Rather we would like to offer the user the possibility of entering information through menu selection as an alternative means of interaction. The central idea is that the system should offer the possibility of menu control leaving the command language as the basis for interaction. This approach introduces some basic requirements:

1. Menus should be easily modified by the user in order to provide the flexibility required in a command language environment.
2. A menu should be called by the user by means of a special key (function key) or by means of a special command typed in by the user.
3. The result of a menu selection should be a string that can easily be inserted into the command line.
4. Two types of menus should be provided, namely pop-up menus and pull-down menus. Recall that pop-up menus pop up on the screen on user request and disappear after the current selection request has been satisfied, while pull-down menus pull down from a menu bar to expand a selected alternative.

An additional requirement for the current implementation of REQUIEM is the following:

5. The menu system must be operational on character-oriented display systems and should be portable.

The implementation of a simple menu system which meets most of the above requirements is discussed in [63]. A menu description is stored in a normal text file. Accordingly, the description can be easily modified by means of a text editor and can be appropriately tailored to meet the requirements of a broad class of users. Moreover, it is argued that the simple menu system can be built on the basis of a small set of abstract screen manipulation functions, like for example a function that clears the entire screen or a function to write a string at a given screen location. This set of functions can be ported to diverse hardware configurations with minimal effort. In this menu system a menu is called by a function that takes as its parameter the name of a file containing the description for this particular menu. This function in turn calls other functions, that read and interpret the menu description from its underlying file, display the menu on the screen, handle user interaction, and take the appropriate measures once the user has finished menu selection.

In order to be able to call a menu upon user request the REQUIEM lexical analyzer must be appropriately extended. Besides the REQUIEM function identifiers and keywords it must be able to identify menu names in a command and call the appropriate function. Additionally, the result of a menu selection must be inserted into the command line (refer to the description of dMac III Plus) so that a syntactically correct REQUIEM statement would be generated. Insertion of the result of a menu selection can be easily performed with the aid of the command editor.

To be of real use the menu system described in [63] should be extended in two directions. First, it should be possible to create menus. For example, in order to provide a list of available relations to the user the application interface should be able to create a temporary menu that holds the names of all the relations in a database application. For this purpose, it seems more appropriate to allow menus to be described by an internal data structure rather than storing them in external files. In the case at hand, appropriate menus would be generated if required. A more complex menu system, that provides amongst other things the above features, is described in [64]. Although the menu system described there is designed for raster screens and makes heavy use of a mouse its underlying design concepts could be adopted for use in REQUIEM.

We conclude the present discussion on user interfaces by stating that in the present chapter we have presented only a quick version of the techniques and problems encountered in the design process of user interfaces. This has certainly influenced the structure of this chapter as many interesting problems and questions have had to be either skipped or briefly mentioned. However, it should be emphasized that no practical guidelines have been formulated thus far for the design and development of user interfaces, and it is questionable whether any will emerge in the near future. The process of developing a good user interface requires not only creativity and a great deal of experience from the developers, but also a cooperative effort between these developers, people engaged in software ergonomics and most importantly the end-users.

16

List of Exercises

16.1 Miscellaneous exercises

1. You might have observed that all numerical data types in REQUIEM are represented by double precision variables or **doubles**. Double type numbers in the standard IEEE format are composed of one high order sign bit, an 11 bit biased exponent, and 52 significant bits. If you wish to clarify how C double numbers are represented refer to [65]. We believe that this size is perfectly adequate for the range of numerical values that you would expect in most applications. However, to cope with such situations where, for example, higher precision or larger number representations are required, a special set of routines must be provided. A practical solution is to develop your own set of mathematical functions for the main arithmetic operations as well as special error-detecting functions. A simple addition would have to accept two numeric strings, i.e. character pointers in C, as operands. Special care should be taken for such conditions as overflow: in this case the simple addition would probably have to be turned into a loop of character shifts followed by an addition. The most appropriate source to look for these concepts and techniques is any good digital logic textbook.

2. In the hashing scheme currently employed by REQUIEM, if two members compute to the same index a collision will be produced. A lot of collisions in the hash table will have a result that eventually degrades performance so that it is worse than had hashing not been used at all. Write a function that calculates the number of entries in a hash table and which (if the table is say more than 40 percent full) introduces an overflow table to accommodate the overflow entries and chains it to the main hash table.

3. As the information contained in the relation header is critical for accessing and manipulating the corresponding relation, care must be taken that the header does not contain any erroneous data. In most cases a file header can be opened, read from, or written to without problem. There are situations, however, when this is not the case. Erroneous data is the outcome of a hardware malfunction that might, for example, occur while reading or writing is taking place, or of a write operation that might run out of disk space. Write a program to monitor such situations and check them explicitly before reading from or writing to the file header comes about. To achieve this introduce an extra buffer to hold the contents of the relation header prior to any disk access operations, and then check whether the corresponding operations were successfully completed.

4. When you expect large amounts of data you can speed up the nested loop join without having to use indices. You must actually try to combine the nested loops join with hashing. The idea is to read in some (perhaps half) of the records from the outer join relation data file and construct a hash table on the join field of these records in memory. Then read entirely through the inner loop join relation data file to find matches using the same hash function. This way you can match each inner record with all the outer records kept in memory at once. All records that match can be stored in a buffer. Once you have read through the entire join data file read the remaining segment(s) of records for the outer file and repeat the same steps.

5. It would be nice if REQUIEM could contain all the information it needs to keep about each individual user. Try to develop your own password support functions. Whenever you log on to the system, the following sequence of actions should take place to validate your password:

1. You must be prompted by the system to enter your user name and then your password.
2. The entry for your password must be found encrypted in the system catalogs.
3. Your password will be encrypted and checked against the one stored in the system catalogs. If the passwords match you will be allowed to log on; otherwise the message "login incorrect" is displayed.

6. With the present implementation of REQUIEM a user can at any time recognize which combination of data and index files implement a relation. Recall that each data file is followed by the suffix ".db" and each index file by the suffix ".indx". To prevent the users from directly inspecting the contents of these files it is necessary to introduce such security mechanisms that are provided by data encryption. The basic idea is that a relation name can be physically stored in the disk and the system catalogs in an encrypted form so that anyone who tries to access it, other than through official channels, will see just an unreadable mess of characters. To program around this you actually require two complementary routines: one encryption and one decryption. You can either utilize the standard encryption/decryption routines provided by Unix such as **crypt()**, **setkey()**, and **encrypt()**, or alternatively you could develop your own personal routines.

7. REQUIEM accepts queries and commands in a lower-case mode. Only the names of relations and attributes can be specified using capital letters. Try to develop two complementary routines, called **fold()** and **unfold()**. The former should accept a string as input and convert its contents into upper-case characters, and the latter should accept a string as parameter and convert its contents into lower-case. This way the user would be able to specify queries in an upper-case as well as in a lower-case mode.

8. In REQUIEM the **in** connective tests for set membership where the set is a collection of values produced by a **select** or **project** clause. In its present form the **in** connective accepts only numeral arguments. Extend the function implementing this operator appropriately to test for membership of character strings. Extend the functions underlying the membership operator to test for the absence of set membership, and name this new construct the **not in** connective.

9. In REQUIEM indices are created only when defining a new relation. Develop a set of functions that permit the creation and destruction of indices at any given time. The statements **create index** and **drop index** should be the only statements in RQL that explicitly refer to indices. The syntax of **create index** may be as follows:

create index on <*attr–name*> **in** <*rel–name*>;

If any data is already placed in the base relation <*rel-name*>, the values of the attribute on which the index is opened must be read from the data file and inserted in the index file in ascending order. Moreover, appropriate entries should be made for the indexed entries in the system catalogs. Indices should be secondary which means that you should precede them by the correct prefix and that you should also dynamically extend the insert and delete index buffers as well as the array limits of the element ix_secnd in the structure indx_attrs. Note that it is useful to allow only a limited number of indexes. Once dropped, an index should have its description removed from the system catalogs and its storage space released.

10. In Chapter 14 we mentioned that the functions **get()**, **store()**, and **put()** do not rely on the indexing mechanism provided by REQUIEM. Actually, these functions are experimental functions used with a previous version of REQUIEM that did not include any indexing facilities, and obviously require appropriate extensions. To incorporate indexing mechanisms in these functions you would probably have to rely on the already existing RE-QUIEM file management functions. To get an idea of how to develop such routines consider the implementation of the parser functions **select()** or **project()**. Both these functions call the index function **scan_ix()** to cater for indexed retrieval.

11. In REQUIEM we use the statement **print** to examine the contents of a relation. However, if the relation file at hand is too long or too broad to fit within the boundaries of exactly one screen, **print** produces the output too fast to be read or it overlays the results on one screenful. What we clearly require is a set of functions to print a stored relation in small, controllable chunks. The result must be a program that will print a relation a screenful at a time, waiting for the response of the user after each screen before continuing to the next. The user must have two options: to continue with the next screen at the right, if the output happens to be outstretched, or with the successor screen at the bottom if the relation is too long. A simple way to prompt the user is not to print the last new line of each chunk. The cursor will thus pause at the right end of the line rather than at the left margin. When the user presses the <return> key, the missing new line will be supplied and the next line appears in the proper place. To implement this program you may need more information or hints; a good source to refer to is [30].

12. The statement **modify** in REQUIEM is used to modify existing attribute definitions. However, this is not enough. What we require is an operation that allows any existing relation to be altered at any time by the addition of a new attribute at the right. To achieve this, introduce an operator called **augment relation** with the following syntax:

augment <*relation–name*> *add* <*attribute–name*>;

For example,

augment supplier *add* status;

This statement should add a *STATUS* attribute to the relation *SUPPLIER*. All existing supplier records must be augmented from four attribute values to five; the value of the new attribute must be *null* in every case. You do not need physically to change existing records until the next time that the relation is the target of an update statement. Do not forget to update the description of the relation in the system catalogs.

13. In an analogous manner define an operator called **remove** to remove an attribute definition from an existing relation. The syntax of this operator may be as follows:

remove from <*relation–name*> <*attribute–name*>;

What you are required to do is to remove the <*attribute–name*> entry from each <*relation–name*> record. Moreover, you must update the description of this relation in the system catalog by removing all <*attribute–name*> entries.

14. It would be very handy if all REQUIEM queries were saved for the duration of a REQUIEM session. This way the results of a query may be displayed at any time during a session. It is therefore necessary that you give each query a unique name. Obviously, names of already existing relations cannot be used for query names. A query name may consist of any sequence of letters or digits. The general format of a query could be:

<*query–name*> ::= <*query–expression*>;

Extend the REQUIEM parser appropriately and introduce a new data structure called **saved_queries** to accept queries posed by the user during a session. Note that space reservations for the save buffer must be accomplished dynamically. The implementation of this operator presents many similarities with the implementation of the **assign** statement. You could also use your imagination to combine these two operations.

15. In Chapter 3 we argued that to perform an operation on an object such as a base relation or view a user must hold the necessary access privilege for that combination of operation and that object. The corresponding operations are **select, insert, update**, and **delete**. Operations like **project, join**, etc. align with **select**. It is assumed that each user has an authorization identifier by means of his/her password and that only authorized users may execute against those objects. These tasks should be performed by the RQL statements **grant** and **revoke**. Their syntax has been already defined in Chapter 3. Extend the REQUIEM parser appropriately by introducing two new functions called **grant()** and **revoke()** to manage the internals of query authorization. You should also introduce a new system catalog to record access privileges and the objects against which those privileges are drawn.

16. An important feature that goes beyond the conventional support provided by a command editor is assistance on the syntactic level. For example, while posing a query the user might make a mistake or even forget the correct query syntax. With the current REQUIEM user interface the user must abort the query and issue a help command to get a description of all possible REQUIEM queries. After having finished that, he/she can then try to enter the correct query. Design and implement a more sophisticated user interface that would allow the user to get situation-dependent help information even during the formulation of a query. The help subsystem that you are required to develop must give the user on-line access to reference material that has been organized specifically for use during the processing of an application program. For example, more user-friendly messaging and supporting help screens could be typically implemented to clarify messages for the user. This can be achieved by providing a certain function key that when pressed displays help information on a specific help window. The window must pop up on request and disappear after you have used the required information. Instead of showing a list of all possible REQUIEM commands, the help subsystem should be able to display on the screen only information concerning the current statement.

17. Extend the current REQUIEM command interpreter to provide a command completion mechanism for commands and keywords. Normally the tab key can be used to request command completion. For example, if the user enters the character sequence:

sel < *tab* >

the system would intervene and expand the string "sel" to the keyword "select." Moreover, in case the user enters an ambiguous command the system must intervene by providing a list of possible alternatives by means of a special menu that directs the user to choose the most appropriate command.

Command completion can be achieved by means of the REQUIEM lexical analyzer. You must merely extend the routines that identify the token type of the current token. If a partial command or keyword is encountered, the scanner could return as a new token type the type *PREFIX*. In the parser routines, the occurrence of the above-mentioned token type must result in calling a routine that provides all possible extensions of the input entry.

Moreover, this kind of expansion must be restricted not only by syntactic but additionally by semantic constraints. For example if the name of an attribute of a given relation is required in a query, the expansion routines should compare the partial token against the attributes of that given relation. Whenever a possible completion has been formed, the expanded token and not the token *PREFIX* must be returned as the result of the completion step.

16.2   Case exercises

18. REQUIEM is primarily a database management system. However, it provides suitable language development tools that – with slight adaptations – are suited for developing programs. By using the scanner, parts of the parser, and the expression compilation and interpretation modules you are in a position to develop a complete interpreter for a programming language comparable in power to say Basic. You will be required to implement arbitrary long variable names, control statements, arrays, and procedures with arguments. This small project is representative of the problems encountered in large programs. Reference [30] is the most suitable source to get ideas on how to develop such a programming language. All you have to do is align the output of the REQUIEM parser and expression compiler with that of the *yacc* parser generator used in this reference.

19. In this book we have repeatedly stressed the fact that REQUIEM is a single user system. In broad terms what this means is that REQUIEM does not offer the possibility for several human operators to access the same database simultaneously. One very important function of such a multi-user DBMS is to control concurrent access to the data, so that one operator's actions do not interfere with another's. In order to be able to organize the control of shared access to the database the DBMS must provide appropriate mechanisms to identify and define sequences of actions, including reads and writes to the database, that are logically linked to one another. This sequence of actions is called a *transaction* and is considered to be an atomic action transforming the database from one consistent state to another. The sequence of elementary actions that make up transactions is, for example, defined by an application program which issues appropriate calls to the DBMS. For example, an application program may define a transaction which transfers money from one bank account to another. This kind of transaction involves several interactions within the database. Such interactions include reading and debiting the amount to the first account or crediting the second account with the given amount. For more information on transactions and transaction processing in general refer to [18].

To prevent transactions that execute concurrently from interfering with each other you must assume that there is a module in the DBMS called the *Lock Manager*, that maintains a lock for each data record in use by a transaction. The lock can be thought of as a control block that includes, among others, the identification of the record with which it is associated and the identification of the transaction holding the lock. A different transaction issued by another application program or user cannot access a locked record unless the lock is released by the first transaction. As there can be only one lock manager, access to it must be controlled by the same mechanism rather than by the lock manager itself. A simple lock manager normally uses semaphores to prevent two or more transactions from accessing shared records simultaneously. In [66] the author presents the implementation of a simple lock manager based on conventional multitasking Unix features. Design and implement this kind of lock management facility for REQUIEM so as to allow the system to handle concurrent transactions successfully. Note that the problem of recovery, which is the topic of the next exercise, is heavily bound up with the notion of transaction processing.

20. Error control and recovery are critical design components for all database management applications. Recovery in a database system means restoring the database to a state that is known to be correct after some failure has rendered the current database incorrect, e.g. a transaction did not commit. We say that a transaction *commits* when that transaction has terminated normally; in that case all its effects should be made permanent. Contrary to this a transaction *aborts* whenever it terminates abnormally; in that case all of its effects should be obliterated. The *Recovery Manager* is the piece of program which is responsible for transaction commitments or aborts. Design and develop a simple recovery manager for REQUIEM which every time that a change is made to the database would write a record containing the old and new values of the changed item into a special file called the *log* file.

It would be possible to produce an ongoing chronology of error conditions by the implementation of a log. The log can reveal a wealth of information if analyzed properly. By its very existence, a log is an audit trail or chronology of events. The implementation of logs also assumes that a disciplined approach to error trapping has been adopted.

If a failure occurs you can restore the database to a correct state by using the recovery manager and the log to undo all the unreliable changes. In that case what your recovery manager is expected to do is to wipe out the effects of the aborted transaction(s). Notice that the effects of a transaction are of two kinds: effects on values that the transaction itself wrote in the database; and effects on other transactions that cooperated with this specific transaction by reading values written by it. Both kind of effects should be obliterated. We stress the fact that the outline given is rather incomplete but we consider it as the minimum necessary for our purposes. In any case, we hope that this exercise gives you a flavor of the magnitude of the problem. In fact the topic of recovery is quite complex, and we suggest that you refer to [18] for more guidance on this particular topic.

A

Appendix A

A.1 The RQL syntax

A.1.1 Data definition statements

```
<DDL-statement>
            ::=   CREATE <rel-name>  ( <attr-def> { , <attr-def> }
                  [, <ref-clause> <ref-clause> ] );
            |     DEFINE <view-name> AS <rql-query>
            |     DROP   <view-name>
            |     MODIFY <rel-name> <interactive>
    <attr-def>
            ::=   <attr-name> ( <attr-type> ( <integer> )
                  [ , <key-spec>] )
    <attr-type>
            ::=   CHAR | NUM | REAL
    <key-spec>
            ::=   UNIQUE | SECONDARY
    <ref-clause>
            ::=   FOREIGN KEY <attr-name> REFERERENCES <attr-name>
                  IN <rel-name>;
```

A.1.2 Data manipulation statements

```
<DML-statement>
            ::=   <query-term> ;
            |     EXPOSE  <retrieve-clause> <expose-clause> ;
            |     DELETE  <del-clause> ;
            |     INSERT  <rel-name> <interactive>
            |     UPDATE  <select-clause> <interactive>
    <query-term>
            ::=   DIFFERENCE  <rel-name>  ,  <rel-name>
            |     INTERSECT   <rel-name>  ,  <rel-name>
```

```
                    |   JOIN      <rel-name> ON <attr-name>   WITH
                                      <rel-name> ON <attr-name>
                    |   PROJECT   <retrieve-clause> [<group-clause>]
                    |   SELECT    <select-clause>
                    |   UNION     <rel-name> , <rel-name>
<select-clause>
            ::=     <sel-attrs> [ <from-clause> ]
                        [ WHERE <pred-clause> ]
<retrieve-clause>
            ::=     <rel-clause> [ over ] <sel-attrs>
                        [ WHERE <pred-clause> | <in-predicate> ]
<rel-clause>
            ::=     <sel-rels> | <nesting-statement>
<from-clause>
            ::=     FROM <sel-rels> | <subquery-term>
<sel-rels>
            ::=     <sel-rel> , <sel-rels>
<sel-rel>
            ::=     <rel-name> [<alias>]
<sel-attrs>
            ::=     ALL | ( <sel-attr> {, <sel-attr> } )
<sel-attr>
            ::=     <attr-name> [<alias>]
<subquery-term>
            ::=     ( <query-term> )
<group-clause>
            ::=     GROUP BY <attr-name> <aggr-clause>
<aggr-clause>
            ::=     WHERE <aggr-func> <aggr-attr> <rel-op> <scalar>
                    |   <aggr-func> <aggr-attr>
<aggr-attr>
            ::=     ( <attr-name> )
<aggr-func>
            ::=     AVG | COUNT | MAXM | MINM | SUM
<del-clause>
            ::=     <view-name> | <retrieve-clause>
<expose-clause>
            ::=     WHEN <attr-name> IS IN
                    PROJECT <rel-name> OVER <attr-name> [ <pred-clause> ]
```

A.1.3   Auxiliary statements

```
<aux-statement>
            ::=     ASSIGN   <rel-name> TO <query> ;
                    |   COUNT    <rel-name> ;
                    |   DISPLAY  [<signed-no> [, <integer> ] ]
                            USING <retrieve-clause> ;
                    |   EXIT;
                    |   EXPORT   <rel-name> INTO <file-name>;
```

```
                    |   EXTRACT    <rel-name>  INTO  <file-name>;
                    |   FOCUS  ON  <rel-name>;
                    |   HELP;
                    |   IMPORT  <file-name>  INTO  <rel-name>;
                    |   PRINT   <print-clause> [  INTO  <file-name> ];
                    |   QUIT;
                    |   SHOW  VIEW   <view-name>;
<print-clause>
                 :: =   <using-clause> <select-clause>
                    |   <retrieve-clause>
<using-clause>
                 ::=   USING <file-name>
   <file-name>
                 ::=   <identifier>
```

A.1.4   Predicate expression statements

```
<pred-clause>
                 ::=   <attr-name> <rel-op> <expresion>
<in-predicate>
                 ::=   <attr-name> [NOT]  IN   <in-list>
<in-list>
                 ::=   ( <scalar> { , <scalar> } )
<expression>
                 ::=   <primary> { <logop> <primary> }
<primary>
                 ::=   <statement> | <assgnt> <relop> <simple-expr>
<statement>
                 ::=   <simple-expr> { <relop> <simple-expr> }
<assignment>
                 ::=   ( <variable> := <simple-expr> )
<simple-expr>
                 ::=   <term> { <addop> <term> }
<term>
                 ::=   <factor> { <mulop> <factor> }
<factor>
                 ::=   <operand> | ( <expression> ) | <nop> <factor>
<operand>
                 ::=   <integer> | <real> | <string> |
                          <attribute> | <variable>
<variable>
                 ::=   $<chars>$
<attribute>
                 ::=   [<rname>.] <aname>
<integer>
                 ::=   <digit> [ <integer> ]
<real>
                 ::=   <integer>.<integer>
<signed-no>
```

```
                  ::=   <addop><integer>
<string>
                  ::=   " <chars> "
<chars>
                  ::=   nil | <chars> { <character> }
<nop>
                  ::=   ~
<logop>
                  ::=   & | |
<relop>
                  ::=   = | <> | < | > | <= | >= | ==
<addop>
                  ::=   + | -
<mulop>
                  ::=   * | / | %
<digit>
                  ::=   0 | ... | 9
```

A.1.5 Miscellaneous

```
<view-name>
                  ::=   <identifier>
<alias>
                  ::=   <identifier>
<rel-name>
                  :: =  <identifier>

<attr-name>
                  :: =  <rel-name> . <identifier> | <identifier>
```

B

Appendix B

B.1　The REQUIEM source listings

file: btree.h *

```
1    /* btree.h - data structures and constants for BTREE modules */
2
3    #define CUR          1  /* getting current block */
4    #define NOT_CUR      0  /* getting non-current block */
5    #define UPDATES      1  /* update indexed attributes */
6    #define NO_UPDATE    0  /* no indexed attribute updates */
7    #define EOF_IX      -2  /* return value for end-of-index */
8    #define IX_FAIL     -1  /* return value for failed operation */
9    #define IX_OK        0  /* return value for sucess */
10   #define NULLREC     -1L /* special return value for file pos of
11                            * index block/data structure */
12   #define MAX_LEVELS   4  /* four index levels permitted */
13   #define MAXKEY      30  /* space to accept max. length of key */
14   #define IXBLK_SIZE  1024  /* no. of bytes in a block on disk */
15   #define IXBLK_SPACE 1016  /* bytes of entry space in blk */
16   #define LEFTN       -1  /* request for left neighbor */
17   #define RIGHTN       1  /* request for right neighbor */
18   #define FOUND        0  /* entry found */
19   #define NOTFOUND     1  /* entry not found */
20   #define FREE_LEVEL  -1  /* marks a block as free */
21   #define MAXKEYS      2  /* max no. of keys per index */
22   #define KEYSIZE     16  /* size of key */
23   #define BNSIZE      10  /* equivalent of ANSIZE in requ.h */
24   typedef long RECPOS;  /* file pos. of index block/data rec. */
25
26   /* call a function using a pointer */
27   #define FUNCALL(pfun)      (* (pfun) )
28   /* get the address of entry in a block */
29   #define ENT_ADDR(pb, off) ((struct entry *)\
30                             ((char *)((pb)->entries)+(off)))
31
32   struct entry { /* entry format in index */
33     RECPOS lower_lvl; /* points to lower level */
34     char key[MAXKEY]; /* start of key value with ficticious size
```

---

*Adapted from W. J. Hunt, *The C Toolbox*, by kind permission of both the author and Addison-Wesley, W. Germany.

```
35                          * whose actual data type is unknown */
36      };
37
38      struct block { /* index block format */
39        RECPOS blk_pos;        /* index file location of block
40                               * or location of next free block */
41        short blk_offset;      /* first unused location in block */
42        short lvl;             /* records level no. -1 for free */
43        char entries[IXBLK_SPACE];   /* space for entries */
44      };
45
46      struct indx_attrs { /* indexed attributes */
47        char ix_refkey[MAXKEYS][24];    /* referenced attributes */
48        char ix_prim[MAXKEYS][BNSIZE];  /* primary attributes */
49        char ix_secnd[MAXKEYS][BNSIZE]; /* secondary attributes */
50        char ix_rel[12];                /* relation name */
51        char ix_foreign;                /* indicates a foreign key */
52      };
53
54      struct ix_disk { /* disk file index descriptor */
55        short nl;              /* no. of index levels */
56        RECPOS root_bk;        /* location of root block in file */
57        RECPOS first_fbk;      /* relative address of first free block */
58        struct indx_attrs ixatts;    /* indexed attribute entry */
59        struct entry dum_entr;       /* dummy entry */
60      };
61
62
63      struct descriptor { /* index level descriptor entry */
64        RECPOS cblock;  /* current block no. */
65        int  coffset;   /* cur.offset within block for indx level */
66      };
67
68      struct ix_header { /* in-memory index descriptor */
69        int ixfile;           /* descriptor for open index file */
70        int (*pcomp) ();      /* pointer to compare function */
71        int (*psize) ();      /* pointer to entry size function */
72        struct ix_disk dx;              /* disk resident stuff */
73        struct block cache[MAX_LEVELS]; /* cache for curent blocks */
74        struct descriptor pos[MAX_LEVELS];
75      };
```

file: btree.c

```
1       #include <stdio.h>
2       #include "btree.h"
3       #include "requ.h"
4
5       /* global variable declarations */
6
7       struct ix_header *pci;    /* refers to index descriptor
8                                 * for current function call */
9       struct block spare_block ; /* scratch block for splits
10                                * and compressing */
11
12      int split_size = IXBLK_SPACE;   /* split block when it contains
13                                      * more than this many bytes */
14      int comb_size = (IXBLK_SIZE/2); /* combine block when it
15                                      * contains fewer than this
16                                      * many bytes */
```

```
17    BOOL err_sig = FALSE;
18    static BOOL insert = FALSE;
19    long get_free();
20    long write_level();
21    long next_ix();
22    long last_ix();
23    struct block *neighbor();
24
25    struct entry dummy_entry = { /* max length of key is 30 chars */
26    NULLREC, { 0xff, 0xff, 0xff, 0xff, 0xff,
27                   0xff, 0xff, 0xff, 0xff, 0xff,
28                   0xff, 0xff, 0xff, 0xff, 0xff,
29                   0xff, 0xff, 0xff, 0xff, 0xff,
30                   0xff, 0xff, 0xff, 0xff, 0xff,
31                   0xff, 0xff, 0xff, 0xff, 0x0,},
32    };
33    /* ------------------------------------------------------------ */
34    int prev_entry(pblk, offset)   /* back up one entry before   */
35         struct block *pblk;       /*  entry at specified offset */
36         int offset;
37    {
38        if (offset <= 0)              /* are we at start of block ? */
39          return(-1);                 /* can't back up */
40        offset = scan_blk(pblk, offset);  /* find previous entry */
41        return(offset);
42    } /* prev_entry */
43    /* ------------------------------------------------------------ */
44    int next_entry(pblk, offset)        /* go forward one entry */
45         struct block *pblk;       /* past entry at specified offset */
46         int offset;
47    {
48        if (offset >= pblk->blk_offset) /* at end of block ? */
49          return(-1);                   /* cannot move forward */
50
51        /* move past entry */
52        offset += (*(pci->psize)) (ENT_ADDR(pblk, offset));
53        if (offset >= pblk->blk_offset) /* at end of block ? */
54          return(-1);                   /* no entry allowed here */
55
56        return(offset);
57    } /* next_entry */
58    /* ------------------------------------------------------------ */
59    int copy_entry(to, from)            /* copy an entry */
60         struct entry *to;              /* to this address */
61         struct entry *from;            /* from this address */
62    {
63        int nsize;
64
65        nsize = (*(pci->psize)) (from); /* get the entry's size */
66        move_struct((char *) to, (char *) from, nsize);
67    } /* copy_entry */
68    /* ------------------------------------------------------------ */
69    int scan_blk(pblk, n)      /* find the offset of last entry */
70         struct block *pblk; /* in this block */
71         int n;                /* starting before this position */
72    {
73        int i, last;
74
75        i = 0;
76        last = 0;
77        while (i < n) {          /* repeat until position is reached */
```

```
78        last = i;              /* save current position */
79        i += (*(pci->psize))(ENT_ADDR(pblk, i));
80     }
81     return(last);             /* return last offset < n */
82  } /* scan_blk */
83  /* ------------------------------------------------------------ */
84  int last_entry(pblk)        /* find last entry in block */
85        struct block *pblk;   /* present block */
86  {
87     /* scan for offset of last entry */
88     return( scan_blk(pblk, pblk->blk_offset)); /* return offset */
89  } /* last-entry */
90  /* ------------------------------------------------------------ */
91  int create_ixf(fn)                 /* create an index file */
92        char fn[];
93  {
94     return(creat(fn, 0600));
95  } /* create_ixf */
96  /* ------------------------------------------------------------ */
97  int read_ixf(start, buf, nrd)
98        RECPOS start;
99        char *buf;
100       int nrd;
101 {
102    long lseek();
103    lseek(pci->ixfile, start, 0);
104    return(read(pci->ixfile, buf, nrd));
105 } /* read_ixf */
106 /* ------------------------------------------------------------ */
107 int write_ixf(start, buf, nwrt)
108       RECPOS start;
109       char *buf;
110       int nwrt;
111 {
112    long lseek();
113
114    lseek(pci->ixfile, start, 0);
115    return(write(pci->ixfile, buf, nwrt));
116 } /* write_ixf */
117 /* ------------------------------------------------------------ */
118 int close_ixf()      /* close index file */
119 {
120    return(close(pci->ixfile));
121 } /* close_ixf */
122 /* ------------------------------------------------------------ */
123 int open_ixf(fn)          /* open an index file */
124       char fn[];
125 {
126    return(open(fn, 2));
127 } /* open_ixf */
128 /* ------------------------------------------------------------ */
129 int make_free(pci)    /* set up the available space list */
130       struct ix_header *pci;
131 {
132    struct block *pblk;
133    RECPOS ptr, fstart;
134
135    pblk = &spare_block;            /* point to scratch block */
136    if (pci->dx.first_fbk == 0) {
137       fstart = ((RECPOS) (MAX_LEVELS +1)) * IXBLK_SIZE;
138       pci->dx.first_fbk = NULLREC; /* no blocks free to start */
```

```
139       ptr = fstart;
140     }
141     else ptr = pci->dx.first_fbk + IXBLK_SIZE;
142
143     write_free(ptr, pblk);
144   } /* make_free */
145 /* ------------------------------------------------------------ */
146   int write_free(rfree, pblk)   /* write out a free block */
147       RECPOS rfree;             /* record no. of block to free */
148       struct block *pblk;       /* use this as scratch space */
149   {
150     pblk->lvl = FREE_LEVEL;     /* mark block as being free */
151     clear_mem(pblk->entries, 0, IXBLK_SPACE); /* zero block */
152     /* point to current 1st block, NULLREC at very first block */
153     pblk->blk_pos = pci->dx.first_fbk;
154     write_block(rfree, pblk);   /* write the free block */
155     pci->dx.first_fbk = rfree;  /* make this block first free */
156   } /* write_free */
157 /* ------------------------------------------------------------ */
158   int init_bio()       /* initialize block input-output */
159   {
160     init_cache();      /* initialize cache buffers */
161   } /* init_bio */
162 /* ------------------------------------------------------------ */
163   int retrieve_block(ix_lvl, rloc, pblk, current)
164       /* retrieve an index block from cache or from index file */
165       int ix_lvl;               /* index level for this block */
166       RECPOS rloc;              /* block's location in index file */
167       struct block *pblk;       /* put it in this block */
168
169       int current;              /* if TRUE put it in cache */
170   {
171     if (chk_cache(ix_lvl, rloc))   /* look in cache first */
172       get_cache(ix_lvl, rloc, pblk); /* and get it */
173     else {
174       read_block(rloc, pblk);   /* not in cache, read it */
175       pblk->blk_pos = rloc;                /* from disk */
176       pblk->lvl = ix_lvl;
177       if (current)              /* current block for level 1? */
178         put_cache(ix_lvl, pblk); /* yes - place it in the */
179     }                            /* cache in header */
180     return(IX_OK);
181   } /* retrieve_block */
182 /* ------------------------------------------------------------ */
183   int update_block(pblk)        /* update an index block in file */
184       struct block *pblk;       /* address of index block */
185   {
186     if (chk_cache(pblk->lvl, pblk->blk_pos))
187       put_cache(pblk->lvl, pblk);
188     write_block(pblk->blk_pos, pblk);
189   } /* update_block */
190 /* ------------------------------------------------------------ */
191   int get_block(lvl, pblk)
192       /* allocate and set up a block, retrieve an index block */
193       int lvl;                  /* index level for this block */
194       struct block *pblk;       /* put it here */
195   {
196     RECPOS rfree;
197
198     rfree = pci->dx.first_fbk; /* get loc. of 1st free block */
199     make_free(pci);            /* produce a free block */
```

```
200        if (rfree == NULLREC)
201          return(IX_FAIL);
202        pblk->blk_pos = rfree;      /* record block's file position */
203        pblk->lvl = lvl;           /* and its level */
204        return(IX_OK);
205      } /* get_block */
206    /* ------------------------------------------------------------ */
207    int put_free(pblk)          /* return a block to the free list */
208         struct block *pblk;
209    {
210      /* when a block is freed ensures that the cache does not
211       * contain out of data information about block */
212
213      scrub_cache(pblk->blk_pos);        /* remove from cache */
214      pblk->lvl = FREE_LEVEL;           /* mark block as free */
215      write_free(pblk->blk_pos, pblk);
216    } /* put_free */
217    /* ------------------------------------------------------------ */
218    int read_block(rloc, pblk)  /* read an index block */
219         RECPOS rloc;               /* block's location in index file */
220         struct block *pblk;        /* store the block here */
221    {
222      int ret;
223
224      ret = read_ixf(rloc, (char *) pblk, sizeof(struct block));
225      return(ret);
226    } /* read_block */
227    /* ------------------------------------------------------------ */
228    int write_block(rloc, pblk) /* write an index block */
229         RECPOS rloc;               /* block's location in index file */
230         struct block *pblk;        /* the block to write */
231    {
232      int  ret;
233
234      ret = write_ixf(rloc, (char *) pblk, sizeof(struct block));
235      return(ret);
236    } /* write_block */
237    /* ------------------------------------------------------------ */
238    int init_cache()            /* initialize block i/o cache */
239    {
240      int i;
241
242      for (i = 0; i < MAX_LEVELS; i++)   /* denote that there is */
243        pci->cache[i].blk_pos = NULLREC; /* nothing in memory yet */
244    } /* init_cache */
245    /* ------------------------------------------------------------ */
246    int chk_cache(ix_lvl, rloc) /* check cache for an index block */
247         int ix_lvl;                /* index level for this block */
248         RECPOS rloc;               /* block's location in index file */
249    {
250
251      if (pci->cache[ix_lvl].blk_pos != rloc)
252        return(FALSE);
253      return(TRUE);
254
255    } /* chk_cache */
256    /* ------------------------------------------------------------ */
257    int get_cache(ix_lvl, rloc, to) /* get a block from cache */
258         int ix_lvl;                    /* index level for this block */
259         RECPOS rloc;                   /* block's loc in index file */
260         struct block *to;              /* if found, copy it there */
```

```
261    {
262       struct block *pblk;
263
264       if (pci->cache[ix_lvl].blk_pos != rloc)
265          return(FALSE);
266       pblk = &pci->cache[ix_lvl];
267       move_struct((char *) to, (char *) pblk, sizeof(struct block));
268       pblk->blk_pos = rloc;
269       return(TRUE);
270    } /* get_cache */
271    /* ------------------------------------------------------------ */
272    int put_cache(ix_lvl, pblk)    /* write index block to file */
273          int ix_lvl;
274          struct block *pblk;       /* address of index block */
275    {
276       struct block *to;
277
278       to = &pci->cache[ix_lvl];
279       move_struct((char *) to, (char *) pblk,
280                   sizeof(struct block)); /* copy the whole block */
281    } /* put_cache */
282    /* ------------------------------------------------------------ */
283    int scrub_cache(rloc)        /* remove a block from the cache */
284          RECPOS rloc;            /* the block's file position */
285    {                             /* = RECPOS scrubs all levels */
286       int i;
287       /* search the cache */
288       for (i = 0; i < pci->dx.nl; i++)
289          if ((rloc == NULLREC) || (rloc == pci->cache[i].blk_pos))
290             pci->cache[i].blk_pos = NULLREC;
291    } /* scrub_cache */
292    /* ------------------------------------------------------------ */
293    int open_ix(f_name, pix, cfun, sfun)
294          char f_name[];          /* file name */
295          struct ix_header *pix; /* control block for index */
296          int (*cfun) ();         /* pointer to compare function */
297          int (*sfun) ();         /* pointer to entry size function */
298    {
299       int ret;
300
301       pci = pix;
302       ret = open_ixf(f_name);
303       if (ret < 0)              /* check for failure */
304          return (FALSE);
305       pci->ixfile = ret;
306
307       /* read header descriptor from disk and place it into pix
308          descriptor structure */
309       read_ixf(0L, (char *) &pix->dx, sizeof(struct ix_disk));
310       pci->pcomp = cfun;        /* record address of compare */
311       pci->psize = sfun;        /* and of entry size functions */
312       init_bio();               /* initialize block i/o and clear cache */
313       go_first(pix);            /* pos at file start(valid current pos) */
314       return(TRUE);
315    } /* open_ix */
316    /* ------------------------------------------------------------ */
317    long write_level(pdum, ndum)
318          struct entry *pdum;     /* dummy entry */
319          int ndum;               /* size of dummy entry */
320    {
321       struct block blk;
```

```
322      int i;
323      RECPOS rloc;
324
325      pdum->lower_lvl = NULLREC;
326      rloc = 0;
327      for (i = 0; i < MAX_LEVELS; i++) {
328        rloc += IXBLK_SIZE;
329        /* make a block of zeroes */
330        clear_mem((char *) &blk, 0, IXBLK_SIZE);
331        move_struct((char *) blk.entries,
332                    (char *) pdum, ndum); /* place dummy in block */
333        blk.lvl = i;
334        blk.blk_offset = ndum;   /* block contains a single entry */
335        write_block(rloc, &blk); /* write the block */
336        pdum->lower_lvl = rloc;
337      }
338
339      return(rloc);
340    } /* write_level */
341  /* ------------------------------------------------------------ */
342    int go_first(pix)                 /* go to first entry in index */
343          struct ix_header *pix;   /* points to an index descriptor */
344    {
345      struct block blk;
346
347      pci = pix;
348      /* start at root level and */
349      first_ix(pci->dx.nl-1, pci->dx.root_bk, &blk);
350      return(IX_OK);
351    } /* go_first */
352  /* ------------------------------------------------------------ */
353    int first_ix(lvl, rloc, pblk) /* set current pos to 1st entry */
354          int lvl;                   /* at this and lower levels */
355          RECPOS rloc;               /* cur. block for level 1 */
356          struct block *pblk;
357    {
358
359      pci->pos[lvl].cblock = rloc; /* set pos of current block */
360      pci->pos[lvl].coffset = 0;   /* and its offset */
361      retrieve_block(lvl, rloc, pblk, CUR); /* get the block */
362
363      /* work down to leaf level */
364      if (lvl > 0)
365        first_ix(lvl-1, ENT_ADDR(pblk, 0)->lower_lvl, pblk);
366
367    } /* first_ix */
368  /* ------------------------------------------------------------ */
369    int go_last(pix)          /* go to last index entry (dummy entry) */
370          struct ix_header *pix;   /* points to an index descriptor */
371    {
372      struct block blk;
373
374      pci = pix;
375      /* start at root */
376      final_ix(pci->dx.nl-1, pci->dx.root_bk, &blk);
377      /* position at last entry */
378      return(IX_OK);
379    } /* go_last */
380  /* ------------------------------------------------------------ */
381    int final_ix(lvl, rloc, pblk) /* set current pos to 1st entry */
382          int lvl;                   /* at this and lower levels */
```

```
383          RECPOS rloc;              /* cur. block for level 1 */
384          struct block *pblk;
385    {
386      int off;
387
388      pci->pos[lvl].cblock = rloc; /* set current block */
389
390      retrieve_block(lvl, rloc, pblk, CUR); /* get the block */
391
392      off = last_entry(pblk);       /* current offset = last entry */
393      pci->pos[lvl].coffset = off;
394      if (lvl > 0)                  /* set lower levels */
395        final_ix(lvl-1, ENT_ADDR(pblk, off)->lower_lvl, pblk);
396    } /* final_ix */
397  /* ------------------------------------------------------------- */
398  int get_next(pe, pix)            /* get next index entry */
399        struct entry *pe;          /* put the entry here */
400        struct ix_header *pix;     /* points to an index descriptor */
401    {
402      struct block blk;
403
404      pci = pix;
405      /* check for dummy entry at end of file */
406      copy_current(0, pe);
407      if (FUNCALL(pci->pcomp) (pe, &pci->dx.dum_entr) == 0)
408        return(EOF_IX);
409
410      if (next_ix(0, &blk) != NULLREC) { /* got next leaf entry? */
411        copy_current(0, pe);            /* then copy it */
412        return(IX_OK);                  /* return successfully */
413      }
414      else
415        return(EOF_IX);
416    } /* get_next */
417  /* ------------------------------------------------------------- */
418  long next_ix(lvl, pblk)          /* get the next entry on a level */
419        int lvl;                   /* level no. */
420        struct block *pblk;        /* curent block */
421    {
422      int off;
423      RECPOS newblk;
424
425      if (lvl >= pci->dx.nl)        /* above top level ? */
426        return(NULLREC);            /* yes - failure */
427      /* get current block */
428      retrieve_block(lvl, pci->pos[lvl].cblock, pblk, CUR);
429      /* move to next entry in block */
430      off = next_entry(pblk, pci->pos[lvl].coffset);
431
432      if (off >= 0)        /* past the end of block? */
433        pci->pos[lvl].coffset = off; /* no - record new position */
434      else {                         /* next block on this level */
435        newblk = next_ix(lvl + 1, pblk);
436
437        if (newblk != NULLREC) {     /* check for begin of index */
438                                     /* make this current block */
439          pci->pos[lvl].cblock = newblk;
440          retrieve_block(lvl,newblk, pblk, CUR); /* put into mem. */
441          pci->pos[lvl].coffset = 0; /* at first entry */
442        }
443        else return(NULLREC);        /* at start of index - can't */
```

```
444      }
445      /* return block no. at lower level */
446      return( ENT_ADDR(pblk, pci->pos[lvl].coffset)->lower_lvl);
447
448    } /* next_ix */
449    /* ----------------------------------------------------------- */
450    long  last_ix(lvl, pblk)    /* get previous entry for a level */
451         int lvl;               /* level no. */
452         struct block *pblk;    /* space for a block */
453    {
454      int off;
455      RECPOS newblk;
456
457      if (lvl >= pci->dx.nl)    /* above top level ? */
458        return(NULLREC);        /* yes - failure */
459      /* get current block */
460      retrieve_block(lvl, pci->pos[lvl].cblock, pblk, CUR);
461      /* back up one entry in block */
462      off = prev_entry(pblk, pci->pos[lvl].coffset);
463      if (off >= 0)            /* past the beginning of block */
464        pci->pos[lvl].coffset = off;  /* no - record new offset */
465      else {                  /* yes - get previous block */
466        newblk = last_ix(lvl + 1, pblk);
467        if (newblk != NULLREC) {/* check for begin of index */
468                               /* make this current block */
469          pci->pos[lvl].cblock = newblk;
470          retrieve_block(lvl,newblk, pblk, CUR); /* put into mem. */
471          /* offset is last entry in block */
472          pci->pos[lvl].coffset = last_entry(pblk);
473        }
474        else return(NULLREC); /* at start of index: can't back up */
475      }                       /* return ptr in curr. entry */
476      return( ENT_ADDR(pblk, pci->pos[lvl].coffset)->lower_lvl);
477    } /* last_ix */
478    /* ----------------------------------------------------------- */
479    int get_current(pe, pix)    /* get current index entry */
480         struct entry *pe;      /* put entry here */
481         struct ix_header *pix; /* points to an index descriptor */
482    {
483      pci = pix;
484      copy_current(0, pe);
485    } /* get_current */
486    /* ----------------------------------------------------------- */
487    int find_key(pe, pb, poff, comp_fun)
488         /* look for a key in a block */
489         struct entry *pe;      /* contains the target key */
490         struct block *pb;      /* look in this specific block */
491         int *poff;             /* store offset where we stop here */
492         int (*comp_fun) ();    /* pointer to compare function */
493    {
494      int i;                   /* offset */
495      int ret;                 /* result of last comparison */
496      struct entry *p;
497
498      i = 0;
499      /* repeat until the end of block */
500      while (i < pb->blk_offset) {
501        p = ENT_ADDR(pb, i);   /* get the entry address and */
502        /* compare to target key */
503        ret = FUNCALL(comp_fun) (pe, ENT_ADDR(pb, i));
504
```

```
505        /* if two primary keys match */
506        if (ret == 0 && p->key[0] == 'P' && insert
507            && strcmp(pci->dx.ixatts.ix_rel,"sysatrs") != EQUAL)
508            if (pci->dx.ixatts.ix_foreign == 'f' ||
509                strncmp(p->key, "P*2", 3) == EQUAL)
510                err_sig = TRUE;
511
512        if (ret <= 0)  /* quit if the target is leq current entry */
513           break;
514        i = next_entry(pb, i);    /* move to next entry */
515     }
516     *poff = i;                 /* store the offset where we stopped */
517     return(ret);               /* result of last compare */
518  } /* find_key */
519  /* ------------------------------------------------------------ */
520  int ins_entry(pb, pe, off)  /* add an entry to a block */
521        struct block *pb;       /* the block */
522        struct entry *pe;       /* the entry to insert */
523        int off;                /* the offset where we insert it */
524  {
525     int n_size;
526
527     n_size = (*(pci->psize))(pe); /* how big is the new insert ?*/
528
529     /* move everything to the end of block */
530     move_up(pb, off, n_size);  /* make room for the new entry */
531     copy_entry(ENT_ADDR(pb, off), pe);  /* move it in */
532     pb->blk_offset += n_size;           /* adjust block size */
533
534  } /* ins_entry */
535  /* ------------------------------------------------------------ */
536  int del_entry(pb, off)         /* remove entry from block */
537        struct block *pb;        /* the block to work on */
538        int off;                 /* new location of entry */
539  {
540     int n_size;
541     /* get entry size */
542     n_size = (*(pci->psize)) (ENT_ADDR(pb, off));
543
544     /* move entries above curr. one down */
545     move_down(pb, off, n_size);
546     pb->blk_offset -= n_size;  /* adjust the no. of bytes used */
547
548  } /* del_entry */
549  /* ------------------------------------------------------------ */
550  int move_up(pb, off, n)     /* move part of a block upward */
551        struct block *pb;       /* the block to work on */
552        int off;                /* place to start moving */
553        int n;                  /* how far up to move things */
554  {                             /* move entries */
555     move_struct((char *) ENT_ADDR(pb, off+n), /* to here */
556                (char *) ENT_ADDR(pb, off),    /* from there */
557                pb->blk_offset - off);         /* rest of block */
558
559  } /* move_up */
560  /* ------------------------------------------------------------ */
561  int move_down(pb, off, n)   /* move part of a block upward */
562        struct block *pb;       /* the block to work on */
563        int off;                /* place to start moving */
564        int n;                  /* how far up to move things */
565  {                             /* move entries */
```

```
566        move_struct((char *) ENT_ADDR(pb, off),    /* to here */
567                   (char *) ENT_ADDR(pb, off+n),  /* from there */
568                   pb->blk_offset - (off+n));   /* rest of block */
569
570    } /* move_down */
571    /* ----------------------------------------------------------- */
572    int combine(pl, pr)          /* combine two blocks */
573        struct block *pl;        /* add the left block */
574        struct block *pr;        /* to the right block */
575    {
576       move_up(pr, 0, pl->blk_offset); /* make room for left block */
577       /* move it in left block contents */
578       move_struct((char *) ENT_ADDR(pr, 0),
579                   (char *) ENT_ADDR(pl, 0),
580                   pl->blk_offset);
581       /* adjust block size */
582       pr->blk_offset = pr->blk_offset + pl->blk_offset;
583    } /* combine */
584    /* ----------------------------------------------------------- */
585    int find_ix(pe, pix)         /* find the first entry with a key */
586        struct entry *pe;        /* points to key to be matched */
587        struct ix_header *pix;   /* points to index header */
588    {
589       int ret;
590       struct entry temp_entr;
591
592       pci = pix;
593       /* make sure that target is < dummy */
594       if (FUNCALL(pci->pcomp) (pe, &pci->dx.dum_entr) >= 0) {
595          go_last(pix);            /* no position at end */
596          return(NOTFOUND);       /* return not equal */
597       }
598
599       ret = find_level(pci->dx.nl-1, pe, pci->dx.root_bk);
600       if (ret == 0) {            /* if an entry was found */
601          copy_current(0, &temp_entr); /* store its record ptr */
602          pe->lower_lvl = temp_entr.lower_lvl;
603       }
604
605       return(ret);
606    } /* find_ix */
607    /* ----------------------------------------------------------- */
608    int find_level(lvl, pe, r)    /* find key within a level*/
609        int lvl;                 /* the level */
610        struct entry *pe;        /* the target entry */
611        RECPOS r;                /* block to look in */
612    {
613       struct block blk;          /* scratch blk, with separate
614                                   * copy for each blk */
615       int ret, off;
616
617       retrieve_block(lvl, r, &blk, CUR); /* retrieve current blk */
618       /* look for the key there */
619       ret = find_key(pe, &blk, &off, pci->pcomp);
620       pci->pos[lvl].cblock = r;   /* make this the current block */
621       pci->pos[lvl].coffset = off;/* and offset in the block */
622       /* search lower levels */
623       if (lvl > 0)
624          ret = find_level(lvl-1, pe, ENT_ADDR(&blk, off)->lower_lvl);
625       return(ret);
626
```

```
627     } /* find_level */
628     /* ------------------------------------------------------------ */
629     int insert_ix(pe, pix)        /* find first entry with a key */
630         struct entry *pe;         /* points to key to be matched */
631         struct ix_header *pix;    /* points to index descriptor */
632     {
633       int ret;
634       struct block blk;
635
636       pci = pix;
637       ret = ins_level(0, pe, &blk); /* insert entry at leaf level */
638
639       if (ret == IX_OK)           /* if insertion was successful */
640         next_ix(0, &blk);         /* move past entry inserted */
641       insert = FALSE;             /* reset insert flag */
642       return(ret);                /* return success or failure  */
643     } /* insert_ix */
644     /* ------------------------------------------------------------ */
645     int ins_level(lvl, pe, pb)    /* insert an entry at this level */
646         int lvl;                  /* at this level */
647
648         struct entry *pe;         /* contains the target entry */
649         struct block *pb;
650     {
651       int ret;
652
653       if (lvl >= pci->dx.nl)      /* do we need a new level ? */
654         return(IX_FAIL);          /* yes - overflow */
655
656       retrieve_block(lvl, pci->pos[lvl].cblock, pb, CUR);
657       /* does it fit into the block ? */
658       if ((pb->blk_offset + (*(pci->psize)) (pe)) <= split_size) {
659         ins_entry(pb, pe, pci->pos[lvl].coffset); /* put in block */
660         update_block(pb);         /* update the index blk in file */
661         ret = IX_OK;
662       }
663       else ret = split(lvl, pe, pb); /* split the block */
664
665       return(ret);
666     } /* ins_level */
667     /* ------------------------------------------------------------ */
668     int split(lvl, pe, pb)               /* split a block into two */
669         int lvl;
670         struct entry *pe;
671         struct block *pb;
672     {
673       int half, ins_pos, last , ret;
674       struct block *pbb;
675       struct entry entr;
676
677       ins_pos = pci->pos[lvl].coffset;/* rem. where insert was */
678
679       if ((lvl+1) >= pci->dx.nl)    /* check for top level */
680         return(IX_FAIL);            /* can't split top level blk */
681
682       /* make a block long enough to store both old and new entries
683        * this block should temporarily serve as a buffer */
684       pbb = (struct block *) calloc(sizeof(struct block) +
685                                sizeof(struct entry), 1);
686       if (pbb == NULL)              /* did allocation fail ? */
687         return(IX_FAIL);            /* yes - exit */
```

```
688
689      /* do insert in big block */
690      pbb->blk_offset = 0;
691      combine(pb, pbb);  /* copy contents of old buffer */
692      ins_entry(pbb, pe, pci->pos[lvl].coffset); /* ins new entry */
693
694      /* find where to split, no more than half entries left blk */
695      /* start of last entry in left half of big block */
696      last = scan_blk(pbb, pbb->blk_offset/2);
697
698      half = next_entry(pbb, last);            /* end of left half */
699      /* allocate disk space for left block */
700      if (get_block(lvl, pbb) == IX_FAIL) { /* check for failure */
701        nfree((char *) pbb);
702        return(IX_FAIL);
703      }
704
705      /* make an entry for the new block on the upper level */
706      copy_entry(&entr, ENT_ADDR(pbb, last));
707      entr.lower_lvl = pbb->blk_pos; /* point entry to left blk */
708
709      ret = ins_level(lvl+1, &entr, pb); /* ins new index entry */
710      /* left block at higher level */
711      /* this makes the lvl+1 position */
712      /* point to the left block */
713      if (ret != IX_OK)  /* higher level failure (overflow) */
714        {
715          nfree((char *) pbb);     /* yes - free big block area */
716          put_free(pbb);           /*      free new index block */
717          return(ret);             /*      return failure code */
718        }
719      /* use pb for right block */
720      move_struct((char *) ENT_ADDR(pb, 0),
721                  (char *) ENT_ADDR(pbb, half),
722                    pbb->blk_offset - half);
723      pb->blk_offset = pbb->blk_offset - half;
724      pb->blk_pos =  pci->pos[lvl].cblock; /* restore blk's loc */
725      pb->lvl = lvl;                        /* and its level */
726      update_block(pb);                     /* and update it */
727
728      /* fix up left block */
729      pbb->blk_offset = half;               /* size = left half */
730      /* entries already in place */
731      update_block(pbb);                    /* update left block */
732
733      if (ins_pos >= half) {    /* curr. entry in left or right ? */
734        /* right - adjust offset */
735        pci->pos[lvl].coffset =  pci->pos[lvl].coffset-half;
736        next_ix(lvl+1, pb);    /* upper level position */
737      }  /* left - make left block current */
738      else pci->pos[lvl].cblock = entr.lower_lvl;
739
740      nfree((char *) pbb);    /* free big scratch block */
741      return(ret);
742    } /* split */
743    /* ------------------------------------------------------------ */
744    delete_ix(pix)                   /* delete the current entry */
745         struct ix_header *pix; /* points to index descriptor */
746    {
747      struct entry temp_entr;
748      struct block b;
```

```
749        int ret;
750
751        pci = pix;
752        /* check for dummy entry at end-of-index */
753        copy_current(0, &temp_entr);
754        if (FUNCALL(pci->pcomp) (&temp_entr, &pci->dx.dum_entr) == 0)
755          return(IX_FAIL);
756        /* not at end - delete it */
757        ret = del_level(0, &b);
758
759        return(ret);
760      } /* delete_ix */
761    /* ------------------------------------------------------------ */
762    int del_level(lvl, pb)              /* delete entry within level */
763          int lvl;
764          struct block *pb;
765    {
766        int ret;
767        struct entry temp_entr;
768
769        ret = IX_OK;
770        /* retrieve current block */
771        retrieve_block(lvl, pci->pos[lvl].cblock, pb, CUR);
772        del_entry(pb, pci->pos[lvl].coffset); /* del entry in blk */
773
774        if (pb->blk_offset == 0) {      /* block now empty ? */
775          put_free(pb);                 /* yes - free block */
776          ret = del_level(lvl+1, pb);   /* del entry for empty blk */
777          copy_current(lvl+1, &temp_entr); /* get new cur. blk ptr */
778          /* reset pos. for lower levels */
779          first_ix(lvl,temp_entr.lower_lvl, pb);
780          return(ret);
781        }
782        /* last entry in block deleted ? */
783        if ( pci->pos[lvl].coffset >= pb->blk_offset) {
784          /* yes - correct upper index */
785          fix_last(lvl, pb->blk_pos, ENT_ADDR(pb, last_entry(pb)));
786        }
787
788        if (pb->blk_offset < comb_size)  /* less than half full ? */
789          ret = compress(lvl, pb);      /* yes - combine with neighb. */
790        else update_block(pb);
791        /* retrieve the  block again */
792        retrieve_block(lvl, pci->pos[lvl].cblock, pb, CUR);
793        /* is position past end of block ? */
794        if ( pci->pos[lvl].coffset >= pb->blk_offset)
795          first_ix(lvl, next_ix(lvl+1, pb),pb); /* move to next blk */
796
797        return(ret);
798      } /* del_level */
799    /* ------------------------------------------------------------ */
800    int compress(lvl, pblk) /* combine a block with the neighbor */
801          int lvl;
802          struct block *pblk;    /* block to be combined */
803    {
804        struct block *pt = NULL;
805
806        if ((lvl+1) == pci->dx.nl) { /* is this the root level ? */
807          update_block(pblk);         /* yes - update the block */
808          return(IX_OK);              /* and return */
809        }
```

```
810
811     pt = neighbor(lvl, LEFTN);    /* get left neighbor block */
812     if ((pt != NULL) && (pt->blk_offset + pblk->blk_offset
813                                       <= IXBLK_SPACE)) {
814       combine(pt, pblk);       /* combine blocks */
815       update_block(pblk);      /* update the right block */
816       put_free(pt);            /* free the left index block */
817       /* cblock(lvl) is OK as is, adjust cur. position */
818       pci->pos[lvl].coffset += pblk->blk_offset;
819       last_ix(lvl+1, pblk);    /* point higher level to left blk*/
820       del_level(lvl+1, pblk);  /* delete ptr. to left blk. */
821       return(IX_OK);
822     }
823
824     /* get right neighbor block */
825     pt = neighbor(lvl, RIGHTN);
826     if ((pt != NULL) && (pt->blk_offset + pblk->blk_offset
827                                       <= IXBLK_SPACE)) {
828       combine(pt, pblk);       /* combine blocks */
829       update_block(pt);        /* update the right block */
830                                /* right blk is cur. one now */
831       pci->pos[lvl].cblock = pblk->blk_pos;
832                                /* coffset(lvl) is ok as is */
833       put_free(pblk);          /* free the left index block */
834       del_level(lvl+1, pblk);  /* delete ptr. to left blk. */
835       return(IX_OK);
836     }
837
838     /* can't combine - just update block */
839     update_block(pblk);
840     return(IX_OK);
841   } /* compress */
842   /* ------------------------------------------------------------ */
843   int fix_last(lvl, r, pe)/* fix higher level index */
844       int lvl;             /* level we're now on */
845       RECPOS r;            /* lower_lvl for higher level entry */
846       struct entry *pe;    /* entry with new key */
847   {
848     struct entry temp_entr; /* last entry in blk deleted/replaced */
849
850     /* update the higher level index */
851     copy_entry(&temp_entr, pe); /* copy key */
852     temp_entr.lower_lvl = r;    /* put in the record pointer */
853     return(replace_entry(lvl+1, &temp_entr)); /* repl. entry */
854   } /* fix_last */
855
856   int replace_entry(lvl, pe)    /* replace current index entry */
857       int lvl;                  /* at this index level */
858       struct entry *pe;         /* new entry */
859   {
860     struct block blk;
861     int ret;
862     /* retrieve the index block */
863     retrieve_block(lvl, pci->pos[lvl].cblock, &blk, CUR);
864     /* is this the last entry ? */
865     if ( pci->pos[lvl].coffset == last_entry(&blk))
866       fix_last(lvl, pci->pos[lvl].cblock, pe); /* fix higher level */
867
868     del_entry(&blk, pci->pos[lvl].coffset); /* rem cur. entry */
869     /* make room to insert new entry */
870     if ((blk.blk_offset + (*(pci->psize)) (pe)) <= split_size) {
```

```
871            ins_entry(&blk, pe, pci->pos[lvl].coffset); /* ins in blk */
872            update_block(&blk);           /* and update the block */
873            ret = IX_OK;
874          }
875          else ret = split(lvl, pe, &blk); /* split the block */
876
877          return(ret);
878
879      } /* replace_entry */
880      /* ------------------------------------------------------------ */
881      struct block *neighbor(lvl, direction)
882            int lvl;                /* level to fetch neighbor on */
883            int direction;          /* left or right neighbor */
884      {
885        RECPOS rnext;
886        int off;
887        struct block *pb;
888
889        pb = &spare_block;
890        lvl++;                /* look in higher level index */
891        retrieve_block(lvl, pci->pos[lvl].cblock, pb, CUR);
892        /* get the offset on next/prev. entry */
893        if (direction == RIGHTN)          /* offset of next entr. */
894          off = next_entry(pb, pci->pos[lvl].coffset);
895        else /* get offset of previous entry */
896          off = prev_entry(pb, pci->pos[lvl].coffset);
897
898        /* at end or beginning ? */
899        if (off < 0)
900          return(NULL);
901        rnext = ENT_ADDR(pb, off)->lower_lvl; /* neighbor's blk no. */
902        /* read it into memory */
903        retrieve_block(lvl-1, rnext, pb, NOT_CUR);
904        return(pb);                 /* return its address */
905      } /* neighbor */
906      /* ------------------------------------------------------------ */
907      int copy_current(lvl, pe)       /* copy current index entry */
908            int lvl;                /* at this level */
909            struct entry *pe;       /* to this address */
910      {
911        struct block *pb;
912
913        pb = &spare_block;           /* get current block */
914        retrieve_block(lvl, pci->pos[lvl].cblock, pb, CUR);
915        /* copy current entry */
916        copy_entry(pe, ENT_ADDR(pb, pci->pos[lvl].coffset));
917        return(IX_OK);
918      } /* copy_current */
919      /* ------------------------------------------------------------ */
920      int find_exact(pe, pix)
921            struct entry *pe;       /* put the entry here */
922            struct ix_header *pix;  /* points to an index descriptor */
923      {
924        int ret;
925        struct entry e;
926
927        pci = pix;
928        copy_entry(&e, pe);          /* make copy for find call */
929        ret = find_ix(&e, pix);      /* get 1st entry matching key */
930
931        /* in case that composite keys match add no new entry */
```

```
932        if (ret == 0 && strncmp(e.key, "P2*", 3) == EQUAL)
933          return(FOUND);
934
935        while (ret == 0) {            /* until keys don't match */
936          if (e.lower_lvl == pe->lower_lvl || err_sig) {
937             err_sig = FALSE;          /* reset flag */
938             return(FOUND);            /* return it if they match */
939          }
940
941          if (get_next(&e, pix) == EOF_IX) /* get next entry */
942             return(NOTFOUND);         /* at end of index - not found */
943
944          ret = FUNCALL(pci->pcomp) (&e, pe); /* compare keys */
945        }
946
947        return(ret);                   /* not FOUND - non-zero code */
948      } /* find_exact */
949      /* ------------------------------------------------------------ */
950      int find_ins(pe, pix)             /* find pos., insert an entry */
951           struct entry *pe;            /* the entry */
952           struct ix_header *pix;       /* points to an index descriptor */
953      {                                 /* returns IX_FAIL if entry present */
954        insert = TRUE;
955        if (find_exact(pe, pix) == FOUND)   /* look for the entry */
956          return(IX_FAIL);                  /* already there - failure */
957
958        return(insert_ix(pe, pix));    /* do the insertion */
959      } /* find_ins */
960      /* ------------------------------------------------------------ */
961      int find_del(pe, pix)            /* find pos., insert an entry */
962           struct entry *pe;           /* the entry */
963           struct ix_header *pix;      /* points to an index descriptor */
964      {                                /* returns IX_FAIL if entry not present */
965
966        if (find_exact(pe, pix) != FOUND) /* look for the entry */
967          return(IX_FAIL);                /* not there - failure */
968
969        /* find_exact has set the cur. position */
970        return(delete_ix(pix));           /* del the current entry */
971
972      } /* find_del */
973
974      int compf(p1, p2)
975           struct entry *p1, *p2;
976      {
977        return(strcomp(p1->key, p2->key));
978      }
979
980      int sizef(p1)
981           struct entry *p1;
982      {
983        return(strlen(p1->key)+sizeof(RECPOS)+1);
984      }
985      /* ------------------------------------------------------------ */
986      strcomp(s, t)
987           char *s, *t;
988      {
989        *t =(*t)&127;
990        for (; *s == *t; s++, t++)
991          if (*s == '\0')
992             return(0);
```

```
993        return(*s-*t);
994    }
```

file: err.c

```
1      /* REQUIEM - error messages */
2
3      #include <signal.h>
4      #include "requ.h"
5      extern char lexeme[];
6      extern char *rmalloc();
7      extern char errvar[];
8      int error_code;              /* global error code variable */
9
10     char *error_text(msg)        /* error text declarations */
11          int msg;
12     {
13       char *txt;
14       char s[40];
15
16       switch (msg) {
17
18       case AGGRPARAM:
19         txt = "wrong aggregate parameter type";
20         break;
21       case ATAMBG:
22         txt = "ambiguous attribute name";
23         break;
24       case ATUNDF:
25         sprintf(s, " undefined attribute #%s#", errvar);
26         txt = rmalloc(sizeof(s));
27         strcpy(txt, s);
28         break;
29       case BADCURS:
30         txt = "cursor mispositioned, reset to origin";
31         break;
32       case BADHDR:
33         txt = "bad relation header";
34         break;
35       case BADSET:
36         txt = "bad set parameter";
37         break;
38       case CDSIZE:
39         txt = "boolean expression too complex";
40         break;
41       case DUPATT:
42         sprintf(s, " duplicate attribute #%s#", lexeme);
43         txt = rmalloc(sizeof(s));
44         strcpy(txt, s);
45         break;
46       case DUPTUP:
47         txt = "wrong insertion operation primary key already exists";
48         break;
49       case FILEMV:
50         txt = "error in moving files";
51         break;
52       case HASHSIZ:
53         txt = "hash table size exceeded";
54         break;
55       case ILLREL:
```

```
56        txt = "illegal relation name start: 'sys'";
57        break;
58     case INCNST:
59        txt = "input entry holds inconsistent information";
60        break;
61     case INDFNF:
62        txt = "indirect command file not found";
63        break;
64     case INDXCRE:
65        txt= "error creating index file";
66        break;
67     case INPFNF:
68        txt = "input file not found";
69        break;
70     case INSBLK:
71        txt = "insufficient disk space";
72        break;
73     case INSMEM:
74        txt = "insufficient memory";
75        break;
76     case IXATRNF:
77        txt = "indexed attribute not found";
78        break;
79     case IXDELFAIL:
80        txt = "index delete failed";
81        break;
82     case IXFAIL:
83        txt = "indexing failed";
84        break;
85     case IXFLNF:
86        txt = "index file not found";
87        break;
88     case KEYEXCD:
89        sprintf(s, " size of key attribute #%s# exceeded", errvar);
90        txt = rmalloc(sizeof(s));
91        strcpy(txt, s);
92        break;
93     case LINELONG:
94        txt = "length of command/viewline line exceeded";
95        break;
96     case LINK:
97        txt = "error in renaming file";
98        break;
99     case MAXATT:
100       txt = "too many attributes in relation create";
101       break;
102    case MAX5:
103       txt = "no more than 5 attributes are allowed in expose";
104       break;
105    case NESTED:
106       txt = "wrong nested command syntax";
107       break;
108    case NJOIN:
109       txt = "join operation failed";
110       break;
111    case NOALIAS:
112       txt = " no aliases allowed  in group clause ";
113       break;
114    case NOEXSTUP:
115       txt = "wrong deletion operation tuple does not exist";
116       break;
```

```
117        case NOKEY:
118          txt= "at least one primary key attribute must be specified";
119          break;
120        case OUTCRE:
121          txt = "error creating output file";
122          break;
123        case QUATTR:
124          txt = "qualified attribute is required";
125          break;
126        case RELCRE:
127          txt = "error creating relation file";
128          break;
129        case RELFNF:
130          if ((strncmp(errvar,"snapshot", 8) == EQUAL))
131            txt = "no intermediate results have been derived !";
132          else {
133            sprintf(s, " relation file #%s# not found", errvar);
134            txt = rmalloc(sizeof(s));
135            strcpy(txt, s);
136          }
137          break;
138        case RELFUL:
139          txt = "relation file full";
140          break;
141        case RLUNDF:
142          sprintf(s, " undefined relation #%s#", lexeme);
143          txt = rmalloc(sizeof(s));
144          strcpy(txt, s);
145          break;
146        case STACKOVRFL:
147          txt = "stack overflow";
148          break;
149        case STACKUNDFL:
150          txt = "stack underflow";
151          break;
152        case SYNTAX:
153          sprintf(s, "syntax error at or near %s", lexeme);
154          txt = rmalloc(sizeof(s));
155          strcpy(txt, s);
156          break;
157        case TOOMANY:
158          txt = "you may specify 2 indexed attributes of a kind at most";
159          break;
160        case TUPINP:
161          txt= "tuple input error: possibly over clause is forgotten!";
162          break;
163        case TUPOUT:
164          txt = "tuple output error";
165          break;
166        case UNATTR:
167          txt= "inapplicable  attribute name encountered";
168          break;
169        case UNDEFTYPE:
170          txt = "undefined attribute type encountered";
171          break;
172        case UNDEFVAR:
173          txt = "undefined variable encountered";
174          break;
175        case UNIQEXCD:
176          txt =  "no. of unique keys exceeded";
177          break;
```

```
178      case UNLINK:
179        txt = "error in purging file";
180        break;
181      case UNOP:
182        txt = "no union-intersect operation is allowed";
183        break;
184      case UPDTERR:
185        txt = "error in  updating indexed atributes";
186        break;
187      case VIEWDEF:
188        txt = "unacceptable view name specifier in view definition";
189        break;
190      case VIEWDEL:
191        txt = "unacceptable view name specifier in view deletion";
192        break;
193      case WRIXCOM:
194        txt = "error in compilation of indexed attributes";
195        break;
196      case WRLEN:
197        txt = "max length of name should not exceed 10 chars";
198        break;
199      case WRONGID:
200        txt = "operation meaningless, operand mismatch encountered!";
201        break;
202      case WRNGCOMB:
203        txt = "wrong foreign key combination, primary already exists";
204        break;
205      case WRNGFGNKEY:
206        txt = "wrong foreign key declaration";
207        break;
208      case  WRNGINS:
209        txt =  "wrong insertion operation";
210        break;
211      case WRNRELREM:
212        txt = " non-existent relation-file";
213        break;
214      case WRPREDID:
215        txt = "wrong identifier in predicate expression";
216        break;
217      default:
218        txt = "undefined error";
219        break;
220      }
221      /* return the message text */
222      return (txt);
223    } /* error_text */
224
225    char *pt_error(errcode) /* store error code and return NULL */
226         int errcode;
227    {
228      error_code = errcode;
229      return (NULL);
230    }/* pt_error */
231
232    int error(errcode)   /* store the error code and return FALSE */
233         int errcode;
234    {
235      error_code = errcode;
236      return (FALSE);
237    } /* error */
238    /* ------------------------------------------------------------ */
```

```
239    int fpecatch()  /* catch floating point exceptions */
240    {
241      signal(SIGFPE, fpecatch);
242      printf("*** CATASTROPHIC-ERROR: overflow, ");
243      printf("please check length of operators ! \n");
244    } /* fpecatch */
```

file: *hash.c*

```
1     #include <stdio.h>
2     #include "requ.h"
3
4     extern float lex_value;
5     struct hash **Hash_Table;
6     int  HTIndex;
7
8     int init_hash()
9     {
10      Hash_Table = (struct hash **)CALLOC(HTSIZE, struct hash);
11    } /* init_hash */
12
13    BOOL db_hash(word, rel_name, aggr_par)
14        char *word, *rel_name;
15        double aggr_par;
16    {
17      return (insert_token(word, rel_name, aggr_par));
18    } /* db_hash */
19
20    BOOL insert_token(word, rel_name, aggr_par)
21        char  *word, *rel_name;
22        double aggr_par;
23    {  /* insert_token */
24      char *copy();
25
26
27      HTIndex = hash(word);
28      if (HTIndex == -1)
29       return (error(HASHSIZ));
30
31      if (Hash_Table[HTIndex] == NULL) {
32        if ((Hash_Table[HTIndex] =
33            (struct hash *) CALLOC(1, struct hash)) == NULL)
34          return(error(INSMEM));
35
36        Hash_Table[HTIndex]->value = copy(word, strlen(word));
37        Hash_Table[HTIndex]->dup_tcnt = 1;
38        Hash_Table[HTIndex]->relation = copy(rel_name, RNSIZE-1);
39        Hash_Table[HTIndex]->aggr_param = aggr_par;
40      } else {
41        Hash_Table[HTIndex]->dup_tcnt++;
42        return(TRUE);
43      }
44      return(FALSE);
45    } /* insert_token */
46    /* ------------------------------------------------------------- */
47    int hash(word)
48         char  *word;
49    {  /* hash */
50      int  HTIndex;
51      int  id_len;
```

```
52       int  Init_HTIndex;
53       int  probe_cntr = 0;
54
55       id_len = strlen(word);
56       if (id_len == 0)
57         fprintf(stderr,"Hash: Word of no length \n");
58       HTIndex = Init_HTIndex = transform_id(word);
59
60       if (Hash_Table[HTIndex] == (struct hash *) NULL)
61         ; /* we've got it */
62       else if/* have we found the correct index ? */
63         (strncmp(word, Hash_Table[HTIndex]->value, id_len) == EQUAL)
64         ; /* done a direct hit */
65       else /* a collision generate new indices */
66         for (probe_cntr = 0; probe_cntr < (HTSIZE / 2);
67              probe_cntr++) {
68           HTIndex = generate_new_indx(Init_HTIndex,
69                                       probe_cntr) ;
70           if (Hash_Table[HTIndex]->value == NULL)
71             break; /* we've got it */
72           else if (strncmp(word, Hash_Table[HTIndex]->value, id_len)
73                    == EQUAL)
74             break;    /* we've got it */
75         }
76       if (probe_cntr >= (HTSIZE/ 2))
77         return(-1);
78       return(HTIndex);
79     } /* Hash */
80  /* ------------------------------------------------------------ */
81  int generate_new_indx(orig_key, probe_no)
82       int orig_key;
83       int probe_no;
84  { /* generate_new_index */
85    return((orig_key + probe_no * probe_no) % HTSIZE);
86  } /* generate_new_indx */
87  /* ------------------------------------------------------------ */
88  int transform_id(word)
89       char word[];
90  {   /* transform_id */
91    int   term;
92    int   word_index;
93
94    term = 0;
95    for (word_index = strlen(word) - 1; word_index > -1;
96         word_index--)
97      term = (257*term) + word[word_index];
98    term = ( term < 0) ? -term : term;
99    return(term % HTSIZE);
100 } /* transform_id */
101 /* ------------------------------------------------------------ */
102 VOID hash_done()
103 {
104   register int i;
105
106   for (i = 0; i < HTSIZE; i++){
107     if (Hash_Table[i] != NULL) {
108       nfree(Hash_Table[i]->value);
109       nfree((char *) Hash_Table[i]->relation);
110       nfree((char *) Hash_Table[i]);
111     }
112   }
```

```
113        nfree((char *) Hash_Table);
114        Hash_Table = NULL;
115      }
116
117      int db_hsplace(buf, name, in_buf, rptr)
118           char *buf, *in_buf, *name;
119           struct relation *rptr;
120      {
121        unsigned cnt = 0;
122
123        if (!(db_hash(buf, name, (double) 0))){
124          cnt++;
125          if (!write_tuple(rptr, in_buf, TRUE)) {
126            rc_done(rptr, TRUE);
127            free(in_buf);
128            hash_done();
129            return (error(INSBLK));
130          }
131        }
132        return (cnt);
133      } /* db_hsplace */
134      /* ------------------------------------------------------------ */
135      int db_hplace(buf, name, in_buf, rptr)
136           char *buf, *in_buf, *name;
137           struct relation *rptr;
138      {
139        unsigned cnt = 0;
140
141        if (db_hash(buf, name, (double) 0)){
142          cnt++;
143          if (write(rptr->rl_fd, in_buf, RELATION_HEADER.hd_size) !=
144              RELATION_HEADER.hd_size) {
145            rc_done(rptr, TRUE);
146            free(in_buf);
147            hash_done();
148            return (error(INSBLK));
149          }
150          RELATION_HEADER.hd_tcnt++;
151        }
152        return (cnt);
153      } /* db_hsplace */
154      /* ------------------------------------------------------------ */
155      sort_table(sort_no)
156           int sort_no;
157      { /* sort_table */
158        struct hash  *exchange;
159        int          base_tcnt;
160        int          cur_tcnt;
161        int          cur_gap_tcnt;
162        int          gap;
163        int          last_in_buff;
164
165        last_in_buff = sort_no;
166        for (gap = last_in_buff / 2; gap > 0; gap /= 2)
167          for (base_tcnt = gap; base_tcnt < last_in_buff; base_tcnt++)
168            for (cur_tcnt = base_tcnt - gap ; cur_tcnt >= 0;
169                 cur_tcnt -= gap) {
170              cur_gap_tcnt = cur_tcnt + gap;
171              if (name_cmp(cur_tcnt, cur_gap_tcnt,Hash_Table) < EQUAL)
172                break;
173              /* otherwise exchange the elements */
```

```
174              exchange = Hash_Table[cur_tcnt];
175              Hash_Table[cur_tcnt] = Hash_Table[cur_gap_tcnt];
176              Hash_Table[cur_gap_tcnt] = exchange;
177           } /* end for */
178     }  /* sort_buffer */
179     /* ------------------------------------------------------------ */
180     int name_cmp(first, second, Hash_Table)
181          int    first;
182          int    second;
183          struct hash *Hash_Table[];
184     {    /* name_cmp */
185       /* if first entry has no value the first is less */
186       if (Hash_Table[first] == (struct hash *) NULL)
187         return(FIRSTLSS);
188
189       /* if second has no value then first is gtr */
190       if (Hash_Table[second] == (struct hash *) NULL)
191         return(FIRSTGTR);
192
193       /* otherwise return the comparison from strcmp */
194       return(strcmp(Hash_Table[first]->value,
195                  Hash_Table[second]->value));
196     }  /* name_cmp */
197     /* ------------------------------------------------------------ */
198     int write_hash(buffer_len, rptr, tkn, tbuf, auxbuf)
199          int buffer_len, tkn;
200          struct relation *rptr;
201          char *tbuf, *auxbuf;
202     {
203       register int tcntr;
204       char format[10];
205       int aggr_len, cnt = 0;
206
207       aggr_len = RELATION_HEADER.hd_attrs[1].at_size;
208
209       /* sort table entries first  */
210       sort_table(HTSIZE);
211
212       for (tcntr = 0; tcntr < HTSIZE; tcntr++) {
213         if (Hash_Table[tcntr] && Hash_Table[tcntr]->value) {
214           if (tkn == FALSE ||
215               eval_tkn(tkn, Hash_Table[tcntr]->aggr_param)) {
216             strncpy(tbuf+1, Hash_Table[tcntr]->value, buffer_len);
217
218             /* leave two places after decimal point */
219             sprintf(format, "%%%d.21f", aggr_len-3);
220
221             /* write the result of the function called in query */
222             sprintf(auxbuf, format, Hash_Table[tcntr]->aggr_param);
223
224             /* catenate second buffer after first entry */
225             sprintf(tbuf+buffer_len+1+(aggr_len-strlen(auxbuf)),
226                                          "%s", auxbuf);
227
228             if (write(rptr->rl_fd, tbuf, RELATION_HEADER.hd_size) !=
229                           RELATION_HEADER.hd_size) {
230               rc_done(rptr, TRUE);
231               hash_done();
232               return (error(INSBLK));
233             }
234
```

```
235              cnt++;
236              RELATION_HEADER.hd_tcnt++;
237              RELATION_HEADER.hd_tmax++;
238          }
239       }
240    }
241    return(cnt);
242  } /* write_hash */
243  /* ----------------------------------------------------------- */
244  int eval_tkn(tkn, qua)
245       int tkn;
246       double qua;
247  {
248    int comp_res;
249
250    comp_res = dcomp(qua, lex_value);
251
252    switch (tkn) {
253    case LSS:
254      comp_res = (comp_res < 0);
255      break;
256    case LEQ:
257      comp_res = (comp_res <= 0);
258      break;
259    case EQL:
260      comp_res = (comp_res == 0);
261      break;
262    case GEQ:
263      comp_res = (comp_res >= 0);
264      break;
265    case GTR:
266      comp_res = (comp_res > 0);
267      break;
268    case NEQ:
269      comp_res = (comp_res != 0);
270      break;
271    }
272    return(comp_res);
273  } /* eval_tkn */
274  /* ----------------------------------------------------------- */
275  dcomp(arg1, arg2)
276       double arg1, arg2;
277  {
278    return((arg1 == arg2) ? EQUAL :
279          ((arg1 < arg2) ? FIRSTLSS : FIRSTGTR));
280  } /* dcomp */
281  /* ----------------------------------------------------------- */
282  hash_data(tmprel_ptr, rptr, slptr, buf, cntr)
283       struct relation *rptr,     /* old rel pointer */
284          *tmprel_ptr;            /* temp rel pointer */
285       struct sel *slptr;
286       char    *buf;
287       int     *cntr;
288  {
289    int    i, abase;
290    struct sattr *saptr;
291    char   *strip_catenate(), *aux_buf;
292
293    /* allocate and initialize an auxiliary  tuple buffer */
294    if ((aux_buf =
295      calloc(1, (unsigned) RELATION_HEADER.hd_size + 1)) == NULL) {
```

```
296          rc_done(rptr, TRUE);
297          return (error(INSMEM));
298        }
299
300        /* create the tuple from the selected attributes */
301        abase = 1;
302        buf[0] = ACTIVE; /* initialize indexes */
303        for (saptr = SEL_ATTRS;saptr != NULL;saptr = saptr->sa_next) {
304          for (i = 0; i < saptr->sa_attr->at_size; i++)
305            buf[abase + i] = saptr->sa_aptr[i];
306
307          /* reset */
308          abase += i;
309        }
310
311        strip_catenate(aux_buf, buf, RELATION_HEADER.hd_size);
312
313        /* eliminate redundant (duplicate) tuples if necessary
314         * and write rest tuples into relation file */
315        (*cntr) +=
316          db_hsplace(aux_buf, tmprel_ptr->rl_name, buf, tmprel_ptr);
317        nfree(aux_buf);
318        return(TRUE);
319
320      } /* hash_data */
```

file: iex.c

```
1        /* REQUIEM - import/export command routines */
2
3        #include <stdio.h>
4        #include "requ.h"
5
6        extern int lex_token;
7        extern char lexeme[];
8
9        int db_import(fmt)
10            char *fmt;
11       {
12         struct scan *db_ropen();
13         struct scan *sptr;
14         struct attribute *aptr;
15         char fname[STRINGMAX+1],avalue[STRINGMAX+1], start_value[STRINGMAX+1];
16         char **key_buf = NULL;
17         int tcnt,astart,i,eofile;
18         int p_cntr = 0, s_cntr = 2;
19         FILE *fp;
20         int error();
21
22         /* check for a command line */
23         if (fmt != NULL)
24           q_scan(fmt);
25
26         /* checks for "<filename> into <relation-name>" */
27         if (next_token() == ID)
28           strcat(lexeme,".dat");
29         else if (lex_token != STRING)
30           return (error(SYNTAX));
31         strcpy(fname,lexeme);
32         if (next_token() != INTO)
```

```
33          return (error(SYNTAX));
34      if (next_token() != ID)
35          return (error(SYNTAX));
36
37      /* open the relation */
38      if ((sptr = db_ropen(lexeme)) == NULL)
39          return (FALSE);
40
41      /* open the input file */
42      if ((fp = fopen(fname,"r")) == NULL)
43          return (error(INPFNF));
44
45      /* import tuples */
46      eofile = FALSE;
47      for (tcnt = 0; ; tcnt++) {
48
49          /* get attribute values */
50          astart = 1;
51          for (i = 0; i < NATTRS; i++) {
52
53              /* get a pointer to the current attribute */
54              aptr = &SCAN_HEADER.hd_attrs[i];
55
56              /* check for the last attribute */
57              if (aptr->at_name[0] == 0)
58                  break;
59
60              /* input the tuple */
61              if (fgets(avalue,STRINGMAX,fp) == 0) {
62                  eofile = TRUE;
63                  break;
64              }
65              avalue[strlen(avalue)-1] = EOS;
66
67              /* store the attribute value */
68              store_attr(aptr,&SCAN_TUPLE[astart],avalue);
69
70              /* update the attribute start */
71              astart += aptr->at_size;
72
73              /* remove trailing blanks */
74              rm_lead_blks(avalue, start_value);
75
76              /* check if indexing is required */
77              if (aptr->at_key != 'n')
78                  check_ix(&key_buf, aptr, &p_cntr, &s_cntr, start_value);
79          }
80
81          p_cntr = 0; s_cntr =2;
82
83          /* store the new tuple */
84          if (!eofile) {
85              if (!store_tuple(sptr, key_buf)) {
86                  buf_free(key_buf, 4);
87                  db_rclose(sptr);
88                  return (FALSE);
89              }
90          }
91          else
92              break;
93      }
```

```
94
95        /* close the relation */
96        db_rclose(sptr);
97
98        /* close the input file */
99        fclose(fp);
100
101       /* check number of tuples imported */
102       if (tcnt != 0) {
103
104         /* print tuple count */
105         printf("[ %d imported ]\n",tcnt);
106       }
107       else
108         printf("[ none imported ]\n");
109
110       /* return successfully */
111       return (TRUE);
112     } /* db_import */
113     /* ------------------------------------------------------------- */
114     int db_export(fmt)
115         char *fmt;
116     {
117       struct scan *db_ropen();
118
119       struct scan *sptr;
120       struct attribute *aptr;
121       char rname[STRINGMAX+1],avalue[STRINGMAX+1];
122       int tcnt,astart,i;
123       FILE *fp;
124       int error();
125
126       /* check for a command line */
127       if (fmt != NULL)
128         q_scan(fmt);
129
130       /* checks for "<relation-name> [ into <filename> ]" */
131       if (next_token() != ID)
132         return (error(SYNTAX));
133       strcpy(rname,lexeme);
134       if (!redirect_to(&fp,".dat"))
135         return (FALSE);
136
137       /* open the relation */
138       if ((sptr = db_ropen(rname)) == NULL)
139         return (FALSE);
140
141       /* export tuples */
142       for (tcnt = 0; fetch_tuple(sptr); tcnt++) {
143
144         /* get attribute values */
145         astart = 1;
146         for (i = 0; i < NATTRS; i++) {
147
148           /* get a pointer to the current attribute */
149           aptr = &SCAN_HEADER.hd_attrs[i];
150
151           /* check for the last attribute */
152           if (aptr->at_name[0] == 0)
153             break;
154
```

```
155          /* get the attribute value */
156          get_attr(aptr, &SCAN_TUPLE[astart], avalue);
157
158          /* output the tuple */
159          fprintf(fp,"%s\n",avalue);
160
161          /* update the attribute start */
162          astart += aptr->at_size;
163       }
164    }
165
166    /* close the relation */
167    db_rclose(sptr);
168
169    /* close the output file */
170    if (fp != stdout)
171      fclose(fp);
172
173    /* check number of tuples exported */
174    if (tcnt != 0) {
175
176       /* print tuple count */
177       printf("[ %d exported ]\n",tcnt);
178    }
179    else
180       printf("[ none exported ]\n");
181
182    /* return successfully */
183    return (TRUE);
184  } /* db_export */
185  /* ---------------------------------------------------------- */
186  int db_extract(fmt)
187       char *fmt;
188  {
189    struct scan *db_ropen();
190    struct scan *sptr;
191    struct attribute *aptr;
192    char rname[RNSIZE+1],aname[ANSIZE+1],*atype;
193    char  buff[TABLEMAX+1];
194    char **prim_buf = NULL;
195    char **sec_buf = NULL;
196    int i, p_cntr = 0, s_cntr = 0;
197    FILE *fp;
198    int error();
199    char *unfold();
200
201    /* check for a command line */
202    if (fmt != NULL)
203      q_scan(fmt);
204
205    /* checks for "<relation-name> [ into <filename> ]" */
206    if (next_token() != ID)
207      return (error(SYNTAX));
208    strcpy(rname,lexeme);
209    /* check for file name provided by user or return stdout */
210    if (!redirect_to(&fp,".def"))
211      return (FALSE);
212
213    /* open the relation */
214    if ((sptr = db_ropen(rname)) == NULL)
215      return (FALSE);
```

```
216
217        /* output the relation definition */
218        printf("\n");
219        strcpy(rname, unfold(rname));
220        templ_line(fp, TRUE);
221        sprintf(buff,"Relation name:%12s ",rname);
222        template(buff, fp);
223        templ_line(fp, TRUE);
224        sprintf(buff,"Attribute names:");
225        template(buff, fp);
226
227        /* get attribute values */
228        for (i = 0; i < NATTRS; i++) {
229
230           /* get a pointer to the current attribute */
231           aptr = &SCAN_HEADER.hd_attrs[i];
232
233           /* check for the last attribute */
234           if (aptr->at_name[0] == EOS)
235             break;
236
237           /* save the attribute name */
238           strncpy(aname,aptr->at_name,
239                   MIN(strlen(aptr->at_name), ANSIZE));
240           aname[MIN(strlen(aptr->at_name), ANSIZE)] = EOS;
241
242           /* determine the attribute type */
243           switch (aptr->at_type) {
244           case TCHAR:
245             atype = "char";
246             break;
247           case TNUM:
248             atype = "num";
249             break;
250           case TREAL:
251             atype = "real";
252             break;
253           default:
254             atype = "<error>";
255             break;
256           }
257
258           strcpy(aname, unfold(aname));
259           templ_line(fp, TRUE);
260
261           /* check for primary key */
262           if (aptr->at_key == 'p' && p_cntr < 4) {
263
264              /* create a key buffer */
265              if (prim_buf == NULL) {
266                if ((prim_buf =
267                    (char **)calloc(4, sizeof(char *))) == NULL)
268                  return (error(INSMEM));
269              }
270              prim_buf[p_cntr] = rmalloc((int) aptr->at_size + 1);
271              strcpy(prim_buf[p_cntr++], aname);
272           }
273
274           /* check for secondary key */
275           if (aptr->at_key == 's' && s_cntr < 4) {
276
```

```
277          /* create a key buffer */
278          if (sec_buf == NULL) {
279            if ((sec_buf =
280                  (char **)calloc(4, sizeof(char *))) == NULL)
281              return (error(INSMEM));
282          }
283          sec_buf[s_cntr] = rmalloc((int) aptr->at_size + 1);
284          strcpy(sec_buf[s_cntr++], aname);
285        }
286
287        /* output the attribute definition */
288        sprintf(buff,"   %s   of type %s  and size  %d",
289                                      aname, atype, aptr->at_size);
290        template(buff, fp);
291      }
292
293      templ_line(fp, TRUE);
294
295      /* print out primary and secondary keys */
296      tab_keys(p_cntr, buff, prim_buf);
297
298      if (i == 1)
299        template("Primary key: ", fp);
300      else if (i > 1)
301        template("Combination of foreign keys: ", fp);
302
303      template(buff, fp);
304      templ_line(fp, TRUE);
305
306      if (sec_buf)
307        tab_keys(s_cntr, buff, sec_buf);
308
309      template("Secondary keys: ", fp);
310
311      if (sec_buf)
312        template(buff, fp);
313      else {
314        buff[0] = EOS;
315        template(buff, fp);
316      }
317
318      templ_line(fp, TRUE);
319
320      sprintf(buff,"No. of tuples currently filled:   %d",
321                                      SCAN_HEADER.hd_tcnt);
322      template(buff, fp);
323      sprintf(buff,"Size of tuple in bytes   %d",
324                                      (SCAN_HEADER.hd_size)-1);
325      template(buff, fp);
326
327      /* force the printing of a blank line */
328      *buff = EOS;
329      template(buff, fp);
330      templ_line(fp, FALSE);
331      printf("\n");
332
333      /* close the relation, free buffers */
334      db_rclose(sptr);
335      buf_free(prim_buf, 4);
336      buf_free(sec_buf, 4);
337
```

```
338        /* close the output file */
339        if (fp != stdout)
340          fclose(fp);
341
342        /* return successfully */
343        return (TRUE);
344      } /* db_extract */
345   /* ------------------------------------------------------------ */
346    int     redirect_to(pfp, ext)
347          FILE **pfp;
348          char     *ext;
349    {
350      /* assume no into clause */
351      *pfp = stdout; /* output redirected to stdout */
352
353      /* check for "into <fname>" */
354      if (this_token() != INTO)
355        return (TRUE);
356      next_token();
357      if (next_token() == ID)
358        strcat(lexeme, ext);
359      else if (lex_token != STRING)
360        return (error(SYNTAX));
361
362      /* open the output file */
363      *pfp = fopen(lexeme, "w");
364      if (*pfp == NULL)
365        return (error(OUTCRE));
366
367      /* return successfully */
368      return (TRUE);
369
370    } /* db_to */
371   /* ------------------------------------------------------------ */
372    int     using(pfp, ext)
373          FILE **pfp;
374          char     *ext;
375    {
376      /* assume no using clause */
377      *pfp = NULL;
378
379      if (next_token() == ID)
380        strcat(lexeme, ext);
381      else if (lex_token != STRING)
382        return (error(SYNTAX));
383
384      /* open the input file */
385      if ((*pfp = fopen(lexeme, "r")) == NULL)
386        return (error(INPFNF));
387
388      /* return successfully */
389      return (TRUE);
390    } /* using */
```

file: impl.c

```
1    /* REQUIEM - command implementor */
2
3    #include <stdio.h>
4    #include "requ.h"
```

```
5
6      extern int      lex_token;
7      extern int      sref_cntr;
8      extern char     lexeme[];
9      extern char     cformat[];
10     extern char     rel_fl[];
11     extern char     *join_on;
12     extern char     *lptr;
13     extern struct ix_header *pci;
14     char            *stck();
15     struct  trans_file *trans_hd = NULL;
16     char    **key_buf = NULL; /* indexed attributes to be inserted */
17     char    **del_buf = NULL; /* indexed attributes to be deleted */
18
19     int help()
20     {
21       FILE          *fp;
22       int           ch;
23
24       if ((fp = fopen("requ.hlp", "r")) != NULL) {
25         while ((ch = getc(fp)) != EOF)
26           putchar(ch);
27         fclose(fp);
28       } else
29         printf("No online help available.  Read the manual\n");
30
31       /* return successfully */
32       return (TRUE);
33
34     } /* help */
35     /* ------------------------------------------------------------ */
36     int db_modify()
37     {
38       struct scan    *db_ropen();
39       struct scan    *sptr;
40       struct attribute *aptr;
41       char           a_size[ASIZE + 1];
42       char           prompt[30];
43       char           *buf_name;
44       struct attribute *new_attrs[NATTRS];
45       int            i;
46       BOOL           change = TRUE;
47       char *unfold();
48       char *getnum();
49
50       /* open the relation */
51       if ((sptr = db_ropen(lexeme)) == NULL)
52         return (FALSE);
53
54       /* indicate that a store in header should take place */
55       sptr->sc_store = TRUE;
56
57       for (i = 0; i < NATTRS; i++) {
58         /* get a pointer to the current attribute */
59         aptr = &SCAN_HEADER.hd_attrs[i];
60
61         /* check for the last attribute */
62         if (aptr->at_name[0] == EOS)
63           break;
64
65         /* set up null prompt strings */
```

```
66          db_prompt((char *) 0, (char *) 0);
67
68          while (TRUE) {
69            if (strlen(aptr->at_name) < 8)
70            printf("%s\t\t###\n ", unfold(aptr->at_name));
71            else
72            printf("%s\t###\n ", unfold(aptr->at_name));
73
74            /* if a change in size is required */
75            sprintf(prompt,"old length = %d new?\t:",aptr->at_size);
76            if (getnum(prompt, a_size, LINEMAX) != "\n")
77          if (isdigit(*a_size))
78            change = TRUE;
79
80            printf("-----------------------------\n");
81            break;
82          }
83
84          /* store the changes in an auxiliary attribute structure */
85          if ((new_attrs[i] = MALLOC(struct attribute)) == NULL)
86            return (error(INSMEM));
87
88          strncpy(new_attrs[i]->at_name, aptr->at_name,
89                          MIN(strlen(aptr->at_name), ANSIZE));
90          new_attrs[i]->at_name[MIN(strlen(aptr->at_name),ANSIZE)]=EOS;
91
92          if (a_size[0] != EOS)
93            new_attrs[i]->at_size = atoi(a_size);
94          else
95            new_attrs[i]->at_size = aptr->at_size;
96
97          new_attrs[i]->at_key = aptr->at_key;
98          new_attrs[i]->at_type = aptr->at_type;
99          }
100
101          /* close rel, write rel header into memory, free scan space */
102          if ((buf_name = calloc(1, RNSIZE + 1)) == NULL) {
103          db_rclose(sptr);
104          return (error(INSMEM));
105          }
106          strcpy(buf_name, SCAN_RELATION->rl_name);
107          db_rclose(sptr);
108
109          if (change)                 /* must perform a file transfer */
110            if (!transfer(buf_name, new_attrs))
111              return (FALSE);
112
113          /* return successfully */
114          return (TRUE);
115      } /* db_modify */
116      /* ------------------------------------------------------------ */
117      int db_focus()
118      {
119        char            rname[RNSIZE + 1];
120        struct scan     *sptr;
121        struct scan     *db_ropen();
122
123        /* save the relation file name */
124        strcpy(rname, lexeme);
125
126        /* make sure that the rest of the line is blank */
```

```
127        if (!db_flush())
128          return (FALSE);
129
130        /* open the relation */
131        if ((sptr = db_ropen(rname)) == NULL)
132          return (FALSE);
133
134        sprintf(cformat, "Current %s focus lies on tuple #%d#", rname,
135            SCAN_HEADER.hd_cursor);
136        rprint(cformat);
137        cformat[0] = EOS;              /* clear command format */
138
139        /* close file and clear relation structure */
140        db_rclose(sptr);
141
142        /* return successfully */
143        return (TRUE);
144      } /* db_focus */
145      /* ------------------------------------------------------------ */
146      int db_display(slptr, c_width, offset)
147          struct sel    *slptr;
148          int           c_width, offset;
149      {
150        struct relation *rc_create();
151        struct relation *rptr;
152        struct sattr    *saptr;
153        char            *aname, *tbuf;
154        int             i;
155        char            filename[12];
156
157        /* create a new relation */
158        sref_cntr++;
159        if ((rptr = rc_create(stck(rel_fl, sref_cntr))) == NULL) {
160          done(slptr);
161          return (FALSE);
162        }
163        /* preserve file name */
164        strcpy(filename, rptr->rl_name);
165
166        /* create the selected attributes */
167        for (saptr = SEL_ATTRS;saptr != NULL;saptr = saptr->sa_next) {
168
169          /* decide which attribute name to use */
170          if ((aname = saptr->sa_name) == NULL)
171            aname = saptr->sa_aname;
172
173          /* add the attribute */
174          if (!add_attr(rptr, aname, ATTRIBUTE_TYPE,
175                                    ATTRIBUTE_SIZE, ATTRIBUTE_KEY)) {
176            free((char *) rptr);
177            done(slptr);
178            return (FALSE);
179          }
180        }
181
182        /* create the relation header */
183        if (!rc_header(rptr, NOINDEX)) {
184          done(slptr);
185          return (FALSE);
186        }
187        /* allocate and initialize a tuple buffer */
```

```
188       if ((tbuf =
189        calloc(1, (unsigned) RELATION_HEADER.hd_size + 1)) == NULL) {
190         rc_done(rptr, TRUE);
191         return (error(INSMEM));
192       }
193       /* reset cursor at current place, and seek tuple */
194       SEL_HEADER.hd_cursor += offset;
195       i = 0;
196       if (!cseek(SEL_SCAN, SEL_HEADER.hd_cursor)) {
197         /* reset cursor to original position */
198         SEL_HEADER.hd_cursor = 0;
199         SEL_SCAN->sc_store = TRUE;
200         done(slptr);
201         rc_done(rptr, TRUE);
202         return (error(BADCURS));
203       }
204       /* read, write tuples where cursor was last positioned */
205       do {
206         /* read tuple from original relation */
207         if (read(SEL_RELATION->rl_fd,
208                   tbuf, SEL_HEADER.hd_size) != SEL_HEADER.hd_size) {
209           done(slptr);
210           rc_done(rptr, TRUE);
211           return (error(TUPINP));
212         }
213         /* write tuple to the temporary file */
214         if (!write_tuple(rptr, tbuf, TRUE)) {
215           rc_done(rptr, TRUE);
216           done(slptr);
217           return (error(INSBLK));
218         }
219         i++;                        /* increment index */
220
221       } while (i < c_width &&
222                 (SEL_HEADER.hd_cursor + i < SEL_HEADER.hd_tcnt));
223
224       /* reset cursor if c_width > 0,
225          indicate that a store should take place in header */
226       if (c_width)
227         SEL_HEADER.hd_cursor += (i - 1);
228       SEL_SCAN->sc_store = TRUE;
229
230       /* finish the selection */
231       done(slptr);
232       nfree((char *) tbuf);
233
234       /* finish the relation creation */
235       if (!rc_done(rptr, TRUE))
236         return (FALSE);
237
238       /* print the resulting tuple on stdout */
239       if (!parse("print", FALSE))
240         return (FALSE);
241
242       /* unlink file */
243       sprintf(filename, "%s.db", filename);
244       if (unlink(filename) == FAIL)
245         return (error(UNLINK));
246
247       /* return successfully */
248       return (TRUE);
```

```
249     } /* display */
250     /* ------------------------------------------------------------ */
251     int db_commit(slptr, no_delete, cntr)
252         struct sel    *slptr;
253         BOOL          no_delete;
254         int           *cntr;
255     {
256       char           response[5];
257       char           prompt[65];
258       BOOL           proceed = FALSE;
259       char *getfld();
260
261       if (strncmp(SEL_ATTRS->sa_rname, "sys", 3) != EQUAL) {
262         sprintf(prompt, "Commit changes ? (<yes> or <no>)\t: ");
263         getfld(prompt, response, 4);
264       }        /* no prompt in case of system applied deletions */
265       else proceed = TRUE;
266
267       if (strcmp(response, "yes") == EQUAL || proceed) {
268         (*cntr)++;    /* increment counter */
269
270         if (no_delete) {    /* update the tuple(s) only */
271           if(!update_tuple(slptr->sl_rels, key_buf, del_buf))
272           return(FAIL);
273         } else {            /* delete the tuple (s) */
274           if (!delete_tuple(SEL_SCAN, del_buf))
275           return(FAIL);
276         }
277       }
278
279       if (proceed == FALSE) {
280         response[0] = EOS;
281         sprintf(prompt, "%s%s",
282                 "Press any character <return> to continue,",
283                 " or <return> to exit : ");
284         getfld(prompt, response, 4);
285
286         if (response[0] == EOS || response[0] == NEWLINE)
287           return (FAIL);
288       }
289       return (TRUE);
290     } /* db_commit */
291     /* ------------------------------------------------------------ */
292     db_remove()
293     {
294       int            i;
295       char           filename[15];
296
297       for (i = 1; i <= sref_cntr; i++) {
298         sprintf(filename, "%s.db", stck(filename, i));
299         if (unlink(filename) == FAIL)
300           continue;
301       }
302     } /* db_remove */
303     /* ------------------------------------------------------------ */
304     static int purge_trans(hd)
305         struct   trans_file *hd;
306     {
307       struct   trans_file *hd_prev;
308
309       while (hd) {
```

```
310          unlink(hd->t_file);
311          hd_prev = hd;
312          hd = hd->t_next;
313          nfree((char *) hd_prev);
314        }
315   } /* purge_trans */
316   /* ------------------------------------------------------------ */
317   int quit()
318   {
319     db_remove();
320     purge_trans(trans_hd);
321     printf("\n ***   You have left the database     ***\n\n");
322     exit(0);
323
324   } /* quit */
325   /* ------------------------------------------------------------ */
326   db_assign(trans_file)
327        char trans_file[];
328   {
329     static struct trans_file *trans_tail = NULL;
330
331     /* append this temp-rel name to the cur. transient file list */
332     if (!trans_hd) {
333       if ((trans_hd = CALLOC(1, struct trans_file)) == NULL)
334         return(error(INSMEM));
335
336       trans_hd->t_next = NULL;
337       strcpy(trans_hd->t_file, trans_file);
338       trans_tail = trans_hd;
339     }
340     else {
341       if ((trans_tail->t_next =
342            CALLOC(1, struct trans_file)) == NULL)
343         return(error(INSMEM));
344
345       trans_tail = trans_tail->t_next;
346       strcpy(trans_tail->t_file, trans_file);
347       trans_tail->t_next = NULL;
348     }
349
350     sprintf(rel_fl, "%s.db", stck(rel_fl, sref_cntr));
351
352     /* transfer files */
353     if (!f_move(rel_fl, trans_file))
354       return(error(FILEMV));
355
356     return(TRUE);
357   } /* db_assign */
358   /* ------------------------------------------------------------ */
359   int new_relation(sref_cntr, rptr, slptr, prptr, rel_fl)
360        int            *sref_cntr;
361        struct relation **rptr;
362        struct sel      *slptr;
363        struct pred     *prptr;
364        char            *rel_fl;
365   {
366     struct relation *rc_create();
367
368     (*sref_cntr)++;
369     if ((*rptr = rc_create(stck(rel_fl, *sref_cntr))) == NULL) {
370       done(slptr);
```

```
371
372        if (prptr)
373           free_pred(&prptr);
374
375        return (FALSE);
376      }
377      return (TRUE);
378    }
379
380    int joined(relat, attrib, r_indx, a_indx, where_flag)
381        char          **relat, **attrib;
382        int           r_indx, a_indx;
383        BOOL          where_flag;
384    {
385      char    *rel1, *rel2, fmt[2*LINEMAX+1], *temp_buf = (char *)0;
386      char    *temp_lptr, relop[5], wh_attr[25], constant[35];
387      rel1 = calloc(1, (unsigned) strlen(relat[0]) + 1);
388      rel2 = calloc(1, (unsigned) strlen(relat[1]) + 1);
389
390      strcpy(rel1, relat[0]);
391      strcpy(rel2, relat[1]);
392      strcpy(join_on, attrib[0]);
393
394      /* make qualified attributes */
395      make_quattr(relat[0], attrib[0]);
396      make_quattr(relat[1], attrib[1]);
397
398      if (where_flag == FALSE)
399        sprintf(fmt, "select from %s, %s where %s = %s", rel1, rel2,
400             relat[0], relat[1]);
401      else {
402        if (!where_in_join(wh_attr, relop, constant))
403          return(FALSE);
404
405        sprintf(fmt, "select from %s, %s where %s = %s & %s %s %s",
406           rel1, rel2, relat[0], relat[1], wh_attr, relop, constant);
407
408        if (strlen(fmt) > 2*LINEMAX)
409          return(error(LINELONG));
410      }
411
412      /* if internally formed query preserve pos of line pointer */
413      if (lptr != NULL) {
414        temp_buf = calloc(1, (unsigned) strlen(lptr));
415        strcpy(temp_buf, lptr);   /* copy contents of line buffer */
416        temp_lptr = lptr;         /* preserve old lptr address */
417      }
418
419      if (!parse(fmt, FALSE)) {
420        buf_free(relat, r_indx);
421        buf_free(attrib, a_indx);
422        nfree((char *) rel1);
423        nfree((char *) rel2);
424        return (FALSE);
425      }
426
427      nfree((char *) rel1);
428      nfree((char *) rel2);
429
430      /* restore line pointer if required */
431      if (temp_buf != NULL) {
```

```
432          strcpy(temp_lptr, temp_buf);   /* recover old buf contents */
433          lptr = temp_lptr;              /* recover old address */
434          nfree(temp_buf);               /* free temporary buffer */
435        }
436
437      return (TRUE);
438    } /* joined */
439    /* ---------------------------------------------------------------- */
440    do_join(slptr, duplc_attr, ref_attr, d_indx, tbuf)
441        struct sel *slptr;
442        char **duplc_attr, **ref_attr, *tbuf;
443        int  d_indx;
444    {
445      char *name;
446      int  i, j, diff, len, abase = 1;
447      char **buff;
448      struct sattr *saptr;
449      BOOL set_dup = FALSE;
450      BOOL intake = TRUE;
451
452      if (!(buff = dcalloc(d_indx)))
453        return (error(INSMEM));
454
455      name = SEL_ATTRS->sa_rname;
456
457      for (saptr = SEL_ATTRS;saptr != NULL;saptr = saptr->sa_next) {
458        if (strcmp(saptr->sa_rname, name) != EQUAL) { /*  2nd rel */
459          for (j = 0; j < d_indx; j++)
460            if (strcmp(saptr->sa_aname, duplc_attr[j]) == EQUAL) {
461              set_dup = TRUE; /* attribute names match */
462              break;
463            }
464
465          /* check if matching attributes hold same data */
466          if (set_dup == TRUE) { /* check for data consistency */
467            set_dup = FALSE;  /* reset duplicate attribute flag */
468            if ((strcmp(join_on, saptr->sa_aname) == EQUAL) ||
469                ATTRIBUTE_TYPE == TCHAR && (strncmp(buff[j],
470                    saptr->sa_aptr, strlen(buff[j])) == EQUAL)) {
471              continue;
472            } else if ( ATTRIBUTE_TYPE != TCHAR) {
473              /* estimate the length difference of ints or reals */
474              diff = ATTRIBUTE_SIZE - strlen(buff[j]);
475
476              if (diff < 0) {
477                if (strncmp(buff[j] - diff, saptr->sa_aptr,
478                            ATTRIBUTE_SIZE) != EQUAL) {
479                  buf_free(buff, d_indx);
480                  return(FAIL);    /* tuple failed test */
481                }
482                else
483                  intake = FALSE; /* no entries permitted */
484              } else if (diff == 0) {
485                if ((strncmp(buff[j], saptr->sa_aptr,
486                            strlen(buff[j])) != EQUAL)) {
487                  buf_free(buff, d_indx);
488                  return(FAIL);    /* tuple failed test */
489                }
490                else
491                  intake = FALSE;   /* no entries permitted */
492              } else { /* diff. > 0 */
```

```
493             if ((strncmp(buff[j], (saptr->sa_aptr) + diff,
494                      strlen(buff[j])) != EQUAL)) {
495               buf_free(buff, d_indx);
496               return(FAIL);    /* tuple failed test */
497             }
498             else
499               intake = FALSE;  /* no entries permitted */
500           }
501         } else         /* char strings with unequal values */
502           return(FAIL);
503       }
504     } else {  /* first relation procesing */
505       for (j = 0; j < d_indx; j++)
506       if ((strcmp(saptr->sa_aname, duplc_attr[j]) == EQUAL) ||
507         (ref_attr[j] &&
508           (strcmp(saptr->sa_aname, ref_attr[j]) == EQUAL))) {
509         len = ATTRIBUTE_SIZE;
510         buff[j] = calloc(1, (unsigned) len + 1);
511         strncpy(buff[j], saptr->sa_aptr, len);
512         buff[j][len] = EOS;
513       }
514     }
515
516     if (intake) {
517       for (i = 0; i < ATTRIBUTE_SIZE; i++)
518       tbuf[abase + i] = saptr->sa_aptr[i];
519
520       abase += i;
521     }
522     intake = TRUE;        /* reset intake flag */
523   }
524
525   buf_free(buff, d_indx);
526
527   return(TRUE);
528
529 } /* do_join */
530 /* ----------------------------------------------------------- */
531 int add_selattrs(slptr,rptr,join_keys,duplc_attr,ref_attr,d_indx)
532     struct sel      *slptr;
533     struct relation *rptr;
534     char            *join_keys, **duplc_attr, **ref_attr;
535     int             *d_indx;
536 {
537   struct sattr *saptr;
538   char key, *aname, *name, **joined_attr;
539   /* referenced attr in first join relation and its semantically
540      equivalent counterpart in second join relation */
541   char semeq_aname[ANSIZE + 1], ref_aname[ANSIZE + 1];
542   BOOL entry, lock, equiv = FALSE;
543   int  i, join_indexed = 0;
544   int  indx = 0;
545
546   if (!(joined_attr = dcalloc((int) SEL_NATTRS)))
547     return(error(INSMEM));
548
549   /* initialize join-keys */
550   join_keys[0] = 'n';
551   join_keys[1] = 'n';
552
553   /* preserve name of first relation */
```

```
554        name = SEL_ATTRS->sa_rname;
555
556        /* create the selected attributes */
557        for (saptr = SEL_ATTRS;saptr != NULL;saptr = saptr->sa_next) {
558
559          /* decide which attr name to use (alternate or normal) */
560          if ((aname = saptr->sa_name) == NULL)
561            aname = saptr->sa_aname;
562
563          /* in case of join must ensure that no repetitive attrs are
564           *   entered into the relation */
565          if (join_on == NULL)
566            entry = TRUE;
567
568          /* no locking required */
569          lock = FALSE;
570
571          /* in case of join, loop thro' the first relation members */
572          if (join_on && (strcmp(saptr->sa_rname, name) == EQUAL)) {
573
574            /* still at first rel, if join-attribute is indexed */
575            joined_attr[indx] = rmalloc(strlen(aname) + 1);
576
577            if (strcmp(aname, join_on) == EQUAL)
578              if (ATTRIBUTE_KEY != 'n') {
579                join_indexed++;
580
581                /* copy key-type */
582                join_keys[0] = ATTRIBUTE_KEY;
583              }
584
585            /* fill-in attributes of first relation */
586            strcpy(joined_attr[indx++], aname);
587
588            /* entry in resulting relation structure should be made */
589            entry = TRUE;
590          } else if (join_on) {  /* second rel, assemble dupl names */
591
592            /* look for potential semantically equivalent attrs */
593            if (equivalent_attrs(aname, slptr->sl_rels->sr_next)) {
594
595              /* make sure whether foreign keys exist */
596              fgn_join(name, saptr->sa_rname,
597                       aname, semeq_aname, ref_aname);
598
599              /* join on foreign keys */
600              if (*semeq_aname &&
601                  strcmp(semeq_aname, aname) == EQUAL) {
602                equiv = TRUE;
603                duplc_attr[*d_indx] = rmalloc(strlen(aname) + 1);
604                strcpy(duplc_attr[*d_indx], aname);
605                ref_attr[*d_indx] = rmalloc(strlen(ref_aname) + 1);
606                strcpy(ref_attr[*d_indx], ref_aname);
607                (*d_indx)++;
608              }
609            }
610
611            for (i = 0;i < indx;i++) { /* loop thro' 1st rel attrs */
612
613              /* if join-attribute is indexed */
614              if ((lock == FALSE &&
```

```
615                     strcmp(aname, join_on) == EQUAL) || equiv) {
616                 if (ATTRIBUTE_KEY != 'n') {
617
618                 /* lock any further entries */
619                 lock = TRUE;
620
621                 join_keys[1] = ATTRIBUTE_KEY;
622                 join_indexed++;
623                 }
624                 equiv = FALSE;
625             }
626
627             /* load duplicate attribute names in buffer */
628             if (strcmp(aname, joined_attr[i]) == EQUAL) {
629                 entry = FALSE;      /* duplicate attr. flag */
630                 duplc_attr[*d_indx] = rmalloc(strlen(aname) + 1);
631                 strcpy(duplc_attr[*d_indx], aname);
632                 ref_attr[*d_indx] = NULL;
633                 (*d_indx)++;
634                 break;
635             } else
636                 entry= TRUE;    /* non-duplicate attr. */
637         }
638     }
639
640     /* if the result is a "snapshot" file do not use indexes */
641     if (strncmp(rptr->rl_name, "snapshot", 8) == EQUAL)
642         key = 'n';
643     else
644         key =  ATTRIBUTE_KEY;
645
646     /* do not add both semantically equivalent attributes */
647     if (semeq_aname && strcmp(aname, semeq_aname) == EQUAL)
648         entry = FALSE;
649
650     /* add non-duplicate attribute names to form a new rel */
651     if (entry)
652         if (!add_attr(rptr,aname,ATTRIBUTE_TYPE,
653                             ATTRIBUTE_SIZE,key)) {
654             nfree((char *) rptr);
655             done(slptr);
656             return (FAIL);
657         }
658
659     }  /* exit from saptr loop */
660
661     /* create the relation header */
662     if (!rc_header(rptr, NOINDEX)) {
663         done(slptr);
664         return (FAIL);
665     }
666
667     /* return successfully */
668     buf_free(joined_attr, indx);
669     return (join_indexed);
670 } /* add_selattrs */
671 /* -------------------------------------------------------- */
672 equivalent_attrs(aname, srptr)
673         char *aname;            /* candidate for foreign key */
674         struct srel *srptr;  /* second join relation */
675 {
```

```
676        int i;
677
678        for (i = 0;SREL_RELATION->rl_header.hd_attrs[i].at_name[0];i++) {
679          if (strcmp(SREL_RELATION->rl_header.hd_attrs[i].at_name,
680                                                aname) == EQUAL) {
681            if (SREL_RELATION->rl_header.hd_attrs[i].at_semid == 't')
682          return(TRUE);
683            else
684            return(FALSE);
685          }
686        }
687        return(FALSE);
688    } /* equivalent_attrs */
689    /* ------------------------------------------------------------ */
690    fgn_join(rname, tname, aname, fst_aname, secnd_aname)
691          char *rname, *tname, *aname, *fst_aname, *secnd_aname;
692    {
693        char fmt[100];
694        struct sel *slptr, *retrieve();
695        extern union code_cell code[];
696        static union code_cell tmp_code[CODEMAX + 1];
697
698        /* preserve code array contents before retrieve operation */
699        structcpy((char *) tmp_code, (char *) code,
700                    (CODEMAX + 1) * sizeof(union code_cell));
701
702       /* the composite relation appears first in the join statement */
703        sprintf(fmt, "syskey over fgnkey, primary where relname \
704    = \"%s\" & qualifier = \"%s\" & primary = \"%s\";",
705            rname, tname, aname);
706
707        if ((slptr = retrieve(fmt)) == NULL) {
708          fst_aname[0] = EOS;
709          return(FALSE);
710        }
711
712        if (fetch(slptr, TRUE)) {
713          /* composite key must appear in snapshot */
714          strcpy(secnd_aname, SEL_ATTRS->sa_aptr);
715          strcpy(fst_aname, slptr->sl_attrs->sa_next->sa_aptr);
716        } else {    /* target rel apears first in join statement */
717
718          /* close composite relation */
719          db_rclose(slptr->sl_rels->sr_scan);
720
721          sprintf(fmt, "syskey over fgnkey,primary where relname = \"%s\"
722            & qualifier = \"%s\" & fgnkey = \"%s\";",
723                tname, rname, aname);
724
725          if ((slptr = retrieve(fmt)) == NULL) {
726            fst_aname[0] = EOS;
727            return(FALSE);
728          }
729
730          if (fetch(slptr, TRUE)) {
731            strcpy(fst_aname, SEL_ATTRS->sa_aptr);
732            strcpy(secnd_aname, slptr->sl_attrs->sa_next->sa_aptr);
733          }
734          else
735            fst_aname[0] = EOS;
736        }
```

```
737
738        db_rclose(slptr->sl_rels->sr_scan);
739
740        /* restore code array contents after the retrieve operation */
741        structcpy((char *) code, (char *) tmp_code,
742                  (CODEMAX + 1) * sizeof(union code_cell));
743
744        return(TRUE);
745    } /* fgn_join */
746    /* ------------------------------------------------------------ */
747    header_buffs(rptr, slptr, tbuf, aux_buf)
748         struct sel *slptr;
749         struct relation *rptr;
750         char **tbuf, **aux_buf;
751    {
752
753        if (!rc_header(rptr, NOINDEX)) {
754          done(slptr);
755          return (FALSE);
756        }
757
758        /* allocate and initialize a tuple buffer */
759        if ((*tbuf = (char *)calloc(1,
760                  (unsigned) RELATION_HEADER.hd_size + 1)) == NULL) {
761          rc_done(rptr, TRUE);
762          return (error(INSMEM));
763        }
764        **tbuf = ACTIVE;
765
766        /* allocate and initialize an  auxiliary buffer */
767        if (aux_buf)
768          if ((*aux_buf = (char *)calloc(1,
769                  (unsigned) RELATION_HEADER.hd_size + 1)) == NULL) {
770            rc_done(rptr, TRUE);
771            return (error(INSMEM));
772          }
773
774        /* initialize hash table and word index */
775        init_hash();
776
777        return(TRUE);
778    } /* header_buffs */
779    /* ------------------------------------------------------------ */
780    create_attrs(rptr, slptr)
781         struct relation *rptr;
782         struct sel *slptr;
783    {
784        char *aname;
785        struct sattr *saptr;
786        char key;
787
788        for (saptr = SEL_ATTRS;saptr != NULL;saptr = saptr->sa_next) {
789
790          /* decide which attribute name to use */
791          if ((aname = saptr->sa_name) == NULL)
792            aname = saptr->sa_aname;
793
794          /* if the result is a "snapshot" file do not use indexes */
795          if (strncmp(rptr->rl_name, "snapshot", 8) == EQUAL)
796            key = 'n';
797          else
```

```
798            key = ATTRIBUTE_KEY;
799
800        /* add the attribute */
801        if (!add_attr(rptr, aname, ATTRIBUTE_TYPE,
802                        ATTRIBUTE_SIZE, key)) {
803          nfree((char *) rptr);
804          done(slptr);
805          return (FALSE);
806        }
807      }
808
809      return(TRUE);
810    } /* create_attrs */
811    /* ---------------------------------------------------------- */
812    int check_union(rptr, slptr, f_rel, name)
813        struct relation *rptr;
814        struct sel *slptr;
815        struct unattrs f_rel[];
816        char **name;
817    {
818      struct unattrs s_rel[NATTRS];
819      struct sattr *saptr;
820      unsigned f_indx = 0, s_indx = 0;
821      int i, j;
822      char *aname;
823
824      /* check if the relations have the same attribute names
825         and types */
826      *name = SEL_ATTRS->sa_rname;
827
828      for (saptr = SEL_ATTRS;saptr != NULL;saptr = saptr->sa_next) {
829        if (strcmp(saptr->sa_rname, *name) == EQUAL) {
830
831          /* preserve names, sizes and types of 1st relation */
832          f_rel[f_indx].size = ATTRIBUTE_SIZE;
833          f_rel[f_indx].name = rmalloc(2 * ANSIZE);
834          sprintf(f_rel[f_indx++].name, "%s%c", saptr->sa_aname,
835              ATTRIBUTE_TYPE);
836        } else { /* preserve name and type of 2nd rel attribute */
837          s_rel[s_indx].size = ATTRIBUTE_SIZE;
838          s_rel[s_indx].name = rmalloc(2 * ANSIZE);
839          sprintf(s_rel[s_indx++].name, "%s%c", saptr->sa_aname,
840              ATTRIBUTE_TYPE);
841        }
842      }
843
844      /* compare two rels according to attribute names, and types */
845      for (i = 0; i < s_indx; i++)
846        for (j = 0; j < f_indx; j++)
847          if (s_indx == f_indx && (strcmp(s_rel[j].name,
848                          f_rel[i].name) == EQUAL)) {
849
850          /* get max relation size */
851          f_rel[i].size = MAX(f_rel[i].size, s_rel[j].size);
852          break;
853          } /* if last attribute of 2nd relation reached, error */
854          else if ( j == f_indx - 1)
855          return (error(UNOP));
856
857      /* create the selected attributes and decide about new
858       * relation size loop only thro' attrs of first relation */
```

```
859      for (saptr = SEL_ATTRS, i = 0; saptr != NULL
860          && (strcmp(saptr->sa_rname, *name) == EQUAL);
861          saptr = saptr->sa_next) {
862
863        /* decide which attribute name to use, in case of aliases */
864        if ((aname = saptr->sa_name) == NULL)
865          aname = saptr->sa_aname;
866
867        /* add the attributes in the union-relation
868         * allowing enough space for the longest common attribute */
869        if (!add_attr(rptr, aname, ATTRIBUTE_TYPE,
870                        f_rel[i++].size, ATTRIBUTE_KEY)) {
871          nfree((char *) rptr);
872          done(slptr);
873          return (FALSE);
874        }
875      }
876
877      /* free union buffer space */
878      free_union(s_rel, (int) SEL_NATTRS);
879
880      return(TRUE);
881    } /* check_union */
882    /* ------------------------------------------------------------ */
883    free_union(data_struct, tcnt)
884        struct unattrs data_struct[];
885        int tcnt;
886    {
887      int             i;
888
889      for (i = 0; i < tcnt; i++)
890        nfree(data_struct[i].name);
891
892
893    } /* free_union */
894    /* ------------------------------------------------------------ */
895    BOOL update_attrs(slptr, tcnt, doffset)
896        struct sel *slptr;
897        int        *tcnt;
898        long        doffset;
899    {
900      struct sattr *saptr;
901      struct attribute *aptr;
902      char       avalue[STRINGMAX+1], old_value[STRINGMAX+1];
903      BOOL       insertion = FALSE;
904      BOOL       updating = TRUE;
905      char       attr_key, *rem_blanks();
906      int        result;
907      char *prompt_input();
908
909      printf("---------------------------\n");
910
911      /* loop through the selected attributes */
912      for (saptr = SEL_ATTRS;saptr != NULL;saptr = saptr->sa_next) {
913
914        /* get the attribute pointer */
915        aptr = saptr->sa_attr;
916
917        /* get and store the old attribute value */
918        get_attr(aptr, saptr->sa_aptr, avalue);
919        rem_blanks(old_value, avalue, aptr->at_size);
```

```
920
921        /* prompt and input attribute values */
922        if (prompt_input(aptr, insertion, avalue) == NULL)
923          return(FALSE);
924
925        attr_key = aptr->at_key;
926
927        /* store the attribute value */
928        if (avalue[0] != EOS) {
929          store_attr(aptr, saptr->sa_aptr, avalue);
930          saptr->sa_srel->sr_update = TRUE;
931          if (doffset != 0)
932          SEL_SCAN->sc_recpos = doffset;
933
934          if ((attr_key != 'n'))
935          update_keys(slptr,saptr,aptr,&doffset, old_value, avalue);
936        }
937
938      }
939      /* update the tuple, and commit changes */
940      result = db_commit(slptr, updating, tcnt);
941
942      /* free  buffers */
943      buf_free(key_buf, 4);
944      key_buf = NULL;
945      buf_free(del_buf, 4);
946      del_buf = NULL;
947
948      /* result obtains three values TRUE, FALSE and FAIL */
949      return(result) ;
950
951    } /* update_attrs */
952  /* ------------------------------------------------------------ */
953    BOOL delete_attrs(slptr, tcnt, doffset)
954        struct sel *slptr;
955        int       *tcnt;
956        long      doffset;
957    {
958      struct sattr *saptr;
959      struct attribute *aptr;
960      char  *rem_blanks(), attr_key,
961            avalue[STRINGMAX+1], old_value[STRINGMAX+1];
962      int result;                /* result of a commit operation */
963      BOOL   update = FALSE;  /* perform deletion */
964
965      /* read tuple from data file if doffset is specified */
966      if (!doffset)
967        doffset = SEL_SCAN->sc_recpos;
968
969      /* loop through the selected attributes */
970      for (saptr = SEL_ATTRS;saptr != NULL;saptr = saptr->sa_next) {
971        attr_key = ATTRIBUTE_KEY;
972
973        /* get the attribute pointer */
974        aptr = saptr->sa_attr;
975
976        /* get and store the old attribute value */
977        get_attr(aptr, saptr->sa_aptr, avalue);
978        rem_blanks(old_value, avalue, aptr->at_size);
979
980        /* signifies tuple deletion */
```

```
981        avalue[0] = EOS;
982
983        if ((attr_key != 'n')) { /* if attribute indexed */
984          if (!update_keys(slptr, saptr, aptr,
985                                 &doffset, old_value, avalue))
986          return(FALSE);
987        }
988      }
989
990        /* preserve the adddress of the data tuple */
991        if (doffset != 0)
992          SEL_SCAN->sc_recpos = doffset;
993
994        /* store changes into data header */
995        SEL_SCAN->sc_store = TRUE;
996
997        /* delete the tuple, and commit changes */
998        result = db_commit(slptr, update, tcnt);
999
1000       /*  free delete buffer */
1001       buf_free(del_buf, 4);
1002       del_buf = NULL;
1003
1004       /* result obtains three values TRUE, FALSE and FAIL */
1005       return(result) ;
1006
1007     } /* delete_attrs */
1008     /* ----------------------------------------------------------- */
1009     semid_attrs(comp_name, fgn_key, qualifier, aname)
1010          char *comp_name;
1011          char fgn_key[][ANSIZE+1],
1012               qualifier[][RNSIZE+1], aname[][ANSIZE+1];
1013     {
1014       int i, j, k;
1015       struct scan *target, *comp, *db_ropen();
1016
1017       if ((comp = db_ropen(comp_name)) == NULL)
1018         return(FALSE);
1019
1020       /* set flag for semantically identical attrs in composite rel */
1021       for (i = 0;comp->sc_relation->rl_header.hd_attrs[i].at_name[0]
1022                                        != EOS; i++) {
1023         for (j = 0; j < 2; j++) {
1024           if (strcmp(comp->sc_relation->rl_header.hd_attrs[i].at_name,
1025                   fgn_key[j]) == EQUAL) {
1026           comp->sc_relation->rl_header.hd_attrs[i].at_semid = 't';
1027           break;
1028           }
1029         }
1030       }
1031       comp->sc_store = TRUE;
1032       db_rclose(comp);
1033       free((char *) comp);
1034
1035       /* set flag for semantically identical attrs in target rels */
1036       for (k = 0; k < 2; k++) {
1037         if ((target = db_ropen(qualifier[k])) == NULL)
1038           return(FALSE);
1039
1040         for (i = 0;target->sc_relation->rl_header.hd_attrs[i].at_name[0]
1041                                          != EOS; i++) {
```

```
1042            for (j = 0; j < 2; j++) {
1043              if (strcmp(target->sc_relation->rl_header.
1044                    hd_attrs[i].at_name,    aname[j]) == EQUAL) {
1045                target->sc_relation->rl_header.hd_attrs[i].at_semid = 't';
1046                break;
1047              }
1048            }
1049            target->sc_store = TRUE;
1050            db_rclose(target);
1051            free((char *) target);
1052          }
1053        }
1054
1055        return(TRUE);
1056    } /* semid_attrs */
```

file: *io_lib.c*

```
1     #include "requ.h"
2
3     writeln(string)
4          char *string;
5     { /* writes the string to stdout ensuring that only one new line
6        * is displayed, resolves the problem of existent or non-existent
7        * newline chars from files*/
8
9        while (*string != EOL && *string != EOS)
10         putchar(*string++);
11
12    } /* writeln */
13    /* ------------------------------------------------------------ */
14    int_convert(ascii_val)
15         char *ascii_val;
16    {
17      /* read past blanks */
18      while(is_blank(*ascii_val))
19        ascii_val++;         /* increment ascii_val to skip blanks
20                               * and get the next letter */
21
22      /* check for sign */
23      if (*ascii_val == '-' || *ascii_val == '+')
24        ascii_val++;
25
26      while (*ascii_val)
27        if (is_digit(*ascii_val))
28          ascii_val++;
29        else
30          return(IO_ERROR);
31
32      return(NO_ERROR);
33    } /* int_convert */
34    /* ------------------------------------------------------------ */
35    read_string(string, max)
36         char *string;
37         int max;
38    {
39      /* reads string entered by user, replaces carriage
40       * return with EOS, if EOF occurs then it returns it,
41       * else it returns the value NO_ERROR
42       */
```

```
43        int i = 0, letter;
44
45        while ((letter = getchar()) != EOL && letter != EOF){
46          if ( letter >= ' ' && letter <= '~'){
47            if (i < max-1){
48              *string++ = letter;
49              i++;
50            }
51            else{
52              printf("***** You're allowed to type in a string");
53              printf(" of max. %d chars ! *****\n", max-1);
54              string = &string[0];
55              return(IO_ERROR);
56            }
57          } else
58            return(IO_ERROR);
59        }
60
61        *string = EOS; /* replace CR or max. len with string terminator */
62        if (i == 0 && letter == EOL)
63          return(EOL); /* return EOL, if only a single line was entered */
64        return((letter == EOF) ? EOF : NO_ERROR);
65      } /* read-string */
66    /* ------------------------------------------------------------ */
67    non_fatal_error(error_message)
68          char *error_message;
69    {
70        int count;
71
72        for (count = 0; count<3; count++)
73          BELL;
74        printf("%s\n", error_message);
75        console_write("Hit <return> to continue:");
76
77        /* wait for return */
78        read_char();
79      } /* non_fatal_error */
80    /* ------------------------------------------------------------ */
81    read_char()
82    {
83        /* reads a char entered from keyboard and discards contents of
84         * i/o buffer until newline char, if it meets EOF it returns it
85         * else it returns the first character. Used to discard
86         * wrong data entered by user */
87
88        int letter; /* letter returned to calling routine */
89        int buffer; /* data remaining in the i/o buffer is read into
90                        buffer, buffer for garbage data */
91        letter = getchar(); /* get response */
92        buffer = letter;
93
94        /* get characters until the i/p buffer is empty */
95        while(buffer != EOL && buffer != EOF)
96          buffer = getchar();
97        return((buffer != EOF) ? letter : EOF);
98      } /* read_char */
99    /* ------------------------------------------------------------ */
100   console_write(string)
101         char *string;
102   {
103       /* writes the string to the console ensuring that a newline
```

```
104        * char is not written */
105
106      while(*string != EOL && *string != EOS)
107        putchar(*string++);
108    } /* console_write */
109    /* ------------------------------------------------------------ */
110    char *getnum(prompt, ascii_val, max)
111        char *prompt;
112        char *ascii_val;
113        int max;
114    {
115      BOOL not_valid = TRUE;   /* FALSE when a valid integer is entered */
116      int c;
117
118      while(not_valid){
119        writeln(prompt);
120        if ((c = read_string(ascii_val, max)) == EOF ||  c == EOL)
121          /* get the i/p */
122          return(ascii_val);  /* num is unaffected */
123        if (isspace(*ascii_val))
124          non_fatal_error(
125      "SPURIOUS-ERROR: Invalid data. You should not start with space!");
126        else if (c == IO_ERROR){
127          read_char();
128          BELL;
129          printf("Invalid data entered. Enter an integer value!\n");
130          continue;
131        }
132        /* convert the string to the corresponding integer value */
133        else if (int_convert(ascii_val) == NO_ERROR)
134          not_valid = FALSE;
135        else
136          non_fatal_error(
137      "SPURIOUS-ERROR: Invalid data entered. Enter a proper integer !");
138      }
139      return(ascii_val);
140    } /* getnum */
141    /* ------------------------------------------------------------ */
142    char *getfld(prompt, individ, max)
143        char *individ, *prompt;
144        int max;
145    {
146      /* Prompts the user to enter a field containing text
147       * of not more than 20 chars. */
148      int c;
149      BOOL valid = FALSE; /* TRUE when valid strings are entered */
150
151      while (!valid){
152        writeln(prompt);
153        if ((c = read_string(individ, max)) == NEWLINE ||  c == EOF)
154          return(individ);
155
156        if (c == IO_ERROR){
157          read_char();
158          BELL;
159          printf("Invalid data entered. Enter a character string!\n");
160          continue;
161        }
162        else if (c == NO_ERROR)
163          valid = TRUE;
164      }
```

```
165      return(individ);
166    } /* getfld */
167    /* ------------------------------------------------------------ */
168    float_convert(ascii_val)
169         char *ascii_val;
170    {
171      /* read passed blanks */
172      while (is_blank(*ascii_val))
173        ascii_val++;
174      /* first convert the numbers on the left of the decimal point
175       */
176      while (*ascii_val)
177        if  (is_digit(*ascii_val))
178          ascii_val++;
179        else if (*ascii_val == '.') /*start the fractional part */
180          break;
181        else
182          return(IO_ERROR);
183
184      if (*ascii_val != NULL){
185        ascii_val++; /* we're now past decimal point */
186        while ( *ascii_val != NULL && strlen(ascii_val) < LINEMAX)
187          if (is_digit(*ascii_val))
188            ascii_val++;
189          else
190            return(IO_ERROR);
191      }
192      return(NO_ERROR); /* just like in int_convert */
193    }; /* float_convert */
194    /* ------------------------------------------------------------ */
195    char *getfloat(prompt, ascii_val, max)
196         char *prompt;
197         char ascii_val[];
198         int max;
199    {
200      BOOL not_valid = TRUE;  /* FALSE if a valid integer is entered */
201      int c;
202
203      while(not_valid){
204        writeln(prompt);
205        if ((c = read_string(ascii_val, max)) == EOF || c == EOL)
206          return(ascii_val);  /* num is unaffected */
207
208        if (c == IO_ERROR){
209          read_char();
210          BELL;
211          printf(" Invalid data entered. Enter a real number!\n");
212          continue;
213        }
214        /* convert the string to the corresponding integer value */
215        if (float_convert(ascii_val) == NO_ERROR)
216          not_valid = FALSE;
217        else
218          non_fatal_error(
219          "SPURIOUS-ERROR: Invalid data ! Enter a real number !");
220      }
221      return (ascii_val);
222    } /* get_float */
```

file: misc.c

```
1     /* Misc. procedures */
2
3     #include <stdio.h>
4     #include "requ.h"
5     #include <sys/types.h>
6     #include <sys/stat.h>
7
8     static double avg_cnt, avg_sum;
9
10    extern BOOL   sys_flag; /* true for system defined relations */
11
12    /* free only if pointer is not NULL */
13    nfree(p)
14        char *p;
15    {
16      if (p)
17        free(p);
18    } /* nfree */
19    /* ------------------------------------------------------------ */
20    char *strip_catenate(to, from, n)
21        char *to, *from;
22        int n;
23    {
24      int i, j;
25
26      i = j= 0;
27      for ( ;  n>0 ; n--)
28        if (from[i])
29          to[i++] = from[j++];
30      return(to);
31    } /* strip_catenate */
32    /* ------------------------------------------------------------ */
33    char *rem_blanks(to, from, n)
34        char *to, *from;
35        int n;
36    {
37      int i, j;
38
39      i = j= 0;
40      for (j = 0 ;  j < n && n> 0 ; j++)
41        if (from[j] != ' ')
42          to[i++] = from[j];
43      to[i] = EOS;
44      return(to);
45    } /* rem_banks */
46    /* ------------------------------------------------------------ */
47    rm_trailblks(s)
48        char *s;
49    {
50      char *ch_ptr;
51
52      for (ch_ptr = s + strlen(s); *ch_ptr == ' ' && ch_ptr > s; ch_ptr--)
53        ;
54      *(ch_ptr) = EOS;
55    } /* rm_trailblks */
56    /* ------------------------------------------------------------ */
57    rm_lead_blks(in_string, out_string)
58        char *in_string, *out_string;
```

```
59    {    int i, j;
60
61         i = j = 0;
62
63         while (in_string[i] == ' ' && i < strlen(in_string))
64              i++;
65
66         for (; i < strlen(in_string); )
67              out_string[j++] = in_string[i++];
68
69         out_string[j] = EOS;
70    } /* rm_lead_blks */
71  /* ------------------------------------------------------------ */
72  char *strip_blank(to, from, len, j)
73         char *to, *from;
74         int len, *j;
75  {
76    int i;
77
78    i = *j = 0;
79    len++;   /* increment to get terminator character */
80    for ( ;  len>0 ; len--)
81      if (from[i])
82        to[i++] = from[(*j)++];
83      else {
84        if (from[i] == EOS)
85          to[i++] = ' '; /* leave one blank between words */
86
87        while (from[(*j)++] == ' ')
88          ;
89        to[i++] = ' '; /* leave one blank between words */
90      }
91
92    return(to);
93    } /* strip_blank */
94  /* ------------------------------------------------------------ */
95  char *strip_semicol(to, from, len, j)
96         char *to, *from;
97         int len, *j;
98  {
99    int i;
100
101   i = *j = 0;
102   len++;   /* increment to get terminator character */
103   for ( ;  len>0 ; len--)
104     if (from[i] && from[i] != ';')
105       to[i++] = from[(*j)++];
106     else {
107       if (from[i] == EOS || from[i] == ';')
108         to[i++] = ' '; /* leave one blank between words */
109
110       while (from[(*j)++] == ' ')
111         ;
112       to[i++] = ' '; /* leave one blank between words */
113     }
114
115   return(to);
116   } /* strip_semicol */
117 /* ------------------------------------------------------------ */
118 char *copy(old_string, length)
119       char *old_string;
```

```
120         int length;
121         /* copy makes a copy of the old string and returns
122          * the address of the copy
123          */
124   {  /* copy */
125     register  char  *new_string;
126
127
128       /* allocate a string able to hold the length of the
129        * string plus the string terminator
130        */
131       new_string = calloc(1, (unsigned) strlen(old_string) + 1);
132
133       /*copy the string and return a pointer to it.
134        */
135       strncpy(new_string, old_string, length);
136       new_string[MIN(strlen(old_string), length)] = EOS;
137       return(new_string);
138   }  /* copy */
139   /* ------------------------------------------------------------ */
140   /* copy structures by bytes */
141   structcpy(to, from, length)
142         char *to, *from;
143         int length;
144   {
145     if (length <= 0)
146       return(FALSE);
147
148     while (length--)
149       *to++ = *from++;
150
151     return(TRUE);
152   } /* structcpy */
153   /* ------------------------------------------------------------ */
154   char **dcalloc(n)
155         int n;
156   {
157     char **p, *calloc();
158
159     p = CALLOC(n, char *);
160     if (p)
161       return(p);
162     else
163       return(NULL);
164   } /* dcalloc */
165   /* ------------------------------------------------------------ */
166   char *fold(str1)
167         char *str1;
168   {
169     char *str;
170     int i;
171
172     str = malloc((unsigned) strlen(str1)+1);
173
174     for (i = 0; str1[i] != EOS; i++)
175       if (is_alpha(str1[i]))
176         str[i] = to_lower(str1[i]);
177
178     str[i] = EOS;
179
180     return(str);
```

```
181    } /* fold */
182    /* ------------------------------------------------------------ */
183    char *unfold(str1)
184        char *str1;
185    {
186       char *str;
187       int i;
188
189       str = malloc((unsigned) strlen(str1)+1);
190
191       for (i = 0; str1[i] != EOS; i++)
192         if (is_alpha(str1[i]))
193           str[i] = toupper(str1[i]);
194
195       str[i] = EOS;
196
197       return(str);
198    } /* unfold */
199    /* ------------------------------------------------------------ */
200    /* moves bytes, allows for overlap */
201    int move_struct(dest, origin, nbytes)
202         char *dest;            /* move data to destination */
203         char *origin;          /* move data from origin */
204         int nbytes;            /* no. of bytes to be transferred */
205    {
206       if ( origin > dest)
207         return(structcpy(dest, origin, nbytes));
208       else { /* origin and destination overlap */
209         dest += nbytes-1;      /* point to end of areas */
210         origin += nbytes-1;
211         if (nbytes <= 0)
212           return(FALSE);
213
214         while (nbytes--)       /* stop when all bytes are moved */
215           *dest-- = *origin--;
216       }
217       return(TRUE);  /* return successfully */
218    } /* move_struct */
219
220    cpy_nosemi(s, t)                /* copy t to s; without semicols */
221         char *s, *t;
222    {
223       while (*t != ';')
224         *s++ = *t++;
225
226       *s = EOS;
227    } /* move_struct */
228    /* ------------------------------------------------------------ */
229    char *s_copy(str)
230        char *str;
231    {
232       register char *s;
233
234       if ((s = calloc(1, (unsigned) strlen(str)+1)) == NULL)
235         return(NULL);
236
237       strcpy(s, str);
238       s[strlen(str)] = EOS;
239       return(s);
240    } /* s_copy */
241    /* ------------------------------------------------------------ */
```

```
242    int cat_strs (result, s1, s2)
243         char result[];
244         char s1[];
245         char s2[];
246    {
247      strcpy(result, s1);
248      strcat(result, s2);
249    } /* cat_strs */
250    /* ------------------------------------------------------------ */
251    char    *stck(rel, arg)
252         char       rel[];
253         int        arg;
254    {
255      sprintf(rel, "snapshot%d", arg);
256      return(rel);
257    } /* stck */
258    /* ------------------------------------------------------------ */
259    make_quattr(rel_name, att_name)
260         char       *rel_name, *att_name;
261    {
262      strcat(rel_name, ".");
263      strcat(rel_name, att_name);
264
265    } /* make_quattr */
266    /* ------------------------------------------------------------ */
267    l_substring(string, result)
268         char *string, *result;
269    {
270      char *bufptr = string;
271
272
273      while((*result++ = *bufptr++) != '.')
274         ;
275      *--result = EOS;
276    } /* l_substring */
277    /* ------------------------------------------------------------ */
278    lsubstring_index(string, substring)
279         char *string, *substring;
280    {
281      int i, j, k;
282
283      for (i = 0; string[i] != EOS; i++)
284        for (j = i, k = 0; string[j] == substring[k]; j++, k++)
285          if (substring[k+1] == EOS)
286            return(i);   /* return index */
287      return(FAIL);                /* substring not found */
288
289    } /* lsubstring_index */
290    /* ------------------------------------------------------------ */
291    buf_free(buf, len)
292         char **buf;
293         int len;
294    {
295      int i;
296
297      if (buf){
298        for (i = 0; i < len; i++)
299          if (buf[i])
300            nfree(buf[i]);
301          else
302            break;
```

```
303
304          nfree((char *) buf);
305      }
306    } /* buf_free */
307    /* ------------------------------------------------------------ */
308    free_pred(prptr)
309          struct pred **prptr;
310    {
311      nfree((*prptr)->pr_rlname);
312      buf_free((*prptr)->pr_ixtype, 10);
313      buf_free((*prptr)->pr_atname, 10);
314      nfree((char *) (*prptr)->pr_opd);
315      nfree((char *) *prptr);
316      *prptr = NULL;
317    } /* free_pred */
318    /* ------------------------------------------------------------ */
319    int set_pred(prptr)
320          struct pred **prptr;
321    {
322      if ((*prptr = MALLOC(struct pred )) == NULL)
323         return(FALSE);
324      (*prptr)->pr_rlname = NULL;
325      if (!((*prptr)->pr_ixtype = dcalloc(10)))
326         return (FALSE);
327      if (!((*prptr)->pr_atname = dcalloc(10)))
328         return (FALSE);
329
330      if (((*prptr)->pr_opd =
331            ((struct operand**)calloc(10, sizeof(struct operand)))) == NULL)
332         return(error(INSMEM));
333
334      return(TRUE);
335
336    } /* set_pred */
337    /* ------------------------------------------------------------ */
338    insert_string(string, substring, loc)
339          char *string, *substring;
340          int loc;
341    {
342      int index_str = 0;       /* index into the string */
343      int t_index = 0;
344      char temp_buf[100];
345
346      /* we can append the substring at the end of current string */
347      if (loc > strlen(string))
348         return(FAIL);
349
350      /* copy the characters in the string prior to the start
351         location to the temporary buffer */
352      while(index_str < loc)
353         temp_buf[t_index++] = string[index_str++];
354
355      temp_buf[t_index] = EOS;
356
357      /* catenate the substring */
358      strcat(temp_buf, substring);
359
360      t_index = strlen(temp_buf);
361      while (temp_buf[t_index++] = string[index_str++]);
362
363      /* copy temporary buffer back into original string */
```

```
364     strcpy(string, temp_buf);
365
366     return(TRUE);
367   } /* insert_string */
368  /* ------------------------------------------------------------- */
369  remove_substring(strng, loc, no_of_chars)
370       char *strng;
371       int loc;               /* location of first char to remove */
372       int no_of_chars;       /* number of chars to remove */
373  {
374    int len;   /* length of string */
375    int loc1;  /* location of 1st char to be removed */
376    int loc2;  /* location of 1st char remaining after removal */
377
378    len = strlen(strng);
379
380    if (loc >= len || loc < 0)
381      return(FAIL);
382
383    /* see whether no. of chars to be deleted GTE string length */
384    if (loc + no_of_chars <= len) /* no */
385      loc2 = loc + no_of_chars;
386    else                          /* yes */
387      loc2 = len;                 /* delete up to EOS */
388
389    /* remove characters now */
390    for (loc1 = loc; strng[loc1] = strng[loc2]; loc1++)
391      loc2++;
392
393    return(TRUE);
394  } /* remove_string */
395  /* ------------------------------------------------------------- */
396  double maximum(arg1, arg2)
397       double arg1;
398       double arg2;
399  {
400    return(MAX(arg1, arg2));
401  } /* max */
402  /* ------------------------------------------------------------- */
403  double minimum(arg1, arg2)
404       double arg1;
405       double arg2;
406  {
407    return(MIN(arg1, arg2));
408  } /* min */
409  /* ------------------------------------------------------------- */
410  double sum(arg1, arg2)
411       double arg1;
412       double arg2;
413  {
414    return(arg1+arg2);
415  } /* sum */
416  /* ------------------------------------------------------------- */
417  double average(arg1, arg2)
418       double arg1;
419       double arg2;
420  {
421    if (avg_cnt == 1)
422      avg_sum = arg1 + arg2;
423    else
424        avg_sum += arg1;
```

```
425
426      avg_cnt++;
427      return(avg_sum / avg_cnt);
428    } /* avg */
429    /* ------------------------------------------------------------ */
430    double count(arg1, arg2)
431         double arg1;
432         double arg2;
433    {
434      return(arg2 + 1);
435    } /* count */
436    /* ------------------------------------------------------------ */
437    init_group()
438    {
439      avg_cnt = 1;
440      avg_sum = 0;
441    } /* init_group */
442    /* ------------------------------------------------------------ */
443    f_move(from, to)
444         char *from, *to;
445    {
446      unlink(to);  /* purge file in case it already exists */
447
448      if (!f_mv(from, to))
449        return(FALSE);
450
451      return(TRUE);
452    } /* f_move */
453    /* ------------------------------------------------------------ */
454    f_mv(from, to)
455         char *from, *to;
456    {
457
458      if (link(from, to) == FAIL) /* give aux. file the rel. name */
459        return (FALSE);
460
461      if (unlink(from) == FAIL)   /* purge file */
462        return (FALSE);
463
464      return(TRUE);
465    } /* f_mv */
466    /* ------------------------------------------------------------ */
467    char  *status(fname, perm)  /* "s" command */
468         char fname[];
469         char perm[];
470    {
471      struct stat sb;
472      char f_name[20];
473      int fd;
474
475      sprintf(f_name, "%s.db", fname);
476      fd = open(f_name, 0);
477      fstat(fd, &sb);
478
479      sprintf(perm, "%o", sb.st_mode & 0777);
480
481      close(fd);
482      return(perm);
483    } /* status */
484    /* ------------------------------------------------------------ */
485    char *path(pathname)
```

```
486           char pathname[];
487     {
488       char *getlogin(), *cuserid();
489
490       if (getlogin() != NULL)
491         strcpy(pathname, getlogin());
492       else
493         strcpy(pathname, cuserid((char *) 0));
494
495       pathname[strlen(pathname)+1] = EOS;
496       return(pathname);
497     } /* path */
498     /* ------------------------------------------------------------ */
499     int fexists(fname)
500           char fname[];
501     {
502       char f_name[20];
503       int fd;
504
505       sprintf(f_name,"%s.db", fname);
506       f_name[strlen(f_name)] = EOS;
507
508       if ((fd = open(f_name, 0)) == FAIL)
509         return(FALSE);
510       else
511         close(fd);
512       return(TRUE);
513     } /* fexists */
514     /* ------------------------------------------------------------ */
515     int rsubstring_index(string, substring)
516           char *string, *substring;
517     {  int loc;
518
519       loc = right_index(string, substring);
520
521       /* substring found, point prior to it */
522       if (loc != -1)
523         loc -= strlen(substring);
524
525       /* return location , -1 if not found */
526       return(loc);
527
528     } /* rsubstring_index */
529     /* ------------------------------------------------------------ */
530     int right_index(string, substring)
531           char *string, *substring;
532     {
533       int i, j, k;
534       int loc = -1;  /* rightmost occurrence of substring */
535
536       for (i = 0; *(string+i) != EOS; i++)
537         for (j = i, k = 0; (*(substring+k) != EOS) &&
538             *(substring+k) == *(string+j); k++, j++)
539           if (*(substring+k+1) == ' ' || *(substring+k+1) == EOS){
540             /* substring found, point past it */
541             loc = i + strlen(substring);
542             break;
543           }
544
545       /* return location , -1 if not found */
546       return(loc);
```

```
547     } /* right_index */
548     /* ------------------------------------------------------------ */
549     int clear_mem(p, c, tcnbyt)
550         char *p;            /* start of memory area */
551         int c;              /* value to write there */
552         int tcnbyt;         /* total no. of bytes to be cleared */
553     {
554       while (tcnbyt--)
555         *p++ = c;           /* clear current location */
556     } /* clear_mem */
557     /* ------------------------------------------------------------ */
558     char *rmalloc(n)        /* check return from malloc */
559         int n;
560     {
561       char *ptr;
562       char *pt_error();
563
564       ptr = malloc((unsigned) n);
565
566       if (ptr == (char *) 0)
567         return(pt_error(INSMEM));
568
569       return(ptr);
570     } /* rmalloc */
571     /* ------------------------------------------------------------ */
572     stf(s, res)    /* convert string to float */
573         char s[];
574         float *res;
575     {
576       float val, power;
577       int i;
578
579       for (i = 0; s[i] == ' ' || s[i] == NEWLINE; i++)
580         ;   /* skip white space */
581
582       for (val = 0 ; s[i] >= '0' && s[i] <= '9'; i++)
583         val = 10 * val + s[i] - '0';
584
585       if (s[i] == '.')
586         i++;
587
588       for (power = 1; s[i] >= '0' && s[i] <= '9'; i++) {
589         val = 10 * val + s[i] - '0';
590         power *= 10;
591       }
592       *res = val / power;
593     } /* stf */
594     /* ------------------------------------------------------------ */
595     requ_init(argc, argv)
596         int argc;
597         char *argv[];
598     {
599       /* create and load system catalogs */
600       if (!fexists("systab")) {
601         sys_flag = TRUE;
602         com_file("cre_cat");
603       }
604
605       /* load views */
606       if (fexists("sysview")) {
607         load_views();
```

```
608        }
609
610        if (argc == 2) {
611          if (fexists("systab") && fexists("sysatrs"))
612            com_file(argv[1]);
613          else {
614            printf("Create the system catalogs first,");
615            printf("and then call a command file !\n");
616          }
617        }
618    }
```

file: requ.c

```
1      /* REQUIEM - main routine */
2
3      #include <stdio.h>
4      #include <signal.h>
5      #include "requ.h"
6
7      extern int error_code;
8      extern char *error_text();
9      extern int fpecatch();
10     extern BOOL   sys_flag;  /* true for system defined relations */
11
12     main(argc, argv)
13         int argc;
14         char *argv[];
15     {
16       requ_header();
17       s_init();
18
19       requ_init(argc, argv); /* create & load system catalogs */
20
21       while (TRUE) {
22         signal(SIGFPE, fpecatch);
23         db_prompt("REQUIEM: ","\t# ");
24         if (!parse((char *) 0, FALSE)) {
25           printf("*** ERROR : %s ***\n",error_text(error_code));
26           cmd_kill(); /* clear command-line and icf environments */
27         }
28
29         if (sys_flag) {
30           if (fexists("syskey"))
31             sys_flag = FALSE;         /* reset system flag */
32         }
33       }
34
35     } /* main */
```

file: table.c

```
1      /* REQUIEM - table output and file format routines */
2
3      #include <stdio.h>
4      #include "requ.h"
5
6      extern struct cmd_file *lex_cfp;
7      static char buffer[TABLEMAX+1];
```

```
 8    int bndx;
 9
10    int    table(fp, slptr)
11          FILE *fp;
12          struct sel *slptr;
13    {
14      int   tcnt;
15
16      /* loop through the selected tuples */
17      for (tcnt = 0; fetch(slptr, FALSE); tcnt++) {
18
19        /* print table head on first tuple selected */
20        if (tcnt == 0)
21          tab_head(fp, slptr);
22
23        /* print the tuple */
24        tab_entry(fp, slptr);
25      }
26
27      /* print table foot */
28      if (tcnt != 0)
29        tab_foot(fp, slptr);
30
31      /* return the tuple count */
32      return (tcnt);
33    } /* table */
34    /* ------------------------------------------------------------- */
35    tab_head(fp,slptr)
36          FILE *fp;
37          struct sel *slptr;
38    {
39      struct sattr *saptr;
40      int twidth,fwidth,i;
41      char *aname;
42
43      /* compute the table width */
44      printf("\n");
45      twidth = 1;
46      for (saptr = SEL_ATTRS; saptr != NULL; saptr = saptr->sa_next)
47        twidth += ATTRIBUTE_SIZE + 3;
48
49      /* print the top line of the table */
50      bstart();
51      binsert(' ');
52      for (i = 0; i < twidth-2; i++)
53        binsert('+');
54      binsert(' ');
55      print_tabline(fp);
56
57      /* print the label line of the table */
58      bstart();
59      for (saptr = SEL_ATTRS;saptr != NULL;saptr = saptr->sa_next) {
60        fwidth = ATTRIBUTE_SIZE;
61        binsert('|');
62        binsert(' ');
63        if ((aname = saptr->sa_name) == NULL)
64          aname = saptr->sa_aname;
65        for (i = 0; i < fwidth; i++)
66          if (*aname != EOS) {
67            if (is_alpha(*aname))
68              binsert(toupper(*aname++));
```

```
69            else
70                binsert(*aname++);
71            }
72            else
73                binsert(' ');
74          binsert(' ');
75        }
76        binsert('|');
77        print_tabline(fp);
78
79        /* print the line under the labels */
80        bstart();
81        binsert(' ');
82        for (i = 0; i < twidth-2; i++)
83          binsert('-');
84        binsert(' ');
85        print_tabline(fp);
86      } /* tab_head */
87  /* ------------------------------------------------------------ */
88    tab_foot(fp,slptr)
89          FILE *fp;
90          struct sel *slptr;
91    {
92        struct sattr *saptr;
93        int twidth, i, fwidth;
94
95        /* compute the table width */
96        twidth = 1;
97        for (saptr = SEL_ATTRS; saptr != NULL; saptr = saptr->sa_next)
98          twidth += ATTRIBUTE_SIZE + 3;
99
100        /* print an empty line */
101        bstart();
102        for (saptr = SEL_ATTRS; saptr != NULL; saptr = saptr->sa_next) {
103          fwidth = ATTRIBUTE_SIZE;
104          binsert('|');
105          for (i = 0; i < fwidth+2; i++)
106            binsert(' ');
107        }
108        binsert('|');
109        print_tabline(fp);
110
111        /* print the line at the foot of the table */
112        bstart();
113        for (i = 0; i < twidth; i++)
114          binsert('\/');
115
116        print_tabline(fp);
117        printf("\n");
118      } /* tab_foot */
119  /* ------------------------------------------------------------ */
120    tab_entry(fp,slptr)
121          FILE *fp;
122          struct sel *slptr;
123    {
124        struct sattr *saptr;
125        int fwidth,i;
126
127        /* print a table entry */
128        bstart();
129        for (saptr = SEL_ATTRS;saptr != NULL;saptr = saptr->sa_next) {
```

```
130          fwidth = ATTRIBUTE_SIZE;
131          binsert('|');
132          binsert(' ');
133          for (i = 0; i < fwidth; i++)
134            if (saptr->sa_aptr[i] != 0)
135              binsert(saptr->sa_aptr[i]);
136            else
137              binsert(' ');
138          binsert(' ');
139        }
140        binsert('|');
141        print_tabline(fp);
142      } /* tab_entry */
143      /* ------------------------------------------------------------ */
144      bstart()
145      {
146        bndx = 0;
147      } /* bstart */
148      /* ------------------------------------------------------------ */
149      binsert(ch)
150          int ch;
151      {
152        if (bndx < TABLEMAX)
153          buffer[bndx++] = ch;
154      } /* binsert */
155
156      print_tabline(fp)
157          FILE *fp;
158      {
159        buffer[bndx] = EOS;
160        fprintf(fp,"%s\n",buffer);
161      } /* print_tabline */
162      /* ------------------------------------------------------------ */
163      int    form(ofp, slptr, ffp)
164          FILE *ofp;
165          struct sel *slptr;
166          FILE *ffp;
167      {
168        char   aname[ANSIZE+1];
169        int    ch, tcnt;
170
171        /* loop through the selected tuples */
172        for (tcnt = 0; fetch(slptr, FALSE); tcnt++) {
173
174          /* reposition the form definition file */
175          fseek(ffp, 0L, 0);
176
177          /* process the form */
178          while ((ch = getc(ffp)) != -1)
179            if (ch == '<') {
180              get_aname(ffp, aname);
181              put_avalue(ofp, slptr, aname);
182            }
183            else
184              putc(ch, ofp);
185        }
186
187        /* return the tuple count */
188        return (tcnt);
189      } /* form */
190      /* ------------------------------------------------------------ */
```

```
191    get_aname(fp, aname)
192        FILE *fp;
193        char      *aname;
194    {
195      int   ch;
196
197      while ((ch = getc(fp)) != '>')
198        if (!isspace(ch))
199          *aname++ = ch;
200      *aname = EOS;
201    } /* get_aname */
202    /* ----------------------------------------------------------- */
203    put_avalue(fp, slptr, aname)
204        FILE *fp;
205        struct sel *slptr;
206        char      *aname;
207    {
208      struct sattr *saptr;
209      char *saname;
210      int   i;
211
212      /* loop through the selected attributes */
213      for (saptr = SEL_ATTRS; saptr != NULL; saptr = saptr->sa_next) {
214
215        /* check the selected attribute name */
216        if ((saname = saptr->sa_name) == NULL)
217          saname = saptr->sa_aname;
218        if (strcmp(saname, aname) == EQUAL)
219          break;
220      }
221
222      if (saptr == NULL) {
223        fprintf(fp, "<error>");
224        return;
225      }
226
227      /* get the attribute value */
228      for (i = 0; i < ATTRIBUTE_SIZE; i++)
229        if (saptr->sa_aptr[i] != 0)
230          putc(saptr->sa_aptr[i], fp);
231        else
232          putc(' ', fp);
233    } /* put_avalue */
234    /* ----------------------------------------------------------- */
235    char *prompt_input(aptr, insert, avalue)
236        struct attribute *aptr;
237        BOOL insert;
238        char *avalue;
239    {
240      char aname[ANSIZE+1];
241      char *val_start; /* points to bof attribute value */
242      char prompt[40];
243      char *unfold(), *getnum(), *getfloat(), *getfld();
244
245      if (!insert) {
246
247        for (val_start = avalue; isspace(*val_start); val_start++)
248          ;
249
250        /* print it */
251        if (strlen(aname) < 8)
```

```
252            printf("%s\t\t: %s\n", unfold(aptr->at_name), val_start);
253         else
254            printf("%s\t: %s\n", unfold(aptr->at_name), val_start);
255
256      }
257
258      /* save the attribute name */
259      strncpy(aname,aptr->at_name,
260             MIN(strlen(aptr->at_name), ANSIZE));
261      aname[MIN(strlen(aptr->at_name), ANSIZE)] = EOS;
262
263      /* set up null prompt strings */
264      db_prompt((char *) 0, (char *) 0);
265
266      /* prompt and input attribute value */
267      while (TRUE) {
268        if (lex_cfp == NULL)
269           if (strlen(aname) < 8)
270              sprintf(prompt, "%s\t\t: ",unfold(aname));
271           else
272              sprintf(prompt, "%s\t: ", unfold(aname));
273
274        if (aptr->at_type == TNUM) {
275           if (getnum(prompt, avalue, aptr->at_size) != NULL)
276              break;
277        } else if (aptr->at_type == TREAL) {
278           if (getfloat(prompt, avalue, aptr->at_size) != NULL)
279              break;
280        } else if (aptr->at_type == TCHAR) {
281           if (getfld(prompt, avalue, aptr->at_size) != NULL)
282              break;
283        } else
284           return(NULL);
285      }
286
287      /* return the attribute value */
288      return(avalue);
289
290   } /* prompt_input */
291   /* ------------------------------------------------------------ */
292   /* routine for printing the extract templates */
293   template(buff, fp)
294        char buff[];
295        FILE *fp;
296   {
297      int i;
298      bstart();
299      binsert('|');
300      binsert(' ');
301      for (i = 0; i < 51; i++)
302        if (*buff != EOS)
303           binsert(*buff++);
304        else
305           binsert(' ');
306      binsert(' ');
307      binsert('|');
308      print_tabline(fp);
309   } /* template */
310   /* ------------------------------------------------------------ */
311   templ_line(fp, simple)
312        FILE *fp;
```

```
313          BOOL simple;
314      {
315        int i;
316
317        bstart();
318        for (i = 0; i < 55; i++)
319          if (simple) {
320            if (i == 0 || i== 54)
321              binsert(' ');
322            else
323              binsert('-');
324          }
325          else
326            binsert('\/');
327        print_tabline(fp);
328      } /* templ_line */
329  /* ------------------------------------------------------------ */
330  int rprint(format)
331        char *format;
332  {
333      int i;
334
335      if (*format == EOS)
336        return(FALSE);
337
338      printf("\n\n");
339      for (i = 0; i < strlen(format) + 6; i++)
340        printf("+");
341
342      printf("\n");
343      printf("+");
344      printf("  ");
345      printf(format);
346      printf("  ");
347      printf("+\n");
348      printf("+");
349
350      for (i = 0; i < strlen(format) + 4 ; i++)
351        printf(" ");
352      printf("+\n");
353
354      for (i = 0; i < strlen(format) + 6; i++)
355        printf("\/");
356
357      printf("\n\n");
358
359      return(TRUE);
360  } /* r_print */
361  /* ------------------------------------------------------------ */
362  requ_header()
363  {
364      int i;
365      char format[65];
366
367      printf("\n");
368      for (i = 0; i <61; i++)
369        printf("+");
370      printf("\n");
371      printf("+  ");
372      printf("REQUIEM: Relational Query & Update Interactive System    +\n");
373      sprintf(format, "VERSION 2.1");
```

```
374        printf("+   ");
375        printf(format);
376        for (i = strlen(format) + 3; i < 60; i++)
377          printf(" ");
378        printf("+\n");
379
380        for (i = 0; i <61; i++)
381          printf("\/");
382        printf("\n\n");
383      } /* requ_header */
384   /* ------------------------------------------------------------ */
385   tab_keys(cntr, buff, key_buff)
386        int cntr;
387        char *buff;
388        char **key_buff;
389   {
390      int i, j;
391
392      for (i = 0, j = 0; i < cntr; i++) {
393
394        if (i == 0) {
395          sprintf(buff , "----- ");
396          j = strlen(buff);
397        }
398
399        if (i+1 < cntr) {
400          sprintf(buff+j, "%s,  ", key_buff[i]);
401          j += 3;
402        }
403        else
404          strcpy(buff+j, key_buff[i]);
405
406        j += strlen(key_buff[i]);
407      }
408    } /* tab_keys */
409   /* ------------------------------------------------------------ */
410   message(cntr, format)
411        int cntr;
412        char *format;
413   {
414
415      if (cntr == 0)
416        sprintf(format, "<   no  tuples  found   >");
417      if (cntr == 1)
418        sprintf(format, "<   only %d tuple found    >", cntr);
419      else
420        sprintf(format, "<   %d tuples found    >", cntr);
421
422    } /* message */
423   /* ------------------------------------------------------------ */
```

C

Appendix C

C.1   A sample session

In this appendix we will describe what steps are necessary to install REQUIEM. For this purpose we have recorded a sample session that illustrates how REQUIEM is compiled and linked and how the system is initialized. Recall that to function properly REQUIEM relies on the existence of the system catalogs. As these catalogs normally do not exist prior to system initialization they must be explicitly created. If during the system start-up phase REQUIEM notices that the system catalogs have not yet been installed, it attempts to open an external command file named cre_cat. This file contains the **create** statements that are required to create the system catalogs. The contents of this file are the definition statements of the system catalogs and are presented at the end of this appendix.

In the remainder of this appendix we shall explain how to install REQUIEM. We shall exemplify this process for computers that run the Unix operating system.* After all source files have been copied into an arbitrary directory, the user simply invokes the Unix command **make**. This is a general-purpose command designed to assist in automating the maintenance of any non-trivial programming packages involving a number of source code files. By default the **make** tool expects to find, in your current working directory, a user-specified file called **makefile** which contains details of the program package that is made up from explicitly named component source files together with an indication of the way that these component files depend on one another (for more information refer to the appropriate Unix documentation). In our case the **make** program is instructed to compile the source files and build a library, named **requ.a**. After the library has been created by the standard Unix commands **ar** and **ranlib**, the source file

---

*If your system does not run Unix do not panic. You must simply compile and link all the source files in section C.1.1 manually.

containing the REQUIEM main command loop (**requ.c**) is compiled and
linked with the **requ.a** library, to form the program package **requiem**.

We are now able to call REQUIEM by simply typing the command
requiem. REQUIEM prints its banner message and automatically creates
the required system catalogs, namely *SYSTAB, SYSATRS, SYSVIEW*, and
SYSKEY. Next REQUIEM prints its prompt and expects the user to type
a valid command. In our sample session we enter the command specifier
symbol @ followed by the name of an indirect command file. This indirect
command file contains **create** statements which define the suppliers-and-
products database schema that we have used throughout this book.

For each created relation, REQUIEM prints an appropriate message.
After the command file has been executed, REQUIEM prints a prompt
and is ready to accept the next command. In our experimental session we
simply edit **print** commands to print the contents of the system catalogs.
We can easily verify that the contents of the catalogs reflect the current
state of *REQUIEM*. Subsequently, we leave REQUIEM by typing the command **quit** (or **exit**). REQUIEM finally prints an appropriate message and
exits.

C.1.1   The REQUIEM makefile

In the following we illustrate the REQUIEM component files which must
be assembled into a concise running package by means of the **make** facility.

```
$ ls
access.c     hash.c      lexan.c      reminder.c   xinterp.c
btree.c      iex.c       misc.c       requ.c
cat.c        impl.c      parser.c     table.c
create.c     io.c        pgm_int.c    view.c
err.c        io_lib.c    quedcmp.c    xcom.c
$ make
cc -g -c access.c
cc -g -c btree.c
cc -g -c cat.c
cc -g -c create.c
cc -g -c err.c
cc -g -c hash.c
cc -g -c iex.c
cc -g -c impl.c
cc -g -c io.c
cc -g -c io_lib.c
cc -g -c lexan.c
cc -g -c misc.c
cc -g -c parser.c
cc -g -c pgm_int.c
cc -g -c quedcmp.c
cc -g -c tabl.c
cc -g -c view.c
cc -g -c xcom.c
```

```
cc -g -c xinterp.c
ar rv requ.a access.o btree.o cat.o create.o err.o hash.o
iex.o impl.o io.o io_lib.o lexan.o misc.o parser.o pgm_int.o
quedcmp.o tabl.o view.o xcom.o xinterp.o
a - access.o
a - btree.o
a - cat.o
a - create.o
a - err.o
a - hash.o
a - iex.o
a - impl.o
a - io.o
a - io_lib.o
a - lexan.o
a - misc.o
a - parser.o
a - pgm_int.o
a - quedcmp.o
a - tabl.o
a - view.o
a - xcom.o
a - xinterp.o
ar: creating requ.a
ranlib requ.a
cc -g -c requ.c
cc -g -o requiem requ.o requ.a
```

C.1.2 Database schema definition and sample run

Here is the user-defined cre_file which creates and initializes the REQUIEM
database system:

file: cre_file:

```
create systab (relname  (char(12), UNIQUE),
           creator (char(20), SECONDARY),
           perms (num(5)),
           deriv (char(5)),
           natrs  (num(8)));

create sysatrs (atrname (char(20), UNIQUE),
           relname  (char(12), SECONDARY),
           type (char(5)),
           length (num(6)),
           index  (char(5)));

create sysview (viewname  (char(12), UNIQUE),
           base (char(12)),
           text  (char(132)));

create syskey (fgnkey  (char(12), UNIQUE),
           relname (char(12)),
           qualifier  (char(12)),
           primary  (char(12)));
```

```
$ requiem

+++++++++++++++++++++++++++++++++++++++++++++++++++++++++++++++++++
+   REQUIEM: Relational Query & Update Interactive System     +
+   VERSION 2.1                                               +
/////////////////////////////////////////////////////////////////


+++++++++++++++++++++++++++++++++++++
+   Relation systab created     +
+                               +
///////////////////////////////////


+++++++++++++++++++++++++++++++++++++
+   Relation sysatrs created    +
+                               +
///////////////////////////////////


+++++++++++++++++++++++++++++++++++++
+   Relation sysview created    +
+                               +
///////////////////////////////////


+++++++++++++++++++++++++++++++++++++
+   Relation syskey created     +
+                               +
///////////////////////////////////

REQUIEM: @cre_file


+++++++++++++++++++++++++++++++++++++
+   Relation supplier created   +
+                               +
///////////////////////////////////


+++++++++++++++++++++++++++++++++++++
+   Relation product created    +
+                               +
///////////////////////////////////


+++++++++++++++++++++++++++++++++++++
+   Relation supply created     +
+                               +
///////////////////////////////////


REQUIEM: print systab;
```

```
++++++++++++++++++++++++++++++++++++++++++++++++++++++++++++++++
| RELNAME       | CREATOR        | PERMS | DERIV | NATRS       |
----------------------------------------------------------------
| systab        | sys            |  600  | base  |     5 |
| sysatrs       | sys            |  600  | base  |     5 |
| sysview       | sys            |  600  | base  |     3 |
| syskey        | sys            |  600  | base  |     4 |
| supplier      | valder         |  600  | base  |     3 |
| product       | valder         |  600  | base  |     4 |
| supply        | valder         |  600  | base  |     3 |
|               |                |       |       |       |
////////////////////////////////////////////////////////////////
```

REQUIEM: print sysatrs;

```
++++++++++++++++++++++++++++++++++++++++++++++++++++++++++++++++
| RELNAME       | ATRNAME        | TYPE  | LENGTH | INDEX      |
----------------------------------------------------------------
| systab        | relname        | char  |   12  | yes  |
| systab        | creator        | char  |   20  | yes  |
| systab        | perms          | num   |    5  | no   |
| systab        | deriv          | char  |    5  | no   |
| systab        | natrs          | num   |    8  | no   |
| sysatrs       | atrname        | char  |   20  | yes  |
| sysatrs       | relname        | char  |   12  | yes  |
| sysatrs       | type           | char  |    5  | no   |
| sysatrs       | length         | num   |    6  | no   |
| sysatrs       | index          | char  |    5  | no   |
| sysview       | viewname       | char  |   12  | yes  |
| sysview       | base           | char  |   12  | no   |
| sysview       | text           | char  |  132  | no   |
| syskey        | fgnkey         | char  |   12  | yes  |
| syskey        | relname        | char  |   12  | no   |
| syskey        | qualifier      | char  |   12  | no   |
| syskey        | primary        | char  |   12  | no   |
| supplier      | supid          | num   |    5  | yes  |
| supplier      | supname        | char  |   20  | yes  |
| supplier      | location       | char  |   20  | no   |
| product       | prodno         | num   |    5  | yes  |
| product       | prodname       | char  |   20  | yes  |
| product       | weight         | real  |   10  | no   |
| product       | finish         | char  |   15  | no   |
| supply        | sid            | num   |    5  | yes  |
| supply        | prno           | num   |    5  | yes  |
| supply        | quantity       | num   |   10  | no   |
|               |                |       |       |      |
////////////////////////////////////////////////////////////////
```

REQUIEM: print syskey;

```
++++++++++++++++++++++++++++++++++++++++++++++++++++++++++++++++
| FGNKEY        | RELNAME        | QUALIFIER     | PRIMARY     |
----------------------------------------------------------------
| sid           | supply         | supplier      | supid       |
| prno          | supply         | product       | prodno      |
|               |                |               |             |
////////////////////////////////////////////////////////////////
$ quit;
```

Glossary

abstract machine To separate the machine-independent and machine-dependent parts of a compiler we can define an intermediate or target language which can mediate between the two separate compiler parts. This target language can be thought of as a machine, usually called an abstract machine, since the front end of a compiler will use it like an object machine.

access method The type of physical file access being performed, e.g. indexed or sequential.

access permissions Specification of the operations that authorized users may apply to relations or views.

application program A program that performs a set of tasks associated with an application supported by a database system.

ASCII A 7-bit standard code used for representing characters.

block The smallest amount of data that can be input from or output to the disk during a single access operation.

buffer The software interface module interposed between a program and a file on disk.

canned query An internal query executed by the system when it needs to perform a fairly complex task involving numerous accesses to the database.

data definition language (DDL) A set of definition statements that is used to describe a database to the DBMS.

data file A collection of records.

data item A unit fact concerning some entity.

data manipulation language (DML) A set of manipulation statements that is used by the user to communicate with the database.

database A repository for structured data.

database management system (DBMS) A set of system modules that receives and satisfies all the data requests from a database.

direct file organization A file organization in which there exists a predictable relationship between the key used to identify an individual item and that item's position in a file.

field A component of a record data structure.

hashing The form of random access where the value of the access key (index key) is converted into a record number by means of a mathematical

transformation. Subsequently, this key is stored in a hash table. Entries
in hashing can be unique or non-unique. In the former case entries are
simply installed in the hash table, while in the latter an instance counter
associated with each entry in table is increased to denote the second or
third occurrence of non-unique keys.

index Associates the value of some field or fields of a record in an index
file with corresponding values in a data file.

index file A file in which each record consists of a data value (key) together
with a pointer. The data value is a value that corresponds to some field
in a data file, while the pointer identifies the records in the data file
containing that value.

leaf node A node in a tree that points to no other nodes.

least recently used (LRU) A replacement technique, whereby the least
recently used block of data is a candidate for replacement.

logical record A collection of data items that logically describe a particular entity.

machine code The bit patterns capable of controlling the operation of a
particular computer.

null value A special attribute value that is used to represent missing information.

P-code Most Pascal compilers generate an intermediate language called P-
code from Pascal expressions by means of actions in the recursive descent
compiler. P-code is the "machine" code for a hypothetical stack-based
machine, which is usually interpreted. P-code has been an aid in trans-
porting Pascal to new environments.

parent node The node at one level higher in a tree that points to the
currently accessed node.

postfix notation A popular type of intermediate code in which the operators appear after their operands. Postfix notation is also known as reverse
Polish notation.

prefix notation A popular type of intermediate code in which each operator appears before its operands. Prefix notation is also known as Polish
notation after the country of its originator.

primary key The field in a record that uniquely identifies it.

random file organization A file organization in which a predictable relationship between the key used to identify an individual record and that
record's location in an external file is implied.

record A data structure in which a collection of data items (fields) can be
accessed by a unique name and describes a particular entity.

relative address A common addressing scheme in which a point or base
address is established at a known address, e.g. the beginning of a record,
so that subsequent points can be located by a displacement value which

is added to the base address.

relative file A common implementation of random file organization available in most high-level programming languages.

root The top node in a tree structure that is pointed to by no other node.

schema A specification (or definition) of a database using the DDL at hand.

secondary key A key field in record other than the primary key, which may be used to speed up access to a data record.

sequential file organization A file organization, whereby components are written and read in sequence (consecutively).

sibling nodes Nodes in a tree structure that are of the same height.

stack machine An abstract machine which uses its primary memory as a stack. This abstract machine has separate instruction and data memories and all operations are performed on values on top of a stack. We regard the bottom of the stack as reserved for variables and the rest of it for working storage. Code evaluation of expressions on a stack machine is closely related to postfix notation for that expression.

subschema A specification of the schema portion that a specific group of users is allowed to utilize.

syntax-direct translation This translation scheme specifies the parsing and consequently the translation of a construct in terms of features associated with its syntactic components. These features may include any quantity associated with a given construct such as a type, storage allocation, scope of the construct, etc. A syntax-directed translation scheme uses a context-free grammar to specify the syntactic structure of a source statement. With each grammar symbol, it associates a set of features, and with each production, a set of semantic rules used for computing the values of the attributes associated with the symbols in the production.

three-address code After syntax and semantic analysis, some compilers generate an explicit intermediate representation of the source program. This intermediate representation can be thought of as a program for an abstract machine. A popular intermediate representation is called three-address code and is an effectively generalized assembly language for a hypothetical machine in which every memory location can simulate a register. Three-address code consists of a sequence of instructions, each of which consists of an operator and three addresses, two for operands and one for a result location.

user In a data processing environment we can typically consider three broad classes of user. First, the end-user who accesses the database from an on-line terminal. The second class of user is the application programmer, responsible for writing application programs that use the database, typically in some high-level language such as C or PL/I. Finally, the third class of user is the database administrator who is the person responsible for the overall control of the database system. In this book we use the term user to denote the database end-user, unless otherwise stated.

Bibliography

1. Stonebraker, M., Kreps, P., Wong E., Held, G., "The Design and Implementation of INGRES," *ACM TODS*, volume 1, no.2, 1976.
2. Astrahan, M., et al., "System R: A Relational Approach to Data Management," *ACM TODS*, volume 2, no.2, 1976.
3. Date, C.J., *An Introduction to Database Systems*, volume 1, 4th edition, Addison-Wesley Publishing Co., Reading, Mass., 1986.
4. Tsichritzis, D.C., Lochovsky, F.H., *Data Models*, Prentice Hall Inc., Englewood Cliffs, New Jersey, 1982.
5. Korth, H.F., Silbershatz, A., *Database System Concepts*, McGraw-Hill, New York, 1986.
6. *Object-Oriented Programming Systems, Languages and Applications*, Conference Proceedings, ACM Press, Portland, Oregon, October 1986.
7. *Object-Oriented Programming Systems, Languages and Applications*, Conference Proceedings, ACM Press, Orlando, Florida, October 1987.
8. *International Workshop on Object-Oriented Database Systems*, IEEE Computer Society Press, Asilomar, Ca., Sept. 1986.
9. Papazoglou, M.P., Hoffman, C., "Towards Versatile Object-Oriented Query Languages," *IEEE Proceedings Languages for Automation*, IEEE Computer Society Press, Vienna, August 1987.
10. Atre, S., *Database: Structured Techniques for Design, Performance and Management*, John Wiley, Chichester, 1980.
11. Perkinson, C.R., *Data Analysis: The Key to Database Design*, North-Holland, Amsterdam, 1984.
12. Kernighan, B.W., Ritchie, D. M., *The C Programming Language*, Prentice Hall Inc., Englewood Cliffs, New Jersey, 1978.
13. Samet, J. (ed.), *Query Languages: A Unified Approach*, report of the British Computer Society, Heyden, London, 1981.
14. Codd, E.F., Date, C.J., "Interactive Support for Non-Programmers, the Relational and Network Approaches," *Procs. 1974 ACM-SIGFIDET Workshop on Data Description, Access and Control*, Ann Arbor, Mich., May 1974.
15. Stonebraker, M.A., "Functional View of Data Independence," *Procs. 1974 ACM-SIGFIDET Workshop on Data Description, Access and Control*, Ann Arbor, Mich., May 1974.

16. Miller, N., *File Structures Using Pascal*, Benjamin/Cummings, Menlo Park, Ca., 1987.

17. Saltzberg, B., *File Structures: An Analytic Approach*, Prentice Hall Inc., Englewood Cliffs, New Jersey, 1988.

18. Date, C.J., *An Introduction to Database Systems*, volume 2, Addison-Wesley Publishing Co., Reading, Mass., 1984.

19. Date, C.J., *Selected Writings*, Addison-Wesley Publishing Co., Reading, Mass., 1986.

20. Teory, T.J., Fry, J.P., *Design of Database Structures*, Prentice Hall Inc., Englewood Cliffs, New Jersey, 1982.

21. Wiederhold, G., *Database Design*, McGraw-Hill, New York, 1983.

22. Database Architecture Framework Task Group, "Reference Model for DBMS Standardization," *SIGMOD Record*, volume 15, no.1, 1986.

23. Codd, E.F., A Relational Model for Large Shared Data Banks, *CACM*, volume 13, no.6, 1970.

24. IBM Corporation, "SQL/Data System General Information," IBM report, no. GH24-5012, San Jose, Ca., 1981.

25. Lacroix, M., Pirotte, A., *Domain Oriented Relational Languages*, VLDB, Paris, 1977.

26. Codd, E.F., "Extending the Relational Model to Capture More Meaning," *ACM TODS*, volume 4, no.4, 1979.

27. Date, C.J., *Referential Integrity*, VLDB, Paris, 1981.

28. Date, C.J., "A Formal Definition of the Relational Model," *SIGMOD Record*, volume 13, no.1, 1983.

29. Papazoglou, M.P., "An Extensible DBMS for Small–Medium Scale Systems," *IEEE Micro*, April 1989.

30. Kernighan, B.W., Pike, R., *The UNIX Programming Environment*, Prentice Hall Inc., Englewood Cliffs, New Jersey, 1984.

31. Date, C.J., *A Guide to the SQL Standard*, Addison-Wesley Publishing Co., Reading, Mass., 1987.

32. Deitel, H.M., *An Introduction to Operating Systems*, Addison-Wesley Publishing Co., Reading, Mass., 1984.

33. Tanenbaum, D., *Operating System Design and Implementation*, Prentice Hall Inc., Englewood Cliffs, New Jersey, 1987.

34. Jaeschke R., *Solutions in C*, Addison-Wesley Publishing Co., Reading, Mass., 1986.

35. Smith, P.D., Barnes, G.M., *Files & Databases: An Introduction*, Addison-Wesley Publishing Co., Reading, Mass., 1986.

36. Bayer, R., McCreight E.M., "Organization and Maintenance of Large Ordered Indices," *Acta Informatica*, volume 1, no.4, 1972.

37. Knuth, D.E., *The Art of Computer Programming*, volume 3, Addison-Wesley Publishing Co., Reading, Mass., 1973.

38. Jarke, M., Koch, J., "Query Optimization in Databases Systems", *ACM Computing Surveys*, volume 16, no. 2, June 1984.
39. Gray, P., *Logic, Algebra and Databases*, Ellis-Horwood, Chichester, 1984.
40. Robie, J., "Fast Data Access", *Byte*, January 1988.
41. Hunt, W.J., *The C Toolbox*, Addison-Wesley Publishing Co., Reading, Mass., 1985.
42. Aho, A.V., Sethi, R., Ullman, J.D., *Compilers: Principles, Techniques, and Tools*, Addison-Wesley Publishing Co., Reading, Mass., 1985.
43. Aho, A.V., Ullman, J.D., *Principles of Compiler Design*, Addison-Wesley Publishing Co., Reading, Mass., 1977.
44. Hunter, R., *Compilers: Their Design and Construction using Pascal*, Wiley, Chichester, 1985.
45. Fisher., R.J., Le Blanc, R., *Crafting a Compiler*, Benjamin/Cummings, Menlo Park, Ca., 1988.
46. Kochan, S., Wood, P.H., *Topics in C Programming*, Hayden Books, Indianapolis, Indiana, 1987.
47. Chamberlin, D., Gray, J., Traiger, I., "Views Authorisation and Locking in a Relational Database System," *Procs. 75 AFIPS National Computer Conference*, volume 44, May 1975.
48. Snader, J.C., "Look it up Faster with Hashing," *Byte*, January 1987.
49. Knott, G.D., "Hashing Functions," *The Computer Journal*, volume 18, no. 3, 1975.
50. Rowe, L., Shoens, K., "Data Abstraction, Views and Updates in RIGEL," *Procs. 1979 ACM-SIGMOD Conference on the Management of Data*, Boston, Mass., June 1979.
51. Stonebraker, M.A., "Implementation of Integrity Constraints and Views by Query Modification," *Procs. 1975 ACM-SIGMOD Conference on the Management of Data*, San Jose, Ca., May 1975.
52. Allen, F.W., Loomis, M.E., Mannino, M.V., "The Integrated Dictionary/Directory System," *ACM Computing Surveys*, volume 14, no. 2, June 1982.
53. Mayne, A., *Data Dictionary Systems; A Technical Review*, NCC Publications, Manchester, 1984.
54. Lanz, K.A., Edighoffer J., Hitson, B.L., "Towards a Universal Directory Service," *ACM SIGMOD*, no.5, 1985.
55. Wertz, C., *The Data Dictionary: Concepts and Uses*, North-Holland, QED Information Sciences, Amsterdam, 1988.
56. Shneiderman, B., *Designing the User Interface: Strategies for Effective Human–Computer Interaction*, Addison-Wesley Publishing Co., Reading, Mass., 1987.

57. Jones, E., *Using dBASE III Plus*, Osborne McGraw-Hill, New York, 1987.

58. Helix Manual, Odesta Corporation, Northbrook, Il., 1984.

59. Curses, *Programmer's Reference Manual for Curses on the Sun Workstation*, Sun Microsystems Inc., Mountain View, Ca., 1986.

60. Unix, *Commands Reference Manual*, Sun Microsystems Inc., Mountain View, Ca., 1986.

61. Pfaff, G.E., *User Interface Management Systems*, Proceedings of the Workshop on User Interface Management Systems, Springer Verlag, Berlin, 1983.

62. Rochkind, M.J., *Advanced C Programming for Displays*, Prentice Hall Inc., Englewood Cliffs, New Jersey, 1988.

63. Ward, R., "A Simple Menu System for MS-DOS & UNIX," *The C Users Journal*, March/April 1988.

64. Hoffman, C., Valder, W., "MenuHandler: An Application Independent Menu Interface," *Proceedings of the German Chapter of the ACM*, Software Ergonomie '87, Berlin, April 1987.

65. Radcliffe, R.A., Raab, T.J., *Data Handling Utilities in Microsoft C*, Sybex, Alameda, Ca., 1988.

66. Rochkind, M.J., *Advanced UNIX Programming*, Prentice Hall Inc., Englewood Cliffs, New Jersey, 1985.

Index